# ATHENS

# ATHENS

## CITY OF WISDOM

## BRUCE CLARK

PEGASUS BOOKS
NEW YORK LONDON

ATHENS

Pegasus Books, Ltd.
148 West 37th Street, 13th Floor
New York, NY 10018

ISBN: 978-1-64313-875-6

10 9 8 7 6 5 4 3 2 1

Printed in the United States of America
Distributed by Simon & Schuster
www.pegasusbooks.com

*In fond memory of some kind Athenian friends who guided me, as a teenager, on my first steps through the city – including John Leatham, Mary Fotiadi and Cristián Carandell.*

# CONTENTS

INTRODUCTION: ROCKS THAT MATTER . . . . . . . . . 1

1   The Beginnings of Greatness, 600–500 BCE . . . . 17

2   Victories of Brilliance, 500–480 BCE . . . . . . . 37

3   Golden Years, 479–432 BCE . . . . . . . . . . . 56

4   Pride and a Fall, 432–421 BCE . . . . . . . . . . 82

5   A Blazing Twilight, 421–405 BCE . . . . . . . . 103

6   A Chastened Democracy, 405–362 BCE . . . . . . 125

7   A Dance of Death with Macedonia, 362–239 BCE . 150

8   Other People's Empires, 239 BCE–137 CE . . . . . 173

9   Polytheists and Barbarians, 138–560 CE . . . . . . 200

10  A Christian Millennium . . . . . . . . . . . . . 224

11  Latin and Greek: the Late Middle Ages, 1216–1460 244

12  Before and After the Bombardment, 1460–1700 . . 268

13  Stones of Contention, 1697–1820 . . . . . . . . . 295

14  A Poet Dreams on a Rock, 1809–33 . . . . . . . 320

15  Hellenism and Its Expanding Hub, 1833–96 . . . . 346

16  Racing to War, 1896–1919 . . . . . . . . . . . . 374

17  Of Loss and Consolidation, 1919–36 . . . . . . . 405

18  The Darkest Decade, 1940–50 . . . . . . . . . . 431

19  A Wedding and Four Funerals, 1960–2000 . . . . . 457

20  Pride, a Fall and an Open Future, 2000–18 . . . . . 489

21  And Greece Travels Onwards . . . . . . . . . . . 514

NOTES ON SOURCES . . . . . . . . . . . . . . . . 536

ACKNOWLEDGEMENTS . . . . . . . . . . . . . . . 598

IMAGE CREDITS . . . . . . . . . . . . . . . . . . 600

INDEX . . . . . . . . . . . . . . . . . . . . . . . 601

# LIST OF MAPS

Athens and Modern Greece . . . . . . . . . . . . . viii–ix

Classical Athens . . . . . . . . . . . . . . . . . . . 18

The Athenian Empire before the Peloponnesian War . . 58–9

Roman Athens, c.150 CE . . . . . . . . . . . . . . 175

Athens and the Latin Empire in the early
        thirteenth century . . . . . . . . . . . . . . 246–7

The Ottoman Empire, c.1550 . . . . . . . . . . . 270–1

Greek Territorial Changes, 1832–1947 . . . . . . . . 347

Greater Athens . . . . . . . . . . . . . . . . . . . 458–9

Athens and Modern Greece

BULGARIA

BLACK SEA

N

*ala*

Istanbul

SEA OF
MARMARA

*Thasos*

*Samothrace*

*Limnos*

E

A E G E A N   S E A

*Lesbos*

T U R K E Y

*Chios*

Izmir

*Andros*

*Tinos*

*Samos*

*Ikaria*

*Mykonos*

*Patmos*

*Paros*

*Naxos*

*Kos*

*Santorini*

*Anafi*

*Rhodes*

F   C R E T E

*Karpathos*

Heraklion

*Crete*

| 0 | | 50 | | 100 miles |
|---|---|---|---|---|

| 0 | 50 | 100 | | 150 km |

# A NOTE ON GREEK NAMES

The rendering in English of Greek places and persons is a minefield, given that for almost any name there can be up to half-a-dozen valid possibilities. I have used the standard English rendering (which is often a somewhat Latinized version) where that is very familiar, for example, Aeschylus, Pericles, Marathon. For less familiar people and places, I have transliterated in a more literal way, for example, Lykourgos, Xanthippos, Kifisia, Fyli. Alas, it is not humanly possible to be completely consistent.

# INTRODUCTION

# Rocks that Matter

When students in the Western world are introduced to global history, they are often told that civilization owes a particular debt to events which unfolded on two stony citadels in different parts of the eastern Mediterranean. At least physically, the two places have something in common. Both these natural formations surge dramatically out of the ground, rising to outcrops which are naturally flattish and can be made flatter still. Both have been defensive strongholds, blessed with secure water supplies, though neither in the end proved unassailable. Despite these common features, their significance has been understood in very different ways.

One is Jerusalem's Temple Mount, seen as the home of monotheism, and the other is the Acropolis of Athens, whose monuments are revered as a testament to human reason, skill and freedom. This book will be about one of those citadels, and the civilization that arose around it, although currents flowing from the two places did eventually swirl together.

The plaza which dominates the Old City of Jerusalem is revered, of course, for its spiritual history, as a locus of carefully orchestrated encounter between man and a single Deity. The other citadel is associated by most modern admirers with a different story, one that focuses more on earthly achievement. The shimmering marble structures which crown the Acropolis are admired as the most tangible survival of a society where mankind, so to speak, stood on its own feet. In today's understanding of things, ancient Athens compels respect as a cradle of humanism.

This was a society, it seems, where instead of bowing meekly before one or more gods, brilliant minds engaged in deliberation whose outcome was genuinely open. A community where weighty matters of war and peace, as well as routine daily administration, were tackled through the interplay of well-trained intellects that knew how to assess arguments and draw conclusions. With approval, modern historians note what seems like an emerging, secular sophistication in the Athenians' understanding of their own collective story: not as a capricious game acted out by divine powers, but rather as an interplay of human motives which may be complex but can ultimately be dissected and described. Contemporary admirers also love the fact that Athens had well-crafted laws and institutions whose very purpose was to transcend the personal vicissitudes of clever, ambitious individuals, and the whims of jealous deities, and instead serve the broad public interest in a consistent way. Days before handing over the presidency to Donald Trump in 2016, Barack Obama visited the Acropolis and observed warmly that 'it was here twenty-five centuries ago, in the rocky hills of this city, that a new idea emerged'. The name of that idea, he enthused, was *demokratia*... in other words a system where *kratos*, the power to rule, came from the *demos*, the people.

As a description of the Athenian golden age and its ideals, all that is more true than false. But it also leaves out an important aspect of the city's legacy: ancient Athens never ceased to be an intensely spiritual place, a space where the transcendental seemed ever-present. True enough, the modern mind fixates on the human achievements of ancient Athens. It marvels at the logistical and practical skill that was required to haul so much shining marble up a steep hill and then fashion the glistening white rock into structures that enchant us with a false appearance of symmetry. Like medieval cathedrals, these monuments required a huge input of human brain-power, applied to engineering, geometry and the properties of stone. But just as the modern mind finds it hard to imagine the spiritual ideals which underpinned those cathedrals, it also underestimates the spiritual aspect of the Acropolis.

In fact, neither ancient Athens as a whole, nor its greatest monuments, was a secular space in the sense we now understand. The finest monument of all, the Parthenon, was not a parliament building but a temple, in the particular sense that the ancient Greeks gave the word: not a place to pray or sacrifice (that happened outdoors, nearby) but a building that housed a sacred statue whose creation and installation was in itself an act of piety.

The whole complex erected on the Acropolis was a giant statement of homage and thanks to Athena, the city's protectress, and to other deities. It was not just the structures on top of the citadel that were invested with holiness. The geological formation was known as the *Hiera Brakhos*, the sacred rock. Democratic debates happened not on the Acropolis but on a nearby hill, the Pnyx, which attracts too few visitors. Moreover, a remarkably high proportion of the democratic assembly's business consisted of micromanaging public religious practices: which sacrifices should be made to which gods and where.

Whatever their penchant for rational investigation, the ancient Athenians resembled and often outdid their fellow Hellenes in having an intense feeling for the numinous. That is what makes their story so interesting and elusive. For them it came naturally to think of certain features of the natural world, from springs to entire mountains, as liminal spots, locations where mankind stood at the boundary between everyday reality and some transcendent world. The best Athenian citizens certainly did have powerful, reasoning, self-critical minds, but they also had a highly charged sense of the spiritual.

It is not hard to see why the Acropolis was always perceived as one intensely liminal place, by virtue of its form and location. It overlooks a well-watered plain, surrounded by four great mountains as well as smaller hills. In ancient times, all these peaks abounded in beautiful vegetation. Mount Hymettus, to the east, was prized for its honey, Mount Pentelikon for its exceptionally pure marble. The sea sparkles at a safe distance: close enough to be convenient, but far enough away to avoid the city becoming a sitting target for maritime invaders. A series of natural, defensible harbours can be made out on the horizon. It seems entirely natural to give thanks for the very existence of a such a magnificent place.

But the way in which holiness, including the sanctity of certain locations, was understood by the ancient Greeks seems like the very opposite of monotheistic. For them, human destinies were guided not by a single, almighty Power but by a perpetual negotiation between human beings and an array of deities. The most important were twelve in number, but the list could easily be lengthened, and each deity had multiple manifestations, linked to particular places, communities or aspects of a turbulent personality. The gods were powerful and immortal, but very human in their passions and failings. The establishment of new cults was a creative, almost entrepreneurial, business. Ancient Greek religion, like ancient Greek politics, was irrepressibly prolix.

The Athenian Acropolis, including its underbelly and its inspiring surroundings, offered plenty of scope for ingenuity in the establishment of cults and focal points for religious energy, places that served to hold society together in common moments of ecstasy. The fortress itself was a honeycomb of caves and springs, and there are perfectly good geological reasons for this. The top layer of the Acropolis consists of limestone, formed more than 100 million years ago by the decaying shells of crustaceans from a long-vanished sea. Beneath there is marl and sandstone, which was formed 30 million years later. Vast tectonic forces, pushing Africa closer to Europe and Asia, forced the limestone above the marl. This limestone, although very hard, is also porous. With its faintly acidic content, rainwater can find places to seep through, until it reaches the impenetrable bedrock below. As a result, the whole rock is latticed with caves, fissures and springs. These have served practical purposes as well as firing the spiritual imagination of countless generations.

We do not know much about the religious practices of – or indeed anything much at all about – the first people who explored this rock and its cavities. But one of the oldest objects discovered in the vicinity of the Acropolis is a plump female figure, dating from before 4000 BCE, which hints at an agricultural society where fertility and reproduction were particularly revered. Almost all the societies that occupied the place in later eras gave greater weight to sky-gods or mountain-gods with masculine characteristics, or else to goddesses who had rather male qualities. Whole theories of religion have been built around this contrast, although it is dangerous to read too much into a single archaeological find.

One thing we do know about those Neolithic people is that they knew where to find and extract water. Some twenty-two shallow wells, dating from 3500 BCE to 3000 BCE, have been identified on the north-western edge of the Acropolis. The societies that dug these wells vanished in the subsequent millennium, but human settlement reappears in the Middle Bronze Age, from 2000 BCE; and sometime between 1400 BCE and 1300 BCE, Athens began playing its part in the great Mycenaean civilization which burst forth in the form of royal courts dotted across the Greek world.

The fortified palace on the Athens Acropolis was not the greatest of these courts, but by 1250 BCE it boasted impressive walls, up to 10 metres tall and 5 metres thick, parts of which can still be seen. These immense piles of stone are known as the Cyclopean walls because later generations felt they could only have been heaved into place by a mythical colossus, like the one-eyed giant or Cyclops described in Homer's epic poetry. Artists' impressions of the palace suggest a magnificent, multi-floored complex where a king was in command of a busy bureaucracy and all kinds of merchandise were imported, processed and exported. But these are all guesses, based on the discovery of the defences as well as the foundations of an impressive edifice.

In all probability, the ruler of Mycenaean Athens did not hold sway even over the surrounding region of Attica, where several different fiefdoms, each with its own burial practices, have been identified. Some of these neighbouring micro-kingdoms grew rich from exporting silver and lead from the mines at Laurion in southern Attica. To judge by the paucity of its artefacts and burial sites, however, Mycenaean Athens did not enjoy such prosperity.

There is one particularly impressive well on the north-western side of the Acropolis, known as the Mycenaean spring. It lay at the bottom of a dizzying 35-metre cleft which had opened up when a piece of rock detached itself from the surface. About 1200 BCE, eight flights of steps, some wooden and some stone, were built to provide access for anyone intrepid enough to climb down. It seems to have been used for a mere twenty-five years before the shaft collapsed.

Over the following century, the entire Mycenaean world implodes inexplicably, ushering in what posterity calls a Dark Age. Only about 3,000 years later, when young Greek resistance fighters were looking for a way to challenge the Nazis who had just occupied Athens, did this extraordinary, vertiginous hole in the Rock regain its strategic importance.

Whatever was happening on the surface of the Rock, it is a fair bet that people never stopped exploring caves or wondering about the divinities or half-divine city founders with which these cavities might be connected. Through those caves, early Athenians found ways to understand how their own lives intersected with those of the gods and demigods.

Now, as in ancient times, there is a path called the Peripatos, which simply means a walkway, that encircles part of the Rock and gives a good view of the principal openings. One, called Cave B, was regarded as the place where Apollo, god of light and prophecy, forced himself on Kreousa, a young mortal woman whose father was the city founder, King Erechtheus. The product of this union was a young man called Ion, the forefather of the Ionian Greeks to whom the Athenians felt connected, although most lived on the other side of the Aegean.

The neighbouring Cave C was a dwelling-place for the greatest of sky-gods, Zeus, the hurler of thunderbolts. So vast was his reach that his presence could be felt deep underground as well as hurtling through the heavens. An adjoining cavity, rediscovered only a century ago, has an association with quite specific events in classical Greek history. It was dedicated to Pan, the sensual, cloven-hoofed goat-god, by grateful Athenians who credited him with sowing confusion in the ranks of their Persian invaders in 490 BCE.

Walk a bit further and there is a cave associated with Aphrodite, goddess of love, and her son Eros. At the eastern end of the Rock, beyond easy reach for a walker, is the largest cave of all, 14 metres wide. This one is dedicated to yet another figure from the city's foundation pageant: Aglaurus, a daughter of King Kekrops, who jumped off the Rock to her death in order to save the city. As we shall see, the mythology of early Athens includes several stories of a king (depicted as a half-snake or with snakes) with two or three daughters who jump off the Acropolis to their deaths, saving the city.

The association with the snakes was a way of expressing the Athenians' belief that they had emerged from the earth, that they were native to the city and had never lived anywhere else. Snakiness is a characteristic ascribed to kings named as Kekrops, or else Erechtheus or Erichthonius.* Kekrops is sometimes presented as a forebear of Erechtheus, and Erechtheus as the grandfather of Erichthonius. But in truth they may all be variants on the same shadowy tradition.

Athenians remembered another early king whom they regarded as a real-life figure even though he surpassed other mortals in his strength and ingenuity. Theseus was a kind of superman, whose

---

* At least in the name Erichthonius, there is a clear hint of the root – *chthon* – which refers to the earth and by extension creatures or people who emerge from the earth.

importance as an Athenian ancestor seemed to increase as the city itself grew in confidence. The story of Theseus is in some ways a grotesque tale of father–son competition in which the hero's mother is relegated to the background.

It starts with Aegeus, an Athenian king who confesses while visiting a fellow monarch, Pittheus of Troezen, that he is unhappy at being childless. Pittheus duly offers the visiting sovereign his daughter Aethra, who soon becomes pregnant, although it is possible that the child she is carrying has been fathered by the sea-god, Poseidon. Aegeus then returns to Athens, having carefully left open the possibility that a son and heir might emerge from his brief liaison. He buries his sandals and a sword under a rock and tells Aethra that when their son grows up, he should move the rock and take the tokens for himself as evidence of his royal parentage. Theseus is raised in Troezen and when he grows up, he duly uncovers the precious objects and heads to Athens to claim his throne. On his journey, he performs six heroic labours, including killing a giant sow and pitching into the sea a bully who made people wash his feet. In the holy city of Eleusis, Theseus sees off a local king who liked to wrestle visitors to the ground and then kill them. But when he arrives in Athens, his father is unimpressed by his feats and fails to recognize him. However, Aegeus' wife Medea does recognize Theseus and in order to prevent him from being acknowledged as heir and assuming the kingdom in place of her own son, she tries to poison him.

So Theseus has to go on proving himself. As every lover of mythology knows, his greatest feat was to settle accounts with King Minos of Crete and slaughter the Minotaur, the subterranean monster who demanded an annual tribute of seven handsome young men and seven maidens, the flower of Athenian youth. Sailing back to Athens, Theseus promised to hoist white sails if his mission was successful. But somehow Theseus forgot, and Aegeus leaped off a cliff into the sea, giving it the name Aegean.

Aegeus had been slow to recognize his son's existence, let alone his merits. But he wanted his son alive, not dead. However, the feeling may not have been mutual. As well as being a poignant tale of filial ambivalence, the story of Theseus may describe something that really happened: from about 1400 BCE central Greece overtook Crete as the epicentre of Hellenic civilization, and it held that position for a couple of centuries before suffering a mysterious collapse.

Athens, like the rest of the Greek world, starts to reappear in recorded history from around 800 BCE as prosperity returns, population levels grow and literacy, with all its benefits, flourishes anew thanks to the adoption of a phonetic alphabet in which the Greek language has been written ever since.

This became the era not of the palace but rather of the *polis*, roughly translated as city-state. One energetic city would spawn many more, as enterprising groups sailed forth and established colonies up to a thousand miles away. Soon there were hundreds of *poleis*, forming a Greek cultural space that stretched from Corsica to the Black Sea. There was no single political unit called Greece, nor would there be for another three millennia. But culturally Greek urban societies, built around an agora or open space where people bargained, socialized and traded, sprang up across the Mediterranean. These micro-communities were not kingdoms, under the sway of a divinely anointed monarch; they had procedures for making decisions which may not quite have been democratic but nonetheless required some compromise and consensus.

This extreme political fragmentation in a culturally uniform space is partly a consequence of the geography of Greece. It is a landscape of barren peaks dividing one patch of relatively fertile soil from another, and of small ports nestling at the foot of towering mountains. In an environment such as this, embarking on a stormy sea, for all its perils, was easier than trekking inland.

Despite this physical and political disunity, there were a number of common features that held the Greeks together, giving them a sense of commonality which might come to the fore in certain circumstances. They all spoke more or less the same language. They all loved the poetry of Homer, which used that tongue in a thrilling way to describe the adventures of fallible, earthly gods and human giants who tested the limits of courage and endeavour. They therefore had a common religious and cultural reference point.

From around 776 BCE onwards they also had the Olympic Games, which were the most famous of the sporting festivals in which any Greek could participate. These were intense but rule-bound competitions, conferring vast prestige on the victor; they were also religious events. Beautifully choreographed acts of worship were as important a part of the proceedings as contests in discus-throwing or foot-racing. And the contests themselves were an act of homage to divine powers.

The whole thing was an offering to Zeus, father of the gods, but that did not preclude the establishment of smaller shrines to other gods as the games developed. At Olympia and other places, Greeks came together, and acknowledged and validated one another, if only through rivalry. This rivalry could take the form of athletic contests between individuals, skirmishing between city-states or even a religious competition over who could attract the most followers to this or that cult.

When compared with other city-states, the one that grew up around the Acropolis of Athens had distinct assets. For a start, it was a region, not just a town. From 800 BCE onwards, the fates of Athens and the surrounding region of Attica, with its mountains and plains, were somehow intertwined. There could be terrible quarrels between one region of Attica and another, intersecting with class warfare. Yet ultimately, people from the town of Athens and the much larger region of Attica felt they belonged to a single political unit. Athens was not merely an urban settlement but the hub of a region, Attica, which jutted south into the Aegean and comprised an area of about 4,000 square kilometres.

It was a kind of micro-country with a great variety of landscapes, including some arable plains and a much larger area where olives and grapes could be produced and transformed. Near the peninsula's southern tip, there were rich seams of silver. The red-clay soil was not especially fertile but was ideal for the production of high-grade pottery, whose adornment became one of the region's fields of excellence.

The Athenians' collective self-understanding rested on a rich and compelling mixture of overlapping and sometimes contradictory stories: stories in which the vagaries of the gods, or of natural forces which are seen as divine, interact with earthly or half-earthly kings. These monarchs were seen as historical figures and common ancestors.

The narratives they used to describe their origins, unfolding in some liminal space between deity and humanity, are a mixture of charming, horrific and revealing. The tale of Theseus was only one among many. The city's main protector was the goddess Athena, standing in equal measure for wisdom, handicraft – including weaving – and military prowess. Scholars have debated whether she gave her name to the city or took her name from it, and concluded that the second is more likely.

From the moment of her birth, Athena was endowed with what traditional societies viewed as male and female characteristics. Her coming into the world was a bizarre affair. Zeus, father of the gods, had been warned that he would be overthrown by his second child. So after impregnating the nymph Metis, he simply swallowed her, to be on the safe side. But soon he was afflicted with terrible head pains. Hephaestus, the god who served as smith and fire-manipulator, was among those who offered to help. But Athena simply burst forth from the father-god's pate, brandishing a spear.

In different locations, and different phases of history, Athena would show varying aspects of her shifting personality. In Homer's *Iliad* she appears as a shrewd helper of the cause of the Achaeans, as the Greeks fighting in the Trojan war are known. In the *Odyssey*, she provides similar assistance to the hero. Several other cities besides

Athens, including Sparta, regarded her as a protector-in-chief, but there was only one city which bore her name. Homer often describes her as *glaukopis*, which could be translated as blue-eyed, grey-eyed, flashing-eyed, or might instead be linked with the owl or *glaux*, the big-eyed bird that was another symbol of Athenian wisdom.

In time of war, as Athena Promachonas ('she who fights in front'), the goddess stood for clever military manoeuvres and prudent strategy, not simply for blood and gore. The crude business of killing was more the domain of her brother Ares, the war-god, for whom the Athenians had less respect. As Athena Ergane ('the industrious') she was patroness of skilled manual workers, both male and female. And sometimes it was her lifelong virginity (as Athena Parthenos) that was stressed.

Although Athens became her principal home, there are tantalizing scraps of evidence, from the dawn of Greek history, that reveal how universal this deity's appeal was. In Knossos, the great Cretan fortress that was abandoned around 1400 BCE, an inscription contains a reference to the goddess, Potnia (Lady) Atana. It is written in Linear B, the earliest script in which a form of Greek was written, deciphered only in the mid-twentieth century.

That raises the question: how did this lady, venerated in so many eras and locations, come to be associated with one city in particular? The Athenians offered different accounts, all of which serve to connect the shadowy world of the gods with their own life and governance. In one story, there was a contest to determine who would be the main protector of Athens.

Central to this narrative is the semi-serpentine King Kekrops. With him as witness, Athena and Poseidon, god of the ocean, competed for the role of chief guardian of the city. Poseidon struck the stony surface of the Acropolis with his trident and a torrent of salt water came gushing forth. Athena offered a more subtle gift.

As Kekrops looked on, she caused a new, hardy kind of tree with small grey-green leaves to sprout forth. Its multiple products, from oil to soap, were a guarantee against poverty and the basis for a thriving export trade. Zeus chose judges to adjudicate the rival claims. By some accounts the entire array of Olympian gods made the choice. In other versions it was Kekrops who took the decision. But the outcome was clear. Athena prevailed, though Poseidon would be worshipped in this place too.

There are as many ways to interpret this story as there are versions of what exactly happened. Perhaps Poseidon's torrent of briny water was an unwelcome reminder of the floods which were a powerful collective memory for all Near Eastern peoples. In any case, the choice of Athena signalled a city whose merits included sophisticated thought, refined culture and the excellence of its products, including fine oil stored in well-made pottery.

The importance of the olive tree and its products in the life and economy of an ancient city can hardly be overstated. It glistened on athletes' bodies, fuelled the lamps which illumined nocturnal processions; it provided a growing population with most of the vitamins they needed. To despatch this oil, and other products, to faraway places, the Athenians would need to master the ocean. But attitudes to the ocean, which could be glassy one moment and terrifyingly rough the next, were always mixed. Even for a maritime power in the making, Poseidon was a god to be feared as much as loved.

There is another, even odder way in which Athenians imagined the connection between the half-serpentine founder of their city and its divine protectress. Athena is said to have visited the divine blacksmith Hephaestus and asked him to make a suit of armour. He was seized with passion for his beautiful visitor, but she rejected his advances and fled. A drop of the lustful deity's seed fell on Athena's leg, and she wiped it away with a piece of wool.

Falling to the ground, this liquid fertilized the earth and brought forth a little boy called Erichthonius, or possibly Erechtheus. Athena took hold of the child and handed him, in a basket, to the three daughters of Kekrops. They peeped at the infant and saw its body was intertwined with at least one snake. In this narrative, it was in horror at the baby's serpentine companion that they jumped off the Acropolis to their deaths.

Athena, being less alarmed by species-bending creatures, raised the child herself. This idea of a king called Erechtheus, dwelling in Athens and under the special protection of Athena, is mentioned in Homer's *Iliad*. It is a fleeting reference, but one that made the Athenians very proud. (It may, of course, have been inserted cunningly by an Athenian hand when the text of the *Iliad* was being finalized.)

> ...Athens, the well-built citadel, the land of great-hearted Erechtheus, whom of old Athena, daughter of Zeus, fostered, when the earth, the giver of grain, had borne him; and she made him to dwell in Athens, in her own rich sanctuary, and there the youths of the Athenians, as the years roll on in their courses, seek to win his favour with sacrifices of bulls and rams...

The outcome of the contest between Athena and Poseidon seems to have been a kind of eternal compromise between the two deities, standing for different facets of the city's greatness, but with Athena in the senior role. In one haunting myth, King Erechtheus, the foster-son of Athena, did battle against a King Eumolpus, who was a son of Poseidon. Erechtheus is killed in an earthquake caused by Poseidon, and thereafter the personalities of Erechtheus and Poseidon somehow fuse. Athena commands the king's widow Praxithea to stay on the Acropolis and serve as priestess for two deities: herself as guardian of the city, and Poseidon-Erechtheus. That explains how, as Athens emerges into recorded history, there are two main religious cults associated with the surface of the Rock: Poseidon-Erechtheus and Athena Polias, meaning city-protectress.

Modern minds have struggled to make sense of Athena. Depending on which theory you accept, she is either a feminist heroine or a crude male fantasy, something between a clever big sister and all-embracing mother to warriors, travellers and craft workers. She intervenes deftly to provide timely help to all manner of enterprising individuals in difficult situations. She is a goddess who likes to succour war-like men, including soldiers, especially when they show courage and ingenuity in helping themselves. She had her favourites among the Greek warriors described in the *Iliad*. In the *Odyssey*, she admired the resourcefulness of the hero and, by appearing in different guises, both male and female, to different people, facilitated his journey back to Ithaca. She is also, in important respects, sexless. Her own arrival in the world, emerging fully armed from the head of Zeus, completely bypassed female reproduction. It is an image that contrasts poignantly with the foundation story of Christianity. In the Christian story, a woman gives birth to a man who has no earthly paternity. Zeus, by contrast, is a man who gives birth to a woman who has no mother, because he has eaten her. As for Athena herself, she seemingly had no interest in being impregnated or giving birth in the usual way. Hephaestus, the lustful blacksmith, was wasting his energy when he chased her.

Sigmund Freud, the father of psychoanalysis, was intrigued by the figure of Athena, and kept a small bronze statue of the goddess on his desk. His lifelong fascination with the city's protectress was fuelled by his first visit to the Acropolis in 1904: he felt overwhelmed by an encounter with the material reality of the stories of ancient Greece which he had learned at school. The bronze statuette featured prominently in his dialogue with a patient, the American writer Hilda Doolittle. It seems that Freud ascribed the escape of his Vienna Jewish family from the Nazis to her protective power. Doolittle, for her part, wondered if atavistic Jewish family loyalty was prompting him to fuse the Acropolis with the Jerusalem Temple Mount.

As the people of Athens, and Attica, grew in confidence, there was a corresponding increase in the splendour of the monuments which they erected to their protectress. For the ordinary people of the ancient city, Athena was the one in whose name they fought; for whose benefit they made fabrics and other artefacts; and the one who inspired them as they deliberated, argued and tried to make sense of the material world.

# I

# The Beginnings of Greatness
## 600–500 BCE

*The shadowy role of the archon – Kylon's attempted coup: the first Athenian power struggle – the reforms of Solon fail to bring stability to Attica – the populist rule of Peisistratos: benign tyrant and instigator of the Panathenaic Games – Spartan intervention ends the turbulent tyranny of his son Hippias – Kleisthenes overthrows a pro-Spartan oligarchy and creates democratic institutions robust enough to endure war and peace*

In the tide of creative energy that swept through Greece from the eighth century BCE onwards, Athens was a latecomer. By the year 600 BCE, seagoing entrepreneurs from Euboea, a long island running parallel to the coast north of Athens, had established flourishing Greek colonies in Sicily. Beautiful lyric poetry was being written, in a world of refinement and prosperity, on the island of Lesbos in the eastern Aegean. Scientific theories were being developed on the adjacent Anatolian mainland. But the Athenians had yet to establish a single colony. If there was one activity at which the people of Athens and its environs seemed to excel from the earliest years, it was statecraft.

The region faced roughly the same political problem as scores of other Greek places. As the population grew and the economy became more diversified, there was tension between well-established old families who controlled most of the land, and emerging groups of merchants, entrepreneurs and farmers, successful and otherwise. In

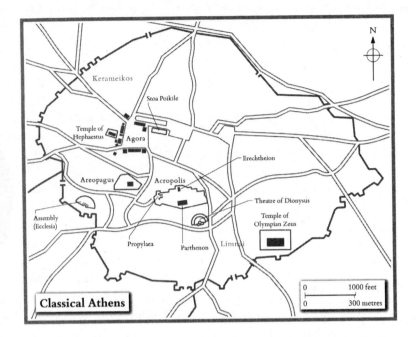

**Classical Athens**

many places, a *tyrannos* or tyrant, claiming to represent the interests of those who were wronged by the existing order, challenged or took over from the older elite. These new rulers were not necessarily harsh or despotic, nor did they claim the mystique of an absolute monarch. Their emergence was a symptom of the growing pains which the entire Hellenic world was experiencing.

In Athens, though, things were often a bit more complicated and interesting. Ingenious ways to finesse the conflicting claims of old and new classes were being devised. Institutions and offices were established, and their function and power evolved rapidly as society's needs shifted.

As early as the eighth century BCE, the daily administration of Athens was assigned to respected individuals called archons. At first they numbered three and were chosen from the ranks of the aristocracy for a period of ten years. Their duties included public ceremonies and the conduct of war. Then the term of office was reduced to a year, and it was established that one archon would be entitled to give his name to each year. The number of archons was increased to nine. It is hard to ascertain their exact duties.

These arrangements consolidated the authority of the city's old families, while also ensuring that no single individual could monopolize power. As we will see, the first clearly recorded event in the history of Athens, the so-called Kylonian affair, brings home several enduring features of the emerging city's life. It shows how venerable dynasties, the equivalent of the Cecils in England or maybe America's Kennedys or Bushes, were a recurring but contentious presence in Athenian affairs, although their position was often challenged by populist strongmen. No less striking is the sanctity that was ascribed to the Acropolis, even though the earliest shrines on the Rock were pretty modest compared with those that would follow.

This primordial Athenian story, in the realm of history rather than myth, concerns an attempted coup by a confident young man called Kylon. He had gained pan-Hellenic glory by winning the foot-race in the Olympic Games in the year 640 BCE, and married the daughter of the tyrant who held sway in the neighbouring town of Megara. In 632 BCE, he attempted to emulate his father-in-law by assembling a gaggle of armed supporters and seizing the Acropolis. But he failed to win support among the townspeople, and the rebels soon found themselves isolated and surrounded. Kylon and his brother slipped away. The insurgents took refuge on the Rock in the shrine of Athena, which was considered sacred space and therefore a place of asylum. Anybody who committed murder in such a numinous spot would be guilty of terrible desecration.

The task of suppressing the rebellion fell to the archon of the year, a man called Megakles who belonged to the greatest of the city's aristocratic dynasties, the Alkmeonids. According to one version of story, the blue-blooded Megakles persuaded the rebels to come down from the hill and face trial. The insurgents made their way down while keeping hold of a rope tied to the statue of Athena, in the belief that they would still be connected to her protective power.

They were confident, in other words, that nobody would harm them as long as they remained, albeit loosely, under the wing of the goddess. But the cord broke and the rebels were duly slaughtered, in some cases by stoning. In 2016, archaeologists working in the port of Phaleron found a mass burial of about eighty healthy young men, many of whom had been shackled together before suffering violent death. These may be Kylon's men.

The story of the rope may be a colourful afterthought. What is more certain is that rebels were killed while they were in a space which they and others regarded as subject to religious protection, whether from Athena or other divine powers. Megakles and other leaders of the wider Alkmeonid clan were put on trial, found guilty of blasphemy and told to leave Athens forever. It was by no means the dynasty's last word, but the perception that they were somehow cursed or tainted would never quite disappear.

What the story tells us is that from the beginning of the city's recorded history, its power struggles were many-sided. In contrast with other parts of Greece, they were never just a binary contest between an old nobility and an autocrat who allowed new money to have its way. From a very early stage, the city had robust institutions designed to accommodate the interests of several parties, and also elaborate religious rules which could constrain people's behaviour. The net result was never easy to predict.

If Kylon is the city's first would-be tyrant, the first personality and effective ruler in Athenian history is a statesman-poet called Solon. He was chosen as archon for the year in or around 594 BCE. Solon's biographers, writing at least 150 years after his reign, attribute to him an unusual combination of talents, from the artistic to the administrative. He was a soldier, a philosopher, a wandering sage and a kind of political genius.

The received facts of his life do not quite add up to a rounded, credible picture of a human being. But we are left with the impression of a thoughtful man who responded judiciously to a critical moment in the city's affairs. His measured actions ensured that Attica did not break up or dissolve into anarchy, although it was a near miss at times.

It seems well-established that before assuming political power, Solon had goaded a war-weary city into fighting and prevailing in a contest with the nearby town of Megara over the island of Salamis. He apparently achieved this through a mixture of military artifice and galvanizing verse.

Having boosted the city's regional standing, Solon defused some of its internal tensions with judicious economic management and political balancing acts. He had inherited a situation where growing inequality might easily have sparked a revolution. As prosperous farms expanded and poor ones collapsed, more and more householders at the bottom of the scale found themselves trapped in debt and forced into bonded labour. Some were sold as slaves to distant places. The countryside was dotted with wooden or stone pillars indicating that a particular piece of land had been mortgaged to discharge a debt.

It is not difficult to imagine how this state of affairs arose, or to think of parallels in other eras of history. As long as it lasts, there is a certain self-stabilizing order in a system which concentrates power in an established aristocratic class, which expects service and loyalty from its underlings but in return offers a kind of protection. Once new money, earned in commerce or manufacture, enters the system, it wields economic power in a more ruthless way and acknowledges no moral obligation to those at the bottom.

The Attica which Solon inherited seems to have been on the cusp of transition from one order to another; that is what makes its political affairs, or what we know of them, interesting. Indeed, throughout the ancient history of Athens, a remarkable variety of classes and subcultures seem to have coexisted, from the grand old families who never left the political scene to freed slaves who thrived in newfangled forms of business. Seeing that greed was on the verge of getting out of control, Solon steered a careful middle line. He did not decree the abolition of all small farmers' debts, but he stopped the use of the human person as surety for a debt, and he somehow raised money to buy back Athenians who had been sold into slavery elsewhere. Solon also made some remarkably bold efforts, for the time, to broaden the range of citizens who took part in political life. He began by acknowledging the reality that new money was creating new political expectations. The starting point of his reforms was a four-way division among male citizens, based on the size of their property and how much agricultural produce it yielded per year.

The richest class were those who produced more than 500 units, equivalent to about a bushel of grain. Then came a class of cavalrymen, producing 300 units or more, who were rich enough to field a warhorse where needed; then a class of yeomen whose land brought forth at least 200 units; and finally a class of labourers and sharecroppers who had to seek employment where they could.

Having laid out these distinctions, Solon created a society that was still far from egalitarian but nonetheless gave more openings to those at the lower end. The humblest category of citizens had no hope of becoming office-holders, but they could participate in an assembly of male citizens where important matters were discussed, and they were eligible to serve as jurors in a legal system which grew steadily in sophistication.

Solon inherited a system where many offices, including that of archon, were restricted to the wealthiest. He duly lengthened the list of functions that could be open to anyone in the top two or three classes. For example, a new council of 400, drawn from the four tribes of Athens, was ushered into existence. Its job was to prepare the business of the assembly.

Most remarkably, Solon created a new kind of appeal court in which a male citizen of any class could participate. Any citizen could volunteer to join the large pool of people from whom juries would be selected to hear particular cases. From the earliest days of Athenian political experimentation, the principle of equality before the law, or *isonomia*, was considered as no less important than that of the popular sovereignty.

Solon also acted shrewdly to boost Attica's position in the commercial networks linking the cities and islands of Greece, while ensuring that trading success brought some local benefits. He encouraged the production and shipment abroad of olive oil, a natural Athenian strength, while suspending the export of other agricultural products, which was causing shortages at home. Skilled craftworkers from other places were encouraged to settle in and around Athens and disseminate their knowledge. This boosted the production and decoration of ceramics, which soon became one of the glories of the city.

Solon was remembered as a man of political feats that were eventually crowned with success, and there is no reason to deny him this accolade. Yet his story contains some odd twists and turns. Immediately after proclaiming his radical changes, he is said to have left the city and gone travelling in the eastern Mediterranean, exchanging nuggets of philosophy wherever he stayed. Herodotus, a pioneer of history and geography with an eye for colour, anecdote and human fallibility, describes Solon's wanderings like this:

> He was on a journey, having departed from Athens for ten years. His supposed motive was a desire to see the world, but in reality he wanted to avoid having to rescind any of the laws which, at the Athenians' bidding, he had crafted for them. The Athenians had no right to repeal these laws without his permission. That was because they had vowed, on pain of suffering a severe curse, to remain subject for a decade to the laws that Solon had imposed.

Like many Greek contemporaries who were searching for wisdom, he went to Egypt and parleyed with the priests of that country's already ancient religion. By one account, Solon received the information that, thousands of years earlier, his home region was at odds with a kingdom called Atlantis which was wiped out by some great disaster. (This might be a memory of a real event in the sixteenth or seventeenth century BCE: the massive volcanic explosion which half destroyed the southern Aegean island of Santorini, sending a tsunami rolling towards Crete, where Minoan civilization was in full flower.)

The wandering Athenian statesman also visited Cyprus and went to Lydia in present-day Turkey, where he reportedly made his most famous pronouncement. Filled by now with Egyptian wisdom, he is said to have engaged in a rather pointed conversation with Croesus, the ostentatiously rich Lydian monarch. Fishing for a compliment, Croesus asked the visitor who was the happiest of men. To the king's frustration, Solon uttered the enigmatic words: 'Call no man happy until he be dead…'

The saying is usually misunderstood. It sounds, at first, like a response of blasé pessimism to the travails of life, to the effect that our troubles will never be over until we are in the grave. But according to Herodotus, to whom we owe this story, Solon was making a much subtler point. The Athenian traveller explained himself by naming some people who had died in a high spiritual state, either in battle or in the midst of noble deeds.

For example, there were two brothers who exhausted themselves bringing their mother to worship at the temple of Hera and expired from their effort. Happiness, in the loftiest sense, does not consist merely of living enjoyably, but also of dying nobly, ideally by giving one's departure from the earth some meaning or purpose. How 'well' we die is something that cannot be determined until it actually happens. Therefore, 'call no man happy until he be dead…'

Properly digested, that is a rather astonishing statement, closer in feeling to the Abrahamic faiths of the Middle East than to anything heard hitherto in the Hellenic world. Perhaps Solon learned more than ancient history lessons from his Levantine travels. His royal interlocutor would soon realize the truth of this aphorism when the ruling Achaemenid dynasty of Persia made a show of their fast-growing strength by defeating Croesus in battle and laying siege to the Lydian capital, Sardis. Persia's King Cyrus then commanded that his captured enemy be burned to death on a pyre. As the flames licked higher, and the hapless Lydian monarch realized the futility of most of his life, he cried the name of Solon three times, and his conqueror was intrigued enough to spare and pardon him.

Like so many things recounted by Herodotus, this seems too good a story to be literally true, but it does tell us many things. It brings home how the Greeks, and the Athenians in particular, imagined themselves to be different from the absolute monarchies which held sway to their east. The Greek world was neither puritanical nor ascetic, but it saw value in self-awareness, self-restraint and temperance. It could borrow nuggets of wisdom, and artistic techniques, from its eastern neighbours, but it had no desire to take lessons in Oriental despotism.

On the other hand, the fact that Solon disappeared from Athens after proclaiming his revolutionary changes may be a sign of a survival instinct, not self-restraint. The reforms he enacted were of lasting benefit to the city, and they foreshadowed even bolder measures. But as far as we can discern, the situation was too volatile to allow such changes to be implemented smoothly or immediately. Having given his home city the benefit of political acumen, he chose the road of temporary self-exile: a path which many Greek politicians, in ancient times and modern, have taken when domestic affairs became deadlocked or dangerous.

To get closer to the real Solon, we can turn to his poetry, which is not the most refined but speaks plainly and from the heart about his love for Athens and the surrounding region. This is the voice of a man who feels horrified at the thought of his home town being torn apart by greed, factionalism and class war.

Not by the doom of Zeus, who ruleth all,
Not by the curse of Heaven shall Athens fall.
Strong in her Sire, above the favored land
Pallas Athene lifts her guardian hand.

No; her own citizens with counsels vain
Shall work her rain in their quest of gain;
Dishonest demagogues her folk misguide,
Foredoomed to suffer for their guilty pride.
Their reckless greed, insatiate of delight,
Knows not to taste the frugal feast aright;
Th' unbridled lust of gold, their only care,
Nor public wealth nor wealth divine will spare.
Now here, now there, they raven, rob and seize.
Heedless of Justice and her stern decrees,
Who silently the present and the past
Reviews, whose slow revenge o'ertakes at last.

To have an even more tangible sense of what was happening in Athens in the era of Solon, it is worth turning not to a text or poem, but to an object, discovered in central Italy but clearly the product of an Athenian artist working in 570 BCE or shortly after. Known as the François vase, after the man who discovered it two centuries ago, this piece of pottery – a krater in the black-figure style that flourished in Attica between the seventh and fifth centuries BCE – stands 66 centimetres high and is adorned by no fewer than 270 human and animal figures, mostly scenes from mythology in which Theseus looms large. We can see the hero celebrating with his fellow Athenians after his destruction of that horrible foreign beast, the Minotaur, whose appetite for young Athenian blood had kept the city in terror. Theseus is also shown fighting alongside his barbarian friends, the Lapiths, against another sort of half-animal, half-human creature, the Centaurs. Their bodies were something between horses and men.

But this refined work of art is not just a dutiful affirmation of a mythological founder king who was moving to the centre of the Athenian imagination. It is proudly signed by the man who made the pot, Ergotimos, and the artist whose deft hand painted those scenes, Kleitias. Athens was already on the way to becoming a thriving hub for creative individuals who were not shy about showing off their talent and competing with their peers. Rival artists in Corinth were adept at depicting animals; the Athenians perfected the representation, at least in outline, of the human form. Perhaps the greatest achievement of Solon was that he sensed and encouraged the potential of Athens as a centre of soft power: a place that could draw in talent from all over Greece and export the resulting products. One of his cleverest political moves was to offer citizenship to skilled artists who settled in Athens.

Solon's reforms, inspired as they were, ultimately failed to bring stability to Attica. Perhaps they had the desired result of easing misery at the bottom of society and giving some release to the energies of a rising middle class. But within twenty years of his archonship, the whole region was again dangerously divided into factions which reflected location, clan loyalties and economic interests.

There was a 'coastal' party at the southern end of the peninsula which stood in the political centre and supported Solon's changes; a conservative 'plains' party, based in the fertile interior, which wanted to roll back the reforms; and a 'frontier' party in the hilly north of Attica, representing small farmers who wanted an even more radical shift in favour of the poor. The centrists were led by Megakles. He was the grandson and namesake of the man who had brought a curse on his family, the Alkmeonids, by killing Kylon's rebels in a holy place. The radical party was led by a hot-headed, ambitious young man called Peisistratus.

By the time he bid for power in Athens, Peisistratus already had a distinguished record as a commander in fighting against neighbouring Megara. His relationship with Solon, thirty years his senior, was mysterious. It seems they were second cousins, and possibly lovers. But by the time Peisistratus reached for the reins of authority in Athens, Solon was a worldly-wise and weary figure, who felt the younger man was inclined to impatience and opportunism.

Opportunistic he certainly was. Peisistratus made his first bid for power by appearing before the assembly of Athenian citizens with a conspicuous wound, claiming there had been an attempt on his life. The assembly gave him permission to field an armed guard. He then used that guard to seize control of the Acropolis, only to be driven off. Whatever it says about Peisistratus, this episode tells us interesting things about Athens in the mid-sixth century BCE: the assembly of citizens had real powers; private armies were taboo; and the Acropolis, where the first huge temple to Athena was probably under construction, was too holy a place for one armed faction to seize.

Peisistratus then formed a coalition with the blue-blooded Megakles and they made a joint bid for power which was successful for a while. The pact between the two strongmen was supposedly sealed when Peisistratus married the nobleman's daughter. He heralded his return to Athens with an eye-catching stunt: storming into town in a chariot with an exceptionally tall woman at his side, who was supposed to represent Athena. The historian Herodotus, who generally loves a good yarn, said it was amazing that anyone was taken in by these vulgar theatrics.

In any case, the deal with Megakles broke down when Peisistratus refused to impregnate his new bride, preferring to guard the legitimacy of his offspring from an earlier marriage. Peisistratus was once again driven out of the city, and went off to make a fortune through mining in Thrace, the untamed north of the Greek world.

In 546 BCE, Peisistratus made his definitive return to his home city: not with a goddess this time, but with money and a small army of mercenaries. He was soon established as the tyrant of the city, a political concept which Athens had hitherto rejected, and continued in that role until his death in 527 BCE. The strange thing is that later generations, in Athens and elsewhere, had nothing but good to say about his time of supreme authority. He was certainly not the worst of despots. Although he was in effective control of Athenian affairs, he did not abolish any of the city's democratic or judicial institutions. On the contrary, he extended them in certain ways, for example by sending travelling courts around Attica so that all corners of the region could benefit from Athenian justice.

Many of the more promising developments that began in Solon's time were continued or accelerated under Peisistratus. The city's prowess as an international exporter of beautifully painted and skilfully made vases grew steadily, overtaking Corinth. Theseus, the mythical uniter of Attica and Athens, became an ever more popular subject for depiction. No less successful were the exports of the exquisite olive oil which those vases often contained.

One affectionately told story about Peisistratus describes his random meeting with a poor farmer, working a barren field on the slopes of Mount Hymettus overlooking Athens. According to Aristotle, this happened shortly after the ruler had imposed a flat tax, which may have been 5 per cent or 10 per cent, on all farms. To the strongman's question about what he was producing, the farmer replied: 'Nothing but stones, and I suppose Peisistratus will be wanting his percentage.' The weary peasant's blunt honesty impressed his political master, who duly relieved him of his tax obligations. The story is in tune with posterity's generally positive view of an untyrannical tyrant who combined administrative skill with common sense.

Peisistratus worked diligently at knitting Athens and the Attica region together as a single political and cultural space. Sometime in the mid-sixth century BCE, it was decided that the annual, city-focused celebration of the goddess Athena would be upgraded, once every four years, into a magnificent festival, which like the Olympics would be pan-Hellenic, in other words open to the whole Greek world. The Panathenaic festival would embrace sports, dance, song and eye-catching processions, culminating on the Acropolis. The change probably happened shortly before Peisistratus took supreme power, but he certainly helped it along and, with his eye for public spectacle, used it to boost the city's prestige.

Religious and folk traditions formerly practised on the region's outer edge were brought to the heart of the city. One of the most fateful moves was the transfer to Athens of the cult of Dionysus, god of wine and intoxication. The original locus of this exuberant deity was a village called Eleutherae on the boundary between Attica and the neighbouring region of Boeotia. His wooden statue was transferred to Athens, and the peasant rituals and songs which celebrated the god were moved to a newly constructed temple of Dionysus on the slopes of the Acropolis. Somewhere in the course of this transfer, a bawdy rural carnival began to metamorphose into one of the great achievements of Greek civilization: theatrical works of ever greater sophistication, complete with hauntingly beautiful poetry and the interplay of sharply drawn characters which can still electrify a modern audience.

Whether or not Peisistratus deserves his reputation as one of history's more benign tyrants, his rule apparently did nothing to impede, and probably did much to encourage, the city's development as a promising vanguard of the Greek world. But while he is fondly remembered, the events that unfolded in the two decades after his death around 527 BCE are recalled with exaggerated horror. Effective power passed to his sons, principally the older one, Hippias, and to a lesser extent the younger one, Hipparchus. In some mysterious way, this family-based administration coexisted, at least for a dozen years, with the progressive political and legal institutions which Solon had established. However, during the Panathenaic festival of 514 BCE there was an attack on the pair in which Hipparchus was killed. During the last four years of power that remained to him, Hippias was embittered, vengeful and – perhaps for the first time – really tyrannical. The two assassins did not fare much better. The younger one, Harmodius, was killed in the initial scuffle; his accomplice Aristogeiton was arrested, tortured and died in custody.

Those are the bare facts, and around these facts a myth developed about the two supremely brave characters who had sacrificed themselves to liberate Athens from despotism. For at least six

centuries, statues of Harmodius and Aristogeiton stood prominently
in the Agora or marketplace of the city. These defiant nude figures,
each brandishing a sword, were fashioned by a top sculptor with
all the skill of the so-called Severe Style, the early classical form of
Greek sculpture which combined fluid and lifelike body movement
with austere facial expressions. When the originals were stolen,
they were instantly replaced by copies. The pair were considered
indispensable torchbearers of Athenian freedom, lauded in poetry
and song as well as fashioned in stone.

Their real story is told in clinical detail by Thucydides, the master
of historical narrative who is best known for recounting the events
of his own era, 100 years later. In an abrupt but vivid flashback,
Thucydides explains what he believes to have happened to Hippias
and Hipparchus. In his view, homoerotic passion, as much as any
disinterested belief in freedom, lay behind the clash of arms that
marred the festival of 514 BCE. With a cold rationalist's disdain
for myths, the historian says he feels compelled to tell the truth
because 'the Athenians are no better than other people at producing
accurate information about their own dictators or the facts of their
own history'.

Harmodius, the historian explains, was a 'most beautiful young
man in the flower of his youth', and Hipparchus conceived a passion
for him. This upset Aristogeiton, a 'man of the middle class' who
was already the lover of Harmodius. Hipparchus, for his part, was
exasperated by the youth's indifference to his advances. He showed
his frustration by delivering a peevish insult to the young man's
family: this consisted of inviting his sister to take part in a public
procession and then disinviting her at the last moment. All this
served to redouble the two lovers' dislike of the city's ruling brothers,
and they gathered up some supporters to make an assassination bid
during the city's most important festival, the Panathenaic one. Their
initial target was Hippias, but at the last moment they decided to
attack Hipparchus, the man they really hated. The partners fell on
him without a thought for their safety, 'acting entirely under the

impulse of rage caused, in the one case by love and in the other by wounded pride'. Hipparchus died instantly, and so did the younger assassin. Aristogeiton managed to escape briefly but 'he was arrested later and died no easy death'.

What happened next could be dismissed as one more easily forgettable episode in a power struggle between the leading families of Attica, a struggle in which ordinary folk were little more than bystanders. But in its final act, the battle for power took a turn which transformed Athens into a state that was quite unlike any other in its ethos and organization.

First, Hippias really did start to behave more like a tyrant as he lashed out, grief-stricken and paranoid, in all directions. Among the targets of his wrath was an erstwhile ally, Kleisthenes, and his fellow members of the Alkmeonid clan. They were expelled from Athens. But a dynasty so wealthy and well-connected could not simply be written out of the Athenian plot. These aristocratic refugees settled near the shrine at Delphi, home of an oracle whose pronouncements were followed with awe across the Hellenic world. Like many a religious institution over the centuries, the oracle combined an extraordinary mystique, a sense of being connected to transcendental realities, with a hard-nosed political edge.

The Alkmeonids won friends in Delphi by using their money to rebuild the temple after a fire. The oracle showed her gratitude by deploying all her influence to encourage the greatest military power in the Greek world to intervene in Athenian affairs and enable the Alkmeonids to march back home.

That power was Sparta, a town on the Eurotas river in the region of Laconia in the southern Peloponnese. Sparta is remembered in history as a counterpoint to the free, extrovert and creative spirit of Athens. With due allowance for the fact that most of our information comes from hostile outsiders, Sparta was an extraordinarily tough and war-obsessed place, though it was not completely without refinement. A very rough modern parallel might be eighteenth-century Prussia.

Where the ethos of Athens was innovative, flighty, irreverent and quick-witted, Sparta was a stolid armed camp, whose male subjects seemingly had no other purpose in life but to train for, and then to wage, war. From the age of seven through adulthood, boys and men were expected to spend most of their lives in the barracks, hardening their bodies and enduring endless tests of their physical and psychological endurance. Even married men were allowed only limited contact with their wives. Perhaps a redeeming feature of the Spartan system was the fact that the city's women had to develop a measure of independence. More than in other city-states, women took part in athletic contests and gymnastics. It was, after all, vital that they be fit enough to breed healthy soldiers.

The task of providing food and other basic necessities was assigned to the subject peoples or helots, inhabitants of the neighbouring regions of Laconia and Messenia, who lived in a kind of permanent bondage. Sparta had no economy or even monetary system to speak of, and no interest in earning money through exports.

Yet Sparta was not exactly a totalitarian state: there was some separation of power. It had two kings and five annually elected ephors who were supposed to represent the public interest and sometimes act as a counterweight to the monarchs. So decision-making was not a simple process. Yet the decisions that needed taking usually concerned the use of force, whether against rival cities in the peninsula or against the unruly helots.

Sparta was on a permanent war footing but it was not expansionist. On the contrary, fear of rebellion among the helots made the city's leaders rather wary of sending their best soldiers to distant places. But in the final years of the sixth century BCE, Sparta had a king who was prepared, within prudent limits, to march out of the city and come to the aid of fellow authoritarians. His name was Kleomenes. As far as we can tell, he was partly inspired by the advice of the Delphic oracle (who had developed a mysterious habit of preceding all other advice with the words 'first, free the Athenians') and partly by some ancient friendship with the Athenians' oldest dynasty.

The Spartan monarch agreed to make common cause with Kleisthenes, the head of the Alkmeonid family, against an increasingly deranged Hippias. The first attempt was driven back, thanks to some horsemen whom Hippias managed to recruit from northern Greece. Then there was a second, more serious, incursion in 510 BCE, and Hippias was forced to take refuge in the sacred precincts on the Acropolis, where attackers could not touch him. But the tyrant now made a foolish mistake. He tried to spirit his five children away to safety, only to see them captured by his enemies, who duly forced him to negotiate surrender terms and leave the city. Hippias took refuge in a town on the north-western coast of Anatolia called Sigeum, which means silent place.

So the grandest Athenian family, with Kleisthenes at its helm, had returned from exile, but it was by no means clear what the consequences would be for the city's political development. Under Peisistratus and his sons, there had been an odd mixture of tyranny and democratic institutions which had somehow worked, as the city expanded and prospered. Or at least it had worked until the tyranny part became unbearable because Hippias had turned paranoid.

In this confused situation, Kleisthenes soon found he had a rival who wanted to turn the political clock back – this was a certain Isagoras, who managed to secure election as one of the city's archons in 508 BCE and set about concentrating political power in fewer hands. He tried to reduce the number of full citizens, reversing the visionary efforts of Solon to make the city an attractive haven that would welcome and enfranchise anybody with practical and artistic skills. Kleisthenes objected and civil war loomed. Isagoras represented old money which feared newcomers and upstarts; his adversary had even bluer blood but was more open to change.

Once again, the Spartan king was drawn into the city's affairs, and predictably enough he took the hard-line side. Kleomenes and Isagoras made a joint drive to throw out the entire Alkmeonid clan, some 700 households. The despotic pair then tried to secure the abolition of the more-or-less democratic council which had been established by Solon to advise the assembly. But at this point, there was a furious reaction among the ordinary citizens of Athens, doubtless including many of the small traders and merchants who had benefited from the city's expansion.

The rebels confined Isagoras and his Spartan supporters to the Acropolis, where the priestess of Athena had harsh words for the visiting monarch, when he approached: 'Spartan stranger, go back. Do not enter the holy place.' The Spartans were trained not to fear other mortals but they were deeply religious. The king eventually abandoned the holy place and negotiated a safe withdrawal for himself and his forces.

That left Kleisthenes in control. History does not tell us much about the personality of this man, but it credits him with extraordinary achievements. He laid the foundations of a deep, democratic change that would regulate the city's affairs during a century of dazzling achievement. His biggest reform was an ingenious piece of political engineering, which served to consolidate the population of Attica and foster a sense of overlapping loyalty to clan, locality and city. Previously the city had four tribes. Now the population was divided into ten tribes, each claiming notional descent from some prehistoric Athenian hero. The tribes did not represent compact pieces of territory. Each one contained members from the three parts of Attica whose feuds had been a perpetual source of instability: the coast, the hilly interior and the city. Each of the new tribes was responsible for mustering its own fighting forces as well as contestants in sporting and cultural festivals. Artificial as they were, these new units rapidly became a strong focus of loyalty.

The region was also divided into 140 localities or demes. Each deme (*demos* in Greek*) had its own mini-assembly which handled local affairs, and was responsible for registering citizens. An Athenian

---

* The word can also refer to the entire body of male citizens of the Athenian city-state.

citizen would henceforth owe loyalty to his deme, his tribe and ultimately to the city, which included its beautiful environs.

Meanwhile the advisory council was expanded from 400 to 500 members, each of the ten tribes supplying a contingent of fifty citizens. In the course of the year, the tribal delegations would take turns to manage the assembly's business. Every afternoon, the delegation would choose one of its number to take formal responsibility for the assembly's business the following day. Nobody could perform this office twice. As a result, thousands of ordinary Athenians gained experience of managing the state's affairs, both ceremonially and in more practical ways.

Those, at least, are some of the features of the so-called Kleisthenic democracy when it was working at full tilt in the early fifth century BCE. Nobody can be sure whether all these changes were conceived and successfully executed by Kleisthenes himself. What seems clear is that despite his own privileged background, he set in motion an effort to involve ordinary men in charting their community's future. At a stretch, his reforms might be compared with the actions of Britain's Tories, led by Benjamin Disraeli, who in 1867 unexpectedly stole the clothes of their Liberal opponents by enfranchising nearly a million working men. There are moments in politics when only the most privileged feel secure enough to share power with others. Whatever may have motivated Kleisthenes, he earned himself a place in history.

## 2

# Victories of Brilliance
## 500–480 BCE

*Persia's emergence as a threat to Athens – the role of Athens in
backing the Ionian Greeks – the first Persian invasion of Greece
– Miltiades masterminds Athenian victory over a superior
Persian force at Marathon, 490 BCE – Xerxes and the second
Persian invasion of Greece, 480 BCE – on the advice of the naval
commander Themistocles, Athens invests in building warships – the
Athenians abandon their city to be sacked by Xerxes –Themistocles
lures the Persian fleet into the strait of Salamis, where it is defeated*

I n the Greek mind, the Medes and Persians were a single nation,
and that was almost true. A great, growing empire burst into
existence around 550 BCE when Cyrus, a Persian prince of the
Achaemenid dynasty, rose up against the Medes, who were the
dominant power in his corner of south-west Asia. Cyrus captured
the Medean capital, Ectabana, proclaimed himself heir to the
throne, and took over the prosecution of the wars which the
Medes had been waging against their other neighbours. He and
his generals were soon fighting successfully on many fronts. They
had a remarkable capacity for assembling multinational coalitions
and deploying them across impressive distances.

As their forces stormed over the known world, the Persians
were exasperated by the Greeks, especially the Athenians. The
conquerors found themselves facing adversaries who were talented,
fickle, hopelessly divided among themselves and yet difficult to

subdue. They had no obvious technological advantage, yet they were unwilling to bow down before the juggernaut of Persian might. As the Persians quickly noticed, individual Greek cities, and indeed individual Greeks, were prepared to bargain with almost anybody if it seemed expedient. But wherever it could be avoided, the Greeks were unwilling to place themselves under the absolute authority of the Persian king, even when relatively generous terms were on offer.

Among the first places targeted by Cyrus was Lydia, whose king Croesus had parleyed so meaningfully with Solon, the wise Athenian. That in turned created ferment a little further to the west, in the Greek cities on the Aegean coast of Anatolia: beautiful, vibrant places like Miletus and Ephesus where powerful thinkers had begun to ask fundamental questions about the nature of the universe. The most important of these cities were inhabited by Ionian Greeks, who shared a dialect and some collective memories and characteristics, including lightness and freedom of spirit, with the Athenians – who were likewise proud to call themselves Ionian.

As his forces ploughed westwards, Cyrus called on the Ionian Greeks to help him by rising up against Lydia, under whose loose domination they had lived. The Ionians refused and they faced the wrath of Cyrus when his campaign succeeded. Still proud, the Ionians asked Cyrus if they might live under his rule, but semi-autonomously. The Persian was in no mood for such concessions, and set about subduing the Ionian cities one by one. The first object of his wrath was the port of Phocaea, whose inhabitants responded with Greek flexibility by migrating en masse to southern Italy and Corsica, where they had already established settlements, and in some cases sailing on to the Greek colony of Massilia (modern Marseilles) on the Mediterranean coast of France.

In 499 BCE, the Ionian Greeks rose up against their Persian overlords. The catalyst for this rebellion was an act of opportunism by a Greek ruler who wielded local power in the city of Miletus, one of the most prosperous of the Ionian states. Aristagoras persuaded his Persian masters that the island of Naxos, in the middle of the

Aegean Sea, might present an easy prey. But an attack on the island failed, leaving its mastermind exposed. Rather than face the consequences of Persian disappointment, Aristagoras called on all his fellow Ionians to make a bid for freedom.

This drew the newly established semi-democracy of Athens into a fateful confrontation with its eastern neighbours. As part of their campaign for freedom, the Ionians crossed the Aegean and tried to rally support from their fellow Greeks on the mainland. The Spartans, wary of far-flung expeditions, refused. Athens, always proud of its Ionian connections, responded positively, and initially the results were spectacular. A joint force of Ionians, Athenians and fighters from Eretria on the island of Euboea marched eastwards in 498 BCE and burned the city of Sardis, the once-illustrious capital which the Persians had recently wrested from the Lydians. That gave the Persians a grievance against Athens which they were determined to avenge. Fighting over the Ionian states raged on for another six years, culminating in a victory for the Persians which left them in comfortable control of the Ionian region, and longing to teach Athens and its Eretrian allies a hard lesson.

All this helps to explain the highly precarious conditions in which the Athenian democratic experiment lived out its first few years. Athens was under threat, and it was far from clear that it had the means to fight back. It was growing steadily in its cultural confidence and commercial success, but it was by no means the pre-eminent military power in the Greek world. That was clearly Sparta. Yet Athens was committed to a political system which the austere rulers of Sparta saw as a permanent provocation.

As the fifth century BCE dawned, dominion over the Persian empire was firmly in the hands of Darius, who was strictly speaking a usurper but enjoyed absolute personal authority over his realm. Stretching as far east as India and as far west as the Danube, it also included Egypt, where the previous ruler, Cambyses, had perished mysteriously. Darius, a distant cousin of Cambyses, had already demonstrated his skill as a power broker by splitting the vast Persian imperium into twenty administrative units while ensuring that his own ultimate power was always respected. To such a confident monarch, the stubborn resistance of certain Greeks seemed like a manageable problem, an irritating detail.

An initial attempt by Darius to subdue the Greek-speaking world enjoyed some success in 491 BCE when his son-in-law Mardonius brought to heel the northern lands of Macedonia and Thrace; but his fleet was destroyed in a storm off Mount Athos, the peninsula in north-eastern Greece that is now famous for its Christian monasteries.

The following year, Darius sent ambassadors to every city in Greece, demanding a formal act of submission. The only ones to refuse were Athens and Sparta, the latter responding by slaying the envoys and virtually declaring war on Persia. Darius felt that his honour depended on bringing these impertinent cities to heel – especially Athens, which had sent twenty ships to join the Ionian revolt, and its Eretrian neighbours, who had taken part in the sacking of Sardis, including its holiest shrines.

In the summer of 490 BCE, a Persian force of warships, cavalry and spear-wielding infantry made its way across the Aegean. It was led by Datis, a Medean nobleman, and Artaphernes, nephew of King Darius. The expedition sent some careful political signals to the various cities and islands of Greece. On the supremely holy island of Delos, birthplace of Apollo and Artemis, Datis offered elaborate sacrifices to Apollo. Although he had a mission to punish the Greeks for their acts of sacrilege at Sardis, he clearly thought it prudent, at this stage anyway, to show respect for Greek religion. Those sacrifices may have had the particular benefit of impressing the priestess of Apollo in Delphi and making her think better of the Persians.

Arriving on the island of Euboea, the expeditionary force began flexing its muscles. It stopped at the port of Karystos, demanded obeisance and quickly subdued the place by force when no surrender was forthcoming. In Eretria, the invaders found a city riven by internal divisions over whether it was worth putting up a fight. After a week-long siege, the defenders gave up the struggle and, as Herodotus puts it, the Persians 'entered the city and plundered and burned the temples, in revenge for the temples that were burned in Sardis; moreover, they enslaved the townspeople, according to Darius' command'. At this point Athens stood virtually alone. The invaders were advised on their route by none other than Hippias, the disgraced Athenian tyrant, who was now a pathetic, scheming old man. Both Hippias and his Persian friends seemed to be confident that they would find sympathizers among the Athenian population, people who looked back with nostalgia to the stable rule of Hippias' father Peisistratus.

Hippias suggested that Marathon, a sickle-shaped bay on the east coast of Attica, would be a good place to land. This was the region which his father had regarded as home, and it was here that Peisistratus had made one of his storming returns to his homeland. To this day, it remains a remarkably quiet, beautiful and inspiring stretch of coast, about 40 kilometres north of Athens and adjoining some rich wetlands which conservationists have battled to preserve.

But the omens for a fresh comeback were poor. As Hippias guided the Persians and their horses onto the beach, there was a grotesque incident. The old man 'happened to sneeze and cough more violently than usual... most of his teeth were loose, and he lost one of them by force of his cough. It fell into the sand and he expended much effort in looking for it but the tooth could not be found.' To the embittered veteran, it was a sign that 'this land is not ours and we will not be able to subdue... my tooth holds whatever share of it is mine'.

The Persians wrongly thought they were getting good advice, from an insider, about the affairs of Athens. The Athenians, meanwhile, received some better advice from a man who understood the Persian mentality very well. Their most important commander had served as an officer in the service of Persia. His name was Miltiades. His uncle and namesake had founded an Athenian colony in the north-eastern Aegean, near the place that enters twentieth-century history as Gallipoli. The younger Miltiades took over the family's fiefdom but in 513 BCE found himself swept up in Darius' invasion of south-eastern Europe and was commissioned by the Persian-led army. One of the Persians' gifts was being able to harness soldiers and officers of many nationalities.

But neither Miltiades nor the Greek-born officers with him were ever reliable servants of the Persian monarch. At a time when the Persians were storming northwards over the Danube, pursuing a tribe called the Scythians, some of their Greek subordinates conceived a plot to leave the Persians stranded by blocking the bridge over the great river which now divides Romania from Bulgaria. The plot was abortive, but it left the Persians wary of relying on Greek help.

Miltiades was part of that plot, or at any rate so he insisted when he decided to return to his native Athens and don Greek colours again. In 490 BCE he was one of the ten men with the rank of 'general' or *strategos* elected by the citizens under the elaborate democratic arrangements which were now receiving their first real test. (At least in ceremonial terms, there was another military figure who ranked even higher than the ten; that was the 'war archon' or magistrate responsible for military affairs. In the year 490 BCE it was Callimachus.) This large panel of commanders was divided over whether it was wise to fend off the invaders at their point of embarkation. Miltiades felt it was the right course, and he was charismatic enough to persuade the others of his view.

After a five-day standoff, the two armies clashed. What we know of the encounter can be summed up in a few lines. The Athenians were laden with protective and defensive metal: heavy armour and shields, as well as spears and a shortish sword. The Persians were lighter on their feet and they were accomplished archers. Miltiades decreed that the Athenian troops should be thin in the centre while thicker on the two wings. Having lined up as instructed, the Athenians astonished the Persians by padding towards them in a measured run. This was a feat of endurance given the weight of their kit, but it was the best way to dodge the Persian arrows. In the words of Herodotus, 'the Persians saw them running to attack and prepared to receive them, thinking the Athenians absolutely crazy, since they saw how few they were and how they ran so fast without either cavalry or archers'.

As Miltiades fully expected, the centre of his army's line broke, giving the Persians an illusion of victory. At that point the two wings closed in on the invaders, sending them fleeing for safety, which was nowhere to be found. Some of the panic-stricken Persians were trapped in a marsh. Most tried to make a dash back to their ships with the Athenians in hot pursuit. The Greeks showed desperate courage as they tried to seize hold of the vessels with their bare hands. By now a still-formidable Persian force, complete with cavalry, had sailed out of Marathon and was heading southwards to Cape Sounion. They were confident, apparently, of landing on the western side of Attica and attacking a city which would be undefended, or perhaps even dominated by people who were ready for a change of regime.

Such was the Athenians' triumph at Marathon that they were able to frustrate all the invaders' hopes. An apocryphal story holds that a fleet-footed messenger, Pheidippides, dashed from the battlefield to the capital, a distance of 35 kilometres, uttered the word *Nikomen* – 'we are victorious' – and immediately died from exhaustion. It is that legendary sprint that has given the world its most famous long-distance run, standardized at 42 kilometres.

In fact it was not one runner but the whole army that hurried back to Athens and reasserted control of the city, in time to deter the Persians from coming ashore from the west. The invaders had hoped they could confuse and overpower the Athenians by landing first on one side of the city and then the other; the Athenians demonstrated to the world, including their astonished fellow Hellenes, that their febrile democracy could defend itself.

There are still unanswered questions about Marathon. One of the most keenly debated is why the battle finally started when it did after five days of standoff. There are two theories, both of which involve secret signals. One holds that the Ionian Greeks who were serving the Persian forces sent a clandestine message of encouragement to their Athenian kinsmen as soon as the Persian cavalry sailed away to the south. Another holds that people in Athens who liked the Persians, because they wanted the return of Hippias and his clan, sent a message of support to the invaders in the form of a flashlight or reflection from the mountain overlooking the beach.

Later generations associated Marathon with two heroic runs. One was that apocryphal dash back to Athens to bring news of the victory. The other, better attested feat is attributed to the same runner, Pheidippides, and it occurred before the great battle. According to Herodotus, he pounded along the mountain road from Athens to Sparta, a journey of 250 kilometres, to request help from the mighty city. The Spartans retorted that they could not set out for several days, because of a religious festival that would culminate only when the moon was full. It may have been an excuse, though the Spartans did take their religion very seriously. Pheidippides said he had encountered a more powerful helper along the route: the goat-footed god Pan, who pledged to aid the Athenians if they paid him proper respect. After the battle, Pan was duly rewarded with a shrine under the Acropolis and an annual ceremony and race in his honour. Behind this story lie two definite facts. For whatever reason, Sparta did decline to provide timely help to the Athenians. This left them to fight almost alone, apart from a small, gallant contingent from the town of Plataea. It is also true that the Athenians held Pan in high esteem, crediting him with the ability to inspire irrational dread or 'panic' in his adversaries.

A deeper point about the Marathon story is that there was only one indisputably heroic piece of running: the purposeful jog of the foot soldiers, proud self-sufficient citizens who had supplied their own clanking kit, as they moved towards a hail of skilfully directed arrows. Only by visiting the beach and seeing the very small space in which the whole drama unfolded is it possible to get a sense of the defenders' courage. The most visible remnant of the battle is a mound or tumulus containing the remains of the 192 Athenian war dead. It is the simplest but most eloquent of memorials, and it helps to explain why, for another two generations or so, a city bristling with talent in every field would continue to regard service at Marathon as the height of civic achievement.

Despite that astonishing victory, the threat to Athens from the eastern empire by no means abated. Only a decade later, an array of Greek forces, dominated by Athenians, would once again confront a formidable and numerically superior force of Persians. This time the fighting occurred at sea, and the geopolitical stakes were even higher. The Persian coalition was even larger but there was at least a semblance of Greek unity, with Sparta and its closest friends more or less lined up with Athens in defence of Greece.

In the run-up to that second confrontation, tumultuous events took place in both Athens and Persia. The Athenians began building a new temple on the Parthenon, offering fresh thanks to their principal divine guardian, Athena, for favouring their cause during the battle on the beach. Whatever the contribution of Pan, the wise lady would always be their main protectress. A second goddess who needed thanking was Artemis, the huntress: a temple to her was duly erected on the Ilisos river on the eastern side of Athens. Every September some five hundred goats would be sacrificed there in gratitude for Marathon. The building would remain an important landmark for twenty-three centuries.

Success at Marathon did not, however, persuade the city's quarrelsome citizens to show any deference to a human leader. Logically, the victory should have guaranteed the position of Miltiades as a revered elder statesman. Instead, he found himself prosecuted and fined so heavily that he was nearly bankrupted.

In Persia, a new ruler took power: Xerxes, the son of Darius.

He had to suppress a rebellion in Egypt before bringing to Greece an expeditionary force of unprecedented size. Comfortably in command of the world's largest empire, he was determined to make this small, stony piece of terrain yield to his power. Against Greek stubbornness, he pitted not only wealth and firepower but a remarkable capacity for logistics and engineering which made it possible to transport men, horses and kit across land and water. A bridge of ships was assembled to straddle the Hellespont, the narrow strait separating Anatolia from the Gallipoli peninsula at the southern extremity of eastern Thrace. Then, some 200 kilometres to the west, in the region of Chalkidike, a canal was dug through one of the three fingers of land that jut southwards into the Aegean.

Advancing towards Athens, in two places the Persian invaders encountered stiffer resistance than they were expecting. One was at the strategic mountain pass known as Thermopylae, where a force led by Leonidas, king of Sparta, put up a kind of kamikaze defence in which hundreds of soldiers sacrificed their lives in the hope of slowing the invaders' progress. Similar acts of self-sacrifice were carried out in the very same terrain by Allied forces in 1941 as they made a fighting retreat in the face of the Nazis' advance on Athens.

In August 480 BCE, while Leonidas was making his last stand, there was a naval encounter over three days – the battle of Artemisium, named for a cape in northern Euboea – whose end result could be called a costly draw. On the second day, a tempest largely wrecked a Persian detachment which was heading south along the island's eastern coast. The following day the two sides clashed again with heavy losses on both sides, and the Greek contingent resolved to retreat southwards and lure the battered enemy into a trap.

Many observers of the battle of Artemisium must have been astonished by how relatively well the Athenian-led fleet was performing against invaders who, with due allowance for storm losses, were still numerically superior. But there was a fresh element in the equation. Once again, the emergent Athenian democracy benefited from the services of a far-sighted strategist who was an outsider in the city's ruling circles. The new man of the hour was Themistocles, a fickle, impatient character with an agile mind who had one overwhelming conviction: the vital importance of maritime power.

Given that Athens had grown rich from marine commerce, Themistocles held that Athens must now be prepared to defend its freedom to trade, and its very existence, against all comers by building up a great navy. In 483 BCE a new seam was discovered in the silver mines in the south-east of Attica. Amid furious political arguments, Themistocles persuaded the city to spend this windfall not on handouts but on a hectic programme of naval construction. The vessels in question were triremes, following a design which had become the standard for warships across the eastern Mediterranean. The concept may have been of Greek origin, or it may have come from the Phoenicians, adept seafarers who now served the Persian monarch.

The construction of these glorious ships is one of the many aspects of ancient Greece about which information abounds, but certainty eludes us. The name reflects the three banks of oars in which the rowers, numbering 170 in total, sat and sweated. By the time of its decisive encounter with the Persians, Athens was able to field 180 triremes out of a total Greek fleet of just over 300. The Persian fleet was said to have numbered 1,200 such vessels, of which between a third and half were probably lost off Euboea before it closed in on the home waters of Athens.

No wreck of a trireme has ever been found. We do not know where the triremes which defended Athens were built. We do, however, know where they were kept, and that is not a trivial piece of information. A Danish-Greek archaeological project has identified the remains of shipsheds, occupying 100,000 square metres or so, in the three natural harbours of Piraeus. Some of the vestiges are hidden by modern apartment buildings, and some lie under the waters of the Zea yacht marina. But thanks to one of the more spectacular archaeological finds of recent times in the Athens area, we now have a sense of the huge civic effort required not just to make these ships but to keep them safe in peacetime from intense heat, waterlogging or mollusc infestation – any of which could destroy them rapidly.

Moreover, illustrations on vases tell us a lot about ancient shipping, as do written descriptions. These enabled a group of Greek and British enthusiasts to construct, in the mid-1980s, a replica trireme named *Olympias* which demonstrated the speed and flexibility of such vessels. They used sails to get from island to island, but under battle conditions they manoeuvred by oar power alone. One trireme could destroy another by using its giant metal beak to ram the enemy ship and break it up. This required dextrous oarsmanship, which soon became an Athenian strong point.

As the Persians sailed southwards after Artemisium, the residents of Athens responded to the looming invasion with an act of self-sacrifice and self-discipline comparable to that of the Russians who abandoned Moscow as Napoleon approached in 1812. Themistocles persuaded the great majority of the population of Athens to leave their city and take shelter on the islands of Salamis and Aegina, or in the port of Troezen, which lies south-west of Athens across the Saronic Gulf. To bring this off, according to Herodotus, the great naval strategist had to convince his fellow citizens to accept his own interpretation of an enigmatic pronouncement by the priestess at Delphi. Although great pain and loss was looming for the Athenians, she said, a 'wooden wall' would keep them safe. Themistocles understood the prophecy to mean that citizens would be protected not by any terrestrial defences, but by his newly built fleet.

But it is clear that the exodus did not involve the entire population. Some may have insisted on staying behind, and some may have been told to do so. In the somewhat confused but still revealing account left by Herodotus, it seems that several categories of people remained in and around the Acropolis as the Persians moved in to trash the sacred citadel. There were the priestesses who guarded the holiest places, although one of the most sacred objects, a wooden statue of Athena, was taken away. There were also diehard defenders who did not believe Themistocles' interpretation of the wooden-wall prophecy. And as in all desperate evacuations, there must have been some who lacked the physical strength to flee.

Xerxes led the assault on Athens. He told his soldiers to take up positions on the Areopagus hill, just to the west of the Acropolis. The skilful Persian archers wrapped rough fibre round their arrows, ignited them and propelled them towards the sacred citadel, in the hope of setting fire to the wooden barricade. But the Rock had determined defenders, who tossed stones and pieces of marble, presumably from the unfinished construction work, at anyone who approached. Finally a number of Persians scaled the Rock from the vicinity of the cave-sanctuary of Aglaurus, a route that would often serve as a passage to the city's holiest heights. Some defenders threw themselves off the Rock in despair; others sought hiding places.

Having reached this supposedly inaccessible plateau, the Persians slaughtered those they found there, burned buildings and smashed statues indiscriminately. The German archaeologists who dug over the place in the nineteenth century invented the term *Perserschutt* or 'Persian rubble' to describe the remnants of this orgy of destruction, which included many fine pieces of black- and red-figure pottery dedicated to Athena. Anything made out of gold, silver or bronze was melted down or, where possible, taken to Persia.

In the super-holy place where Athena and Poseidon had fought their contest to be supreme protector of the city, the invaders showed little respect; they ignited the olive tree which was supposed to have sprung up at the goddess' behest. How did they know their way around the Acropolis? Herodotus is adamant that among the Persian army, there were bitter Athenians who still felt nostalgia for the days of Peisistratus and his sons. Apparently they saw a foreign invasion as the best way of restoring their own domination over the city.

Whether it was because of his own subliminal respect for all things sacred, or whether in deference to his Athenian friends, Xerxes seems to have had a moment of self-doubt. Perhaps these acts of defilement had gone too far; perhaps he felt a need to re-establish the sacred character of the Rock. As Herodotus tells us, he summoned the Athenian exiles who accompanied him and asked them to go up to the Acropolis and perform sacrifices in the time-honoured way. These returning exiles soon had the sense that the divine forces which had always attended this numinous place still lingered here:

> It happened that the olive tree was burned by the barbarians with the rest of the sacred precinct, but on the day after its incineration, when the Athenians ordered by the king went up to the holy precinct, they saw a shoot of about a cubit's length had sprung from the stump.

Meanwhile, news of the great citadel's destruction had an electrifying effect on the Greek forces that were lining up not far away to resist the Persian advance by land and sea. But there were differences over tactics. To commanders from the Peloponnese, it no longer seemed worthwhile to fight for Athens or even for its immediate environs. Their interest lay in making a last stand at the isthmus that connected their great tooth-shaped peninsula with the rest of Greece. This collapse of Hellenic unity horrified Themistocles. In a series of frantic deliberations with his fellow Greeks, he used all his powers of persuasion, manipulation and trickery to cajole them into changing their minds.

For the Athenian commander, it was essential to persuade both the Persians and his fellow Hellenes to fight in the narrow strait which divides the island of Salamis from the mainland. As with Marathon, fighting in a confined space would give the defenders an advantage. Like modern Marathon, modern Salamis is an under-valued visitor attraction, frequented by Athenians of modest means but neglected by tour operators. However, anyone who sets foot on the island, reachable by a shuttle ferry from a grimy industrial part of Piraeus, can instantly see why Themistocles wanted to entice the Persians into that narrow stretch of water.

He did so with what military planners call a psy-op – a psychological operation – that was both neat and ingenious. One of his most trusted aides, a certain Sicinnus, was sent over to the Persian camp on the mainland and delivered a message to their commanders. It was cunningly calculated:

> The Hellenes are terrified and plan to flee, and you can perform the finest deed of all if you do not allow them to escape. They do not all have the same intent and they will no longer oppose you. You will see them bickering among themselves, with some on your side and others not.

In other words, the Persians were persuaded that they could bottle up the entire quarrelsome Greek coalition by sealing the Salamis strait at both ends. They set about patrolling the eastern side of the strait, while landing forces on the tiny islet of Psyttaleia which lies in the middle. They confidently expected that bodies and wrecks would soon be washed ashore on this small speck of land. Meanwhile, Egyptian ships were sent on a circuit of the island to seal off the other entrance.

All this was good news for Themistocles. The Persians were falling into his trap, and his fellow Greeks were being placed in a situation where they had no choice but to fight. Scholars still argue over what the Persians did during the night before the great battle. Either they entered the strait in the darkness and began lining up for a clash at dawn with foes whom they believed to be demoralized and disorganized. Or they may have stayed outside the strait until daylight made it easier to navigate.

On the morning of 29 September, there was a titanic encounter between the two armadas. Xerxes observed the proceedings from a golden chair planted on Mount Aigaleo on the western side of

Athens. He was expecting to see the final triumph of the force he had laboured so hard to transport to Greece, and the final humiliation of the Greek enemy which had eluded his power. But he saw no such thing. Far from being a disorganized rabble, the Greek crews (especially the Athenian contingent which occupied the left flank) were rested and eager for a fight. The Persians were exhausted after long manoeuvring in difficult waters. The Athenians were no doubt galvanized by the sight of smoke rising from their ravaged homes. Immediately opposite the Athenians were the Phoenicians, who were the most skilled boatmen on the Persian side, but that did not faze the defenders.

Aeschylus, writing only eight years later, uses a drama to deliver the freshest and most coherent account of what happened next. A heart-stopping description of the battle is put into the mouth of a messenger, bringing the news to the horrified Persian queen, Atossa. This is the high point of his play *The Persians*, the only extant Greek tragedy to deal entirely with contemporary events rather than mythological ones.

> The night went by, and still the Greek fleet
> gave order for no secret sailing out.
> But when the white horses of the daylight
> took over the whole earth, clear to be seen,
> the first noise was the Greeks shouting for joy,
> like singing, like triumph, and then again
> echoes rebounded from the island rocks.
>
> ...There was no Greek panic in
> that solemn battle-song they chanted then,
> but battle-hunger, courage of spirit;
> the trumpet's note set everything ablaze.
> Suddenly by command their foaming oars
> beat, beat in the deep of the salt water,
> and all at once they were clear to be seen.

First the right wing in perfect order leading,
Then the whole fleet followed out after them,
and one great voice was shouting in our ears:
'Sons of the Greeks, go forward, and set free
your fathers' country and set free your sons,
your wives, the holy places of your gods,
the monuments of your own ancestors,
now is the one battle for everything.'

That morning battle hymn to Apollo has gone down in Hellenic history as an expression of wild, collective exuberance: a cry of irrational joy at the prospect of defending that which is most beautiful and precious, whatever the odds.* The words can, of course, be sceptically deconstructed. Whatever the outcome of Salamis, the wives of the Athenian citizen-warriors would not in any modern sense be free. And the money to build those freshly varnished ships had been made not by free people but by slaves toiling to extract silver.

On the other hand, the oarsmen who manned the ships, rushing at the enemy with all the strength they could muster, were free individuals in a sense that was hardly understood elsewhere in the ancient world. They were citizens with an established right to a say in their city's affairs. They were conscious participants in the chain of decisions which had led them into the waters where their community was now fighting for its life. For the sailors on the Persian side, including the Ionian Greeks, nothing like that could be said. They served at the whim of a sovereign who could be merciful or cruel.

Aeschylus describes the events that followed:

Our Persian voices answered roaring out,

---

* The most famous citation of this battle cry in modern times was by the Greek strongman General Ioannis Metaxas, as the nation's army was setting out to fight the forces of fascist Italy in Albania in 1940.

and there was no time left before the clash.
Ships smashed their bronze beaks into ships,
it was a Greek ship in the first assault
that cut away the whole towering stem
from a Phoenician, and another rammed
timber into another. Still at first
the great flood of the Persian shipping held,
but multitudes of ships crammed up together,
no help could come from one to the other,
they smashed on another with brazen beaks,
and the whole rowing fleet shattered itself.
So then the Greek fleet with a certain skill
ran inwards from a circle around us,
and the bottoms of ships were overturned,
there was no seawater in eyesight,
only wreckage and bodies of dead men,
and beaches and rocks all full of dead.
Whatever ships were left out of our fleet
rowed away in no order in panic.
The Greeks with broken oars and bits of wreck
smashed and shattered the men in the water
like tunny, like gaffed fish. One great scream
filled up all the sea's surface with lament,
until the eye of darkness took it all.

All manner of strange things happened in the heat of this terrible
battle. Herodotus acknowledges that seamen on the Persian side
were in general brave, perhaps because they knew their king was
watching. Artemisia, queen of the Persian-controlled city-state of
Halicarnassus, was probably the only female commander of a ship.
She found herself being pursued by a Greek vessel, to which she
responded by ramming one of her own side's triremes, and this
prompted the attacker to conclude she must have switched sides,
and hence to back off. Xerxes approved of this act of pretended

treachery, observing that 'my men have become women and my women men'.

The Phoenicians complained to the king that defeat reflected betrayal by their unsteady allies, the Ionian Greeks. But as he watched the fighting Xerxes came to a different conclusion. He observed that his Ionian subjects, who were experienced mariners, were fighting bravely, and executed some of the tell-tale Phoenicians.

It can be argued quite plausibly that the two central features of the Salamis story (the disinformation so artfully spread by Sicinnus, and the joyful battle cry of the Greek fleet) are nothing more than literary devices. But that does not change the central fact that Themistocles, through a mixture of ingenuity, deviousness and charisma, made sure that the battle was fought on his terms, in a place where his new navy had the best chance of prevailing. And we are surely not wrong to interpret the battle cry of the Athenians as a collective cry of confidence and determination from a newly established political community whose best days lay ahead.

Today's Salamis is a messy place, not a well-groomed historical theme park. The tumulus commemorating the battle is surrounded by large and small boat-repair yards, and the island's authorities visibly struggle to cope with the detritus left by Athenians who come for day trips or summer sojourns. Not many foreigners stay long enough to appreciate the wonderful small museum or the virgin forest in the island's south. But from any elevated point on the eastern side of the island one can look towards Athens and imagine the smoke pouring from the Acropolis, and the bodies and wreckage bobbing about in the clogged sea, and quickly gain a sense that in this place, history took a fateful turn.

# 3

# Golden Years
## 479–432 BCE

*An alliance of city-states defeats the Persians at Plataea in 479
BCE, ending the second Persian invasion of Greece – the Athenians
build defensive walls around their city – the emergence of Kimon
and then Pericles as leading Athenians – ostracism as a guide to
Athenian politics – Athenian successes in distant and local wars
– the construction of the Parthenon as a democratic project –
debates over the Parthenon frieze and its mythological meaning*

To the ordinary Athenians who faced the task of rebuilding
their city after its near-annihilation, the future must have
seemed precarious. For the children in particular, war had
left a deep and lasting trauma. They had cowered on the island of
Salamis, or in some other place of safety, watching smoke billow into
the blue Attic sky from the city's holiest rock. Doubtless some took
a private vow to restore the honour of Athens when they came of
age. In fact, they were about to enter what later generations would
regard as the height of Greek civilization, a glorious half-century
when Athens was recognized as a shining beacon among Hellenic
cities. But nobody would have guessed at the time.

Salamis had proved that the Persians, for all their wealth, numbers
and sophistication, were not unbeatable on the sea. Moreover,
Athens could confidently claim the role of leading maritime power
among the Greeks. But it took one more big battle to stave off the
immediate threat to the heart of the Hellenic world. That took place

in the summer of 479 BCE, near the Boeotian town of Plataea north of Athens. This was the place whose men had served gallantly as the sole allies of the Athenians at Marathon.

Xerxes and his entourage had limped out of Greece over the previous winter, taking many troops, but he left behind his general, Mardonius, with what seemed like enough residual strength to give his Greek enemies some well-deserved punishment. The range of forces under the command of Mardonius was impressively broad: it included soldiers from the centre and north of the Greek world (from Thebes and the surrounding region of Boeotia, plus Phokis, Thessaly and Macedonia) and horsemen from as far east as India and Bactria (modern-day Afghanistan).

Mardonius established a fortified camp in terrain that would suit his cavalry. A large Greek coalition of Spartans, Athenians and others faced them down for eleven days, and then began retreating. The Persians chased them, at which point the Greeks turned and fought, decimating the lightly armed Persian foot soldiers and killing Mardonius. Those Persians who had stayed back at the camp were surrounded and slain. The Greek retreat may have been real or feigned, but not for the first time, the Persians had overestimated the disarray in their enemy's ranks. For a couple of generations, at least, their defeat put paid to any external threat to the Greek heartland.

Furthermore, the battles of Salamis and Plataea had affirmed a sort of division of labour between Sparta and Athens. The Spartans, as the architects of the victory at Plataea, had consolidated their position as the strongest land power in Greece; the Athenians, with artful tactics at Salamis, had established their supremacy at sea. That might have been the basis for an uneasy coexistence. Some prominent figures in both cities hoped that it would be. If the two city-states had stood alone, it might have been possible for them to achieve a happy symbiosis.

But things grew harder as each place became the nucleus of a large, volatile alliance. It was inevitable that the two blocs' interests would clash. At times it was the small allies who stirred things up,

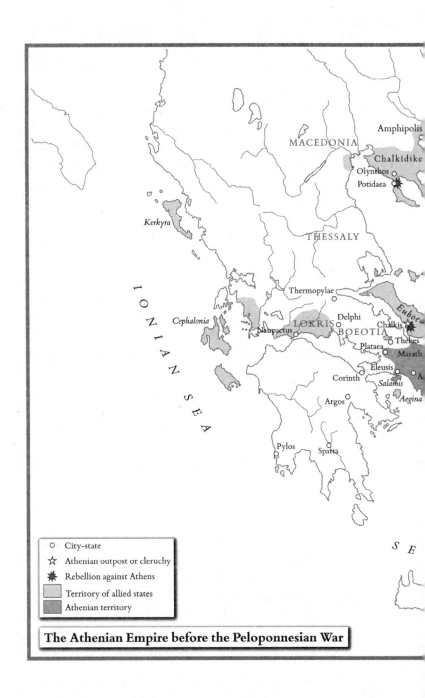

The Athenian Empire before the Peloponnesian War

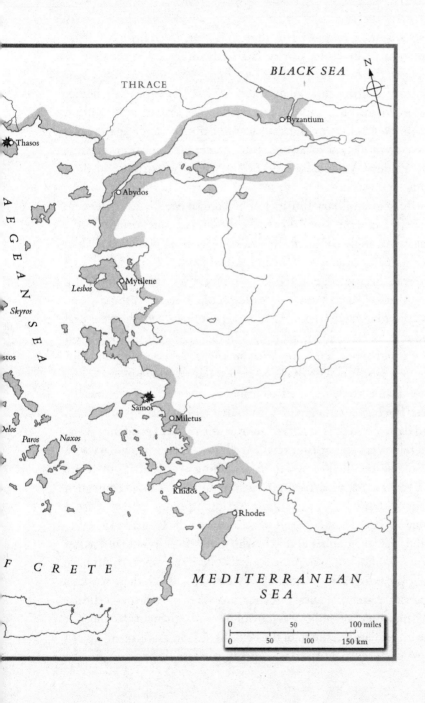

BLACK SEA

N

THRACE

○ Byzantium

✳○ Thasos

○ Abydos

*A E G E A N S E A*

*Lesbos* ○ Mytilene

*Skyros*

*stos*

✳
*Delos* ○ Samos

*Paros* *Naxos* ○ Miletus

○ Knidos

○ Rhodes

*F* *C R E T E*

*MEDITERRANEAN*
*SEA*

| 0 | | 50 | | 100 miles |
|---|---|---|---|---|
| 0 | 50 | 100 | | 150 km |

just as, some two and a half thousand years later, little countries could turn the Cold War to their advantage by manoeuvring between the American and Soviet camps. There was hardly a year in the mid-fifth century BCE when Athens was at peace, whether it was skirmishing with other Greek cities, imposing its will on disobedient allies or fighting wars of opportunity against the Persians in distant locations. But thanks to Marathon, Salamis and Plataea, Athenians could be sure that the existence of their homeland was not in question.

The city's military fortunes ebbed and flowed, and there were plenty of setbacks. But Athens, like the United States prior to 2001, was increasingly confident that its own territory was unassailable. With an ever more powerful and skilled navy, it could advance its interests on the edge of the known world without fear of being annihilated. Thanks to its increasing sense of security, the city saw an upward trend in its economic and geopolitical heft, in its cultural and intellectual achievements, and in the exuberant sophistication of its internal politics. Some Athenians felt a perverse admiration for the iron self-discipline of the Spartans, but their own lively spirits created an entirely different atmosphere, one that was irrepressibly free. The power struggles that unfolded within the city of Athens, and between Athens and its rivals over the so-called great fifty years, are relentless and at times hard to follow, even for scholars who devote academic lifetimes to investigating every detail. There are two main written sources for the period. One is the master-historian Thucydides, who was not quite a contemporary: he was born a couple of decades after the great victories over the Persians. The other is the lively biographer Plutarch, who lived 500 years later but writes with a confidence and immediacy that compel respect. Both have their prejudices. But fortunately we can cross-check these writings against the archaeological evidence uncovered over the past century.

Thucydides describes a colourful piece of Athenian chicanery in the immediate aftermath of the Persians' defeat. His account gives a sense of the deep gulf that was opening up rapidly between the two main cities of Greece. When the Spartans saw that the Athenians were rebuilding and increasing their fortifications, they became highly suspicious. Themistocles, still admired across the Greek world for his role at Salamis, went to Sparta, supposedly to offer reassurances. He then prevaricated, insisting that discussions could not begin until some other senior Athenians came to complete his delegation. This playing for time was part of a plan. As the Spartans waited, the women and children of Athens were working furiously to construct walls out of anything hard they could find, not even caring whether important works of art were being thrown in. As Thucydides puts it:

> ...even today one can see that the building was carried out in a hurry. The foundations are made of various kinds of stone, sometimes not shaped so as to fit, but slapped down just as each one was brought [to the site]... There are lots of pillars taken from tombs and fragments of sculpture combined with the rest...

Some of these 'fragments of sculpture' were discovered in 1922. They include a work known as the 'Hockey Players', a marble relief depicting two young lads using sticks with curved ends to vie for control of a ball, watched by two pairs of friends standing on either side. It is a tantalizing vignette of life around 510 BCE, and it adorned the base of a funerary statue, presumably for a wealthy young man. Other pieces of high art that were chucked into the crude masonry include a pair of sly, mysterious sphinxes, discovered only in 2002, when the Athens metro was being dug.

But to a city that was frantically trying to protect itself, the hardness of these objects was the only thing that mattered, not their beauty. The walls themselves, every bit as makeshift as Thucydides describes them, can be observed in several places in modern Athens: in the Kerameikos cemetery (where they can be compared with walls from other eras) and in the basements of ordinary modern buildings, such as a bank on Eolou Street.

When the Athenian leaders turned up in Sparta, they whispered to Themistocles that the walls were now defensible, and he conveyed this unwelcome news to the Spartans. He had made sure that some Spartans were being held hostage back in Athens, as surety for his own party's safe return. The Spartans had no choice but to accept this fait accompli, bite their lips and let their guests depart.

Behind these solid defences, the city was able to flourish and grow. The arts of ship-building and naval warfare, at which Athens excelled, were steadily refined. Performances of drama, music and dance became ever more sophisticated. Ship-building and staging cultural events had one thing in common: both required the free collaboration of hundreds of individuals, and the combination of public funds with private donations. This sort of synergy became a hallmark of the city. Meanwhile, Athens imposed its authority on scores of smaller cities, especially those in the Aegean and on the Anatolian coast, by a mixture of prestige and brute force.

Perhaps the most striking feature of Athenian life, when compared with all other states which had previously existed, was this: it really had something recognizable as open-ended political contests. Matters of policy and personnel were settled in free deliberations in which all citizens had a say. Those who wanted to hold high office or influence decision-making had to use their powers of argument in debates, and the outcome was not predetermined. The winners did not get their way by fawning on a capricious monarch or by recruiting armed claques to terrorize their opponents. Persuasion was needed, and it was anybody's guess who would be the more successful persuader. The political process was open and self-aware. Citizens conducted their affairs under certain agreed rules. It was also understood that these rules could be changed, but that too could only happen under carefully laid-down procedure.

The decades after Salamis saw some ruthless power struggles between the city's leading commanders and politicians. They were men with powerful egos and a keen sense of the wrongs inflicted on their forebears. Rivalries between great dynasties could cascade down the generations, just as they do in modern Greek politics. But these power struggles were conducted within an agreed framework, in contrast with the previous century, when would-be rulers of Athens had organized coups and invasions with foreign assistance. The political fights that followed Salamis were somehow contained within the Athenian political system. A law-based state in the modern understanding of the word was beginning to emerge.

There were several constraints on any individual who was seeking supreme power. One was the gradually growing authority of the assembly of free male citizens whose assent was needed for every important decision in internal administration or the conduct of war. (This was counterbalanced during the two decades after Salamis by the power of the Areopagus, a body of retired magistrates where old money predominated.)

The other constraint was the judicial system, which by modern standards was both laughably simple and paradoxically sophist-icated. All trials were by jury, and jurors were selected by lot from Athenian citizens who had offered their services and were paid for their trouble. The process of selecting jurors was complex enough as to make the fixing of trials almost impossible. All prosecutions were private; there was no professional class of lawyers or state prosecutors. When functioning at its best, this Athenian demo-cracy had a system of accountability which would put many of today's imperfect states to shame. While the majority of public offices were allocated by lot, important positions (especially those which involved a lot of public money) were chosen by annual election. The holders could then be held to account for the way they did their job. But this system was also open to abuse. One of the easiest ways to cut an over-mighty personality down to size was to prosecute him for misappropriating public funds, or for military incompetence, and abusive prosecutions were a popular political tactic.

The third instrument for the conduct of power struggles was ostracism: an extraordinary and fascinating feature of the Athenian system. It worked like this. At the start of each year, the electorate would vote on whether the atmosphere would be improved by throwing out one dislikeable character. If the answer was yes, there would be an unpopularity poll two months later and the person who got the most votes had to leave for ten years. The system flourished for about seventy years, coinciding with the golden age of Athenian democracy. We know of ostracism not only from ancient writers, but also from physical evidence: the pieces of broken pottery on which ordinary Athenians scratched the names of the person they wanted to see ejected from the city. The word 'ostracism' comes from the *ostraka* or sherds on which names were incised by citizens.

Over the past century, about 11,000 *ostraka* have been discovered. The great majority, nearly 9,000, were found by German archaeologists in the late 1960s in a single deposit. They were piled up in a riverbed, left dry by the wall-building project. As far as we can reconstruct the process, part of the Agora was roped off, with separate entrances for each of the ten tribes. Individuals would then toss into vessels the sherds on which they had inscribed the name of the person they wanted out. The city grandees known as archons were responsible for counting; this lent credibility to the process. Powerful individuals could organize campaigns for the ostracism of their rivals, but there was also something random and whimsical about the process. People could vote for the expulsion of anybody they liked, for any reason they liked. A few *ostraka* are beautiful. In one, the inscription is fired with the skilled techniques of black-figured pottery; another contains a snatch of poetry. But the majority are amateurish, often complete with mistakes and obscenity.

The sherds used for scribbling are of such variety that they provide a glimpse into Athenian life. There are ordinary kitchen items as well as beautifully glazed tableware; the smallest are no bigger than a thumb, the largest the size of a paperback book. There are salt cellars, parts of soup bowls, bits of a frying pan, roof tiles, small troughs. Sometimes a pot was deliberately broken, sometimes bits of pottery, fashioned centuries earlier, were picked off the ground. From written sources, we know of thirteen individuals who were ostracized, but archaeology suggests that the number of people targeted was vastly greater than that. Many of the people named on sherds are utterly unknown, but the victims and potential victims include almost all the main players in the city's power struggles. The archaeological evidence, fragmentary as it is, provides vital assistance with cross-checking the information of ancient writers.

Under intensive scrutiny, the spidery scribblings on broken pots can offer many insights into the passions and whims which informed the daily conduct of democratic life. They also help to explain how the fortunes of some key individuals fluctuated. Consider the fate of Themistocles, the strategic genius who led the Greeks to victory at Salamis. He used ostracism and then fell victim to it. An outsider to the city's elite by virtue of his humble birth and foreign mother, he exploited the procedure in the 480s BCE as he was agitating for the diversion of new silver revenues to the construction of ships. His rival, the cautious aristocrat Aristides, was ostracized in 483 BCE. Themistocles had clearly orchestrated this decision, though one of the most famous stories about ostracism, told by Plutarch, reminds us that regardless of high politics, there was always an element of caprice.

It describes an illiterate farmer who comes to the Agora and asks the first person he sees to scratch the name Aristides. The person happened to be Aristides, who politely complied and then asked the farmer what grievance he had. 'None in particular,' came the reply. 'I am simply bored with hearing that man called just.' Just or not, Aristides was recalled in the city's hour of need for defenders against the Persians, and he played an honourable role in the fighting at Salamis. But the unity between Greek city-states was short-lived, and so too was the truce between prominent Athenian individuals. For perhaps a year or two after Salamis, it seems that Themistocles, Aristides and other city grandees worked together to advance the city's interests. They collaborated in outwitting the

Spartans when building the city's makeshift walls. But it was a fragile collaboration. In 478 BCE it was Aristides who, as a representative of Athens, oversaw the ceremony on the holy island of Delos in which scores of Greek cities and islands pledged to work together to keep the Persian threat at bay, by pooling their military and financial resources. The sanctity of Delos gave an aura of solemn purpose to this enterprise. Over time it became a mechanism through which Athens exercised dominion over its allies, who were really subjects, or, in Cold War parlance, satellites.

Meanwhile, the prestige of Themistocles began declining rapidly, and within a decade he had been ostracized. The Spartans tried to implicate him in a corruption scandal in which one of their own generals was already mired. In a weird twist of fate, the great naval strategist finally sought asylum with his Persian enemies, who made him governor of the region of Magnesia in Asia Minor, which roughly corresponds to Manisa in modern Turkey.

Once again the evidence from the broken sherds is crucial. Stefan Brenne is a self-effacing German scholar who has spent twenty-five years piecing together and analysing the *ostraka* found in the Kerameikos cemetery. He believes the ostracism of Themistocles took place in 470 BCE, a year or two later than most other historians have guessed. After careful study, he believes the great majority of the *ostraka* in the Kerameikos deposit can be dated to the unpopularity contest of the previous year, in which an aristocrat called Megakles was expelled, he thinks, for the second time. So we know more about the personal politics of the year 471 BCE than for any other moment of ancient Athenian history.

In that single year, more than 100 other candidates were named, most of them gathering only a handful of hostile signatures, which presumably reflected petty personal quarrels. Although Themistocles was a candidate in 471 BCE, he only topped the unpopularity poll the following year, in Brenne's view. His work has often involved piecing together fragments that came from a single pot, perhaps deliberately broken by a group of friends who turned up to vote, often in different ways. 'When I look at an ostrakon, I can hear the voters discussing what insults to write,' says Brenne. About half the Kerameikos sherds target the blueblood Megakles, known (the graffiti suggest) for spending on horses and his pushy mother. It seems he was so obnoxious that he was thrown out twice, initially in 486 BCE. He was clearly the 'winner' in 471 BCE, but many other sherds name Themistocles, who topped the dislikeability poll a year later.

The system was at once crude and sophisticated. It dimly foreshadowed the revolving door of modern two-party systems, but only on a microscopic scale. The victim might be readmitted in a national emergency, but otherwise the penalty for returning early was death. In most ways, though, this was a mild way to release public discontent. The victim was not deemed guilty of any crime, so there was no long procedure of self-defence. He lost no assets, and could enjoy income from his property while in exile. A well-connected blueblood could live out his exile comfortably in another Greek city-state. Once the decade was over, he could re-enter politics.

One drawback of the system was that Athens risked forfeiting great talent. The exiled Themistocles defected to the Persians. But as safety valves go, ostracism worked well. The fact that it was limited to one person precluded any wider factional purge. The careful counting of the sherds by the city's archons, revered figures who rotated annually, meant that verdicts were accepted. When the system of ostracism was functioning smoothly, it served many purposes. It was a warning to all prominent types not to overreach, and to any challengers that they must tread carefully. The mood in the weeks between any decision to hold an ostracism and the vote was electric, as satirists and gossip-mongers spread salacious tales.* But once the vote was over, things calmed down.

Through the study of *ostraka*, cross-checked against written sources, we can also trace the rise and fall of the commander-politician

---

* According to Brenne, the rambunctious comedies of ancient Athens, where any bigwig could be lampooned, form a single genre with the scribblings on *ostraka*.

who dominated Athenian affairs for a couple of decades after Salamis. His name was Kimon: an earthy, unrefined character, who in Plutarch's revealing turn of phrase 'lacked entirely the cleverness and fluency of speech' which was associated with Athens and its environs. In a pattern that recurred in Athenian politics, Kimon grew up with a sense that he and his family had been wronged. His kin had done the city great service, only to be rewarded with punishment and disgrace.

Kimon's father was Miltiades, who had led the Athenians to their historic triumph at Marathon. That should have been enough to gain him a place in the city's pantheon. But instead the career of Miltiades ended very badly, because of a disastrous expedition against the island of Paros, supposedly part of a drive to punish places which had succoured the Persians. He failed to take the island, suffered a terrible leg injury and was prosecuted for treason on his return. Escaping the death penalty, he was landed with a fine of fifty talents and died in a debtor's prison, leaving the financial liability to his son. One result of all this was that, in the early stages of his career, Kimon's personal finances were quite strained. He lived with his half-sister Elpinike, and had to endure rumours that their relationship was incestuous. The household's problems eased when Elpinike married Kallias, one of the wealthiest men in Athens.

But Kimon's sense of grievance did not go away. As he struggled to rebuild the family fortunes, Kimon had another disadvantage. His mother was a Thracian princess; he carried the blood of people whom the Athens viewed as semi-barbarians. That seemed only to intensify his desire to fight real barbarians, while avoiding unnecessary quarrels with fellow Hellenes, such as the Spartans, whose austere militarism he admired. As soon as the anti-Persian alliance was sealed on Delos, Kimon began leading expeditions on the alliance's behalf that were designed to eliminate all trace of the Persian aggressor from the lands where Greeks lived, or anywhere nearby.

In Thrace, the land of his maternal forebears, he captured the town of Eion, prompting the Persian general he defeated to kill

himself and his family. Then he conquered Skyros, a small island which is vital to control of the northern Aegean, and replaced the old, piratical natives with new land-hungry Athenians. Returning to Athens, he brought with him a skeleton which was supposedly that of the city's founding hero, Theseus. A cheapish trick, some people must have said, but it enhanced his popularity among ordinary Athenian folk. His military successes, and the booty they brought in, not only eased his own financial problems but enabled plenty of humbler Athenians to grow richer too.

Although he was no great enthusiast for democracy, Kimon understood the mentality of ordinary soldiers and sailors, and made sure their interests were well served. In domestic Athenian affairs, Kimon belonged to the camp which favoured keeping intact the present political system, with the privilege it gave to established wealth. Their opponents wanted to deepen the democratic system in Athens, and enhance the distinctiveness of the city as it stood up to the non-democratic parts of the Greek world, such as Sparta. Kimon preferred arbitrary acts of generosity to any systemic change. He was not a man of refinement, though he did his bit to beautify his home city. He built a wall around a sacred olive grove which would later become Plato's Academy.

His downfall came in the late 460s BCE, when his pro-Spartan (but never treacherous) sentiments came to the fore, and caused him severe embarrassment. There was a terrible earthquake in Sparta, and the city's oppressed subjects, the unlucky helots, took the opportunity to rebel. Sparta asked the Athenians for help, and Kimon successfully proposed that he lead an expedition to assist in quashing the uprising. But when the Athenian troops arrived, the Spartans at the last moment declined their help. This was considered a dire humiliation for Athens and for Kimon in particular.

Kimon's absence, and his discomfiture, were a perfect opportunity for his political adversaries in Athens, the 'democratic' camp which wanted to tilt the balance of power within the city in favour of ordinary, poorer citizens. The leaders of this faction were a man called Ephialtes, who was mysteriously murdered, and his younger protégé, a brilliant aristocrat in his mid-thirties called Pericles. In 461 BCE, Kimon was ostracized, amid a cacophony of personal calumny and gossip. This is the background to one of the most famous of the newly discovered *ostraka*. Crudely scratched on the base of a pot, it screams: 'Kimon, son of Miltiades, take Elpinike and go!' To anyone who knows modern Athenian history, this sounds weirdly familiar. In the early 1960s, when young King Constantine was struggling to assert his authority, with his strong-willed German-born mother Queen Frederica looming in the background, anti-royalist crowds would chant: *Den se thelei o laos, par' tin mana sou kai bros!* ('The people don't want you, take your mother and go!')*

When Kimon duly went, he was replaced at the helm of Athenian affairs by a man who was in many ways his polar opposite. Thanks to some talented teachers, Pericles had been feasting since childhood on the cultural and intellectual achievements of the Greek world, especially that of the Ionian school of philosopher-scientists. The influencers of this budding statesman included Protagoras, Zeno of Elea and the brilliant Anaxagoras from Klazomenai, the modern Turkish port of Urla, a man who had thought deeply about the basics of astronomy and physics. Contact with these great minds instilled in him a sort of cerebral agility which would come in handy for anyone entering the hurly-burly of Athenian democracy.

But at least in Plutarch's pen portrait, Pericles was not one to use his rhetorical or intellectual skills frivolously. On the contrary, he was reserved both in his social life and in his appearances in the assembly, so that whenever he did speak out on some grave matter of state, his carefully chosen words carried enormous weight. For all their differences, both Kimon and Pericles had grown up with a powerful calling to repair an unjust injury to the family's honour. In fact they were on opposite sides of a single dynastic feud. Kimon's father was prosecuted and ruined by Xanthippos, who was Pericles'

---

* At least the first line of this demotic Greek slogan would have been perfectly understandable to Kimon.

father. Then, in 484 BCE, Xanthippos himself was ostracized: he is the target of several of the most recently unearthed *ostraka*. That act of expulsion was part of Themistocles' campaign to build up the Athenian navy and eliminate opponents of this policy. The young Pericles, it seems, must have imbibed a keen sense of how risky public life could be, even (or perhaps especially) if you were well-connected and possessed natural charisma – the sort of charisma that reminded people of Peisistratus, the tyrant who had dominated the city a century earlier. As Plutarch explains:

> Since he was rich, of brilliant lineage, and had friends of the greatest influence, he feared that he might be ostracized, and so at first had naught to do with politics, but devoted himself rather to a military career, where he was brave and enterprising.

In another famous passage, Plutarch describes Pericles the politician as a man who preserved his dignity by eschewing the exuberant social life to which Athenian men of his class felt they were entitled.

> On one street only in the city was he to be observed walking – the one which led to the market and the council-chamber. Invitations to dinner, and all that sort of amicable social intercourse, he refused, so that during the long period that elapsed while he was leader of the state, there was not a single friend to whose house he went to sup, except that when his kinsman Euryptolemus gave a wedding party, he attended until the libations were made... and then got straight up and departed.

Self-disciplined Pericles certainly was, but that description could be a slight exaggeration of the statesman's steely puritanism. In his youth, at least, he may have had some fun. As it happens, only one of his apparent possessions has been unearthed in modern times: a drinking cup with six names, including that of Pericles and his brother Ariphron, scratched uncertainly on the side. The cup had been presented to a certain Dramiton, possibly a tavern-keeper, maybe as a memento of an enjoyable night of carousing. It was found in 2014 in the northern Athenian suburb of Kifisia, and most archaeologists see no reason to doubt its authenticity.

But there is also plenty of evidence to support the picture of Pericles in maturity as a calculating, cerebral politician who deliberated carefully and generally made the right calls. Kimon was a soldier's soldier who shared the fruits of his conquests with his troops and ultimately with his city. Pericles firmly played the democratic card. He believed in using the city's growing wealth not on random acts of generosity but in ways that permanently devolved power to the humbler citizens of Athens.

By successfully proposing a system of daily payments for jury service, he made it worthwhile for poor farmers in the Athens region to leave their fields and apply their minds to thorny legal issues. This consolidated the role of Athens as the Greek world's capital of justice, comparable to modern London. With a guaranteed wage for the oarsmen who manned scores of triremes, Pericles also gave poor city-dwellers a stake in the city's naval adventures. In the immediate aftermath of Kimon's ostracism and the advent of his rival, Athens seemed to embark on a surge of strategic adventurism on many fronts. An expeditionary force, initially sent to Cyprus, was diverted to Egypt, where it was deployed in support of a rebellion against the Persian empire. Dates for these events are still debated, but the military adventure in Egypt, which ended badly, probably lasted from 460 BCE until 455 BCE.

At the same time, Athens took a more assertive stance in the internal conflicts of the Greek world. It took under its wing, and fortified, the neighbouring port of Megara, thus enraging the powerful, adjacent city of Corinth. It fought and subdued the island of Aegina, another long-standing rival. There is a famous stone inscription that reveals the military ambitions of the Athenians in the early 450s BCE. It lists the 177 casualties suffered by a single

Athenian tribe, and notes that they were incurred within twelve months on six different fronts: Cyprus, Egypt, Phoenicia (modern Lebanon), Aegina, Megara and Halieis (a small Peloponnesian port). The words 'IN THE SAME YEAR' are then spaced out to drive home the point. The year in question was probably 459 BCE.

In the post-Cold War Pentagon, American strategists used to concern themselves over whether they had the capacity to fight two major wars and a minor one simultaneously, and the superpower's forces were scaled accordingly. A similar degree of confidence seemed to fill the Athenians at the height of their prowess, but in truth their ability to fight in multiple arenas had its limits. Part of the genius of Pericles the politician lay in quickly identifying those limits, adjusting policy and minimizing the damage either to his own prestige or that of the city.

In the year 457 BCE, the Athenians confronted not just the forces of Sparta's allies, against whom they usually prevailed, but the land army of Sparta itself. The clash occurred at Tanagra, north of Athens. After a long, hard day of fighting with heavy casualties on both sides, Sparta was the winner, but the outcome was no disgrace for Athens. Pericles himself was said to have fought bravely. Despite his professed admiration for all things Spartan, Kimon volunteered (unsuccessfully) to come back and fight for his home city. However, many of Kimon's friends did fight and die in Tanagra. The overall outcome was not disadvantageous for Pericles. The Spartans were free to march home, but crucially, they had failed in one of their strategic objectives, which was to obstruct the building of long walls connecting the inland city of Athens with its two ports: the older harbour of Phaleron and the newer one at Piraeus, which was emerging as the base for the Athenian navy. Within a couple of years, the Athenians suffered another reminder of the limits of their power. After a five-year campaign, the forces they had sent to Persian-aligned Egypt were besieged and trapped on an island in the Nile. A smaller armada sent to relieve the Greeks also ran into a trap. Scores of Athenian ships were lost. But Pericles responded to this disaster in a way that was creative, to put it mildly. He used the Egyptian fiasco as an excuse to transfer the treasury of the Athenian-led alliance from the holy island of Delos to Athens itself, and to the Acropolis.

The association of cities and islands known as the Delian League, which had begun as a voluntary pact to protect Greeks from Persians, thus became an Athenian empire, in whose ranks the imperial metropolis would tolerate no dissent. More clearly than ever, the Greek world was now divided between an Athenian-dominated realm which took in the islands and coastal cities of the Aegean, and a Spartan commonwealth which controlled most of the Peloponnese, leaving central Greece as a zone of contention. Athens was liberal in its domestic governance but ruthless in controlling its empire; Sparta was militarized and authoritarian but the alliance it led was more loosely articulated.

Kimon returned from exile around 450 BCE, taking advantage of the principle that ostracism implied no long-term disgrace. As the American historian Donald Kagan puts it, the veteran commander instantly followed his oldest, deepest calling, which was to say, 'let's go fight the Persians'. He led an expeditionary force to Cyprus and laid siege to the Persian-held harbour of Kition, but then sickened and died in mid-campaign. His passing was kept secret, and the forces he had commanded still managed to honour his memory by scoring a victory at the Cypriot port of Salamis, named after the illustrious island near Athens.

But it was clearly beyond the ability of the Athenians to establish any long-term dominion at the eastern extremity of the Mediterranean. Once again, Athens in the era of Pericles demonstrated its ability to cut its losses. Kallias, the wealthy brother-in-law of Kimon, was directed to Persia to negotiate a peace in which Athens gave up its Egyptian ambitions, while the Persians promised not to despatch ships into the Aegean.

Even in Greek affairs, Pericles strongly believed that Athens should act with prudence and pick its fights carefully. The territory of Boeotia, immediately to the north of Attica, was a perpetual field of strife involving the large city of Thebes, which was an ally of Sparta, and many smaller towns whose loyalties shifted. In 447 BCE several Boeotian towns revolted against Athenian domination. A swaggering Athenian called Tolmides insisted that the revolt must be suppressed, while Pericles said this was one battle his city did not need to fight. Tolmides and his forces were soundly defeated by the army of the Boeotian League that same year.

Then anti-Athenian rebellions broke out in places which Pericles *did* care about: the island of Euboea and the perpetually troublesome little trading centre of Megara. Each held the key to important trade routes, and Pericles managed to quash both uprisings. As the final chapter in that round of inter-Greek fighting, known as the First Peloponnesian War, a Spartan army led by a young king, Pleistoanax, marched almost all the way to Athens. Pericles mysteriously parleyed with the inexperienced monarch and persuaded him, probably with a bribe, to go home again. That cleared the way for the Athenians to negotiate a thirty-year truce with the Spartans, obliging each side to respect the integrity of the other's empire, and to submit any disputes to compulsory arbitration. At least on paper, Athens had made peace with its two main adversaries, the Spartans and the Persians, and it was now free to flourish unimpeded as a cultural and commercial superpower.

Peace brought its problems for Pericles, both as an apostle of democracy in his own city and a mastermind of imperial hegemony. For the poorer citizens of Athens, the chance to pull an oar and earn a decent wage was an important economic safety net. In the wider Greek world, the handsome tributes that flowed into the coffers of Athens were justified, in theory, by the need to ward off a Persian threat. A bit like NATO in 1990 after the collapse of communism and the Soviet bloc, the Athenian empire was in danger of being an alliance without an enemy.

This was the backdrop to the fateful decision by Pericles, in the early 440s BCE, to launch another sort of collaborative effort. The rebuilding and decoration of the temples on the Acropolis, which had been lying in ruins since the Persian ravages of the year 480 BCE, was one of the most spectacular civil projects, both in its execution and its end results, that had ever been launched in human history. Its undertaking was something more than a piece of political or economic gamesmanship. The Athenians who had seen the Acropolis smouldering and experienced the frantic struggle to rebuild and refortify the city, felt it was now time to proclaim its glory to current and future generations.

Thanks to the wealth, talent and energy that was now concentrated in Athens, and thanks to the physical security afforded by lengthy walls, they now had confidence to make that proclamation to the world. The Acropolis would not simply act as a repository for the alliance's accumulated treasure; it would be turned into abiding testimony to the city's greatness, and as an emphatic statement of gratitude to her divine protectors. Like the Kremlin under the early Romanovs, the new Parthenon was planned as a place of mystery, piety and political aggrandizement. At its heart was a giant gold-and-ivory statue of Athena which also served as a bank; the gold ingots which formed the raiment of the goddess could be detached and, in dire emergency, used to fund the city's needs. Moreover, the money was there. The allies of Athens were supposed to contribute to the joint defence effort with either ships, materiel or money, and the vast majority made their contribution in cash. The funds transferred from Delos to Athens in 454 BCE amounted to 8,000 talents; the allies were expected to top this up with a further 600 talents every year. In the following decade it was decreed that one-sixtieth of this money would be reserved 'for Athena', or in other words for the adornment of her temples. This amounted to a licence to build and decorate gloriously.

Work on a new Parthenon temple began around 447 BCE, and was completed over fifteen years. In medieval and modern Europe, it took centuries to build cathedrals of comparable ambition and complexity. The rapid construction of the Parthenon is a testimony to the Athenian talent for marshalling skills and resources, whether for military, religious or cultural purposes. All such enterprises require a minimum of accountability in the use of public funds, and an ability to combine state funds with the donations of wealthy individuals.

None of this was achieved without intense controversy. But in comparison with most previous monument-building in human history, which depended on the whim of an all-powerful monarch, this project was something new. It was undertaken by a contentious democratic community, in which competing ambitions somehow had to be channelled constructively.

The new Parthenon was comparable to some of the Greek world's existing temples, but in important ways it was uniquely ambitious. For example, Olympia boasted a huge temple to Zeus, complete with a statue by Pheidias, artistic director of the Parthenon works. But that temple was in limestone. The Parthenon would be entirely built from marble – and not just any imported marble, but the fine-grained material from Mount Pentelikon. Building the Parthenon involved quarrying and transporting 100,000 tonnes of marble on a tortuous journey by cart from a low peak whose shimmering pale outline framed the north-eastern side of the city. New roads had to be built to reach deep inside the mountain, and a ramp constructed on one side of the Acropolis to transport the materials. Plutarch, with his five centuries of hindsight, is mindful of the social and economic consequences of this huge harnessing of public energy and skill. He describes how Pericles

> boldly proposed to the people projects... of construction, and designs for works which would draw on many different skills and take a lot of time, in order that citizens who stayed at home, no less than the seamen and guards and soldiers, might have a reason for receiving a share of the public wealth.

He adds that:

> the materials to be employed were stone, bronze, ivory, gold,
> ebony and cypress-wood; the skills needed to... fashion those
> materials were those of carpenter, moulder, bronze-smith, stone-
> cutter, dyer, worker in gold and ivory, painter, embroiderer,
> embosser, to say nothing of the providers... of the materials,
> such as factors, sailors and pilots by sea, and, by land, wagon-
> makers, trainers of yoked beasts, and drivers. In addition there
> were rope-makers, weavers, leather-workers, road-builders and
> miners.

Constructing the Parthenon was far more, of course, than a
technical challenge. It was also a sublime work of art and worship.
Among its aims was to reinforce the Athenian democracy by
reminding citizens of their common origins in a single set of
foundation stories. The pediments at either end of the building
feature crucial moments in the sacred narratives to which Athenians
traced their origins. On the eastern side, the birth of Athena,
emerging with a full panoply of armour from the pate of her father,
Zeus; on the western side, an image of the contest between Athena
and Poseidon, with the goddess prevailing but still leaving a big
role for the sea-god.

These twin themes perfectly suited a city that was now firmly
established as both a terrestrial and a maritime power. The temple
was quite literally built on past accomplishments, but it surpassed
them to an enormous degree. The new Parthenon was erected on
the same platform as the previous, half-built one, which had been
started as a thank-offering for Marathon and then burned by the
Persians. However, it was much wider, as well as slightly shorter,
and this gave a substantially larger interior, encompassing a shrine
to Athena which had previously been outdoors. In the early stage
of its construction, the new Parthenon took shape as a temple in
the relatively austere Doric form, but at some point a decision was

made, presumably by the assembly, to incorporate some aspects of the more florid Ionian style.

Behind the forty-six columns that are visible from outside, the building incorporates a second row of columns which are Ionian in design, topped by a frieze forming a continuum around the building. The very fact that the design was changed in mid-construction is a testament to its emergence out of a noisy democracy. Building the Parthenon was an idea conceived by Pericles, but it required the consent of the citizens, and in the early stages there were some loud naysayers. A character who confusingly bore the name of Thucydides (but was not the historian) insisted that spending so much money on a temple was the equivalent of dressing up the city like a courtesan. Pericles managed to secure his critic's expulsion, while broken sherds show that there was a countervailing but unsuccessful attempt to force Pericles out.

The technical excellence of the Parthenon's construction has only recently been grasped by the modern world, thanks to a restoration project begun in 1975, which involves rebuilding the columns by repairing and supplementing the drums of marble. All the lines look perfectly straight because of cleverly executed illusions.

The floor of the temple appears flat but in fact it swells upwards. The columns slope inwards, and they bulge in the middle. To achieve these effects, each of the drums had to be designed separately: there is no such thing as a replaceable part. The drums fit together neatly, helped by the fact that they often fused over time, making the Parthenon relatively resilient to earthquakes. As modern marble sculptors reproduce the fluting which adorns every single drum, they have realized that the final stages of carving must have been executed when the drums were already in place. When they began experimenting, these modern imitators discovered that the carving could only be done manually. Some processes can only be mastered by trial and error.

Bringing the white rock to the Acropolis was hard enough. Freshly quarried pieces of marble were hauled to the citadel on horse-drawn wagons which made a journey of five or six hours from Mount Pentelikon and then used a specially constructed track to reach the summit. Marble was conveyed to the site in exactly the quantities that were immediately required; otherwise the area would have become impossibly congested.

Stones yield many secrets, but they do not reveal everything. The majority of the surviving sculptures from the Parthenon come not from the exterior but from the 160-metre frieze which ran round the second, interior set of columns. Some 128 metres of the frieze are extant. Most of it is to be found, controversially, at the British Museum, and some at the Acropolis Museum in Athens, which also offers visitors an impressive reproduction of the entire original.

The frieze clearly shows a procession which splits in two at the south-western end. There are horses, knights, chariots, musicians playing lyres and flutes, and water-carriers. There are cows and sheep being led for sacrifice, and carriers of honeycombs and cakes which were used to lure the animals to their place of slaughter. But what does it all signify? No ancient texts have survived which might throw light on what Pericles and his favourite sculptor Pheidias had in mind when they conceived this narrative in stone. In 1787, two British antiquarians, James Stuart and Nicholas Revett, made an intelligent guess: the sculptures were a depiction of the city's greatest public event, the Panathenaic festival in the highly elaborate form which was acted out every four years.

But that raises as many questions as it answers: is this work a stylized portrayal of the festival as it was performed in the fifth century BCE, or does it hark back to the foundation myths on which the festival was based? Especially enigmatic is the central scene, in which a folded cloth is being exchanged between an adult figure of indeterminate sex and a young, partially naked figure, whose gender has also been vigorously and almost farcically debated: are those shapely buttocks male or female? A powerful school of conventional wisdom holds that this scene shows one of the key moments in the Panathenaic festivities: the delivery of a new woollen dress, specially woven by young women, which will be draped over the wooden statue of Athena as a kind of birthday offering.

Joan Breton Connelly, a distinguished American classicist, has put forward an alternative theory. First, she makes the case that one of the most important stories told by Athenians about the foundation of their city has been neglected in modern times because a play on the subject by the tragedian Euripides had largely been lost. Or, to be precise, most of the play was missing until the 1960s, when 120 lines of the text were discovered on a piece of recycled papyrus which had been used to wrap an Egyptian mummy. The play tells the story of King Erechtheus being advised by an oracle that he must sacrifice one of his daughters if he is to prevail in a forthcoming battle. In Connelly's view, the cloth-exchange scene shows Erechtheus giving a funeral shroud to his daughter who is about to forfeit her life for the good of the city. Also depicted, she believes, are two other daughters who sacrifice themselves in solidarity with their sister, and their mother Praxithea, who becomes a priestess after the death of her entire family. Connelly makes an unchallengeable case for the importance of the Erechtheus story. She also demonstrates that all conventional wisdom about the frieze rests on shaky ground. Whether she is right about the central scene in the Parthenon frieze is a question that remains open. There are things about the Athens of Pericles that neither texts nor stones will ever fully elucidate.

# 4

# Pride and a Fall

## 432–421 BCE

*Pericles' funeral oration for the young men lost in the war with Sparta – the Athenian plague of 430 BCE – conflicts erupt across Greece, ushering in the thirty years of the Peloponnesian War – Sophocles'* Oedipus Rex *and Aristophanes'* The Acharnians: *great dramatic literature in an age of crisis – the death of Pericles – the peace of Nikias, 421 BCE: a ceasefire after ten years of grinding warfare – the puzzle of Aspasia – differing readings of the Socratic dialogue* Menexenus

The fashioning and adornment of the Parthenon, with all its brightly coloured sculpture, was completed in 432 BCE. In the same year, work was finished on another splendid marble structure. This was the Propylaea, or gateway to the Acropolis. For a person or a procession arriving at the citadel, its steep steps serve (as they still do) as preparation for a breathtaking sight of the great temple to Athena. For anyone leaving the citadel, it offered a view westwards that trained the eye towards Salamis, the place where Athenian naval power and cunning had saved Hellas.

Less than two years after that, the message proclaimed by these sculptures was delivered in words. Whatever the medium, the statement was broadly the same. It was a cry of delight over a city whose citizens rejoiced in their common ancestry and their common birthright of freedom: a freedom, as it happened, which included the right, perhaps even the duty, to dominate others.

The great manifesto of liberal democracy, and indeed liberal imperialism, was delivered by Pericles in the form of a funeral oration for the first cohort of young men who had died in the terrible war with Sparta which had begun about a year earlier. Athens had been skirmishing, directly or indirectly, with Sparta and its allies for decades. But only in 431 did a conflict begin in which the very existence of Athens, Sparta and their respective empires was in the balance. That is why the year 431 BCE is compared with 1914 in modern history.

The first winter of that war seemed a proper moment for a great piece of rhetoric from Pericles, or at any rate from the historian Thucydides, who passionately admired Pericles and ascribes to him sonorous words whose accuracy we cannot gauge. Thucydides certainly does an admirable and convincing job in setting the scene for the speech, attended by an exceptionally large crowd from the city and its surroundings. In a stirring passage, he describes how

> That winter, the Athenians organized a public funeral for the first cohort of men who had been slain in the war. They followed the dictates of tradition: a couple of days before the ceremony the bones of the dead are displayed on a specially erected structure and people can make offerings to their own dead, as they wish. Then there is a funeral procession in which cypress coffins are transported on wagons, one for each tribe... Everyone who desires, whether an alien or a citizen, can take part in the procession, and women relatives of the fallen can make their lamentations at the grave. The remains are laid in the public burial place which is in the finest of districts just beyond the city walls. When the bones have been buried, a man chosen by the city for his brilliance of mind, and his overall good name, delivers an appropriate oration. Pericles pronounced the following words, from an elevated platform so that as many as possible could follow him.

The 'public burial place' was probably in or near the numinous archaeological site now known as the Kerameikos cemetery. Amid the hubbub of modern Athens, it is an area of extraordinary calmness, bisected by the hastily erected Themistoclean wall, and is still watered by the Eridanos river, although the latter is little more than a trickle these days. This place was one of the nodal points in the spiritual life of ancient Athens. Processions passed through here on their way to taste the unearthly secrets of Eleusis, about 18 kilometres down the coast, where mysterious rites imparted to the initiates some deep truth about the afterlife. It was also the spot where participants gathered for the more local but even richer pageant, the Panathenaic festival, which involved climbing up to the Acropolis and paying homage to Athena. So the setting for the great oration, as described by Thucydides, is almost as evocative as the language of the speech. But the words are pretty impressive too.

The arresting figures of speech with which Pericles praised his city can still tingle the spines of people who read them 2,500 years later. His tone is a mixture of idealism, humanism, egalitarianism, sensitivity to nuance and sheer, insufferable arrogance. It expresses a political philosophy that would not resurface in human affairs until the French and American Revolutions. He makes little effort to comfort the bereaved. Instead he emphasizes what a privilege it is for anyone to die in the service of such a marvellous, unique city: a place that should inspire passionate love in those who serve it.

> We enjoy a political system which does not emulate the institutions of our neighbours. On the contrary we stand as a good example to others, rather than copying anybody else. Our constitution is known as a democracy because it vests power not in the hands of the few but in the many. In the adjudication of private disputes, everybody can enjoy equality before the law. When it comes to placing one person [in authority] over another in some responsible position, merit is what counts, not membership of a particular class.

It is hard to overstate the degree to which this philosophy overturned all previous understandings of the purpose of government. In Athens, those who wielded administrative power did not do so by virtue of divine right, by dynastic inheritance or by personal charisma. Power was delegated to them, on a provisional basis, by the people under fixed rules:

> We submit to those whom we have appointed to positions of authority, and we adhere to the laws themselves, especially the ones which serve to protect the weak, as well as the unwritten norms whose violation is generally regarded as shameful.

When Pericles said this, he was acknowledging that his own position as de facto master of Athens was entirely reversible if the people so decided. This is a tough-minded and sophisticated presentation of a political theory which the modern world can recognize, one that anticipates thinkers such as David Hume and John Stuart Mill who lived a couple of millennia later. Also remarkably modern in tone is the statesman's vision of a balance between individual freedom and public duty, between modest private affluence and the higher ideal of contributing to the city's fortunes. George Orwell, despite his biting critique of his country's inequality and imperialist hypocrisy, found something to admire in the British tolerance of eccentricity and private pursuits, the sense that 'an Englishman's home is his castle'. Pericles foreshadows this in his celebration of the 'privacy' enjoyed by Athenian citizens, in combination with an overwhelming sense of public duty.

> We behave liberally in politics and also in our relations with one another in everyday life. We do not become irritated with our neighbour for seeking enjoyment in some particular way, nor do we respond with looks of disdain which, although doing no real harm, can still lead to hurt feelings. We avoid giving offence in our private dealings, while in public life we are constrained by the law which commands our deep respect.

Just as the Athenian self-understanding was finely balanced, the Parthenon and its sculptures were based on a delicate equilibrium, reflecting the much-used geometrical ratio (4 to 9) and the homage being paid both to human endeavour and divine encouragers.* Its presentation of Athena and Poseidon reflects a balance between terrestrial skill and craftsmanship, from weaving to olive-growing, and maritime prowess. In the speech, too, contrasting themes are held in perfect tension. A spirit of nativism, underpinned by the notion that Athenians are uniquely indigenous to the territory they now inhabit, is balanced by a cosmopolitan internationalism which rejoices in the fact that 'all the good things from all over the world flow into us, so that it seems just as natural to enjoy our own foreign goods as our own local products'.

Many a disgruntled subject of the Athenian empire must have responded rather cynically to Pericles' high-flown rhetoric. Imagine the feelings of an Asian or African anti-colonialist of the 1950s, or indeed those of a Mexican of the twenty-first century who is dubious about American-inspired free trade deals. A wealthy metropolis has every reason to rejoice in the fruits of international commerce when it can shape the terms of that commerce by virtue of its financial and – ultimately – military strength. But the partners in those transactions may feel differently.

Apart from Athena and Poseidon, the other equilibrium, between the private and the public, is a recurring theme in the speech. A respect for privacy is balanced with a sense of civic duty, a commitment not only to avoid harming the city through reckless law-breaking but to bring benefit to the polis. Being an entirely private person is considered contemptible, a kind of free riding on the benefits of citizenship.

At one point, there is a back-handed recognition of the intense jealousy that can exist between those who are competing to sponsor

---

* Efforts have been made to show that a 'golden' mean, based on the number 1.62, recurs in the Parthenon as is said to be the case in other great monuments like the Pyramids. But this has never been successfully proved.

the finest ships, the fastest Olympic charioteers or the most brilliant public spectacles. Funeral orations, Pericles admits, can go awry if they merely serve to upset people who feel their own achievements are being upstaged.

> Eulogies of other people are bearable only up to a certain point, the point where listeners are convinced that they too could achieve the feats being described. Once this point is passed, the hearers grow envious and sceptical.

However utopian the vision of Athens presented by Pericles, that part rings entirely true. To judge by the evidence of ancient texts, ranging from history to comedy, this was indeed a city whose fortunes were advanced, and also compromised at times, through perpetual competition between men with powerful egos, in a process sometimes abetted by women who could make their influence felt only through backstage manipulation. If Pericles was commanding the attention of his fellow citizens on this solemn occasion, it was because earlier in his life he had done quite successfully in exactly that kind of competition: he had ostracized one of his severe critics and avoided being ostracized himself.

For all its moments of dishonesty, there is something thrilling about Pericles' ode to a democratic city. Consciously or unconsciously, many leaders of modern times have followed his speech as they galvanized fellow citizens into believing that their own societies deserved to flourish and prevail over enemies, not because they were strong but because they were uniquely virtuous. Abraham Lincoln was invoking Pericles in his Gettysburg address over those who had fallen in the Civil War: 'We here highly resolve that these dead shall not have died in vain, that this nation, under God, shall have a new birth of freedom, and that government of the people, by the people, for the people, shall not perish from the earth.' Winston Churchill had his Periclean moment when, heralding the Battle of Britain, he proclaimed a fateful choice: either 'all Europe may be free and the life of the world may move into broad, sunlit uplands', or else the whole world could 'sink into the abyss of a new Dark Age'. And George W. Bush was channelling the Athenian statesman when, after the terrorist attacks of September 2001, he told his compatriots that America had been attacked by people who had been provoked by the country's outstanding merit: its democratic freedom. 'They hate what they see right here in this chamber – a democratically elected government. Their leaders are self-appointed. They hate our freedoms – our freedom of religion, our freedom of speech, our freedom to vote and assemble and disagree with each other.'

In different ways, Pericles and his Anglo-Saxon imitators were saying: people are attacking us because we are so good, and in particular because we practise the virtue of freedom, and it is in the name of that freedom that we will fight back. The liberal democratic vision presented by Thucydides, like those of all his successors, is of course an idealized one. It takes little account of the fact that liberal freedoms enjoyed in an imperial metropolis are financed, quite literally, by less fortunate folk at the periphery of the realm. But in the case of Thucydides, the dramatic effect is enhanced by the way he juxtaposes a soaring description of a city flourishing in law-governed freedom with a nightmarish vision of the collapse of that very order, just a few pages later. As presented by Thucydides, the Athenian plague that began in 430 BCE is one of the most lurid accounts we possess of a society and its institutions collapsing under the shock of a raging disease. He describes how a wealthy, vibrant city was struck by a horrific malady which caused panic, despair and a loss of faith in sacred values and institutions. Symptoms such as raging body heat, retching, convulsions and disfigurement suggest typhus, smallpox or Ebola fever. 'The catastrophe was so overwhelming that men, not knowing what would happen to them, became indifferent to every rule of religion or law,' he observes.

It is a nightmarish vision of suffering and anomie. Yet para-doxically enough, much of the latest scholarly writing about the subject emphasizes the obverse point: the remarkable resilience of the Athenian way of doing things. In other words, scholars are taking the bare facts presented by Thucydides and other sources and coming to the very opposite conclusion.

If we are to believe Thucydides, all the civic virtues and self-restraint which have been so carefully enumerated a couple of pages earlier are suddenly going into reverse. As Pericles describes it, the brilliance of Athenian democracy rested both on well-enforced laws and a kind of inner moral compass that prompted people to observe their religious duties and treat one another with at least a degree of respect. First among those religious duties, and high on the list of duties in any civic religion, lies the appropriate burial of the dead. Suddenly, we are told, people had neither the capacity nor even the desire to observe those decencies.

> Many lapsed into shameless methods of burial because so many people in their households had perished that they did not have the materials needed for a funeral. Some would take advantage of other people's [newly-made] pyres, putting their own dead in first, and stoking the blaze. Others would toss the body they were carrying onto one that was already alight and then scarper.

In short, we are led to believe, people were casting aside whatever dictates of conscience or modesty had guided them in the past, because they had become selfish and hedonistic, with an alacrity that cast doubt on whether that modesty had ever amounted to much in the first place. 'It was generally agreed that what was both honourable and valuable was the pleasure of the moment and everything that might conceivably contribute to that pleasure.' Neither divine nor human punishment seemed to offer any deterrent against licentious behaviour.

> Observing that all kinds of people had the same fate, people judged that piety and impiety amounted to the same thing. Also

nobody anticipated living long enough to be called to account
and made to pay the [earthly] penalty for any misdeeds.

If we were to follow Thucydides to the letter, we would have
to accept that Athenian democracy soared to its zenith, and then
collapsed into anarchy, within the space of barely two years. Part of
the reason why Thucydides presents this change so abruptly lies, in
all probability, in his own political bias. It is generally agreed that
he was an admirer of Pericles, but not of the radical democracy
which Pericles had introduced. He is keen to make the point that
Athens generally chose the best course as long as Pericles was in
charge, and that things started to go really wrong after the guiding
hand of Pericles was removed. As Thucydides explains, one of the
direst consequences of the plague is that it spelled doom for the
statesman: first political, then physical. The historian recounts how,
not surprisingly, the general unhappiness in the city prompted
people to turn against Pericles and blame him for the conduct of
a war which was leading to multiple disasters.

That in turn provides the cue for Pericles, as presented by
Thucydides, to make a passionate speech in self-defence. He is
said to have 'summoned an assembly with the aim of putting fresh
courage' into the city's faint-hearted citizens and given them a
thorough scolding for their ingratitude to him. First, he insists, the
city had no choice but to wage war, and he was the best qualified
person to lead that war. Secondly, his policies were the right ones,
and if consistently pursued, they would lead Athens to success.
Athens should use to maximum effect its greatest asset, sea power:

> With your navy as it is today, there is no power on earth... not
> the King of Persia not any people under the sun... which can
> stop you sailing where you wish.

At this point, Pericles (or perhaps his admiring chronicler) can
drop the pretence that Athens stands out from other Greek cities

purely by virtue of her moral superiority, in other words her love of freedom, equilibrium and democracy. Athens, the statesman declares bluntly, is in command of an empire, and the present generation has an obligation to maintain that realm even if its acquisition had been morally dubious.

> Nor is it any longer possible for you to give up this empire, though there may be some people who in a mood of sudden panic and in a spirit of political apathy actually think this would be a fine and noble thing to do. Your empire is now like a tyranny: it may have been wrong to take it; it is certainly dangerous to let it go.

If Pericles did indeed utter those words, they failed in their immediate purpose. He was recalled from his position as *strategos* or commander, a post to which he had been elected for each of the past fifteen years and many of the previous fifteen. The following year, the people relented and re-elected him, but he succumbed to the plague, as did his two legitimate sons. In a final act of gratitude to the statesman, the fickle populace agreed to his request to confer citizenship on the son he had borne to a foreign woman, his mistress Aspasia.

Apart from admiring his literary skills, what sense can we make of the dramatic way in which Thucydides presents the glorious ascent and dismal crash of the world's first experiment in rule by the people? Did things really degenerate so rapidly, in just a couple of years, and was the plague the principal cause? There is no doubt that Athens was profoundly damaged by the disease, which claimed between a quarter and a third of its population and recurred over four years. It turned out to be the first in an interlocking series of dire events that would unfold over three decades: military miscalculations, an incessant internal conflict between democrats and oligarchs, violent coups d'état, murderous juntas and eventual surrender to Sparta in 404 BCE.

Nor can there be any doubt that even when it was observing the rules more or less correctly, the Athenian political process, and Athenian public affairs generally, grew coarser and more cynical over this period. The age of statesmen gave way to the era of tub-thumpers. And yet many of today's classical scholars would still emphasize a different point. The immediate aftermath of the plague offers proof not of the fragility of Athenian life and culture, but of its astonishing resilience.

The decade of many-fronted conflict which followed the plague is known as the Archidamian War. Terrible as it was, the loss of population did not fatally affect the city's ability to fight. In 429 BCE, an Athenian naval commander called Phormio pulled off a remarkable victory against a larger squadron of Peloponnesian ships, near his base at Naupactus at the mouth of the Gulf of Corinth. It was remembered as a typically Athenian display of maritime dexterity and derring-do.

Over the years that followed, conflict erupted in one corner of the Greek world after another, with Athens supporting the notionally 'democratic' faction in local disputes against the 'oligarchs' who were aligned with Sparta. The one consistent pattern is that Athens and its armies behaved rather badly, acting more like calculating imperialists than virtuous promoters of democratic change. But there was no obvious failure of Athenian capacity or competence. Even when it behaved ruthlessly, the city observed its own democratic procedures.

In 428 BCE, the oligarchic leaders of four towns on the island of Lesbos staged a revolt against Athenian hegemony. After suppressing the revolt with help from local democrats, the Athenians held a debate, memorably described by Thucydides, about how to treat the islanders. With chilling ruthlessness, a new political strongman called Kleon convinced the assembly to put the entire male population of the island to death, and a ship was despatched to convey the necessary orders.

Within the next twenty-four hours, however, the Athenian

assembly had second thoughts. A more moderate speaker, Diodotus, convinced the citizens that it would be wiser to take a softer line and punish only the guilty. The argument was couched not in moral language, but in terms of expediency. Savage punishment, the more liberal camp argued, would alienate the allies and make them resist more desperately. It is an argument between rival schools of imperialism that foreshadows the debates heard in Victorian Britain between Disraeli's Tories and Gladstone's Liberals. A ship was sent racing to Mytilene to enforce the more restrained line that the city eventually adopted, but despite its message of clemency up to 1,000 residents of the island were executed for taking part in the rebellion.

For all its horror, the Athenian pestilence and its aftermath was not, in the end, a world-changing event comparable to the plague that started in 540 CE, which recurred over two centuries and destroyed the Roman world; or the Black Death, starting around 1350 CE, which broke up the feudal society of medieval Europe. Indeed, there is evidence that the Athenian system coped well with the plague; anomie was short-lived. Consider the fate of Pericles himself. It is true that as anger surged, he was deposed and prosecuted; but it seems important that this was done by a rules-based procedure, not by a crazed mob.

No less impressive is the continuity in the city's artistic life, including annual drama festivals which required extensive and costly organization. As is pointed out by Jennifer T. Roberts, a contemporary American scholar of the war with Sparta, the Athenians were presented in 429 BCE with Sophocles' tragedy *Oedipus Rex*, a milestone in world literature. Apart from inspiring the psychoanalysts of the twentieth century, it drove home some very topical points to an audience battered by war and disease. This masterpiece, in whose staging more than 1,000 people might have been involved, is hardly suggestive of a city in hopeless disarray. Its portrayal of a king who is trying to assuage the wrath of Apollo, which took the form of a deadly plague, would have resonated with Athenians who half suspected their city had likewise offended the god of light and prophecy.

Even more astonishing, as evidence of the city's stubbornly democratic and liberty-loving culture, is a play called *The Acharnians* (inhabitants of the rural area of Acharnai, north of Athens), which is the earliest surviving comedy by the master humorist Aristophanes, presented in 425 BCE. In the opening scene we are introduced to Dikaiopolis, a frustrated, flatulent old farmer who is sitting on the Pnyx hill waiting for a debate in the Athenian assembly to begin. He vents his weariness at the continuation of the war with Sparta, and exclaims how much rather he would be spending his days back on his property trading his vinegar or garlic. In due course he makes a kind of private peace with the Spartans, but he is soon set upon by neighbours who are furious over the damage inflicted on their fields by the Spartan army and are determined to wreak revenge. As the plot unfolds, it becomes clear that Dikaiopolis is a proxy for Aristophanes himself, who is fighting back after being prosecuted by Kleon, the city's leading war hawk, over the supposedly seditious message of his previous farce, *The Babylonians*.

This outrageous slapstick probably tells us much more about the real nature of Athenian democracy, both its staying power and the threats it faced, than any of the rhetorical pirouettes performed by Pericles. It shows that within the Athenian state, there was real tension between the city and the surrounding countryside, as well as between conflicting rural factions. The war strategy of Pericles had consisted of ordering the whole population to hunker down behind the city walls, which extended all the way to the sea. Country-dwellers had to abandon their farms and seek temporary accommodation behind the mighty defences. In effect, Athens became an unsinkable aircraft carrier, secure and impregnable and with assured access to the harbours that were needed to launch naval expeditions and import vital food. Whatever happened outside the walls was deemed to be of secondary importance. There was a certain cold logic in this calculation.

But overcrowding inside the city was clearly a huge factor in bringing on the plague. Even in those days, the spread of infectious disease must have seemed like the dark side of globalization, one that laid bare the dangers of open commerce and human intercourse. Similar talk was heard at the time of the Black Death, and the Covid pandemic of the early twenty-first century. Was this, then, the main reason why people turned against their revered statesman? On the one hand, the role of Pericles in creating conditions that favoured the plague seems like an understandable, even an objectively justified, reason for people to resent him. On the other, it is worth recalling that people in the ancient world did not have much idea of how disease spread, and they were inclined to attribute such disasters to the wrath of Apollo. In the view of Professor Roberts, a more likely reason for the temporary downfall of Pericles was simply unhappiness over the conduct of the war.

But the rural ferment depicted in the comedy is certainly plausible enough. Whatever its other consequences, the chosen strategy of sheltering inside the walls meant that the city was not even trying to stop Spartan forces from ravaging the nearby fields. That turned some country folk into pacifists and others into militarists, bent on punishing the aggressors. Indeed the seemingly random ravings of Dikaiopolis throw some light on the solemn rhetoric pronounced by Pericles five years earlier. In an atmosphere of real tension between city-dwellers and farmers, whose experience of the war was so sharply different, the statesman must have felt a strong imperative to stress the universality of the privileges that went with being an Athenian citizen. The point Pericles wanted to emphasize was roughly this: contrary to what many people, especially disgruntled and displaced farmers, now thought, all Athenian voters were stakeholders and beneficiaries in an enterprise of outstanding nobility, in whose service it was an honour to lay down one's life.

These were lofty ideals, but there is one line in Pericles' oration which is horrifying to a modern sensibility, and that too may have an explanation which reflects the expediencies of the moment. It is his exhortation to the women of Athens to show modesty and restraint.

> If I am to speak of womanly virtues to those of you who will
> henceforth be widows, let me sum them up with one short
> admonition: to a woman, it is a great glory not to show more
> weakness than is natural to her sex, and to be mentioned as little
> as possible among men either in praise or in blame.

In other words, decent women should be neither seen nor heard.
According to Edith Hall, a British classicist, a possible explanation
is that Pericles was afraid of an uncontrollable reaction at that
particular moment from women who were accustomed to act as
ritual mourners. In private Greek funerals, bereaved women were
expected to engage in acts of ceremonial lamentation, including
washing the dead, breast-beating, gouging of their own cheeks,
punching the ground with fists and the singing of dirges.*

In organizing a magnificent state funeral, Pericles was removing
all this activity from the private sphere, and he may have felt nervous
of the female mourners, kept at a distance from the bodies, whose
reactions might have been impossible to restrain. Professor Hall, who
clearly does not want to make too many excuses for Pericles, adds that
whatever the context, his words to the bereaved 'forcibly remind us
that classical Athens was a militaristic state and a brutal patriarchy'.

We can never be sure whether Pericles was really afraid of the
lobby of mourning women, but he may well have been. Even in
the most patriarchal of societies, bereaved soldiers' mothers can be
a mighty force, as was demonstrated by the movement of Russian
women whose sons had perished in the Chechen War of 1994–6.

Ironically enough, though, the site of the oration in the
Kerameikos cemetery is not far from one of the most moving
depictions of feminine dignity which has survived from ancient
Athens: a marble grave stele, erected in the memory of a lady
called Hegeso, whose sensually robed, seated figure is shown in

---

* Intense, formalized mourning existed until very recent times in modern
Greece: see Margaret Alexiou's classic work: *The Ritual Lament in Greek
Tradition* (Cambridge University Press, 1974).

conversation with her maidservant as they both hold a jewellery box. It is an outstanding example of disciplined grace and skill in the portrayal of human beings. Such elaborate funerary monuments enjoyed a strange revival at the time of the Peloponnesian War, which seemed to intensify the impulse (at least among those who could afford it) to celebrate individual human lives. The sculpture is in Pentelic marble, like the ones adorning the Acropolis. However brutal its patriarchy, this was a society which in some contexts knew how to celebrate and honour women, and interactions between women, albeit ones who were divided by class. The Kerameikos cemetery and its 'street of the dead' where the monument to Hegeso stands (in reproduction because the original is now in the National Archaeological Museum) has become a landmark for any visitor to Athens who wants to commune with the ancient city in a quieter atmosphere than the now-bustling Acropolis can offer.

Around 1994, when the Kerameikos metro station was being constructed, about ninety apparent victims of the plague, ten of them children, were discovered. The one thing that has not been discovered, because no serious attempt has been made, is the grave of Pericles. Before their deaths in the late twentieth century, two eminent Greek archaeologists confided to Euphrosyne Doxiadis, an art historian, in separate conversations that they were certain where the statesman's grave was located. It was to be found, they said, underneath the swirling smog and melting asphalt of Pireos Street, an artery which leads from a roughish part of downtown Athens to the port of Piraeus. These days, a German-owned hardware store roughly marks the spot. However, until the masters of Greek archaeology can convince the state that it is worth the expense of burrowing underneath the avenue and creating a small flyover, the statesman's tomb is likely to remain undisturbed.

Whatever the hidden agendas of the great Periclean speech, it is clearly true that Pericles and the other, much more ruthless men who stepped into his shoes wanted the freest possible hand to pursue the war as they thought best. For the Athenians, taking the war to the enemy usually meant playing to the city's strategic strength, which was its superiority in naval power. On that matter, the influence of Pericles was felt long after his death.

Very soon after his passing, a new commander called Demosthenes (not to be confused with the great orator of that name who lived a century later) led some increasingly successful maritime expeditions and set up well-defended outposts which ringed the Peloponnese. Manning and equipping ships must certainly have become harder after Athens' huge population loss in the plague, since there were fewer free citizens who were willing and able to make a living by pulling an oar, but foreigners and slaves seem to have filled the gap. To explain the city's resilience, Josiah Ober, a scholar of ancient Greek politics, emphasizes the 'democratic advantage' enjoyed by Athenians, in common with other societies based on free speech and a wide-ranging franchise. A robust democracy, as the professor describes it, is one where citizens see advantage in pooling their knowledge and energy, and would not cheat the system even if they could.

Ancient Athens broadly meets that test, and there are plenty of modern states which do not. Athenian democracy at its best also cherished truth-telling, and the principle that whenever expression is free, good information will drive out bad. Enough of that tradition survived to endow the city with an impressive ability to bounce back after a devastating loss of life. In the post-plague years, dominated by demagogues, these democratic virtues clearly waned, but they did not vanish. The undiminished competence of the Athenian navy was one sign of the city's political health.

But as every year of war with Sparta went by, its conduct became more cruel. In some ways, it can be argued, democratic Athens waged a dirtier fight than authoritarian Sparta. The Athenians landed a heavy blow by establishing an outpost on the tiny island of Sphakteria, near the port of Pylos on the south-western edge of the Peloponnese. It was a place made famous by Homer's allusions to 'sandy Pylos' as the stronghold of King Nestor.

The Athenian garrison attracted helots or second-class subjects of Sparta who were glad to desert. Sparta became nervous of a general uprising among its underlings and tried fighting back, but it lost a battle at Pylos in 425 BCE and a group of Spartan soldiers were trapped on Sphakteria, giving the Athenians some vital leverage. The Athenian commander Demosthenes was still unable to inflict a definitive defeat, and his younger rival Kleon persuaded the city assembly to let him have a try. He managed to capture 300 fully armed Spartan infantrymen, a severe blow to a city where the elite warrior class was quite small in number. Athens made it known that the captives would be killed if the Spartans made any more forays into Attica. The Spartans reacted dynamically, overcoming their shyness of distant expeditions.

Brasidas, a Spartan commander as tough as Kleon, marched on the northern Greek colony of Amphipolis, adjacent to some silver mines which were a vital source of revenue for Athens. The historian Thucydides, who could fight as well as write, led an expedition which tried and failed to stop the Spartans taking control of Amphipolis. Thucydides was punished for this reversal with exile, a fate that gave him plenty of time to complete his great chronicle of the war. The fighting around Amphipolis claimed the lives of both Brasidas and Kleon, leaving both Sparta and Athens yearning for a break. The Athenians surrendered their hostages, and the Spartans relinquished the towns newly captured by Brasidas. The resulting ceasefire in 421 BCE was called the peace of Nikias after the Athenian commander who negotiated it.

After a decade of grinding warfare, the Athenians had probably lost some of their appetite for perorations of collective self-praise, although they were by no means a spent or entirely demoralized force. However, the story of Pericles and his oration, with its glorious appeals to freedom and its lapse into nasty sexism, does have one curious postscript, in the form of a mysterious text that was written four or five decades later.

The puzzle concerns the role, real or perceived, played in Athenian politics, and perhaps Athenian public discourse, by Aspasia, the woman whom Pericles passionately loved. Just a handful of facts about Aspasia are generally accepted. She was born around 470 BCE in Miletus* – a port which had flourished commercially long before Athens. As a non-citizen and newcomer to Athens, her formal status was low. Ironically, it was Pericles who had diminished the position of foreign women in his home city by pushing through a law which restricted citizenship to the offspring of two Athenian parents. But Aspasia seems to have turned her outsider's role to advantage. She had none of the entitlements of a citizen (which for a woman were pretty modest) but was bound by none of the conventions.

As the only love of Pericles' life (his formal marriage to an Athenian woman seems to have been passionless) she clearly commanded a huge share of his attention. In literature written by resentful Athenian men, she is described as a kind of courtesan or geisha, a woman who paid flattering attention to high-status males and groomed female apprentices to perform similar services. Some described her as a madame or a brothel-keeper pure and simple.

It was alleged that she had convinced her partner Pericles to make a storming intervention when, in 440 BCE, her home city of Miletus became involved in a conflict with the adjacent island of Samos. (Whether that holds good is impossible to tell: there were plenty of other reasons of state to bring the Samians to heel, including the risk that Persia might be sucked into the dispute.)

The rollicking satire of *The Acharnians* would not have been complete without a dig at Aspasia. The real catalyst for the huge inter-Greek war, burbles Dikaiopolis, came when hoodlums from the port of Megara stole some prostitutes from the house of Aspasia. It was this impertinence, he adds, which prompted Pericles to slap a trade embargo on the Megarians: an action which (in real life, not just comic fantasy) was one of the sparks for the great conflict.

---

* Aspasia's upbringing in a cradle of early metaphysics and scientific enquiry (her home city had produced thinkers like Thales, Anaximander and Anaximenes) may be a clue to the influence she exercised over Pericles.

Of all the scraps of literary evidence concerning Aspasia, none is more puzzling than a short dialogue entitled *Menexenus*. In the early part of the fourth century BCE, the great philosopher Plato scribbled prolifically about the life and thought of Socrates, presenting him as a brilliant, eccentric sage who frequented the streets and salons of Athens but wrote nothing himself. One of these Platonic texts features Socrates in conversation with a man called Menexenus, a politically ambitious Athenian who happened to bear the same name as the sage's little son. Socrates treats his friend to a recitation of an oration for the war dead which, he says, he has learned from Aspasia.

The oration that Socrates reels off is in some ways slightly more conventional than the famous one ascribed to Pericles; it makes pious references to the gods, and to the earliest episodes in Athenian mythology, and it glosses skilfully over some of the uglier chapters in the recent history of Athens. Somewhere in the middle of this, Socrates mentions, as though it was a well-known fact, that Aspasia was the real author of the greatest speech delivered by her statesman lover, which is also considered one of the greatest speeches of all time: in other words the Periclean oration for the war dead.

Could that be so? *Menexenus* is such an elusive text that many scholars have simply ignored it. Among those who have wrestled with it, there are numerous different readings. Some see the text as a satire on the whole genre of pompous funeral speeches; others see it as a way for Plato, who was no friend of democracy, to attack the memory of Pericles, which many other people saw as sacrosanct.

Peter Adamson, a professor at Munich University, sees the oration spouted by Socrates as a literary construct whose imagery is chosen in deliberate counterpoint to the more famous one offered by Pericles. In that speech, Pericles had urged the men of Athens to fall in love with the city as though she were a female lover. In *Menexenus*, by contrast, Socrates portrays the soil of Attica as a nurturing *mother* to her fighting men, while the city's political institutions are seen as playing the role of a father. The mention of

Aspasia, the consort of the city's political father, could be a way of highlighting Attica's motherly function.

These are all intelligent, ingenious ways to read the text. But it might just be that the sonorous words of Pericles, including his advice to Athenian women to avoid being seen or heard, were in fact written or co-written by a woman – who was not Athenian or in any sense a beneficiary of Athenian democracy.

# 5

# A Blazing Twilight

## 421–405 BCE

*Alcibiades and his personality – his friendship with Socrates
– the* Symposium *as a portrait of Athenian decadence –
the Sicilian expedition and the desecration of the Herms
– Alcibiades' shifting loyalties and their effect on the
Peloponnesian War – Lysander destroys the Athenian fleet
at Aegospotami, 405 BCE, leading to Athenian surrender
– culture and drama as Athens slides towards defeat*

In the final two decades of the fifth century BCE, Athens saw flashes
of moral and artistic brilliance, stunning military disasters, bitter
internal conflicts and a surge of public passions which the safety
valves of democracy could not always cope with. On two separate
occasions, the democratic system was interrupted as cliques of
powerful men seized power and began terrorizing their rivals.

Depending on how you look at it, the whole story is either
a sign of democracy's limitations, or else an indication that rule
by the entire (male) citizenry was remarkably enduring. After
all, it did bounce back into existence with impressive speed after
each of the bloodstained interludes. At the end of it all, Athens
had lost her walls, her empire and her claim to be the strategic
master of the Greek world. But the city was still not finished as
a competitor in the eternal contest between Greek city-states, or
as a laboratory for bold political experiments.

In the imagination of later generations, and probably even at the time, two personalities stood out from the Athenian crowd during those turbulent years. One was a charismatic, seductive schemer with an appetite for all life's pleasures, the other a disturbing, disinterested other-worldly thinker about the meaning and mysteries of our existence on Earth. The latter, Socrates, was a squat, snub-nosed man, notorious for his ugliness and scruffiness in a city that prized male beauty and grooming. The younger man, Alcibiades, was endowed with devastating good looks, of a sort that 'flowered at each age and season' of his life, according to Plutarch, although we are not told many precise details of his appearance. While the middle years of the golden Athenian century will always be associated with the austere, reserved figure of Pericles, the final part was dominated by a man from the same aristocratic stock with a diametrically different way of demonstrating his cleverness.

The stories told about Alcibiades as a child suggest insufferable arrogance and narcissism, underpinning a boundless confidence that all rules could be rewritten in his favour. Struggling to prevail in a wrestling contest, he sank his teeth into the hand of his opponent, who accused him of biting 'like a woman', to which the cocksure lad snapped back, 'No, like a lion.' When a cart threatened to roll over the game of dice that he and his friends were playing, he lay face down in the road and forced the carter to stop. He refused to learn to play the flute, on the grounds that it would disfigure his face.

Anecdotes aside, there are some concrete facts about his origins that throw light on the character of Alcibiades. He was only three when his father, Kleinias, died in the battle of Coronea in 447 BCE after a distinguished military career, which had included sponsoring and commanding a warship in a fight with the Persians. The little boy was fostered by a kinsman – none other than the virtual master of Athens, Pericles. On his mother's side the lad descended from the Alkmeonid clan of patricians who were both founders of the city's democracy and the inheritors, supposedly, of a curse.*

---

* See page 27.

Losing a parent, especially a distinguished parent, at a tender age, and then being reared with a feeling of being rather special, can have complex results. Sometimes it can instil a powerful sense of ambition and entitlement: Alcibiades is a perfect example. As a youth he was clever and charismatic and made no attempt to hide his gifts. That makes the story of his entanglement with Socrates all the stranger. If Socrates was known for one thing, it was disarming humility, his bizarre insistence that whatever other people might know, he knew nothing at all. So in this and several other ways, the two men were at opposite ends of a spectrum.

Yet the lives of these contrasting Athenians were closely intertwined, first and foremost on the battlefield. Just as the great war between Athens and Sparta was starting, when Alcibiades was about twenty, he served with his city's forces who were besieging the northern Greek outpost of Potidaea. That campaign was remembered in Athens as an exceptionally harsh endurance test, in part because of much colder winters than any Athenian was used to, and also because of an early outbreak of pestilence. Alcibiades found himself at close quarters with the eccentric sage. As Plutarch puts it,

> … Socrates lodged in the same tent with him, and stood next to him in battle. Once an intense skirmish took place, in which they both behaved with outstanding courage. When Alcibiades received a wound, Socrates threw himself in front to protect him and beyond any question saved him and his arms from the adversary… [When] the generals appeared eager to award the battle honours to Alcibiades, Socrates… was the first to give evidence for him, and pressed them to crown him and award him a complete suit of armour.

This ill-matched military pair crossed paths again, after the rout of the Athenians by Sparta's Boeotian allies at Deleon, north of the city, in 424 BCE. This time Alcibiades was mounted, as would be expected of a young man wealthy enough to keep thoroughbreds for sport and battle. He espied the bedraggled but still dignified Socrates, who was walking and leading others to safety. Alcibiades stayed long enough to shelter his friend from danger, even though the enemy was pressing hard and cutting off the retreat of many soldiers.

But the most famous encounter between Socrates and Alcibiades was nowhere near a killing-field. It unfolded in a camp, upmarket literary salon, amid the security and refinement which the Athenian elite continued to enjoy even when war was raging not far away. The story's details are probably an artificial device, possibly fusing and embroidering a multitude of real-life conversations and scenes. But Plato's *Symposium* gives a flavour of the life and banter of the Athenian cultural elite at the zenith of their achievements, marked by a bizarre mixture of genius, debauchery, idealism and cynicism.

Indeed, if there are two scenes that capture life in Athens during the twilight of the city's supreme glory, the *Symposium* is one. The other is the hauntingly dignified execution (or, in a sense, assisted suicide) of Socrates in 399 BCE, after a trial in which he was held to account for his alleged misdeeds against the city. These included the mentoring of dangerous men, the late General Alcibiades very much included.

In the *Symposium*, an all-night party is thrown at the home of a talented poet, Agathon, who has just won the first prize in the annual competition for tragedy. This means the notional setting for the gathering is 416 BCE, although the description of Alcibiades would fit an earlier stage in his life. In any case, if we take the dating at face value, five years have passed since Athens and Sparta proclaimed a draw in their titanic military contest, but the region's peace has already been shattered several times over, thanks to political manoeuvres in which Alcibiades was deeply involved, and all-out war is on the horizon. None of that has changed the fact that brilliant poetry is still being penned and judged, witty comedies are still cutting bigwigs down to size, and sculptors are continuing to fashion beautiful monuments and temples.

The apparent setting of the *Symposium*, in a private dwelling accessible from the street, is worth noting. As visitors to ancient Athens sometimes observed, private houses in the city were relatively modest when compared to the magnificence of public spaces. This was a world, and a climate, in which many of life's most meaningful moments were enjoyed out of doors. But the homes of the rich were certainly not slums either. Agathon's house is not a villa in its own grounds; it probably takes the form of a courtyard with two main reception rooms, one for men, the other for women.

As can be observed in modern Greek urban spaces, from the Plaka of Athens to the whitewashed lanes of the Aegean ports, a modest-looking house accessed from a narrow, winding street can turn out to be remarkably elegant and spacious once you are inside. Whether large or small, an ancient Athenian house often enclosed a walled garden. The majority of houses were made of mud and they were in perpetual need of rebuilding as they crumbled. That explains why so few have survived. In a wealthy house, the floors at least were made of stone.

The men's reception room, known as the *andron* or *andronitis*, had beautifully carved couches arranged round the walls. In a luxurious house, the floor of this room might consist of a mosaic, depicting some classical scene. (Alcibiades showed off his unusual wealth by convincing a distinguished painter, one who was more used to public than private art, to decorate his Athenian home with murals.) As in later Ottoman houses, there are separate quarters where women hold sway, cooking and weaving. Women keep well away as men settle down to the serious business of social life, which involves witty, bantering conversation, ample but relatively simple food and lashings of wine, suitably diluted so that its consumption can be stretched over a long evening.

The *Symposium* describes a world dominated by men who are assumed to be bisexual. They have wives and marital duties, which are not trivial: marriage provides legitimate heirs, and adultery is a serious crime. But these arrogant males also expect to be able to enjoy themselves, more casually, with individuals of either sex. And relationships between older men and adolescent youths are regarded as part of the younger party's growing-up process. The incorrigibly eccentric Socrates, the son of a stonemason, is comfortable in this society but he also stands above it. In a world of preening dandies, the philosopher is notoriously indifferent to his dress, and he usually goes around barefoot, gathering dust.

The evening described in the *Symposium* is, however, an exception. Aristodemos, a follower of Socrates, encounters the master in the street and is surprised to see him looking well-scrubbed and sporting smart evening shoes. Socrates explains that he has spruced himself up in honour of his host, Agathon, who has just won a well-deserved award. Socrates cheerfully suggests that his pupil invite himself along to the celebration. Within this cosy circle, gatecrashing a party is permissible. They proceed together for a while, and then Socrates feels the need to stop for a think, so he sends Aristodemos on alone. By the time the philosopher eventually arrives, dinner is in progress. The assembled wits decide to drink gradually, to work themselves into the mood for a philosophical debate. The flute-girl is told to go away and play in the women's quarters. Then the all-male fun can begin, and they begin a debate on the nature of love.

The conversation features plenty of mildly comic whimsy, but there are moments when it soars to a much higher level, almost heavenward. An amusing contribution is made by Aristophanes, the comic poet. Behind all the banter, some human and political rivalries, with the potential to turn deadly, are lurking. In 423 BCE, with war raging, Aristophanes had staged an uproarious farce, *The Clouds*, that featured an absurdly caricatured Socrates, floating in a basket and speculating about useless scientific questions. Other characters include Strepsiades, a grumpy older man, and his extravagant son Pheidippides. The exasperated father tries to persuade his lazy offspring to enrol in the 'Thinkery' – a school supposedly run by Socrates, where you could learn to argue any side of any case. Finding his son reluctant, Strepsiades samples for himself the weird stuff that Socrates is peddling.

All good clean fun, one might think, except that some highly sensitive issues are being touched on. Ultimately the nature of this 'fun' would be a matter of life or death. Aristophanes' caricature of Socrates, which misrepresents both his style and his interests, would be used as evidence at his trial. More immediately, the playwright Aristophanes was struggling for his own survival after a prosecution launched against him by the arch-hawk Kleon for allegedly defaming the city.

By lampooning Socrates and associating him, falsely, with the real-life caste of people who took money to argue difficult cases, Aristophanes may have been trying to save his own skin and curry favour with some political hardliners who thought democracy had gone too far. By one interpretation, Strepsiades is a proxy for Pericles (recently dead and still too venerable to be attacked directly) and Pheidippides for the statesman's profligate foster-son Alcibiades.

But in the *Symposium*, there are no openly expressed hard feelings between Aristophanes, Socrates and the other members of the Athenian cultural elite. They all seem happy to drink together and think together, with no obvious fear of sinking together. As his contribution to the debate about love, Aristophanes speculates that the first human beings had two faces, four legs and four arms, until they were split in half by a jealous Zeus. That is why we spend our lives looking for our 'other half' – who may be of the opposite or the same sex, depending on the characteristics of the original quadruped we emerged from.

When the turn of Socrates comes round, the tone changes dramatically. He delivers an eloquent hymn of praise to the progressively higher planes at which love can operate. From sexual attraction to one human body; to an appreciation of human beauty in general; to a love of beautiful minds and knowledge; and lastly to a love and understanding of beauty pure and simple: 'And finally, [the seeker] will see something wonderful, beautiful in its nature…'

This ideal of spiritual ecstasy is at the heart of the vision that Plato would develop over the following decades. We will never be sure how much of this sentiment really came from Socrates and how much is Platonic projection. In any case, according to the account in the *Symposium*, even Socrates does not claim to be the originator of these lofty thoughts. He says he has heard them from a mysterious wise woman called Diotima. This is a social world from which the feminine is all but excluded, and yet it finds a way of re-entering, even when the flute-girls have been banished.

Suddenly the party is interrupted by sexual ambivalence of another kind. A loud commotion is heard on the street, then knocking on the door. This turns out to be a band of tipsy revellers, led by the most glamorous man in Athens, Alcibiades, whose hair is decked out with ivy, violets and ribbons. He marches in and, amid apologies for his drunken state, garlands Agathon the host, while simultaneously launching into a stream of flirtatious banter with his old friend and mentor Socrates: 'Trust you to be sitting next to [Agathon] the handsomest lad in the room...'

With his tongue loosened but not confused, Alcibiades launches into a hymn of adoration, not for love in general but for Socrates, an ugly old man whose disturbing brilliance moves him as nobody else can. 'When I hear him, my heart turns over, more than if I were in a religious frenzy, and tears flow from my eyes...' Amid all the foolish chatter, there is something touching about Alcibiades' outburst. This was a supremely arrogant young man whose looks, wealth and confidence could command the attention of almost anybody else in Athens. But his greatest fascination was with a man he could not subdue or control: a pug-faced brainbox, who was fond of him but saw through his nonsense, a man who insisted on looking below the surface to the deep things of life. Socrates moved and disturbed him as nobody else did.

In fact, the *Symposium* is not the only encounter between Alcibiades and Socrates which Plato describes. He actually devotes a whole dialogue, *First Alcibiades*, to a conversation between the two men, in which Socrates probes the younger man's desire for worldly achievement and acquisition, and gently indicates how vain these aspirations are. But that work is obviously a literary device. The *Symposium* probably isn't literally true either, but it portrays a world that undoubtedly existed, and gives a flavour of a certain style of interaction.

To imagine the world of Alcibiades and his drinking companions, it may be helpful to call to mind the self-indulgent decadence of upper-class Britain in the late eighteenth century, or the wild, spoiled Oxford students of the 1930s, described by Evelyn Waugh. Or the high jinks enjoyed by upmarket secret student societies such as the Skull and Bones club, which future US president George W. Bush joined as a Yale undergraduate.

To be fair, Alcibiades did much more than sound off at raucous parties. Having grown up in the household of Pericles, he had failed to imbibe the statesman's gravity and sense of purpose, but he did inherit the assumption that he was born to a commanding role in shaping the city's destiny. Money helped. He married Hipparete, the daughter of a notoriously rich Athenian: her dowry added to his already substantial fortune.

During and after the negotiations that led to a shaky peace between Athens and Sparta in 421 BCE, he played a supremely devious role as he outmanoeuvred his rival Nikias, an older and more moderate figure, for the role of dominant personality in Athenian politics. Given that his family had close connections with Sparta, Alcibiades had initially expected to play some part in brokering the peace. Once those hopes were dashed, he churlishly set about sabotaging the accord. Nikias wanted the settlement to hold, but Alcibiades worked craftily for the opposite result. As part of his effort to undermine the peace, he encouraged the city of Argos to challenge Sparta's domination of the Peloponnese.

Around 420 BCE, at the behest of Nikias, a Spartan delegation came to Athens, armed with authority to negotiate any issues which the treaty had left unresolved. Alcibiades persuaded the visitors to play down their own rank, deny having any mandate to negotiate sensitive matters and instead place their faith in his intimate knowledge of Athenian affairs. When that advice was followed, he then denounced the envoys for being two-faced and untrustworthy.

But when in 418 BCE the Spartans beat an Argive army at Mantinea in the central Peloponnese, in one of the largest battles of the war, Alcibiades somehow escaped any blame. The rivalry between the impulsive Alcibiades, whose swaggering insouciance won him many admirers, and the more cautious Nikias led to the final use of ostracism in Athenian political history. A politician called Hyperbolus, an opportunistic loudmouth who sounds like a lesser version of Alcibiades, proposed that an ostracism be held. Perhaps he dreamed of stepping into the gap if the arch-boaster Alcibiades could be removed. In any case the two titans of city politics, Alcibiades and Nikias, felt they were both in danger; they briefly joined forces and saw to it that Hyperbolus got the largest number of negative votes. After that, ostracism fell into disuse. The idea that the whole body politic could be cleansed by the removal of one person seemed to belong to a more innocent age.

If we are to believe Plato's description, Alcibiades was still capable of behaving like a spoiled, precocious youth when he was well past thirty and already playing an influential role in the affairs of the city. Whatever we think of Plato's timing, he was probably right about one thing: Alcibiades could, almost in the same breath, be as playful as a child and as cleverly calculating as a snake.

In 415 BCE, the two strongmen of Athens clashed once again, and the stakes were higher than ever. The city faced a fateful decision over whether to become deeply embroiled in the affairs of a huge, wealthy island 900 kilometres to the west: Sicily. The western Sicilian city of Segesta, which had recently entered an alliance with Athens, asked for help to ward off an attack by a neighbouring town, Selinus, which in turn was being assisted by the mighty city of Syracuse, aligned with Sparta.

Alcibiades enticed the assembly with visions of the vast strategic prize that lay within the city's grasp, while Nikias urged citizens to remember how difficult expeditionary warfare could be. The speech of Alcibiades, as reported by Thucydides, mixes boasting about his own munificence as a benefactor of the city with exhortations to imperial glory. Benjamin Disraeli, who urged Victorian Britain and indeed Queen Victoria herself, to rejoice in having an empire, would recognize some of the Athenian imperialist's sentiments. So perhaps would the hard-line American foreign-policy pundits who advocate pre-emptive strikes on potential enemies.

> There seems no reasonable argument to induce us to hold back... or to justify any excuse to our allies in Sicily for not helping them. The reason why we made them our allies is not that we wanted them to send troops here but so that they should be a thorn in the side of our enemies in Sicily... This is the way we won our empire and this is the way all empires have been won, by coming vigorously to the assistance of all those who seek it, regardless of whether they are Greeks... One does not only defend oneself against a superior power when one is attacked; one takes measures to prevent the attack from materializing. And it is not possible for us to be like housekeepers and calculate how much empire we want to have.

The *demos* was fired up with patriotic fervour and voted to send sixty ships to Sicily. Nikias retorted that if there was to be an expedition at all, more vessels would be required. The assembly duly upped the number to 100. They also reckoned that a broad range of military talent would be needed: Alcibiades, Nikias and another general, Lamachus, were all named as commanders. The armada set out from Piraeus in a frenzy of patriotic enthusiasm.

One day in May, shortly before the ships left, something extraordinary happened. Monuments known as Herms, which were dotted across the city and formed an important part of its sacred geography, were desecrated. With a bearded face at the top and phallus protruding lower down, these stone pillars represented Hermes, the deity responsible for boundaries, journeys, messages, transitions. They were supposed to ward off harm and guarantee success in all manner of enterprises. Their destruction would have been a bad enough omen at any time, and in a city full of febrile jingoistic passions it became a source of near-hysteria. In the course of investigations, an even worse blasphemy was discovered. It turned out that a group of drunken young men had mockingly imitated the supremely sacred mysteries that took place every year at Eleusis. This was a place where initiates gained a new understanding of mortality, thanks to a mixture of intoxicants and rituals whose details were kept highly secret. Control of the Eleusinian mysteries, which commanded awe throughout the Greek world, was one of the secret spiritual weapons of Athens. It connected the city to the threshold between life and death. It was alleged that this horrible act of blasphemy had taken place at the house of Alcibiades and that he might even have participated in it.

Who exactly mutilated the Herms, and who mocked the mysteries, are questions that will never be answered. However, one thing is clear: for anyone who wanted to sabotage the Sicilian expedition by spreading despondency in the city, such talk would have been a highly effective form of psychological warfare. Ordinary Athenians cared deeply about the elaborate system of private and public rituals that governed their lives.

The preening arrogance of the Athenian upper classes, confident in their own ability to govern human affairs and discern life's mysteries, had a counterpoint: the religious feeling of humbler folk of Athens, who believed that proper attention to gods, shrines and rituals was essential to keeping the city going. A young dandy endowed with wealth, beauty and brainpower probably felt little obligation to bow before any power, divine or human. Such arrogant types generally think they can make up the rules as they go along. Athens had plenty of those, and Alcibiades was only the prime example. But at the other end of the spectrum were decent, ordinary, superstitious people who felt the city's divinities needed placating and were easily persuaded that disasters were a punishment for sacrilege.

Over the next decade, the fortunes of the Athenians, the Spartans and even the Persians, who re-entered Greek affairs by lending their support to Sparta, fluctuated wildly. So too did the personal loyalties of Alcibiades. When it was all over, and Athens was forced to sue for peace on humiliating terms, some felt that he was ultimately to blame for tempting his home city into risky adventures. Others insisted with good reason that wherever his advice was consistently followed, it led whichever camp he happened to be in at that moment to brilliant success. Alcibiades was one of the commanders of the armada which left Athens for Sicily, amid fanfare, in mid-415 BCE. But as soon as he arrived at the port of Catania, he was summoned back to Athens to stand trial for alleged blasphemy. He promised to head back towards his home city in a ship of his own, but early in the voyage he gave his escorts the slip and defected to Sparta, where he immediately started giving his new masters some excellent military advice. In his fresh capacity as Spartan strategist he helped to tilt the fighting in Sicily against Athens and its local allies. Indeed he became a hawk in the Spartan camp. Unless the Spartans made a dynamic intervention and supported Syracuse, which was the main pro-Spartan outpost in Sicily, the Athenians might spread their wings and establish a west Mediterranean empire including North Africa: that was the warning Alcibiades gave, and it was heeded.

Whether thanks to his advice or not, the Sicilian expedition ended within two years in total disaster for the Athenians, even though they had brought in reinforcements. About 7,000 citizen-soldiers from Athens were taken prisoner and rounded up into a quarry, where they were left in a semi-starving state and most died within a few months. The defeat of the Athenians in Sicily, with the loss of 100 or so ships, was described by Thucydides as the most momentous development in the war: 'at once the most glorious to the victors and the most calamitous to the conquered'.

With perfect knowledge of the weak spots of his birthplace, Alcibiades also convinced his Spartan hosts to encroach on their adversary's hinterland. A Spartan fortress was established at Decelea, just 18 kilometres north of Athens. For the Athenians this was a multiple blow. Many farmers lost access to their own fields. Slaves toiling in the silver mines in southern Attica began escaping to the Spartan stronghold. Athens was more reliant than ever on being able to import foodstuffs by sea. Meanwhile, several of the imperial city's allies and commercial partners on the other side of the Aegean began revolting, especially after Alcibiades egged them on.

Having given the Spartans all this invaluable help, Alcibiades then fell out with them. Or to be precise, he fell out with King Agis of Sparta by seducing his wife Timaea and apparently siring a child. Convinced that his life might be in danger if he stayed among the Spartans, he made yet another switch of loyalty and headed for the court of Tissaphernes, a Persian satrap of Lydia who was already financing the Spartan war effort.

Seemingly loyal only to himself, and gripped by a lively spirit of vindictiveness, he began pointing out to Tissaphernes ways in which he could bring the Spartans to heel and make them more reliant on him. The Persian interest, he told Tissaphernes, was best served by a policy of divide and rule. Persia should let the Athenians and Spartans exhaust one another through endless fighting, and hence open the way to a resurgence of Persian power.

Of course, Alcibiades was no more faithful to his new Persian friends than he had been to his Spartan ones. He was already dreaming of a return to Athens. His home city, having endured two decades of war, was torn by internal divisions between democrats and those who advocated rule by a much smaller number, in other words the oligarchs. From his base in the west of present-day Turkey, Alcibiades pondered how to exploit those divisions. As it happened, some of the finest Athenian soldiers and sailors, along with their commanders, were near at hand, on the island of Samos.

This presented multiple opportunities for meddling, and Alcibiades set about taking advantage of the situation with a dizzying set of manoeuvres. He hatched a plot to which most of the Samos-based officers assented. There would be a coup d'état in Athens, replacing democracy with a restricted group of decision-makers; Alcibiades would be invited to return; and with the help of Tissaphernes, Athens would be drawn into the Persian sphere of influence and receive financial support from its old adversary.

In the end, that particular plot did not quite succeed, in part because Tissaphernes was unwilling to play his part. But one element in the plotters' fantasy came to pass: a coup d'état *did* take place in Athens, albeit not exactly along the lines which Alcibiades and his co-conspirators had envisaged. A self-appointed committee of 400 seized power, while promising in due course to hand over to a somewhat broader group of 5,000 citizens.

At that point, precisely as authoritarian rule took hold in Athens, Samos and its officer corps suddenly became a stronghold of the democratic cause. For a couple of years, the collective consciousness and strategic energy of the Athenian city-state were divided between two places: Athens itself and Samos, where pro-democracy officers claimed to be the more authentic representatives of the Athenian tradition. For a very rough modern parallel, think of the right-wing pro-American dictatorship that wielded power in twentieth-century Athens for seven years (1967–74) while a separate Greek administration, non-aligned and tilting leftwards in world affairs, held sway in Cyprus.*

Such was the infinite flexibility of Alcibiades that he instantly reinvented himself as a wise friend of the Samos democrats, advising them and at times restraining them as they plotted against the

---

* In the end, it was impossible for two poles of Greekness to coexist: in 1974 the former tried to annihilate the latter, triggering a Turkish invasion of Cyprus and a disaster for Hellenism.

dictators in Athens. So extraordinary are his gyrations that they merit being spelled out. Months earlier, Alcibiades had been colluding with would-be oligarchs on Samos to subvert democracy in Athens. Now he found himself eagerly making common cause with democratically minded officers on the same island who promised to bring him back to the imperial capital and restore universal franchise to the Athenians. That says something about the fickleness of the officer corps, not just about Alcibiades.

For all his duplicity, Alcibiades in maturity was a very competent strategist. He used his de facto command of the best Athenian ships on the eastern side of the Aegean to good advantage. Thanks to him, a pro-Spartan fleet suffered a series of devastating blows as it tried to block the Athenians' access to vital grain routes in the Black Sea. In the naval battle of Abydos, fought in 411 BCE, his fellow commanders went ahead of him and engaged their adversaries in a long, inconclusive fight, right in the narrows of the Hellespont strait. Only in the evening, when Alcibiades arrived with eighteen ships, did the fighting tilt against the Spartans.

Another sweet moment for Alcibiades as a middle-aged commander came in the battle of Cyzicus, waged the following year on the southern shore of the sea of Marmara. As it advanced on a Spartan-controlled harbour, his armada of Athenian ships split in two. Alcibiades led twenty ships straight towards the enemy base and then feigned flight when the Spartans gave chase. Once they were all in the open sea, Alcibiades turned and fought, while a larger contingent of Athenian ships appeared out of nowhere and cut off the Spartans' retreat. It must have seemed as though the Alcibiades effect was magic.

A few months after that, full democracy, with all its turbulent passions, was restored to Athens. But in the absence of any great strategic guide like Pericles, the Athenians did not regain their collective common sense. It would have been sensible at that point for the all-but-exhausted city to exploit its temporary advantage and make peace with Sparta and its allies, but a stubborn instinct prompted Athens to fight on.

**1.** The killing of the tyrant Hipparchus in 514 BCE, depicted on a two-handed jar or stamnos, was idealized in Athenian history as a blow for freedom and democracy.

**2.** A moving monument to slain heroes: the burial mound at Marathon, which contains the ashes of 192 Athenians who died while defending their city from a Persian invasion in 490 BCE.

**3.** By scratching names on sherds, Athenians could vote to expel a fellow citizen for ten years. This one excoriates Kimon, who was a great military commander like his father Miltiades.

**4.** The Parthenon frieze, sculpted between 443 BCE and 437 BCE, was a showpiece of the building programme on the Acropolis, which celebrated the cultural, economic and naval glory of Athens as the dominant power in the Aegean.

**5.** This enigmatic scene in the Parthenon frieze may depict the presentation of a new robe to Athena: another theory says the daughter of King Erechtheus is receiving a death-shroud before sacrificing herself for the city.

**6.** Pericles, the statesman of the Athenian golden age, was called 'squill-head', apparently because of his unusually shaped pate. A blue-blooded democrat, he guided the city with fine political judgement and passionate belief in the Athenian claim to historical greatness.

**7.** Soldiers in the traditional Evzone uniform parade outside the Greek parliament where a quote from Pericles adorns an unknown soldier's grave: 'For gallant men, the whole earth is a grave'.

**8.** The marble memorial to Hegeso, a wealthy Athenian lady who died in the late fifth century BCE, is an outstanding example of funerary art. She is shown with her maidservant handing her a jewellery box.

**9.** The relationship between Socrates, the wise man of Athens, and his brilliant, decadent and erratic pupil Alcibiades has never ceased to fascinate.

**10.** The memorial to Dexileos, a young cavalryman who died fighting for Athens in 394 BCE, contains a political message: his family are signalling that despite their wealth, they are loyal to the city's democratic tradition.

**11.** Built by King Attalos II of Pergamon (in western Anatolia) around 150 BCE, this stoa or colonnade was reconstructed by the American School of Classical Studies in the 1950s, giving a boost to a war-damaged city.

**12.** Saint Paul's appearance on the Areopagus rock around 51 CE is remembered as a seminal moment in world history: the monotheism of the Middle East was introduced to the sophisticated polytheists of Greece.

**13.** The surviving west wall is a tantalizing reminder of Hadrian's Library, commissioned in 132 CE by a Roman emperor who passionately loved Athens. A stately courtyard with 100 columns, the library was a place for music and lectures as well as reading.

**14.** Emperor Julian is denounced in Christian annals because he tried during his short reign (361–63 CE) to introduce the old Hellenic religion. Like his main Christian adversaries, he studied in Athens.

VEDUTA DEL CAST: D'ACROPOLIS DALLA PARTE DI TRAMONTANA

**15.** During their siege of the Acropolis in September 1687, the Venetians directed intense artillery fire towards the Parthenon. When a cannonball ignited a Turkish powder store, the finest of all ancient Athenian monuments was blown sky high.

**16.** Watercolours produced by Irish-born traveller Edward Dodwell, in collaboration with a painter called Simone Pomardi, portray late Ottoman Athens as a small but fascinating settlement, clustered around the Acropolis.

**17.** Established by French Catholics in 1658, the Capuchin monastery incorporated the ancient Lysicrates monument and became a handy lodging for visitors to Athens, including Byron.

**18.** Completed in 1847, the Royal Palace built for King Otho dwarfed the existing war-damaged settlement of Athens but reflected the fantasies of grandeur imposed on the new Greek kingdom by its Bavarian overlords.

Indeed, many things might have been saved if only the Athenians had decided to sue for peace after the spectacular series of victories in the north-eastern Aegean which Alcibiades had engineered. The city's artistic prowess was remarkably unscathed. Above all, the great accumulation of engineering and aesthetic talent which made the Parthenon possible had not dissipated, even though the exigencies of war affected the pace and scale of construction.

Only in 406 BCE was the Erechtheion, the last of the great marble temples which adorn the Acropolis, completed. It provided a supremely dignified protection for some of the sacred objects and locations which were part of the common heritage of all Athenian people. These included the *xoana*, an ancient olive-wood effigy of Athena which was adorned with a newly woven dress in the city's most important annual ritual; the spot where the sea-god Poseidon's trident struck the ground during his competition with Athena; and the very olive tree that Athena brought forth as her (winning) entry for the contest for guardianship of Athens.

The temple is an ingenious piece of architecture which somehow achieves a sense of harmony despite an uneven rock surface. The showpiece of the Erechtheion consists of the six robed maidens known as the Caryatids who seem to be bearing the weight of the monument, despite their delicacy and refinement. Scholars have debated the political meaning of the Erechtheion, along with the smaller Athena Nike temple, another late addition to the Acropolis. Do these buildings reflect a conservative or even reactionary spirit, in contrast with the democratic exuberance which informs the Parthenon and the Propylaea? In truth, it is very hard to make definite links between aesthetics and politics, especially in view of the time lags involved. An aesthetic trend can easily outlive the political developments that gave rise to it.

Building the Parthenon can be described as a democratic project, in the sense that it celebrated the common heritage of all Athenian citizens, and it was guided by a statesman, Pericles, whose vision was both democratic and imperialist. But the Parthenon affirmed that common citizenship by reference to ancient symbols and myths, so it is hard to make an absolute distinction between democracy and conservatism. Perhaps the one certain thing is that the guiding hand of Pericles is absent in the later Parthenon buildings which were undertaken after his death. There is an irony here. The Acropolis monuments were planned as a celebration of the leading role which Athens had played in warding off the Persian threat to the whole Greek world. By the time the Erechtheion was completed, Athens and Sparta were competing rather pathetically for Persian help, or at least to avoid Persian disfavour. But the sculptors and marble-workers who built and fashioned the Parthenon had lost none of their brilliance or energy when the later buildings were completed.

Alcibiades, for his part, bided his time before heading home. Only in 407 BCE did his peregrinations come full circle; he arrived in Athens to a hero's welcome and an assurance that all charges for blasphemy against him had been dropped. He soon demonstrated that he was not merely a respecter but a champion of the city's traditional religious practices. He conducted the procession from Athens to Eleusis, using a land route for the first time in several years. Most recent processions had made the journey by sea for fear of the Spartan forces which occupied swathes of Attica; but Alcibiades brought soldiers along to protect the pilgrims.

This sweet return, like so much else with Alcibiades, was short-lived. In 406 BCE he led a large force across the Aegean. He was bent on recovering for Athens the Ionian lands which he had encouraged, only a decade earlier, to defect to Sparta. By now the Spartans had a far more competent and dynamic leader in Lysander. Having arrived near Ephesus, on the west coast of modern Turkey, Alcibiades briefly left the fleet in the hands of his helmsman, with orders not to attack. But these orders were ignored: Antiochus the helmsman did attack, and was soundly defeated. In earlier life, Alcibiades had been adept at dodging blame and grabbing credit; now his sharp antennae told him that he could not avoid bearing responsibility for this reversal, even though it was not entirely his fault. He scarpered northwards to the Hellespont region, where he had tasted an earlier series of triumphs and had plenty of friends.

In the absence of the most dazzling of Athenian leaders, the final outcome of the war between Athens, Sparta and their allies was determined by another two bloody sea battles: one a success for Athens, albeit with a very nasty aftermath, and the second a victory for Sparta. The first took place in the tiny Arginusai islands between Lesbos and the mainland in 406 BCE. In an impressive demonstration of an iron will to fight on, the Athenians had redoubled their efforts to build ships and recruit new oarsmen. Slaves and non-Athenians were enticed to row and fight with an offer of citizenship. The Athenians were spurred on by news that one of their commanders, Konon, had been blockaded in Lesbos. They assembled a force of 150 vessels, roughly matching the Spartan fleet. This naval competition brings home how much had changed in three decades of inter-Greek warfare. The land-lubbing Spartans had become adept at maritime warfare, with help from their Persian friends, and they had lost their shyness of deployments far from home.

The Athenians eventually prevailed, but a storm prevented them from rescuing the survivors from twenty-five ships which had been disabled. In a city where war had already taken a cruel toll, this was horrifying news. Thousands of men had been abandoned in the heaving waters as they clung desperately to the whatever bits remained of their vessels. All eight of the generals involved in the battle were deposed; two fled and the six who returned were tried and executed. Among those put to death was Pericles the younger, son of the statesman.

So much for the Athenians' last great victory. The sting of defeat then prompted the Spartans to reappoint Lysander, and give him a mandate to exact revenge. In 405 BCE he swept northwards through the Aegean, seizing several towns from Athenian control, and finally headed north-east to the straits that lead to the Black Sea. The Athenians despatched 180 ships to try to stop him choking off enough to rear a lion cub, it needs to find ways of accommodating this dangerous big cat. Or perhaps it was the other way round; scholars cannot quite agree on who said which line in this snatch of underworld gossip. But one thing is perfectly clear. Even in the kingdom of the dead, people could not stop talking about the beautiful, brilliant bad boy of Athens.

to the Hellespont region, where he had tasted an earlier series of triumphs and had plenty of friends.

In the absence of the most dazzling of Athenian leaders, the final outcome of the war between Athens, Sparta and their allies was determined by another two bloody sea battles: one a success for Athens, albeit with a very nasty aftermath, and the second a victory for Sparta. The first took place in the tiny Arginusai islands between Lesbos and the mainland in 406 BCE. In an impressive demonstration of an iron will to fight on, the Athenians had redoubled their efforts to build ships and recruit new oarsmen. Slaves and non-Athenians were enticed to row and fight with an offer of citizenship. The Athenians were spurred on by news that one of their commanders, Konon, had been blockaded in Lesbos. They assembled a force of 150 vessels, roughly matching the Spartan fleet. This naval competition brings home how much had changed in three decades of inter-Greek warfare. The land-lubbing Spartans had become adept at maritime warfare, with help from their Persian friends, and they had lost their shyness of deployments far from home.

The Athenians eventually prevailed, but a storm prevented them from rescuing the survivors from twenty-five ships which had been disabled. In a city where war had already taken a cruel toll, this was horrifying news. Thousands of men had been abandoned in the heaving waters as they clung desperately to the whatever bits remained of their vessels. All eight of the generals involved in the battle were deposed; two fled and the six who returned were tried and executed. Among those put to death was Pericles the younger, son of the statesman.

So much for the Athenians' last great victory. The sting of defeat then prompted the Spartans to reappoint Lysander, and give him a mandate to exact revenge. In 405 BCE he swept northwards through the Aegean, seizing several towns from Athenian control, and finally headed north-east to the straits that lead to the Black Sea. The Athenians despatched 180 ships to try to stop him choking off their food supplies. Right in the straits, at the mouth of a rivulet called Aegospotami (literally 'Goat-River') Lysander destroyed the Athenian fleet and put an end to the city's pretensions to be a dominant force in Greek affairs. All the shipwrecked sailors and soldiers were slaughtered, in revenge for atrocities the Athenians had committed.

After a hungry winter, the Athenians surrendered in 404 BCE to Lysander, who insisted on dismantling both the city walls and, at least for a short time, the democratic system as well. It must have seemed as though a great city was on the verge of extinction.

The story of Alcibiades and his involvement in Greek affairs does not quite end there. As the Athenian fleet sailed towards its doom at Aegospotami, it had passed near his newly adopted home. He offered its commanders some good advice, pointing out that the ships were in a strategically weak spot and would do well to move to the comfortable nearby harbour of Sestos. This advice was ignored, with terrible results.

Observing his homeland's defeat, Alcibiades crossed the strait and planned to head inland, hoping to seek help from the Persian king. Pharnabazus, the Persian viceroy who was closest to the Spartans, then saw an opportunity. He sent an assassination squad to annihilate the man he regarded as the most dangerous of characters, the one Athenian who had never been neutralized. The house where Alcibiades was staying with his mistress Timandra was set on fire. He rushed out, brandishing a dagger, but was cut down in a hail of arrows. He had at least gone down fighting. In some ways, his own personal end was more dignified than the termination of his city's role as a powerful regional force.

According to Xenophon, an adventurous Athenian general with a flair for writing simple Greek prose, flute-girls played as the walls of Athens were dismantled under the watchful eye of Spartan commanders and their Athenian collaborators. The defences which had turned the city into an unassailable island, enabling Athens to embark on far-flung imperial adventures without fear of reprisal, were all but reduced to rubble.* Through every round of inter-Greek fighting in the past century, the Spartans had made no secret of their desire to destroy those walls, while the Athenians, even when suffering temporary reverses, had always managed to preserve them.

In reality, even at that moment of abasement Athens was by no means a nonentity in Greek affairs, least of all in cultural matters. But there is poignancy as well as great refinement in one of the last dramatic productions of the century, a comedy by Aristophanes entitled *The Frogs*. For bawdy slapstick, some prefer his *Lysistrata*, written in 411 BCE, a glorious farce in which the women of Athens and Sparta try to bring about peace with a sex strike. But *The Frogs*, produced in 405 BCE, when the city's final humiliation loomed, stands out for its supreme sophistication combined with an unmistakable sense that a brilliant era was coming to an end.

It describes how Dionysus, worried at the dearth of tragic poets in Athens, goes to the underworld to see if he can bring the master playwright Euripides back from the dead. He finds himself holding a competition between the venerable Aeschylus, the father of tragedy who had fought and hymned the liberation wars against Persia; and the more modern, jaded and worldly figure of Euripides. In the final scene, reference is made to the third great tragedian, Sophocles, who is expected in Hades after his recent death. The first two wordsmiths mock each other's styles and turns of phrases in a way that only an audience with a highly detailed understanding of literary nuance would appreciate.

At one point Dionysus asks the first two sages the question that Athenians could not help asking, in between mourning their war dead and worrying about the next meal: 'Concerning Alcibiades, what opinion does each of you have… [the city] longs for him, but hates him, and yet she wants him back.' Euripides is among the haters, describing Alcibiades as a man who was swift to do the city harm. Aeschylus is more ambivalent, saying that if the city is rash

---

* Not completely so, as anyone can see by inspecting the basements of certain buildings in central Athens.

enough to rear a lion cub, it needs to find ways of accommodating this dangerous big cat. Or perhaps it was the other way round; scholars cannot quite agree on who said which line in this snatch of underworld gossip. But one thing is perfectly clear. Even in the kingdom of the dead, people could not stop talking about the beautiful, brilliant bad boy of Athens.

# 6

# A Chastened Democracy
## 405–362 BCE

*The death of Socrates in 399 BCE and its moral and political import – Athenian commanders Xenophon and Konon do well in foreign wars – the revival of Athens as a player in contests involving Sparta, Thebes and other cities – Thebes defeats Sparta at Leuctra in 371 BCE – a battle at Mantinea (362 BCE) weakens all sides – Athens regains a sea empire but Persia is the arbiter in Greek affairs – Athenian eloquence, drama and philosophy flourish anew, partly by trading on old glories*

In the cultural and spiritual history of the world, the death of Socrates ranks as a milestone. Along with the crucifixion of Christianity's founder, it is recalled as a heart-rending case of capital punishment being inflicted on a good man who accepts it with peace and dignity. We are told how, as the sun descended on the Athenian hills and the hour came for a potion to be quaffed, Socrates remained quite calm, despite the agitation of his friends and jailers. His serenity was the counterpoint to their grief and bewilderment.

The conditions of his incarceration seem to have been fairly benign, allowing him access to his friends and family, and the possibility – if he chose – of a sneaky escape. To the disappointment of his friends, however, he had no interest in that option, preferring instead to undergo the death sentence which a jury of 501 fellow citizens of Athens had imposed on him. He was charged with not duly acknowledging the gods which the city worshipped; introducing new gods; and with corrupting the youth of the city.

The final chapters in the life of Socrates are described by Plato in four separate dialogues, each amounting to a masterly, self-contained piece of writing. Details of the sage's death are given in the text entitled *Phaedo*, after the student who tells the poignant tale. We learn that the great thinker's followers howled while their teacher held forth with perfect composure about the threshold he would soon cross. When his disciples asked how they should bury him, their teacher said the matter was of no importance, because the corpse they were despatching would not be the real Socrates. The sage then washed and bade farewell to his three sons as well as the women in his family, including his long-suffering wife Xanthippe. Then he was left with his pupils once more. In Plato's words:

> Soon the jailer, who was the servant of the Eleven, entered and stood by him, saying, 'To you, Socrates, whom I know to be the noblest and gentlest and best of all who ever came to this place, I will not impute the angry feelings of other men, who rage and swear at me, when, in obedience to the authorities, I bid them drink the poison – indeed, I am sure that you will not be angry with me; for others, as you are aware, and not I, are to blame.'

The jailer explains the gentlest way to let the poison work. After drinking the carefully mixed hemlock brew, Socrates should walk up and down until his legs were feeling heavy. Then he should lie down and let the venom work its way upwards through his body, eventually reaching the heart, and the end would come.

The thinker's last words, to his favourite pupil, Crito, have always been a teasing conundrum. This perceived religious sceptic said to his disciple, 'we owe the sacrifice of a cock to Asclepius [the god of healing]; pay it and don't forget...' One of many interpretations is that Socrates saw death itself as a kind of healing for which gratitude was due. That was especially applicable to the departure of a philosopher whose fundamental mission on earth, as presented in the *Phaedo*, was to prepare for death. Plato concludes his account on a note of awe: 'Such was the end… of our friend; about whom I may truly say, that of all the men of his time whom I have known, he was the wisest and most just and the best.'

The trial and death of Socrates bring to an end the spectacular fifth century BCE, in which Athenian power, wealth and political energy soared, only to decline over thirty years of particularly brutal warfare between the Greek city-states. The thinker's death also looms powerfully over the decades that followed, a time when Athenian democracy and military prowess, as well as the Athenians' passion for eloquent discourse, experienced a revival, while never quite regaining the exuberance of the Periclean age.

If the haunting narrative of Socrates' final moments leaves some puzzling questions, so too does the story of his trial. At first sight, it all seems like a lamentable act of judicial murder which makes a mockery of all the features of the ancient Athenian system that we most admire: freedom of speech, freedom of thought, and a penal procedure that was designed to be fair and incorruptible. Ostracism had offered a remarkably humane, and reversible, way of removing from the scene individuals who had suffered a dip in their popularity. The fate of Socrates appears to be at the other extreme.

Yet there is no doubt that due procedure, of a sort, was rigorously followed, and this was not a transaction whose results were fixed in advance. The 501 jurors consisted of randomly selected male Athenians, aged thirty or above, representing a range of economic and social classes. Socrates was given ample opportunity to speak in his own defence. He was found guilty, and sentenced to death, by a majority of fifty-nine or sixty votes. He then had the chance to counter-propose a different penalty, which might have been accepted if he had offered a substantial one, such as permanent exile. Instead he teasingly asked for free food at public expense, then suggested a provocatively low fine of 100 drachmas; his friends, standing surety, raised the amount to 3,000 drachmas. This was rejected by a bigger margin of 141 votes, an outcome which Socrates accepted with perfect serenity.

Such is the poignancy and spiritual power of these events that modern admirers of classical Athens have long yearned to locate them geographically. Roughly half a century ago, American archaeologists seemed to have solved that mystery with two exciting discoveries. In June 1970, Professor Leslie Shear discovered part of a colonnade on the north side of the Agora, abutting the modern railway leading to Piraeus. The site was identified as the Royal Stoa which served as the centre of religious, ceremonial and to some extent judicial power in ancient Athens. This was the place where an indictment against Socrates was composed at the insistence of three aggrieved citizens.[*]

Then in 1976 came a more sensational announcement: the apparent identification of the prison where Socrates was held, a building on the edge of the Agora, complete with washing facilities and phials which might have contained poison. This was immediately adopted as the most likely site, displacing another location which had previously been a popular guess: a row of natural cavities at the bottom of the Pnyx hill.

In the dialogue *Euthyphro*, Plato describes the scene in which Socrates was summoned to the Stoa. Instead of worrying about his own fate, the philosopher plunges into an intellectual discussion with a fellow citizen who was also on the verge of judicial proceedings, after a grisly chain of events on his family estate. Euthyphro is about to bring a murder charge against his father, who has arrested one of his workers for killing a slave on the estate, and then had him tied up and thrown into a ditch, where he died of exposure. Socrates questions whether putting one's own parent in the dock is an act of piety.

The location of the Royal Stoa, the setting for this dialogue, has been reinforced by subsequent investigations. However, the

---

[*] It was wrongly reported at the time that the site of the philosopher's trial had been found. That remains uncertain; the proceedings may have taken place outdoors near the Stoa.

proposed site of the prison has lost credibility as a new generation of archaeologists argue that the paltry remains were more likely part of a shopping centre near the Agora entrance. The Stoa, meanwhile, has confirmed and revealed many important features of Athenian public life before and after the thinker's execution.

It was the working headquarters of the citizen who was chosen by lot each year to fill the post of 'king archon' and hence oversee the city's religious and cultural life. This did not imply that the holder of the office was a king (democratic Athens had no monarchs) but it meant he was temporarily appointed as a kind of master of all ceremonies in a society that attached huge importance to public rituals. The king archon was the second most senior of the nine archons who were randomly chosen each year; the only one who outranked him was the archon who gave his name to the year. Because the staging of dramatic performances, like the great annual festival in honour of Dionysus, was considered a religious activity, it unfolded at least partly under the supervision of the king archon.

The archaeological evidence confirmed all this. For example, one of the inscriptions found in the Royal Stoa records the king archonship of a man called Onesippus, and it notes that on his watch, a man called Nikochares won the annual prize for comedy. We know from other sources that, in 388 BCE, the great Aristophanes prevailed over Nikochares in the comedy-writing competition; but as the inscription (apparently dated somewhere between 400 BCE and 380 BCE) tells us, there must also have been years when Nikochares came out on top. The Athenian era of supremely brilliant tragedies came to an end around 405 BCE, when Sophocles and Euripides, two great writers in that medium, died; but the writing of first-rate comedies clearly continued well into the following century.

The Royal Stoa and its staff were involved in setting up the Socrates trial because the charges against him were of a religious nature. He was accused of endangering the city's future by tinkering with state-established forms of worship. That was a serious matter. To the ordinary Athenian who was not a scientist or a philosopher, it probably seemed obvious that religious rites, sacrifices, processions and festivals, executed in all their complexity, played a vital role in maintaining the city's welfare. After all, it was exactly because of those popular beliefs that the enemies of Alcibiades were able to corner him, by charging him with terrible acts of blasphemy which were also tantamount to treason. So the idea of Socrates meddling with the established religion was grave in itself, and in the eyes of the jurors who condemned him, it might have portended further disasters for the city if it went unpunished.

Still, both at the time and in every subsequent era, suspicions abounded that political and personal expediencies were at work in the prosecution of Socrates, not just religious concerns. What were those expediencies? This is an awkward question for anyone who holds classical Athens in high esteem as the birthplace of free thought and free speech. The people who prosecuted Socrates included some who, in the city's internal conflicts, had supported the democratic faction, in other words they favoured keeping the universal male franchise. They regarded Socrates as a foe of democracy, and they had reasons for taking this view. All this is rather confusing for any modern observer who is trying to make easy black-and-white distinctions.

In truth, Socrates did express views that were sceptical about democracy, as he was about every arrangement for governing human affairs. If he believed in one thing, it was the profoundly subversive idea that every proposal should be examined from first principles, with a presumed starting point of zero knowledge. High on the list of proposals that needed challenging, from his viewpoint, was the notion that people generally knew best what was good for them. So whatever the trial and despatch of Socrates may signify, this is not a simple story of a democratic hero being annihilated by cynical tyrants.

The speech made by Socrates in his own defence, as presented by Plato in his *Apology*, is one of most startling texts we have inherited from ancient Greece. The philosopher is utterly unfazed by the prospect of being executed, and issues an eloquent warning to the jurors that they will damage themselves far more than they damage him if they decide to hasten his exit from earthly life.

His stance is one of formal, almost pedantic modesty, resting on an insistence on knowing absolutely nothing. To a sceptical listener this attitude can easily tip over into provocative arrogance. He does not disclaim an enigmatic pronouncement by the Delphic oracle that no man is wiser than Socrates. He merely parries it by saying that on investigating the matter, he found the so-called expertise with which many people are credited is in fact worthless or over-rated. He at least was aware that he knew nothing, while others laboured under the illusion of their own cleverness.

In many ways, Plato's *Apology* is the mirror image of the camp drinking party which reportedly took place about twenty years earlier. In the *Symposium*, much is made of the ability of Socrates to fascinate arrogant young men who were not easily impressed by anyone or anything. Alcibiades, confident of his ability to seduce or buy off anyone of either sex, is maddened by the mysterious other-worldly charisma of his mentor and wartime protector. Socrates also seems to have had a bantering but highly charged relationship with the comic writer Aristophanes, who fiercely lampooned him, precisely over his supposed ability to distract young men from their families and other sensible concerns.

By the time of his trial, these jokes have turned very sour. Socrates protests that the real motives behind his prosecution are precisely the false allegations that were so hilariously spelled out in *The Clouds* by Aristophanes. In other words, he is unfairly accused of encouraging useless enquiries into the nature of the physical world, though that had never been his focus; and he is equated with the Sophists or silver-tongued teachers of rhetoric who in exchange for money can demonstrate how to prevail with a weaker argument.

It is also clear that Socrates' influence over young male minds has long since ceased to be a joke. Everybody present at the trial knew which of his young mentees had played the biggest role in

Athenian affairs. One was Alcibiades, whose legacy had never ceased to be a matter of hot contention. To his detractors, he had brought Athenian democracy low by convincing the city to risk everything with its expedition to Sicily. (His admirers would retort that the outcome of the expedition would have been very different if Alcibiades had not been hounded out of the city, and provoked into switching sides, just as the adventure was starting.)

The other notorious pupil of Socrates was Kritias, the sinister aesthete who had conducted a nine-month reign of terror after he seized power, with Spartan support, following the Athenian defeat of 404 BCE. At the time of the trial, there were still bitter memories of the savagery of Kritias and his henchmen – the pro-Spartan oligarchy known as the Thirty Tyrants, imposed on the city by the victorious Spartan general Lysander.

Socrates tries, at least implicitly, to defend himself from the charge of being a teacher who had culpably and knowingly cultivated monsters. When he tells the story of the Delphic oracle being consulted, he is careful to mention the name of the enquirer as Chaerophon, one of his few friends (apparently a contemporary rather than a pupil) who was known to be of democratic sympathies. While treating his immediate adversaries with ill-disguised contempt, Socrates speaks with greater bitterness about the longer-term campaign of calumny against him which, he complains, was highlighted by the biting mockery of Aristophanes: 'The right thing for me to do first is to defend myself against the first false accusations made against me... leaving till after that the accusations and the accusers that have come along later.' He laments that his listeners, since they were children, had their ears filled with the nonsensical notion that 'there is a Socrates... who dabbles in theories about heavenly bodies, who's already searched out everything beneath the earth and who makes the weaker argument the stronger'.

On this narrow question, about the nature of his favourite mind-games, Socrates certainly had a point. Since the mid-fifth century BCE, with some encouragement from Pericles, Athens had become a centre for two kinds of intellectual activity that were quite separate in nature. One involved speculation about the nature of the material world; another involved using words and arguments in such a clever way that they could win either side of any debate. In the perception of ordinary folk, these categories probably blurred. Socrates could plausibly insist that he did not fall into either camp. His strongest impulse was something different: he wanted to follow any line of thought to its logical conclusion, however awkward the result; and he claimed to be guided in this process by a kind of inner divine voice. He was neither traditionally religious nor an atheist.

Even today, many see the prosecution of the great philosopher as a political move by an embittered camp of democrats. The horrors perpetrated by Kritias must have been a source of pain to every single Athenian. If the number of killings is correctly assessed at 1,500, then every citizen must have known some victim of the death squads. Moreover, according to new laws for the settlement of Athens' internal feuds – imposed under Spartan guidance in 403 BCE – there could be no prosecutions which directly addressed wrongs suffered under the tyranny, or even demands for the return of confiscated property. Like Argentina's return to democracy starting in 1983, this was a transition based on amnesia and, at least notionally, on mutual pardon.

For aggrieved democrats, Socrates and his provocatively unconventional style offered a handy scapegoat. They could not challenge the tyrants themselves but they could go after a philosopher who was at least indirectly associated with them. Socrates had not actively supported the despotism of his pupil Kritias, but he had not actively worked against it either, or so it seemed. For some, the mere fact that he stayed in Athens throughout, as opposed to going into exile nearby and working to overthrow the tyrants, was suspicious.

Even in ancient times, the real significance of the trial of Socrates was fiercely contested. A thoroughly political interpretation of the trial is offered by Xenophon, the aristocratic soldier of fortune who ranks, along with Plato, among the main chroniclers of the barefoot thinker's life and death. As Xenophon (himself a pupil of Socrates) puts it:

> Among the associates of Socrates were Kritias and Alcibiades; and none did so much harm to the state. For Kritias in the days of the oligarchy took the prize for greed and violence. Alcibiades, for his part, exceeded all in licentiousness and insolence under the democracy.

Xenophon does not try to deny the dreadfulness of Socrates' pupils, or the fact that some people held the philosopher to blame. But he argues that both pupils were opportunists who took cynical advantage of the sage, in ways that were hardly his fault. They extracted whatever knowledge they could from the wise old man, but had no interest in following his humble, enquiring personality.

> They knew that Socrates was living on very little, and yet was wholly independent; that he was strictly moderate in all his pleasures; and that in argument he could do as he liked with any contender... Is it to be supposed that the two men wanted to adopt the simple life of Socrates, and with that aim in mind sought out his company? Did they not think by associating with him they would gain the greatest skill in thought and action?

As long as the two wrongdoers were under the direct influence of Socrates, their teacher had some success in restraining their worst impulses. But both pupils fell back into evil ways as soon as they left the philosopher's side: that at least is the case put up by Xenophon. He notes that Alcibiades was simply too attractive for his own good.

> On account of his great beauty, [he] was pursued by many great ladies, and because of his influence at Athens... he was spoiled

by many powerful men: and as athletes who win an easy victory are apt to slacken their training, the cheap triumph he won with the people led him to neglect himself.

In any case, none of this could be blamed on Alcibiades' teacher. Neither Plato nor Xenophon could dodge the fact that their hero Socrates had been the mentor of at least one exceptionally wicked man, Kritias; both had to find ways to dissociate Socrates from that monster. When it comes to Alcibiades, whose record is more ambivalent, the two biographers chose different strategies to defend Socrates from the charge of being a bad teacher. Xenophon argues that Alcibiades was a formidable general and statesman who lamentably ignored the benign influence of Socrates. Plato plays down Alcibiades' importance, presenting him as an immature and over-rated character.

The one person who was not especially concerned with defending Socrates was, it seems, Socrates himself. Nor was his surrender to the highest penalty a pointless act of self-sacrifice. By forfeiting his life with such dignity, Socrates brought a certain calmness to the internal affairs of the city. Over the next seventy years or so, there was much warfare between Greek city-states, allowing Athens to make a partial resurgence. But we do not hear of any bloodshed between different Athenian factions.

That is a remarkable fact. In the final years of the fifth century BCE, as Sparta drove home its victory, Athens had come close to the verge of definitive collapse, not simply through the loss of its empire and trade, but because bitter internal strife was becoming unmanageable. The dictator Kritias had, in the name of the Sparta-loving aristocracy, turned vengefully on the middle and lower classes. The 'democrats' such as the nouveau-riche former general Anytus who helped take Socrates to court, were equally ruthless, bent on revenge rather than reconciliation between different segments of society.

However, as Athens recovered strength in the early fourth century BCE, a new consensus emerged. Democratic, rule-based procedures, designed as a way of managing disagreement and change, once again became a hallmark of the city, something in which Athenians could take pride. It was widely felt that the interludes of dictatorship in 411 BCE and 404–403 BCE had been shameful episodes. Citizens of all classes were keen to proclaim their loyalty to the city and its democratic system.

As far as we can reconstruct them, democratic procedures also became more sophisticated. The final years of the fifth century BCE had delivered some hard lessons. They had shown up the terrible mistakes that can be made by a democracy that accepts no checks or balances. No less chastening was the experience of what happens when democracy is suspended, and a tiny, kleptocratic clique allows itself free rein to arrest, kill and loot.

In the fourth century BCE, the political system made a clearer distinction between a law (*nomos*) which expressed a general rule and a decree (*psephisma*) which dealt with a specific matter such as honouring an individual. Changing the laws became an elaborate procedure, a bit like amending the constitution in a modern democracy. The job of considering a proposed change in the law was shared by the whole assembly and a smaller body of citizens, with the role of *nomothetes* or legislator selected by lot from the pool of male citizens who were at least thirty and eligible to be jurors. Something like a trial took place in which arguments were heard in favour of the existing law, as well as the case for alteration. In another innovation, a citizen who stood up in the assembly and proposed an action which contradicted an existing law, or was based on false or misleading information, might be prosecuted, even in theory put to death. Harsh as that sounds, legal historians see this new Athenian system as an early foreshadowing of the judicial review of legislation which today's democracies practise: think of the activist role played by America's Supreme Court. As far as we know, these judicial sanctions probably came into force towards the end of the fifth century BCE, and only became really effective in the fourth.

Whatever its precise workings, democracy was a system in which Athenians of the early fourth century BCE took renewed collective satisfaction, and they were embarrassed by the fact that it had not always functioned smoothly. A careful study of public inscriptions and epitaphs in that period has shown how very anxious citizens were to dissociate themselves, in life and death, from the periods of tyranny. One example of this is the memorial to Dexileos, a gallant and promising cavalryman who perished in battle at the age of twenty. It is a magnificent piece of sculpture. Fashioned from the marble of Mount Pentelikon, it stands nearly 2 metres high. In the scene commissioned by his grieving family, the brave Athenian boy masters his rearing horse and wields a spear with supreme confidence. His weapons, reins and stirrups are now missing, but we can imagine them easily. His enemy cowers below in helpless nakedness.

The sculpture was discovered in 1863 in the area of the Kerameikos cemetery, and it is now displayed in the small museum at the site: a replica is on view in the spot nearby where it actually stood, as part of a row of memorials on one of the main roads out of Athens. Historians have drawn some important conclusions both from the high-relief sculpture itself and from the elaborate inscription, which reveals that Dexileos was one of five horsemen who perished during or around the time of a battle on the Nemea river, against the Spartans, in 394 BCE.

The boy's family, scholars believe, were keen to stress the time of his birth, which was 415 or 414 BCE. This implies that he was born in a democratic Athens, and he was not of an age to have colluded with either of the interludes of dictatorship, in 411 BCE or 404–403 BCE. Those sanguinary episodes are sometimes described as a conspiracy by the rich, the class from which the cavalry was drawn, against their poorer fellow citizens. But in designing this memorial, a grand military family was mixing proud remembrance of their son with an implicit assurance that they and their class would remain loyal to the wider body of citizens. The sculpture itself is an extravagant exercise which implicitly asserts the right of the wealthiest people to make a prestigious contribution to the city's defences, through the costly business of training sons to fight on horseback. But it also promises that these glamorous equestrians will be loyal to the city.

That assurance was needed because, as far as we can tell, there was still a spectrum of opinion in Athens. There were probably some rich people who still sympathized with Sparta and had mixed feelings about the restored democracy. And there were convinced democrats who were furious over the Spartan attempt to suppress the Athenian experiment in rule by the people, and longed to take revenge on Sparta. But if the death of Socrates (along with several other trials that year) had a moral effect, it was that of shaming the warring classes of Athens into a kind of truce.

Why, it might be asked, was young Dexileos sent galloping to war again, so soon after his home city had been defeated, disarmed and virtually knocked out of the contest for power in Greece? The answer is that Athens had been drawn in, a little queasily, to a new maelstrom of inter-Greek fighting, albeit only in a supporting role.

To understand how this happened, we have to step back to the immediate aftermath of the Spartan triumph of 404 BCE, which seemingly left Athens exhausted, depleted and unlikely to resurface as a serious military or naval force for a long time to come. The city had lost virtually all her ships, her empire and the cream of her fighting men. But this apparent annihilation of one of the two main contenders for power in Greece certainly did not signal any lasting peace, either among the Hellenes or further afield. On the face of things, Sparta was easily the most powerful force in the Greek world. But Persia and its monarchs had refined the art of acting as arbiters in the internal Greek contest, where necessary by stirring up one Hellenic city against another. Moreover, the interplay between Greek and Persian power struggles worked in both directions. Greeks become actively involved in contests between rival Persians. In this multi-sided conflict, defeated Athens did not initially have much to offer; but individual Athenians could play an important role.

As the century turned, two commanders from Athens distinguished themselves, but neither was serving his own city. One was Xenophon, who was an accomplished soldier as well as a lively historian. In 405 BCE, the death of Persia's King Darius had triggered a power struggle between the four sons he had sired with his half-sister. Artaxerxes II took the throne but his royal brother Cyrus the Younger was jealous and enjoyed the favour of their mother. Cyrus decided to call in the favours he had done to his Greek friends, the Spartans. He recruited a force of more than 10,000 Greek mercenaries, with a Spartan general in charge. Xenophon, an Athenian cavalryman, joined the expedition. The forces assembled by Cyrus clashed with his brother's near the village of Cunaxa on the Euphrates river in spring 401 BCE. The Greek troops were the best in the field, and their mere presence frightened the Persians arrayed nearby. But Cyrus was killed and the Greek contingent was left exposed, especially after their commanders were tricked into accepting a dinner invitation from a Persian grandee and then killed. The stranded Greeks elected new generals, among them Xenophon, who duly led his men home in an exhausting, perilous trek over deserts and snowy mountains which he would later describe in one of the seven books of his much-loved work, the *Anabasis* (*Ascent*). In one of the great vignettes of Greek literature, the homesick soldiers gave a cry of joy when, after negotiating a pass in the peaks of (present-day) north-eastern Turkey, they glimpsed the Black Sea. '*Thalassa, thalassa*', they whooped, uttering the word which has been Greek for 'sea' for at least the last 3,000 years. We do not know exactly which parts of the Peloponnese they came from; Xenophon cannot have been the only Athenian. They still had a long journey home, but it could now be made by sea, which for all its perils was easier to traverse than rocky peaks.

Besides Xenophon, the other competent, footloose commander to emerge from a humiliated Athens was Konon. In 405 BCE, he was the only commander to get away intact from the fiasco of Aegospotami, where most of the Athenian fleet was wiped out. He led a contingent of eight triremes which not only escaped but managed to capture a set of sails from the Spartan enemy's headquarters. He then fled prudently to Cyprus, where King Evagoras was in the process of establishing a Greek mini-state in defiance of the Persians.

A decade later, Konon saw an opportunity to make himself useful both to the Persians and to his native Athens. Drawing on Greek sailing and ship-building skills, and on money from Persia's King Artaxerxes, Konon began assembling a fleet. The purpose of this new navy was dear to his own heart, and to that of his Persian paymaster. Both for the monarch and for a homesick Athenian admiral, it seemed a good time to cut the Spartans down to size.

Sparta, for its part, was still pondering how to capitalize on its victory in the great inter-Greek war which had ended in 404 BCE. Or at least some Spartans were. Among the ruling institutions of that mysterious, militarized state, including a pair of hereditary kings who by no means always agreed, there was a variety of opinion. Some were wary of far-flung military adventures, because of the opportunity they provided for Spartan officers to misbehave.

They were also nervous of the corrupting effect of the money that such adventures might haul in. Like communist societies at their purest, the Spartan system did not allow for the private accumulation of wealth. Strict codes of honour and discipline were supposed to be drivers of human behaviour, and the countervailing incentives provided by private lucre could only complicate things. Indeed that may explain why Sparta chose not to destroy Athens completely when it could easily have done so in 404 BCE. According to one version of the story, Sparta's allies Corinth and Thebes were in favour of annihilating Athens, but Sparta objected on the grounds that Athenians of a previous generation had defended the Greek world so bravely. But an alternative explanation is that some

Spartans were nervous of the cascade of wealth that crushing and looting Athens would haul in.

In any case, by the mid-390s BCE it was Sparta's more assertive streak that was coming to the fore. King Agesilaus, a bold commander, joined an expedition against Persia. He aimed to liberate and harness militarily the Greeks on the western coast of Anatolia, whose freedom mainland Greece (and Sparta in particular) had in years past been willing to trade away; and then he wanted to take as much Persian land and wealth as possible. He was not the last Greek king to march into Anatolia in a spirit of excessive confidence. He pulled off victories as far east as the regional capital of Sardis.

But the expedition started inauspiciously. In an un-Spartan act of self-aggrandizement, he launched his armada from the harbour of Aulis, a mythologically resonant place on the coast north of Athens, and set about offering sacrifices just as Agamemnon, the hero of the Trojan war, had done when embarking from that very spot. (Unlike Agamemnon, he did not sacrifice his daughter.) Aulis was in the territory of Boeotia, the region dominated by Thebes; and the Thebans put a stop to this pretentious ceremony.

This was a dark moment in relations between Sparta and its long-standing Theban ally, and much worse was to come, as the Persians responded asymmetrically to the Spartan challenge and set about recruiting an anti-Spartan coalition. As well as financing Konon's navy, envoys from Persia offered generous financial incentives to any Greek city that was prepared to bring Greece's newly dominant power to heel. That is probably the main reason for the Corinthian war, in which the gallant Dexileos met his end. Sparta faced a Persian-backed coalition of Athens, Corinth, Thebes and Argos.

In 394 BCE, Konon and his newly assembled naval force wrecked the Spartan fleet off the port of Knidos in the south-eastern Aegean. The victorious armada then sailed round the islands, driving away Spartan garrisons, until the ships reached Piraeus and were given a hero's welcome: this was not quite an Athenian navy but it was a navy created and led by an Athenian. The crew were put to work rebuilding the long walls that encompassed the port of Athens. The so-called Konon Walls are still easy to spot on the edge of the Piraeus seafront.

Nearly a century after Salamis, the Athenians were eager to re-enter the business of maritime warfare, waged from an impregnable base. In the short term, this could only be in tactical co-operation with Persia, not against it. But very soon Athens was not merely welcoming Konon's friendly vessels, she was building ships of her own. By 390 BCE, Thrasyboulos, one of the heroes of the democratic camp in Athens, was confident enough to sail to the north Aegean with forty ships and seal friendship with the island of Thasos and with local chieftains in Thrace. He then swung south-east and collected tribute from the settlement of Aspendos on the Eurymedon river, near Antalya in modern Turkey. This was the place where an earlier Athenian hero, Kimon, achieved one of his greatest triumphs. But the old democratic dog Thrasyboulos was less lucky. After gathering in the expected money, he was murdered one night in his tent by some aggrieved locals.

Sparta became alarmed by all this activity, and sent eighty ships racing north to choke off the supply of grain from the Black Sea to Athens. Old patterns were re-emerging. Athenian ships were sailing far and wide and reopening trade links with distant locations. Any severing of those routes would hit Athens hard. By now, the two historic Greek rivals were becoming nervous, and they made separate appeals to the Persians for help in stopping the war. The Persians were cynical about the Greeks and their machinations, and they did not want any faction in Greece to become too strong. The result was the so-called King's Peace of 387 BCE, mandated by Artaxerxes. It allowed Athens to keep three newly regained colonies, but generally forbad new alliances or blocs in the Greek world. Sparta was made guarantor of this new order.

If this was a sincere effort to stabilize Hellenic affairs, it failed. In 382 BCE Spartan forces marched to the northern edge of the Greek world to put an end to an emerging alliance of cities, and on the way back they engineered a coup in Thebes, installing an oligarchic regime which was backed up by a permanent Spartan garrison.

But in 379 BCE, patriotically minded Thebans struck back. In a spectacular plot, the Spartan-backed despots of Thebes were surprised during a drunken party by raiders dressed in female garb. With remarkable speed, Thebes had been liberated, and the Spartan garrison had to limp home, where two of its leaders were executed. For the Thebans, long despised by the Athenians as dullards, this act of self-emancipation unleashed a surge of political and military energy. A charismatic general and thinker, Epaminondas, rode that wave, developing new military tactics and using money wisely to expand the class of hoplites or infantrymen who could afford their own armour. This exuberant atmosphere swept through the whole region of Boeotia, on which Thebes had often struggled to impose its will.

Athens, for its part, responded cautiously to the Theban spring. When it emerged that two Athenian officers had been of decisive help in the Theban coup, they were prosecuted in their home city, and the one who was incautious enough to attend the trial was executed. That signalled a cold Athenian attitude to resurgent Thebes. But then there was another apparent act of military freelancing, and another trial, which changed the situation. An impulsive Spartan officer called Sphodrias led his men in a clumsy assault on Athens and its environs. His plan was to march into the Attic interior and then seize Piraeus. But he was intercepted after an overnight yomp which took him only as far as Eleusis, well to the west of his target. Back in Sparta he was put on trial for acting without proper instructions. King Agesilaus secured his acquittal, using the old argument that boys will be boys. He may have had private reasons for showing leniency to this particular boy: the king's son and Sphodrias' son were said to be lovers.

The acquittal was seen in Athens as a very hostile act, enough to make Athenians swing, temporarily at least, behind Thebes. For a while, Athens and Thebes seemed to work together in an impressive double act. The Athenians supported the Theban effort to challenge Spartan mastery of the Greek mainland, while Athens played to her historic strengths by reassembling a sea-based federation, albeit in a relative emollient spirit that avoided the arrogance of the city's earlier maritime empire. The charter of that new alliance, inscribed on a stone monument, has been discovered. Reassembled from twenty pieces, it stands in the Epigraphical Museum of Athens, a little-known neighbour of the magnificent National Archaeological Museum.

In the new arrangement, there would be no draconian moves by the imperial centre to impose terms on its allies. A council of allied representatives would sit permanently in Athens, and its decisions would carry equal weight with those of the Athenian citizens meeting in their own assembly. Athens promised not to claim land or property on the territory of its partners, or to plant clusters of its own citizens. The most telling feature of the charter is its stated purpose: to ensure 'that the Spartans may allow the Greeks to live in peace'. The alliance attracted members across the Aegean, and even in the Ionian Sea, where Kerkyra (Corfu) signed up. At its height this Second Athenian League comprised seventy islands and ports, of which half had been partners of Athens in the mighty Delian League a century earlier. Athens had retained an ability to assemble seagoing coalitions, and had learned a few lessons. Thebes showed its new friendship with Athens by joining.

But it was not long before the kaleidoscope turned again. Through the 370s BCE, the Spartans made repeated attempts to bring their Theban adversary to heel, even as some war-weary Greeks made fresh efforts to get Persia involved in imposing a settlement. In 371 BCE, a huge Spartan-led force of infantry and cavalry marched to Leuctra, south-west of Thebes. Here they suffered a shattering defeat, and Cleombrotus, the co-monarch of Sparta, was killed. Sphodrias, sometime raider of Attica, was part of the king's escort, and he perished too. The Thebans used a new military formation, involving layers of armed soldiers up to fifty deep, to devastating effect. Of the 700 full Spartan citizens who took part, 400 perished. The British classicist A. R. Burns likened the Spartan defeat to that of the kingdom of Scotland at Flodden Field in 1513, when it lost a king and 10,000 men in a clash with England.

Reports of the Theban triumph were received stoically in Sparta, where a sporting festival in honour of Apollo, the Naked Games, was in progress and relatives of the dead made a point of showing no public emotion. Among the Athenians, the news was heard with a degree of suspicion: it implied that Thebes rather than Sparta had become their main challenger. Within a couple of years, Athens was attempting to prop up its old Spartan enemies as they tried to resist the Theban tide. But that torrent was powerful. Democratic uprisings occurred in many parts of the Peloponnese, as fear of Spartan punishment melted away. Epaminondas led his triumphant Theban forces on a march round the Peloponnese, freeing one region after another from servitude to Sparta. He curbed Spartan power in a way that Athens, at the height of anti-Spartan fury, had only dreamed of doing. Sparta never revived.

But there are limits to every historical tide, especially in the affairs of Greek city-states. The final act in the contest between Thebes and Sparta occurred in July 362 BCE in Mantinea, a flood-prone valley surrounded by towering peaks in the heart of the Peloponnese. In 370 BCE, profiting from the decline in Spartan power, Epaminondas of Thebes had established the Arcadian League, comprising a cluster of towns to the north of Sparta which were now hostile to the region's old master. But the League had overreached itself by taking over the sanctuary of Zeus at Olympia, a holy place which all Greeks revered. In protest, the small town of Mantinea seceded from the League. That set the stage for a clash pitting Thebans and Arcadians against Spartans, Athenians and Mantineans. Epaminondas once again used deep columns of densely packed infantry to good effect, and his side prevailed. But the Theban commander himself, and two of his most trusted lieutenants, both potential successors, perished; the indefatigable King Agesilaus, strongman of Sparta for the previous forty years, remained alive. Both sides had been fatally weakened. Every participant in the conflict between Greeks was looking battered, with Athens on balance doing best, although still a shadow of its fifth-century self.

Even as the Athenians manoeuvred their way through endless fights between rival cities, life in Athens itself not only continued but regained confidence. Both then, and to every subsequent generation, it seemed clear the peak of Athenian achievement was already in the past. But that did not prevent a revival that was based, in part, on the self-conscious resurrection of old glories. Athenian culture became a product for export.

At the height of the city's imperial pride, Pericles had declared that Athens was, by its very democratic existence, a school for the rest of the Greek world. In its somewhat chastened fourth-century state, Athens became a school in a slightly different sense. Take the field of drama, one of the city's strong suits. After a lull of thirty years or so, intensive competition for tragedy-writing prizes resumed around 370 BCE, but the plays of that period do not survive, so we cannot assess their quality. What we do know is that the older dramas penned by Aeschylus, Sophocles and Euripides were performed as reruns across the Greek world, from Sicily to Asia Minor. Magnificent theatres were constructed to host these shows. And in Athens itself, fifth-century favourites were restaged from 386 BCE onwards, along with new offerings. In comedy, meanwhile, the biting, sexually explicit political satire of Aristophanes gradually gave way to lighter domestic farces.

When contemplating the glory years after Salamis, it seems possible to admire the achievements of Athens as a single narrative, with literature, sculpture, political innovation and military prowess reinforcing one another. The spirit of Pericles is expressed in the performances he sponsored, in the monuments he had commissioned, in the constitutional changes he brought about and in the battles he won. All these were great, interlocking public achievements. This was an era when individuals competed hard, but mostly over how best to serve the city. In the fourth century BCE, by contrast, Athenian talents were expended in a more prolix way. Facility with words and ideas, above all the art of rhetoric, were refined to new levels. But these gifts were often used for private rather than public purposes. Even philosophy itself, along with other disciplines of the mind, was taught in a more systematic and sometimes calculating style, in contrast with the artless generosity of Socrates.

A characteristic figure from this period, confusingly enough, bore the name of Isocrates, though he had no particular connection with his near-namesake. Having lost the family fortune in the Peloponnesian War, he needed money, and made some by writing speeches for court cases. In 392 BCE, he opened a school that charged fees for instruction in the art of persuasion. Because of his weak, strangled voice, he rarely gave speeches himself, but he was good at writing them for others. Isocrates served a broad range of clients but he had opinions of his own, in which nostalgia for past Athenian prowess loomed large. His heroes were Solon the law-giver, Kleisthenes the architect of democracy and Themistocles the ship-builder. What he liked about Themistocles and his era was that back in those days, the most important cities in Greece had been united against the alien invader instead of squabbling among themselves.

In the fourth century BCE, the flavour of commercial and private life in greater Athens is best captured in the speeches of lawyers. If you knew where to go and were able to attend court, you could get a ringside seat in some extraordinary cases of shipping fraud, a practice that always goes hand in hand with vigorous maritime commerce.

Indeed, some features of life of greater Athens show remarkable continuity. Modern Piraeus has become the hub of a world-leading commercial fleet and the scene of some colourful trials involving the seamier side of merchant shipping. In a dingy Piraeus courtroom in spring 1985, details emerged of one of the biggest maritime fraud cases in history. The Greek crew of a super-tanker, the *Salem*, admitted that five years earlier they had scuttled the vessel off West Africa. They had secretly delivered $60 million worth of oil to the apartheid regime in South Africa, in defiance of sanctions, and then sunk the ship in a deep maritime trench as part of an insurance scam. Rescuers wondered why the crew seemed so well-prepared to abandon ship.

A similar story was told in a maritime fraud trial in Athens about twenty-four centuries earlier. Two shady characters from the Greek colony of Massilia (modern Marseilles) borrowed money in the Sicilian city of Syracuse against a cargo of grain that was destined for the Athenian market. Then, while the ship was on the open sea, two or three days from land, one of the rascals distracted fellow passengers by chatting to them on deck while another allegedly went below and began cutting a hole in the bottom of the ship. But the noise disturbed the crew, who caught the villain in the act. The would-be scuttler jumped overboard, attempting to escape in the dinghy, but he missed and suffered a 'bad end to a bad lot', as the trial lawyer put it. His accomplice still tried to bribe the crew to go ahead with the scuttling, but they refused and the old boat limped into Cephalonia.

At the other extreme of the spectrum between sleaze and refinement, the greatest philosophical works bequeathed by classical Athens were written in the fourth century BCE. Plato was not only the most famous pupil and chronicler of Socrates, he was a powerful thinker and teacher in his own right. Starting in 388 BCE, he spent some turbulent years as tutor to the son of a Sicilian tyrant, Dionysios. But his hosts were supporters of Sparta which was intermittently at war with Athens, and at one point they tried to pack him off to a slave-market in Aegina. It was after that experience that Plato founded his Academy, which in one form or another would remain a seat of learning for another 900 years. It was located about 1.5 kilometres from the western edge of Athens, in a wooded park which had been planted by the commander Kimon a century earlier. Women as well as men from across the Greek world were admitted to study a range of subjects including mathematics and geometry as well as philosophy.

Meanwhile Plato developed his own ideas about man, the universe and human society: ideas which have never ceased to fascinate, even if they disturb. His thinking is on the boundary between the mystical and the rigorously rational; it is idealistic in several senses, seeing the creatures and objects of everyday life as mere hints at some sublime but mostly hidden realm of existence. His ideal society, with its intellectual or military elites, and its curbs on foreign travel, seems at the opposite extreme from the open egalitarianism proclaimed, albeit rather hypocritically, by Pericles.

Plato was obviously traumatized by recent events and dreaming of an alternative. He was stunned by the death of his master Socrates, but also chastened by the Thirty Tyrants and their reign of terror, which had brought home how quickly a clever, self-appointed elite could slide into tyranny. His response was not to romanticize about the recent past, but rather to let his mind wander into another plane of existence altogether. Such was the dangerous beauty of his intellectual journey that people have never stopped reading him.

Compared with Plato's soaring flights of fancy, the patriotic sentimentalism of Isocrates was rather banal. But his Panhellenic dreams would soon, in an unexpected way, come true. The quarrelsome Hellenic commonwealth would be forced to forget its own squabbles as a new power imposed its will on the tired old city-states. It would then propagate Greek culture, and Athenian culture in particular, across the known world. That power was Macedonia.

# 7

# A Dance of Death with Macedonia
## 362–239 BCE

*The rise of Macedonia under Philip II – its rivalry with
Athens and other Greek cities – wars over the sanctuary at
Delphi, which Philip turns to his advantage – ferment in
Athens as the Macedonian threat looms, culminating in
Athenian defeat at Chaeronea in 338 BCE – Athens in the
early Hellenistic era, with two overlords called Demetrius –
philosophers such as Zeno of Kition exemplify Athens' continuing
intellectual importance, even as its strategic power vanishes*

These days, it takes at least five hours to make the car journey
northwards from Athens to the ancient settlement of Aiges,
known in modern times as Vergina. In many ways the two
places feel even further apart, yet both are vital to an understanding
of classical Greece and its legacy. Starting in 2022, with the planned
opening of a new museum dedicated to Alexander the Great and
the royal house of Macedon, the remoter spot may be destined
to join the Acropolis of Athens as one of the main attractions for
history-loving visitors to Greece. So it is worth considering how
the two places, separated by nearly 400 kilometres, differ from one
another, and how they interconnect.

The two-storey palace at Aiges (looking only at its central part,
enclosed by handsome stucco columns) was about three times bigger
than the Parthenon: it lacks the refinement of the Athenian temple
but it is still an ingenious enough piece of construction. Not much

more than the foundations are visible now, but part of its façade has been re-erected from original pieces in one of the courtyards of the new museum down the road, a flamboyant piece of reconstruction which befits an extravagant royal world. Aiges, the royal capital, is in the heart of Macedonia, with forbidding forested mountains on one side and flat plains stretching towards the sea on the other. It enters history as a place governed not by citizens but by hereditary sovereigns who knew how to fight, manipulate and seek out the weak points of more comfortable and effete places in the Greek world and well beyond.

Travelling between Athens and Aiges brings home a sharp contrast in atmosphere, physical as well as political. The Attic sunshine lends itself to open-air, open-ended deliberation, be it over weighty matters of state or just everyday chatter, on the price of figs or the meaning of love. The Macedonian interior is much harsher and colder, a land of flinty stock-breeders and equestrians where only the hardiest will thrive. Its monarchical system recalled the world of Homer more than it resembled the noisy politics of places further south. The palace at Aiges did have a place of assembly, an inner courtyard where as many as 8,000 could muster, but these gatherings took place under the watchful eye of a king.

For snobbish Athenians, Macedonia was at the edge of the Greek world. Its people spoke a rough dialect which they could barely understand. If the political system of Athens, with all its checks and balances, was the epitome of sophistication, that of Macedonia seemed crude. In Athenian eyes, Macedonia was a ramshackle tyranny topped by a thin layer of royal charisma, closer to Persia than to any form of governance worthy of Greeks. The members of Macedonia's ruling dynasty seemed to deal as cruelly with one another as they did with the rest of the world.

Licentious as they were, Athenians and most other Greeks believed in a social order where a man had only one legitimate wife, and one set of legitimate children, at a time. The Macedonians practised polygamy and used it as a form of statecraft. It was true that Aiges boasted a theatre, but that was a piece of high culture imported recently from Athens. Far from being intimidated by the sophistication of their southern neighbours, the Macedonians seemingly felt that anything could be acquired through money or brute force. That included philosophy and artistic achievement.

All this brings home the shock that reverberated through the Greek world when, in the late fourth century BCE, its centre of gravity jerked abruptly northwards from Athens, and other independent city-states, to Macedonia. This development brought down the curtain on whatever remained of Athenian freedom: the liberty of its male citizens to govern themselves and chart their own course in foreign and military affairs. The Athenian institutions staggered on, intermittently, but they had lost most of their energy and power. What did not come to an end was the high esteem in which Athenian learning, art and thought were held. On the contrary, the culture of Athens became a kind of priceless intangible asset which the conquering Macedonians spread eastwards with lasting effects for the history of humanity.

The defeat of Sparta at Mantinea in 362 BCE brought an end to a period in which there were three main contenders for power in the heartland of Greece. Sparta lay in ruins, and its particular model of militarized aristocracy was exhausted. Thebes had lost its two finest commanders. Athens, by comparison, was having a modest upturn, as head of a new maritime confederation, albeit with nothing like the wealth and reach of the empire it had commanded a century earlier. No single polis could now expect to dominate the Greek mainland.

Into the stalemate between war-weary cities, there came a thunderbolt in the person of Philip of Macedon. He was twenty-three when he took the throne, a survivor in a lethally hazardous world. His older brother had been killed, along with 4,000 compatriots, while fighting the Illyrians, an even wilder people living further north. His younger brother was slain in a palace intrigue.

Philip had spent part of his childhood as a kind of upmarket hostage with the masters of Thebes, and he eagerly observed the military tactics and formations which had allowed that city to dominate Greece for a couple of decades. He also saw for himself how a well-organized state could spend money on building up a powerful military. All these lessons, Philip found, could be applied to Macedonia, with impressively swift results. A primitive, cashless economy based on livestock was turned into an effective apparatus for transforming freshly grabbed resources into strategic power. He developed a national army of professional soldiers who earned decent money and were fiercely loyal to their king. Hitherto Greek wars had been waged either by citizen-soldiers who were longing to go back to their fields and workshops or by mercenaries who would fight for anyone. A decently rewarded standing army was something new.

The young king also brought about revolutionary changes on the battlefield. The Thebans, as he well knew, had introduced some successful refinements to the old formation known as the phalanx. He went further. The biggest change was the introduction of a much longer spear, known as a *sarissa*, which could measure 6 metres or more. It had a lethally sharp iron head and at the other end, a bronze spike which could if necessary be planted in the ground and obstruct enemy advances. With both arms needed to carry these immense pikes, the Macedonian front line could only carry a smallish shield round their necks. The new Macedonian army had many other contingents, including the cavalry that one would expect from a nation of horsemen; lightly armed infantry which could dart in and out of strategic places; and shield-bearers. And Philip clearly knew how to co-ordinate this array of forces.

As soon became clear, Philip was a crafty practitioner of armed diplomacy who could threaten, sweet-talk and cajole. He could exploit the fears, weaknesses and internal divisions of his adversaries, and was shameless about lying. The Athenians discovered that to their cost, rather quickly, as their interests clashed with those of Philip on the northern Greek coast.

The Athenians had conquered the town of Pydna in 363 BCE, and they were aiming for an even bigger northern Greek prize: the city of Amphipolis and the nearby gold mines. Philip made a deal with the southern interlopers: if they would return Pydna to Macedonia, he would take control of Amphipolis and then lease it to the Athenians. The king was soon in control of both places and promptly broke his promise; the mines were soon adding to his war chest.

As Philip smugly observed, the Athenian position was being weakened by rebellions within its naval alliance. In four member-states (Chios, Rhodes, Kos and Byzantium) local cliques took power from democratic governments and declared a rupture with the mother city. Athens fought back, unsuccessfully. At one point Chares, an Athenian commander who was running short of funds, entered the service of Artabazus, Persian satrap of an area of north-western Anatolia which had revolted against King Artaxerxes III in 356 BCE. But this nearly triggered a broader clash between Athens and Persia, for which Athens was not prepared; so the Athenians had to sue for peace on humiliating terms, letting their disloyal allies go and withdrawing from Anatolia.

Far from inspiring any desire for revenge on the streets of Athens, the result of all these setbacks was to boost pacifist sentiment: a feeling that instead of reviving old imperialist dreams, any spare public money should be spent on improving life for the ordinary folk of Athens, whether by providing entertainment or simply giving welfare handouts. A new politician, Euboulos, came to the fore. He was the prime mover of a fund whose notional purpose was to offer the poor a chance to attend drama festivals without having to pay. Over time it became an all-purpose pool of money for the poor, a sort of cash cow which politicians competed to squeeze without much regard for the city's long-term health. All this was a far cry from the popular imperialism of the previous century. In those days, the city's financial needs were amply met by revenue pouring in from the empire. That in turn made it possible to offer ordinary Athenians a wage for manning a warship. As a result, imperial adventures were attractive to the poor, while the rich were sometimes more sceptical.

In the new political order, with no (or much less) imperial bounty to count on, Athens had to levy new taxes from its citizens to fund any far-flung expeditions. Not only the rich but citizens of average means were likely to be targeted. But one thing did not change. Given that the rich were expected to pay the highest taxes, there was always a constituency of wealthy types whose interests were best served by pacifism.

That temptation was especially strong if the looming challenger was an anti-democratic power whose political ideas included the concentration of power in the hands of fewer people. During the fifth century BCE, part of the Athenian elite had leaned towards accommodation with authoritarian Sparta. In the fourth century, there were plenty of wealthy people in the city who saw advantage, direct or indirect, in the rising power of Macedonia. To put it crudely, it seems that Philip could always find some Athenians who were susceptible to bribery, and were not immovably attached to democracy.

Even as he prepared for a final reckoning with Athens, Philip found plenty of opportunities to test his mettle in a series of inter-regional wars which plagued central Greece. The notional cause of these wars was quarrels over control of the oracle of Delphi, an institution whose perceived wisdom was held in high esteem among all Greeks and which commanded considerable wealth.

The territories in the immediate vicinity of the great Delphic shrine to Apollo, especially the region of Phokis, made repeated attempts to gain control of the holy place, its land and resources. Delphi's priests and priestesses appealed for protection to the association of Greek states, known as the Amphictyonic League, who were supposed to be their guarantors. Back in the sixth century BCE, when Sparta was in its heyday as a deeply religious as well as highly militarized power, it often acted as protector of the oracle.

With Sparta in decline, the priests had to look for other protectors. The result was a fight with many rounds, which came to a head in 356 BCE, when a general from Phokis captured the sanctuary of Apollo at Delphi. As far as we can judge, Philip allowed the cities of central Greece to exhaust themselves until the moment was ripe for his own storming intervention.

In the hottest of these holy wars, a decisive moment was the Battle of the Crocus Field in 352 BCE: the crack troops of Macedonia joined cavalry from Thessaly, their southern neighbours, to chase into the sea a force from Phokis, which had previously been faring well under an unusually fine general. Although historians are not completely sure of the date, this is sometimes described as the bloodiest encounter which had ever taken place on Greek soil, with 6,000 Phokians killed. The Athenians then acted cautiously to shore up the defeated party. They sent ships to rescue desperate swimmers and they established a secure base for some Phokian forces at Thermopylae – then as in other eras a mountain pass associated with courageous last stands.

Philip could have confronted Athens, but the moment was not yet ripe. Instead he made another indirect challenge to Athenian power by advancing through parts of northern Greece which were strategically important. In 348 BCE he challenged the modestly flourishing town of Olynthos by demanding that it immediately hand over two half-brothers of his who were potential rivals for his throne. The real threat posed by Olynthos was its aspiration to lead a group of smaller *poleis* on the three drooping fingers of land which make up the Chalkidike peninsula. Olynthos and its neighbours refused Philip's ultimatum and appealed to Athens, which did send help, but only of a rather half-hearted kind. This was Philip's cue to raze Olynthos to the ground, with some help from local townspeople who had turned traitor. Most of the residents who survived were sold as slaves. It was Philip's way of telling the world that any place which resisted him might pay a terrible price. Similar tactics were used in Ireland by Oliver Cromwell.

Early in the eventful year of 346 BCE, the Athenians concluded that there was no choice but to make peace with Philip, and they sent a delegation to his administrative capital, Pella. (Aiges and its palace were Macedonia's ceremonial headquarters.) Philip played the visitors with the masterly self-confidence of a man who knew he held all the cards. He agreed quite rapidly to the idea of a peace treaty. The Athenians asked him to surrender Amphipolis, the northern town adjacent to gold mines, but it soon became clear that that was utterly unrealistic. The Athenians also floated the idea of a face-saving 'common peace' involving many Greek parties, but that was not realistic either. A bilateral peace deal was struck on Philip's terms. But when a second Athenian delegation visited Pella to extract a formal peace oath from Philip, he kept them waiting for three months, and invited the visitors to join him on a minor military campaign in the locality. All that turned out to be a distraction from Philip's real intentions.

Soon after the Athenian ambassadors returned to their home city, news came that Philip was fully in control of Thermopylae and was well-poised, if he chose, to march even further southwards. But that did not mean he planned to attack Athens. Instead, Philip first focused on consolidating his prestige in the Greek world which had once regarded him as a rough-hewn outsider.

The Crocus Field victory had by no means settled the endless contest over the holy sites of Delphi, which was really a contest for resources between regions and cities of central Greece which could not stop quarrelling. The Thebans raised their heads; they felt provoked by the fact that some Phokians were holding out at Thermopylae, and they invited Philip to intervene. Philip's forces marched southwards, without saying exactly what they planned to do. They did not take orders from Thebes or anybody else. Then the main obstacle to their progress suddenly vanished. There was a mysterious change of leadership among the Phokians and they suddenly lost the will to defend their stronghold. Athens and Sparta, which had been preparing to help with that defence, were left embarrassed.

Having neutralized the unruly Phokians, Philip swiftly took control of the league of Greek states which was supposed to oversee the sanctuary at Delphi. The holiest place in the Hellenic world, the dwelling place of Apollo, was now under the sway of a man who had been regarded, only a decade or so earlier, as an uncivilized interloper. Athenians were divided in their response to these events. Some saw Philip's spectacular advances as a deadly threat to their city's interests which could and should be resisted. Some accepted, or said they accepted, Philip's claim that he admired the refinement of Athens and hoped to live in peace with the city. In 343 BCE, after all, the king had given proof of his respect for Athenian thought by hiring Aristotle, the brainiest product of Plato's philosophy school, as a tutor for his teenage son Alexander.

Over the next few years, Athens did start to act more assertively, if not always judiciously. It sent fresh settlers to its outposts in the north-eastern Aegean, and ignored Philip's demands that this stop. It struck an alliance with Chalkis, the main city of the island of Euboea, and tried to rally other cities into this anti-Macedonian axis. It made a clumsy appeal to the king of Persia for help against Macedonia, which was turned down. In what Philip considered an unbearable provocation, Athens struck a strategic deal with Byzantium, one of the entry points to the Black Sea.

While still insisting that he preferred peace to war, Philip made yet another march southwards in 338 BCE. A fresh quarrel over Delphi provided the pretext. The king took on the combined forces of Athens and Thebes at Chaeronea, midway between Thebes and Delphi. It was a hard-fought encounter, in which the Macedonians fielded an impressive array of their superbly trained army: about 30,000 infantry and 2,000 cavalry. Philip prevailed, and in the process he wiped out the elite Theban force known as the Sacred Band, consisting of pairs of soldiers who were also lovers.

Philip occupied and garrisoned Thebes but he treated Athens with remarkable leniency, allowing the city to keep her navy and her prized colony of Samos. This might have been because he dreamed of using the Athenian navy in a forthcoming attack on Persia; but we will never know, because two years later, Philip was assassinated during a wedding feast in Aiges and his son Alexander, aged eighteen or nineteen, became king of Macedonia.

The fate of the known world, Athens included, was now in the hands of this brilliant young man, a combination of Macedonian ruthlessness and the Athenian polish he had learned from his teacher. By the time Alexander died in Babylon thirteen years later, he had established an empire that stretched from the Adriatic Sea to India. Among their many effects, his conquests cast a wash of Greek cultural influence across South Asia, mingling with many pre-existing cultures, be they Semitic, Persian or Buddhist. The word Hellenistic conjures up the process by which Greek (and above all, Athenian) thought, art and statecraft cross-fertilized with those of North Africa and South Asia.

As a result, the work of Athenian authors, playwrights and sculptors would be appreciated and copied in places thousands of miles from the city. But the immediate effect was to turn Athens itself into a kind of geopolitical backwater, whose very survival depended on the mercy and forbearance of the mighty Macedonians. It took a while for Athenians to realize this. Over the next century, Athens would alternate between meek submission to Macedonian domination and bursts of spirited resistance which left the city worse off.

Throughout the long dance of death between Macedonia and independent Athens, one remarkable character stood out. That was the Athenian orator, agitator and politician Demosthenes, who is remembered as the personification of principled opposition to the ever-expanding northern power. Depending on your perspective, he was either a brave Athenian patriot who was prepared to make the supreme sacrifice for his magnificent city, and urged others to do likewise, or else a busybody who provoked and alienated a rising power under whose protection, if not subjugation, Athens was destined to live.

Whatever the assessment, the orations of Demosthenes are literary masterpieces, and they have inspired speech-writers ever since. His style is different from the preening self-confidence of Pericles, or the other-worldliness verging on arrogance displayed by Socrates when facing execution. Like a well-composed painting, every speech of Demosthenes contains subtle variations of tone to marshal a torrent of arguments in support of a single point. He ranges over a vast canvas but never rambles, and he makes well-aimed appeals to patriotism, honour and conscience.

Much of the knowledge we have of politics in fourth-century Athens is derived from the speeches of Demosthenes. Thanks to him, we know of raging political arguments over whether or not public welfare funds should be diverted for military purposes. We also know that the system whereby wealthy individuals financed dramatic performances and the construction of warships was still alive and well when independent Athens was entering its twilight. Having earned money by writing speeches for private law-cases (including the shipping fraud mentioned in the previous chapter), Demosthenes was himself rich enough to sponsor public causes and encouraged others to do so. Thanks to him, there was one last burst of building for the Athenian navy. Foreshadowing Winston Churchill, he warned that standing up to Macedonia might involve the expenditure of blood and treasure, but was nonetheless the right thing to do.

Demosthenes was among the Athenians who fled for his life after Chaeronea, but this was not held against him. He was chosen to give a funeral oration for the men his city had lost. When news came of Philip's assassination, he gave a provocative display of rejoicing by appearing in public with a garland on his head and in gleaming white robes, although he was supposed to be in mourning for his newly deceased daughter. When young Alexander began warming up for world conquest by sallying forth against the tribes to his immediate north, Demosthenes spread rumours of the new king's death. This prompted the Athenians and their Theban neighbours to prepare for a new uprising. Alexander made it plain that he was still alive by razing Thebes to the ground and threatening to do the same to Athens.

Reckless Demosthenes may have been, but the orator's way with words never failed him. In 330 BCE, six years after Philip's death, he gave his most brilliant speech, entitled 'On the Crown'. The occasion seems petty. The orator is defending a fellow politician, Ktesiphon, who wanted to award him a gold crown and got into trouble, in the form of a malicious prosecution, as a result. But Demosthenes uses the moment to defend his entire record as an anti-Macedonian politician. In a flood of eloquence, he contrasts the lily-livered treachery which most Greeks have shown in the face of Philip's advances with the principled resistance which he, with intermittent success, had urged on the Athenians. Aiming his barbs with precision, he suggests to the Athenians that they are unworthy of their noble forebears:

> Philip had one great factor on his side. Among the Greek peoples there emerged a contingent of traitors, corrupt and god-forsaken men, more that anybody could remember. These he took as helpers... deceiving some, offering inducements to some, leading astray others in every possible way... Given that all the Hellenes were in this state, ignorant of this growing evil, you must ask yourselves, men of Athens, what policy was fitting for this city to adopt? Should she have thrown away her pride and dignity? Should she have... abetted Philip in gaining the realm of Hellas, thus extinguishing the brave, righteous legacy of our forebears?

In 324 BCE, Demosthenes was found guilty on a charge of financial corruption and went into exile. However, when news arrived of Alexander's death the following year, he was summoned back to his home city and triumphantly received. His defiant policies were once more in the ascendant. Athens began recruiting mercenaries and encouraging other cities to join an anti-Macedonian campaign, in what is known as the Lamian War. The newly assembled army marched north and initially had some success against Antipater, the Macedonian commander who controlled the Greek part of the empire. But in August 322 BCE, the Macedonians prevailed at Krannon in Thessaly, and the central and southern parts of Greece were at their mercy again. Both sides had fielded an impressive display of cavalry, but the southerners' leadership was disorganized.

Exactly like Philip of Macedon, and many others before and since, a conqueror who could have destroyed Athens held back from doing so. The city was worth more with its magnificent monuments and cultural institutions intact than as a ruin. But, like the Spartan victors of eighty years earlier, Antipater insisted on the replacement of the Athenian democracy with an oligarchic system, with voting restricted to the wealthy. A Macedonian garrison was deployed in Piraeus, depriving the Athenians of their own port.

Antipater also sought the execution of Demosthenes and other members of the anti-Macedonian faction. The orator managed to escape, as far as the island of Poros in the Saronic Gulf, where he was found sheltering in a temple of Poseidon. He asked his captors for permission to write a last note to his family, and instead sucked poison from his pen. Later generations were not sure what to make of him as a statesman, but they loved his prose.

Demosthenes is the most famous Athenian to have emerged from the city's final period as an independent power, but it can be argued that the contribution of another orator, a somewhat lesser-known figure, was far greater. In addition to making speeches, Lykourgos was an administrator, a builder, a careful manager of public money and a priest. He restored the city's finances after its humiliation on the battlefield at Chaeronea in 338 BCE, and used the money to showcase the artistic glories of the golden age. Important parts of his legacy are visible today. The stone seats of the theatre of Dionysus, at the foot of the Acropolis, were his project. He standardized the texts of the three great playwrights (Aeschylus, Sophocles and Euripides) and commissioned statues of them. He completed work on the Panathenaic stadium, which became the venue for the athletic contests which marked the great festival held in honour of Athena every four years. Gold statues of Athena Nike (Athena as Victor) which had been melted down during the war with Sparta eighty years earlier were refashioned. Gold and silver vessels, as well as gold jewellery, were produced for the Panathenaic procession, one of the high points of the city's religious calendar.

Lykourgos would have seen all these projects as a religious duty, not just an act of municipal pride. As a member of a priestly family which enjoyed the honour of offering sacrifices at the city's most important altars, and derived a handsome income from that job, he had a natural interest in enhancing the city's theatrical and sporting facilities, all of which had the ultimate purpose of honouring the gods. He and his sons took turns to serve on the Acropolis at the temple to Poseidon, the sea-god who was fused with the semi-mythical founder, King Erechtheus; some of his female relatives had the even more prestigious role of looking after the statue of Athena Polias (Athena, protector of the city) which was the centrepiece of the Parthenon.

The one speech by Lykourgos that survives has none of the power and elegance of Demosthenic prose. Yet Lykourgos did more for Athens than his more eloquent compatriot. He prepared the city for a long period in which it could not act freely but could still enjoy the respect that its past glories merited. Athens would no longer be a strategic force, but it still commanded huge reserves of soft power, above all as a centre of artistic and intellectual activity. That intellectual activity continued unabated as the city's fortunes were brought low through subjugation to the Macedonians. Philosophy, after all, is an occupation which requires no special equipment. Buildings in Athens which were once associated with the city's military and municipal pride became more famous as places where barefoot thinkers held forth to anyone who would listen.

Take for example the handsome colonnade known as the *Stoa Poikile*, or Painted Stoa. When it was constructed in the mid-fifth century BCE, on the north side of the Athenian Agora, it mainly served as a gallery of military art. It was adorned with superbly painted scenes of great triumphs on the battlefield, including the triumph at Marathon, and mythological fights, like the victory of Theseus over the terrifying women warriors known as the Amazons. The building's foundations and the lowest part of the walls have been traced by archaeologists, but nothing remains of these paintings except vivid descriptions. By the year 300 BCE, the cool space behind the handsome columns was best known for something quite different. It was the place where a scrawny, swarthy philosopher called Zeno shared his ideas about the universe and the purpose of human life with eager pupils from all over the Greek world. He thus founded a school of philosophy known as the Stoics which would enjoy great influence over several centuries – and this was only one of several such schools that flourished in Athens.

In some ways, Zeno was an even more unconventional figure than Socrates, who at least had an ordinary wife and family. Zeno lived without worldly attachments, a path he had chosen. Born in Kition in Cyprus to a family of wealthy traders with roots in present-day Lebanon, he had plenty of experience of material pleasures. But it seems that his life was transformed after escaping a shipwreck on the journey from the Levant to Piraeus. This prompted him to read Xenophon's life of Socrates, a work which became his source of inspiration. Later, without entirely following their example, he was influenced by an even stranger group of ascetics, the Cynics, who believed in renouncing wealth and bringing shame on themselves through weird behaviour.

The teaching offered by Zeno about morals and metaphysics was impressively systematic, more so than that of Socrates. The hemlock victim had insisted that he had no particular interest in how the universe worked; by his own lights he was just an ugly old man who liked to ask simple questions about life and society. Zeno's ideas harked back to the Ionian philosopher-scientists of three centuries earlier, who had gazed up at the skies over the eastern Aegean and pondered the greatest conundrum of all: how had it all come to be, and what were the building blocks of creation?

For Zeno, the Universe and God were the same thing, an integrated, reason-governed whole, and a virtuous human life must be governed by reason too. Another way he described ultimate reality was based on images of conflagration; the divine energy that drives the universe forward is fire, an all-knowing, all-consuming blaze. Humans must crackle with similar flames. Zeno consciously blurred the boundaries between the mystical and the scientific. The course he offered included practical elements, like rhetoric and grammar, which might be useful in court. But his lessons on physics had a spiritual dimension; he invited pupils to study the divine nature of creation.

Zeno established one intellectual community, that of the Stoics. Another, no less influential, was founded by Epicurus, who was born on the Aegean island of Samos to Athenian parents in 341 BCE. His ideas continue to win converts today, and they dovetail quite nicely with the pragmatic, secular individualism of the modern West. Anybody who has studied modern humanism, read a book by Alain de Botton or practised mindfulness will find something familiar about Epicurus.

Epicurus, like Plato, was wealthy and conventional enough to mark out a dedicated physical space for his school. He set up shop in a place called the Garden, somewhere between the Agora and Plato's Academy. For Epicurus, wise humans should strive for serenity and happiness by limiting their desires and overcoming an irrational fear of death, whose promise of total extinction should be a kind of comfort. He could accept the existence of deities but believed they had no interest in human affairs; it followed that humans should not waste their energy cowering at the prospect of divine punishment. People should lead decent lives because it will guarantee them peace of mind, not through fear of some retribution from above.

Influenced by Democritus, an earlier philosopher-scientist, he conceived a universe without beginning or end whose fundamental constituents were atoms, literally that which cannot be cut or divided. Between those atoms, he intuited, there is empty space, and the way in which atoms will roll about in that gaping void is impossible to predict.

On the charge (false, as it happens) of engaging in this kind of idle speculation, Socrates was lampooned on stage and ultimately put on trial; yet a century later, it seems perfectly permissible to probe these questions in the Athenian public square. Conquerors were imposing their will over thousands of miles of territory but they did not, apparently, have the desire – or the capacity, perhaps – to micromanage what went on inside feverishly active minds.

Indeed those conquerors and their quarrelsome successors had plenty else to occupy their minds. The vast dominions which Alexander had subdued were swiftly convulsed by war between rival commanders. As of the year 300 BCE, the claimants were Kassander, ruler of the European empire; Antigonus (*Monophthalmos* or One-Eyed), who held the Asian part; and Ptolemy, based in Egypt. For anyone who aspired to reassemble and dominate Alexander's realm, Athens was a coveted prize, because of its geographical position and glittering heritage. Among the people who controlled Athens through this turbulent era were two characters who both happened to bear the name Demetrius, although they had little else in common.

One was born in Phaleron, the older of the two ports serving Athens, around 350 BCE, and his birthplace became his nickname. For a decade starting in 297 BCE he exercised power at the behest of the Macedonian tyrant Kassander, and part of his brief was to stamp out Athenian democracy, in the sense of universal male franchise, and entrench a new property-based system. But he was a man of personal culture, a skilled orator and a writer on history and literature.

As a well-educated Athenian despot, Demetrius of Phaleron had something in common with Kritias, the man who ruled Athens with a rod of iron between 404 BCE and 403 BCE; but the new master of the city seems to have been a bit gentler. In such a diminished state, Athens could no longer afford spectacular theatrical performances, and the creative energy of its playwrights had ebbed. Demetrius of Phaleron duly encouraged Athenians to go back to their roots with public recitations of Homer, something Alexander the Great would have endorsed. Ordinary Athenians resented the restriction of their political rights, but Demetrius also reined in the rich by limiting the amount they could spend on aggrandizing themselves, for example with extravagant funeral monuments. A whole category of magnificent marble sculpture disappeared as a result.

Demetrius of Phaleron conducted a census of Attica, whose results are usually given as follows: 21,000 full voting citizens, 10,000 resident foreigners, and 400,000 others including women, children and slaves. A more recent interpretation of the scanty evidence suggests that the figure of 21,000 refers only to those citizens who were wealthy enough to compete for the highest offices. Another 10,000 or so may have been citizens of lower rank. In any case, all this is a reminder that ancient Athens was similar to today's Gulf monarchies: a place where only a small proportion of residents were citizens with full civil rights, although some non-citizens could be very prosperous.

Some accounts of this first Demetrius suggest that he was gratuitously vain (encouraging the dedication of 350 statues in his honour) and sexually licentious, even by the standards of the age. But these alleged details may reflect a confusion, even among ancient historians, with the second Demetrius, who came from an entirely different world.

The first Demetrius was a refined Athenian who suited the purposes of the city's Macedonian overlord; the second was a Macedonian commander himself, an active player along with his father in the contest for Alexander's vast dominions. He is known as Demetrius *Poliorketes*, the Besieger, thanks to his skill at terrorizing embattled cities with enormous battering rams, a talent that was used to spectacular effect against the island of Rhodes.

The Besieger was the son of Antigonus *Monophthalmos*, one of Alexander's generals. The pair had fought together in Alexander's eastern dominions, for example in two battles near the Persian city of Isfahan. Demetrius was then only about twenty. At twenty-two, he was left alone to defend the newly Hellenized regions of Syria, turning in a mixed performance.

According to Plutarch, that indefatigable chronicler of ancient lives, Antigonus and his son made an impressively close-knit duo of rough Macedonian fighters, and they were not shy about demonstrating their affection in public.

> Demetrius was exceedingly fond of his father... On one occasion, when Antigonus was busy receiving some ambassadors, Demetrius came home from hunting; he went up to his father and kissed him, javelins in hand. Antigonus called out to the ambassadors, as they were going away... 'Carry this report about [the two of] us, that this is the way we feel towards one another...'

With their fortunes in the eastern realms waning after a defeat in Babylon, the fighting pair turned their attention westwards, towards Athens. In 307 BCE the young Besieger sailed into Athens with an armada of 250 ships and was hailed by the city – initially, at least – as a liberator from the other Demetrius.

What Athens experienced was not so much a takeover by the Besieger as a jointly managed operation by the father and son, who were also engaged in a much wider contest with their rivals on many fronts. It was under paternal orders that the Besieger made his dashing appearance in Athens, after first driving off the Macedonian garrison which had guarded Mounichia, one of the smaller harbours serving the city. For the next twenty years, the Athenians found themselves in the eye of the storm of inter-Macedonian contests. The Besieger made not one but three dramatic appearances.

As far as we can make out, the Athenian reaction to these events was a mixture of resignation and resentment. At times, the city seemed obsessively nostalgic for the glory days of its emergence as a free democratic power, nearly two centuries earlier. Yet it was painfully obvious how much had changed since then, and in their hearts the Athenians probably knew this. Formally, the Besieger was overturning an oligarchic regime (that of Demetrius of Phaleron) and reintroducing at least the outward forms and procedures of the old democracy. But the hero-worship he and his father fostered was far from democratic in style. The spirit of the times was very different from the stubborn self-reliance which had characterized Athens when it emerged as a champion of civil rights and Greek freedom. The Besieger and his father behaved like Oriental demigods, and expected to be treated as such.

Months after his son took over, Antigonus ingratiated himself with the Athenian population by sending a large consignment of grain and ship timbers: the city could hope to build at least a modest navy again. A powerful Athenian politician, Stratokles, took up the role of organizing an appropriate display of fawning gratitude towards the father and son, who had suddenly become the city's benefactors. A further shower of honours was conferred on friends and agents of the two Macedonian strongmen, as twenty surviving inscriptions demonstrate.

Given that he was also fighting, with fluctuating fortunes, on other fronts, the Besieger spent only four relatively short periods as a resident and de facto overlord of Athens: 307–306 BCE and 304–303 BCE, and then (in the role of reconqueror) 295–294 BCE and 291–290 BCE. But these truncated stays were enough for the Besieger and his father to be hailed, in effect, as new gods, worthy of worship as well as admiration.

To regain Athens in 295 BCE, Demetrius had to live up to his nickname and impose a naval blockade on the rough, populist tyrant who had taken control. He was called Lakhares, and he had melted down some of the gold on the great statue of Athena in the Parthenon to feed his fighters. By this stage Demetrius had lost his father, in a battle in north-western Anatolia in 301 BCE. But he seemed more than capable of battling on alone.

When he re-entered the city Demetrius ordered the hungry, anxious citizens to assemble, under armed guard, in a theatre; they half expected to be massacred. Instead the Besieger simply scolded them for following Lakhares, ordered up fresh grain supplies and planted a garrison not merely by the harbour but on the Hill of the Muses next to the Acropolis. To Athenians who knew their history, this was humiliating; not for a couple of centuries had external forces imposed their will on the heart of the city.

But the Besieger's acts of haughtiness went much further still. His chosen place of residence in Athens was the Acropolis itself, in the back section of the Parthenon. He encouraged the idea that the protecting goddess was his older sister. However, in contrast with the Virgin Athena whose likeness glinted from the Parthenon's interior, his own behaviour was anything but chaste. As Plutarch notes with disapproval, he virtually turned the place into a harem; he maintained his mistress Lamia at public expense and did far more immoral things than that. That did not deter the assembly from approving a series of adulatory measures which would have been utterly scandalous in the days when Athens was a real, proud democracy.

Gilded statues of the Besieger and his father Antigonus were erected alongside the famous tyrant-slayers, whose act of regicide in 514 BCE was still revered (and idealized) as the founding moment in the era of rule by the people. Next, the assembly chose to dedicate an altar to the pair, complete with an annually chosen priest whose job was to carry out the appropriate sacrifices. This was the kind of thing the city did only for its favourite gods, Athena and Dionysus.

It was still the custom to weave a new robe for the wooden statue of Athena Polias (that is, Athena as guardian of the city) when the Great Panathenaic festival took place every four years. Now it was decided that likenesses of Antigonus and his son would be woven into the cloth, along with the more familiar scene of the Olympian gods triumphing over the giants.

In another, extraordinary piece of tinkering with a time-honoured practice, it was decreed that there should be two new tribes in Athens, in addition to the ten which had existed since the great democratic reforms of 508 BCE. They would be named for the city's new legendary champions, Antigonus and his son Demetrius. All the established tribes were named after mythological or semi-historical figures like Ajax or Erechtheus. The new Macedonian heroes, founders of a dynasty known as the Antigonids, were being elevated at least to that level.

Our knowledge of this period is heavily reliant on Plutarch and his life of Demetrius the Besieger, which draws in turn on the insights of Duris, a ruler of Samos whose prolific historical writings survive in fragments. Both Plutarch and Duris seem to have felt that by showering such veneration on Demetrius and his father, the Athenians were revealing how far they had fallen, morally, since the days when they beat the Persians at Marathon and showed their disdain for Oriental theocracy. With their fawning gestures, Plutarch notes, the Athenians risked making Demetrius into an 'odious and obnoxious' character.

That judgement about the Athenian spirit was not quite fair. In 287 BCE, a coalition of rival commanders invaded Macedonia and took Demetrius prisoner; he died in Syrian captivity. In 268 BCE an Athenian called Khremonides won the assembly's approval for a full-blown revolt against Macedonia in alliance with Sparta. This almost felt like a return to old Greek times. But the battered old cities which had once vied for dominion over the Greek world were not really acting alone; they were counting on support from the latest of the Hellenistic kings of Egypt. Nor did the rebellion last long. In 263 BCE, a Spartan king was killed in battle and the Athenians sued for peace.

The city was promptly taken over by Antigonus Gonatas, son of the Besieger. He deployed garrisons all over Attica, including the vicinity of the Acropolis. Although his base was Macedonia, he dominated Athens until his death in 239 BCE, whereupon his son, yet another Demetrius, ruled for another decade. Antigonus Gonatas (whose second name suggests something to do with kneeling or knees) was mostly famous not as overlord of Athens but as the Macedonian king who fought off invasions of his homeland by the Galatians, a people apparently akin to the Celts. But he did have one strong Athenian connection. He had a keen interest in philosophy and was a devotee of Zeno, whose lectures he loved to attend whenever he visited Athens. More than once he tried to persuade Zeno to come north to Macedonia and offer the kingdom the benefit of his wisdom. Zeno said he was too old and ill to make the journey but sent two pupils to become part of the king's entourage; one of those envoys was later appointed by Antigonus as an administrator of Corinth. So there was a connection, however improbable, between the world of bitter power struggles among rough-hewn Macedonian power brokers, and the world of ragged Athenian philosophers who paced about under the blue sky, asking brilliant questions about life and the universe.

8

# Other People's Empires
## 239 BCE–137 CE

*Athens beautified by Hellenistic kings and benefactors,
including the Attalid kings of Pergamon – Sulla's siege of
Athens in 86 BCE – civil wars of Republican Rome, in which
all the contestants are philhellenes – in the first century CE,
the Apostle Paul preaches monotheism but wins few converts
– Augustus and Hadrian transform the Athenian skyline –
Hadrian builds a new city on the river while appropriating
the region's oldest symbols, traditions and sites – Hadrian's
dreams of a new Greek commonwealth based on Athens*

S et aside, for a moment, the great monuments on the Acropolis. Amid the honking horns, clouds of dust and polyglot chatter of modern Athens and its small historic centre, there are plenty more surviving or half-surviving structures that recall the glories of the classical era. But most of this masonry was in fact erected several centuries later, and tells a somewhat different story.

Moreover, its construction was decreed not by Athenians but by monarchs from elsewhere who were entranced by the city's past and wanted a share. Some of these builders were Hellenistic rulers from places to the east who had emerged in the wake of Alexander's conquests; others were Roman emperors who were determined to co-opt the city's prestige by making their own contribution to the skyline.

Take, as a start, the Agora, which enters world history as the heart of an emerging democracy in the great fifth century BCE. This was the place where business was prepared for the citizens' assembly, ahead of their deliberations on the nearby Pnyx hill. As we have seen, it housed the headquarters of the 'king archon' who oversaw ceremonial and spiritual life. But in the city's democratic heyday this open space was not very impressive to look at. It was fringed by an odd mixture of buildings, and from a newcomer's viewpoint its most striking feature was the throng of purposeful citizens, all bent on pursuing their various political, judicial or commercial ends.

Four centuries later, by the year 100 BCE, it was a different story. The Agora was neatly framed by magnificent colonnades, representing variations of the architectural style that was developed in the Periclean age. There was a great irony here. Buildings that recalled the democratic energy of four centuries earlier were being constructed with ever greater panache. But the noisy, unpredictable business of rule by a vast body of male citizens, representing many social classes and interests, was fading into the past. In their public life, Athenians still went through the motions of democratic procedures, but under foreign domination the democratic spirit had long been extinguished. Athens had become a kind of upmarket theme park, whose magnificence would grow over the centuries as one monarch after another, from Anatolian despots to Roman aesthetes, tried to put a fresh stamp on the place.

One early product of this exuberant building spree is visible to any modern visitor to Athens. It is the Stoa of Attalos, a gleaming row of columns whose total length is nearly 120 metres. This two-storeyed structure neatly fills the eastern side of the Agora. What we see now, of course, is no miraculous survival from antiquity. Rather, it is a very accurate reconstruction, cleverly incorporating many original pieces, of an edifice that was erected around 150 BCE. The modern rebuilding was carried out with American philanthropic funding in the mid-1950s, and it spruced up the appearance of a city centre that was recovering from a decade of war.

By the norms of modern archaeological ethics, holding that intervention should be as discreet as possible, such a reimagining of

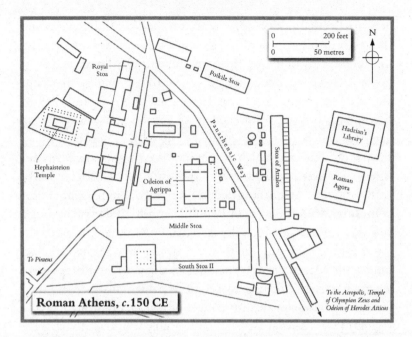

Royal Stoa

Poikile Stoa

Hephaisteion Temple

Odeion of Agrippa

Stoa of Attalos

Panathenaic Way

Hadrian's Library

Roman Agora

Middle Stoa

To Piraeus

South Stoa II

Roman Athens, c.150 CE

To the Acropolis, Temple of Olympian Zeus and Odeion of Herodes Atticus

the past would be frowned on. But it seems right that visitors should be able to enjoy one monument from classical Greece, refashioned in all its glory: not the pinnacle of ancient Greek achievement but still eye-catching enough.

The original Stoa was built by King Attalos II of Pergamon. By the mid-second century BCE, the kingdom of Pergamon occupied an impressive swathe of present-day western Turkey. Its capital is now the Turkish town of Bergama. The kingdom and its ruling dynasty, known as the Attalids, had been gaining power from the third century BCE onwards. Close cultural relations with the venerable city of Athens had played their part in Pergamon's ascent; so too had a tactical alliance with a much greater rising power, Rome. Pergamon had assisted Rome in its contest with the Macedonian kings who still held sway in their northern Greek fastness.

The story of Pergamon and its Athenian connections is worth telling. It gives some idea of how the old city's historical prestige and intellectual power never ceased to make a difference, even though it had lost most of its economic and military importance. One of the early kings of Pergamon, Eumenes I, who reigned from 263 BCE to 241 BCE, encouraged one of his erstwhile subjects to study at the Athens Academy, established by Plato, and then to become its director. Both Eumenes I and his son Attalos I were generous benefactors of the Academy and of the school established by Aristotle. Given the high esteem in which these places were held across the eastern Mediterranean, this was a very prestigious link.

By 200 BCE, Athens was caught up in the looming geopolitical contest between the Roman Republic and Macedonia, although this was a situation which the Athenians had sought to avoid. In a war lasting from 214 BCE to 207 BCE, the Romans had tried to punish the Macedonians for seeking an alliance with Rome's great enemy, Carthage. Athens managed to keep out of that war. But then something odd happened. A couple of youths from Acarnania, a region of west-central Greece that was allied to Macedonia, were stoned to death because they committed the terrible sacrilege of sneaking, without the proper preparation and permission, into the final stages of the mind-altering rituals at Eleusis. The Acarnanians appealed to Macedonia's King Philip V for help in getting back at the Athenians, who were masters of Eleusis and its mysteries, and hence ultimately responsible for the youths' harsh fate. Philip responded by encouraging the Acarnanians to lay waste to the Athens region.

In the wake of those dire events, King Attalos I, who was himself smarting from a military reverse at the hand of Macedonia, visited Athens and received a tumultuously warm reception from a desperate-sounding Athenian populace, with priests and priestesses lining the street on both sides as he entered the Dipylon gate. With little difficulty he persuaded the Athenians to join the anti-Macedonian cause. The Athenians, in keeping with their newly acquired habit of adding friendly rulers to the list of their gods, sealed the friendship by establishing a cult of King Attalos.

As an immediate consequence of all this, the Athenians paid quite a heavy price for plunging into the campaign against the northern power. King Philip V sent his general, Philokles, to cause havoc in Attica, while a Roman force of twenty ships and 1,000 men sailed in to assist the Athenian defences. The Romans ravaged the town of Chalkis, a Macedonian stronghold, and Philip hastened southwards to join the fray. He defeated the Athenians and their allies in an encounter just outside the main Dipylon gate, but stopped short of attacking the great conurbation itself. He tried instead, with disappointing results, to get the Achaeans of the northern Peloponnese on his side, and made further, devastating raids on the region around Athens. But the city itself remained intact, and in 197 BCE the whole strategic picture changed.

There was a reckoning between the once-invincible army of Macedonia and that of Rome. It was a battle with philhellenes in both camps. The Roman commander, Titus Quinctius Flamininus, was an admirer of Greek culture who spoke Greek fluently and knew the landscape well. As the two armies clashed on the hills of Cynoscephalae in Thessaly, the Macedonians deployed their distinctive phalanx formation, especially deep on the right-hand side. Flamininus, observing this, sent elephants thundering up the slope to attack on the other flank, and for the first time since the formation's inception more than a century earlier, a Macedonian phalanx was defeated. The bravery of one Roman tribune, who attacked the Macedonians in the rear, clinched the result. After Philip's defeat at Cynoscephalae, Athens was no longer in the Macedonian sphere of influence, and it had to start adjusting to the hegemony of Rome. Largesse from the wealthy and broadly pro-Roman monarchs of Pergamon must have helped that process along.

From the early years of the third century BCE and into the second, the kings of Pergamon had vied with the Hellenized rulers of Egypt, a waning power, for the position of chief benefactors of Athens. One spectacular result of this competition can be seen at the foot of the Acropolis in the form of a portico erected by Pergamon's King

Eumenes II in 197 BCE, running west of the Theatre of Dionysus for 163 metres.

For Pergamon's rulers, friendship with Rome (and enmity with Macedonia) turned out to be a way of growing even richer. In a four-year conflict starting in 192 BCE, Pergamon defeated the Seleucid kingdom,* its neighbour to the east, and was rewarded with a huge increase in its territory. Rome was pleased to see western Anatolia in friendly hands. The rulers of Pergamon busied themselves creating a 'new Athens' in their own capital, while acting generously to beautify the old Athens. That, roughly, is the background to the erection of the Stoa which, in reconstructed form, now fills the west side of the Agora.

For all the generosity it attracted, simply remaining in existence was often a challenge for a smallish city like Athens which had to manoeuvre between endlessly shifting alliances and personal rivalries. The leadership of Rome was bitterly contested by powerful characters during its final years as a republic. Despite the passion for Athenian letters felt by Rome's would-be masters, Athens found itself manoeuvring desperately to avoid being caught in the slipstream. In the words of a modern Greek history of Athens,† 'a sturdy but rudderless, defenceless little ship of state was struggling exuberantly to negotiate the nightmarishly powerful tides that pulled it hither and thither'.

Sometimes the Athenians played up to their reputation as a society of unworldly thinkers, in a spirit of self-caricature. Or perhaps they were forced to do so under pressure from outsiders. In 155 BCE a delegation travelled from Athens to Rome to appeal against an unfavourable decision in a boundary dispute on the north side of Attica. The ambassadors were the leading Athenian philosophers of the day, representing three prominent schools of

---

* The Seleucid dynasty (312–63 BCE) ruled large parts of western Asia following the division of the Macedonian empire after the death of Alexander the Great.
† *I Athinaiki Peripeteia* (2 volumes), co-authored by George and Lambros Koromilas.

thought. There was Karneades, head of the Academy; Diogenes of Babylon, leader of the Stoics; and Kritolaus, chief of the wandering school of thinkers known as the Peripatetics. Only the Epicurean school was not represented, presumably because of its doctrine of non-involvement in political affairs. It was the job of the Senate to receive foreign embassies, and the ambassadors made their case to the senators in Greek, rendered into Latin by a senator, Gaius Acilius, who would later write a history of Rome in Greek.

The envoys probably did not get much satisfaction in the petty matter which had brought them to Rome; but they took the chance to convey to the Romans the intellectual sparkle of the Aegean. Among their Roman hosts, the most Greek-minded were able to show off their familiarity with matters Hellenic. To an ever-increasing extent, a deep knowledge of the language and culture of Greece was an indispensable status symbol for an ambitious Roman, just as fluency in French was cultivated by the elite of Tsarist Russia. As the prime mover of the Greek spirit, Athens was the beneficiary.

But the luck and staying power of the Athenians was not infinite. On 1 March 86 BCE, an army led by Sulla, one of the most powerful figures in the late Roman Republic, broke down the defences of Athens and then rampaged around the city. That much we know for certain, but how much damage the Roman soldiers really did to the great city and its environs has been hotly disputed, both in ancient times and more recently.

Sulla's troops had been laying siege to the city throughout the previous winter. The leaders of Athens had made the foolish mistake of siding with Mithridates VI, an ambitious and expansionist monarch whose home territory was Pontus, in the north of present-day Turkey, and who had been at war with Rome in 89 BCE. Having occupied the neighbouring kingdom of Cappadocia, in 88 BCE Mithridates carried out a slaughter of Roman citizens living in Anatolia which, depending whether you believe Appian or Plutarch, cost the lives of 80,000 or 150,000 men, women and children. Mithridates continued to expand his territory, proclaiming a campaign of liberation against Roman domination. Athens was one of the places which found that proposal seductive.

It is worth asking why some prominent Athenians were so keen on Mithridates, imagining he could bring back the good old days of independence. For those who knew their history, there was certainly plenty of reason to feel nostalgic for a past when the trappings of democratic procedure had real substance. As they could see, whatever remained of the political system in the city was steadily degenerating. To take one example, there was still in theory an annual ritual, as there had been for most of the past five centuries, of electing an archon who would give his name to the year. But between 91 BCE and 88 BCE, the same archon held that post for three straight years. Such consecutive terms would have been an unthinkable violation of the rules in the time of Pericles.

As was fitting for a city whose trademark was philosophy, the Athenians sent an eminent thinker, Athenion, to the court of Mithridates to ascertain how the king could help them.* The envoy on his return whipped up a burst of naïve enthusiasm, saying the Asian despot was ready, unlikely as it sounded, to restore political freedom to Athens.

Tensions between Athens and Rome reached boiling point when the holy and commercially important island of Delos refused to follow Athens, its notional mother city, in allying with the Asian king. Mithridates responded by sending to the island one of his commanders, Archelaus, who massacred thousands of people, mostly Italians. The marauding general also seized some of the island's sacred treasure, which was despatched to Athens in the care of Aristion, who was then declared 'tyrant' of the city.

---

\* There is confusion about the philosopher-envoy's identity. The contemporary polymath Posidonius (*c.* 135–51 BCE) names him as Athenion, while three later writers (Pausanias, Appian and Plutarch) identify him with Aristion, the future tyrant.

Soon Aristion, in Athens, and Archelaus, in the port of Piraeus, were digging in to defend the heart of Attica against an expected Roman onslaught. By this time the 'long walls' connecting Athens with Piraeus had decayed, and the two conurbations were distinct. Sulla duly organized separate assaults on each place; Athens was soon reduced to a state of hunger.

The Roman general is said to have chopped down the handsome trees which adorned the two main philosophy schools on the outskirts of the city, Plato's Academy and the Lyceum. To bombard Piraeus, he used rubble from the long walls to erect a mound, and wood from the academies to make his siege engines. The walls of Athens were penetrated on the north-western side, allowing the Romans to march on the Agora. The best-known accounts of the attack, written by Plutarch and Pausanias about 200 years after the event, insist that the Roman soldiers massacred and plundered so freely that the streets ran red with blood. But writers closer to the event insist that Sulla, while punishing Aristion, treated ordinary Athenians with restraint.* On the defending side, Aristion apparently burned the concert hall built by Pericles, to prevent its timber being used to make new siege equipment.

Once Athens had been subdued, Sulla turned his attention to Piraeus, where he forced Archelaus to sail away. He also burned down the arsenal, a handsome building erected in the late fourth century BCE, which had once contained rigging for the city's warships. Its traces, including evidence of a conflagration, were rediscovered in the late 1980s by archaeologists working near Zea harbour, which is now a bustling marina.

But it remains an open question whether Sulla did the minimum, in military terms, to bring Athens and Piraeus to heel; or whether he was positively sadistic. Dylan Rogers, an American scholar, has given a fair assessment of the conflicting evidence. Certainly there was some significant damage in Athens. One symbolically resonant building was

---

* Strabo, Diodorus and Posidonius.

lost: the Pompeion, where celebrants gathered for the Panathenaic procession, ready to bring a wool garment to adorn the statue of Athena on the Acropolis. The building, whose extensive remains can now be seen in the Kerameikos cemetery, was never restored.

Some of the splendid, newish colonnades which encircled the Agora were also damaged, especially the South Stoa. As a result, that end of the giant square ceased to be a commercial and social meeting place and was occupied by workshops instead. The Stoa of Attalos was apparently unharmed. Buildings concerned with religion and political administration were left intact, as was the Acropolis. This was not a war of annihilation, and Sulla could make a better claim than Mithridates that his real aim was to restore the old Athenian way of living and governing.

One thing did not change: the Roman elite's ever more passionate engagement with Greek philosophy and art, and their love affair with Athens in particular. During the bitter power struggles that raged through the final century of the Roman Republic, the characteristic that all the combatants had in common was an attachment to Greek culture and language. The story of Athens over the next three centuries is the story of Rome's engagement with the city as a lodestone of refinement, romance and wisdom.

Cicero, the Roman orator who was one of the towering statesmen of his age, was one early example of this passion. As a young man, we are told, he studied in Rome under a Greek philosopher who had served as head of Plato's Academy but had taken refuge (presumably from Sulla's wars) in Italy. This exposure to the Hellenic mind, and to the memory at least of Plato's genius, filled the young Roman with an 'extraordinary zeal' for intellectual enquiry. In 79 BCE, he went to pursue his studies in Athens, where he found another famous teacher. As Plutarch tells the story:

> On coming to Athens he attended the lectures of Antiochus of Ashkelon, and was charmed by his fluency and grace of diction, although he disapproved of his [teacher's] innovations in doctrine.

Cicero [intended]... in case he was altogether driven out of a public career, to change his home to Athens, away from the forum and the business of the state, and spend his life in the quiet pursuit of philosophy.

Even when he was battling hard for influence at the top of the Roman tree, a part of Cicero's heart remained in Athens, where he would happily have sat in the shade of the cypresses debating the deepest questions. One of Cicero's lifelong Roman friends, Titus Pomponius, did manage to spend twenty years in Athens, and gained the nickname of Atticus as a result.

Cicero's letters to Atticus, aching with nostalgia for the blazing Greek sky, are an important part of his written record. Cicero asks his friend to procure sculptures and other works of art to decorate his Italian villa. Just as fine pieces of European painting and furniture came to adorn wealthy American homes, this westward flow of Athenian artefacts served as one of the many channels for the dissemination of Greek taste and sensibility.

Indeed, to understand Cicero, it may help to think of an American politician whose best days were spent as a young scholar in England. It is also worth remembering a famous quotation by Harold Macmillan. At the height of his friendship with President John Kennedy, the prime minister suggested that Britain could play Greece to America's Rome. In other words, the new Rome would guarantee the peace of the Western world with its military might, while Britain offered the subtlety and sophistication to help America, and individual Americans, to wield that power with wisdom. It is not a stupid comparison.

It is also telling that Cicero's mentor came originally from the eastern end of the Mediterranean. The ancient coastal town of Ashkelon is now a suburb of Tel Aviv. In the seamless world fashioned by Alexander in a single decade of conquest, intellectual currents flowed quickly between different regions, with Greek as a common language. Athens was a nodal point in the transmission of new intellectual impulses, but it was not always (indeed, not usually) the birthplace of the transmitters.

As well as being famous in Athens, Antiochus had founded a philosophy school in Alexandria, to which he fled when Athens was engulfed by war. But by the time of Cicero's arrival, just seven years after Sulla's depredations, it was again perfectly safe for Antiochus to hold forth in Athens, and for the eager young Roman to listen, and voice some qualified disagreements.

Just as Mithridates had offered to liberate Athens from Roman domination, Sulla claimed to be liberating Athens from the puppets of the Asian king. If by liberation Sulla meant allowing the intellectual life of Athens to flourish and grow, albeit largely for the benefit of well-bred Romans, then perhaps the conquering commander had a point.

In any case, whatever the physical consequences of Sulla's assault on Athens, it seems to have made virtually no difference to the intimate relationship between Romans and Athenians. It may or may not be true that Sulla burned down the well-pruned groves that adorned the philosophy schools, but he certainly made no difference to the schools of thought that such institutions harboured.

Passing through Athens in the year 51 BCE, Cicero stayed with a man called Ariston who was the brother of his Athenian teacher. The other house guest was a certain Marcus Iunius Brutus who would, just seven years later, be a co-conspirator in the murder of Julius Caesar. If he had arrived just a few months later, Cicero's visit would have coincided with the completion of a magnificent new Odeion, replacing the one destroyed during Sulla's assault. This time the benefactor was an Anatolian king: Ariobarzanes of Cappadocia, whose mother had been an Athenian and who had apparently studied at the earlier Odeion.

Another important visitor to Athens in that period was the Roman commander Pompey, Caesar's famous rival. He was given a tumultuously warm and obsequious reception, with the city gates decorated and inscribed in the visitor's native Latin, not in the

Athenian Greek which clever Romans learned. Pompey's mission to Greece was a delicate one: he had been given a mandate to clear the Aegean of pirates, including the privateers and slave traders based on Delos who had recently carried out a massacre of local Italians. Athens had probably taken a cut from the nasty people-trafficking which had eclipsed the reputation of Delos as a place of sanctity. But this was conveniently forgotten as Pompey offered Athens the generous sum of fifty talents for the restoration of any war damage from Sulla's attack, as well as specific grants for the maintenance of the philosophy schools. Acting as a benefactor to Athens was a boost to Pompey's reputation in his native Italy.

Athens would play a part in every stage of the great drama which wracked the Roman Republic in its final decades of life. Recalling the principal scenes in that drama, it was January 49 BCE, when the popular and successful commander Julius Caesar crossed the Rubicon river and advanced on Rome, declaring war on his main rival, Pompey, who fled to Greece. In August 48 BCE, Caesar and his loyal supporter Mark Antony defeated Pompey at Pharsalus in central Greece, following which Pompey eventually sought sanctuary in Egypt – only to be assassinated there on the orders of King Ptolemy XIII, who was seeking to find favour with Caesar.

In March 44 BCE, Caesar was murdered in Rome by a group of conspirators, including Brutus and Cassius, who said their purpose was to restore constitutional freedom and thwart a looming dictatorship. Caesar's friends vowed revenge. Then, in October 42 BCE, Mark Antony and Octavian, Caesar's adopted son, buried their own differences and vanquished the forces of Brutus and Cassius at Philippi in northern Greece; both of the defeated men committed suicide after the battle. In 41 BCE Mark Antony went to Egypt and met Queen Cleopatra VII, last descendant of the Macedonian kings who had ruled that country since Alexander's conquests.

They entered a passionate relationship and political partnership. Antony thus broke his dynastic marriage to Octavian's sister, and conflict between the two strongmen was inevitable. In 31 BCE, the forces of Octavian defeated those of Antony and Cleopatra at Aktion on the western coast of Greece, partly because Cleopatra withdrew the forces under her command in mid-battle, prompting Antony to run after her. The lovers fled back to Egypt, but Octavian hunted them down, and both Antony and Cleopatra took their own lives. A plot by Cleopatra to survive and make a separate peace with Octavian failed. In the year 27 BCE, Octavian took supreme power in Rome, under his new name of Augustus. He did not officially use the title *imperator* (emperor), but in practice, the Roman Republic was over and the Roman empire had begun.

In every single act of this narrative, there is an Athenian dimension. In a recurring pattern, the Athenians tended to back the losing side, only to be spared from any punishment because of the historic renown of their city. At Pharsalus, many of them fought for Pompey, a benefactor of his beloved Athens, against Julius Caesar; but Caesar acted far more leniently with the Athenians than he did towards other people who had opposed him. At one point, Caesar asked an Athenian delegation which came to parley with him: 'How many times will you destroy yourselves, how often will your ancestral glory save you?' Brutus, one of Caesar's assassins, was a devotee of Athenian philosophy, and paid a visit to his old teachers in the final years of his life, resulting in his meeting with Cicero.

Many Athenians sympathized with the idealistic plot against Caesar, comparing it with the acts of tyrant-killing from their own history. But they escaped punishment from Mark Antony, because he too was a passionate philhellene who had spent several important phases of his life in Athens. For that very reason, he and his Hellenized Egyptian queen enjoyed the support of Athenians when they squared off against Octavian. But when Octavian was transformed into the new Emperor Augustus, he followed the same philhellenic script as Julius Caesar. In other words he was keener on endowing and beautifying Athens than on punishing it, though his feelings towards the city were mixed.

A proof of his largesse can be found in the pillared gateway which marks the entrance to a new Roman Agora that was completed in 11 BCE, to the east of the much older Agora where Socrates had taught, thought and met his end. The gateway is dedicated to Athena Archegetis, in other words to one of the many manifestations of the city's patron goddess. An inscription offers thanks for the endowments offered by two supremely important Romans who had themselves attained divine status: 'Gaius Julius Caesar the God' and his equally deified son, the new sovereign Augustus. Although Julius Caesar had been stabbed to death by self-proclaimed lovers of Greece, the funds he had bestowed three decades earlier were still bearing fruit.

Augustus gave a free hand to his ally and son-in-law Marcus Agrippa in an ambitious effort to turn Rome into a Greek-style city of marble, while also imposing an exuberant layer of freshness on the Athenian prototype. Several new features were added to the monuments on the Acropolis. Agrippa and Augustus, like so many visitors, were entranced by the delicate beauty of the Erechtheion, with its six robed maidens or Caryatids appearing to hold up a roof. The Roman pair restored at least one Caryatid which had suffered damage and made casts of the sculptures, which were duly copied, on a somewhat smaller scale, in the new 'Augustan' Forum in Rome.

At the entrance to the Acropolis, a monument to King Eumenes II of Pergamon, celebrating his victory in a chariot race, had stood on a tall tapering pedestal since 178 BCE. At Agrippa's behest, that piece of vanity sculpture was torn down and a monument honouring his good self was erected instead. The monument does not survive but the inscription does: 'The city [dedicates this] to Marcus Agrippa, son of Lucius, three times consul and benefactor...'

A more important legacy of Augustus and Agrippa was the addition of the first new temple on the Acropolis for nearly half a millennium. It stood not far from the east entrance to the Parthenon, an elegant round structure nearly 8 metres in both height and diameter: its dedication was to the city of Rome, personified as a god, and to the divine emperor Augustus. Although dwarfed in size by the Parthenon, this clever construction would have caught the eye. What Augustus meant by meddling with the most sacred of citadels has been debated. A peculiar story is told by the Roman historian Cassius Dio, writing about two centuries later.

> From the Athenians, [Augustus] took away [the island of] Aegina and [the city of] Eretria, from which they had received tribute, because, as some say, they had espoused the cause of Antony; and he furthermore forbade them to make anyone a citizen for money. And it seemed to them that a thing which had happened to the statue of Athena [in the Parthenon] was responsible for this misfortune; for this statue on the Acropolis, which was placed to face the east, had turned around to the west and spat blood.

Whatever we make of that bizarre tale, it suggests that Augustus harboured feelings towards Athens that included bitterness as well as respect. By having himself worshipped, alongside Athena, on the Parthenon, and by placing copies of the Caryatids in his showpiece building project in Rome, he was making a gesture of triumph as well as deference towards things Hellenic.

In the year 51 CE, two civilizations came together in Athens, with fateful consequences for history. One was the Greco-Roman culture of which the city was a showpiece, with its new or newly restored monuments, its mansions and gardens and its sophisticated academies of philosophy and rhetoric. The other was the stark, desert-rooted world of Abrahamic monotheism, which brought passion and simplicity to the encounter between man and his Creator.

This is how the encounter is described in the seventeenth chapter of the Acts of the Apostles:

Now while Paul waited for them at Athens, his spirit was stirred in him, when he saw the city wholly given to idolatry. Therefore disputed he in the synagogue with the Jews, and with the devout persons, and in the market daily with them that met with him. Then certain philosophers of the Epicureans, and of the Stoics, encountered him. And some said, What will this babbler say? Other some, He seemeth to be a setter forth of strange gods: because the preached unto them Jesus, and the resurrection (anastasis). And they took him, and brought him unto [the] Areopagus, saying, May we know what this new doctrine, whereof thou speakest, *is*? For thou bringest certain strange things to our ears: we would know therefore what these things mean. (For all the Athenians and strangers which were there spent their time in nothing else, but either to tell, or to hear some new thing.)

Then Paul stood in the midst of Mars' hill (the Areopagus) and said, *Ye* men of Athens, I perceive that in all things ye are too superstitious. For as I passed by, and beheld your devotions, I found an altar with this inscription, TO AN UNKNOWN GOD. Whom therefore ye ignorantly worship, him declare I unto you.

God that made the world and all things therein, seeing that he is Lord of heaven and earth, dwelleth not in temples made with hands; Neither is worshipped with men's hands, as though he needed any thing, seeing he giveth to all life, and breath, and all things; and hath made of one blood all nations of men for to dwell on all the face of the earth, and hath determined the times before appointed, and the bounds of their habitation; that they should seek the Lord, if haply they might feel after him, and find him, tohugh he be not far from every one of us: For in him we live, and move, and have our being; as certain also of your own poets have said, For we are also his offspring. For as much then as we are the offspring of God, we ought not to think that the Godhead is like unto gold, or silver, or stone, graven by art and man's device.

And the times of this ignorance God winked at; but now commandeth all men everywhere to repent: Because he hath appointed a day, in which he will judge the world in righteousness by *that* man whom he hath ordained; *whereof* he hath given assurance unto all *men*, in that he hath raised him from the dead. And when they heard of the resurrection of the dead, some mocked: and others said, We will hear thee again of this *matter.*

It is one of the most vivid scenes in Christianity's founding text. With the zeal of the penitent convert still blazing, Paul is on a journey round the eastern Mediterranean, preaching first to fellow Jews, who differ sharply, often violently, over his claim that the Hebrew scriptures have been fulfilled by the new faith. In Athens, we are told, things are different: he is coming to the thought capital of the Hellenistic and Latin world and debating with its cleverest representatives. He challenges both the popular religion of the polytheists and the highbrow speculation of the philosophers, and his pitch is shrewd. It follows the golden rule that a sales message must include references and resonances that the listener recognizes.

We are told that Paul spoke on the Areopagus, in other words the rocky hill just to the west of the Acropolis. This was the seat of the city's highest court, whose remit had been confined, since the era of Pericles, to murder trials. By the time Paul came, it seems likely the court had moved elsewhere, probably to the Agora. So the text is ambiguous. It might simply be telling us that he literally spoke on that famous outcrop, which also looms large in mythology as the place where Orestes was tried and acquitted for the revenge killing of his murderous mother, Clytemnestra. Or else it might be saying that Paul spoke to a session of the city's highest court, or even that he faced a kind of trial.

In any case, what he said is a shrewd mixture of the old and familiar and the dangerously new. When the Jewish visitor teasingly described the Athenians as 'very fearful of the gods', he chose a word, *deisidaimon*, which could be used either neutrally, to describe a religious person, or it could have a negative sense of being superstitious or irrationally cowed by invisible forces. In any case, this state of nervous piety is exactly what the sophisticated creeds like those of the Epicureans and the Stoics are supposed to free people from. Paul tells the clever philosophers they have failed to remove god-fearfulness from Athenian hearts, and then takes them on more directly. In place of the hedonist atheism offered by the Epicureans, or the nature-worshipping pantheism of the Stoics, he counters with an uncompromising, universalist monotheism. Although Islam is generally hostile to Paul, the rejection in his Athenian speech of all religious trappings, in the form of temples, carvings and other artefacts, would be recognizable to a purist Muslim, as would the claim to be rescuing mankind from a state of ignorance whose main characteristic is chaotic polytheism. While the Stoics and Epicureans insist that death is the end, Paul is adamant that the resurrection of Jesus portends resurrection for all. His Athenian listeners initially assume that *Anastasis* (the Greek word for resurrection) is a new-fangled deity, coupled with Jesus. Paul retorts that for him, *Anastasis*, or rising again, means what it says.

He makes this provocative case in terms that would be deeply familiar to his audience. His words contain two quotations from Greek poets, and they are well chosen. The reference to a God 'in whom we live and move and have our being' comes from Epimenides, a half-legendary visionary and bard who is supposed to have lived in Crete in the seventh or sixth century BCE but had special links to Athens. He is said to have advised wise Solon on his redesign of the Athenian state and in return received a sprig of sacred olive that betokened friendship between Athens and Knossos, his Cretan home town. The snatch of verse quoted by Paul was first addressed to Zeus: it tells how the foolish Cretans had made a tomb for the king of the gods, assuming him to be mortal. 'But you are not dead, you abide forever,' the poem goes on. Paul also quotes from a much later Greek poet, Aratus, who died in 240 BCE and wrote catchy lines about astronomy and meteorology. The fragment used by the Christian missionary makes a neat bridge between popular religion and higher forms of devotion: 'every street, every market-place is full of [the] god, even the sea and the harbour are full of this deity, everyone everywhere is indebted to him, *for we are indeed his offspring*'.

Well-judged as his pitch obviously was, Paul made very few converts in Athens. In the brassy, turbulent, cosmopolitan city of Corinth, 80 kilometres to the west, he would soon acquire a group of eager if ill-disciplined disciples to whom he wrote several important letters. The two surviving ones are part of the spiritual canon of the Western world. But there is no Pauline letter to his small Athenian flock.

Athens continued to be a stronghold of the old-time religion of twelve gods and rising, along with the highly sophisticated forms of art and literature which gave expression to that religion and made Athens into a hub of high culture. By general agreement there were two Roman emperors who really made their mark on Athens: Augustus, whom we have already encountered, and Hadrian, who ruled Rome more than a century later. Both were enchanted with Greek art, and determined to improve their own imperial capital by adorning it with Hellenic features. Both also felt that restoring Athens to its former glory, and adding to those glories, would be an important part of their legacy.

For Augustus, philhellenism was a coldly adopted style and policy choice. For Hadrian, a more complex character, it was more like an obsession, combined with a strategic vision. He was an aesthete, a dilettante, and a gobbler-up of knowledge and experience. He could be cruel as well as sentimental. According to one biographer: 'He was, in the same person, austere and genial, dignified and playful, dilatory and quick to act, niggardly and generous, deceitful and straightforward, cruel and merciful, and always in all things changeable.'

He is remembered with horror in the annals of the Jews as the emperor who not only suppressed a great Jewish uprising but tried to wipe out the spiritual legacy of Jerusalem by establishing a new,

Roman colony in its place and mandating the worship of Zeus on the Temple Mount. However, the eighteenth-century British historian Edward Gibbon called Hadrian one of Rome's virtuous emperors: he took charge of the empire at the apogee of its power and probably left it in more robust shape, albeit slightly smaller. Hadrian believed in abandoning the most far-flung acquisitions of the realm and consolidating what remained, above all by creating a single cultural space. To a large extent that culture was formed from Greece, and above all Athens.

Born in 76 CE into a privileged Spanish-Roman dynasty with lucrative olive holdings, Hadrian was groomed for high office by his father's cousin, the Emperor Trajan. During his education in Rome, which abounded with clever Greek teachers, his passion for Hellenic literature and art earned him the nickname *Graeculus*, the little Greek boy. We next hear of Hadrian visiting the city of his dreams in the year 112 CE, by which time he was in his mid-thirties, an ambitious protégé of the imperial family, and a man whose career seemed to stop and start in mysterious ways. This was a time, apparently, when a well-connected Roman could visit Athens in the confidence that honours would be showered on him, and he was not disappointed. He was made archon for that year, and a statue was erected to him in the Theatre of Dionysus, where the base of the likeness still sits, inscribed in Latin and Greek: it is our main source of information about Hadrian's early career, as an officer, possibly a reluctant one, in the service of the empire.

We do not know how long Hadrian stayed in Athens. He may have continued drinking from the fount of Hellenic wisdom for another five years, until the final events of Emperor Trajan's reign began unfolding. After receiving a summons to battle in the eastern provinces, Hadrian found himself in Syria, in effective command of the Roman armies, as Trajan headed westwards in a state of sickness. Trajan died in Cilicia (southern Turkey) in August 117 CE. It was not obvious who would take the throne next, but Hadrian enjoyed decisive support from Trajan's wife, Plotina.

As emperor, Hadrian was an indefatigable traveller, but visits to his beloved Athens were especially close to his heart. He arrived in autumn 124 CE and immediately set about a programme of economic and constitutional reforms, including a grain subsidy for the city and the creation of a new *phyle* or tribe which was named after him. He spent the winter touring the Peloponnese and returned in spring to preside over the festival of Dionysus, decked out in local costume. But his commitment to Athens was more than folkloric. There was one area in which Roman know-how clearly surpassed that of Greece, and that was water engineering. A magnificent aqueduct was duly constructed to serve the practical, recreational and aesthetic demands of a thirsty, growing city. Its creation took about fifteen years, and it remained in use until the twentieth century. Running mostly underground for almost 20 kilometres, it was hacked through solid rock by hundreds of workers who were probably slaves. Starting at the foot of Mount Parnes to the north of the city and picking up other sources along the way, it delivered water by gravity to a new reservoir on the slopes of Mount Lycabettus. Impressive remains of the aqueduct's upper reaches were found during the building of the Olympic village for the games of 2004.

Among monuments erected by Hadrian that still stand, vestigially at least, the most famous is probably his library, abutting Monastiraki Square and the modern Flea Market. It was more than a book collection, although one side of it comprised two storeys full of books (papyrus scrolls, to be exact) and reading rooms. Hadrian's Library was a cool, restful, enclosed space which included gardens, a pond and places where philosophers could walk, talk and teach. Just one row of columns in the Corinthian style, adorning one wall, can now be seen, but they give a hint of the opulence and grace of the original structure.

Hadrian's gift to Athens went far beyond individual buildings. In a sense he founded a whole new city, designed as the centre of a new Greek commonwealth. But Hadrianic Athens aspired to revere the past as well as proclaim the new. The urban space he created near the banks of the Ilisos river was a self-conscious throwback to the most glorious moments of Athenian history, both factual and mythological. At the heart of this development was the completion at long last of a grandiose exercise in sacred architecture. During his 125 CE visit, Hadrian decreed that work would finally be finished on the Temple of Olympian Zeus, construction of which had begun in the era of the tyrant Peisistratus some 650 years previously.

The project had been abandoned by the citizens of democratic Athens in the fifth century BCE, apparently on the grounds that such a huge house of worship reflected an authoritarian spirit. (The Parthenon, for all its magnificence, was ultimately an offering to Athena; this place felt more like an exercise in self-aggrandizement.) Much later Antiochus Epiphanes, the Hellenistic king of the Levant, tried finishing the construction, but this effort collapsed with his death in 164 BCE. Then, in 86 BCE, when Sulla ravaged the city, he took away some of the unfinished columns and reused them in the temple to Jupiter (the Latin counterpart to Zeus) on Rome's Capitoline Hill.

Another two centuries passed before Hadrian mustered the resources and will needed to accomplish the construction, adding many features of his own. When it was finished around 131 CE, it measured 110 metres by 44, and was surrounded by more than 100 columns. Fifteen columns still stand today, while one has dramatically collapsed, its spilled drums offering an eloquent warning to grandiose enterprises which fly too near the sun. It broadly followed the design which Antiochus had been trying to use, based on Corinthian columns, topped by an elegant flourish of foliage. Inside the temple there was a likeness of Zeus fashioned from gold and ivory. In other words, it used the same materials as the figure of Athena which glinted from the heart of the Parthenon. To judge by other statues of Olympian Zeus, it probably showed the god seated on a throne, brandishing a sceptre and an image of victory. 'Olympian' was one of the many roles in which the chief god appeared. It also happened to be a divine appellation which Hadrian conferred on himself. By realizing this centuries-old project, the emperor was creating a new spiritual reference point for the Hellenic world, placing not only the senior deity but his own imperial person at its centre.

Just as the Parthenon, looming above, was the beating heart of the old city, this new monument was conceived as the centre of another political order. It was surrounded by a wide-paved plaza, dotted with statues of Hadrian. The inscriptions on the bases of these statues indicate the context in which they were presented: a recurring phrase is 'to the saviour and founder, Emperor Hadrian the Olympian'.

This reflects his determination to make Athens the centre of a constellation of Roman-Greek cities, held together by common participation in Greek culture and loyalty to the Roman realm. In his youth, Hadrian had playfully equated himself to Dionysus, the god of wine, intoxication and imagination. At the height of his imperial greatness, his pretensions were greater still.

The multiple statues and inscriptions had been offered as an act of gratitude, or submission, by cities which had joined his new Panhellenion or Panhellenic League, whose symbolic centre was the freshly erected temple. Meetings of the confederation would take place a short distance away, near the Ilisos river, at a shrine to Zeus and his consort Hera.

An apparent dividing line between the old Athens and the one created by Hadrian is provided by another landmark of the modern city, Hadrian's Arch. Standing 18 metres tall, it is made of marble from Mount Pentelikon, though of a lesser quality than the shiny stuff used on the Acropolis. In the final bend of the road running north into the centre of Athens, the arch appears on the right with the Temple of Olympian Zeus in the background. As noted by the travel writer Pausanias, who lived in the second century CE, there was a rough line connecting several important points: the south-east corner of the Acropolis; the ancient Prytaneion where much of the city's bureaucratic business was done; the Arch of Hadrian and the great Temple on the river. In establishing this new landscape, Hadrian was sending a message of both brassy innovation and profound conservatism. The modern Lysikratous Street runs along the first part of that route.

The Arch is presented as an offering to Hadrian from the grateful Athenians. There are inscriptions on each side which appear to proclaim a neat division of the city: to the north-west, 'Athens, the ancient city of Theseus'; and to the south-east, the new riverside settlement which was 'the city of Hadrian, not of Theseus'. However, there is an alternative interpretation of the first inscription. It might be saying: 'This is the former city of Theseus…' In other words, Hadrian might be claiming both halves of the city, or indeed representing himself, among his many other claims, as the new Theseus.

What is certain is that locations associated with the life of Theseus (the original, mythological one) abounded on both sides of the arch, and these stories were cultivated by Hadrian and his admiring contemporaries. For example, near the Temple of Olympian Zeus, there was another fine place of worship, reputed to be very old indeed. It was said to be where Theseus arrived in the city, with long fair hair and a long tunic. Enraged when the temple's builder mocked his 'womanly' appearance, Theseus seized one of his tormentor's oxen and threw it higher than the temple's unfinished roof, or so the story goes. Much nearer the Acropolis, the Prytaneion was said to be the building where Theseus had gathered in all the tribes of Attica and fused them into a single state. Pausanias, always a great booster of Hadrian, is keen to remind readers of these magnificent Theseus moments, and their association with the new emperor and refounder. Hadrian and his cheerleaders were not trying to replace the heroes of the past but to cover the new realm in old stardust.

The exact functions of Hadrian's Panhellenion or all-Greek league of cities, headquartered in Athens, are still debated. But this was clearly an important institution and remained so for more than a century. Like the British Commonwealth, it was a club in which ceremonies, sporting contests and common veneration for cultural symbols played a big role. Reverence for the shrines of Eleusis and their mind-bending power was clearly part of the glue which held the federation together and enhanced the prestige of the Athens region. The league comprised at least twenty-eight cities, including eleven in the northern Peloponnese, ten in Asia Minor, and the remainder in Crete, North Africa and northern Greece. Worshipping (including the worship of the emperor) was clearly one of its main activities, and in Greece cultural and sporting festivities could be a form of worship. If the Panhellenion had a permanent staff, it was a priestly bureaucracy: its most senior official was described as 'archon of the Panhellenion, priest of the god Hadrian Panhellenios, and master of the games at the Great Panhellenia'.

Hadrian was concentrating all the holiness of Hellas in a single place, which was Athens, or strictly speaking New Athens, a refounded conurbation on the banks of the Ilisos that drew power from the illustrious sites of old Athens but also had the energy of a brand-new foundation. One explanation for this action is that he sensed the subversive power of Christianity and was determined to keep alive the old polytheistic faith, which was one of the defining characteristics of Hellenism. But the scanty written evidence suggests that Hadrian was somewhat more lenient towards the new faith than his predecessor Trajan, an outright persecutor, had been. Hadrian's advice to a provincial governor was that simply being Christian did not merit any punishment; Christians should not be touched unless they committed some other offence. Moreover, people who made 'slanderous attacks' against them deserved retribution.

Laura Nasrallah, one of America's leading New Testament scholars, sees an uncanny parallel between the early Christian commonwealth described in the Book of Acts and Hadrian's effort to unite the cities of the Greek east into a single cultural and religious space. Hadrian's Panhellenion was a way of affirming both the power of the Roman empire and the bonding effect of a common Hellenic heritage, playing up the connection of certain places with the Greek past. Nasrallah sees the Acts of the Apostles as a proclamation of a similar transnational association of places, each of which enjoyed the prestige of association with Christianity's opening scenes. Even as Hadrian created his Athens-centred community based on Greek nostalgia and emperor-worship, a sort of shadow community was growing up in roughly the same geographical space, and using the same lines of communication.

# 9

# Polytheists and Barbarians
## 138–560 CE

*In the second century CE, Herodes Atticus continues Hadrian's ambitious building programme, showcasing Athens' cultural and literary glories – Eleusis thrives under several emperors but suffers a raid – barbarians ransack parts of Athens (267 CE), but a riotous student scene continues – in the 350s CE, the Christian theologians Gregory and Basil, plus the future pagan Emperor Julian, study together in Athens – as a new Christian imperial capital takes root in Constantinople, Athens remains a hub of polytheist learning despite another barbarian attack in 396 CE – wealthy neo-Platonist teachers thrive in Athens for another century until the closure of their schools*

Only after Hadrian's death in 138 CE did his plan to make Athens the shining capital of a Greek commonwealth, flourishing under Roman peace, really come to fruition. The building works and cultural initiatives started by the emperor were continued by an energetic Greek who commanded both huge wealth and stratospheric connections in Rome. Among the array of people who transformed the appearance of Roman Athens, he is unusual in being from the region himself.

Herodes Atticus was born in Marathon in 101 CE, and his grandfather Hipparchus was one of the richest people in the Roman empire. Herodes was a member of the Imperial Senate and in 143 CE he became the first Greek to hold the lofty rank of *consul ordinarius.*˙ In other words, he personified the fusion of Roman power with Greek prestige, intellectual prowess and in his own case, personal wealth. He was clearly a protégé of Hadrian, who made him prefect over a cluster of cities in Asia Minor around 134 CE. Hadrian's successor, Antoninus Pius, invited Herodes Atticus to act as tutor to his adopted sons, who included a future emperor, Marcus Aurelius. So the period when Herodes Atticus enjoyed huge influence at court spanned three Roman imperial reigns.

Hadrian had endowed Athens with a new library, gymnasium and stoa, as well as completing a grandiose temple; to this Herodes Atticus added an Odeion or concert hall which, in restored form, is very much a feature of present-day Athens. Although his cedar-wood roof has long disappeared, the Herodes Atticus theatre is in current use as the venue for a grand summer festival of music and drama. The flamboyant builder also provided Athens with a stadium to surpass the one in Olympia. This structure was restored in the late nineteenth century to serve as the location for the first modern Olympics.

In keeping with the nostalgic spirit of the times, Herodes Atticus claimed links with the historical and mythological past. His pretensions were not quite as audacious as those entertained by the Greek-obsessed Roman emperors, but they were bold enough. Emperor Hadrian had tried to fuse his own divinity with that of Zeus, and compared himself at least subliminally to the mythological hero Theseus. Herodes Atticus claimed genealogical descent from Zeus and Theseus. More in the realm of the plausible, his ancestors included Elpinike, one of the powerful women of fifth-century BCE Athens. He also gave that name to his daughter.

Both Hadrian and Herodes Atticus were encouragers of an intellectual and literary movement called the Second Sophistic which tried to refocus Greek thought and letters on the Athens

---

* Great prestige was attached to these 'ordinary consuls' – consuls elected to start the year – since the Roman dating system defined a year by the names of two consuls who took office as it began.

region where they had flourished 600 years earlier. The conquests of Alexander the Great, and the reigns of his various successors, had sprayed a kind of Greekness, often in heavily diluted form, from North Africa to the Hindu Kush; now a new imperially driven project was trying to refocus on the historic source of Hellenic high culture, and drink the water at its purest. Stories, real and legendary, of Athenian feats against the Persians were reread and retold in obsessive detail. A prime exponent was the orator Aelius Aristides, born in north-western Anatolia in 117 CE but trained in Athens and Egypt. He rehashed the stories of Athens at its imperial peak as laid out by Thucydides, while carefully changing certain details. Where Thucydides had written of Athenian bravery and resourcefulness, Aristides describes the city of Pericles as fair-minded and (against all evidence) gentle in its dealings with weaker parties. The ruthlessness with which Periclean Athens treated wavering allies did not get much mention in this highly sanitized rendering of the past.

As Sarah McHugh, a young British scholar, shows in her doctoral thesis on Roman Attica, this rewriting served an ideological purpose. First it presented Athens in her mightiest days as a benign force, the 'mother of the free' as the British patriotic hymn puts it. Step two in this argument is that, while remaining under Roman sway, the city could now become an equally benign cultural power, propagating the Athenian genius with crystal clarity.

In this spirit, scholars tried to revive the old Attic dialect of Greek, supposedly spoken more purely in the countryside around Athens than in the city. One of Plato's works was studied with particular zeal: the *Phaedrus*, in which Socrates and a pupil of that name take a stroll through the shady and numinous landscape on the banks of the Ilisos river, in other words the very place where Hadrian had planted a new city that simultaneously claimed to be very old.

As a symbol of late Roman Athens, a city which would continue to attract young, precocious minds even when the world was crumbling into chaos, one project of Herodes Atticus stands out. He established a school in one of the luxurious villas he owned in Kifisia, then as now a desirable northern suburb of Athens. It included lecture halls and open-air spaces for teaching, as well as leafy groves and fountains that provided relief from the summer sun. The leading novelists, travel writers and historians of the day were welcome guests. As evidence of this combination of gracious living and learning, Sarah McHugh has unearthed a description by the little-remembered Roman grammarian Aulus Gellius of staying as a guest of Herodes on the city's shady outskirts.

> Both in the torpor of summer and under the extremely warm autumnal sun, we shielded ourselves from the trying heat thanks to the shade of the ample groves, with their long, gentle promenades, as well as the cool situation of the house, with its elegant baths and abundance of sparkling water.

An estate agent promoting the charms of a villa in modern Kifisia might take useful hints from this smug and flowery language. The establishment described by Aulus Gellius had many imitators: places that combined opulent Athenian living with serious instruction and boosted the prestige of the founder. A kind of posh finishing school, although the parallel is not exact. Over the years, life in Athens would become more precarious, but the zeal to learn and teach would not diminish, and competition for pupils would intensify. But clouds were always discernible on the horizon, even in the time of Hadrian and Herodes, when imperial confidence was running high.

In that era of wealth and stability, Athens itself may have been unassailable, but its outer reaches were not. Around the year 170 CE, the sanctuary at Eleusis, west of the city, was ransacked by barbarians. Much about this raid is shadowy: who exactly attacked, when they came and how much damage they did. The invaders are generally referred to as Costobocci, one of the peoples vying for power on the north-eastern fringe of the Roman province of Dacia, roughly speaking modern Romania. However, in one inscription, they are called Sarmatians, a group who spoke a Persian-related tongue. The incident seems to have given Emperor Marcus Aurelius a chance to show, by reconstructing the sacred buildings, that he was as dedicated to this supremely holy place as his predecessors were. There is an inscription, dated 176 CE, honouring a venerable old priest who had served in Eleusis for fifty-six years. It credits him with initiating two emperors into the holy rites (Antoninus and Marcus Aurelius) and with performing them 'in the presence of' Hadrian, who must have been through his own initiation much earlier. (Having tasted the secrets as a youth, Hadrian apparently made repeated visits as an honoured spectator and had his young companion Antinous, the great passion of his life, initiated in turn.) Another inscription praises the priest in charge for managing to spirit the holiest objects to safety in Athens when the barbarians came. It must have been a terrifying moment.

The barbarian raid prompted Aelius Aristides, that great propagandist of Athenian culture through the years, to pen a flowery oration which mixed the usual romantic references to the region's noble past with an unusually frank statement about the present day. Even in the direst emergencies, the Athenians of yesteryear had always managed to protect Eleusis, he wrote: was it not a disgrace that this time, the unlettered enemies had been allowed to break through?

> O Eleusis, of old it was more pleasant for me to sing of you!... As I come to speak, I grow numb, I turn back, I am compelled to speak because I cannot keep silent... O you who have betrayed the Mysteries, who have revealed what was hidden, common enemies of the gods beneath and above the earth. Oh you Hellenes... who stood idly by at the approach of so great an evil! Will you not now, dear sirs, get control of yourselves? Will you not even save Athens?

Behind this mannered language there was a hard truth. The Athens of late Roman times, along with the holy and historically resonant places in its vicinity, enjoyed a unique sort of prestige which the emperors found fascinating and politically useful. But a city with no defence forces of its own was also extremely vulnerable; its safety depended on the willingness and capacity of the Roman overlords to defend it, and that was never completely guaranteed. On the other hand, the Athenian will to exist as a spiritual and cultural centre would prove remarkably tough.

The next time the barbarians came, in the year 267 CE, the consequences were much more serious. By now the Roman empire as a whole was in a more precarious state, with war raging in the north for the past couple of decades. The new invaders of Athens were the Heruli, a Germanic tribe. Scholars used to believe that they wrought utter devastation on Athens, bringing its political and economic life to a standstill. These days, thanks to diligent perusal of the archaeological evidence by new researchers like Lambrini Chioti, it is possible to take a more nuanced view. The Heruli swept through Athens from the west, torching and plundering many of its most precious buildings, but they had little desire to linger in the city. Indeed the warriors' dash through Athens seems to have been only one episode in an astonishingly active year. From a base on the north coast of the Black Sea they briefly seized the outskirts of Constantinople, then retreated; a second expedition took them through several islands of the northern Aegean and around the Peloponnese before they reached Athens.

Among the worst-hit Athenian targets was the old Agora, where several august structures were burned and rendered useless, and there was probably some serious damage done to monuments on the south slope of the Acropolis, such as the Stoa of Eumenes and the newish Odeion of Herodes Atticus. Dwelling places in that area below the Acropolis were likewise torched, but residences in other parts of the city seemed remarkably unscathed. The city fathers swiftly set about protecting the inner section from any future incursion: a new wall was erected with the Acropolis at the bottom end; it embraced the area immediately to the north but not the old Agora. Indeed bits of the old Agora buildings, such as the once-magnificent Middle Stoa, were cannibalized to make up this fortification.

Despite this humiliation, the city did not grind to a halt, either for the poor or the rich. The export of lamps, which had recently been one of the city's prize products, continued apace, and the burned-out shells in the Agora were taken over by small workshops and metal-bashers. More remarkably, as Chioti has observed, some luxurious baths (a feature of Roman rather than Greek living) were installed or improved in various parts of the city, including the location now occupied by the National Gardens. There are no reports of terrible damage in the 'new Athens' on the banks of the Ilisos, founded by Hadrian. But interestingly, some buildings in that part of town had already, even before the Heruli came, been dismantled to provide material for an earlier fortification effort, the so-called Valerian wall,* which tried to draw a large circle round the city. Generally, Chioti believes, the city's centre of gravity moved eastwards because of the heavy damage to its western side.

The local Athenians, resurfacing in the record, did make a respectable effort to fight their corner during and after the Herulian raid. A contemporary historian called Dexippus recalls the speech to the city's defenders by their leader (who may well have been Dexippus himself) in some elevated spot in the city's environs.

> Wars are decided by courage rather than numbers. We have no
> mean force. Two thousand of us have gathered in all, and we
> have this very strong position as a base from which to damage
> the enemy. If they come up against us we shall resist – we have
> an excellent defence against their weapons in this abrupt wooded

---

* This construction was named, long after the event, for Emperor Valerian, who ruled from 253 CE to 260 CE. It now seems that the fortification effort was slightly later, in the reign of his successor Gallienus.

position. If they assault us from different directions they will be thrown out – fighting against men who are unseen... We, protected by the wood, will be able to shoot accurately from a position of advantage, and will apply ourselves safely, in minimal danger.

Garth Fowden, a historian who has studied Attic geography as well as literary evidence, reckons the rallying point was on Mount Aigaleo, the sprawling stretch of highland west of Athens from where King Xerxes had watched the battle of Salamis. Although the range is now badly deforested, it would have been well covered with trees in late Roman times, and above all the defence unit would have been able to spot and co-ordinate with the Roman naval forces that were sailing in. Neither Romans nor locals were able to stop the Heruli trashing Athens, but the raiders do seem to have been well and truly punished, with a devastating ambush, as they made their way out of the city towards Boeotia.

It would be fair to say that classical Athens never fully recovered from the damage wrought by the Heruli, but that does not mean it ceased to function. One sign of the city's realism and resilience was the speed with which an inner redoubt was erected; another was the city's recovery as a centre of intellectual activity and education. About eighty years after the Herulian raid, the classrooms of Athens made a contribution to the intellectual and spiritual history of the Western world by incubating two of the clerics who laid out some of the fundamentals of Christian doctrine; and at roughly the same time, the anti-Christian emperor Julian who is known in ecclesiastical history as 'the apostate' and correspondingly excoriated.

It was not just the city of Athens whose centre was moving eastward. The same could be said of the entire Roman empire. As the threat from external enemies grew, and internal strains intensified, the Roman realm was wracked by civil war between rival claimants to supreme power. At times there were two or four co-emperors.

In 324, Constantine the Great became sole emperor, after defeating his rivals Maxentius and Licinius, and founded a new capital in the Greek city of Byzantium, which he rebuilt as Constantinople. Before that, it had seemed possible that the empire would divide between a weak, indefensible west, where Christianity flourished in the absence of other effective institutions, and a Greek east, where many were still devoted to Hellenic religion as well as culture. Constantine made a creative response by establishing a capital that would be Christian (or at least Christian-friendly) in religion, Greek in culture and Roman in its organization. The place he chose was in a strategically vital location at the entrance of the Black Sea.

Within a year of founding Constantinople, the emperor convened a council of Christian bishops at Nicaea which attempted to settle the theological differences that were roiling the church. He is remembered by Christians as the first emperor who practised their faith; he and Licinius had jointly proclaimed their tolerance of Christianity in Milan in 313. Under Constantine's influence, the new religion enjoyed ever-greater favour, even though he was only baptized on his deathbed in 337. At the same time, polytheism was still permitted and continued to flourish in many places.

For Athens, the capital of the old Greek religion and culture, all this had complex implications. For the past 300 years or so, Athens had benefited from a mixture of mostly stable Roman power and Roman philhellenism. Now the strongest centre in what remained of the empire was a rival pole of Greekness, and that new Christian metropolis was, on the face of things, at spiritual loggerheads with the old polytheist elite of Athens.

Initially, however, strategic relations between the new city of Constantinople and Athens were good. The imperial city had nothing to fear from Athens militarily, and much to gain culturally. Whatever Constantine's private beliefs, he was certainly not so opposed to the old religion of Greece as to cut all connection with its adherents. As George Deliyannakis, a scholar of late antiquity, puts it, 'in the period immediately after his victory over Licinius, Constantine attempted to win favour with the pagan aristocracy of Athens. Correspondingly, the Athenian elite hoped to derive some benefits for the city and themselves.'

The city fathers of Athens gave the new emperor the symbolic title of *strategos* (general) in charge of the hoplites (armed infantry) and the sovereign rewarded this favour by supplying the city with ample amounts of wheat. Constantine quickly started building up his own capital as a hub of Hellenic culture, but initially this was not done at the expense of Athens itself. Instead, the opportunistic Constantine seized various resonant objects from other locations. For example, he took away from Delphi the victory monument, known as the Serpents' Column, which celebrated the battle of Plataea, the great land victory over the Persians in 479 BCE.

This warm relationship with the new imperial capital helped Athens to maintain its status as an intellectual powerhouse, where ambitious young men would sit at the feet of equally ambitious teachers and hone their ability to think, write and speak. Battered as it was by the ravages of the Heruli, the city was simultaneously a great metropolis of the spirit and a hardscrabble place where competition between different schools, and rowdiness among students, could easily get out of hand. By the mid-fourth century, Athens was making intellectual history. But to capture the mixture of roughness and refinement it offered, it is worth going back a little and contemplating a story of educational life in Athens as the fourth century dawned. It relates to the early steps in the career of a great wordsmith and teacher known as Prohaeresius, or else by his original Armenian name of Paruyr. He was a protégé of a brilliant pedagogue called Julian of Cappadocia,* who was so respected that 'youths from all parts flocked to him and revered the man for his

---

* Not to be confused with Emperor Julian, or with the Cappadocian church fathers.

eloquence and noble disposition'.

Julian had one main competitor, a man from Sparta named Apsines. There was a brawl between supporters of the two teachers, and the Spartan's pupils left those of his rival badly injured. But quite unfairly, it was the Cappadocian's battered students who were prosecuted for causing the disturbance. The Roman proconsul or governor of the region, whose duties included that of magistrate, insisted that the Cappadocian should himself be put on trial. He also specified that 'all the accused be placed in chains, like men imprisoned on a charge of murder'.

Apsines came to the trial to back his protégés, who were led by Themistocles, a young thug. The Roman's sympathies began to shift. The accused, 'with hair uncut and in great physical affliction', were a sad sight. The proconsul would not allow Apsines to speak on behalf of his bullying students. The loutish Themistocles had laid out his side's basic complaint, and he was then challenged by the governor to elaborate. Instead he clammed up, 'changed colour and bit his lips in great embarrassment'. At that point it was the turn of the Cappadocian sage and his boy supporters to defend themselves.

Teacher Julian asked that young Paruyr be freed from his chains and allowed to speak. The lad made a brilliant peroration, including a 'pitiable account of their sufferings' and words of praise for his master. The listeners, including the governor-magistrate, were transfixed: in fact, 'shaking his purple-edged cloak' he applauded the young orator with schoolboy enthusiasm and even Apsines, leader of the other camp, joined the clapping.

It was into this mouthy Athenian world that two young men from the heart of Asia Minor arrived around 351. One is known in history as Gregory of Nazianzus, or Gregory the Theologian; the other, who arrived a little later, is Basil the Great, a pioneer of eastern Christian monasticism. When Basil died in 379, his classmate offered a famously nostalgic account of their days as fellow students and bosom friends in Athens.

When as time went on, we acknowledged our mutual affection, and that philosophy was our aim, we were all in all to one another, housemates, messmates, intimates, with one goal in life, and an affection for one another growing warmer and stronger. Love for bodily attractions, since its objects are fleeing, is as transitory as the flowers of spring... But the love which is godly and restrained, since its object is stable, is more lasting.

Their friendship had been sealed, apparently, when Gregory saved Basil from the worst of a hazing ritual which involved a noisy gang marching a newcomer to the bathhouse, then pretending that the bathhouse was closed and pounding furiously at the door. Only when the student gained entry and performed his ablutions was he fully accepted as one of the gang.

Basil apparently escaped this teasing. In another test of the greenhorn's nerves, he was subjected to a torrent of aggressive argument by some 'crafty and cunning' Armenian youngsters, and expected to talk back. Gregory admits that he initially went along with this game, but then stepped in to protect Basil. As Gregory tells it, the frat-boy ethos in Athens reflected 'young men hard to keep under control' who acted like excited spectators at horse races: 'they leap, they shout, they raise clouds of dust... they beat the air'.

The two students went on to become princes of the church. Both were deeply involved in fighting the doctrine of Arianism which from a mainstream Christian perspective downgrades the divinity of Christ. Basil became bishop of Caesarea (modern Kayseri) in central Anatolia in 370 and used his authority to appoint Gregory to the less prestigious see of Sasima, a smallish town in the region of Cappadocia which was the home region of both prelates. For a time their relationship soured.

But the death of Basil in 379 gave Gregory a chance to make posthumous amends and emphasize their lifelong bond. Both men played a seminal role in theological history by developing the argument that the Holy Spirit, the mysterious, inspirational power of God, was a co-equal member of the Holy Trinity.* One modern theologian has playfully found parallels, conscious or otherwise, between Gregory's account of his youthful comradeship and Plato's *Symposium*, and in particular the discourse of Alcibiades on his love for Socrates. But the former relationship, at least, was what we would now call Platonic.

For better or worse, many of today's observers are more interested by another young man who studied in Athens in the 350s, coinciding with Gregory and possibly also with Basil. This was the anti-Christian Flavius Claudius Julianus, a nephew of Constantine the Great, who became emperor in 361. The American author Gore Vidal wrote a bestselling novel that tells the story of this unique and colourful figure in the transition from polytheism to Christianity. As presented by Vidal, who made a meticulous study of the evidence, Julian is a sardonic, sophisticated personality with a passion for the traditions of ancient Greece, who knew he was fighting a losing battle to save them. Julian spent only a couple of months in Athens, in the spring and summer of 355, but Athenian memories would be as decisive for him as they were for the Christian blood-brothers. As well as following classes from the same venerable teachers (including Paruyr/Prohaeresius) as the Christian lads did, young Julian was initiated into the Eleusinian mysteries by a priest, Nestorios, who felt he was at or near the end of a noble line.

Having fought quite successfully in the empire's western European reaches, Julian became sole emperor and marched into Constantinople on 11 December 361. He set about restoring the pagan sanctuaries of Greece. His attitude to the Christian religion, which he had renounced, was subtle rather than relentlessly hostile: he forbad Christians from being teachers of Hellenic culture, on the grounds that this tradition should only be shared by those who believed in it. Julian was killed in battle in June 363 while fighting

---

* Basil of Caesarea and Gregory of Nazianzus are known, along with Basil's brother Gregory of Nyssa, as the Cappadocian fathers of the church, credited with elaborating the idea that God consists of one essence (*ousia*) and three *hypostases* (ways of existing) or Persons.

the Persians, but he managed to give a boost to the old Hellenic cause in Athens and elsewhere which outlasted his own short span.

Julian's memory is honoured by Jews, who remembered the fact that he allowed them to start rebuilding their Temple; and condemned by the early church, which probably overstated the damage he did to the Christian cause. Saint Gregory of Nazianzus claimed to recall Julian as an unstable Athenian student, 'with his shoulders always in motion and bobbing up and down like a pair of scales, his eyes rolling and glancing from side to side with a certain insane expression'. For those who have a soft spot for Julian, such barbs will fail to convince.

Indeed, to modern readers of the old texts, including Vidal, the self-effacing Basil comes over as an easier-going character than Gregory. But both clerics left a huge mark on theology, as advocates of Trinitarian understanding of God in all its deep paradoxicality. As for the royal Julian, he remains a compellingly sympathetic figure for modern anti-clericalists or indeed for all sorts of people, perhaps including some religious believers, who are exasperated by the way monotheism's masters have used their earthly power over the last millennium and a half. Only very narrowly did he escape the murderous intrigues of the Constantinian dynasty into which he was born. By the time he became emperor, life had endowed him with much worldly wisdom. Vidal portrays him as a sharp observer of his peers, including the Galileans, to use his contemptuous name for Christians.

For all the huge differences between the Christian duo and Julian, it is always worth noting what these three alumni of Athens had in common, as products of a single intellectual and religious culture. Whatever Julian stood for, he was no cold rationalist. Among many other influences, he was touched by Iamblichus, the thinker who had 'succeeded in transforming Platonism from a philosophy with mystical connotations into a mystery religion'.* He had a yearning

---

* See Polymnia Athanassiadi, *Julian and Hellenism: An Intellectual Biography*, first published by OUP 1981, p. 136.

for the transcendental. He believed that ascetic discipline, including celibacy, could lead to great spiritual insights. He believed he was guided and protected by his own particular divinities, namely Zeus and the sun-god Helios. He thought these gods had a mother, and that she had a partner, Attis-Logos; and that the power of all these beings was truly universal. It wasn't just a local or national cult. Not unlike his Christian adversaries, he believed that several divine manifestations could share a single essence. Like his foes, he believed he was propagating a belief system which had meaning for humanity as a whole; he found the religion of the Galileans too provincial and narrow. In different ways, the Christians and Julian (and perhaps all the philosophers who saw themselves as heirs to Plato) were aspiring to give universal significance to narratives and practices which had first arisen in very local contexts.

To put it mildly, the gap between Julian and the Christians was not trivial; but they were all responding to the same teachers, the same reading material and historical circumstances. They were seeking answers to the same questions.

In Athens, at least, this search continued to suffer from rude interruptions. In or around 396, barbarians swooped once more. This time, the identity of the attackers is fairly clear: they were led by Alaric, commander of the Visigoths, the people who would later sack Rome. But there is still intense debate about how much harm they did to the Greek city. Zosimus, a polytheist author of the sixth century, insists that little or no damage was done, and offers a startling explanation.

> When Alaric advanced with all his forces against the city, he saw Athena, its protecting goddess, walking along the wall, in the same form as she is portrayed among the statues of the gods… in armour ready to attack those who oppose her. Before the walls he saw Alaric standing in a heroic posture, just as Homer

represents him engaging the Trojans... Being struck with awe by this spectacle, Alaric desisted from his attempt on the city and sent heralds with proposals for peace... After an exchange of oaths, Alaric entered Athens with a small number of troops [and] was entertained with all possible politeness, after which he received some gifts and left, leaving the city and Attica unharmed.

In the realm of academic history, scholars are not convinced that Alaric was so lenient in his treatment of Athens. Yet there is one big and wide-open question: how much destruction did the Parthenon suffer in the late Roman period, and when? Was the main damage done in the Herulian raid, or by Alaric? As with the events leading up to the battle of Salamis, this is a matter on which the literary and physical evidence is scanty, and the leading authorities are divided down the middle.

What physical evidence does make clear is that at some point during the Roman period, seventy-nine of the ninety-two metopes (smallish sculptures immediately above the columns) were brutally defaced, to the point where it is hard to guess what they represented. It is also apparent that a fire badly damaged the interior of the Parthenon; that blaze may have coincided with the wrecking of the carvings, or it may not.

One theory holds that all this damage was done in the Herulian attack of 267. It may, in that case, have been repaired by Emperor Julian during his brief reign as part of his revival of the Hellenic religion. Another school of thought finds it more likely that Alaric and his men were responsible for the assault on the city's most famous temple, the worst it had suffered since it was constructed in the Periclean era. One striking fact is that pieces of the Doric columns which once stood in the Parthenon's interior have been found in a wall of the ancient Agora that was erected after 400 CE. They were in good condition when they were reused, so it seems unlikely they were dislodged from their initial location as far back as 267. It seems quite probable that these prize pieces of marble became available for other purposes because of Alaric's depredations. Alison Frantz, the great American scholar who put forward this theory, believed that the damage to the Parthenon was repaired by a Roman prefect called Herculius who is known to have endeared himself to the Athenians, in the early fifth century, by overseeing an ambitious programme of new building and reconstruction.

There is another scrap of evidence, literary this time, which may throw light on what Alaric's warriors did and why. According to Eunapius, the fourth-century polytheist historian to whom we owe a lot of our knowledge of this period, Alaric's army was assisted on its journey southwards by men 'wearing brown clothes'. These may well have been monks professing Arian Christianity, in other words denying the full divinity of Christ. For such monastics, polytheism and the Nicene form of Christianity, which was now the eastern Roman empire's official faith, were both wrong beliefs. It is possible that these monks urged Alaric on in his destruction of the sanctuary at Eleusis, as well as the pagan holy places of Corinth and Olympia. In the view of Charalambos Bouras, a Greek historian and conservator who died in 2016, it also seems likely that 'when Alaric marched into Athens... the frenzy over destroying ancient temples had not abated' and they headed for the Parthenon.

However, Manolis Korres, who like Professor Bouras is a prime mover of conservation work on the Acropolis, inclines to the opposite view: he thinks the worst wrecking of the Parthenon's interior and exterior happened in the Herulian raid. Lambrini Chioti, who may know more than anybody about the Herulian episode and its aftermath, tends to agree but accepts that the question remains open.

The intact state of some metopes, the rather inaccessible ones on the south side of the Parthenon, may lend weight to the notion that the seventy-nine damaged ones were hit by an army on the move, be it in 267 or 396. If at some point there had been a cold-blooded decision by the *local* authorities to deface these sculptures, they would surely have finished the job. In any case the leaders of Athens were proud pagans until well into the fifth century.

As Christianity gained power and adherents across the eastern Mediterranean, the relative importance of Athens, being a bastion of the old religion, declined. But it is astonishing to find that there was one final burst of building in late Roman Athens, in the early fifth century. Whatever happened elsewhere, the city remained a haven for wealthy, entrepreneurial professors of Platonism, who could also be mystics and priests. This was confirmed by some remarkable archaeological finds in the post-1945 rehabilitation of the city.

Perhaps the most handsome street in today's Athens is a thoroughfare named after Dionysius the Areopagite, one of the few people in the city who quickly accepted the apostle Paul's Christian message. With its splendid marble-fronted mansions, the road has become even more desirable since it was closed to traffic in 2000, allowing visitors a pleasant walk over cobblestones to the entrance to the Acropolis.

In 1955, when the course of this street was being shifted, a discovery was made by archaeologists who had to labour quickly because the roadworks were considered pressing. What they found was one of the most luxurious residences that can be dated to the late Roman period in Greece. It comprised twenty-two rooms, grouped around two courtyards. One especially opulent room had a multicoloured mosaic floor and a small horseshoe-shaped swimming pool. The compound included a mini private bathhouse, with cold, warm and hot rooms, a late addition to the original edifice.

Even more exciting, it was possible to name, with fair confidence though not certainty, the person who lived in this swish residence: a philosopher, priest, healer and sage called Proclus who served as head of the neo-Platonic Academy in the fifth century and spent much of his long life as a master of thought in Athens. Thanks to a biography written by a grateful pupil, we know quite a lot about him. He personified the durability of Athens as a centre of polytheistic thought and practice at a time when, in theory,

Christianity was imposing itself across the eastern Roman empire. As Frantz puts it, 'Athens was quite naturally the last and most determined outpost of paganism in the Roman empire.'

Proclus was said to find the location of his dwelling place 'extremely congenial' because it was close to the altar of the healing-god Asclepius, and to the theatre and shrine of Dionysus, another establishment that was rebuilt, with pagan embellishments, in this defiantly backward-looking era. The Proclus mansion was also conspicuous from the Acropolis. Proclus did more than gaze enjoyably at the healing-place; he is said to have prayed a sick woman back to health by offering prayers to Asclepius at his local place of worship.

What ideas about the ultimate nature of things did Proclus propagate from his well-appointed headquarters? Like so many people before and since, he kept warm the intellectual legacy of Plato, who had taught in Athens some 800 years earlier. But unlike some modern interpreters of Plato, Proclus regarded the cult of the great giant of classical thought as a spiritual calling, not just a mental exercise. Plato's Dialogues were regarded as religious texts. Today we admire Plato for using human reason to delve into ultimate questions without being hidebound by any theological dogmas. For at least a millennium after he lived, Plato was often viewed differently. He was treated as though he was the founder of a religion, not a system of rational thought.

Like other thinkers whom we now describe as neo-Platonic, Proclus had a theory of reality which put *to Hen*, 'the One', at the centre of everything. The One was not itself a being, but it caused everything to exist. Because of their common source in the One, there was a unity between all particular things. Proclus added the concept of intermediate powers called *henads*, who caused particular things to be. This had the convenient effect of finding a place for the traditional Greek gods, like Apollo, who could be understood as *henads*.

Extensive remains of three almost equally fine residences (plus another of which only the apse survives) were discovered around 1970 on the lower, northern slopes of the Areopagus. Like the presumed house of Proclus, these dwellings included central halls and courtyards which would have lent themselves well to educational and religious gatherings. One possibility is that these buildings were used as places of instruction by master philosophers who thrived even later than Proclus – for example Damaskios, who is credited with giving the Academy a final boost and attracting the finest thinkers from across the domain of Hellenism.

Proclus, and whoever else may have occupied the mansion below the Acropolis, built up an impressive collection of sculpture, totalling eleven pieces ranging from the fourth century BCE to the third century CE. As the archaeologists discovered, eight of these pieces had been thrown down wells. Frantz thought the house was abandoned by polytheist owners, fleeing the new Christian order, who nourished 'the hope that the climate might one day change and that the pagan ornaments might be restored to their place of honour'.

But it was not to be. The archaeological evidence indicates that the house, at least for a few decades before its final destruction and desertion, had Christian occupants. A cross was inserted in the floor mosaic in the dining room and the pool was used for baptism. A torso of Athena was used as a step block. One very real possibility is that the polytheists left the house of Proclus around 529, the year when Justinian, Christian ruler of the eastern Roman empire, is said to have closed the philosophy schools of Athens.

Indeed there are many general history books which treat this imperial decision as a melancholy landmark in the annals of the West: the rational deliberation of the ancient Greeks was suppressed and would not resurface for a millennium. It is true that around that time, Christianity was imposed as the imperial religion, including in places like Athens where many had resisted. But the belief systems which Christianity replaced were not based on cold, disinterested, empirical enquiry. In certain ways they were not all that different from Greek Christianity.

In standard world history, another twist is often added. As a result of this cruel imperial decision to close the schools, seven of the eastern Roman world's finest thinkers went and took refuge with the ruler of Persia, their own empire's enemy. This is adduced as further evidence of cruel Christian theocracy.

But how certain is that? There is no doubt that the teaching of polytheistic philosophy and religion in Athens came to an end in the course of the sixth century. What precisely happened in or around 529 is a matter which has been debated by historians who study that period. In the chronicles of John Malalas, a Byzantine historian of debatable accuracy, it is recorded that in 529:

> the emperor issued a decree and sent it to Athens ordering that no one should teach philosophy nor interpret [?]astronomy,* nor in any city should there be lots casting for dice; for some who cast dice had been discovered in Byzantium indulging themselves in dreadful blasphemies... their hands were cut off and they were paraded around on camels.

Teaching philosophy is not considered quite as shady or deplorable an activity as playing about with dice, but it is mentioned in the same breath.

As for the journey of the seven philosophers, it is attested by a minor Byzantine writer, Agathias, who names them (they include Damaskios, the last head of the Athenian Academy, and at least two other eminent figures†) and adds that King Chosroes of Persia insisted that they be allowed safe passage home as part of a peace settlement with Justinian.

One is justified in feeling a certain scepticism about Agathias' account. Chosroes I came to the throne in September 531, and struck a peace deal in 532, so the philosophers' sojourn in Persia,

---

* In one reading, the word for astronomy is replaced by 'nomima' – legal things.

† Simplicius of Cyrene and Eulamius of Phrygia.

if it happened, was a rather short one. Some modern scholars doubt whether Chosroes would have taken such an interest in intellectual freedom, and they insist that there were plenty of places in Justinian's realm where these thinkers could have lived safely. But it is tantalizing to imagine these eminent representatives of polytheistic thought seeking refuge and freedom of expression among their country's enemies, just as Soviet dissidents did. Perhaps that is why this tallish story endures.

One titbit of evidence suggests the teaching of Platonism went on in Athens as late as 560. It comes from a philosopher called Olympiodorus, a pupil of Proclus. Writing in that year, he makes a revealing observation about their intellectual movement's ultimate master, Plato himself: 'Perhaps Plato made a practice of taking no fees because he was well-off. That is why the endowments have lasted until now, in spite of many confiscations.'

This suggests that the Byzantine imperial authorities were making life very difficult, but not completely impossible, for those deep-pocketed characters who, even in the mid-sixth century, were still determined to teach polytheism in Athens. In some ways, however, the exact dates hardly matter. On one point, the archaeological evidence is absolutely clear. Around 580, Athens succumbed to Slavic invaders whose depredations covered the city's fine structures and institutions in a thick layer of debris and dust. Whatever the fate of the pagan Athenians themselves, their ability to engage in fine metaphysical speculation and clever talk was terminated, at least for a while.

Depending on their own point of view, modern writers about the late flowering of thought and rhetoric in Roman Athens, and in the Greek-speaking eastern Roman empire, tend to lean one way or the other. They either praise the Hellenic holdouts against Christian bullying, or they admire the Church fathers for using the subtleties of the Greek language and thought to articulate Christian doctrine in a robust and coherent way which would stand the test of centuries.

A point that many play down is the common ground between the

Christian teachers and the polytheist ones. This was not a contest between logical enquiry and the straitjacket of revealed religion. Both the Christian fathers and the polytheists wrestled with the same paradox. They were precociously intellectual, taking pleasure in stretching their own minds and those of their listeners. They were all skilled and at times self-indulgent users of language: specifically the Greek language as it had developed at the peak of Athenian military and artistic achievement, 800 years earlier. For example, along with his other talents, Gregory of Nazianzus could knock out verse which copied the diction and metre of the Attic golden age. This was just one of the accomplishments an Athenian education instilled in Christian and pagan alike.

At the same time, all the great alumni of the Athens schools, be they monotheist or polytheist, were seekers of transcendental enlightenment. Dextrous as they were with words, they were adamant about their limits. They felt that the divine realities they were approaching ultimately could not be expressed in any words, even beautiful and grammatically correct Greek ones, or reduced to human concepts, or fully understood by the human mind.

Platonist philosophers like Proclus spoke of the utter inaccessibility of the One, *to Hen*, which brought everything into existence but was not itself an existing thing. The Christian alumni of Athens, like Basil and Gregory, also developed a theological system in which God in His essence was unknowable. They might experience God but not understand Him.

For them it was this essence, or *ousia*, that held the three Persons of the Trinity, and indeed everything else, together – but no word, concept or flight of the human intellect could get near it. Statements about God might be true as far as they went, or at least not untrue; but they could never express the full truth, which would always elude expression. Precisely because, at a certain point in the quest for the divine, all words, categories and concepts seemed to fail, there was an intense yearning – common to both Christians and non-Christians of the era – to seek transcendental moments of an ineffable kind. Ascetic discipline, psychological preparation and elaborate ritual all played their part in gaining this experience. Control of access to such experiences could easily be abused, just as access to cultural knowledge and the intellectual side of religion could easily become a thing to be fought over. (That, alas, is an abiding feature of almost all forms of religion.) None of this implies that the differences between the Christians and neo-Platonists were unimportant, but in several different senses, they were all speaking the same language. Damaskios, often called the last neo-Platonist, may have lost his teaching licence in Athens, but his works continued to be read with interest in Christian Constantinople.

Whatever the exact order in which things happened, we can be sure of one thing. Sometime in the mid-sixth century the Athenian theatre of a many-fronted contest between pagans and Christians saw victory for the latter, even as the city's worldly fortunes declined to the point of near-annihilation.

10

# A Christian Millennium

*A shadowy half-millennium after 500 CE – the Parthenon's
adaptation to Christian use – arguments over the damage
which it and the Hephaisteion suffered through conversion
– Byzantine Athens as a Christian pilgrimage centre –
Michael Choniates: a Christian bishop who loved and
loathed Athens – the city's capture by the Franks in 1204 –
possible connection of Athens with the Shroud of Turin*

In the twilight of the polytheistic age, Athens was a lively, chaotic
place where pugnacious youths were trained in subtle philosophy
and clever rhetoric. In the era of Byzantine Greek Christianity, the
city – and the Parthenon in particular – would take on a different
role as a place of pilgrimage both for humble folk and kings. The
transition between these two states occurred over five murky
centuries when Athens is rarely mentioned in the annals of history.

After the reign of Justinian, whatever remained of the city's
worldly importance diminished to vanishing point as Constantinople became entrenched as the hub of a multinational but Greek-
flavoured empire. In the seventh and eighth centuries, when the
whole empire at times had to fight for its life on several fronts, the
half-ruined town of Athens took a share of the pain. However,
the Athens region was one of the few parts of Greece south of
Thessalonica which escaped Slav domination, and it may even have
attracted a modest influx of people fleeing other Greek places where
life was even worse.

In the winter of 662–3 the Byzantine Emperor Constans II made Athens his temporary headquarters as he campaigned against the Slavic tribes installed nearby. That led to a little upswing in the city's fortunes, attested by the coins from that monarch's reign in the Agora. But as Alison Frantz points out, a degradation in municipal water supplies, detected by archaeologists, is a grim indication of general decline. Of fifteen wells in use near the Athenian philosophy schools during the early sixth century, only four were still operating in the following century. Many running-water systems, a field in which Roman technology excelled, went out of use over the course of the sixth century.

In the obscurity of the eighth century the town did produce one extremely powerful woman, a ruler who changed history; but she exercised that power in Constantinople, not her native Athens. Irene was born into a prestigious Athenian dynasty, the Sarantapichos family, but we know little about that clan, or indeed about what it meant to enjoy local prominence in that shadowy time. What we do know is that in 769 she married the Byzantine emperor Leo IV, who ruled jointly with his father, and she was therefore crowned empress.

She had strong views on the religious question which was bitterly dividing the empire: whether holy icons or religious images should be used in prayer. To their supporters, icons were windows onto heaven which could bring the worshipper closer to God. To the icon-breakers or iconoclasts, such images were no better than pagan idols. Leo at least moderately favoured the iconoclasts, whose cause had generally prevailed since about 720; his Athenian wife sympathized with those who venerated images, and over time succeeded in having them reinstated. She reflected the sentiments of her home region. In 727, central Greece and some Aegean islands had staged a short-lived rising against an earlier emperor in protest over his anti-icon policies.

After Leo's death in 780, Irene held office as regent with her son Constantine VI until 790. When he reached maturity, they quarrelled. In 797 Irene had the – by now unpopular – emperor blinded and killed, whereupon she became the sole ruler, and was soon on the verge of a dynastic marriage which might have transformed European history. In 800, she agreed to wed Emperor Charlemagne, king of the Franks. He was the dominant figure in western Europe, and had just been crowned Holy Roman Emperor by Pope Leo III.

If the wedding had gone ahead, Christendom's east–west split might possibly have been avoided; but she was overthrown before the ceremony could take place. Force of nature and epoch-making figure though she certainly was, there is little evidence that Irene took much interest in her Athenian home patch. But she used Athens as a convenient place to exile her brothers-in-law in 797.

Did anything at all remain of the intellectual tradition of Athens in that era? Only the tiniest scraps of written evidence exist. Theodore of Tarsus was a Greek-speaking prelate who as Archbishop of Canterbury from 668 to 690 laid the administrative foundations of the English church. He was described in a papal letter of 748 as a Greco-Latin philosopher, 'educated in Athens and ordained in Rome'. So perhaps some teaching did continue in the shadow of the Acropolis. But that description might simply be a way of saying that Theodore was deeply versed in Greek letters, a field in which Constantinople was now dominant. In some people's minds, Athens may have been an idea, a cultural concept, rather than a physical place.

By the turn of the first millennium, Byzantine power had recovered under the Macedonian dynasty of emperors, and Constantinople was reaffirmed as the most prosperous and culturally vibrant city in Europe. Athens at this stage was little more than a modest provincial outpost, though it would have felt some slight benefit from the general upturn.

Yet the spiritual fascination of the Parthenon was powerful and enduring. By now it was well-established as an important church and shrine to the Theotokos or Mother of God. Once again, we have to acknowledge that the transition to that new state of affairs, and even the date of its conversion to Christian worship, are somewhat elusive. But it had certainly become a church by the year 600, and some traces of the building's early Christian existence survive.

Among the most striking written vestiges of life in the era of the Christian Acropolis are more than 230 inscriptions, from formal announcements to untidy scribbles, that have been deciphered on the marble columns. Before 600, plenty of inscriptions were planted on the citadel, but on dedicated slabs. Sometime after that year, they started appearing on the Parthenon itself. They include 104 prayers, addressed either to God or the Virgin Mary, who was the protectress and guardian of the Rock and the city. Another sixty-four are epitaphs which provide basic details of bishops of the city whose names would not otherwise survive. Also mentioned are the names of humbler clergy and church servants such as cantors. As the Byzantine scholar Anthony Kaldellis points out, 'there is no comparable body of epigraphy from any [other] building' in the Greek Christian world, probably not even in Hagia Sophia, the great church of Constantinople, whose Christian inscriptions have never been published.

The topic of the writing on the Parthenon ranges from the spiritual to the colourfully personal. There is one inscription in which a man asks the Virgin Mary to visit affliction on a love rival – 'the man sleeping with my girlfriend' – ideally, in the specific form of a hernia. The supplicant also begs to be transformed into a doctor so he can rip off the bandage from the hernia-stricken rogue. Another is a clever piece of poetry spelling out the writer's name, Ioannes. There are also three ship images, comparable to those scratched by grateful pilgrims in the Holy Land. They could be offers of thanks for a successful voyage to Athens, or supplications for the future safety of loved ones at sea.

For lovers of liturgical poetry, the more formal inscriptions offer a unique insight into the development of Orthodox Christian worship in all its intricacy. As fixed for the last millennium or so, Greek Orthodox rites are a mixture of the cathedral tradition developed in Constantinople's Hagia Sophia and the monastic services first heard in ascetic communities around Jerusalem. The hymns and singing instructions carved on the Parthenon, with their variations for different days of the week, seem to be a stepping stone towards the full cathedral office of the Eastern Church, with its endless ingenious variations on well-known Hebrew Psalms.

At the heart of the church it seems there was a prized image of the Virgin. No copy of that image survives, but it was very possibly some version of the familiar style known as *Odigitria* ('She who guides') in which the Virgin points to her divine Son with one hand as she cradles him with the other. The apse of the building was decorated with a separate image of the Theotokos, a mosaic from which 188 fragments are now to be found in the British Museum. Many other vestiges from the Christian Parthenon, including a marble cross which stood near the altar, can be seen in the Byzantine and Christian Museum of Athens.

The intensity of the epigraphs, from the solemn to the scatological, reflect the growing appeal of the Mother of God in her Athenian manifestation. In 848, a general called Leon who had overseen the Byzantine province of Hellas* was buried on the Acropolis, near the Parthenon: a respectful epitaph was carved on one of the columns. At a minimum, that shows the prestige of the Christian Parthenon, as locus of the Holy Virgin, was riding high. It could also be a sign that the officer felt a personal devotion to the Athenian Theotokos, as more and more people did.

Apart from the Parthenon, another piece of evidence for the spiritual intensity of Byzantine Athens is the Church of the Holy Apostles, in the middle of the archaeological park which has been created in the ancient Agora. It was built on the ruins of a nymphaion, a small shrine to the female divinities that were

---

* Hellas was a 'theme' (a civilian-military Byzantine province) that covered southern Greece.

believed, in the ancient religion, to gather round a spring. Its first Christian use was as a baptistry. Then, around 1000 CE, it was transformed into a full-blown domed church by an architect with a genius for mixing two early Byzantine styles, square and octagonal. More seamlessly than usual, a narthex or entrance was tacked on. The frescoes now visible in the narthex date only from 1700, but they add to the atmosphere of a numinous place.

The Church of the Holy Apostles is one of two buildings in the Agora that have stayed relatively intact since their original construction. The other one is a much older edifice on the north-western side of the Agora – the temple of Hephaestus, erected in the early fifth century BCE. Like the Parthenon, it was built of shining Attic marble. The Parthenon is a brilliant mixture of the Doric and Ionian architectural styles; the Hephaisteion is a purer example of the Doric order. Its well-preserved condition, apart from the aesthetic delight, is a boon to historians. It means that when archaeologists discover even tiny fragments of Doric temples in other places, they can confidently reconstruct the proportions of the entire building.

But by the turn of the second millennium CE, this house of worship was well-established as a Christian church, dedicated to Saint George. In a switch that also occurred in the Christianized Parthenon, the orientation of the building was reversed, so as to create an entrance on the west and a rounded end or apse on the east, the direction which worshippers of Christ always faced. On a smallish scale, which makes everything a bit easier to understand, the Hephaisteion exemplifies some of the changes that occurred when a building changed religion, and the arguments that the process can trigger centuries later. As a polytheist temple it had metopes featuring stories of the mythological heroes Heracles and Theseus; they have suffered damage, but they are still recognizable, and they still stand above the columns in their original place. How much of the damage is deliberate is impossible to tell. Those who blame the Christians say many heads, particularly of the heroes, seem to have been knocked off. On the other hand, the building's reuse clearly guaranteed the preservation of the structure: there was no risk of marble slabs being deployed elsewhere, as would certainly have happened if the monument had simply fallen into desuetude. It is arguable that the story of Theseus did live on, at least as a faint echo, through the building's long span as an infrequently used Christian temple, which ended only in 1833. The church bore the mysterious title of Saint George Akamatis, and that could be a reference to Akamantos, the child sired by Theseus with a Cretan princess.

A tourist walking down the gentle slope of the Agora today sees a Christian church, the Holy Apostles, and a classical temple, the Hephaisteion, two venerable and remarkably intact buildings. In Byzantine times, a visitor would have seen the same buildings and perceived two churches, recalling only dimly that one of them had formerly served a different purpose.

Among the emperors who restored the fortunes of Byzantium and boosted the role of Athens as a centre of Christian veneration, an outstanding figure was Basil II, who ruled from 958 to 1025 and is known in Greek parlance as *o Voulgaroktonos*, the slayer of the Bulgars. He also advanced the empire's interests and frontiers, through an adroit mixture of wars and diplomacy, at the expense of Slavs, Arabs and Georgians. To give thanks for these successes, he came to Athens and knelt before the Parthenon's image of the Virgin Mary. The occasion for his trip in 1018 was a four-year campaign against the Bulgars which pushed the empire's boundary up to the banks of the Danube. It was unusual for Byzantine emperors to make pilgrimages unless a sacred site happened to lie on their route. But it seems clear that Basil went on a long detour to pay homage to the *Panagia Atheniotissa*,* to use the title that would soon become established for the Virgin as she appeared in the Parthenon. The visit was a big injection of prestige for Athens. One of its indirect consequences was the refounding of the monastery at Daphni, about

---

* Scholars are uncertain whether this refers to a specific icon, to a style of icon, or in general to the veneration of Mary on the Acropolis.

11 kilometres west of Athens, whose stark, severe images of Christ and the saints are some of the most powerful works of religious art that survive from that period. The refoundation was once thought to have been carried out on Basil's orders; now it is dated later, to around 1080, and linked with a general upturn in the spiritual standing of the Attica region which the emperor's visit had set in motion.

Despite its recognition as a UNESCO world heritage site in 1990, Daphni remains one of the undervalued treasures of the Athens area. Most of what the visitor now sees is a superb example of art and architecture from the eleventh century, but the location goes much further back. It was originally a temple to Apollo, located halfway along the road to Eleusis; one of the Ionic columns which held up that structure is still intact, while the rest were taken away by Lord Elgin, a British diplomat of the early nineteenth century, in one of his lesser-known acts of appropriation. It is still a magnificent site, where the attainments and spiritual yearnings of many eras can be felt. At least in religious and aesthetic terms, Athens of a thousand years ago was no backwater.

Especially after 1100, the pilgrims' enthusiastic descriptions of the Parthenon put special emphasis on a light which was said to glow perpetually with no need for replenishment. One such mention comes from the Anglo-Saxon traveller Saewulf, who passed through Greece in 1102 on his way to visit the Holy Land shortly after the First Crusade. He describes Athens as a place where Saint Paul preached, and converted Dionysus the Areopagite, and adds: 'There is a church there of the Blessed Virgin Mary in which oil in a lamp is always burning and never running out.' It is not clear whether this is an eye-witness account or something he was told while staying nearby.

The study of the Christian Parthenon, and of other Christian monuments which stood in Athens at the same time, is a rarefied and controversial business. For better or worse, this segment of the city's past receives only a tiny fraction of the attention which is devoted to the classical era, and a similar emphasis is evident in the material now offered to tourists. One fifty-page guide to the Acropolis, on sale at the entrance, devotes two lines to the citadel's 1,000 years as a Christian monument and almost all the rest to the 800 or so years when the Parthenon housed a gleaming statue of Athena, starting around 430 BCE.

Among those who do study the Christian era, there is little middle ground. Manolis Korres, a revered authority on all phases of the Parthenon's history, makes the argument that as pagan-to-Christian adaptations go, the conversion of Athena's temple was a relatively seamless one. However, Professor John Pollini of the University of Southern California is in the opposite corner. He has no patience with what he regards as special pleading, and insists that much more damage was done by the Christians than conventional wisdom generally allows. After studying the surviving Parthenon sculptures in the British Museum and the Acropolis Museum, he is convinced that what he calls gratuitous desecration of the polytheist artwork by Christians was cold-blooded and systematic. He doubts the theory that this destruction was either a crime of passion by Alaric's Gothic invaders, sweeping through in 396, or even a functionally necessary price paid for the building's conversion. What he suspects is a storm of ideologically inspired destruction which may have taken place several centuries after those events, possibly under the influence of iconoclasm.

As we have seen, three main groups of sculpture adorned the Parthenon: the triangular pediments crowning the front and back; the small metopes immediately below; and the enigmatic, panoramic frieze which ran all the way around the top of the inner columns. When the Parthenon changed use, the western pediment, depicting the contest between Athena and Poseidon, was spared, while the centre of the eastern pediment was removed to make way for an apse, as was one key part of the frieze: the central slab whose meaning would generate controversy in the twenty-first century. This is the section interpreted by the American classicist Joan Breton Connelly as an act of sacrifice of the daughters of King Erechtheus.

It was not destroyed: it was built into one of the fortification walls of the Acropolis and rediscovered only a couple of centuries ago, in time to be despatched, contentiously, to England along with many other Parthenon sculptures.

The rest of the frieze was mainly left in place, apart from the bits that were removed to make room for windows. As already noted, the worst damage was done to the metopes: those on the north, west and east were badly damaged, leaving only those on the south. In fact, one of the northern metopes was left comparatively intact, and according to one theory, it was spared because it depicts a scene similar to the Christian Annunciation: the angel Gabriel informing Mary that she will bear a child.

Controversy flared when the new Acropolis Museum, opening its doors in 2009, presented the Annunciation hypothesis as proven fact. In truth, it is only a theory, put forward by a German archaeologist, Gerhard Rodenwaldt, in 1933. He found it strange that 'not a blow of a chisel' touched that particular metope when those around it were destroyed, and suggested that decisions about the fate of various metopes were made and executed when the building was surrounded by scaffolding for the purpose of its conversion to a church. In fact, the theory is hard to sustain. The so-called Annunciation metope did suffer chisel blows, albeit less severe than other sculptures; and any scaffolding needed to convert the church (which did not fill the entire expanse of the old Parthenon temple) would not have been in the right place to hack away at the metopes.

Whatever happened to the metopes, Pollini argues that deliberate damage was done to the frieze. Moreover, he says, this harm was not done for any practical reason, but from icily hostile intention or through fear of the demons that might lurk in pagan sculpture. For example, his inspection of a section of the north frieze, with a scene of elders or branch-bearers apparently taking part in the Panathenaic procession, leads him to suspect 'concentrated bashing of the facial features with some sort of blunt instrument'. In some cases, he says, heads and facial figures were the primary target, even though streaming hair was left intact. The part he describes was taken down to make room for one of the church's windows, but Pollini is convinced that gratuitous damage was done to the figures, during or after the removal. Ultimately, there is no incontrovertible evidence as to when or why or by whom any of this vandalism was carried out. Nor are there any written sources which can shed much light on the matter.

Anthony Kaldellis, author of a sympathetic study of the Christian Parthenon, argues that what remained intact is more significant than what was, in some circumstance or other, destroyed. He is especially impressed by the endurance of one of the Parthenon's magnificent pediments: the western one, showing the contest between two Olympian gods over who would be the main protector of Athens. It was below this Olympian scene that followers of the monotheist faith crowded in, over ten centuries, paying their homage to the Virgin Mary who had taken over as the new protectress of the citadel and by extension the whole city. The pediment remained for the entirety of the building's Christian existence, and its eventual destruction in the seventeenth century was an accident of war, not an act of religious zeal.

One devotee of the light that was said to emanate from the Parthenon was Michael Choniates, the last Greek archbishop of Athens. He is an outstanding figure in the city's annals, embodying its charms, transcendental power, contradictions and wildly fluctuating fortunes. He was one of two talented brothers who were born in north-western Anatolia and received a first-class education in Constantinople. Nikitas, the elder one, became the best-known historian of his era. Michael Choniates was also a prolific wordsmith, penning orations, homilies and letters which give an idea of his passionate and temperamental nature. His appointment to Athens around 1180 was in worldly terms a severe disappointment. Precisely because he was well versed in the city's classical glories, he was bitterly disillusioned by its economic and cultural decline, by the poor educational level and uncouth dialect of its inhabitants, and the corrupt way it was administered, with opportunistic locals and greedy bureaucrats locked, as he saw it, in a compact of sleaze. But he developed an absolutely passionate love for the Parthenon, which was his spiritual base. This was not, of course, because of its ancient dedication to Athena but more because of its contemporary role as a luminous temple of the Christian Mother of God.

Like the church fathers who studied in Athens 800 years earlier, he was deeply familiar both with ancient Greek literature and with the Christian and Hebrew scriptures. That gave him a vast store of metaphorical resources. It also presented him with an acute dilemma. In a sense, a similar dilemma has been faced by everybody, whether from Greece or much further afield, who has looked for a coherent way of capturing the vicissitudes of Athens down the ages, one that somehow incorporates the Periclean glory, the hard realities of later eras and the hope of better things. Given the evidence of decline from the Periclean peak, many have asked themselves: should the very word 'Athens' be used only to refer to some elevated state of mind or soul, some artistic sensibility, which happened to flourish on the Acropolis but no longer has any particular connection with that spot? This was one solution to the problem, but it offered no help to a cleric who was obliged to inhabit and make peace with the Athens of his own time. The dilemma was particularly acute for an educated Christian intellectual, who on one hand insisted that his own faith transcended all others, and on the other had to admit that Hellenic culture's greatest heights were attained before that new faith appeared.

Choniates found some very creative answers to those puzzles. Precisely because he was so steeped in high Hellenic culture, he deplored the fact that his own Athenian flock hardly lived up to the nobility of the people who had once inhabited the city. But in spiritual terms, he insisted, the city had taken a leap forward since the time of Pericles. It had moved on from the 'false virginity' of Athena to the Christian Mother of God who connected the citadel and the city with heaven.

In his Inaugural Address to the Athenians, many of whom were probably baffled by his flowery rhetoric, he used the theme of light to drive home the point that a false and artificially stoked flame had been replaced, in the Christian era, by a brilliant and true one. Recalling the New Testament story of the foolish virgins, acting as attendants at a wedding, who fail to keep fuel in their lamps, he declares:

> … They say that the lamps of the sinners fade. And this Acropolis was liberated from the tyranny of the false Parthenos Athena: no longer is the fire on her altar fed indefatigably. Now it is the ever-shining torch of the eternal Parthenos and Mother of God that is held up on this peak as though from heaven itself. It does not illuminate only the city and the land beyond Attica, but as much of the earth as the sun traverses.

To express his awe of the holy light beaming from the Parthenon he used two images from the Book of Exodus. The illumined Parthenon was a beacon comparable to the pillar of fire which guided the children of Israel through the desert. It also recalled the burning bush through which God spoke to Moses. That was a very carefully chosen metaphor. For eastern Christians, the bush which blazes but is never consumed is an image of the Mother who gave birth without losing her virginity. Listeners versed in the Bible would have picked up the allusion.

The emergence of Athens as a place with a special bond with the Virgin Mary is all the more striking because a vastly bigger city, the imperial capital of Constantinople, made a similar claim. Her 'protecting veil' was believed to have saved that great metropolis from invasion at moments of great peril. The most famous Greek Orthodox hymn, the Akathist, uses images of great beauty to address the Virgin Mary and praise her 'invincible power' as a guardian of the 'City' – meaning first and foremost the one on the Bosphorus.

Moreover, that hymn also contains lines which seem directed *against* Athens and the values for which that city supposedly stood. These lines mock the worldly cleverness for which Athens was once famous. They affirm that in multiple senses, the Theotokos embodies a divine wisdom, mysteriously accessible to humble fishermen but baffling to silver-tongued orators: a sagacity that trumps the smartness of all earthly philosophical debates of the kind that were first heard amid marble stoas and flickering male-only dining rooms. As the hymn to Mary declares:

> Orators most eloquent do we behold mute as fish before you,
>     O Theotokos;
> For they are at a loss to explain how you could be a virgin and
>     yet give birth.
> But as for us, marvelling at this mystery, we cry with faith:

> Rejoice, Vessel of the Wisdom of God.
> Rejoice, Treasury of His providence.
> Rejoice, you who proves the philosophers fools.
> Rejoice, you who proves the logicians illogical.
> Rejoice, for the subtle debaters are confounded.
> Rejoice, for the inventors of myths are faded away.
> Rejoice, you who break the webs of the Athenians.
> Rejoice, you who fill the nets of the fishermen.

In view of this anti-Athenian rhetoric, it is all the more startling that the Parthenon established its own claim to be a hearth of the Mother of God. In the worldly calculus of economic and political power, Byzantine Athens commanded no more than a fraction of the capital's weight. In spiritual affairs, and especially in its claim to a connection with the Mother of God, the lady who brought divinity to earth, medieval Athens came a very respectable second.

Nor, to this day, have Athenians taken personally the barbs against their city which the popular hymn seems to contain. Its weekly recitation on Fridays in Lent draws to church people who rarely attend any other service. And in spring 2020, with churches closed by the coronavirus pandemic, pious Athenians simply chanted it heartily from their balconies.

Kaldellis, a professor at Ohio State University, has made the contrarian argument that the relative importance of the Parthenon was greater during the Christian epoch than during the Periclean era when it was built. During that polytheistic period and for centuries afterwards, the Parthenon was one among many fine monuments in Athens. Indeed we are not precisely sure what liturgical function it may have served, in addition to housing a gold-and-ivory statue, and the imperial treasury. Of the various monuments on the Acropolis in the time of Pericles, the Erechtheion had a much clearer religious role, as the home of a more modest but much older wooden statue which marked the end point of the Panathenaic procession. In the Christian era, by contrast, the glowing Parthenon literally dwarfed all the city's other spiritual attractions, which included many small churches that were architectural gems.

Michael Choniates knew all that, and constructed arguments which fused the greatness of Hellenism, of which Athens was the cradle and Constantinople was now the capital, with the higher truth of Christianity. With the subtlety of his Byzantine mind he reconciled the poor condition of Athens in his own time, which he may have exaggerated for effect, with its unmatched historical prestige. He also riffed on the theme that Athens, while going downhill economically, had soared upwards spiritually by replacing a false polytheistic religion with a true one.

Although the parallel is not exact, similar dilemmas were certainly faced by the cultural masters of Iran when their nation embraced Islam in the second half of the seventh century CE. They had to reconcile their confidence in the greatness of Persian civilization with the superior status of a new monotheistic religion, and they had to make the claim that Persian culture could provide new ways of interpreting the universal religion. Exponents of Christian

Hellenism like Choniates had to make the case for the excellence of the Greek language and heritage while also professing that a new faith superseded all other religious yearnings. The archbishop, being human, adjusted his emphasis according to the moment. In letters to friends, he could be pretty frank about the doldrums of ordinary life in twelfth-century Athens.

'To what depths of ignorance art thou sunk?' Choniates once exclaimed about the misery and squalor of the material and human culture of Athens. It was now a place where tax-collectors 'look over our barren soil with measures petty enough to check the prints left by fleas… the hairs on our heads are counted – how much more the leaves of vines and plants'. Athenians might have forgotten about the glories of the Periclean age, but Choniates, being schooled in the classics, could not. For example, the Painted Stoa, initially a military art display where the triumphs of Marathon and Salamis were depicted, and later a hub for philosophers, was in a state of ruin. 'Sheep graze among the meagre relics,' lamented the archbishop. Archaeological evidence, as well as a document listing properties around Athens as of roughly 1100, confirm that many fine classical buildings were buried, neglected or cannibalized. American archaeologists, while unearthing the Painted Stoa, found a humdrum storage vessel resting on a step of the colonnaded classical building. Clearly people in medieval times had forgotten what grand public purposes the original building had served.

Elsewhere in the Agora, during the Byzantine era, modest houses were built around courtyards and wells, sometimes constructed from the bits of the grander classical buildings lying beneath. The very fact that these cleverly built and ancient wells were being used at all suggested a modest uptick in activity. But it was certainly true, as Choniates suggests, that parts of the sprawling ancient city defined by the Themistoclean wall, and then by the Roman-era Valerian wall, had relapsed into agricultural use. The 1100 document suggests that within those walls, on the north-west, there was a ground for the popular sport of tzykanion, similar to polo. On the other hand, sections of the old city still played host to a modestly flourishing scene of craftsmanship and commerce. Between the Acropolis and the Hill of the Muse, there was a district of dye-workers, who probably sent their shellfish-based extract to Thebes, where it was used in the production of dazzling silks. Elsewhere in Athens, pottery and ceramics were made for export, and the city and port reclaimed some of their old role as a commercial entrepot.

For all the ambivalence of his feelings about Athens, in the early years of the thirteenth century Michael Choniates found himself defending the city, and the Acropolis in particular, from a ruthless warlord. At any rate, he sounds like a ruthless character from such evidence as we possess; we do not have his side of the story. It was a time when the imperial masters in Constantinople were facing challenges both from petty local warlords and much broader geopolitical forces. There were local rebellions in central and northern Greece, and this emboldened Leo Sgouros, a regional governor and tax-collector based in Nauplion in the northern Peloponnese, to defy the emperor's authority and seize control of nearby Argos and Corinth. A man given to explosions of violence, Sgouros was no respecter of clerical authority. He asked the bishop of Corinth to dine with him, then had his hapless guest blinded and thrown from the city's high citadel.

Fearing a similar fate, Michael Choniates hoped the authorities in Constantinople would come to his aid, but everybody in the capital was preoccupied by the danger from the advancing Franks: soldiers from western Europe who had marched eastwards under the Crusaders' banner, supposedly to reclaim the Holy Land, but would prove as threatening to their fellow Christians as they were to the 'infidels' of Islam. The participants in this Fourth Crusade had strayed a long way from their original purpose of reconquering Jerusalem. Strapped for cash, the Crusade's leaders became entangled first in a Venetian military adventure in the Adriatic (which led to their excommunication by the pope), then in a Byzantine palace conspiracy in which they agreed to help restore a previously deposed emperor. Thus was the stage set for one of the darkest episodes of the Christian Middle Ages.

Deeply preoccupied by his own, more local challenges, Choniates went on a desperate, thankless mission to seek help from the imperial capital, where he found that people had too many other problems on their minds. He returned only to find that Thebes had already fallen to Sgouros' troops. Only with difficulty could he get back to Athens. In 1203, Sgouros laid siege to the city and took control of its lower ground. The inhabitants, led by Choniates, fought back successfully from the Acropolis, using engines of their own. After setting fire to the Agora, Sgouros moved northwards in search of easier targets.

This inter-Greek fighting was soon overshadowed by a disaster of much greater magnitude. On 12 April 1204, a black day in the collective memory of the Greeks, the Crusaders burst into Constantinople, then a city of around 350,000 people, and spent three days running amok: they smashed their way into churches, palaces and homes, seizing what they could carry and killing thousands of their fellow Christians.

One graphic description of these horrors was left by Nikitas Choniates, brother of the Athenian bishop. The invaders installed a Fleming, Count Baldwin, as Latin Emperor of Constantinople. Once ensconced in the capital, the Franks marched through Greece: they laid siege to a bishop in Corinth, where he became the latest cleric in that turbulent city to tumble fatally from the high fortress. They also invested the Athenian stronghold of Choniates, leaving him no choice but to surrender.

The lands in Greece were then divided up among Frankish knights, and Athens and Thebes fell to a certain Otho de la Roche, a squire from Burgundy. He established a Duchy of Athens, whose administrative centre was in Thebes, a relatively prosperous town, while its greatest spiritual centre was the Parthenon, which duly became a Catholic church, dedicated to Notre Dame, Our Lady of Athens. Choniates sought exile in the island of Kea, struggling to retain control of at least some of the buildings and lands which had belonged to the Orthodox, while many church properties were taken over by the Catholics. The internal affairs of the Orthodox community were still run by the Greek Church, but they became second-class subjects of the new order, dominated by a French-speaking court which followed the medieval pursuits of hunting and archery as well as feasting and dancing.

Frankish power – in Greek, *Frangokratia* – prevailed in Constantinople for only six decades, until 1261, but in Athens the era of *Frangokratia* (in the general sense of rule by a succession of Catholic and west European knights and soldiers of fortune) lasted much longer. It was terminated only by the advance of the Ottomans, who conquered the great city on the Bosphorus in 1453 and Athens three years later. Considering its duration, *Frangokratia* left little trace on the culture, language and landscape of Athens and its environs. A so-called Frankish tower, dating from fairly late in that period, used to loom up from the entrance to the Acropolis, but it was torn down in the nineteenth century.

Obscure as it is, Frankish Athens features in one of the mystery stories of medieval Christian Europe: the fate of the Holy Shroud, a linen cloth believed by some to have wrapped the body of Jesus, which is now preserved in Turin and periodically exposed to visitors by the Catholic authorities. At least this much is known. The religious treasures of Constantinople prior to the Frankish conquest included one and possibly two prized pieces of linen which were said to bear the imprints of the body of Jesus Christ. On the other hand, the securely recorded history of the Shroud now in Turin does not begin until it emerges in a village in France around 1350.

If the carbon-dating tests conducted on pieces of the Shroud in three laboratories in 1988 are accurate, then there is nothing surprising about that medieval date. It corresponds roughly to the likely period of the Shroud's construction, which the laboratories estimated at 1290 at the earliest. However, if, as some respectable scientists still insist, the carbon-dating is flawed and the Shroud is in fact older, then it is plausible that it featured among the treasures that were grabbed from Constantinople in 1204 and spirited away by the marauding Franks. Or, as another possibility, a different piece of sacred linen could have been nabbed by the Franks and then brought westwards.

A western visitor who spent time in Constantinople before the conquest said a sacred shroud was kept in a well-known church, that of Saint Mary of Blachernae, and exhibited, and indeed somehow made to 'stand up', every Friday. It so happens that Otho de la Roche, the future Duke of Athens, fought in the Blachernae district. It seems very possible that he removed the precious cloth, taking it initially to his new Athenian duchy and then back to his native France. In 1205, a Byzantine prince, Theodore of Epirus, wrote to Pope Innocent III with a litany of bitter complaints about the looting of Constantinople. In a letter whose authenticity is (like almost every aspect of the Shroud's story) vigorously debated, he is said to have lamented:

> In April last year a crusading army, having falsely set out to liberate the Holy Land, instead laid waste the city of Constantine. During the sack, troops of Venice and France looted even the holy sanctuaries. The Venetians partitioned the treasures of gold, silver and ivory, while the French did the same with the relics of the saints and, most sacred of all the linen in which our Lord Jesus Christ was wrapped after his death and before the resurrection. We know that the sacred objects are preserved by their predators in Venice, in France and in other places, [and] the sacred linen in Athens.

If any native Athenians were aware of the temporary presence in their midst of this sacred object, the records offer us no clue. This was a period when ordinary town-dwellers were largely bystanders in their own history.

# 11

# Latin and Greek:
# the Late Middle Ages
## 1216–1460

*The Catalan Company of mercenaries seize Athens in 1311 –
the kingdoms of Sicily and then Aragon become overlords of
the town – the Catalans are ousted in 1388; the Florentine
dynasty called Acciaiuoli take control of Athens – Ottoman
influence over the town culminates in formal takeover in
1456 – Italian travellers' tales from 1395 and 1444*

Back in the age of Socrates and Alcibiades, a contest between Athens and Sparta played out on the coasts of Sicily. In the Middle Ages, this process was reversed, as a conflict which flared up in a Sicilian city proved to have big, messy consequences for the Greek world, which was a disordered enough place already.

The new Sicilian saga began on Easter Monday 1282, near a church outside Palermo where evening prayers were in progress. A violent incident involving a Frenchman and a Sicilian woman triggered a general uprising – known as the Sicilian Vespers – in which more than 10,000 French people living on the island were killed. This was an act of rebellion against the French-born King Charles, who wielded power at the southern tip of Italy and was a member of the royal house of Anjou in the Gallic heartland. To help them in a campaign which lasted twenty years, the Sicilians recruited the kings of Aragon, a Spanish dynasty that was gaining confidence after reconquering Iberian lands from the Muslims who had controlled them for centuries. A series of treaties, culminating in the Peace of Caltabellotta in 1302, left the Spanish-protected Sicilians in control of the island while the French retained the adjacent part of the mainland. But peace had one complication. King Frederick, the Spanish-born ruler of Sicily, had no further use for the mercenaries he had recruited from his homeland. These battle-hardened soldiers had no interest in returning to Iberia, and were minded to go east in search of more wars to fight.

To understand parts of southern Europe in that era, it may be helpful to think of places like Angola, Congo or Afghanistan in the grip of modern civil wars. Imagine a territory endlessly fought over by warlords and private armies with no fixed loyalties, a situation which did not prevent the existence of little pockets of prosperous life in places where one side had for the time being prevailed. A warlord could be subject, at least in theory, to broader structures and authorities, but in practice, that warlord's charisma and ruthlessness would always determine the facts on the ground. When peace was declared, there was no guarantee that soldiers would obey orders to put down their weapons, especially if they no longer had homes to return to.

Of the wild cards in the Mediterranean power game, none was wilder than the Catalan Company. Left high and dry in 1302 by peace between the houses of Anjou and Aragon, they found another master in Byzantium, where the emperor was hard pressed by the rising power of the Turks. The company had the advantage of a charismatic leader, Roger de Flor, who had learned resourcefulness in a hard school. He was orphaned when his father, a falconer in the service of the Holy Roman Empire, perished in battle. Aged eight, Roger boarded a ship of the Knights Templar, a powerful Catholic military order, and he made himself useful in several battles. He later offered his services, unsuccessfully, to the army of Anjou which had killed his father, and was finally hired by a Spanish king to fight in Sicily.

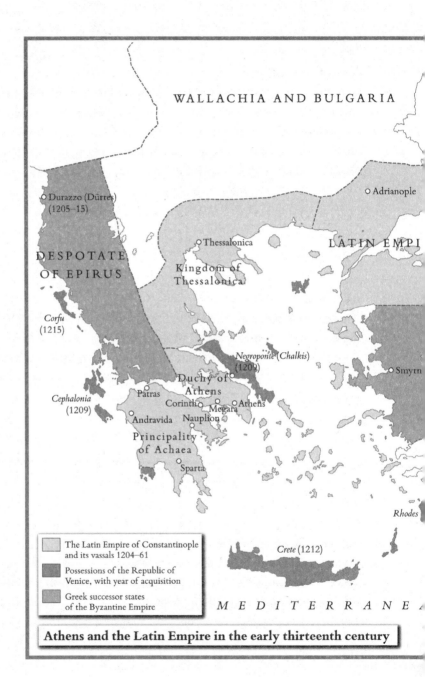

WALLACHIA AND BULGARIA

○ Durazzo (Dürres)
(1205–15)

○ Adrianople

○ Thessalonica

LATIN EMPI

DESPOTATE
OF EPIRUS

Kingdom of
Thessalonica

*Corfu*
(1215)

*Negroponte (Chalkis)*
(1209)

○ Smyrn

Duchy of
Athens

*Cephalonia*
(1209)

○ Patras

Corinth○ ○ Megara ○Athens
○ Nauplion

○
Andravida

Principality
of Achaea

○
Sparta

*Rhodes*

| | The Latin Empire of Constantinople and its vassals 1204–61 |
| | Possessions of the Republic of Venice, with year of acquisition |
| | Greek successor states of the Byzantine Empire |

*Crete* (1212)

M E D I T E R R A N E A

**Athens and the Latin Empire in the early thirteenth century**

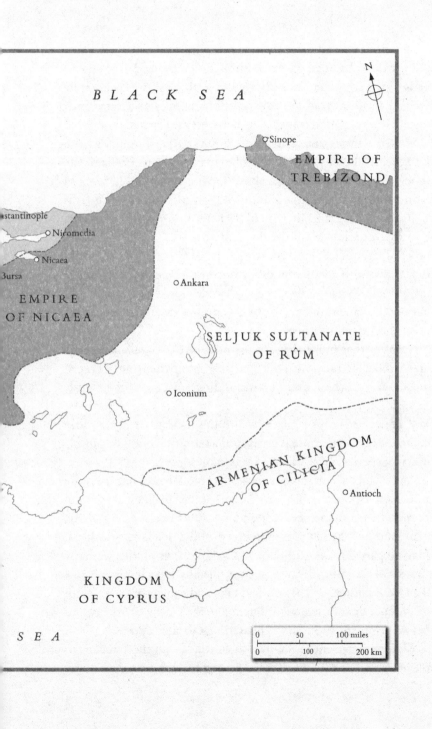

BLACK SEA

N

○ Sinope

EMPIRE OF
TREBIZOND

Constantinople

○ Nicomedia

○ Nicaea

Bursa

○ Ankara

EMPIRE
OF NICAEA

SELJUK SULTANATE
OF RÛM

○ Iconium

ARMENIAN KINGDOM
OF CILICIA

○ Antioch

KINGDOM
OF CYPRUS

SEA

| 0 | 50 | 100 miles |
| 0 | 100 | 200 km |

As long as he and his men were being paid, de Flor performed well for the realm of Byzantium, inflicting a heavy defeat on one faction of Turks, the Karasids, in October 1303. A year later, he relieved and liberated the town of Philadelphia in what is now western Turkey. But tensions grew between the Catalans and other parts of the Byzantine army, especially the Alans, nomads from the north Caucasus who spoke a language close to Persian. The imperial house grew uneasy about having such a large force of Latin troops in its heartland. In April 1305, Michael IX – who was co-emperor of Byzantium with his father, Andronikos II – ordered Alan mercenaries to kill de Flor and attack his army during an imperial banquet. Deprived of their leader, the Catalans fought back and saw off an attempt by Byzantine forces to wipe them out in Gallipoli. By 1309, the Catalans had devoured the resources of that peninsula and moved westwards into northern Greece; from there, they edged southwards.

It was at that point that the fortunes of the Catalans became intertwined, fatefully, with the French knights who (from a base in Thebes) ruled Athens and its surroundings. Walter V of Brienne, the new Duke of Athens, hired the company to wage war against the Greek overlords of Thessaly, and the Iberian soldiers swiftly obliged. Recruiting those Iberians was a tempting but rash gamble by an inexperienced ruler, as soon became clear.

Walter had only just taken over in succession to his cousin, Guy de la Roche, a respected nobleman who succumbed to illness at the royal court in Thebes in October 1308 and was duly buried at the dynastic mausoleum in the Daphni monastery on the outskirts of Athens. (Having passed from Orthodox to Catholic control, this was now a powerful Catholic institution, controlled by French Cistercians.) The Greek masters of Thessaly had taken advantage of Guy's death to renounce their formal subordination to the Duchy of Athens, and they were initially successful in reasserting Orthodox power.

Walter entered into a six-month contract with the Catalans to roll back the Greek advances, in return for handsome amounts of gold, and this was initially very successful. The new Duke of Athens was duly commended by the pope for his success against the 'schismatic' Greek Orthodox.

After benefiting from their military prowess, Walter naïvely imagined he could dispense with the services of his Iberian shock-troops. Having picked out 200 horsemen and 300 foot soldiers to keep, he told the remaining Catalans, who numbered several thousand, to relinquish control of the castles they had seized and leave his realm. Predictably, they refused, and Walter began rallying Frankish forces from other parts of Greece to help him see off the private army from Barcelona.

All sources agree that, in March 1311, a battle took place between the two sides, in which the Catalans prevailed despite being outnumbered. Walter was killed; he and his fellow Frankish knights had counted on their equestrian skills, but the Catalans had cleverly placed themselves next to some marshy ground which impeded the horses of their foes. Only recently have scholars concurred on the location of this clash, at a place called Halmyros, which literally means 'salty', in southern Thessaly. The end result of the battle is not in question. Catalan forces took over the Duchy of Athens, and they and their successors held it till the 1380s. Soldiers looted the court of Thebes, as many locals fled for their lives to Negroponte (modern Chalkis or Chalkida), on the island of Euboea, which was then a Venetian stronghold. Walter's widow, Joanna of Châtillon, surrendered the city of Athens, a place of spiritual rather than economic importance. In a bitter blow to Frankish pride, many a rough Catalan fighter settled down with a war-widowed French noblewoman whose 'wash-basin he was unfit to carry' – in the words of one Catalan chronicler.

Quite a lot is known about how the Catalans took power in Athens, but the way they exercised it is shadowy. In 1312 they gave themselves a skein of respectability by inviting their old master, King Frederick II of Sicily, to be their overlord, and to appoint a member of his family to whom they could pronounce an oath of fealty. The king's son Manfred, a minor, was nominally elevated to the Duchy of Athens, and a Spanish knight called Berenguer Estañol was sent with five galleys to oversee the duchy's administration. In an interesting historic reversal, he came from the Catalonian port of Ampurias, whose name (derived from the Greek *emporion*, trade) recalls its foundation by Greek colonizers, in 575 BCE.

The Catalan system of governance lacked the glitter and grandeur of the feudal, French-speaking order (with its castles, minstrels and jousting contests) that it replaced, but it was probably effective enough. A 'marshal' who was always a member of the Catalan company held the highest military rank, while a vicar-general headed a civilian administration, helped by local *castellanos* in every town and district.

As for the Greek Orthodox people of the duchy, they were second-class subjects (barred from acquiring, selling or freely disposing of property), and only by stealth could they exercise any influence over public affairs. But the social boundary was not hermetically sealed. Some high-ranking Catalans took Greek wives, and these ladies were allowed to keep the Orthodox faith. In the later Catalan period some high-ranking posts were held by Greeks. Some Catalans must have converted to Greek Orthodoxy, given that the Catholic Church expressed its disapproval of such switching.

There was severe tension, at first, between the Catalans and the papacy, which was temporarily established at Avignon* in southern France, and subject to the influence of the French families which had been ousted from Athens by the Iberians. Successive popes urged the Venetians, entrenched in neighbouring parts of Greece, to harass the Catalans. Another papal tactic was the imposition of an interdict, a ban on the church's holiest rites, on these unruly members of the flock. In 1330, Pope John XXII denounced the Catalans as 'schismatics, sons of perdition and pupils of iniquity' whose ejection from the Duchy of Athens would be a virtuous act.

---

* Conflict between the papacy and the French monarchy led to seven successive popes residing in Avignon between 1309 and 1376.

This emboldened the Burgundians to hope for the reconquest of their Athenian prize, but they were frustrated by the Catalans' skilful preservation of good relations with Venice. Venice calculated that it could live with the Catalans as an assertive land power in central Greece so long as they did not also aspire to become a naval force. Hence in 1319, Venice successfully demanded that a plank must be taken out of every Catalan vessel in Piraeus harbour, while the ships' tackle was to be deposited in the 'castle of Athens' – in other words the Acropolis.

In 1335, a Catholic Archbishop in Patras pronounced the excommunication of the Catalan leaders of the duchy. However, in the words of Kenneth Setton, a historian of medieval Greece, 'the Catalans seemed to have a higher regard for their dominion in Greece than for their future in heaven'. The Catholic Archbishop of Thebes, who understood local realities well, refused to carry out the papacy's anti-Catalan policy, and was unsuccessfully invited to present himself at a papal court in Avignon.

In practice, the staying power of the Catalans, under Sicilian protection, showed up the limits of the papacy's reach. So too did the collapse of an attempt by the Burgundian claimant, Walter VI de Brienne, to regain Athens; it failed 'beneath the walls of the Acropolis', as Setton puts it, proving that a natural stronghold in the hands of superbly experienced fighters is very hard to challenge, whatever the rights and wrongs of legal and spiritual arguments.

But it was a gallant enough effort. Walter brought an army of French knights and Tuscan infantrymen across the Adriatic and fought some successful battles in north-western Greece on behalf of the House of Anjou, which had claims in the region. However, by the time he reached Athens, his funds were running out, and he may have been disappointed to find that local Greeks offered him no assistance.

By the mid-fourteenth century, the Catalans were becoming less terrifying to their neighbours and more divided among themselves. In the 1360s, Roger de Lluria, a Catalan commander based in

Thebes, mounted a coup d'état and renounced the authority of the monarch in Sicily. Sensing isolation in the Christian world, he accepted help from the Turks, prompting a cry of outrage from the pope, as well as other Christian fiefdoms in Greece. But by 1364, Lluria had expelled the Turks, made peace with the Sicilian king and reassured the pope.

In 1372, Thebes was the venue for a meeting of the Christian rulers of Europe and the Levant, called with the supposed purpose of countering the Islamic challenge. But history was moving in the other direction: from the late fourteenth century onwards, the Turks would increasingly be the arbiters in an ever more intricate contest between squabbling Christian powers and chieftains for control of the Greek heartland.

While Turkish power was concentrating minds throughout the eastern Mediterranean, some new forces joined the struggle for control of the Greek lands. The Catalans had to contend with another group of mercenaries from western Europe, as wild as they had been seventy years earlier. The newcomers were the Company of Navarre, originally from the Basque Country at the western end of the Pyrenees. They were sent to the Balkans by the Royal House of Navarre, one of whose members claimed the throne of Albania. They helped capture the Albanian port of Durrës in 1376, but like the Catalans, they soon found themselves heading southwards, wandering the region in search of new paymasters.


A more durable presence in Greece was the Italian dynasty whose surname, Acciaiuoli, hinted at one of the sources of their wealth. In Florence, they were bankers and makers of steel (*acciaio* in Italian); in Naples they reached high rank at court; and as contenders for the strongholds of Hellas they were calculating pragmatists and clever diplomats whose principal failing was family quarrels. In the early fourteenth century, the leading scion was Niccolò Acciaiuoli, who held high office in the Neapolitan court, enjoyed the friendship of poets like Petrarch and Boccaccio, and worked to consolidate the possessions of the Neapolitan royals, and of his own family, in southern Greece. After his death in 1362, his heir and distant kinsman Nerio Acciaiuoli took up the family tradition of seeking opportunities for power in Greece, using funds from the clan's Italian branches.

In the mid-1370s, Nerio managed to take possession of Megara on the western edge of the Duchy of Athens. He then hired a commander from the Company of Navarre to help him capture Thebes. But as Nerio would soon discover, any relationship with Navarrans was likely to be fickle and short-lived.

Meanwhile the Athens-based Catalans, determined to defend the Acropolis at least, held an assembly and resolved that of the various nobles and sovereigns who claimed title over Athens, they should put their faith in a monarch from their original home, King Pedro IV of Aragon. (Not all Greece-based Catalans agreed with this; one faction preferred to stay under Sicilian authority and collaborated with the Company of Navarre as it wreaked havoc across Boeotia.)

For a few years at least, relations between Athenians and Aragonese became rather intense. A delegation from Catalan-controlled Athens travelled to the court of Aragon in Zaragoza to declare loyalty and put to the king a strange ragbag of requests from various parties in the town. The wish list, and the king's response, throw some helpful light onto how things were in the shadowy world of Iberian Athens.

One beneficiary of Pedro's decrees was a rising star in the affairs of Attica: a property owner and warrior called Dimitrios Rendis, who by origin was either Greek or more likely *Arvanitis*. Then as now, this refers to a population group whose ultimate origins were Albanian, but who were both Orthodox and in varying degrees Hellenized.

The king gave him and his heirs the title of chancellor of Athens. Rendis was given tax breaks and privileges which only members of the Catalan ruling class had hitherto enjoyed; and he was confirmed in possession of extensive lands on the west side of Athens, which now form a grimy industrial suburb that still bears his surname.

The delegation from Athens also conveyed requests from Catholics who asked him to make bequests to their church easier. The king refused, arguing that at a time of such insecurity, piling extra resources on the church was too great a luxury. He also refused the Athenians' proposal that their town be formally separated from the rest of the Duchy.

In his correspondence with his Athenian subjects, King Pedro made a revealing outburst of praise for the Parthenon, calling it 'the most precious jewel that exists in the world, and such as all the kings of Christendom would imitate in vain'. This was one of the first declarations by a medieval ruler that the artistic accomplishments of the classical world might surpass those of the Christian era. His queen, Sibilia, was more interested in the Christian Parthenon; she knew that this great church housed many treasures, and dreamed of bringing some of them to Aragon. In November 1379, she wrote to a bishop in Athens asking about the 'very many relics both of the blessed Mary and other saints' which the Parthenon contained.

Apart from wise pronouncements, King Pedro despatched some military help to his Athenian subjects, as soldiers commanded by Nerio Acciaiuoli closed in on the Acropolis. A small force sailed into Piraeus and somehow reached the citadel. But it was not enough to tilt the balance in the defenders' favour. After a two-year encirclement, the Iberian commander gave in to the Italian opportunist, and the Catalans were forced out of Greece.

Unlike the Catalans, who initially kept interaction with the locals to a minimum, the new master of Athens set about making friends and allies in the Greek population. He set up his own headquarters on the Acropolis, turning the Propylaea into a ducal palace. Dimitrios Rendis survived the change of guard, although he had played a prominent role in the Catalans' defence. Clearly this was a time when the de facto influence of Greeks was rising at the expense of their Catholic overlords. Nerio spoke Greek and made it the language of administration. Any Italians who joined him in the region were encouraged to assimilate; among those who did was a branch of the great Medici family who Hellenized their name to *Iatros* (doctor).

Without giving up Catholic control of the Parthenon, Nerio invited the Greek Patriarch in Constantinople to assign an Orthodox bishop to Athens. That was an important concession to local sentiment. He married one daughter to a Greek grandee in the Peloponnese and another to an Italian count, a member of the Tocco family which held sway in the Ionian Islands.

But his position was still precarious. Although he wanted to normalize relations with the Venetians, he was soon at odds with them over the port of Nauplion, where his Greek son-in-law was in control and had no intention of giving up. Nauplion and the surrounding area of Argos had remained in Burgundian hands until recently, when a French heiress, with no close relations, left the region to Venice. The republic was keen to take possession of this bequest.

Acting on the Venetians' behalf, the Navarre company invited Nerio to negotiations over the Argos region, and kidnapped him. As William Miller puts it, 'the law of nations was mere waste-paper to the men of Navarre; Nerio was arrested and imprisoned in a Peloponnesian jail'.

This triggered a diplomatic brouhaha between Venice and Florence, with the powerful Acciaiuoli network using all its connections, including clerical ones, to secure their cousin's freedom. But hard cash as well as high-level connections were required. Silver plate was peeled off the door of the Parthenon, and the precious stones donated to the church by the faithful had to be traded before he could return as master of the Acropolis.

Nerio spent his final months as master of Athens in a desperate attempt to shore up his own legitimacy. The royal house of Naples, where his family had gained influence, formally conferred on him the title of Duke of Athens, with no overlord except the Neapolitan king.

He died in September 1394, causing much confusion with a remarkable will. As though he was contrite for having robbed the treasures of the Parthenon, he piled beneficence on that Catholic place of worship. The doors were to be re-covered in silver, all its treasures were to be restored and its clerical staff expanded, from the twelve existing clerics. At least twenty priests were to be hired to say prayers for his body, which should be laid to rest inside the great church. (It has never been found.) To fund the ever-expanding place of worship, he bequeathed all his holdings in the town of Athens, along with his large stud farms, for the cathedral's use.

There were generous and well-calibrated bequests to his various progeny. His favourite daughter Francesca, already mistress through marriage of the western Greek islands, received castles in Corinth and two other places. Her older sister Bartolomea, married into the Greek family that controlled much of the Peloponnese, was less well treated but granted some relief on her husband's debt. To his common-law son Antonio he left the administration of Thebes and other nearby towns.

His mistress Maria Rendi (presumed to be Antonio's mother, although that is not certain) was confirmed in her existing holdings, including the western bits of Athens that bear the family name. Despite his careful calculations, his will had some unintended consequences. Francesca and her husband Carlo Tocco (but particularly, it seems, Francesca) soon found themselves organizing the defence of Corinth against other members of the family. They included her half-brother Antonio and her sister Bartolomea's Greek husband. Carlo and Francesca managed to spirit away quite a lot of possessions, from jewels to well-bred horses, to their home island, Cephalonia. The power of Francesca's character is evident in the slightly misspelled signature (in Greek capital letters) that she appends to a document around that time, drawing on Byzantine imagery to call herself queen of the (east) Romans.

Jean Froissart, the French chronicler, gives a lyrical description of the court of Cephalonia where the Athenian-born Francesca presided, with ladies highly skilled at making silken clothes and chatting freely with the nymphs who inhabited the island. As is pointed out by Dionysios Stathakopoulos, an insightful modern historian of the Byzantine era, her robust role in the defence of Corinth indicates that she 'could do much more than… needlework or conversing with fairies'.

In all these inter-Christian squabbles, the Turks were hovering in the background. Aggrieved parties sought Turkish help, and Turkish diplomacy consistently tended to support the weaker party in any dispute between Christians, in the hope of maximizing its own influence. Francesca's defence of Corinth was organized with Turkish help, and the sultan received some fine horses in return. Another party which ran to the sultan was the Greek archbishop of Athens, Makarios. Although he owed to Nerio the fact that he was entitled to live in Athens, the prelate was clearly frustrated by the Italian's immense generosity to the Catholic establishment in the Parthenon. At least according to the Venetian version of events, Makarios persuaded the Turkish commander Timurtash to make an assault on Athens. As with so many attackers, he easily overran the town itself, but was stopped short by the defences of the Acropolis. One of Duke Nerio's lieutenants, Matteo de Montona, offered gallant resistance, while also making a desperate appeal to the Venetian stronghold of Negroponte, 70 kilometres to the north, for help.

The Venetians agreed to take control of Athens – not it seems, through any romantic love of the Athenian past, or any real interest in the town itself, but more because holding Athens would make it easier to retain their other possessions in the region. For the next seven years or so, the Acropolis would remain under the precarious, and in many ways reluctant, control of the Serene Republic.

It was around this time that a traveller from another part of Italy passed through Athens and left a revealing description. Niccolò da

Martoni spoke of a town 'nestling at the foot of the castle hill [which] contains about a thousand hearths' but no place of accommodation. The top of the hill he found much more interesting. He was impressed by the ducal palace fashioned out of the Propylaea, with thirteen columns, and dazzled by the Church of Saint Mary, in other words the Parthenon, where he counted sixty outer columns and eighty more inside (only a slight exaggeration), and was given a guided tour by one of the many clergy. Da Martoni was enchanted by the icons, relics and religious treasures which he inspects and venerates at the Parthenon. As he confirms, there was a prized icon of the Virgin Mary, ascribed like many Marian images in the Hodigitria style to the hand of Saint Luke himself. He was also shown part of the head of Saint Makarios, relics of Saint Denis of France and a copy of the Gospels in gold letters that was reputedly transcribed by Saint Helen, mother of Constantine, the first Christian emperor. He was impressed by the four jasper pillars holding up a dome which covered the altar, and by the doors of the cathedral which were presented, fantastically, as trophies from the Trojan war. His guide pointed him to a nick in the Parthenon wall, said to be the source of the mysterious, unfading light emanating from the building.

In another feature that anachronistically mixed classical and Christian associations, the visitor was shown a cross reputed to have been scratched on a column of the Parthenon by one of the city's first Christian converts, Dionysios or Denis the Areopagite, at the moment of the Crucifixion.

Elsewhere in Athens, da Martoni inspects many correctly and falsely labelled talismans of the past. He sees the Temple of Olympian Zeus, which people insisted on calling the 'house' of Hadrian, although it was really a sacred structure whose construction that emperor had completed. When he viewed the culmination of Hadrian's great aqueduct, at the bottom of Mount Lycabettus, locals told him what must have been a well-established legend: this was the place where Aristotle and other philosophers drank to gain wisdom. Although it was little more than a village, Athens was taking shape as a palimpsest of medieval and classical, Christian and polytheistic, real and fantastical.

For a maritime power associated with wealth and glitz, the Venetians expended only minimal resources on administering Athens. It was decreed that the town would have a governor, assisted by a notary, an assistant, four servants, two grooms and two horses. It was very difficult to find takers for the post, given that this was still a very hazardous corner of the world, with the surrounding seas infested by pirates and probing attacks on land by Turkish and other forces. Indeed Turkish sources assert that their forces briefly captured Athens in 1397, although this may have amounted only to a raid on Attica.

Meanwhile, Antonio Acciaiuoli was feverishly plotting a return to Athens, charting a skilful course between the clashing interests of Venetians and Turks. In 1402 he made a surprise assault on Attica and fended off an attempt by the locally based Venetians to thwart his plans. By early 1403 he had starved out the defenders of the Acropolis and was master of the citadel. The Venetians put a price on his head, and there followed a period of feverish negotiations over whether his possession of the Acropolis should be legitimized.

The Turks' ability and will to support him temporarily collapsed after the Ottoman army was defeated near Ankara in 1402 by the great Mongol commander Tamerlane. Sultan Bayezid was captured, but his eldest son Suleyman escaped the battlefield, travelled westwards and began negotiating a tactical peace with the Venetians. As part of this bargain, the Turks were willing to give up their support for Antonio.

Antonio, however, was able to exercise plenty of countervailing influence in Italy, not least through his brother, a cardinal who had the ear of the pope. In the end, a compromise was struck which saved the honour of all sides. The Ottomans promised to restore Athens to Venice but did nothing to bring this about, so Antonio was left firmly in control. Antonio agreed formally to be a vassal of Venice, making an annual gift of Theban silk to the Church of

Saint Mark. But he did not keep that promise either. He settled down to a thirty-year reign as master of Athens, and it was an open secret that he held this position not really by grace of Venice but by kind permission of the Turks.

Antonio seemed to enjoy his lordship of Athens; he encouraged Florentine friends and cousins to visit and enjoy the pleasures of riding, hawking and partridge-shooting. Antonio teamed up with Turkish forces to take Nauplion from the Venetians, and grabbed Corinth from its Greek masters (in other words, his brother-in-law's family) in 1423. Like his father, he settled down with a local lady, a Greek noblewoman called Maria Melissene. He built himself a handsome residence by the Ilisos river, near the site of Emperor Hadrian's new Athens.

Unusually for a master of the Acropolis in that era, he died in his bed at an advanced age, in 1435. But then another round of family feuding broke out. His will named as successor his nephew, Nerio II. But to take power the new ruler of Athens had to fight his aunt-by-marriage Duchess Maria and her local allies, led by a Greek family called Chalkokondyles. One member of that family, Laonikos, had literary talents and has been described as the Herodotus of medieval Greece, in other words a chronicler with an eye for colour.

In a familiar standoff, Nerio II and his allies were in control of the lower town, while the duchess and her friends held the Acropolis. George Chalkokondyles appealed to the Turks, who apparently preferred the claim of Nerio II, described as a weak and uncertain figure who may have been glad of Turkish tutelage. In any case, while those negotiations were going on, prominent figures in Athens tricked the duchess into leaving the Acropolis and allowed Nerio II to become master of the city. The ousted duchess tried to negotiate a deal with Constantine Paleologos, the Greek prince based in the Peloponnese who would later be Byzantium's last emperor, under which he would make a claim for the Duchy of Athens, while she would retire to the Peloponnese. But that initiative failed, not least because public opinion in the small settlement of Athens seemed to favour the Acciaiuoli.

Once firmly established, the new Duke Nerio gave the town another two decades of peace under light Turkish oversight. His brother Antonio II manoeuvred him into ceding control of the Acropolis for a couple of years (1439–41) and he moved temporarily to his home city of Florence, where negotiations were in progress over a possible union between the Orthodox and Catholic churches. Returning to Athens, he had to manoeuvre between the Greek forces which were quite firmly established in the Peloponnese and the Turks who were the region's rising power. In 1444 he allied briefly with Constantine against the Turks but soon had to come to terms with them. Two years later, the Turkish sultan Murad helped him recapture Thebes.

In any case, the most consequential event for Athens during its final years under Latin rule had little to do with the caprices of its Florentine masters. In 1436 and again in 1444, the town received visits from a remarkable man who has been described, albeit loosely, as the father of Greek archaeology. He is known as Cyriacus of Ancona, a merchant's son from that port on the Adriatic coast who became a compulsive wanderer around the venerable cities of the eastern Mediterranean, as well as a chronicler of any signs of ancient glory that were still visible. He reflected the Renaissance spirit of reverence for the classical past. Coming to Athens, he showed little interest in the town's present-day life or in the Christian treasures which had fascinated other recent travellers. But he was enthralled by the sculptures from the Periclean age which were still visible on the Parthenon and in a few other places in Athens. Arriving at the Acropolis in April 1436, he wrote in his diary:

I came to Athens, the celebrated city of Attica, where I saw, first of all, large walls everywhere in a state of disintegration because of their antiquity. In the city and in the surrounding fields there were marble buildings beyond belief – houses, sacred shrines – as well as different works of art, noteworthy for their remarkable execution and huge columns, but all in heaps of shattered ruins…

He was one of many visitors in the post-classical era to have puzzled over the Parthenon frieze and wondered, in the absence of any written evidence from antiquity, what it might portray. His reading told him that this was the work of master sculptor Pheidias, or at least his school; and the visitor's best guess for the subject matter is that it 'fashioned with extraordinary skill… Athenian victories during the time of Pericles'. He made a careful count of the Parthenon's pillars, more accurate than the one made by da Martoni four decades earlier: he found twelve at each end and seventeen on each side. He was equally transfixed by the pediments at either end, which after a millennium of Christian worship were still in large part visible and comprehensible. His attempts to draw the Parthenon and its sculptures were crude but also revealing of what his mind's eye was seeing.

His rendering of the pediments, now in a Berlin museum, have served as a vital clue for those trying to establish how those sculptures originally looked, even though he is selective in his depiction. He shows that the west pediment portrays Athena emerging triumphant in the contest to be chief protector of Athens, but his sketch fails to include her rival for the position, Poseidon. As for Athena, she looks more like an Italian Renaissance lady than a Greek goddess. Observing the 2,500-year-old edifice in the Agora which was in active use as a Christian church, he writes of 'a splendid temple of Mars, still standing intact with its 24 columns'.

In other words, he focuses on the polytheist past (wrongly identifying the dedication as Mars/Ares rather than Hephaestus) and barely notices the monotheist use which the building now served. That is in absolute contrast with visitors of a century or two earlier, for whom the Hephaisteion, as we now call it, was a Christian church with a mildly interesting former life. Deep inside, near the icon-screen, Cyriacus spotted a round, partly hollowed-out marble column which originally stood elsewhere. Its Christian use as a baptismal font was of no concern to the keen antiquarian, but he took careful note of the inscription listing some of the *prytaneis* or officers of the democratic assembly in ancient times.

On the other side of the Agora, Cyriacus offers an intelligent glimpse of the Tower of the Winds, an octagonal water clock and weather vane topped by fine sculptures of the divinities which personify the gusts that blow down from different directions. 'On it are eight winged figures of the winds, with their attributes, at the top of each angled wall, marvellous pieces of sculpture.' Elsewhere he is confused like other visitors by the tall stories told by local guides, accepting the description of the Temple of Olympian Zeus as Hadrian's 'palace'. However, just like today's archaeologists, he is a diligent copier and interpreter of epigraphy, for example those on Hadrian's Arch (dividing the city between its ancient founder Theseus and the Roman emperor who refounded it) and on the Lysicrates monument, which celebrate a prize won by the poet of that name.

In another gift to posterity, Cyriacus studied the Philopappos mausoleum on the Hill of the Muses, celebrating a Hellenistic-Syrian ruler of the second century CE. He made careful note of an inscription which had disappeared by the time, two centuries later, when a new wave of antiquarian Westerners descended on Athens.

In his indifference to the contemporary condition of Athens, and indeed to anything other than the golden classical past, Cyriacus foreshadowed many later travellers. Indeed it might be said that over the years, influential visitors to Athens divide into two categories. There are those like Cyriacus who are interested in one particular era of history, and filter out everything else. Then there are those like da Martoni who are interested in the present, the past and the skein of connections between them – including the efforts of successive generations to interpret, however creatively, the visible traces of yesteryear.

*

Very soon, a kind of curtain, albeit not an iron or impenetrable one, would come down between the Catholic West and the whole Greek world. That became inevitable after the epoch-changing month of May 1453, when the shrunken but symbolically all-important city of Constantinople fell to the twenty-one-year-old Ottoman sultan Mehmet after fifty-three days of siege. The eastern Roman or Byzantine empire thus formally came to an end after more than a millennium of existence; that left the Peloponnese as the only swathe of territory that remained in Greek Orthodox hands.

As conqueror of the queen of cities, and master of the southern Balkans, Mehmet was bound to make an assault on southern Greece, and he could hardly do that without turning his attention to Athens, which was already in his sphere of influence, although under the day-to-day control of colourful Italians.

Whatever happened, Christian-ruled Athens was not destined to last long. But its end was probably hastened by the antics of its ruling family. Following the death of his first wife, Duke Nerio II married a Venetian noblewoman called Chiara Zorzi, whose father had estates not far from Athens, in southern Euboea. They had a son called Francesco, who was still a minor when the duke died. The duchess became regent, an arrangement which the Turkish sultan at least provisionally accepted. Then she fell in love with another blue-blooded Venetian with Greek connections, Bartolommeo Contarini. Awkwardly, Contarini had a wife in Venice, but such was his determination to live regally on the Acropolis that he poisoned her.

The new duke and duchess were pleased to have the comforts of courtly life in Athens to themselves, but it seems that Athenians grew tired of their bloodstained regime and denounced the couple to Sultan Mehmet. At the same time, a fresh candidate for the Duchy of Athens appeared, a member of the Acciaiuoli family called Franco. Contarini and his stepson had to go to the Turkish court to explain the situation; the boy disappeared in mysterious circumstances and it was Franco who received the sultan's blessing as the legitimate ruler of Athens. He lost no time in arresting and killing his errant aunt. It was then Contarini's turn to complain to the Turkish ruler that he had been horribly wronged; and this messy situation provided an excuse for the sultan to impose his direct authority on Athens. He instructed Omar, son of Tourakhan, who was governor of Thessaly, to attack the city.

In a familiar pattern, Omar swept through the lower town but had to halt at the Acropolis, where a handful of Venetians held out in conditions of near-starvation. In the end, the besiegers induced Franco to leave with a seductive offer; he could leave in peace, taking an ample amount of treasure with him, along with his wife and three sons, and enjoy a no less stately life in the castle of Thebes. The Florentine family duly quit the citadel, as did the last Catholic archbishop to preside over the Parthenon, Niccolò Protimo.

Exact dates are disputed, but these events seem to have happened in 1456, three years after the Turkish triumph in Constantinople. Two years later, after a campaign to subdue Greek realms in the Peloponnese, Mehmet the Conqueror rode into Athens. A powerful tradition holds that he was given the keys to the city by the abbot of the monastery of Kaisariani, an important Greek Orthodox institution which flourished, and still flourishes modestly, on the slopes of Mount Hymettus. Mikhail Kritovoulos, a Greek writer of Ottoman sympathies, describes the arrival of Mehmet in Athens with these words:

He was greatly enamoured of that city and of the wonders in it, for he had heard many fine things about the wisdom and virtue of its ancient inhabitants, and also of their valour and merits and the many wonderful things they had done when they fought against both Greeks and barbarians. He was eager to see the city and learn the story of it and of all its buildings, and of the Acropolis... of the places where the heroes had conducted the city's government and accomplished those deeds. He desired to learn of every other locality in the region, of its present condition, and also of the facts about the sea nearby, the harbours, the arsenals, in short everything. He saw it, and was amazed, and especially the Acropolis as he went up into it. And from the ruins and remains, he reconstructed in his mind the ancient buildings, being a wise man and a philhellene... and as a great king. He conjectured how they must have been originally. He noted with pleasure the respect of the inhabitants of the city for their ancestors, and he rewarded them in many ways. They got from him whatever they asked for.

We are being told here that Mehmet combined reverence for the classical Greek past with at least some regard for the city's present-day inhabitants. It is likely that the arch-antiquarian Cyriacus was a member of Mehmet's mission; the Italian had offered advice to the sultan at other crucial times, including the siege of Constantinople. But if we are to believe Kritovoulos, the sultan took a more balanced view than his antiquities adviser. Of course, the deceptively naïve story of Mehmet's appearance must be taken with many pinches of salt. Part of its purpose is to impress on the reader that the author, at least, remembers how Athenians of old fought against external aggressors, be they Persians or Spartans.

An open question is how soon the cry of the muezzin was heard on the Acropolis and elsewhere in Athens. It seems possible that the Parthenon reverted briefly from Latin to Greek Orthodox worship before it was transformed into a mosque. Here again, squabbles and conspiracies among the Christians might have been the catalyst for change. After his negotiated departure from Athens, Duke Franco Acciaiuoli enjoyed two years of comfort in Thebes, until suspicious reports reached Turkish ears: some Athenians might be plotting to reinstate Franco as ruler of their city.

To test his loyalty, the Turks demanded that Franco take part in a planned attack on his fellow Italians and kinsmen on the island of Cephalonia. Franco tried desperately to find an escape route in the form of some gainful employment in his home region of north Italy; when that failed he sulkily joined the Turkish force, but that did not save him. He sought a moment of respite in the tent of the commander Zagan Pasha, who distracted him with conversation and then killed him. That marked the end of the Italian dynasty's presence in Attica, and it may have been the cue for the Parthenon's adaptation to Islamic worship. Yet another theory holds that a Venetian landing in Attica in 1466 was the trigger for the Parthenon's change of use.

In any case it seems likely that by 1470 or so, the muezzin's call to prayer had replaced Christian hymns to the Virgin Mary as the sound which rang out from the gleaming marble pillars.

# 12

# Before and After the Bombardment
## 1460–1700

*From 1500, Athens enjoys a modest upturn – the (real) life of
Saint Filothei, philanthropist and martyr – the destruction
of the Parthenon in the Venetian siege of 1687, followed by an
evacuation of the town – western European and Ottoman travellers
describe the city, and make crucial records of ancient sculptures
while they are still intact, on the eve of the Venetian onslaught*

By the early 1500s, the Ottoman town of Athens was growing steadily, both in size and prosperity. The town's population was overwhelmingly Greek Orthodox Christian. It enjoyed a high degree of self-regulation, as long as its ultimate loyalty to the sultan, and willingness to pay taxes, was not in question. But in one obvious respect, this was clearly a place under foreign occupation.

The Acropolis served as the garrison and place of residence for Turkish administrators and soldiers, and the Parthenon was the place where they prayed. The building's adaptation for Muslim worship involved less structural change than its Christian transformation had required a millennium earlier. But a minaret was erected at the south-western end, and it became a prominent feature of the Athenian skyline. From the point of view of the Greek Orthodox resident living in the lower town, the Acropolis was forbidden territory, just as it had been under Catholic Frankish rule. In the days of Latin dominion, tall residential buildings up to three storeys high abutted the entrance to the Parthenon, reaching more than halfway up the pillars. Under the Turks, the space around the Parthenon was similarly crowded, but the houses were lower. Under both regimes, the Propylaea served the needs of foreign masters: as a palace, or as a place of fortification or storage of military materiel.

One of the main differences was that under the Ottomans, the Greek Orthodox living in the lower town were able to expand their economic activities, grow demographically and build their own churches. In the first two centuries after the Ottoman takeover up to 200 places of worship may have been built, many of them on top of the late-Roman wall which no longer marked the boundaries of the town. These included a handsome church dedicated to Saint Dionysios the Areopagite, the city's first Christian convert, which stood at the foot of the Areopagus hill. The church itself probably lasted only a century or so, before being destroyed in an earthquake around 1600. But the site remained important as the residence of the Greek Orthodox archbishop, who was the most powerful member of his community.

In other respects, considering the turbulent state of the region, it can be argued Ottoman power sat fairly lightly on Athens, at least for the duration of the sixteenth century. Even as the Ottomans did battle with Western powers, a handful of west Europeans continued to live in the city without impediment. The Ottomans almost certainly felt more secure after capturing Euboea, and its capital Chalkis (Negroponte), from the Venetians in 1470. Immediately after its own submission to Ottoman rule, Athens was designated as the capital of one of the five *sanjaks* or provinces into which the sultan divided Greece. But once Chalkis became Ottoman, it became capital of a newly defined *sanjak*, within which Athens had the lower status of *caza* or district. That change may have worked to the advantage of Athens as it reduced the number of bureaucrats who were billeted on the city. Sometime in the early 1600s, there was another big change in the arrangements linking Athens to the sultan. The city was subordinated to the 'black eunuch' or *kizlar agha*, who occupied a supremely influential post in the palace as

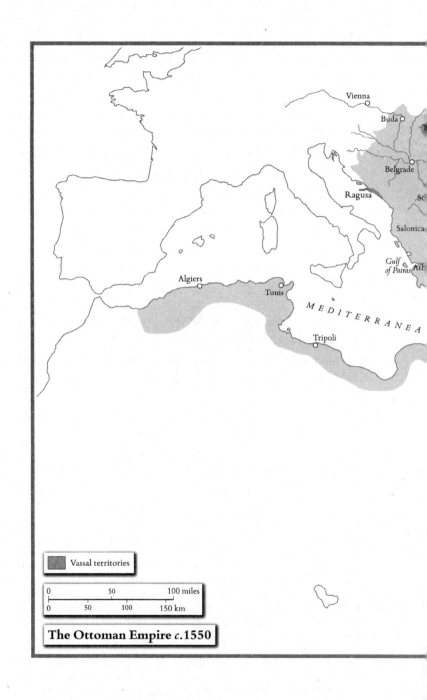

Vienna

Buda

Belgrade

Ragusa

Sć

Salonica

Gulf
of Patras   Ath

Algiers

Tunis

Tripoli

MEDITERRANEA

Vassal territories

| 0 | | 50 | | 100 miles |
|---|---|---|---|---|
| 0 | 50 | 100 | | 150 km |

**The Ottoman Empire *c.*1550**

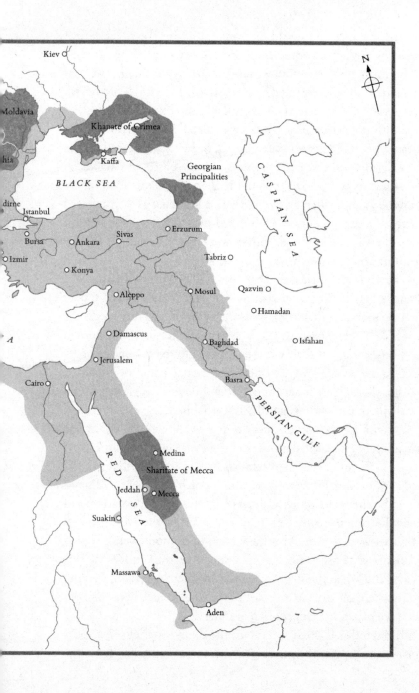

Kiev

Moldavia

Khanate of Crimea

hia

Kaffa

Georgian
Principalities

BLACK SEA

dirne

Istanbul

Erzurum

Bursa    Ankara    Sivas

Izmir

Tabriz

Konya

Qazvin

Aleppo         Mosul

Hamadan

A

Damascus

Baghdad         Isfahan

Jerusalem

Cairo

Basra

PERSIAN GULF

Medina

Sharifate of Mecca

Jeddah    Mecca

Suakin

RED SEA

Massawa

Aden

CASPIAN SEA

N

overseer of the closed world of women serving the sovereign. A *voivode* or governor represented the mighty eunuch in Athens, but this intimate connection with the court meant that prominent Athenians who felt aggrieved by the intermediate levels of Turkish bureaucracy could take their complaint directly to Istanbul, as Constantinople was called by its new rulers. That was on balance a more advantageous arrangement than being subjected to the tax-gathering whims of the *sanjak* governor based in Chalkis. A colourful story was told to explain the change of status achieved by Athens. A young Athenian woman called Vasiliki was the preferred consort of a certain sultan, who asked her what favour he might grant; she was loyal enough to her home town to request for it a direct link to the eunuch.

Meanwhile, in their everyday affairs, the Greek Christians of Athens largely looked after themselves. They would develop over time an elaborate system of class distinctions which dimly recalls the era of Solon, 2,000 years earlier. The grandest families were known as archons, and from their number a small group of *demogerontes* – leaders of the people – were elected every year. In descending order, the other classes were independent householders; shopkeepers who were divided into various guilds; and smallholders, who included farmers, market-gardeners and honey-producers. By 1570, the population of Athens had grown in just over a century from 10,000 to 15,000. Throughout the Frankish period, the population had fitted comfortably in the maze of streets north of the Acropolis and defined by the late-Roman wall erected after the barbarian raid of 267 CE. During the early Ottoman years, it expanded to the north and north-west. Some of the new neighbourhoods were peopled by Albanians whose influx was encouraged by the Ottomans. This was a period when the Aegean Sea was infested by pirates, making life anywhere on the Greek coast precarious. But Athens enjoyed a measure of safety from those marauders.

Although this is often forgotten, the town experienced a spurt of growth exactly at the moment when it was vanishing from the sight of western Europeans. The Florentines had lost their Greek foothold, and the Venetians were confined to the islands; there was no particular reason to pass through Greece on the way to the Holy Land, and the seas were not safe. When Athens 'disappeared' behind the Ottoman veil, it almost (for a century or so, at least) ceased to exist in western European eyes. Indeed George Tolias, a French-trained Greek historian, identifies a school of European writing and cartography which presents Athens as a ruin, a once-glorious phenomenon of which not a single vestige survives.

Things changed after the battle of Lepanto in 1571, in which a Catholic coalition defeated the fleet of the Ottoman empire in the Gulf of Patras and set a limit to Ottoman naval expansion. (This was also the last battle fought with rowing vessels which recognizably descended from the triremes of ancient Greece.) It did not change the status of Athens, but it made Athens seem less far away. It also whetted the keenness of west Europeans to drag the Greek Orthodox into their own (Protestant-Catholic) religious contests.

The German scholar Martin Crusius, a professor at Tübingen University, was one of several Teutonic Lutherans who felt a keen fascination with all things Greek, and nurtured a hope that the Greek Church, whose Patriarchate was located in Istanbul, might be won round to the Protestant cause. As a Hellenist, he was curious to know what had befallen Athens, but his method of information-gathering did not involve visiting that place or even contacting anyone who lived there. Instead he wrote to Istanbul, addressing Greeks who held prominent posts on the staff of the Patriarchate. He asked them to provide some details, from their own observations, of how the Athenians were faring. One of his correspondents, Theodosius Zygomalas, was a fine scholar who came originally from Nauplion and had been to Athens several times; he told his German contact as much as he could about the shadowy topic he was exploring. Crusius duly produced some basic maps, annotated in Greek and Latin. Among the aims of this work was simply to demonstrate that, contrary to what many people in western Europe thought, Athens did actually continue to exist. Indeed it had a certain dynamism as the third biggest town in Ottoman Europe after Salonica and Edirne. But few Europeans saw that for themselves.

Still, the picture of an Athenian society that was quietly flourishing, almost unknown to the West, needs to be repainted. A countervailing image is provided by the most important Athenian personality of the century. She was the first woman to exercise real agency in the modern history of the town. Her humanitarian and educational work earned her many enemies, a martyr's death and a place of honour as the saintly patroness of the city, canonized under her monastic name of Filothei.

Her worldly name was Revoula Benizelou, and she was born in 1522 into the Benizelos dynasty, who were among the richest of the town's ruling families or archons. According to her saintly life, she was the only offspring of parents who had waited long for parenthood. When she was fourteen they married her off to a much older man, of similarly high social status, who mistreated her but did not live long. Within three years she was a widow. She resisted parental pressure to remarry and instead devoted herself to charitable work. By 1549, after the death of her parents, she was in command of much wealth and founded a convent near the family residence in central Athens which offered training in weaving, handiwork and domestic skills. Her establishment grew rapidly and she set up communities at two other locations on the north side of Athens.

What made her work controversial was that it offered shelter to women who had been confined to harems, serving the sexual needs of Ottoman bigwigs. She also stood ready to give a home to women who were domestic slaves of rich families, or those who had incurred social disgrace by becoming pregnant out of wedlock. Her network of refuge and protection extended to several Aegean islands, including Andros and Kea. Inevitably, this activity incurred hostility. In order to pay debts and protection money, she had to appeal to powerful friends in Venice and at the Patriarchate in Constantinople. Things came to a head, it seems, in the 1580s after she took in four women in flight from bondage; they were then discovered under her protection. She was beaten up and imprisoned and friends had to pay the governor to secure her freedom. One night in October 1588, a group of paid thugs broke into her convent in Patesia, on the north side of Athens, where she was engaged in evening worship. They injured her so badly that she died of her wounds the following February. Within a few years the Patriarchate recognized her as a saint and people began venerating her earthly remains, which now occupy a place of honour in the metropolitan cathedral of Athens. What makes the life of Filothei interesting is the documentary evidence which supports the piously recounted story of her life. For example, she writes in February 1583 to the Venetian Senate:

> ... the Agarenes [Muslims] have denounced us... because of the liberation of Christian captives who fell into our hands; and because of some Muslim women who were found in the convent, after believing in Christ, and becoming nuns. The Agarenes discovered all that and they wanted to destroy the monastery, and take the virgins into their possession.

The previous August, she had written that 'the Muslims came and searched the convents; they found a former slave of the governor (of the sanjak) whom we were keeping under guard with a view to freeing him; and three women of Turkish origin who had become nuns'.

It was this incident, apparently, that led to the temporary break-up of her communities and her imprisonment, whereupon she and her fellow nuns were put under harsh pressure to become Muslim or else be killed. Huge sums of money were needed to secure her release. She sent a male monastic, Seraphim Pangalos, to Venice to plead their case for financial assistance. Apart from Filothei's correspondence with the grandees of Venice, the Catholic bishop of the Ionian islands confirms in a separate letter to the Serene Republic that she was a person born to great privilege who had made huge personal sacrifices for her charitable and religious work. She was known for liberating slaves, for enabling Muslim women to renounce their religion if they chose and for giving a home to 'sinful women who were pregnant, and were hidden in the monastery to avoid punishment by the Turks...' In August 1583, the Venetian Senate agreed to these petitions and sent a generous donation to help Filothei through her difficulties.

There is another part of the saint's literary record which is more surprising from the point of view of conventional hagiography. It consists of a denunciation of the Athenians (and she clearly means her fellow Greek Christians) for a remarkable litany of perceived vices. It is addressed to a senior cleric on the staff of the Patriarchate who has been to Athens, and had apparently helped extract her from some awkward situation for which Greeks rather than Turks were to blame. 'The Athenians have raged against me,' she expostulates, before reeling off an astonishing series of abusive terms, in high literary Greek, to describe her fellow citizens.

They were 'a vulgar race, useless and dishonourable... weak-willed, unholy, shameless, corrupt, mentally disturbed, with mouths ready for slander, whingeing, miserly, ill-spoken, trouble-making, petty-mouthed, small-minded, prattling, arrogant, lawless, treacherous, nosy, keenly interested in the misfortunes of others'.

The style of this invective suggests that it was not composed without help. Filothei's letters to the Venetians are couched in homely language, complete with spelling mistakes. The missive to Istanbul is almost a caricature of the mannered rhetoric which was taught in late-Roman Athens and more recently in Byzantium. So Filothei can hardly have written it alone, and it is possible that the recipient, a church bureaucrat, helped her to compose it.

But the sentiments may have been perfectly sincere. For the Athenian men who were living more or less comfortably under

Ottoman rule, Filothei was rocking the boat, disturbing the social order. It is easy to imagine why relations deteriorated. In any case the story of Filothei tells us a lot about early Ottoman Athens, and the terms on which the Greek majority coexisted with the imperial order. There was clearly no impediment to the Benizelos family's enjoyment of its wealth.* The church and its institutions also enjoyed a degree of freedom, including the right (not always accorded under Muslim rule) to found new Christian communities and places of worship. But this right depended on a certain self-restraint: the pillars on which Islamic authority was built, including slavery and the ban on apostasy, must not be shaken.

In any broad-brush account of the story of Athens, the Ottoman takeover of around 1460 is, understandably enough, treated as the defining event in the middle of the second Christian millennium. But there is another contender, an incident whose effects, at least on the physical patrimony of Athens, were far more dramatic. Indeed, for the cultural historian, the event in question must rank as one of the greatest and most pointless tragedies in the annals of civilization.

On the moonlit evening of 26 September 1687, a mortar bomb lobbed by a Venetian-led army penetrated a small window in the roof of the Parthenon, and ignited the powder-keg below. One of the finest monuments ever conceived by the human spirit was blown sky-high. In place of a standing edifice, a ruin was left. Six of the mighty columns on the south side fell, eight on the north side. Much of the frieze, with its enigmatic scenes of people and animals in procession, crashed to the ground. Despite multiple changes of use, the building and its sculptures had remained remarkably intact between its completion around 438 BCE and that fateful night. More than 300 Turkish soldiers, as well as civilians who were sheltering in

---

* The family's handsome townhouse, incorporating many features of Ottoman architecture, has been restored and is now a landmark in the Plaka district of Athens, billed as the oldest continuously standing house in the city.

the fortress, lost their lives as marble flew in all directions. Many of the Ottoman homes adjacent to the Parthenon were destroyed as a fire raged for two days. Astonishingly, the surviving Turks did not immediately surrender. Only after forty-eight hours, when their hopes of reinforcement faded, did they quit the Rock in return for a promise of safe passage, which was kept.

The great citadel had seen catastrophic incursions, including the barbarian onslaughts of 267 and 396, at least one of which involved arson in the Parthenon's interior. But through those twists of fate, the outer structure of the temple and its sculptures had proved impressively resilient, vindicating the confidence of Pericles that it would stand as an enduring testament to the brilliance of his Athenian generation. During the early Middle Ages, the various sieges involving Byzantine, Latin and Ottoman forces meant that the Acropolis was under attack for a combined total of ten years or so, but in none of these assaults was the Rock ever taken by force. (Defenders could be starved into surrender, but it was almost impossible to physically eject them, as repeatedly became clear.) Until the Venetians threw their bomb, no such destructive power had been visited on the Acropolis since the Persian assault of 480 BCE which preceded the battle of Salamis.

Some facts about the bombardment of 1687 are disputed; others are broadly agreed. The Parthenon was blown up in the course of a siege by a multinational but Venetian-led army, with Francesco Morosini in command. He had endured the humiliation of losing the island of Crete to the Ottomans in 1669 and the city fathers had given him a mandate to restore their honour and his own. The Athenian siege was one theatre, and one episode, in a much wider contest between the Ottoman realm and a shifting constellation of European and Christian powers. After their victory in Crete, the Turks stormed northward and captured cities from the Poles and Russians. But the tide seemed to turn in September 1683 when Poland's King Jan Sobieski defeated the Turkish army which had been threatening Vienna. That was the cue for the formation of a 'Holy League' comprising Austria, Poland and Venice, with the declared aim of expelling the Turks from Europe. Morosini's contribution was a ramshackle but generally effective assortment of mercenary contingents, mainly of German and Scandinavian origin.

As it confronted the Ottoman empire, the Serene Republic of Venice at least dimly resembled ancient Athens in its standoff with the Persians. On the one hand there was an extrovert, commercially successful city-state, with sophisticated internal governance, which controlled a far-flung network of ports and islands; on the other a militarized, authoritarian land-based empire. But there was one difference. Venetian strategy was based on using its wealth to pay other people to fight its wars; it had no equivalent of the ancient Athenian citizen-soldier.

The terrible cultural crime which occurred in 1687 surely owed something to the ramshackle nature of the coalition, and confusion over its purpose. In 1684, Morosini was put in charge of all the republic's forces and embarked on an expedition to Greece. The mercenary component was placed under the command of a German, Count Otto Wilhelm von Königsmarck, with long experience in the Swedish army. Initially they were very successful in driving Turkish forces out of the Peloponnese. By August 1687, the coalition had assembled in Corinth and began considering an assault on Ottoman Athens. The Greek Orthodox population of Athens had very mixed feelings about this prospect, even though they would not, ultimately, have much say in the matter. At the end of August, the Venetian camp received a member of the Capuchin monastery in Athens, a French Catholic fraternity which had recently established itself in the city. This institution was already becoming an important go-between in communication between the city's permanent population and curious Westerners, be they antiquarians, diplomats or soldiers.

The intermediary said the Athenians were prepared to pay the Venetians good money to hold off storming the city. An annual sum of 40,000 reals was duly agreed. Then in early September an

Orthodox prelate, Metropolitan Iakovos, came to hammer out precise details of the payment.

After much haggling, Morosini promised that there would be no attack. He was in any case dubious about the military case for seizing Athens; he anticipated, with foresight, that the Venetians would not be able to hold the place long, and the Turks would soon reassert their authority with a vengeance. Meanwhile, in the latest enactment of a familiar script, the Athenians turned out to be very divided in their reactions to foreigners who were contending for control of the town. A delegation came from Athens with the message that the population fully supported an expedition to dislodge Ottoman power, and would make their own contribution to the military effort. Urged on by the more gung-ho contingents in his own ill-mixed army, Morosini marched onwards. As soon as it became obvious that a siege was in prospect, the Turks in Athens hunkered down in the Acropolis (where many of them lived anyway) and withdrew whatever forces they had in other parts of the town. They reinforced the defences on the western side of the Rock, where the Propylaea was mainly intact despite some damage from an explosion in 1640. The exquisite ancient temple of Athena Nike, which had jutted out from the Propylaea since 420 BCE, was dismantled to provide material for the defences. (Happily it was reconstructed from its constituent parts in the 1830s and the job was completed in 2010.)

On 21 September, a Venetian-led force consisting of 10,000 men and 871 horses arrived in Piraeus harbour. Prominent Athenians made furious calculations as to where their best interests lay. They sent messages to the Venetians to assure them they would welcome a change of master, while taking care to hide their property from looting by either side. A small Venetian force took over the lower part of the town and met no resistance.

Having failed to persuade the Turks to surrender peacefully, German gunners put their artillery in place: fifteen cannons on the Hill of the Muses, nine on the Pnyx and five mortars on the

Areopagus. On 23 September, they began pounding the great citadel. At least 700 projectiles left traces on the west façade of the building, as conservators found in the twentieth century. The cannon fire seemed to be doing real damage, but the mortar bombs made very little impact. The Italian officer in charge of the mortars was accused of gross incompetence; but at some point, a mortar bomb apparently rolled through a window and caused unspeakable catastrophe.

In eye-witness accounts of the siege, and among historians interpreting those accounts, there is much disagreement over whether the blowing up of the Parthenon was a deliberate act or an accidental one. In fact, that distinction may be meaningless. With the technology of 1687, it was not possible to rain mortar bombs on a marble fortress with the certainty of penetrating it through a small vent; nor could one cover the place with fire with any confidence that a bomb would *not* get through. In his first despatch to his native Venice, Morosini himself coyly describes the process in which cannon and mortar were directed at the Acropolis. He explains that the effects of the mortars were limited at first, until the 'fortunate shot' which happened to ignite a 'good quantity of powder' and start a fire which crackled for two full days. He omits any mention of the fact that one of the world's most glorious monuments has been reduced to a smouldering, putrid wreck. A week later, he writes with greater frankness: he describes delegating an officer to take charge of the Parthenon and remove more than 300 corpses of both sexes, who had perished as a result of the 'prodigious bomb' which had caused 'the desolation of the magnificent temple of Minerva (Athena) which had been converted into a mosque'. Morosini seems torn between taking satisfaction over his military achievement, expressing embarrassment over the human and cultural disaster which has occurred, and fretting about the pointlessness, in strategic terms, of the feat he has just pulled off.

A different perspective is offered by a German officer, a certain Lieutenant Sobiewolsky, who was serving under Morosini. Along with other sources, he says the Venetians initially tried burrowing underground to mine the Acropolis, but realized this was impossible. They directed intense fire at the Parthenon after receiving a vital piece of intelligence. In a vivid and plausible account, Sobiewolsky writes:

> There came a deserter from the castle with the news that the commander of the fortress had all the stores of powder and other precious things brought to the temple... of Minerva, and that all the people of rank were there because they believed the Christians would not do any harm to the temple. Upon this report, several mortars were directed against the temple, but none of the bombs was able to do damage, particularly because the upper roof of the temple was somewhat sloping and covered with marble and thus well protected. A lieutenant from Lüneberg, however, offered to propel mortar bombs into the temple... and one of the bombs fell through (the roof of) the temple and right into the Turkish powder-store, whereupon the middle of the temple blew up and everything inside was covered with stone, to the great consternation of the Turks.

Independent evidence confirms that there was a contingent from Lüneberg, a small town in Saxony, among the gunners. But perhaps there was, in the end, some contrition on the part of the leaders of the expedition over the loss to the world's heritage. We get a hint of that from one of the most revealing accounts of the siege, and the events that preceded it, penned by an observant Swedish woman. Her name was Anna Akerhjelm; she was lady-in-waiting to Countess of Königsmarck, whose husband was deputy commander of the expedition. Arriving in Piraeus harbour on 6 September, she had an instant sense of the ambivalent feelings that were swirling among the Athenians as the prospect loomed of a change of masters. As their boat entered the harbour, Anna and her dozen companions ran into a French resident of Athens, Jean Giraud, who was serving as British consul and was bobbing about on a British-flagged vessel. Giraud invited the visitors onto his boat and gave them a quick, cautious account of the situation. The Turks were taking refuge in the Acropolis, but the Athenians were cautious about siding with the Venetians because they were resentful of the 'tribute' Venice was asking them to pay. At a certain point, Giraud urges his new friends to switch to speaking in German because the ship's crew might be eavesdropping. Anna and her party then sailed back to Corinth, where Morosini and Königsmarck were encamped, and were no doubt intrigued by this valuable intelligence.

On 21 September, with open conflict looming, she reports sailing back into Piraeus. Her party must have made a foray into the town of Athens, now firmly under the invaders' control. She finds that Protestant members of the expeditionary force have already set their sights on one of the town's mosques as a Lutheran house of prayer. Her journal breaks off as the armed clash comes to a head, but on 18 October, she writes to her brother about the wrecking of the Parthenon, insisting that it was perpetrated with a heavy heart. 'How repugnant it was for His Excellency (Königsmarck) to destroy the beautiful temple which has existed for 3,000 years, and which is called the temple of Minerva! (Such feelings are) in vain… the bombs had their effect, and the temple can never be replaced in this world.'

The same letter gives some tantalizing details of the dramatic events that have just unfolded. After surrendering on 28 September, the Turkish civilians were evacuated from the town but they had to leave behind some finely embroidered garments which they could not carry as far as the ships waiting to take them away. She confirms that the local Greeks, while willing to give the Venetians a cautious welcome, 'salted away all their possessions' for fear of greedy soldiers. Exploring the maze of streets which now form the Plaka, she and her party enjoyed the hospitality of a Catholic priest in the Capuchin monastery, incorporating the Lysicrates monument that people associated, falsely, with the orator Demosthenes.

The visitors also enjoyed the hospitality of some local Greeks, who plied them with orange and lemon juice, fresh almonds and marmalade. In general Anna finds Athens 'superior to other Greek towns with very attractive houses belonging to both Greeks and Turks…' Athens in 1687 seems to have found room for genteel conversation over sweetmeats as well as artillery barrages and horrific acts of destruction.

In some ways, the hospitable Athenians were offering the newcomers more kindness than they deserved. The disasters visited on the city did not end with the blowing up of the Parthenon. Over the winter of 1687, the occupation of Athens became unsustainable, exactly as Morosini had foreseen, as the German soldiers complained that they were being cheated of their promised financial rewards. The occupiers failed to keep their promise to protect the people of Athens and its environs from crime; indeed some of the occupying soldiers turned to robbery, confirming the Athenians' worst fears. In a recurrence of an ancient pattern which Thucydides would have recognized, people in the villages of Attica had to flee for safety into the walled town because random violence (mainly from Muslim bandits, it seems) made life impossible. This led to an outbreak of disease in Athens.

On the last day of 1687, Morosini convened a council of war at which various desperate options were considered. Given that the occupation could not continue, he suggested evacuating the entire town and levelling it to the ground, along with all the monuments on the Acropolis. The local Athenians would be transported away for their own safety and the city's natural defences would not be subject to easy recapture by the Turks. Not since Salamis had the city been abandoned by its inhabitants; and that first evacuation was undertaken by the city's own leaders, as part of an elaborate stratagem to outwit an invader. This time it was a foreign occupier who was proposing to take the townspeople away. The local Athenian leaders offered to fund the defence of the city themselves, but this was rejected by Morosini.

Meanwhile the Venetian Senate authorized Morosini to remove whatever he could of the Parthenon sculptures. He focused his attention on the west pediment, depicting the contest between Athena and Poseidon; this was still in place but badly damaged, with some figures knocked out of balance and ready to fall. But the attempted extraction did not go well. As he reported to his Venetian masters in March: 'An effort was made to remove the large pediment, but it collapsed from a tremendous height and it is a wonder that no accident happened to a labourer.' Morosini abandoned the idea of a systematic dismantling of the sculptures, but some of his men took what they could find. His secretary San Gallo took away a female head, which is now in the Louvre. Another Venetian took part of the frieze (a horse and two riders) and that found its way to the Art History Museum in Vienna. A Danish officer pocketed two heads from fallen metopes, and they can now be seen in Copenhagen. Around the same time, a much sadder removal took place: the great majority of the population accepted an invitation to board Venetian vessels and seek safety and shelter elsewhere. They were brought to Salamis, to the islands around the Peloponnese or much further west to the Ionian isles. Just like the Athenians who cowered on Salamis in flight from the Persians more than 2,000 years earlier, they had no idea when, or to what sort of town, they would return.

The exodus of 1688 was not exactly a forced population transfer, but it was comparable, perhaps, to the flight westwards of some Soviet civilians as the Red Army advanced in 1945. The people involved saw that their home patch was about to change masters at least temporarily, and they knew they were in danger of being branded as traitors regardless of what they had actually done.

These uprooted Athenians did not find any calmness in exile. They were forced to make desperate calculations as fighting sputtered on between Ottomans and Venetians in other parts of Greece. The Ottomans released, and unleashed, a warlord from southern Greece, Limberakis Yerakaris, who had taken their side in the battle with

Venice over Crete but was later imprisoned in Istanbul for piracy. This rough character managed to land some heavy blows on the Venetians in various Greek places, but his biggest success was in persuading the Athenians to return to their home town under the sultan's authority. To secure a safe return, the exiled people of Athens wrote flowery letters to the Orthodox Patriarch, and to the sultan himself. The missive sent on the Athenians' behalf to the Patriarch was couched in careful classical Greek, combined with a deferential tone. From the Patriarch's point of view, the wandering folk of Athens were technically apostates who had deserted the Orthodox faith by coming under the wing of the Venetian Catholics. But he graciously forgave his errant children, and a new chapter in the era known as *Tourkokratia*, Turkish rule, began in Athens.

A recurring feature of Athenian history is that in some uncanny way, precious objects, sculptures and inscriptions have been recorded, drawn and studied with particular attention just before they disappeared from view. The fact that they were about to be lost was not always obvious, but perhaps in some cases the recorders had some intuition of what lay ahead. As a result, later generations at least have a clear idea of what was lost. The catastrophe of 1687 is no exception to that rule.

During the decades prior to the explosion, both the Acropolis monuments and Athens in general received an unprecedented level of attention from visitors bent on investigating and reporting to the world whatever remained from antiquity. In very different ways these visitors also made it their business to describe the contemporary condition of Athens, and somehow integrate what they saw with a glorious historical and mythological past, as well as with their own personal beliefs.

Some of these visitors openly represented foreign powers with an interest in boosting their influence in the region; others were making more private and precarious journeys, although that did not mean they were completely unconnected with officialdom or high politics. In worldly terms, the most important visit was that of the French ambassador to the Ottoman empire, Charles-François Olier, the Marquis de Nointel, who came in 1674.

His large entourage made meticulous drawings of the Parthenon sculptures, which have been an invaluable resource to historians. These images are often ascribed to one particular member of the mission, called Jacques Carrey, but that is far from sure. In truth we cannot tell which artist or artists wielded their crayons with such skill. The resulting work can be seen in a single album in the Bibliothèque Nationale in Paris.

With equal uncertainty, Carrey is credited with a magnificent painting of Athens and its surroundings, with the diplomatic visitors in the foreground and the islands of the Saronic Gulf glinting in the far distance. Athens itself is shown as an extensive and compactly walled town at the foot of the largely intact Acropolis where a minaret peeps up. More than 5 metres long, the memorial of that stately mission now hangs in the Museum of the City of Athens. Nointel had been sent to Istanbul in 1670 with a mandate from King Louis XIV to secure trade privileges for France and reduce the influence in the eastern Mediterranean of older powers like Venice. The ambassador seems to have brought greater zeal to the investigation of the ancient past and Middle Eastern culture than to his diplomatic duties.

The following year, Athens received an Anglo-French cluster of somewhat less grand but still significant visitors. The best known are a French Protestant doctor, Jacob Spon, and his English acquaintance George Wheler. They had met while travelling in Italy, and decided to venture eastwards together. For the first part of their trip, they were accompanied by two more Englishmen: Francis Vernon, who had been posted to Paris as a diplomat but found a stronger calling in architectural history, and his friend Sir Giles Eastcourt. The four journeyed down the Adriatic in easy stages, reaching Corfu in July 1675 and Zakynthos in August. At this point they split up, and the enterprise became more hazardous. Spon and Wheler made their way to Constantinople, where Spon was able to make useful connections with the powerful French embassy, and eventually looped back to Athens in early 1676.

Vernon and Eastcourt went straight to Athens, arriving in late August and embarking on a tour of the Peloponnese which Eastcourt did not survive. On 24 September 1675, while staying in the town of Aigion in the Gulf of Corinth, he fell ill and died. Grief over his companion did not distract Vernon from his self-appointed task, which was to spend six weeks in Athens continuing his meticulous, if rather cold and laconic, reporting on the ancient monuments. He then sailed eastwards again, braving the hazards of an Aegean winter which included an attack by pirates who took many of his papers, though luckily not his journal.

Reaching Smyrna by the end of the year and Constantinople in April – to use the place-names Vernon would have employed – he journeyed on relentlessly, till he reached the Persian city of Isfahan where he was murdered, apparently in a row over a pen-knife. The human emotions that swirled around his dangerous expedition are lost to posterity, but his letters and journal give a conscientious account of what he saw in Athens. He made a decent attempt to measure the Parthenon, seeing the building in its ancient glory and largely ignoring the Christian and Muslim modifications. He diligently describes the Hephaisteion, the Tower of the Winds and the monument of Lysicrates, which he associated with Hercules: a better guess than the fanciful connection with the orator Demosthenes. His effort to document ancient Athens was begun with his friend Eastcourt, and another Englishman, Bernard Randolph, during the few days they all spent together. They committed an act of petty vandalism by carving their names on the Hephaisteion, but it is mainly thanks to Vernon that we have a fairly precise idea of the dimensions of the cella or inner chamber of the Parthenon where the gold-and-ivory statue once stood.

Presumably in a state of deep shock over the death of his companion, but unshaken in his commitment to enquiry, Vernon resumed work only a few weeks later. He came to Athens neither as a predator nor as a colonialist, but in search of useful knowledge. He was in tune with the enquiring, scientifically curious spirit of the age. As Joan Connelly argues, we owe Vernon one more debt: while puzzling over the humans and animals processing in the Parthenon frieze, he had the intuition that this was not just a well-rehearsed religious ceremony, but a celebration of victory, whether contemporary or mythological or both.

We have a much more rounded impression of the two other travellers, Spon and Wheler, who got home safely and published far more expansively on the results of their journeys. They were spurred on by competition with a French rival, writing under the name of Guillet, who had published a description of Athens without actually visiting the place. Spon was the more erudite classicist, while Wheler had a keen eye for the natural world and agriculture, noticing the beekeeping which has always been practised on Mount Hymettus. Wheler was interested in the modern Greek language, to which he offered a helpful introduction.

Parts of Spon's antiquarian observations are simply copied, in English translation, by Wheler. In many ways, their reports on Athens are best treated as a single text, rendered in different languages and slightly different versions. As Protestants, both the Frenchman and the Englishman took a keen but critical interest in the Orthodox Church as it flourished in Athens. This was a time when Protestant–Catholic contests were still active in western Europe, and the Orthodox were seen as a prize to fight over.

In the end that sectarian contest would cast a shadow over Spon's life. In 1685, the Catholic realm of France revoked its toleration of Protestantism and Spon was forced to move to Switzerland, where he died in poverty at the age of thirty-eight. Wheler, knighted and ordained in the Church of England, was the only member of his Greek travel party who lived to a happy old age.

More than previous travellers, Spon and Wheler saw ancient Athens and the town's present-day reality as part of a single narrative, unfolding in a distinctive, beautiful and benign landscape. That distinguishes their account from western European writings about Athens in the sixteenth century, in which the town was described as a ruin, a place where settlement had literally ceased to exist. In this spirit, Spon and Wheler whisk readers through the foundation tale of Athens, vividly recounting ancient stories like the suicidal leap of Aegeus, father of Theseus, who falsely believed his son to be dead. Wheler brings some nice turns of phrase to his succinct description of the rise and decline of classical Athens. The Athenians 'held the sovereignty of Greece for threescore and ten years; but kept it no longer, by reason of the Lacedemonians (Spartans) and Thebans emulating their greatness and stirring up factions and divisions against them'. They accurately describe the treatment of Athens under Alexander, his successors and then under the Romans, noting the 'particular affection' harboured by Emperor Hadrian, who 'with great munificence harboured the city to its former beauty' with the construction of a library, a stadium and a 'building of vast magnificence', which was the Temple of Olympian Zeus.

No less accurately, they record the barbarian raids of 267 and 396, as well as the role of the first emperor Constantine as the 'great friend or benefactor' of Athens, despite its refusal to adopt the new Christian religion. After the reign of Justinian, it is conceded, 'there is a deep silence… either for want of historians who, in those times, were few and obscure – or that it pleased Divine Providence to give them such a long period of privacy and peace'. They are confused about the Byzantine period but quite accurate on the contest between Florentines and Venetians which preceded the Ottoman takeover. Summing up the present situation, Wheler says the Athenians

> … have been ever since under the Turkish tyranny; and they are
> likely so to continue until God shall restore them to liberty; which
> is far beyond the reach of human policy to conceive how, or by
> what means it should be; so long as Christendom is so disunited

in itself and that Divine Providence, for our sins, permitteth the Turkish arms and superstition so mightily to prevail.

But that did not mean, he hastens to add, that life among today's Greek Orthodox Christians in Athens lacked interest or vigour. After listing and briefly describing the eight residential districts, he notes:

> *To these the castle being added*, Athens is not so despicable a place that it should deserve to be considered only a small village, according to the reports of some travellers; who perhaps have seen it only from the sea, through the wrong end of their perspective-glass.

It is true that from anywhere on the coast, the Acropolis would have soared into view, obscuring the settlement branching out on its far side. Wheler firmly corrects that misapprehension.

Yet another witness to Athens and the Acropolis on the eve of the Parthenon's destruction is Evliya Çelebi, who is often described as the greatest travel writer of the Ottoman empire. He journeyed continuously for four decades, slaking an endlessly curious mind, with interests that ranged from architecture to sociology to the supernatural. His account of Athens, based on a visit around 1668, blends Islamic references with classical and Christian ones with an exuberance that some modern readers find almost comical, although there are plenty of serious reasons to study his text as a case of Greco-Islamic synthesis. For example, he sees the Temple of Olympian Zeus as the dwelling place of Suleyman (the Islamic rendering of Solomon) and his queen, whom he names as Belkis. Suleyman is also given credit for the foundation of Athens. In keeping with the Islamic tradition (or one strand of it, at least) he pays homage to the philosophers of Athens, and imagines them in conversation with their counterparts from the golden Abbasid era of Baghdad.

Like some Christian chroniclers of Athens, he has vulnerable moments when words almost fail him, but if anything, he is more confident that his own faith ultimately transcends all other traditions and can therefore confront the evidence of past civilizations without fear. As he marvels at the sculptures on the Acropolis, he exclaims:

> The human mind cannot indeed contemplate these images – they are white magic, beyond human capacity. [Even] one with the intellect of Aristotle would be dumbfounded at the sight of these creatures and proclaim them to be a miracle, because to a discerning creature they seem to be alive.

As is demonstrated so convincingly by the American classicist Joan Connelly, the subject of the Parthenon frieze really is, in an important sense, anybody's guess. No written text from ancient times offers any definite idea as to what the sculptors, or their ultimate patron Pericles, had in mind. As he contemplates these amazing artefacts, Evliya Çelebi puts scholarship and tradition aside and scours the brightest and darkest corners of his imagination. He finds indirect affirmations of his own religion while also feeling freed, for a moment, from that faith's anxiety about figurative art.

> In sum, whatever living creatures the Lord Creator has created, from Adam to the Resurrection, are depicted in these marble statues... Fearful and ugly demons, jinns, Satan the Whisperer, the Sneak, the Farter; fairies, angels, dragons, demons, earth-beasts; the angels that bear up the throne of God and the ox that bears up the earth; sea-beasts, elephants, rhinoceri, giraffes, horned vipers, snakes, centipedes, scorpions, crocodiles, sea-sprites; thousands of mice, cats, lions, leopards, tigers, cheetahs, lynxes; ghouls, cherubs, Gabriel, Israfil, Azrael, Michael; the Throne, the Bridge, the Scales; and all the creatures that will arise in the plain of the resurrection and be assigned their place – those in the fires of hell depicted grieving and mourning and

tormented by serpents and demons; and those in the gardens of paradise depicted in marble enjoying the pleasures of the maidens and the young men.

Like the Byzantine prelate Michael Choniates, the Muslim and the Protestant travellers of the seventeenth century are wrestling with a common dilemma as they contemplate the glories of classical Athens. They were confronted with the fact that a uniquely brilliant civilization, attested by monuments and the written word, had flourished in this place long before the divine revelation of the One God by whose lights they now lived.

It is Evliya Çelebi who lays into the problem with the greatest gusto, being utterly confident in his Islamic sensibility, and in Islam's interpretation of events prior to its own emergence. Untroubled by any impulse to investigate the past empirically, he sweeps Islamic, Abrahamic and classical Greek traditions into a single exuberant synthesis. There is a revealing contrast between the reactions of Wheler and Evliya to the religious aura of the Parthenon's interior, where both intuit the high-church Christian rituals whose vestiges were still evident in the decoration and furnishings. In one of his caustically Protestant moments, Wheler describes the interior of the Parthenon as a place of darkness, where low lighting served to facilitate the practice of deceptive rituals. Rather than anything Islamic, he seems to sense the Catholic and Orthodox Christian sacraments which had been celebrated in the building for ten of the previous twelve centuries.

> The heathens loved obscurity in their religious rites and customs... because by that means [they hid] the pomps they exposed to the people... and the defects of them, with all their juggling and cheating.

Evliya Çelebi perceives almost the opposite. He too must have picked up the local Christian traditions which described the Parthenon as a place of perpetual, mysterious light, and he tries to offer a physical explanation. In one of his wild historical concoctions, he ascribes the furnishings to 'Plato the Divine', who on one wall of the interior had placed 'paper-thin slabs of marble, otherwise known as fire-stones...': 'As the sun rose, the stones turned red-hot from the heat of the sun, igniting naphtha-soaked wicks that lit the carbuncle lamps and illuminated the interior... The infidels revered this mechanism as a talisman, calling it a lamp of Divine Light.'

Both perceive the temple as a place where human ingenuity has invoked the visible presence of God's mystery, or at least its appearance. The Protestant sees darkness while the Muslim, as a confident if rather creative exponent of his own creed, sees light.

# 13

# Stones of Contention
## 1697–1820

*Turkish–Greek co-operation over honey and history – Stuart and Revett, pioneers of British antiquarianism – Hadji Ali Haseki's cruel domination of Athens – French efforts to control Athenian antiquities, dislodged by Britain – Ambassador Elgin uses Anglo-Ottoman amity, and hostility to France, to secure the Parthenon sculptures*

At the heart of the Ottoman relationship with Athens was honey, above all monastic honey. Beekeeping was among the most important economic activities in Attica, and Orthodox monasteries were the most active producers.

As the eighteenth century began, the most venerable and prestigious of the honey-making monks were to be found at Kaisariani on Mount Hymettus, where an abundance of thyme and other scented herbs made for delicious produce. Although it now belongs to the Greek culture ministry rather than the church, the cool and well-preserved monastery is still considered one of the finest Byzantine sites in the Athens area, and one of its oldest (at least occasionally) functioning places of worship. People were praying there, and bees buzzing, at least from the twelfth-century era of Archbishop Michael Choniates.

Over the following centuries, two more honey-making religious fraternities were established in the region. One was founded amid the marble rocks of Mount Pentelikon, and flourishes as a monastery to this day; another was close to the heart of Athens, on Mount Lycabettus. It is a little jewel called the Petraki monastery and now serves as a kind of spiritual headquarters for the Greek ecclesial hierarchy. As a reward for their sweet produce, all three of these establishments enjoyed a privileged status, including tax breaks, under the Ottoman system. For the sultan and his entourage, delivering honey to the high and mighty in Istanbul was one of the principal functions of Athens, one of the main reasons for its continued existence. As the town gradually recovered from the Venetian–Ottoman war, these arrangements mattered.

The abbots of Kaisariani were not just skilled traders and diplomats. In at least two cases, we know that they were highly trained men of letters and educators. Theophanes Kavallares, who became abbot in 1728, was a member of a powerful Athenian family; his forebears had founded a well-known church near the Acropolis, dedicated to Saint Dimitrios, around 1600. For at least a decade before his monastic appointment, he had been one of the most respected pedagogues among the Athenian Greeks. His teaching work was sponsored by the Greeks of Venice.

Another learned Athenian cleric with western links was Gregorios Soteres, who studied classics in Italy before returning to his home town in 1717 and setting up a school adjacent to the old site of Hadrian's library, whose shell now contained a church dedicated to the Virgin Mary. The school attracted hundreds of pupils, and Kavallares joined the staff. Unfortunately, the endowment was not big enough to sustain such an ambitious project for long, and the school had to merge with another establishment around 1750.

Both those learned abbots made an important, if indirect, contribution to a rather gripping account of Athens past and present. Although very little known, it surely rates as one of the most revealing documents to emerge from Ottoman Greece. While it has some elements of an exotic traveller's tale, and of a flight of pious imagination, the text is underpinned by an intelligent and well-informed interest in real historical events. This account was written in Ottoman Turkish by a mufti of Athens, Mahmud Efendi, who acknowledges the help he received from the two 'very profound' abbots of Kaisariani, named above, as well as from another learned Greek cleric, George Kontares.

Mahmud had family roots in Athens, Thebes and Chalkis, and Greek may well have been his native language. He studied with the best Islamic teachers in Istanbul, and being sent back to his home region as mufti may have been a professional disappointment for him. But he certainly made the best of his stay in Athens, even as he lamented over the half-ruined Parthenon. Mahmud's book is entitled *Tarih-i Medinetu'l-Hukema* (*History of the City of the Sages*). The only known copy is in the Topkapi Palace Library in Istanbul, and it is known to Anglophones only through a partial translation made by Gülçin Tunali, a Turkish scholar, as part of her doctoral thesis.

As with the much more famous account of Evliya Çelebi, Mahmud seeks to blend Greek history and mythology with Islamic and Abrahamic traditions, as well as the landscape and lore of Athens as he experienced them. Where Evliya Çelebi had identified Solomon as founder of the city, Mahmud ingeniously fuses the person of Solomon with Solon, the early law-giver of Athens who was a historic figure.

Of the two Ottoman chroniclers, Mahmud engages far more deeply with classical Greek history and tradition. He gives a detailed and coherent account of the Athenian story from Theseus to the golden age and then to the Hellenistic and Macedonian periods. He is not far in spirit from the Frenchman Jacob Spon, who was such a well-drilled classicist, or indeed from George Wheler, that doctor's observant English companion. In all cases, the writers perceived that the events of classical times and the reality of contemporary Athens were part of a long, undulating narrative. There is little attempt to distinguish myth from proven and concrete historical events, like the battles of Marathon or Salamis; but nor is there an attempt to exclude any era from the Athenian story. With the pride of a man who grew up not far away, the mufti makes a gallant effort to describe the political system of ancient Athens, using Ottoman terms for things like poll tax, public order, justice and tyranny. Mahmud devotes many pages to the Parthenon, showing a clear understanding of the building's technical ingenuity and of the challenge of hauling so much white rock up to the citadel. The Ottoman writer appreciates that Pericles was neither a dictator nor a sultan nor a Byzantine emperor; he knows the statesman had to use rhetorical power to persuade his fellow Athenians to allocate the funds for such an ambitious effort. But Mahmud presents the proceedings in Ottoman terms, as though the project under discussion was an Islamic *hayrat*, or endowment.

Even more ingeniously, Mahmud compares the beauty of the Parthenon to Solomon's Temple in Jerusalem. The Ottoman writer puts into the mouth of Pericles the argument that, although Solomon's greatest achievement could never be surpassed, people in Greece needed a spiritual focal point which was nearer and more convenient.

> In noble Jerusalem the sainted Solomon... has built a rare valuable temple and all, high and low, are desirous of going to worship in it. However the Greek population of Rumeli [present-day central Greece]... has formidable difficulties in reaching [Jerusalem] to worship in the Temple. We must build [another] outstanding and magnificent temple...

In a few deft lines, Mahmud manages to put the Parthenon on the list of supremely sacred buildings and pilgrimage sites, along with the Islamic monuments of Jerusalem (standing where the temple once stood) and Hagia Sophia, the great Christian church which the Ottomans had made into a mosque. Although the Parthenon's role as a place of worship was diminished by Mahmud's time, he had apparently sensed something awesome about the marble structure itself, despite its dilapidation. The importance of Mahmud's work has been highlighted by Elizabeth Key Fowden, a historian who has studied Islam's relationship with the classical and Christian inheritance. As she puts it, his writings on the Parthenon are an 'extraordinary example of Muslim creative engagement with the Hellenic past'. With much help from Greek friends, this Ottoman Turkish writer had constructed not only a new version of Athenian history but a new architecture and ecology of monotheism and its sacred spaces.

The Turkish–Greek collaboration underpinning Mahmud's work says something about the Ottoman world in the early eighteenth century. The Balkan region enjoyed a sluggish peace, and Greeks played a role in its administration, for example as de facto masters of present-day Romania. This favoured a calm, regimented atmosphere in Athens in which the conservative structures of Greek Christian society meshed neatly with those of the Ottoman overlords.

Ioannes Benizelos, an Athenian man of letters who lived in the eighteenth century, writes that the town's everyday business was handled efficiently as long as prominent families like his own held sway. The Greek town fathers would meet every Monday at the palace of the metropolitan bishop to consider any matters that could be dealt with by the Christian community alone; on Fridays they would call on the most senior Ottoman officials, the voivode (town governor) and cadi (Islamic judge). If they were frustrated by any decisions made by their local Turkish masters, the Greeks of Athens could if necessary make an appeal to higher authority in Istanbul. A powerful position in the Eastern Church – that of Patriarch of Jerusalem, whose incumbents resided mostly in Istanbul – went twice in a row to Athenian candidates. That gave the town fathers of Athens a friend who had the ear of the sultan's entourage.

As the years went on, the atmosphere darkened inside and outside the Ottoman realm. There was increasing competition between the powers of western Europe over the cultural prizes and resources which lay within the sultan's grip. High on the list of those cultural assets were the antiquities of ancient Greece and

Athens in particular. At first, the contest was simply over access to, and detailed knowledge of, those classical treasures. Over time, it would turn into a battle for physical possession of those objects and ultimately into a fight for the land where they had been created. In 1748, two opportunistic and artistically talented Britons, well-established as expatriates in Italy, made a proposal to fellow members of a charmed circle to which they had recently gained access.

One, James Stuart, had grown up poor in London after the death of his father, a Scottish sailor. The other, Nicholas Revett, was the second son in a family of Suffolk gentry. For both men, settling in Rome and developing their skills as artists and art historians had been a liberating experience. Stuart made a living by acting as guide to English visitors. Using their foothold in a coterie of London-based aesthetes, the Society of Dilettanti, the pair floated the idea that it was now time for them to extend their quest to Greece. The terms of their proposal 'for publishing an accurate description of the antiquities of Athens' are quite revealing.

> ... Athens, the Mother of elegance and politeness, whose magnificence scarce yielded to that of Rome, and who for the beauties of a correct style must be allowed to surpass her, has been almost entirely neglected... Unless exact copies of them be speedily made, all her beauteous Fabricks, her Temples, her Palaces, now in ruins, will drop into Oblivion; and Posterity will have to reproach us, that we have not left them a tolerable Idea of what was so excellent, and so much deserved our attention; but we have Suffered the perfection of an Art to perish, when it was perhaps in our power to have retrieved it.

Just as the grandees of ancient Rome had sought a slice of Athenian refinement to decorate the public and private spaces of Italy, an emerging British elite was looking for a similar dose of prestige. Part of the subliminal message delivered by the two artistic entrepreneurs was that masters of a new world empire should benefit from the sublime artistic achievements of an older empire, that of Athens. For the time being, the expected benefit would consist not of physical objects but of knowledge – about the architecture and sculpture of Athens in its golden age, which could duly be copied in much colder climes. Neither the two aesthetes nor their sponsors took any interest in any more recent phase of Greek history, or in the political future of Greece. If the duo were at all interested in present-day realities, it was mainly because such knowledge was necessary for them to survive and work as antiquarians. With that caveat, Stuart did leave some intelligent, revealing observations about Athens as he found it when he and Revett settled there in 1751.

> The air of Attica is extremely healthy. The articles of commerce [it] produces are chiefly corn, oil, honey, wax, resin, some silk, cheese and a sort of acorns called *velanede* by the Italians and French… The principal manufactures are soap and leather. Of these commodities, the honey, soap, cheese and leather, and part of the oil are sent to Constantinople; the others are chiefly bought by the French, of which nation they reckon that seven or eight ships are freighted here every year…
>
> The inhabitants of Athens are between nine and ten thousands, about four-fifths… are Christians. The city is an archiepiscopal see and the archbishop maintains a considerable authority among the Christians, which he usually strengthens by keeping on good terms with the Turks in office. He holds a kind of tribunal, at which the Christians frequently agree to decide their differences, without the intervention of the Turkish magistrate.

Stuart and Revett were well-connected and savvy enough to gain the necessary access to the classical monuments and to establish good relations with local Ottoman officialdom. But during their stay, the Ottoman peace foundered, and on at least a couple of occasions they had to make rapid departures from the town. In

1752, a particularly greedy Chief Eunuch (the grandee in Istanbul who controlled the administration of Athens) was executed by the sultan. The eunuch's Athenian point-man Hassan Aga had to flee, and an official was sent from Istanbul to enquire into any abuses which had occurred in the town. This mission merely inflamed the situation and the two antiquarians were advised by British diplomats to leave. A year later, a new voivode of Athens, Sari Mouselimi, was proving unbearably harsh, and when some prominent figures in the town called on him to protest, he had several killed on the spot.

As a result, there was fresh rioting, with many deaths on both sides. The voivode's residence was set on fire; he reacted with phlegm by cutting his way through the crowd, sabre in hand, and taking refuge with the garrison on the Acropolis. All this provided an excuse for the pasha of Negroponte (modern Chalkis) to impose a collective fine on Athens and briefly imprison the town's metropolitan bishop. However, the bishop was powerful enough to exercise some moderating influence and secure an order from the sultan which barred the pesky pasha from Athens.

At some point Stuart had an extraordinary adventure which was only made public in 1804, long after his death, via an Irish Anglican bishop, Thomas Percy. As the cleric tells the story, about three years into Stuart's Greek sojourn, the Grand Vizier in Istanbul was toppled. This obliged his representative in Athens to rush home and sweet-talk the new order. Stuart decided he should accompany the 'bashaw' (an Anglicization of pasha) back to Istanbul and duly joined the official convoy. In the words of the Irish prelate, who claimed to have heard every detail from Stuart, 'they had not proceeded far before he plainly saw that the great Bashaw had conceived a dislike to him… and exerted all his cunning to get rid of his fellow-traveller'.

Stuart managed to drop out of the convoy and take refuge in a nearby town, only to find out by eavesdropping that the keepers of the local inn had similarly murderous intentions. This prompted yet another crafty escape, until he fell in with two mounted men from

Epirus who 'being a sort of Christians' were willing to protect him and escort him to the nearest port. Even if the story has gained a little colour in the telling, it feels like an accurate rendering of life in the remoter Ottoman provinces. In their more regular work as recorders of art, the two Britons made an impressive duo. Revett had trained as an architect and imparted some of his knowledge to Stuart, who in addition to having drawing skills was an accomplished painter and turned out copious depictions of Greek scenes, which still make a fascinating record. In the presentation of the promised fruits of these labours, Stuart proved both wildly fickle and, ultimately, brilliant.

He and Revett returned to England in 1755, and the first volume of their work, *The Antiquities of Athens*, did not appear until 1762, at which point Revett dropped out and threw himself into other Greek expeditions. A second volume appeared in 1789, a year after Stuart's death, and his heirs produced a third one in 1794 and a fourth in 1816. In the final decade of his life, Stuart led a dissolute existence in London, drinking heavily, marrying a woman of twenty when he was sixty-seven and delivering only the most erratic services to the aristocratic clients who were clamouring for his architectural eye. But the net result of these truncated labours remains astonishing. With hundreds of gouache paintings as well as exquisitely presented, scrupulously accurate engravings and etchings, Stuart fully earned his nickname of 'Athenian', adding to archaeological knowledge and transforming British taste. There are a dozen famous buildings and interiors in England which bear his hand, including the neoclassical Spencer House in London, off Saint James's Street.

At the Shugborough estate in Staffordshire, he created a near-perfect replica of the Tower of the Winds, the Athenian building which in Ottoman times was used as an Islamic *tekke* or house of prayer where the swirling, mind-altering dances of the dervishes took place. In eighteenth-century England, no less than in Rome of the first or second century CE, it was firmly established that perfection in art and architecture consisted of imitating, as closely as possible, the pillars, pediments and architraves of Athens at the height of her achievement. On returning to London, Stuart was both distracted and spurred on by a Gallic rival, Julien-David Le Roy.

The Frenchman spent only three months in Athens, in 1755, and within three years delivered the results of his investigation, a book entitled *Les Ruines des plus Beaux Monuments de la Grèce*. Stuart responded with scathing criticism, arguing that many of Le Roy's depictions, for example of the sculptures on the Tower of the Winds, were inaccurate. 'The figure of Boreas* bears little resemblance to the original; the position of the head, the leg and the arms are very different from it.' Le Roy retorted with no less spleen, saying his English rivals were too obsessed with precise empirical observations, while his concern was to capture the spirit of great monuments and show how they fitted into a broader cultural and historical landscape. The Frenchman's work served to fan philhellenic sentiment in his home country, just as Stuart and Revett stirred up a Greek craze in Britain.

Around 1760, there was a change in the way Athens was ruled. The town was no longer under the sway of the black eunuch, and became a *malikane* or tax-farm. Under this system, the right to gather taxes in a particular area was auctioned out and awarded to the highest bidder. In theory a tax-farming contract was for life, though in practice it could change hands fairly often, and it could be shared between several people. The governor, or voivode, of Athens (a post still subject to annual renewal) might or might not be the same person as the holder of the *malikane*. This change weakened the link between Athens and the sultan and made it harder for prominent Athenians to take their grievances to the highest level in Istanbul. The new system might have been more tolerable but for the emergence of a cruel master of the town who dominated its affairs for the last quarter of the eighteenth

---

* The north wind.

century. He was known as Hadji Ali Haseki: the last part of his name describes the job he did in his early life, as a bodyguard to important people.

Among those he served were the sultan and his sister, Esma Sultan. He developed a close, probably physical bond with this lady. She bought, or helped Hadji Ali Haseki to buy, the *malikane* rights over Athens. By the mid-1770s he had established himself as the strongman of the town. In a recurring pattern, he sought to build tactical alliances with the town's richest and most powerful residents while mistreating and enraging people (Muslims as well as Christians) a little lower down the social scale. This was not of course the first time in Athenian history that a malign outsider had bought off the rich. Whether the outsiders were Persian, Spartan, Macedonian or Roman, there were always some privileged Athenians who saw advantage in foreign domination.

By his own odd lights Haseki was a defender of the town's interests, against the wiles of the Ottoman governors of Negroponte, who saw Athens as part of their turf, and against the irregular Albanian fighters who posed a more deadly threat. The emergence of this challenge reflected both the broader currents in the region and some personal feuds which Haseki had picked. He had dismissed a tough Albanian character from his job as one of the security chiefs of Athens. The aggrieved man, Yialohouri, recruited hundreds of ethnic kin to help secure his return.

This was not difficult, given that there were plenty of armed Albanians on the loose, especially since the Ottomans had encouraged them to fight a Greco-Russian uprising in the Peloponnese in 1770. Faced with threats from Yialohouri to set fire to Athens, Haseki conferred with leading Greeks and Turks in the town and they agreed to oppose the incomers by force. In a skirmish near Halandri, about a quarter of them were killed and the remainder forced to retreat northwards. Dimly channelling the spirit of Themistocles, Haseki immediately ordered the townspeople to start building a wall, using any materials at hand, including

sculpted pieces of marble. The Agroterra temple to the goddess
Artemis, which had stood on the banks of the Ilisos river since
the fifth century BCE and was now a church with paintings, was
demolished to provide material for the barrier. As often happened,
this beautiful structure was captured just before its destruction, in
a fine painting by Stuart.

Despite all this zeal, the wall-builders struggled to keep up with
their foes. While work was still at an early stage, news came that a
much larger force of 6,000 Albanians was on its way. Haseki allowed
many Athenians to take temporary refuge on Salamis; finally the
invaders were bought off. Work on the wall restarted, and it was
eventually completed in barely 100 days. Parts of it still stand, up to
3 metres high and less than a metre thick, running for 10 kilometres.
But the successful execution of this desperate project did not make
Haseki into a popular hero. He demanded that the Athenians,
whose toil had built the wall, pay him for his own expenses, such
as the import of expert supervisors. He also placed loyal guards at
the gates; the wall would serve to keep the unruly townspeople in
as well as rogue Albanians out.

Within months of the wall's erection, a plague broke out and
killed hundreds of children. Like Demetrios the Besieger in the
fourth century, Haseki was a ruthless overlord of Athens who
kept returning and returning, despite dogged attempts to remove
him from the scene. He began a fresh term as voivode in 1779,
expelling many of his Muslim opponents and further alienating the
Christians. An Athenian delegation went to Constantinople and
threw their ploughshares before the Grand Vizier, saying Haseki
had made life in and around the town unbearable.

After a brief exile in Cyprus, Haseki began plotting to regain
mastery of Athens. For a couple of years he managed to reclaim the
*malikane* or tax-collecting rights, although the post of voivode had
to be ceded to a rival. By late 1782 he regained full control of Athens,
thanks to local allies that included a faction of the Greek Church
and a powerful local Muslim called Makfi. Haseki finally turned

against Makfi and sent his agents in pursuit when this hitherto valuable ally fled the city. Makfi was brought to Athens in chains in February 1785 and then drowned in the hold of ship, a punishment Haseki devised.

Such tyrannical behaviour appalled both the leading Greeks and Muslims in Athens. Sixty prominent figures, including the new Metropolitan of Athens, went to Constantinople to complain. Something like a class uprising, cutting across ethnic divisions, occurred in Athens. Liberal-minded Muslims, inspired by leaders called Bellos and Bekir, burned the house of Baptista Vretos, a local supporter of Haseki. At a big public meeting, citizens denounced the wealthy grandees who had sided with the tyrant and demanded a fairer system of municipal self-government. Just possibly, some faint echoes of the revolutionary spirit sweeping through France were drifting eastwards. A bit like a Greek city-state in the Periclean age, Athens now had an oligarchic party as well as a democratic one, and plenty of outsiders sought to manipulate the balance of power.

From 1786 to 1788, Haseki found it prudent to stay in Constantinople, and his star seemed to be waning when his benefactress Esma Sultan died. But this master manipulator was not slow to make fresh connections at court, and by the beginning of 1789 he had secured his restoration to the tax-farming privileges of Athens and to the post of voivode as well. As the news reached Athens, his faction rapidly gained the upper hand and imprisoned its adversaries, including Bellos and Bekir and the Orthodox archbishop. When Haseki arrived in Athens, he went further, killing many of the Christians and Muslims who had opposed him. Some twenty-four citizens of intermediate rank were told they would be impaled unless they or their friends could raise a ransom. The entire Christian population had to find 400,000 piastres in cash or olive oil: Haseki began collecting this tribute immediately, killing or imprisoning many who failed to pay, and seizing the chance to confiscate olive trees and presses. Panagis Skouzes, one of the Athenian writers who describes this period, gives a ghoulish account of the debtors' prison, where men were packed too closely to sit down.

The flogging of inmates who had failed to pay was a frequent occurrence. A falanga, applied to the soles of the feet, was in perpetual readiness to be used on male prisoners. Female inmates were tied to a column and whipped with no less severity. Friends would toss morsels of bread to the half-starved captives. So dreadful was the hygiene in the male prison that black vapour seemed to exude from the window, Skouzes writes. Haseki used his kleptocratic powers to build up a handsome estate,* replete with olive trees, on the western side of Athens. He eventually fell from power not because of any local resistance, but rather thanks to a shift in the murky politics of the Ottoman elite. A new pasha with good connections at court arrived in Chalkis and demanded that Haseki raise some forces for the Ottoman defences; when Haseki refused, there was an armed clash which warded off any threat to Athens but also angered the sultan, who in 1792 expelled both grandees from their fiefdoms. Haseki was sent north to Thessalonica, but he soon found his way back to Constantinople and began intriguing again. His star was still high, but waning just a little. After falling foul of the head of the imperial bodyguard, he was exiled to Chios but returned yet again to the Ottoman capital. He summoned a delegation of local grandees from Athens and demanded a payment of 200,000 piastres.

However, by 1795, his Athenian opponents were gaining confidence and a delegation of them arrived in Constantinople. One of them, an Orthodox abbot called Dionysios Petrakis, managed to gain the confidence of one of the top ladies at court, Valide Sultan. Haseki tried to poison Petrakis but the cleric survived. This redoubled the determination of Haseki's Athenian adversaries to ensure he did not return to the city. After presenting their case to many senior people in Constantinople, including their own church's Patriarch, they had the satisfaction of seeing the despot

---

* The land is now occupied by an agricultural university, whose scrubby greenness offers mild relief in an otherwise grimy urban landscape.

expelled to the island of Kos and then executed. The tyrant's head was displayed outside the Topkapi Palace in Istanbul, but Athens was left embittered and impoverished, and the after-effects did not disappear immediately.

The great honey-making monastery of Kaisariani, which had always been politically adept, managed to dodge expropriation only by resubordinating itself to the metropolitan bishop of Athens. The upheavals suffered across the southern Balkans, and in Athens in particular, in the late eighteenth century can to some degree be understood as a process internal to the region. In Athens, there were signs of a class struggle between the wealthy and powerful and the town's humbler inhabitants, with Christians and Muslims in both of the two main camps. But the whole atmosphere in the region was affected by intensifying competition among external powers for the resources and land of south-eastern Europe. The two processes, of internal class conflict and strategic competition, were mutually reinforcing and therefore escalated rapidly.

In February 1770, Russia's Admiral Alexei Orlov had landed in the Peloponnese and begun stirring up a revolt against Ottoman power which spread to Crete; it fizzled out in the summer of the following year, with Russians and Greeks accusing each other of being half-hearted. The after-effects were more enduring. As a countermeasure the Ottomans encouraged Albanian irregulars and mercenaries to run amok in many parts of Greece, which in turn disrupted trade routes, leaving many Athenian merchants in severe financial difficulties and unable to pay their French business partners. In the 1780s, the last ambassador of royalist France to the Ottoman empire, the Comte de Choiseul-Gouffier, pointedly urged the Turkish authorities to make the Athenian traders pay their debts or face confiscation.

This tactic seems not to have secured much money, even after three members of the Greek Orthodox community in Athens were hanged by way of example. In any case, Choiseul-Gouffier wanted more than cash from the Ottoman lands. He was a passionate admirer of ancient

Greece, even though his observations of the Orlov revolt made him sceptical of the modern Greeks' willingness to fight. Well before his ambassadorial appointment in 1784, he had been conducting and sponsoring investigations into the ancient artefacts of the eastern Mediterranean, especially Greece. Among his carefully chosen assistants in this endeavour was a talented painter and historian called Louis-François-Sebastien Fauvel. It was in 1780 that the classically minded aristocrat gave the twenty-seven-year-old painter what must have seemed a thrilling assignment, to travel round all sites connected with ancient Greece, and to document and depict them. The count had already made his own tour, and was preparing to launch a glossy book, but did not feel he had enough material.

The expedition did not quite achieve its intended purpose; the aristocrat produced his handsome book without waiting for his scout to report. However, the mission filled Fauvel with a passion for the physical remnants of the classical world, and gave him some practice at negotiating the hazards of remote Ottoman places. The partnership between the nobleman and the painter was established. As soon as he was named ambassador to Istanbul, the count instantly had the idea of sending Fauvel to Athens with a mandate to make casts of sculptures and collect artefacts. The ambassador instructed his country's long-standing consul in Athens, Monsieur Gaspari, to secure from the local Turkish authorities whatever permits the painter might need. Fauvel was soon busy on the Acropolis, making casts of the sculptures. He also ventured to other Greek locations, including the island of Santorini, before settling down to some intensive work in and around the Acropolis in 1787–8. He clearly did much more than simply investigate. On four occasions, crates of antiquities were despatched to France, either directly or via ports like Izmir.

It was during his excavations at the Erechtheion, where he found a mosaic floor from the Christian era, that he received a famously blunt instruction from his aristocratic master. 'Take away what you can, do not neglect any means, my dear Fauvel, of plundering in

Athens and its surroundings everything that can be plundered...
press on, spare neither the living nor the dead.' That is one notorious
segment in the correspondence between the two Frenchmen.
The doctoral thesis of Alexandra Lesk, an archaeologist based in
Canada who has devoted an academic lifetime to studying the
Erechtheion, throws some further light on the creative way in which
they interpreted Ottoman permits, in order to serve their own
acquisitive purposes. Fauvel apparently gained leave to investigate
the Erechtheion (which meant removing a wall* and burrowing
deep underground) as part of a search for the spring of water which
Poseidon was supposed to have brought gushing forth during his
contest with Athena. Choiseul exhorted him to use the permission
as a 'pretext' to spirit away not merely some bas-relief sculptures
but an entire Caryatid (one of the six exquisitely carved maidens)
if the chance arose. Fauvel did snitch some bas-relief works and a
cast, at least, of one of the Caryatids.

Both the ambassador and his henchman were indignant
over changes made to the building during its conversion into a
church, which presumably happened around the same time as the
transformation of the Parthenon. 'This temple has been defigured in
every way by the Christians,' grumbled Fauvel, who did nonetheless
take a fancy to two green pillars from the Byzantine Christian
period. He persuaded a local Muslim to spirit some fragments
from the Erechtheion down the hill to the lower town under a
heap of manure. In and around the Parthenon, the painter did
even better. He managed to remove from the Acropolis and
despatch to France two metopes and a section of the Parthenon
frieze, 5 metres long. (These objects did not have to be detached
from the temple; they were already in or under the ground as a
result of the 1687 catastrophe.) The French Revolution severed
the connection between the lordly envoy and his underling. The
count was summoned back to Paris by his country's new masters

---

* At the east end of the Porch of the Maidens.

but thought it prudent to flee to Russia and serve the tsar.

The upheaval in France made less difference to Fauvel, who settled in Athens as an independent collector and trader of antiquities. He grabbed for himself a set of artefacts that were due to be sent to his boss (in lieu, he said, of three years' pay he was owed) and began building up a kind of private museum which became a showpiece of the small town's expatriate scene. Although he was now a freelance antiquarian, his scope for action still depended on cordial relations between France and the Sublime Porte.* These collapsed in 1797 when France took over the Ionian Islands, challenging Turkish control of the adjacent mainland, and then invaded Ottoman Egypt. The sultan reacted by setting aside his long-standing rivalry with the tsar and forming an anti-French alliance. (In 1798, as in 2018, Russian–Turkish rivalry could suddenly evaporate when both powers felt under pressure from the West.)

Within days of the outbreak of war between the Ottoman empire and France, in September 1798, moves were made in Athens to arrest French subjects and sequester their assets. Fauvel was among those apprehended; a year later he was transferred to a notorious prison in Istanbul, and any hope of keeping his precious collection of antiquities must have been fading fast. On the contrary, the property of French people in Athens was being auctioned at fire-sale prices. To the Greek merchants who had been ruined at the insistence of their French creditors, this must have seemed like sweet revenge.

When France fell out of Ottoman favour, Britain immediately stepped into the breach. The cultivation of this volatile but strategically important friendship was assigned to Thomas Bruce, the seventh Earl of Elgin, who was also master of an impressive family seat called Broomhall in the Scottish county of Fife. He arrived in Istanbul as British ambassador to the Porte in November

---

* The term denotes the central government of the Ottoman empire, and is a translation (via French) of the Turkish words for the monumental gate through which visiting dignitaries passed on their way to an audience with Ottoman officials.

1799 and stayed just over three years. By the time he left, the lion's share of the sculptures attached to the Parthenon, and many other magnificent objects from the Periclean age, had been prised away and were at least earmarked for transport to Britain, where Elgin initially hoped they would adorn Broomhall.

In other words, Elgin achieved what Fauvel only dreamed of – not merely the transfer northwards of knowledge and designs from classical Greece, but the removal from Athens of physical objects that brilliantly exemplified that genius. How exactly he achieved that, and when exactly he conceived that plan, is a mysterious and insidiously fascinating story.

As soon as he was sent to the Porte, Elgin declared that one of his goals would be promoting, in one way or other, the cause of artistic refinement in his home country. In keeping with the general mood among the elites of Europe, he was convinced by his artistic advisers that ancient Greece, and Athens in particular, were indispensable sources of that refinement.

He almost hired a twenty-four-year-old painter, J. M. W. Turner, as his personal artist, and had negotiations not failed over money, he might have been content with having antiquities depicted in oil. The artistic heritage of at least two countries would in the event be much richer now. Instead, Elgin recruited Giovanni Battista Lusieri, a landscape painter serving the royal house of Naples, plus at least five more artists (four Italian, one Russian) to serve his diplomatic mission. Another important adviser was Philip Hunt, a shrewd and worldly cleric who besides being chaplain to the embassy in Istanbul was entrusted with many diplomatic missions. Such was Hunt's opportunism that at one point, he suggested that Elgin might haul off all six of the maidens adorning the Erechtheion, if only a naval ship could be found. In the event, only one was taken away to London.

Elgin said later that he initially planned only to record and mould the sculptures on the Acropolis, so that they might be reproduced more accurately back home: this was roughly what James Stuart and his backers had had in mind half a century earlier. The ambassador insisted that the idea of physically exporting Athenian artefacts only came to him when he saw local conditions and understood how vulnerable those artefacts were. Elgin borrowed evidence from Stuart's oeuvre to explain why he felt compelled to go much further than Stuart had. As the earl noted, the 'old temple on the Ilisos river' which Stuart had painted so beautifully in the 1750s was torn down thirty years later to reuse the stones in a new city rampart. Was such vandalism not grounds for saving the antiquities of Athens, while there was still time, by removing them? Elgin even claimed to have met Turks who had admitted grinding down precious pieces of Athenian marble to make mortar.

Elgin's account of his motivation does not convince. He did not go to Athens until 1802, by which time the removal of sculptures from the city, under Lusieri's supervision, was at an advanced stage. However, it does seem likely that the scale of Elgin's plan broadened progressively over time. This was not because of an increasingly pressing need to 'save' anything, but because of the ever-greater opportunities provided by the diplomatic climate of 1801, when Britons and Ottomans fought side by side to dislodge the French from Egypt. Elgin himself noted that growing Anglo-Turkish ties brought steadily more enticing opportunities for the antiquarian: 'In proportion with the change of affairs in our relations towards Turkey, the facilities of access were increased to me and to all English travellers; and about the middle of the summer of 1801 all difficulties were removed.'

Still, there is some mystery over when the transition was made between the harmless activity of drawing the monuments or taking casts, and the deeper and darker purpose of detaching sculptures from the Parthenon and despatching them to England. The official correspondence is illuminating but it leaves gaps. In the first few weeks of 1801, the artists hired by Elgin made quite good progress in their narrow purpose of documenting the Athenian antiquities. But in February, Mr Logothetis, the English consul in Athens, wrote to Elgin to say that no more work on the Acropolis, even of a purely artistic nature, would be possible without a *firman* or decree from the sultan. Some document was probably sent in response to this plea, but it proved insufficient.

Then, in March 1801, two parties set out from Britain's Istanbul embassy to Athens. Lusieri sallied forth with the English traveller Edward Clarke and another friend; meanwhile Hunt, along with a British Arabist, Joseph Carlyle, took a different route, visiting the monasteries of Mount Athos on the way. The records suggest a rivalry between the two groups, but they were all heading to Athens with the common mandate of promoting British antiquarianism in every possible way.

By early May, all were at the walls of the Acropolis; Lusieri would stay for many years, while Hunt headed fairly swiftly back to Istanbul, having worked out the lie of the Athenian land, physical and diplomatic. By mid-May, Lusieri in Athens was writing to Elgin in Istanbul about the urgent need for a clear *firman* from the sultan. Routine access to the Acropolis had always involved offering a gift to the *disdar* or commander of the small Turkish garrison. But for anything more ambitious to happen, the consent of the voivode or city governor was needed, and he in turn needed authority from Istanbul.

It seems clear that on his return to Istanbul, Hunt began some intensive, very private discussions about broadening the scope of the 'artistic' project: they would not merely record antiquities or even gather up objects which were on, or just under, the ground; they would do something almost too shocking to mention openly even in private letters.

In a memo on 1 July 1801, Hunt noted enigmatically that a *firman* should cover three things: drawing and moulding sculptures; securing the right 'to erect scaffolding and to dig where [the artists] may wish to discover the ancient foundations'; and finally the 'liberty to take away sculptures or inscriptions which do not interfere with the works or walls of the citadel'.

Within a matter of days, the desired *firman* was issued: not by the sultan himself but by the deputy to the grand vizier, an official with whom Ambassador Elgin clearly had a warm working relationship. It was exactly what Hunt had been hoping for, leaving aside a certain ambiguity in the final, all-important sentence, at least in Italian, the only language in which the text is still extant.

After pleasantries about the amity between Britain and Turkey, it first laid down that no obstacle should prevent the simple activity of visiting the Acropolis or modelling the figures there. Nor should there be any impediment to the erection of scaffolding or to excavating the foundations 'in search of inscriptions among the debris'. And finally, it was stated that 'no one should meddle with their scaffolding or implements, nor hinder them from taking away some pieces of stone [*qualche pezzi di pietra*] with inscriptions or figures'. To put it mildly, this mandate was interpreted creatively.

Around the same time, Elgin wrote a letter to Lusieri in Athens that was full of odd innuendo. Mr Hunt was on his way and 'will show you much better than I can describe the proofs of the efficacious measures that we have taken – I refer to him for all the details'. Elgin goes on to discuss his interest in procuring fresh marble for his house in Scotland, which is, as he acknowledges, a different matter from 'the value that is attached to a sculptured marble, or historic piece'.

There is no explicit suggestion in the letter that a plan has been formed to detach sculptures from monuments and export them to Britain on a huge scale, with the purpose of decorating Elgin's mansion. Instead there are hints that some sensitive news will soon be conveyed orally by Hunt, when he came to deliver the latest *firman*.

Hunt's next trip to Greece, in July, was not undertaken with the sole aim of activating a project to remove sculptures; he was also engaged on a sensitive mission to places including the Peloponnese where he suspected a forthcoming French attack. The crafty cleric explained to a friend that exploring antiquities and 'attempts to procure such as are interesting and portable' would be a 'secondary object' of his trip. But then, many human activities have multiple purposes, and it can be difficult, sometimes impossible, to discern which is really the main aim, even with the full benefit of hindsight.

In any case, on 31 July, the first of the remaining metopes was yanked off the Parthenon and hauled to the ground, as Lusieri issued orders. Apart from the new *firman*, the way was cleared for this activity by news recently arrived from Egypt: a British–Ottoman coalition had forced the French garrison to Cairo to surrender. The Ottoman defence minister, Hadji Ibrahim Effendi, was the patron of the voivode in Athens. The minister clearly drove home to all concerned the message that Anglo-Ottoman friendship must be reinforced in all possible ways. By September 1801, the Italian was confident he would soon be able to 'get possession of all the fragments' he could find and wrote to Elgin asking for a dozen saws of different sizes, of which three or four should be '20 feet in length'. Among the purposes of these tools was to reduce the weight of the famous and controversial eastern segment of the frieze, which might or might not depict the presentation of a dress to Athena.

Lusieri sent frank reports about his progress. In September 1802, he wrote to Elgin that he had 'pleasure of announcing to you the possession of the eighth metope, that one where there is the centaur carrying off the woman'. He adds: 'This piece has caused much trouble in all respects and I have even been obliged to be a little barbarous.'

Indeed such was the 'barbarism' that it shocked the Turkish *disdar*. Edward Clarke, an English traveller and clergyman who was visiting Athens at that very time, described how

> We saw this fine piece of sculpture raised from its station between the triglyphs; ... a part of the adjoining masonry was loosened by the machinery; and down came the fine masses of Pentelican marble, scattering their white marble with thundering noise among the ruins... Observing, the Turkish commander took his

pipe out of his mouth, dropped a tear and said to Lusieri, *Telos!*

Lusieri's extractions were not completed till 1805, a couple of years after Elgin had left his post. In total he took about half the surviving Parthenon frieze, around 75 metres of the 160-metre total, plus fifteen of the ninety-two metopes and seventeen figures from the pediments, as well as pieces from the other monuments on the Acropolis: the Erechtheion, the Propylaea and the temple of Athena Nike.

Transporting the sculptures to Britain proved much more complicated than extracting them from the Acropolis temples, especially after the diplomatic climate worsened from Britain's viewpoint. France made peace with the Ottomans, who were disappointed by a new British alliance with Russia. As a result, Fauvel was free to return to Athens, full of bitterness over British actions. As he saw things, it was British pressure on the sultan that had led to his own incarceration and to the ruin of many French citizens in Athens. Fauvel was appalled, and jealous, over the British depredations on the Acropolis monuments, and immediately did his best to obstruct the despatch of precious artefacts to England. There was also a more specific bone of contention: a consignment of antiquities, including a metope from the Parthenon, which Fauvel had despatched to his own homeland in a French corvette, was intercepted by the British, and the objects were added to Elgin's haul.

Elgin himself was intercepted en route northwards, and held prisoner by the French for three years. Only in 1806 did he reach his native shores, and he immediately set about gathering up his collection. One part was lying in various English ports, including some artefacts that sank off the Greek island of Kythera and had to be salvaged. Many more cases of precious sculptures had yet to leave Athens, and Fauvel did everything possible to obstruct their departure. In 1808, the indefatigable Lusieri wrote to the new British ambassador in Istanbul, Sir Robert Adair, asking for a *firman* authorizing the release of the artefacts from Athens. This became easier after Britain and the Ottomans made a renewed alliance in 1809, and the Ottoman authorities did eventually issue the necessary instructions to the voivode in Athens. Thanks to some research that was presented in 2015 by Eleni Korka, in collaboration with Seyyed Mohammed Taghi Shariat-Panahi, the relevant correspondence can now be studied in all its revealing detail. At least on this occasion it seems clear that the sultan, the grand vizier and his deputy were involved in the transaction.

A letter sent by the grand vizier's deputy to the voivode in Athens reads in part:

> The [new] ambassador of England... pleads for the transport of the aforementioned stones with images. These stones are not acceptable in Islam, but they are acceptable in the European countries. There is no harm in conceding a permit for the transport of the aforementioned stones. The transport and safe passage of these stones should not be hindered.

There is a subtext to this correspondence which is also present in almost all the documents relating to the Parthenon marbles. The removal and despatch to a foreign land of precious sculptures, especially for private purposes, is perceived in many quarters as a shady undertaking; arguments therefore have to be constructed to show why, in this particular instance, the export of such artefacts is permissible. On this occasion the arguments chosen, with just a hint of desperation, have to do with the Muslim antipathy to the representation of the human form. But no such antipathy had prevented other Muslim observers of the Parthenon, from Evliya Çelebi to Mahmud Efendi, from recognizing the temple of Athena as a place of beauty and holiness that was worthy of protection.

# 14

# A Poet Dreams on a Rock
## 1809–33

*E. D. Clarke, antiquarian and writer – Byron arrives in Athens, denounces Elgin, has a new vision of Hellenism – the Acropolis under siege – Greek takeover in 1822, with an ugly aftermath – quarrels and dramas among Greek commanders: Androutsos, Gouras and Makriyannis – Turkish recapture lasts from 1827 to 1833, long after the Greek cause has prevailed elsewhere*

Among those who study the foreign antiquarians of late-Ottoman Greece, there are mixed memories of Edward Daniel Clarke, an English clergyman whose main interests were history and mineralogy. As we have seen, we owe to him some vivid descriptions of the process by which sculptures were extracted from the Parthenon, and of the negative reactions among local people, both Greek and Turkish. On the other hand, he himself took away no fewer than seventy-six cases of Greek antiquities, including a Roman-era sculpture of a maiden from Eleusis that is now in the Fitzwilliam Museum in Cambridge. It was snatched in 1801 in the face of furious resistance by local people who believed the statue represented the ancient goddess Demeter. In other parts of Greece, Demeter had blended with Saint Demetrios, the Christian warrior-saint. But the Eleusinians were adamant that Demeter remained female and that she protected their crops. Indeed, they accurately predicted that the ship carrying the sculpture would sink – it happened off Beachy Head in 1802. However, the cargo was successfully retrieved.

It is to Clarke that we owe many telling details of the stripping of the Acropolis monuments. He toured the Parthenon under Lusieri's guidance and experienced for himself the evident 'dissatisfaction' of the Turkish *disdar*. Indeed, 'Lusieri told us that it was with great difficulty he could accomplish that part of the undertaking, from the attachment the Turks entertained towards a building which they had been accustomed to regard with religious veneration, and had converted into a mosque...'

One particular detail – the fact that an especially heavy-handed operation to haul down a metope had driven the *disdar* to visible tears – made a strong impression on another adventurous Englishman, who warmly thanks his friend Clarke for the information in a note appended to one of his many writings about Athens. This was a man who would utterly transform his country's understanding of Greece, while emerging as one of the most famous and controversial personalities in Europe. His name was George Gordon Byron. Like Elgin, he had roots in the Anglicized Scottish aristocracy and he attended Harrow, the elite school north of London. But there the resemblance ends.

Indeed Byron's personality was altogether an unusual one. Regardless of the rank he was born to, he always saw himself as an outsider. He was raised in Aberdeen, in quite modest circumstances, by his widowed mother before inheriting a peerage and an English stately home, though hardly enough money to maintain it, at the age of ten. His mother was by turns adoring, abusive and intensely ambitious for her only child, who was gifted with good looks, charisma and a perfect feeling for words.

He was only twenty-one when he rode into Athens on Christmas Day, 1809, with his friend John Hobhouse and a retinue of servants. They had made an exhilarating Balkan journey which had begun at the court of Ali Pasha, the politically astute warlord who controlled the north-western edge of mainland Greece. They approached their destination via the fastness of Fyli, where a democratic uprising had been organized in the final years of the Athenian golden age. As they were emerging from the ruined fortress, the young Britons saw the Acropolis rising above a dense cluster of red roofs and minarets, encased in an undulating stone wall. They were instantly entranced.

Byron and Hobhouse took up residence for ten weeks with a Greek lady whose late husband had been British vice-consul. Their lodgings overlooked a courtyard with a small grove of lemon trees. It was located in a street called Agias Theklas in the district of Psirri, whose scruffy alleys have only recently been redeveloped for edgy tourism. The Hephaisteion was just a few minutes' walk away, and other antiquities only a little further.

For Byron, the sojourn with the bustling Theodora Makri was the first of part of a more extended exploration of Athens which lasted until spring 1811. He and Hobhouse went to Izmir and Istanbul in spring 1810. Byron returned to Athens in mid-July, and more definitively in late August when he settled in for the autumn and winter in the Capuchin convent, which had long since lost any real monastic function but served as a kind of upmarket hostelry, school and social gathering point for expatriates.

With the fresh eyes of youth, Byron and Hobhouse loved the town and almost everything about it: not just the multilayered past, but the lively, gossipy world of Greek merchants, Turkish bureaucrats and Westerners with a ragbag of ambivalent purposes. It helped, of course, that they were privileged representatives of a powerful country. When they were insulted by a 'renegade Spaniard' while on a trip to Piraeus, they reported the matter to the voivode and the offender was thrashed on the soles of his feet till he was screaming and incontinent. 'Autocracy has its advantages' was the foolish comment of Hobhouse.

In contrast with so many others who passed through Athens, Byron did not view the place a means to an end, a place to be endured for the sake of gaining useful knowledge or precious objects. He instantly felt that the town, even in its battered late-Ottoman state, had a charm and beauty of its own. Ascending to the Acropolis, he could see the gaping holes on the Parthenon where the frieze had been taken down and the metopes extracted. Unlike many recent visitors to the place, he was not obsessively interested in the sculptures as such, but he had an aversion to the arrogance which their removal seemed to reflect. He had already formed an opinion on the matter when the first consignment of sculptures – what he mockingly described as 'mis-shapen monuments, and maimed antiques' – arrived in London in 1807 and found a temporary, unsatisfactory home in Elgin's London residence. Viewing the Parthenon in its mutilated condition, Byron vowed to take further revenge on his compatriot, in verse.

His other thoughts, on watching the sun slide over the mountains, were of Socrates, who must have observed the same scene on the last evening of his life, before quaffing the fatal brew as darkness fell. 'All that we know is that nothing can be known,' Byron murmured to himself, recalling the philosopher's most famous maxim. Where others saw Athens as a source of valuable stones, the wild, gifted twenty-one-year-old understood Athenian civilization as a flowering of the human spirit which had been fostered by a uniquely benign environment: sparkling seas, scented olive groves and cypress trees, protective mountains that offered up their marble, herbs and honey. As Byron intuitively grasped, the Attic spirit and its fruits could not be removed from their environment without losing some of their elan. Being young, wild and impulsive probably sharpened that understanding, and gave him an advantage over older antiquarians whose minds had already grown fusty with book-learning.

For all his antipathy to Elgin, Byron was in general forgiving of human foibles, having plenty of his own, and correspondingly wide-ranging in his choice of Athenian companions. He and Hobhouse instantly made friends with Fauvel, who was firmly ensconced in Athens, and enjoyed his private collection of ancient artefacts, including some very shocking ones. Fauvel became their guide on many excursions. The young Britons thoroughly relished the cross-dressing of the pre-Lenten carnival, then as now an occasion when Athenians could unleash their wilder fantasies. In late-Ottoman times, local Greeks would dress up as their Turkish overlords. Closer to real life, Byron enjoyed the company of the voivode, who had an un-Islamic taste for liquor.

It was on one of his many excursions around Attica that he saw the battlefield where the Athenians prevailed over the Persians in 490 BCE, a place where the simple facts of geography, more than any artefact or monument, bring history alive. That would inspire some of his most famous lines of poetry, whose deceptive simplicity recalls ancient Greek verse at its finest.

> The mountains look on Marathon –
> And Marathon looks on the sea;
> And musing there an hour alone,
> I dream'd that Greece might still be free.

The sensual environment stimulated not only Byron's political imagination, but his voracious bisexual energy. Leaving Athens in spring 1810, he penned a beautifully turned poem that professed his love for Teresa, one of his landlady's three daughters: 'Maid of Athens, ere we part, Give oh give me back my heart.' Writing to his old schoolmaster Henry Drury he describes feelings of infatuation for all three daughters, 'I am dying for the love of three Greek girls.' But in truth it was Athens itself he was in love with, not any of its particular inhabitants. More intense, and certainly more physically expressed, was the passion he conceived for a teenaged Franco-Greek youth, Nicolo Giraud, during his stay at the convent. He was apparently either the brother-in-law, or at least a close relation, of Lusieri, the wily Italian who was still trying to outwit Fauvel and despatch the last of Elgin's trophies to Britain. Athens was full of intrigues and interconnections which Byron relished.

In that letter to his teacher Drury, Byron declared, with a youthful penchant for airy and arrogant generalization: 'I like the Greeks, who are plausible rascals – with all the Turkish vices, without their courage. However, some are brave, and all are beautiful, very much resembling the busts of Alcibiades.' Byron himself had more than a passing resemblance to Alcibiades, a character who had walked roughly the same streets, with the same charm and tipsy swagger – ostensibly in search of social and sexual entertainment, but always open to the possibility that the human spirit might rise to higher things than that.

Much as they liked the hedonistic cosmopolitanism of the late-Ottoman scene, Byron and Hobhouse picked up intimations of a longing for a change that would not be satisfied by riotous parties or cheeky cross-dressing. En route to Athens they had stopped at the town of Vostitsa (modern Aigion) on the Gulf of Corinth, and stayed with a young man who despite being only twenty-three held a position of authority in the local administration. Andreas Londos was, formally speaking, an office-holder in the Ottoman system, but as his British guests discovered, he was a passionate Greek patriot. The young man was a keen gymnast whose energy, and penchant for spontaneous displays, seemed to say something about his people's pent-up frustrations. Hobhouse was astonished when, during an evening chess game, Londos 'jumped suddenly from the sofa, threw over the board and clasped his hands', repeating with tears the name of Rigas, a great martyr for freedom whose memory he revered.

Rigas Velestinlis was a man worth weeping over, and the history of the Balkans might have been very different if more people like him had lived. Born in 1757 into a family of prosperous merchants in Thessaly, he exemplified the modest but growing movement known as the Greek enlightenment: an impulse that sought to improve educational standards and bring the best ideals of the French Revolution to the south-east of Europe. He dreamed of an uprising by all the peoples of the Balkans, including Muslims and Turks, against the theocratic power of the sultan. He entered into communication with Napoleon and was on his way to Venice to meet a general from the French leader's coalition when he was betrayed, arrested and jailed by the Ottoman authorities in Belgrade, where he and five companions were strangled by their jailers. Before expiring, he is said to have declared: 'I have sown a rich seed; the hour is coming when my country will reap its glorious fruits.' In 1797, the last full year of his life, Rigas had written a song, urging freedom-loving people to quit the Ottoman-held towns and take to the mountains. Among its most stirring lines was: 'It is finer to live one hour as a free man than forty years as a slave and prisoner.' Young Andreas could have little direct knowledge of the final moments of Rigas' life (he would have been eleven or so when the hero perished) but it was evident to the British travellers that the martyr's idealism still crackled through the Greek world.

For Byron, this impassioned outburst of patriotism, in its most utopian form, was only one among the extraordinary variety of sentiments, scenes and subcultures that he would experience in and around Athens. In the winter of 1810–11, without the companionship of Hobhouse, the poet was even freer to navigate his own way through the bohemian society of his temporary home. As he described it: 'Here I see and have conversed with French, Italians, Germans, Danes, Greeks, Turks, Americans, etc etc etc, and without losing sight of my own, I can judge of the countries and manners of others.' Every so often, he was confronted with the darker side of Ottoman theocracy. That is well illustrated by a mysterious and horrible incident of which two versions, both put about by the poet, exist. When returning to Athens from a trip to Piraeus he came across a procession carrying a sack in which a young woman had been sewn up. He was told that under Islamic law she had been condemned to death by drowning for immorality. In one version, Byron realized that the woman was a person with whom he had enjoyed sexual relations, wrongly assuming her to be a Greek Christian; the sentence had already been carried out and the sack held a corpse. The other version, spread by Byron's friend Lord Sligo, was that the poet intercepted the party while they were en route to carry out the sentence, and that he persuaded them to spare the young woman's life. She was turned over to the voivode, who was in turn persuaded or induced by Byron to free her on condition that she left Athens.

For Byron, Athens was a place of sexual liberty and experimentation of which he could not have dreamed in England; but for others the body was in the most literal and ghastly sense constrained. Still, there is something elusive about this story and neither version completely convinces. For all its dark side, the sheer beauty of the Athenian environment thrilled Byron in a way recognizable to many northern Europeans who had mulled the details of Greek history in chilly classrooms and suddenly experienced the brilliant light and landscape where that genius emerged. Soon after settling into the monastic lodgings in August 1810, Byron wrote to an English friend:

> I am living in the Capuchin Convent, [Mount] Hymettus before me, the Acropolis behind, the temple of Jove [i.e. Olympian Zeus] to my right, the Stadium in front, the town to the left… eh, Sir, there's a situation, there's your picturesque! Nothing like that, sir, in 'Lunnun', not even the Mansion House.

In other words, faced with a choice of Greek-inspired architecture in the chilly streets of his home metropolis, and the sun-blessed prototype, he had no hesitation in preferring the latter. Still, leave for England he eventually did, in April 1811, in part because of the financial problems that made it uncertain whether he could hold onto his newly inherited family seat. He made the first leg of the voyage, as far as Malta, on the naval transport ship which was also carrying the final consignment of Elgin's marble acquisitions, along with Lusieri, the man who had obtained them. Other passengers included two Greeks whom Byron intended to use as servants in his stately home, and his young Franco-Greek protégé Nicolo, who by agreement with his parents was left at a monastic school in Valetta – from which he was expelled a year later.

In the documentary evidence of Byron's passionate liaison with this young man, intimations of death are a weirdly recurrent theme. From the moment they meet in the wild atmosphere of the Athenian lodging house, with the idea that Nicolo should teach the visitor Italian, Byron is nonplussed by the boy's plea that they should not merely live and travel together but *morire insieme*, die together. As the poet makes clear in a coded letter to a friend in England, the relationship becomes physical during an excursion to the honey-making monastery on Mount Pentelikon, a place dedicated ironically enough to the 'Bodiless Powers of Heaven', in other words the angels. But there is nothing bodiless about this partnership; Byron hints to a female friend that he almost expired *in flagrante* during an expedition to Patras, where he and Nicolo both contracted a fever that was severe but apparently no killer of passion.

On returning to England, Byron wrote a will, later cancelled, which left a fabulous sum of money (£7,000) to his young friend. As for Giraud, one of his last (unanswered) communications to Byron, written from Athens in 1815, contains the pathetic line: 'If only I were a bird and could fly... to you for one hour, I would be happy to die at the same time. Hope tells me that I shall see you again, and that is my consolation for not dying immediately...'

When Giraud did, in fact, die is a mystery. Byron was destined to live another nine years, before succumbing to illness on a Greek battlefield, but he never returned to Athens. By the time of his death on 19 April 1824, he had dazzled and scandalized London society with his long narrative poems; entered a passionate affair with his half-sister and a short-lived marriage; lived for seven years in Italy; and finally, starting in August 1823, made a powerful intervention in the Greek revolution which had been raging for two years. First in the island of Cephalonia and then in the besieged stronghold of Missolonghi, which held the key to central Greece, he made some well-calibrated acts of support, using his money and diplomatic skills. He worked with Alexander

Mavrokordatos, the most sophisticated of the revolutionaries, to reconcile the insurgency's endlessly warring factions, and made generous disbursements from his own, by no means unlimited, resources. By exposing himself to the hazards, including scanty medical attention, of such a foreign field, he can truthfully be said to have died for Greece. In the eyes of posterity, that more than cleanses any stains left by the erratic, manipulative side of his character. Rather than any physical passion, it was passion for a new country, a country at whose birth pangs he had assisted, that cost Byron his life.

As for his feud with Elgin, that found eloquent expression in several poems, one of which gloatingly ascribed to goddess Athena's revenge a series of misfortunes which befell the noble diplomat. These included the breakdown of his health (including the atrophy of his nose); the failure of his marriage; and the collapse of his finances, which forced him to sell his sculptures to the British nation, a transaction that was agreed after an impassioned parliamentary debate in 1816.

Like much else in Byron's vast oeuvre, his poem about the Curse of Minerva (i.e. Athena) wavers between the sublime and the merely clever. It begins with his own dreamily ecstatic response to the descending Attic sun, as observed by himself – and 2,200 years earlier, by the soon-to-die Socrates.

> Slow sinks, more lovely ere his race be run,
> Along Morea's hills the setting Sun;
> Not, as in northern climes, obscurely bright,
> But one unclouded blaze of living light; ...

Then its tone turns really savage, comparing Elgin unfavourably to Alaric, the Gothic warrior who ransacked Athens (and probably burned the Parthenon) in 396 CE. Where the barbarian warrior might claim the traditional rights of conquest, the Scottish lord was merely a scavenger.

Be ever hailed with equal honour here
The Gothic monarch and the Pictish peer:
Arms gave the first his right, the last had none,
But basely stole what less barbarians won.
So when the Lion quits his fell repast,
Next prowls the Wolf, the filthy Jackal last:
Flesh, limbs, and blood the former make their own,
The last poor brute securely gnaws the bone.

With another twist of the knife, Byron suggests that not merely Athena but the love-goddess, Aphrodite or Venus, played a part in dishing out to Elgin his just deserts. His wife (who had often claimed that her charms had been decisive in getting the sculptures despatched to Britain) was accused of committing adultery, prompting Elgin to divorce her in 1808.

When holding forth about Greece, Byron could be lofty and idealistic, or else brutally frank and cynical about the messiness of Hellenic reality. And in the uprising which began in 1821, there was plenty of messiness, starting with the extraordinary mixture of forces that took up arms against the sultan. There were wealthy and well-educated Greek intellectuals from the diaspora, schooled in Paris, Venice or Vienna, who were fired up by the enlightenment and dreams of progress. Inside Greece there were chieftains, warlords and Christian landowners, whose pre-modern worldview was not so very different from their Ottoman masters, except that they wanted to be the masters instead. There were fighting sea captains from the Aegean islands who had gained prosperity, toughness and sophistication by plying their trade across the eastern Mediterranean. Among the commanders of the uprising on land or sea, as many spoke Albanian as Greek; that was also true of the forces deployed by the Ottomans to repress the insurgency.

Still, at least in its starting point, the revolt was well co-ordinated and well-timed. In 1814, three young Greek merchants in Odessa set up a secret fraternity called the *Philiki Etairia*, or Friendly Society. They in turn recruited a carefully chosen handful of individuals, including clerics and local bigwigs in the Peloponnese and a general in the tsarist army, Alexander Ypsilantis, whose origins were in the Greek elite of Istanbul. Greeks have long commemorated the uprising on 25 March but in fact it began in the preceding weeks and months, and the Peloponnese emerged quickly as the scene of the fiercest fighting. The insurgents struck the Ottoman empire at a moment when it was vulnerable, preoccupied by tension on its eastern boundary, and on the Adriatic by the uprising of Ali Pasha. Even so, the objective chances of success did not initially seem very high. All the leading powers in Europe had interests in south-eastern Europe, but that did not mean they were prepared to risk everything by unequivocally backing one nationalist cause. Indeed, when the uprising started, no European power, not even Russia, which saw itself as the protector of the Orthodox Christians, was openly prepared to support a free Greece. Whatever their differences with the sultan might be, European states were reluctant to set a precedent by backing a secessionist movement against an established power.

But in history, many anti-state rebellions have started small, only to demonstrate that new realities can be created rather quickly. Atrocities take place, the stakes rise, public opinion becomes outraged and people with political and financial influence demand intervention. Simply allowing the old state of affairs to be re-established is no longer the line of least resistance. Instead of hoping the rebellion will go away, outside powers start competing for a slice of influence in the new order. That very broadly describes what happened in Greece in the 1820s, and it bears some comparison with what happened in the Balkans in the 1990s, as the Western powers tried to mitigate and manage the conflicts that arose when communist Yugoslavia broke up. In all cases, a relatively small and poor stretch of territory preoccupied much bigger and richer countries. That was not because those bigger countries had any vital interest at stake; it was more because none wanted to be excluded from influence over the region. As a result, they were willing in the end to co-opt an independence war, simply to be sure of having some share of the post-independence bounty.

Massacres served to concentrate minds. In September 1821, thousands of mostly Muslim civilians, as well as Jews, died when Greek revolutionary forces stormed the Ottoman bastion of Tripolitsa in the Peloponnese. Then the following April, as many as 50,000 Christians on the once-prosperous Aegean island of Chios were slaughtered by Ottoman troops, provoking outrage across western Europe and inspiring a famous work by the French painter Eugène Delacroix. In high places in Russia, there was horror in April 1821 when the Orthodox Christian Patriarch in Istanbul was dragged out of his church and hanged, despite the fact that he had condemned the uprising. Even if some half wished it would, this was not an independence war that would simply die down, as the foreign ministers of Europe gradually came to acknowledge.

Among the many fronts in the independence war were battles over the Acropolis. As with the war as a whole, these Athenian clashes had their sordid episodes and their inspiring moments. There were displays of great courage and demonstrations of terrible, gratuitous cruelty. The fundamental facts about the citadel never changed. This was a rock which was almost impossible to capture by frontal assault – and also a place which cannot be defended for an indefinite period if the besieger has effectively cut off supplies of food and water. From the start of the uprising, the Acropolis saw one siege after another.

The story of the first begins in spring 1821 when about 1,200 Athenian Muslims took refuge with the small Ottoman garrison on the Acropolis. Who exactly were these Muslims? In speaking of this or any other phase of the Greek independence war, terms can be confusing. For practical purposes, followers of Islam who might be Turkish, Albanian or Greek by origin and/or language are often lumped together and described as 'Turks'. The people ranged against them go under the catch-all term Greeks, although their most salient characteristic was adherence to Orthodox Christianity. Neither category was hermetically sealed, and that makes any description of the independence war more complicated.

As the occupants of the Acropolis were bombarded from nearby strategic points, the Ottoman authorities despatched two commanders with the same name to break the siege. Omer Bey from Karystos in Euboea arrived with up to 800 infantry, and the other, Omer Vrioni, came from further north with 1,500 light cavalry and musketeers. He had been a prominent figure and treasurer in the semi-independent statelet run by Ali Pasha.

By 30 June, the garrison on the Acropolis had been relieved and resupplied with food, water and ammunition. Some interesting diplomatic background to this period has been unearthed by Şükrü Ilıcak, a Turkish-born historian whose Harvard University doctorate focuses on Ottoman reactions to the independence war. As he demonstrates, the fate of the Acropolis was of extreme concern to the British government, not because of any particular interest in the military outcome, but more out of a desire to preserve whatever remained of the antiquities.

Britain's ambassador, Viscount Strangford, told the Ottomans that as one monarch to another, King George IV would be personally grateful for the sultan's efforts to preserve the Athenian citadel and the monuments testifying to its ancient glory. In elaborate, diplomatic French, the message was formally conveyed to a sultan 'so distinguished in his tastes and his attachment to art and literature, of which Athens is the cradle'. Cynics might say this reflected a peculiar version of philhellenism which, like the designers of the neutron warhead, wanted to keep buildings intact but had little concern for the survival of people. As Ilıcak correctly notes, 'the Acropolis was in fact heavily shelled by both the Greek revolutionaries and the Ottoman armies in the following years'.

The intervention of Omer Vrioni, who stayed in Athens for three months, was sufficient to keep the Turkish garrison safe in the face of a spasmodic series of Greek attacks over the winter of 1821–2. However, by the following summer, the other Omer and the foot soldiers he had brought from Euboea had grown weary and thirsty; in June he asked for the sultan's leave to abandon the Acropolis. The question was whether this could be done in a way that preserved the lives of more than 1,000 Muslim civilians who were living on the citadel.

In contrast with the sordid tale of European competition to grab Athenian antiquities, the next chapter in the story speaks rather well of the Western consuls who still functioned in wartime Athens, and who tried (a bit like the UN agencies which observed the Bosnian conflict) to mitigate the suffering of civilians, even when this involved awkward bargaining with the warring parties. To be precise, just three consulates were operating in Athens: those of France, the Netherlands and Austria. Their role is told in impressive and clinical detail by George Waddington, an English cleric who was resident in Athens. In general, his prejudices are pro-Christian and anti-Muslim, but that does not prevent him writing with reasonable objectivity and giving discredit where it is due.

As he describes it, the three consuls negotiated hard to ensure that at least some of the Muslim civilians encamped on the Acropolis were allowed to get away alive. The French consul in Athens was none other than Fauvel, the cynical and urbane antiquities collector. In this episode he behaved well. Waddington describes the dilemma of the fighters and civilians camped out on the Acropolis who were counting on foreign powers to get them out alive:

> With little hope of the efficacy of such influence, but afflicted by their own misery, which they witnessed hourly, and by the loss of about a third of their force which had already perished from want or sickness, they agreed at last to... articles of capitulation.

The articles were remarkably precise. They laid down that those abandoning the Acropolis must leave behind all weapons, and bring only a minimal supply of clothes and kitchen utensils, plus half the jewellery or precious stones in their possession, not including anything which had been plundered. They would then have a choice of staying in Athens or leaving for Asia Minor in European vessels, with 'biscuits and cheese' for the journey.

This seemed to portend a humane and dignified end to a contest over the Acropolis which had been sputtering on for more than a year. It had begun in April 1821 when fighters from Salamis and various parts of Attica descended on Athens and helped the local Greek Christians to take full control of the lower town. Those Greek forces obtained 'one or two small pieces of artillery' which they installed on Philopappos hill and attempted 'with singular lack of skill and efficiency' – Waddington's words – to deploy them against the garrison on the Acropolis. They also made preparations to blow up the fortifications which surrounded a water source on the south side of the Acropolis; this triggered a wave of rumours across the town that a terrible explosion might soon bring down the entire Rock. (An explosion of sorts did occur, but to no particular effect.)

Waddington describes the atmosphere during this phoney Athenian war with admirable sharpness. The Greeks, entrenched in the lower town, had advantages over the Muslims; they were able to grow food inside the town walls, including on some land which had been owned by Muslims. The latter meanwhile were struggling to find food and water for themselves and the many horses and donkeys they had taken to the citadel. But when a group of Muslim men and women tried to make an early-morning sortie into the lower town to grab some food, they were ambushed and about twenty-five of them were killed.

The atmosphere changed rapidly when Athenians heard that Omer Vrioni was on his way from the north with a force of several thousand. Most of the Athenian population took the ancient recourse of fleeing to Salamis, leaving an empty town which Vrioni easily occupied, to the great relief of the Turks and Muslims ensconced on the Rock. As Waddington was told by his

Greek informants, Vrioni then used his control of the entire town to launch 'Greek hunts' across Attica – capturing all manner of Christian civilians, including aged shepherds, monks, women and children, who would be brought to the door of the chieftain's headquarters and then slaughtered.

But the Turkish advantage only lasted as long as Vrioni remained. The warlord, 'having consumed all the resources of the country' and made sure the Acropolis was well supplied, went on his way in November 1821, and this immediately allowed the Greek and Christian forces to start clawing back some advantage. Although deprived of Vrioni and his forces, the Muslim forces rashly continued to send irregulars out on 'Greek hunts', and in the course of one such expedition, in mid-November 1821, the Greeks fought back and slew twenty-five of the hunters. That was a signal for the Athenians still sheltering on Salamis to return – and for some of them to make a desperate attempt to scale the Acropolis from the western side, an operation in which about 200 were killed. They did however manage to take control of the well on the south side, leaving the 1,600 or so soldiers and civilians on the Acropolis, along with their beasts of burden, very thirsty. According to the Greek lore which Waddington records, the Turks prayed hard for rain but their prayers were unanswered, even when it was pelting down in other parts of Attica.

This was the background to the capitulation agreement of June 1822, involving safe passage guaranteed by the European consuls. At this point Waddington's account becomes even more coldly precise. About 1,140 Turks came down from the Rock and were accommodated initially in a mansion belonging to the town administration. The consuls began an urgent search for ships to take them away. But on 10 July, a rumour swept through the Greek Christian community that a powerful Turkish force was heading southwards towards Athens, and it had already passed Thermopylae. This triggered a furious Greek reaction, prompting a crowd of soldiers and citizens to storm the building where the hostages were being kept, and kill about 400 of them. Others, mostly women, were taken prisoner and effectively enslaved. Still others managed to find refuge in the nearby foreign consulates. Some representatives of the embryonic Greek government, based in the Peloponnese, were so horrified that they fled, 'finding that they had no influence' in the face of an 'enormity of which they resolved not to be spectators'. Before leaving, these hapless representatives addressed a 'spirited appeal' to the Athenian populace to respect the integrity of the foreign consulates.

Two days later, a couple of French naval ships arrived in Piraeus. At that point hundreds of Muslims were sheltering in the three consulates. A French naval commander managed to escort many of them to his vessels, despite the efforts of Greek soldiers to stop them. Other civilians were shipped away in batches over the following year, so that by July 1823, a total of 537 had been taken away to Izmir. It was the Austrian consulate which played the biggest part in sheltering hostages, accommodating 347, while it was the French ships that did most to ensure their safe passage, evacuating a total of 448.

The episode clearly troubled some Greek Christians, and Waddington considers various arguments that he heard 'in palliation of its criminality' during many anguished discussions. He mentions that when the Muslims and Turks first holed up in the Acropolis, they took nine Greek hostages. When Greeks in turn established control of the lower town, they captured forty local Muslims – but were persuaded to let them shelter in the consulates. Then, as skirmishing intensified, the Greek hostages were killed, and locals unsuccessfully called on the consuls to release the people under their protection, so that they in turn could be slain. In the tit-for-tat war over civilian life, there was a score to be settled, from the Greek point of view. Waddington also heard the mitigating argument that most of the prominent people in Athens, including the town fathers and the archbishop, were absent when the 400 were killed. Yet another argument, which may tell an emotional truth but almost certainly not a factual one, held that the man who unleashed the massacre was from Chios, where his family had been among the tens of thousands slain by the Ottomans. Having considered all these points, Waddington concludes that he cannot completely exonerate the Greek authorities. Regardless of what they could or could not have done on 10 July, the fact was that they accepted the consequences of the massacre. The women who were enslaved on that day remained enslaved, unless they were ransomed. In many cases the consuls had to pay for the captives' liberty.

Following the turbulent events of July 1822, the Acropolis remained in Greek hands, and therefore at least notionally subject to the Greek government in Nauplion, for another five years. But life on the Rock was far from stable. Further extraordinary events played out among the commanders who wielded authority amid the marble pillars.

The citadel's first master was the charismatic, mysterious figure of Odysseas Androutsos. To understand him, it helps to have a sense of the world in which he was raised. Androutsos had spent his teenage years as a protégé of Ali Pasha, the swashbuckling lord of north-western Greece whose amoral charisma had fascinated Byron and Hobhouse during their first weeks in the Balkans. Ali Pasha was notionally an Ottoman subject and a Muslim, but in truth he was almost impossible to classify, whether by language, religion or political affiliation. His native language was Albanian but the language of his court was Greek, and he fostered the educational and religious activities of the Greeks. In 1820, his rebellion against the sultan caused a distraction to the Ottomans which greatly assisted the Greek revolutionaries further south. After two years of fighting he was tricked into leaving his fortress; he was then killed and beheaded. His bloodstained head was presented to the sultan in Istanbul. This fulfilled the prophecy of an Orthodox Christian mystic that the great chieftain would 'go to Constantinople with a red Beard'. The remains of his body were buried at the Fethiye Mosque in a mausoleum which still stands as one of the landmarks of the lakeside town of Ioannina in Epirus.

This was the locale in which Androutsos grew up. In the acerbic words of Waddington, 'he was removed at a very early age to [Ioannina] and received his education in the service of Ali Pasha, a school where it was easy to become instructed in every possible vice. Distinguished by the gracefulness of his person, he was first introduced to the notice of his master by his extreme agility.' In fairness he seems to have imbibed virtues as well as vices, including the ability to retain the loyalty of his own soldiers in a chaotic situation. He participated in his master's final campaign for survival and then did good service in the early years of the Greek uprising. He joined the Friendly Society as it was planning the Greek uprising and tried, along with others who shared his Ioannina background, to forge a Greek–Albanian alliance. It was the stance of Omer Vrioni, who after briefly joining the alliance took the Ottoman side, that made such a coalition impossible.

When in 1822 Androutsos was named commander both of Athens and of eastern Greece, his forceful personality initially helped to unite the Greek (or at least pro-Greek) cause. However, as feuding between the various leaders of that cause intensified, the situation became awkward. Androutsos quarrelled bitterly with the more Europeanized Greeks who dominated the provisional government which had been established in Nauplion. This prompted him to open negotiations in 1825 with the pro-Ottoman chieftain, Omer Bey of Euboea. He proposed that he should shift base to Thebes and then retake Athens, but this time in the name of Ottoman power. Omer Bey was clearly attracted to the proposal, but it was regarded with suspicion by the sultan: the idea of contracting out the recapture of Athens to a semi-independent chieftain seemed humiliating. But the sultan's governor for central Greece, Reshid Mehmed Pasha, was authorized to consider the proposal further. By the end of March 1825 Resid had cautiously agreed to the plan, and its effects were rapidly felt, as communities to the west and north of Athens began declaring loyalty to the Ottomans. But the Greek revolutionaries (or at least the faction which had broken with Androutsos) made a counter-attack from Athens and the Peloponnese; they clashed with those of Androutsos and Omer Bey in nearly forty days of heavy fighting. Seeing that reinforcements promised by the Ottomans were nowhere in sight, Androutsos tried retreating to Megara, but he was captured and brought back to Athens and imprisoned in the Frankish Tower, looming over the entrance to the Acropolis. He was then brutally killed.

On the Greek side, and in Greece to this day, there have always been plenty of people who insist that he was not a traitor: on the contrary, they affirm, he was just a man of the people who fell foul of the more conservative forces in the Greek coalition, including Peloponnesian landowners, and families who had attained wealth and power in Istanbul. It was these grandees who falsely accused him, so his supporters have always said. In 1967 his body was reburied in the port of Preveza by General Thrasyvoulos Tsakolotos, who had commanded the pro-government forces in the 1946–9 civil war. To this day, church services are held in his memory at which local Greek bureaucrats and clerics sing his praises and deplore the cruel way in which, according to admirers, he was killed. It is alleged that after trying over several days to torture him into confessing his guilt, his enemies strangled him in his cell. They then tied a cord round his body and threw it down onto what remained of the ancient temple of Athena (on the right-hand side of the Acropolis entrance) to create the impression that he had tried escaping when the rope broke. Whatever the truth, Androutsos, like his father-figure Ali Pasha, is deeply revered in his homeland on the north-western edge of Greece, a territory where distinctions between Greek and Albanian, Christian and Muslim, grew fuzzy at times but the image of a brave warrior was always sharply defined.

There is one more event in the battle for the Acropolis which stands out in the Greek collective memory. This one concerns not a brutally botched evacuation, nor an internecine killing – but a song, sung in the middle of a desperate battle which was tilting towards defeat.

The death of Androutsos left two main commanders in charge of the citadel. One was Ioannis Gouras, who was one of the adversaries of Androutsos and played a key part in his despatch. The other was Ioannis Makriyannis, a man who for the Greeks epitomizes the pluck, wisdom and unlikely verbal gifts of a fighter with minimal formal education. Paradoxically, this rough-hewn figure is especially admired among the Hellenic intellectuals, although he was no intellectual himself. He was born in modest circumstances near Doris in central Greece, the district from which the Spartans and other Doric Greeks claimed to originate. As a young man he prospered in trade and was drawn into the secret deliberations of the Friendly Society, at least until he was imprisoned for six months by the Ottomans. What marks him out is that after most of the fighting was over, he taught himself to read and write and penned a set of memoirs in untutored and colloquial but lively Greek which have been hailed as a literary masterpiece. One of the most poignant sections of those memoirs describes a scene in which he and his fellow commander, Gouras, facing an intensifying Turkish assault on the Acropolis, put aside their quarrels and are reconciled, an event which called for a makeshift celebration.

> Then Gouras sat down, and the others, and we ate bread; we sang and made merry. Gouras and Papacostas urged me to sing because we had not sung anything for a long while – it was a long time since the selfish ones had set us apart in quarrel to achieve their evil ends. Then I sang a song:

> The sun has set
> Son of Greece, it has set –
> And the moon has gone
> And the clear morning-star which follows
> In the wake of the Bear.

These four were talking, in secret talking;
The Sun turns and tells them, turns and laments:
Last night when I set behind a low hill
I heard women's tears and men's lamentation
For the bodies of heroes stretched on the plain
All in a mess of blood
Those hapless ones, for their country they have died.

The indefatigable Gouras sighed and said, 'Brother Makriyannis, may God bring good out of this, you have never sung so movingly before…' I told him: 'It was because we had not sung for such a long time.'… Fighting broke out and there was a lot of shooting. I waited a while and we engaged in battle. Then they came and told me… 'Run, Gouras has been killed in his post. He was shooting at the Turks. At the instant when he fired, they shot him in the brain, and there was never a word out of him.' We carried him on our shoulders and placed him in a cell. His family prepared him and we buried him.

The unselfconscious mixture of war, tragedy and song has reminded many critics of the world of Homer, where heroes quarrel and reconcile dramatically, with mysterious forces involved, and respond in song to the darkest and lightest of moments.

At this point in the saga, as told in Greek lore, a female authority figure makes an appearance: Asimo, the widow of Gouras. She was the daughter of a chieftain who had a feud with Androutsos, and she seems to have played a part in that man's disgrace. Then, after Gouras was killed in September 1826, she took temporary command of his forces and made them swear an oath to honour his memory by fighting to the death. Soon enough a male commander, Nikolaos Kriezotis, arrived to take charge of the Acropolis garrison – and promptly married Asimo. She and her household made their home in the marble splendour of the Erechtheion, but in January 1827, the great temple received a direct hit from a Turkish projectile which damaged the northern entrance and killed the entire family. Although she is often revered as a doughty warrior, those who still sympathize with Androutsos say she might have got her just deserts for encouraging her husband to deal so harshly with his fellow commander.

Makriyannis recounts all these dramatic events, at least in outline, although he seems not to know the names of the great monuments on the citadel he is defending. At one point in the fighting, he admits, he suggested to Gouras that they simply blow themselves up along with 'the temple' – presumably the Parthenon – if that was the only alternative to surrender.

> And when the Turks come on and we cannot stand our ground... we'll go back fighting into the temple... and there we will lay a mine all round and send ourselves and the Turks and the temple into the air... [Otherwise] where shall we live to hide from the shame of the world, you above all, who have told all the foreign travellers and the people of this town that you could fight on in the citadel for two or three years.

Still, admirers of Makriyannis stress that the hoary soldier had a keen intuitive understanding of the ancient Greek heritage, whatever his lack of education. In a famous vignette in his memoirs, he recalls coming across two young soldiers who were preparing to sell a couple of well-preserved ancient sculptures to foreign collectors. He forbad them with words that have become legendary: *Di' afta polemisamen*, we fought for those things.

In the course of 1827, the tide of war in Athens moved in one direction while in the Greek world as a whole, it moved in the very opposite way. The old adage about the Acropolis – that it cannot by seized by storm but it can be taken by attrition – was once again proved right. The Greek defenders could not hold out indefinitely against the steady Turkish bombardments which had killed the Gouras family and also badly injured Makriyannis. Nor were the

Greek efforts to relieve the citadel with forces from elsewhere very effective. By early 1827 an adventuring Irish-born commander, Sir Richard Church, had been placed in charge of the depleted insurgent army. He tried to insist that the revolutionary leaders, Greeks and foreign philhellenes, must bury their multiple differences before he could accept the post. In the vicinity of Athens, however, there persisted a huge and disastrous disagreement between the various commanders as to which tactics to adopt. This culminated in a chaotic march towards Athens across the plain from the port of Phaleron. The 2,500 attackers were intercepted by the Ottoman commander Reshid, who killed 1,500 of them. A month later, the Greek defenders negotiated a peaceful surrender of the citadel and it returned to Ottoman control.

At that moment, the Ottoman cause appeared at least to be faring well in other places. Since 1825 a large swathe of the western Peloponnese had been taken over by Ibrahim Pasha, son of the man who ruled Egypt as a vassal of the sultan. It was anticipated that he might completely expel or enslave the Christian population of southern Greece and replace them with subjects of his own.

Exactly that prospect was preoccupying the foreign ministers of Europe. If they let the situation drift, it looked as though the Ottomans might quash the Greek cause completely. But that no longer seemed like an acceptable or attractive outcome, even to those powers that were initially sceptical about the uprising. On 6 July 1827, Britain, France and Russia signed a treaty calling for the creation of a virtually independent Greek state, albeit retaining some loose relationship with the sultan. The external powers also awarded themselves the right to impose an armistice along these lines. Soon they began using their naval power to confine the Egyptian fleet under Ibrahim to its base in Navarino Bay in the south-western Peloponnese. Then they resolved to enter the bay and demand that the Egyptian take his fleet back to Alexandria. On 20 October, there was a fateful clash. An Egyptian vessel naïvely fired at a ship carrying emissaries who wanted to parley. That was the cue for the allied navies to annihilate the Ottoman fleet, sending perhaps 3,000 sailors and seventy vessels to the bottom of the sea. From that moment, it was a settled matter that there would be an independent Greece; the provisional Greek government, based in Nauplion, would rule in reality as well as theory. What form that new state would take, what its territorial extent would be, was a matter for frantic negotiation. But a new polity had been blasted into existence, just as surely as the NATO allies would use their firepower to bomb Kosovo into political existence in 1999.

Yet in Athens, in contrast with what was happening everywhere else in Greece, Ottoman control of the Acropolis drifted sleepily on, and this situation would not change for another six years. The last of the garrison marched out of the citadel on 31 March 1833 – by which time Greece had a monarch, and plans were afoot to turn the half-ruined and war-weary town of Athens into a capital fit for a king. As George Finlay, an English resident of the town, describes it, the outgoing party included 'little bands of ten and twelve, with dirty ragged clothes, [plus] two richly caparisoned horses, a mule and a man pulling a ram by the horns'.

# 15

# Hellenism and Its Expanding Hub
## 1833–96

*The advent of King Otho in a war-torn city – German-trained architects design a new capital: Schaubert, Kleanthes and their rivals – the cleaning up of the Acropolis monuments – neoclassical architecture and the Periclean fashion – the Pacifico affair and the Anglo-French occupation – the reaction of visitors to the Parthenon, including Florence Nightingale – Otho replaced by George I – the role of diaspora Greeks in endowing Athenian monuments*

One of the most delightful features of modern Athens is the tiny neighbourhood of Anafiotika on the northern slopes of the Acropolis. Here there are cleverly terraced roads, steep, winding lanes and white-washed houses decked out with exuberant bougainvillea. The visitor suddenly feels transported to one of the Cycladic islands.

That feeling is well-founded, because this little settlement was created by people from the islet of Anafi, a minute sliver of land in the mid-Aegean, east of Santorini, whose present population is less than 300. In a modern city full of sharp edges and stark urban landscapes, this spot seems human and cosy. It feels like a place where a community has grown organically, creating a setting where families can live in coolness and modest comfort. Ironically enough it used to be viewed as an undesirable shanty-town, well into the twentieth century. On arriving in 1840, the Cycladic incomers were initially encouraged to settle on flattish ground which today forms

N

BLACK SEA

WESTERN
THRACE

Occupied by and claimed
by Greece, 1914–16

EASTERN
THRACE

Istanbul

MACEDONIA

SEA OF
MARMARA

Thessaloniki

Imbros

EPIRUS

Tenedos

THESSALY

AEGEAN SEA

IONIA

Smyrna/Izmir

IONIAN SEA

Athens

DODECANESE

| 0 | 50 | 100 miles |
|---|---|---|
| 0 | 100 | 200 km |

MEDITERRANEAN SEA

Kingdom of Greece, 1832

Ionian Islands, ceded by United Kingdom, 1863

Conference of Constantinople, 1881

Treaty of Bucharest, 1913, and Florence Protocol, 1914, after the Balkan Wars

Western Thrace, under Bulgaria until 1919

Acquired through the Treaty of Sèvres, 1920,
returned to Turkey through the Treaty of Lausanne, 1923

Dodecanese, ceded by Italy, 1947

**Greek Territorial Changes, 1832–1947**

the mid-point of Akademias Avenue; a decade later, some had the idea of grabbing the space on the slopes of the Acropolis, where African workers had lived in Ottoman times. The move was illegal, but in practice irreversible.

Then consider another, even more familiar landmark of central Athens: the vast, square and relatively featureless pale-yellow structure in the neoclassical style which dominates the city's central plaza, Syntagma or Constitution Square. The building's foundation stone was laid in February 1836 in the presence of King Ludwig of Bavaria, who was financing the construction, and his son, the newly installed King Otho* of Greece, who was destined to occupy this stately pile. Also in attendance were representatives of the three powers which had ushered the new kingdom into existence and kept a close eye on its development: Britain, France and Russia.

By 1843, the palace was ready for Otho and his equally German queen, Amalia, to occupy. It had been constructed with impressive speed, using marble from Mount Pentelikon and wood from Euboea. Yet it could hardly be described as beautiful. A simple triangular pediment and colonnade adorn the otherwise rather monotonous, three-storey façade. It bears an odd resemblance to the palace of Aiges,† the ceremonial headquarters of the fighting kings of Macedonia which would be unearthed nearly 200 years later: both buildings signal power rather than elegance or refinement. The new building stood in utter contrast to the nearby, half-ruined settlement, which had probably dwindled to 4,000 souls at the depths of its wartime doldrums. This brand-new fortress must have seemed in its early days like an entirely alien imposition, what we would now call a flying saucer.

It was designed by Friedrich von Gärtner, one of many Teutons who laid the foundations of the new capital. The fanatically philhellenic King Ludwig tussled with him over how elaborate

---

* The young king, born with the German name Otto, Hellenized it to Othon, usually rendered in English as Otho.
† See Chapter 7.

his son's residence should be. Although Ludwig generally liked to commission showy, elegant buildings in the Greek style, back in Munich, he wanted this particular edifice to be austere and simple. At one point, Ludwig took a red pencil and crossed out Gärtner's suggestions for some fancy external decoration, prompting the architect to cry out, 'That leaves only a barracks, Your Majesty!' As a glance at this big, plain building makes clear, the king largely got his way.

The tiny homes of Anafiotika are practical, pretty and well adapted to their rocky environment. The palace – now Greece's parliament – is surreally gaunt and forbidding. Yet the history of the two places is intimately connected. Anafi was one of several Cycladic islands from which craftsmen willingly migrated to help with the exciting project of providing the new kingdom with a dignified capital. The construction workers of Anafi were particularly adept at erecting walls on hard, unforgiving rock, and this skill was badly needed by foremen working on the palace. The builders also wanted homes for themselves and their families. Although this was not envisaged in any of the grandiose plans that were being formulated for the new city, the islanders simply improvised houses in the only way they knew how.

In many ways, the story of modern Athens oscillates between those two extremes. On the one hand, there are buildings, avenues and squares whose dimensions and designs were decreed from above, often reflecting an interpretation of Hellenism that had developed, or been refined, far from Greece itself. On the other hand, there are little slices of social reality that have flourished in a more natural way, as groups of people from a certain village or island or burned-out war zone decamped en masse. In the process of moving, these groups brought their own understanding of communal and private space, an understanding that may have emerged over long years in a rocky island, an Epirote mountainside or a town in the interior of Anatolia.

There is a comic-opera quality about the Greco-German machinations which led to the reshaping of Athens as a capital worthy of a Bavarian-born king. As of 1829, when the last skirmish of the independence war took place near Thebes, it was by no means clear what form the future Greek state would take, how extensive its territory would be, or where its capital would be located. The administration of the embryonic state was at that time firmly established amid the elegant Venetian architecture of Nauplion, with Ioannis Kapodistrias, a Corfiot who had briefly served the tsar as foreign minister, as Greece's first president. Skilled diplomat though he was, he was unable to establish his authority over the unruly coalition of forces which had waged the revolutionary war, from enterprising shipowners to clan leaders in the Peloponnese who had never paid dues to the Ottomans and did not intend to start paying taxes now. He took the risky step of jailing the Peloponnesian chieftain Petrobey Mavromichalis. On 9 October 1831, as he was about to enter a church, he was assassinated by Petrobey's son and brother. The rickety Greek polity was soon collapsing into civil war. One of the killers was lynched and the other tried and executed. Some saw Kapodistrias as a martyr, while others compared the assassins with the two tyrant-slayers of ancient Athens, Harmodios and Aristogeiton.

In early 1832, the British, French and Russians settled on a new formula for governing Greece: they would offer the throne to Otho, the second son of Bavaria's King Ludwig, who would be represented by a trio of emissaries from Munich until he reached the age of twenty-one in 1835. Paradoxically enough, this was more acceptable to the various Greek factions that any local ruler could have been. The glamour of a sovereign who was connected with the other crowned heads of Europe seemed to augur well for the new state, and for its ambitions to grow larger. All the various contenders for influence over the new polity, whether inside or outside its borders, began considering how they could win the ear of the young monarch.

Even then, it was not an immediately settled matter where the new capital would be. Plenty of people thought the handsome, historic port of Nauplion would serve better than the war-battered alleys of Athens. In Nauplion, there was, confusingly enough, a newspaper with the name of *Athina*; but the name referred to the goddess, not the town – of which the paper took a thoroughly sceptical view. It declared: 'Those who would like to see the capital in Athens want... to give us, instead of a wealthy, splendid and commercial capital [like Nauplion] the worthless and barren Attica, which all the Greek world, educated by long revolution and not by archaeological phantoms, rejects unanimously.' But it was soon clear that influential people thought otherwise, including the kingdom's foreign protectors and the leading figures in Rumeli, the region north of the Gulf of Corinth. They all preferred Athens, and their view prevailed.

The new monarch of Greece made a series of theatrical appearances. The first was in February 1833, when he sailed into Nauplion, escorted by more than seventy ships from various nations, all bedecked with flags and firing endless celebratory shots. Accompanied by the three Bavarian regents, the smartly uniformed seventeen-year-old rode at the head of a procession into his provisional capital while the leaders of Greece's various factions received him with awe and unaccustomed unanimity. By this stage, plans to refashion Athens were already underway and the design had been entrusted to a couple of German-trained architects. Over the following months the king began the process of shifting his headquarters. In May, he visited Athens by land; in September he sailed into Piraeus, to be greeted by prominent Athenians who were apparently determined to invoke the ancient city's protecting deities. Recalling Athena, one gave Otho an large owl; another presented him with an olive branch; and a third made a speech, expressing confidence that 'through you... our struggles will be crowned, now that Athena along with Demeter and Hermes have returned our city'. The king then travelled to Hadrian's Arch, where a laurel wreath proclaimed that 'Athens, once the city of Theseus and Hadrian, is now the city of Otho'. In December,

Otho took up residence in Athens. The occasion was marked with a Christian service at the ancient temple which was then known as Saint George's but would soon revert to being a classical monument, the one now called the Hephaisteion. Right from the start of the kingdom's existence, there was confusion, sometimes deliberate confusion, between the newer religion and the older one.

Another recurring feature of Athenian history is that people who made their mark on the city, whether as actors or influential observers, often came in pairs. The latest duo were architects who had met while studying in Berlin under a great Hellenist professor. One, Stamatis Kleanthes, was from northern Greece but had been educated in Bucharest and Leipzig before moving to the Prussian capital. That was where he became friendly with a fellow student, Eduard Schaubert, who was from Breslau (Wrocław in present-day Poland). Together, the young men decided to make an impression on the Mediterranean, bringing southwards again the grand Greek styles which had become so fashionable in northern Europe. In May 1832, before the formal decision to transfer the administration to Athens had been taken, they secured a commission to lay out a vision of the Athenian future which would be 'equal to the fame and the brilliance of the city and worthy of the century in which we live'. By the end of the year, it had been formally accepted and endorsed by royal decree. The plan was based on the assumption that a town of 6,000 people, where most houses lacked roofs, would grow rapidly to 35,000 or 40,000 and would need scope to expand further. This was right: by 1900 the population had exceeded 100,000.

Within a couple of years, the plan had been discarded and a much more senior Bavarian architect, Leo von Klenze, was asked to remake it. But in certain essential features, the design dreamed up by the two friends for a city of broad converging avenues was retained and put into practice, and its outlines can still be discerned. As Kleanthes and Schaubert imagined things, much of the existing small town on the north side of the Acropolis would be pulled down and turned over to archaeological work. Immediately to the north of that, there would be a simple grid of wide boulevards, forming an isosceles triangle culminating in the space that we now call Omonia (Harmony or Unanimity) Square. Running due south from Omonia would be an arrow-straight road leading to the Acropolis: that is today's Athinas Avenue, now a long, scruffy road whose lower end features a lively food market.

The plan also called for an avenue running south-west from Omonia Square to the sea; then as now, that road was known as Pireos. Today it is a fast-moving and mostly rather grimy highway, where a new branch of the Benaki Museum helps a little to relieve the harshness. Running south-east of Omonia, the plan provided for another broad boulevard, heading towards the remains of the ancient stadium. Today, Stadiou is one of three wide avenues which run in parallel between areas defined by the city's two central squares, Syntagma and Omonia.

In the imagination of Kleanthes and Schaubert, cultural life – in the form of a library and cathedral – would flourish on the eastern side of Athinas, and political life and administration on the western side. A central feature of their vision, but one that was firmly rejected, called for a palace surrounded by stately gardens to be constructed in and beyond Omonia Square. Today's Omonia, a place where migrants hang out, shady transactions are negotiated and low-budget tourists are accommodated, is lively but far from stately.

The triangular grid is the most enduring legacy of the young architects and their ambitious plan. Its other parts ran into objections because they called for widespread demolition of existing structures whose owners would have to be compensated. In summer 1834, King Ludwig arrived and entrusted further work on the redesign of Athens to his adviser, von Klenze, a man who was also responsible for creating some astonishing neoclassical structures in Munich – such as the Monopteros, a small circular imitation of an Ionic temple, set amid the rolling lawns of the English Garden.

(Indeed his work invites the question: does the *flamboyant* mimicry of ancient Greece sometimes work better in northern Europe than in Greece itself?)

Von Klenze scaled down the younger architects' plan, but in one respect he too was overruled. It was his idea to put the palace on the site of the (then unexcavated) Kerameikos cemetery. If that plan had been adopted, some important archaeological finds would never have been made, but the royal residence would have had a fine view of the sea. Yet another, even bolder proposal was floated by Karl Friedrich Schinkel, the professor in Berlin who had mentored Kleanthes and Schaubert: to build a palace on the Acropolis, adjacent to the Parthenon.

In the end, the palace was located on the low hill, right in the centre of things, just a few minutes' walk from the existing settlement. In favouring that proposal, while also giving his son's residence a somewhat fortress-like appearance, Ludwig may have had political calculations in mind. The new king needed to be close to his people, but also able to protect himself from them if necessary.

That consideration was far from hypothetical. In autumn 1843, the German-trained but Greek-officered army rose up in polite but firm opposition to their sovereign: cavalry and infantry marched to the palace and chanted their demand for a constitution. They were happy for the young Bavarian to remain as monarch, but he should be a constitutional one. Otho had no choice but to agree, but he did so willingly enough. Strikingly it was not idealism that catalyzed this political change, but rather a crisis in the kingdom's financial relations with its foreign supporters: the sort of crisis that would be a recurring feature of the new Greek state, including in the early twenty-first century. The European powers had endowed Greece with a loan of 60,000 francs, and the kingdom kept having to take out new loans to service the debt. In 1843, with the international scene darkening, the powers adopted a tougher policy. They forced Otho to adopt harsh austerity measures, and rejected the king's initial offer as not stringent enough. The king finally had to accept some quite demeaning terms and as a result lost some legitimacy at home. Something quite similar unfolded during the economic crisis that hit Athens in 2009, with one Greek leader after another forfeiting all credibility because of the tough dictates of the country's creditors.

Back in the 1840s, the idea of forging a coherent state and a functioning capital out of a handful of grandiose buildings, adjoining a small hardscrabble town, must have seemed wildly ambitious, but also strangely exciting. Indeed, for some of the kingdom's founders, remaking Athens as a suitably dignified capital was only a stepping stone in an even more ambitious endeavour. They felt that Athens, however well-endowed with suitably imposing Greco-German architecture, could serve at best as a temporary headquarters for Hellenism. The aim of the Greek state must be to gather in all the scattered children of Hellenism, and the only fitting headquarters for this neo-Byzantine realm was Constantinople. Ioannis Kolettis, who was prime minister until 1847, was a strong advocate of this view.

But for some visitors to the emerging city, the mere idea of making Athens into a decent, well-functioning metropolis of modest dimensions clearly seemed pretty fanciful. One sceptic was the great English satirist William Thackeray, who passed through Athens in 1844 and complained bitterly of the dust and bedbugs.

> The shabbiness of the place actually beats Ireland, and that is a strong word. The palace of the Basileus (king) is an enormous edifice of plaster, in a square containing six houses, three donkeys, no roads, no fountains... The king goes out to drive (revolutions permitting) at five... the two dozen soldiers who have been presenting arms slouch off to their quarters: the vast barrack of a palace remains entirely white, ghastly and lonely: and save the braying of a donkey (which long-eared minstrels are more active and sonorous in Athens than in any place I know), all is entirely silent round the Basileus' palace.

As he compares this strutting pomp and ceremony with the street life of ordinary Athenians, Thackeray's pen grows ever sharper. The town, he says, is

> ... little better than a rickety agglomeration of larger and smaller huts, tricked out here and there with the most absurd cracked ornaments, and cheap attempts at elegance... Athens may be about as wealthy a place as Carlow or Killarney – the streets swarm with idle crowds, the innumerable little lanes flow over with dirty little children, they are playing and paddling about in the dirt everywhere, with great big eyes, yellow faces and the queerest little gowns and skull-caps.

Eloquent as they are, these caustic comparisons between palace and people fail to take account of something else that was going on in Athens: an activity that was thrilling for all those involved, and would palpably affect the emerging city's whole atmosphere. That was the transformation of the Acropolis (and in due course other ancient sites) into a standing exhibition whose purpose was not to enforce a regime but simply to showcase, for the benefit of all, the glories of ancient Athens at their zenith.

It was a Bavarian officer, Christopher Neezer, who took the surrender of the Ottoman garrison in 1833. He left a startling account of the Rock's condition:

> I entered the Acropolis and saw heaps of tumbled marbles. In the midst of the chaotic mass of column capitals, fragments of columns, marbles large and small, were bullets, cannon balls and human skulls and bones, many of which were near the slender Caryatids of the Erechtheion.

The team went to work on the Acropolis was mostly Teutonic – German or Danish – but they included one passionate Hellene, Kyriakos Pittakis, a war veteran who although deficient in formal training would be remembered by posterity as the first modern Greek archaeologist.

They were cleansing the site in several different senses: not just removing the detritus of war, but taking away everything that detracted from the monument's old-and-new role, which was the one defined by Pericles. In other words, celebrating a city which must serve as an 'education' to the city-states of Greece, and demonstrate the achievements of one generation to its countless successors. It followed that virtually all vestiges of the Byzantine, Frankish and Ottoman periods in the city's life must be taken away. The Frankish Tower, which loomed over the entrance, was one of the last things to go: it was knocked down in 1874.

Mending the beautiful Ionic asymmetry of the Erechtheion was among the top priorities. Of the six female figures which held up the South Porch, one – known as Maiden 3 – had been taken away by Elgin, while its neighbour, Maiden 4, had been knocked out during bombardment; this had caused most of the porch to collapse, and it was duly shored up in a somewhat makeshift way. In what must have been an exhilarating rediscovery, Pittakis identified the head and body of Maiden 4 and was able to reunite them. He also discovered sections of another figure, Maiden 6, disproving the theory that she had been hauled off to Rome in the time of Augustus or Hadrian. Meanwhile most of the Erechtheion's North Porch had caved in as a result of the shelling which killed the family of Gouras, the commander, in 1827. There too some ingenious propping up had to be done.

In a bold but perfectly legitimate piece of recreation, German and Danish archaeologists disinterred and put together the constituent parts of the temple of Athena Nike, built optimistically by the ancient Athenians in the midst of the Peloponnesian War. This exquisite little edifice had been largely destroyed by the Ottomans during the war of 1687 as part of their frantic effort to fortify the Rock against the Venetians. All in all, the Acropolis works were a mixture of enthusiastic rebuilding and ruthless stripping away.

It was von Klenze, the man who had colourfully Hellenized parts of Munich, who expressed the new governing principle: all features of the citadel which have no 'archaeological, structural or artistic interest' must be taken away. His royal master, Otho, laid this down with even greater emphasis: 'All of the vestiges of barbarism must be eradicated from the Acropolis and from all of Greece and the remains of the glorious past shall shine forth with a new splendour as a firm base for a glorious present and a glorious future.'

There was no doubt which glorious past he had in mind: it was the fifth century BCE. That principle was applied systematically to the Acropolis, and somewhat more mildly to the town as a whole. Dozens of small Byzantine and Ottoman-era churches and shrines (many of them already in poor condition) were torn down, but some important ones were spared: for example the beautiful little Kapnikarea, standing in the middle of Ermou (Hermes) Street. This Byzantine gem, dating from the eleventh century, faced demolition under von Klenze's plan but was saved at the intervention of King Ludwig. (It had another narrow escape from removal in 1863, and it was only preserved thanks to strong protests from worshippers.)

The small mosque in the interior of the Parthenon, erected by the Ottomans after the catastrophe of 1687, was removed in the 1840s; it appears in a daguerrotype image of 1839 (one of the oldest photographs of any monument) but not in later images. Of the seven mosques in the lower town, just two survived, and are now used as exhibition space; another (the *Küçük Camii* or Small Mosque) lasted until the 1920s and its foundations are still visible, near the Roman Agora.

King Otho's manifesto, read carefully, is much more than a nostalgic or self-indulgent look backwards. It was in equal measure a call to glories yet to come. This vision was common to all those involved in the founding of the Greek kingdom, be they Greeks, Teutons or from anywhere else. The idea was roughly this: once the golden age of the fifth century BCE was exposed in all its glory, the latest cohort of Athenians could be expected to leap forward into a similarly brilliant and exciting future.

This was not, of course, the only time in history that the heritage of the Periclean age had been revived for some newfangled purpose. Emperor Hadrian had built on that legacy, in several senses, as a way of forging a pro-Roman but culturally Greek commonwealth with Athens at its centre. Choniates, the Byzantine bishop, had showcased the Parthenon as a way of proving his argument that ancient Greek excellence and the new revelation of monotheism could literally inhabit the same space and somehow lend each other strength. The more imaginative of the Ottoman chroniclers of Athens had suggested something similar as they tried to fuse Greek glory with Islamic history.

But the early masters of the modern Greek state were more single-minded in juxtaposing the very old with the very new, and allowing almost nothing in-between. The legacy of that curious juxtaposition is still palpable in contemporary Athens. The clearance, excavation and reconstruction on the Acropolis went hand in hand with the construction of fresh neoclassical buildings in other parts of Athens, a short walk away. Perhaps there is another way to describe this process. The transmission of ancient Greek style, already such a powerful trend in Europe, took a new twist, and in comparison with what had gone before, it was surely a turn for the better. Instead of taking things or ideas from Athens to promote Hellenism elsewhere, the new impulse was to re-Hellenize Athens. In the recent past, antiquarians from northern Europe had prowled over the Acropolis, looking for things they could extract, whether it be designs, casts, measurements or actual objects. Now the insights and inspirations gained by working on the Acropolis were being reapplied, successfully or otherwise, in the immediate vicinity as the new city of Athens took shape.

The roster of artists and archaeologists who laboured on the Rock overlaps heavily with the list of designers of modern Athens. For example, the team which worked on reconstructing the Athena Nike temple included Schaubert, the Prussian who had co-conceived the new city, and Christian Hansen, one of two Danish brothers who endowed the reborn city with some magnificent neoclassical buildings. Three of those buildings can be seen amid the traffic fumes and melting tarmac on the avenue known as Panepistimiou (University) Street, one of the arteries that connect the city's two main squares. If they look a bit uncomfortable now, they must have appeared quite extraordinary when they arose out of the debris of newly independent Athens. The University of Athens, designed by Christian Hansen, features a long colonnade and murals, perhaps giving a hint of what the coloured Stoa of the ancient Agora might have looked like. On closer inspection, the murals are a romanticized depiction of King Otho reviving the arts and sciences of Greece, executed by a German artist, Karl Rahl.

The formal foundation of a university, in 1836, was one of the first acts of the Greek kingdom. There were faculties of medicine, law, theology and 'general sciences' ranging from philosophy to mathematics. After functioning for a few years in a mansion in the Plaka which was also the workplace of Schaubert and Kleanthes, it moved into its imposing neoclassical setting in 1841, and the building received many further adornments in the course of the century. Next to it stands the Academy of Athens, with a perfectly executed Ionian façade, plus a pediment inspired by the Parthenon. Statues of Apollo and Athena stand on high pedestals, towering over seated likenesses of Plato and Aristotle. The Academy was designed in 1859 by Christian's brother Theophil, who also (two decades later) conceived the adjacent National Library of Greece, featuring Doric columns a bit like the Parthenon, with symmetrical sets of marble steps making an elegant entrance. These three buildings are a superb technical achievement, which relieves an otherwise harsh vista. Yet they seem bunched too close together and uncomfortably located in the middle of the swirling traffic. Ideally, any such building should stand alone with an appropriately graceful approach. Perhaps the Athenian Agora in the Roman era, brimful of perfect imitations of an architecture which had flourished 500 years earlier, appeared similarly crowded.

The kingdom of Greece was exciting, volatile and inherently unstable, and all these aspects were palpable in the capital. Objectively, this was a poor, underdeveloped state. In geopolitical terms it was reliant on its British, French and Russian creators, while the aesthetics of its capital owed much to Teutonic sensibilities. Every so often something would happen which brought home those realities in a painful way. Yet the kingdom and its governors, whatever their origin, were possessed from the beginning with a strong will to survive and thrive, and a keen appetite for territorial expansion. The country's actual state was perpetually at odds with its dreams, and to cynics, it often seemed as though dreams were being offered as a substitute for improvements to the actual state of affairs. Only the more prudent members of the Greek political class seemed to grasp the need to mend the existing situation before any aggrandizement could be contemplated. In the later nineteenth century, the main fault line in Greek public debates would reflect exactly that dilemma.

On the Athenian spectrum, a model of circumspection was provided by Charilaos Trikoupis, remembered as one of the kingdom's most competent prime ministers, serving intermittently between 1875 and 1895. His most memorable public statement was the grave news, delivered to parliament in 1893, that the country had become insolvent – mainly thanks to a crash in the price of its chief export, currants. Viewed as a whole, his leadership was marked by pragmatic improvements to the kingdom's infrastructure, in the form of railways, ports, roads and canals. His rival, Theodoros Deliyannis, tried to excite the electorate with hopes of successful military adventures. Moreover, even for Trikoupis, consolidating the kingdom's economy was a sensible prerequisite to further expansion, not a promise of eternal restraint. In the background of all their debates was an almost unspoken calculus that everybody understood. A leader who added substantially to the national territory would be forgiven by the electorate and by future Greek governments for any other actions, however misguided.

Moreover, as Athenian decision-makers and voters toyed with these dreams, they took it for granted that Hellenism, the greatness of Greek style and thought, would act as a vital energizing force: not just an aesthetic delight or an inspiration to the soul, but an engine of expansion. After all, Hellenism had so often been used as a source of power, whether in Alexander the Great's time or in the Roman era or the Byzantine empire. More recently, many European countries had transformed Hellenic refinement into an instrument of their own greatness. They had used Greek architecture, Greek ways of thinking, Greek literature as devices to enhance their own prestige. For the grandees of London or Paris who had encouraged young artists to seek out the artefacts of ancient Greece, draw them with greatest possible precision, copy them in their homeland or simply remove them from Greece, there was a common, underlying assumption. Adopting the Greek style was not merely a matter of producing aesthetically pleasing objects or pondering subtle philosophical concepts. It was also an affirmation of might. It said: 'I am powerful, and therefore it behoves me to adopt these cultural forms' – and moreover, 'the mere fact of adopting these forms will make me more powerful'.

Given all that, it was hardly surprising that the overlords of the young Greek kingdom invested in Hellenism – classical Hellenism – with a certain purist zeal. Apart from reproducing ancient architectural styles, the new educational institutions of Athens served to inculcate the ideology of the new state. Students arrived from all corners of the Greek and semi-Greek world to be drilled in the neo-Hellenic national ideal. The medium of instruction was a linguistic construct that was midway in complexity between ordinary demotic Greek and the highly inflected tongue of the ancients. The name of the language was *katharevouza*, which literally means 'purifying'. Just as unwanted excrescences were removed from the Acropolis, shameful loanwords from Turkish or other languages were squeezed out of speech and writing – at least in formal contexts.

By half cleansing both the language and the urban landscape of all but ancient influences, the guardians of the kingdom clearly hoped to increase the role of Athens as a pole of attraction for the wider Hellenic world. But that was still a formidable task. At the moment of its creation, Greece had around 800,000 inhabitants, no more than a quarter of the total number of people across Europe and the Ottoman empire who identified as Greek by virtue of language, religion or both. Those numbers were both a challenge and a stimulus.

Byron had conceived the outrageous thought of Greece being free: in other words, the enterprise of Hellenism would be taken over and directed by people who were proud to call themselves Greek, rather than by those who hoped simply to gain something from Hellenism. For the governors of the new Greek state, it seemed self-evident that they were destined to be not merely free but increasingly powerful. They loved to accuse one another of being lackeys of foreign interests, but that very accusation carried the implication that it was possible and morally right for a free Greece to be something different.

The very fact that Greece had a multiplicity of masters at least created a lively degree of uncertainty, and gave its rulers some room to manoeuvre. The kingdom's three protectors were the spiritual hegemon, Russia, which aspired to protect the interests of all Orthodox Christians; France, which hoped to be the new nation's most important cultural and commercial partner; and Britain, the world's most important centre of maritime power and finance. Russia was often at loggerheads with the Ottoman empire, and this gave heart to people in Greece who wanted to expand their state at the expense of the Turks. Britain and France were generally aligned with the Ottomans, and therefore wanted Greece to show restraint. This created a perpetual dilemma: should Greece encourage the irregular fighters who were challenging Ottoman rule in places to its north – the fertile fields of Thessaly – or to its south, notably the island of Crete? King Otho soon found that territorial opportunism was a way to shore up his legitimacy and prove that a Hellenic heart was beating under his Bavarian exterior.

For religious reasons, the sympathies of many Greeks were with Russia. But with its strategically vital harbours and coasts, Greece would always come under pressure to side with the leading naval power in the Mediterranean. Through the nineteenth century and until the Second World War, that was Britain; thereafter it was the United States. In several different ways, people in Athens would feel the impact of British naval power during the first couple of decades of the kingdom's existence. One episode began at Easter-time in 1847. It was triggered by one of the darkest features of popular Christian culture in Europe, the habit of using the Paschal celebrations as an occasion for anti-Semitic demonstrations. At its most subtle, Christian theology urges worshippers to see humanity as a whole as responsible for the Saviour's execution; at its crudest, Christian folk tradition encourages believers to focus their ire either on the Jews in general or on one Jewish individual, notably Judas Iscariot. To this day, Judas bonfires are a feature of Easter celebrations in Crete.

However, on this occasion the Judas-burning custom was banned in Athens in deference to the feelings of one of the Rothschild family who was staying in the city. A group gathered at the spot where the bonfire usually took place and looked for some other target for their collective passion: they settled on the home of David Pacifico, a Jewish merchant who had served as consul for Portugal but was a British citizen. He lived in a relatively grand residence which had once housed one of the Bavarian regents.

Pacifico complained afterwards that a mob of three to four hundred people had surrounded his house, battered down the door with stones, wrecked the furniture, stolen money, jewellery, ornaments and linen and abused his wife and children. The incident led to angry exchanges between British officials and the Greek government, and it quickly became entangled in other Greco-British disputes. Lord Palmerston, the Liberal foreign secretary, felt that Greece's leaders, in league with diplomats from other countries, were dragging their feet over the issue because they resented Britain's role as an advocate of constitutional reform in Greece. In modern terms, Palmerston believed in correcting and reforming the behaviour of small countries, up to and including regime change.

In February 1848 Pacifico demanded compensation amounting to just over £30,000. A few weeks later he reported that violent intruders had broken into his house a second time, and that one of them was the prime minister's son. By November 1849, Palmerston had decided that the might of the Royal Navy was the only way to make Greece comply. The commander of the British fleet in the Mediterranean was instructed to sail towards Athens, and Her Majesty's envoy to Greece was told to press his demand, courteously at first, but if necessary by seizing the tiny navy of Greece 'if that can be done handily' and sealing up harbours. His tactics were soon criticized as heavy-handed by political opponents in London as well as by other European powers. The Greek foreign minister asked the French and Russians to help by arbitrating in the dispute, and those countries immediately urged Greece to reject Britain's maximum demands.

By January, the Royal Navy had seized Otho's own ship, plus a schooner and several gunboats, and blockaded the main harbours of Greece. This prompted diplomats from France, Russia and five other countries to protest over British interference with commercial shipping. Lord Palmerston was excoriated in the British parliament for upsetting important European powers. The facts of the case were obscured by a widespread feeling of antipathy to the foreign secretary's bombastic style. Benjamin Disraeli, for the Tories, denounced Palmerston for having deployed the navy in all its might to support the 'somewhat ludicrous and suspicious claims' of Pacifico. In the end, Pacifico did receive compensation but it was well short of his original demand. Palmerston managed to win a vote of confidence in the House of Commons, with the most famous speech of his career, recalling that Saint Paul had asserted his rights (to a fair trial) by declaring that he was a Roman citizen; the entitlements of a British citizen, he insisted, should be no less inalienable.

Back in Athens, Otho gained some popularity thanks to the perception that he was standing up to British bullying. However, a couple of years later, Athens experienced a second show of military and naval power, this time by France and Britain acting together. The Crimean War, the bloodiest inter-European clash of the mid-nineteenth century, broke out in 1853. Its background was Russia's ambition to trim the Ottoman empire, and perhaps even raise the Christian cross over Constantinople, plus the determination of London and Paris to shore up the sultan-caliph. The immediate spark was a Franco-Russian squabble over physical control of Bethlehem, birthplace of the prince of peace. Sentiment in Greece, from the king downwards, was intensely and opportunistically pro-Russian, and there was keener than ever appetite for probing raids on Ottoman territory. London and Paris insisted that Greece remain neutral and hold off from sending fighters into Ottoman lands; King Otho resisted these demands. A Franco-British naval force not only blockaded Piraeus but occupied the entire port. It remained there from 1854 to 1857, staying a full year after the Crimean War ended, in part in order to enforce a new settlement of Greece's debt.

As occupations go, this was a relatively genteel one. Relations between the ceremonial, political and military leaders of Greece and the Anglo-French forces seem to have remained fairly cordial. One bizarre consequence was a scene that was depicted in a sketch in the *Illustrated London News*: officers of the Greek, British and French forces, along with Athenian grandees, were invited to a banquet inside the Parthenon, lasting from 2 p.m. till dusk. The Athenian press gave a mixed reaction. One of the sharpest comments came from a newspaper called *Aion*:

> Was it necessary for so-called Greeks to feast in a place which [even] the Turks respected, making into a place of worship for their God and building a mosque inside it? What idea will the English and French officers have of us when they see us Greeks, feasting alongside them, in the very place that they robbed of its adornments, which they now keep in their own cities…?

For patriotically minded Athenians, this must indeed have been a bitter pill to swallow, not least because the Acropolis had only twenty years previously become accessible to the town's Greek Orthodox people for the first time since 1200. This had intensified popular attachment to the monuments, and popular indignation over their despoliation. But the dinner only lasted a single afternoon, and as the announcement hastened to assure local people, the Acropolis would be free to visitors as soon as dusk fell. The great majority of the foreigners who toured the citadel around that time came not in uniform but in peace, and they were almost invariably exhilarated by what they saw.

Something of the thrill and the poignancy of a visit to the newly cleansed Acropolis in the mid-nineteenth century is conveyed by Aubrey de Vere, an Anglo-Irish critic and writer who toured Greece and left some revealing descriptions. He is entranced by the Parthenon and, while deploring Elgin's actions, finds that just enough is left of the pediments and frieze to trigger a meditation on Athena, a figure whose 'virgin estate, serene valour resisting all aggression… her sacred and practical wisdom, we trace in the mythic idea a faint approximation to one yet more exalted, that of the Christian Church as contemplated in the mind of early Christendom'.

But he feels the damage done by Elgin is more palpable in the Erechtheion, not only for antiquarians but for the ordinary Athenians to whom he has spoken:

The loss of this caryatid, when Lord Elgin carried it off, occasioned more disturbance of the heart at Athens than the removal of the frieze of the Parthenon... The strength of their feeling is attested by a belief which prevails to this day among the people, a belief that on the night of her second captivity her five remaining sisters were heard to lament with loud sobbings her fate and their own loss. All night long, as the story goes, the voice of lamentation was echoed among the pillars and wafted eastward over the sea; nor was it till the next morning that the sacred breasts of the mourners were revisited by their ancient peace... and the beams of the rising sun dried the tears on their stony faces.

There was another Anglophone visitor to Athens who was similarly fascinated by the Acropolis. Like de Vere she wrestled with its spiritual message and wondered how, if at all, it could be reconciled with monotheism. That visitor was also intensely concerned with the Pacifico affair, although chiefly famous for humanitarian work during the Crimean War. Her name is Florence Nightingale, the pioneer of modern nursing.

With her powerful, restless mind and an advanced classical education of a sort that was not granted to many women of her generation, Nightingale had pronounced views on spirituality, ancient civilization and modern politics. In common with Byron, she was entranced by the Attic landscape and tried to understand how it had fostered such a supremely refined civilization. In contrast with Byron, she had little time for the modern Greeks or for the modern town. She was a passionate liberal imperialist, and – unlike many of her compatriots – strongly admired Palmerston for using the British navy to press for the righteous cause of Pacifico's compensation. In fact she was dining next to Edward Wyse, the British envoy to Athens, on a naval ship on 27 April 1850 when news came that the Greek government had agreed to the latest set of British proposals. She despised the French and Russians for encouraging Greece to resist London's demands. 'The unmannerly threatenings of Russia have fallen as harmlessly as her snows, and [the] polished arrows of French chicanery have only glanced from the shield of truth and steadfastness,' she gloated. Nightingale also had harsh words for *The Times* of London, which in a spirit of anti-Palmerston venom, had claimed that Pacifico's house had never been as grand as he claimed, and that London's demands on his behalf were excessive.

More striking still are the spiritual and philosophical reflections which her trip to Athens conjured up. A landmark in her life was the rescue (from some urchins who were playing with it) of a baby Athenian owl, a little personification of Athena's wisdom; she brought the creature back to England and had it stuffed when it expired. Visiting the Areopagus, she was reminded not only of its Christian associations (as the site of Saint Paul's sermon) but of the mound's ancient status as the home of the Eumenides – or furies – who punished evildoers, creatures mentioned by Aeschylus, whose tragedies she rated higher than Shakespeare.

Her visit to Greece came shortly after a tour of Egypt where, at the archaeological site of Luxor, she had a powerful spiritual experience. She had the sense that the religion of ancient Egypt was, despite appearances, fundamentally monotheist, and she believed that it had eventually infiltrated Greece via Pythagoras and Plato. In other words, she felt there were two religious traditions in classical Greece: the world of the twelve Olympian deities, and the worship of one God which was intuited long before Paul preached Christianity. All these reflections were stimulated by her wanderings around the Acropolis and its surroundings.

Her own religious practice was an idiosyncratic Anglicanism. She admired the Greek bishop who had led the uprising against the Turks in 1821 but otherwise had little time for Greek Orthodoxy, calling it a dead religion. In her almost Unitarian faith, there was little understanding of elaborate rituals or sacraments. But she had a strong gut feeling for the mystical, and this was fuelled by the experience of wandering over the Acropolis, especially at night. It was 'impossible that earth or heaven could produce anything more beautiful', she wrote after seeing the Parthenon lit up by the moon.

Forty years earlier, when Byron and Hobhouse ascended the Rock they had to bribe the *disdar* and then use their imagination to get a sense of the Parthenon, half-hidden by a cluster of tumbledown houses. Stripping the citadel down to its Periclean essentials, as the German, Danish and Greek archaeologists had so enthusiastically done, was in violation of everything we would now regard as archaeological ethics, but the net result would have an electrifying and unpredictable effect on all manner of people.

In the political and military annals of Greece, the story of the nineteenth century is punctuated by the replacement of King Otho by another monarch. The fifty-year reign of King George I began in 1863 and ended with his assassination. Like Otho, he was an outsider chosen by foreign powers, a teenager at the time of his accession, and also, despite those handicaps, a leader who proved capable of promoting the Hellenic cause, inside and outside the kingdom, rather vigorously.

Otho had gained some popularity in the eyes of his people by provoking the Ottomans even when he was under strong pressure from Britain and France to exercise restraint. But the defeat of Russia in the Crimean War, and the Anglo-French occupation, showed up the limits of that tactic. In 1859, when war broke out between Austria and Italy, Otho's aptitude for populist foreign policy seemed to fail him. The Greeks sympathized with the Italian cause, while the king favoured his fellow Teutons, and suffered a slump in his popularity. His ability to handle Greece's political class also wavered. The neoclassical university was notorious for turning out underemployed graduates, but it also produced some smart politicians who could no longer be manipulated predictably by the king, or indeed by Greece's foreign protectors. Early in 1862 things came to a head when Otho clashed with his prime minister,

Admiral Constantine Kanaris, who was proposing some sensible reforms: the monarch pretended to agree but quietly made sure they were not implemented. In August, while the king and queen were on tour, the middle-ranking officers rose up against him and prevented the royal couple from landing in Piraeus. The protecting powers, including Britain, did nothing to challenge Otho's removal, and they set about finding another sovereign for Greece.

They found one in Prince William George, second son of the king of Denmark. This was a second choice: people in Greece would have preferred the British Prince Alfred, Queen Victoria's second son, but he declined the honour. But in Greece and elsewhere, the new monarch was still felt to be a promising figure who might play a more reliable role in diplomatic affairs than his predecessor had done. This impression was confirmed when he received a massive vote of confidence from Britain, with the transfer from British to Greek sovereignty of the Ionian Islands, including Corfu, in 1864. But for those who could read the signals, there were also some indications that under its new master, Greece would maintain and even sharpen its expansionist appetite. Unlike Otho, who after some deliberation was merely styled King of Greece, the new monarch was enthroned as King of the Hellenes – in other words, the sovereign of all self-identified Greeks inside or outside the country. Greeks of the diaspora could count on his protection, and possibly dream of living one day in his expanding realm. This impression of an assertive, extrovert spirit was reinforced in 1864, when a new constitution gave expatriate Greeks the right to parliamentary representation in Athens. As it turned out, King George eventually bequeathed a territory which had doubled in size.

So much for the switch of monarch. Many historians of Athens would argue that a more important change occurred around the middle of the nineteenth century, although it was a gradual process and cannot easily be pinpointed in time. This concerned not the name of the Greek monarch, nor even the intensity of the kingdom's desire to expand, but the willingness of at least certain members of the wealthy and dynamic Greek diaspora to invest in and foster Athens as a centre of Hellenism.

This was by no means a foregone conclusion, given that by many standards, the Greek mercantile class outside the kingdom was faring far better than people in the notional homeland. To some footloose Greeks, Athens was an irrelevant backwater. Under the reforms which the Ottoman empire adopted under pressure from its western friends, Greek and other Christian subjects of the sultan were flourishing commercially and benefiting from an early wave of globalization. The half-Christian port on Turkey's western coast known as Smyrna or Izmir was of far bigger commercial importance than any harbour in Greece; Istanbul was a vastly greater city, whether in population or strategic heft, than the new-old town of Athens.

From the Athenian viewpoint, the important thing was that some wealthy Hellenes from the diaspora were prepared to finance and adorn their city, much as American Jews proudly foster projects in Israel, and the Armenians in California are glad to act as benefactors of projects in Yerevan.

As the century progressed, Greeks of the diaspora played an ever more important role in endowing Athens with magnificent buildings. Even when the architects were Teutonic or Danish, the funding often came from the deep pockets of entrepreneurs who had flourished far from Greece. In several cases, the benefactors' own origins were ambivalent; their family roots were on the northern edge of the Greek world where Greek identity merges with others, just as it did in antiquity. For these tycoons, bankrolling Athens was an emphatic way of affirming their Greekness.

Thus George Averoff (1815–99) came from the mountain town of Metsovo in north-western Greece: a stronghold of Vlach, a Latin-based language whose speakers have always been loyal to the Greek cause. He made a colossal fortune in Egypt and Sudan through banking, property dealings and the cotton trade, a substantial part of which was ploughed back into beautifying Athens. Evangelos

Zappas (1800–65) was born in present-day Albania and in his youth served the fiefdom of Ali Pasha; he went on to grow rich in Romania, in part by buying up monastic land. One legacy of Zappas, which he did not live to see completed, is the Zappeion Palace, a splendid neoclassical exhibition hall, in the middle of a park, that presents an ingenious alternation of internal and external space. It was Zappas who financed the first attempts of the modern Greek kingdom to hold athletic contests that roughly corresponded to the games of ancient Olympia, and the initial restorations of the stadium built in the Roman era. But when the time came to present a revived Olympic movement to the world, inviting all comers to relive the classical ideal of noble competition, the vast coffers of Averoff had to be opened to remake the marble arena in all its ancient glory.

# 16

# Racing to War
## 1896–1919

*The 1896 Olympics – a disastrous war with Turkey in 1897
– crisis of confidence for the kingdom – Venizelos takes
control in 1910 – his collaboration with the Anglo-Irish
journalist Bourchier – Greece triumphs in the Balkan Wars,
divided by the First World War – Athenian gun battles of
December 1916 – Venizelos steers Greece into the Entente
– Greeks briefly gain access to Istanbul's holiest place*

I t was one of the most electrifying moments in the history of sport. On Friday 10 April 1896, two kings – those of Greece and Serbia – and about 80,000 ordinary folk sat waiting to watch the final moments in a contest with a glorious historic association. It was not just the result of this particular race that hung in the balance, but the outcome of a bold experiment: the revival after a gap of twenty-three centuries of an athletic festival that epitomized the highest human ideals.

The first modern Olympics had begun enthusiastically, five days earlier, with 241 athletes from fourteen participating countries. But the show's success was never guaranteed: some events had drawn few spectators, and the sailing contest was cancelled at the last minute. Equally precarious was the standing of the smallish capital of a young kingdom which nonetheless aspired to be an important city. Apart from antiquities, it boasted an array of exotic, even ostentatious buildings – yet traces still existed of the half-ruined, straggling Ottoman settlement which older residents still remembered. What impression would the visitors take away?

Neo-Olympic passion was coming to a head with the recreation of the run which may possibly have been made by a sprinter called Pheidippides to tell the Athenians of their army's victory at Marathon. In fact, as discussed in Chapter 2, it is more likely that the whole Athenian army rushed back to the city, securing it from a possible attack on the west coast of Attica. Whatever the exact historical facts, the route of 40 kilometres, skirting round Mount Pentelikon, carried huge emotional resonance. There were seventeen starters, including the Australian Edwin Flack, America's Arthur Blake, France's Albin Lermusiaux and Gyula Kellner of Hungary. The remainder were from the host country. The first three were deemed promising, as respective winners of the top three places in the 1,500-metre event on 7 April. But long-distance runs bring their surprises. At the Marathon's halfway mark, the Frenchman was in the lead but shortly after he collapsed. Flack was in front for a while, barely noticing the fact that an unknown local was hard on his heels. Then the Aussie runner dropped out. As the afternoon wore on, the spectators, almost entirely Greek, were feeling desperate for news. At one point a German arrived on a bicycle to say that Flack was leading. Then a mounted army officer galloped in with a report that a Greek had taken the lead, and spirits soared. Around 5 p.m., a stocky, sweat-stained figure came into view, and the crowd exploded, chanting 'Ellin! Ellin! Ellin! A Greek! A Greek! A Greek!' Crown Prince Constantine and his brother Prince George leaped down from their seats and jogged alongside Spyridon Louis as he completed the final straight. The surprise winner was the offspring of a farmer from Maroussi, then a village and now a suburb of Athens; the father and son made a modest living by selling water in the city centre. According to one story, the only reward he asked from the king was an extra beast of burden to convey their canisters to the parched Athenians. Hitherto he had been forced to jog along beside his father's horse as they trundled their way into the city. Thanks to Louis, the hosts of the games could walk taller in the world. And the visiting athletes had plenty of happy memories to savour.

As *The Times* of London laconically reported:

> At the Olympic games... the first three places in the race from Marathon to Athens, a distance of 40 kilometres, were won by Greeks. This result aroused great popular enthusiasm. The kings of Greece and Servia were present in the Stadium... The final heats in the 100-metre and the hurdle races, as well as the high jump, fell to American competitors, whose success seemed to be very popular.

The Athens Olympics duly passed into legend, the future of the modern festival was assured, and the prestige of the city rose accordingly. In the words of Roderick Beaton, a British scholar of modern Greek culture and history, 'foreign visitors could not fail to be impressed by the seamless superimposition of the very new upon the foundations of the very old'. That comment is fair in a broad sense, as an observation about Athens, but it can also be taken more narrowly. A literal superimposition had occurred several times over. The first solid structure at the games' venue was the limestone arena erected by Lykourgos around 330 BCE for the Panathenaic contests: this sporting and religious festival in honour of goddess Athena had probably been held at the same location for a couple of centuries before that, with spectators sitting on the bare hillside. When the wealthy Herodes Atticus covered the benches in marble around 140 CE it was both a gesture of homage to the past and also a showy and patriotic display of new wealth.

A strangely similar process unfolded in the nineteenth century: first the bequests of the Zappas family were used to refashion the stadium and host pan-Hellenic (i.e. Greek-only) contests in the 1870s. Then, at a congress in Paris in 1894, the decision was taken to host the first international Olympics in Athens, despite grave uncertainty over whether the funds existed to organize such an extravaganza. Only after passing the hat rather desperately around the wealthy Hellenic diaspora could such a costly undertaking be contemplated. The contribution of George Averoff, who gave 900,000 drachmas (amounting to perhaps two-thirds of all spending on the games) to refurbish the stadium was deemed outstandingly generous.

It was not only the marble seats (which were not quite completed) that dazzled visitors. The whole modern city of Athens seemed to have proved itself as a worthy capital of a promising European state: unusual enough to be teasingly exotic but also capable of playing host to the athletes and sports fans of the world in decent comfort and style. As the journalist and historian William Miller described it, Athens around the turn of the twentieth century was a place where

… more than anywhere else, the very old and the very new are placed in sharp contrast… more classical than Constantinople or Salonika, Athens is also more European than Sarajevo or Belgrade… The pace and development… have been extraordinary. When it became the Greek capital… it contained only 162 houses; at the last census it contained a population of 111,486 or, including two suburban villages, 128,735 – a total surpassed by two cities alone in eastern Europe, Constantinople and Bucharest. Marble palaces, covered with the crimson blossoms, now line the Kephesia Road; the broad boulevard of University (Panepistimiou) Street fringed by a row of costly public buildings, represents Athenian Culture, just as the wide thoroughfare of Stadion (Stadiou) is the centre of modern trade… The wide, shadeless streets and the glare of the marble houses may not be so well suited as narrow lanes and Turkish buildings to the heat of summer; it might have been better if the plan of modern Athens had been made in Byzantium rather than in Germany… But undoubtedly, it can boast houses… which no European capital would scorn to own.

As Miller suggests, Teutonic architects, as well as artists and archaeologists, continued in the late nineteenth century and beyond to play a prominent role in moulding the urban landscape of Athens. Yet somehow the terms of the transaction gradually changed. Just as the Greek monarchy was progressively Hellenized, the creative German talents that shaped the environment began to work on local terms. Rather than dipping into the Athenian scene from a great height, the new generation of Teutons had to adapt their lives to Athenian reality and make Greece their adopted homeland. One of them was the extraordinary antiquarian and entrepreneur Heinrich Schliemann. He had made a shady fortune in the Californian gold rush, and then profiteered in Russia during the Crimean War. He then threw himself into uncovering the remains of the Homeric era in Troy and Mycenae – and demonstrated to a sceptical world that the heroes of epic poetry really existed. In Athens, he commissioned an exotic quasi-palace, adjacent to Constitution Square, which now houses the Greek Numismatic Museum. The designer was his compatriot Ernst Ziller, a talented and energetic architect who – like Schliemann – took a Greek wife and threw in his lot with the young Hellenic kingdom.

Initially Ziller worked for Theophil Hansen, the Danish architect who was also very active in Vienna. Ziller was more exclusively Greek in his focus. Like the Hansen brothers and Schliemann, he had a penchant both for discovering new things about ancient Greece and also for fresh construction inspired by ancient style. In the 1860s he was involved in the unearthing of the Panathenaic – i.e. Olympic – stadium. He went on to provide Athens with some of its most spectacular private and public buildings, including the Royal Theatre (now the National Theatre of Greece) on Agiou Konstantinou Street and the Crown Prince's palace (now the official residence of the President of the Hellenic Republic). Ziller understood that, paradoxically enough, the neoclassical style needed to be re-Hellenized – fully adapted to the climate and environment of Attica – before it could look comfortable in the revived city. He also combined the neoclassical with a dash of Renaissance and Baroque styles. Although he and Theophil Hansen remained lifelong friends, admirers say Ziller had a better sense of the Athenian ambience. His final contribution to the city's aesthetics was his own magnificent grave in the First Cemetery of Athens, where wealthy modern Greeks are remembered by their families just as the heroes and heroines of ancient Athens were immortalized on marble slabs.

So, thanks to Greek tycoons and imaginative Teutons, the Olympic spectators found themselves in a city where the contemporary and the antique were combined in ways that were spectacular, playful and sometimes a little over the top. But that did not mean that visitors could be sure of perfect, problem-free comfort. Guidebooks of the time have much to say about the hazards of bedbugs and mosquitoes, and the advisability of big protective nets.

Even at the time of the Marathon delirium there were small dark clouds on the horizon for the few who cared to look. From the moment the Athens games were planned, their financial consequences had been a source of grave concern to Prime Minister Charilaos Trikoupis, that Cassandra-like advocate of fiscal prudence who had shocked parliament in 1893 by declaring the country bankrupt.

The games went ahead, thanks mainly to the personal sway of their prime mover Pierre de Coubertin, a Frenchman with a vision of the moral and spiritual benefits of sport, who had the ear of the Greek royal family. Still, Trikoupis issued a warning before leaving office that the cost of the games must not be shouldered by the state. On 11 April, the day after the Marathon excitement, news came that the elderly politician had died in the south of France.

Respected as he was, the news cast only a pale shadow over the rest of the games, which came to a satisfactory conclusion on 15 April, as King George handed out prizes: a silver medal and an olive branch from ancient Olympia for every winner. There was a Victory Parade, led by Spyridon Louis wearing the pleated white skirt or foustanella which was now established as Greece's national costume. This followed a more private celebration hosted by the king, an upmarket picnic for 250 people near Daphni monastery on 12 April. Sole and beef were on the menu, and the monarch gave a speech in French and Greek that lauded the games as a milestone in the young kingdom's history that would greatly boost its international standing: 'I am sure the champions from abroad, when they leave Greece, will advertise the progress of our country and the great works which were completed in a fairly short space of time to ensure the success of the Games.' King George went on to conclude that Athens had earned a place as a worthy host not just of one modern Olympiad but of all future re-creations of the games: 'Greece can justly hope that the foreigners who have honoured her with their presence will point to our country as the stable and permanent seat of the Olympic Games.'

The picnic's royal hosts showed particular courtesy to the American visitors, drawn from Princeton University and the Boston Athletic Association, a club in which Harvard University jocks loomed large. They returned the compliment a couple of days later with a letter to Crown Prince Constantine which voiced the opinion that, in view of 'the proven ability of Greece to competently administer the Games', it was now clear that 'the Games should never be removed from their native soil'. That letter and its sentiment were duly highlighted in *The Times* of London, whose Irish-born Balkan correspondent, James David Bourchier, was busy establishing himself as a well-connected player in the affairs of south-eastern Europe. Indeed, Bourchier filed many despatches about the Olympics, all of which emphasized the role played both by the Greek royals and the Greek diaspora in managing successfully to host this spectacular contest in a relatively small European capital. In one report, for example, he spelled out rather bluntly the financial challenges and the role played by benefactors. His writing reflects the secret knowledge, and the private purposes, of a consummate insider.

RACING TO WAR 381

... It was felt, however that the festival could not be worthily celebrated at Athens, without a renovation of the ancient stadion [*sic*] and the funds obtained by subscription were wholly inadequate for such a purpose. Considerable anxiety prevailed until a telegram arrived from Alexandria announcing that M. Averoff, a wealthy Greek of that city, was prepared to defray the cost of this gigantic undertaking. From that moment, all misgivings with regard to ways and means were laid aside.

That might have eased the financial problems, but there were still some organizational challenges – and in solving these, as Bourchier was keen to emphasize, the royal princes had played a vital role. Born into an Anglo-Irish family in 1850, Bourchier knew how to flatter, and his high-ranking Greek friends appreciated the publicity he gave them. His late vocation to journalism had already taken him to some unusual places and led to some extraordinary contacts. After teaching at Eton College, he arrived in the Balkans around 1890 and quickly learned the languages of Greece and Bulgaria. He filed some astonishing despatches about moonlit rides over the Cretan mountains in the company of dashing rebels. Among his strongest Cretan contacts was a keen revolutionary intellectual called Eleftherios Venizelos. The fact that Bourchier knew both Venizelos and Greece's royals so well would prove to be a significant factor in Balkan history.

For all the sweetness of the moment, the exuberance of the Marathon spectators proved to have an unfortunate side. Within months, Greece was showing a capacity to overreach and miscalculate. Pressure to march to war and expand the kingdom was coming not from wily politicians or a cynical monarch, but from ordinary citizens and soldiers. A so-called National Society was agitating for military adventures. It was backed by young army officers and headed by Spyridon Lambros, head of the University of Athens, which had always had a powerful role in propagating the vision of a greater Greece. In the autumn of 1896, the society was urging the king to try the nation's strength against the Ottomans. There were two obvious arenas for such a test. One was Crete, which had recently been wracked by violence between its Greek Orthodox population and pro-Ottoman Muslims – despite the efforts of the sultan, and the combined European powers, to keep the situation under control. The other was the territory immediately to the north of the kingdom: Ottoman Macedonia, where competition between pro-Greek and pro-Bulgarian communities (formally defined by the bishops to which particular villages owed loyalty) was escalating ominously.

Since 1878, Crete had supposedly been subject to an internationally guaranteed regime which combined loose Ottoman sovereignty with generous autonomy. Through the 1880s, Ottoman envoys had failed to give the island's Greek population the benefits of this regime, prompting successive rebellions. Then in 1894 the Ottomans appointed an ethnic Greek governor who infuriated the Muslim population. By the beginning of 1897 intercommunal conflict between Orthodox Greeks (who longed for union with Greece) and Muslims was exploding again, and the Christian quarter of the port of Chania was set on fire. The navies of the European powers patrolled nearby, trying erratically to contain the violence.

All this pushed patriotic, interventionist fervour to boiling point in Athens. In response, a small unit of the Greek navy, under Prince George, approached the island on 12 February 1897 but was dissuaded from landing by the international armada. Two days later an adventuring Greek colonel, Timoleon Vassos, did set foot on the island with a couple of battalions and claimed the island for Greece. Within a week they had defeated a 4,000-strong Ottoman force, but they were warned by the foreign powers to keep away from Chania. The port was occupied by the European nations who were trying to act as pig-in-the-middle – bombarding Greek rebel positions, at one point, but also pledging to stop any reinforcement of the Ottoman side. Many Greeks concluded that as soon as the foreigners lost their will to hold the ring in Crete, as would surely happen, the island would slide into Hellenic control.

By the beginning of April, the government – like so many Greek governments – was caught between international pressure to show restraint on all fronts and domestic pressure to hoist the flag higher. At the beginning of April war was declared on the Ottoman empire, and the army marched northwards. The conflict lasted just over a month and it was a disaster. While Greece and its capital were benefiting from German aesthetics, the Ottoman army had been re-equipped and retrained by German army officers. It managed to push the defeated Hellenes deep inside their territory. The port of Volos and the town of Larisa were captured. All the Thessalian farmland which Greece had been awarded in an international settlement in 1881 was overrun. In the end it was great-power diplomacy which saved the day for the Greeks. The sultan was persuaded to halt his advance, and settle for only the smallest territorial adjustments at Greece's expense, in return for a large financial settlement. The powers had to guarantee the payment to the sultan and then reclaim the money from Greece by means of an International Financial Commission which virtually took charge of the kingdom's economy – much as the pesky troika of bureaucrats from the European Union and the International Monetary Fund would do when Greece became insolvent in 2010. It was a bitterly humiliating outcome. It was the only really dark blot on the otherwise successful record of King George I as a national leader, and it dented the reputation of his son, Crown Prince Constantine.

The whole disaster also compromised the credibility of the small Hellenic kingdom, with its showy little capital, as a linchpin of the Greek world. In other places, Greeks were thriving. In the early twentieth century there were well over 200,000 of them living in Istanbul, accounting for perhaps a quarter of the city's population. In the Ottoman administrative region of Aydin, which included the commercially important port of Smyrna (Izmir), there were 300,000 Greeks out of a total of 1.2 million people. This was a time when many subjects of the kingdom migrated – not just to the New World but to the flourishing cities of the Ottoman empire, where so many of their compatriots were toiling and making money.

In the early years of the twentieth century, attention in Athens was also much taken up by an ever-bloodier three-way contest between Greeks, Bulgarians and the Ottoman authorities over the future of Macedonia. As in Crete, the European powers tried to pacify the situation by proposing autonomy under loose Ottoman sovereignty. But none of the powers was acting in a disinterested way; each had its private purposes and calculations over the future of the Ottoman lands. Meanwhile, at least a segment of the Greek elite came to the view that Hellenism had more to fear from Slavic expansion than from Ottoman power. They concluded that rather than trying to grab territory from the Ottomans, the focus should be on maximizing Greek influence within the Ottoman empire, which in financial terms was already strong. To the Bulgarian contestants in the struggle for Macedonia, it sometimes seemed that Ottomans and Greeks were working in quiet synergy.

More broadly, it might be said that from the turn of the twentieth century, two conflicting impulses were at work in the geopolitics of the Balkans. Each had its advocates in Athens and the wider world of Hellenism. One was the aspiration to reform and rearrange the internal equilibrium of great cosmopolitan empires, in particular the Ottoman one. The other was the narrower nationalist impulse which wanted to advance the interests of one new nation at the expense of every other.

As of 1908, the two trends were still finely balanced. Early that year, a secretive and powerful movement of Greeks was founded with the aim of boosting the political and cultural weight of the Greeks inside the Ottoman empire, especially in Istanbul and the still Ottoman Balkans. Although it had some well-placed supporters in Athenian officialdom, its success could have scotched the aspiration of Athens to be the hub and reference point for Greeks everywhere. Not for the first time in history, Athens would have been eclipsed by Constantinople. One founder, Ion Dragoumis, was the Greek consul in Istanbul; the other, Athanasios Souliotis-Nikolaides, was an army officer who liked to undertake sensitive diplomatic missions. Members of this so-called Constantinople Organization were carefully chosen, and they underwent an initiation ritual that bound them to secrecy. They soon established a network which worked very effectively across the region. It encouraged the huge Greek community in Istanbul to assert their collective interests by boycotting Bulgarian shops and businesses, and educating their children in Greek schools rather than (as some did) Catholic ones. It became the dominant force among the Istanbul Greeks, putting a stop to that community's incessant quarrels.

If the organization's vision had come about, the Ottoman empire might possibly have been refounded as a Greco-Turkish confederation, with Istanbul as its eternal capital. On 23 July 1908 there was another brief surge of utopian optimism when a group of Ottoman officers called the Young Turks staged a coup d'état in Salonica and outlined their dream of a progressive polity where all groups – even Greeks and Bulgarians – could live in amity. One of their leaders, Enver Bey, appeared on a balcony alongside the Greek metropolitan bishop, a mufti and a Bulgarian representative and they all embraced one another. But the movement's flash of cosmopolitan idealism was short-lived. Within a matter of weeks, the trend towards competitive nationalism was reasserting itself all over the region, and the Young Turks were swinging to a harder chauvinist line. They were pushed onto the defensive by the Austrian annexation of Ottoman Bosnia in October 1908; by Bulgaria's declaration of full independence; and by a proclamation of union with Greece in the Cretan Assembly.

Among the Istanbul Greeks, the dream of competing for influence within the Ottoman empire lived on a bit longer. The Constantinople Organization took part in the Ottoman elections organized by the Young Turks in late 1908, and its leaders were disappointed (without entirely giving up on Ottoman democracy) when they secured only twenty-seven seats in the new legislature, about half the number they expected. The next spring, the organization helped the Young Turks resist a counter-coup by conservative Ottoman forces led by the sultan. But by this time, the idea of decent relations – let alone true amity – between different ethnic groups within the Ottoman or any another empire was receding. Nationalism was reasserting itself, and this brought Athens and the Greek kingdom back into the frame. This did not necessarily imply that Greece would follow a policy of isolationism or autarky. In the calculus of nationalism, it was perfectly thinkable for one nation to ally tactically with another, but such partnerships were fickle and based on ruthless, short-term expediency. An especially brilliant calculator was about to enter the Athenian scene.

In the early months of 1909, the overwhelming preoccupation for the Athenian political class was how to handle the fast-evolving situation in Crete. The Cretan Greeks were ever more insistent in their demand to be incorporated formally into the kingdom. But many people worried about what the Young Turks, or indeed the British or other diplomatic players, might do in response. Greece's established leaders, including the monarch and the prime minister George Theotokis seemed paralyzed by apprehension. The king considered abdicating and Theotokis resigned in July; only with difficulty was the opposition leader Dimitrios Rallis persuaded to take the seemingly poisoned chalice of power.

Among army officers, especially junior ones, there was a different mood. On 28 August, a group of them gathered in Goudi, an elevated location on the eastern side of Athens, below Mount Hymettus, and set up camp in defiance of their superiors. They quickly forced Rallis to step down in favour of a more amenable successor, who agreed to a shake-up of the military. Uncertain what to do next, the coup leaders had the brainwave of inviting to Athens the most charismatic figure on the Greek scene: Venizelos, political leader of the Cretans, a man who combined charm, intellectual accomplishments (he enjoyed translating Thucydides) and the cheerful ruthlessness of a mountain warrior.

The Cretan acted judiciously and methodically. He paid an initial, three-week visit to Athens, met the Military League which had staged the coup, and mapped out a plan to restart Greek politics. There would be a caretaker government and then elections to a Constituent Assembly, which eventually took place in August 1910. With breezy confidence that he was ultimately indispensable, he stayed away from Athens until after a few days after the assembly met. On 18 September 1910, he arrived in Piraeus in a chartered steamship and then addressed an enthusiastic crowd in Constitution Square. Within a month he had been named prime minister, and two months after that, he and his supporters achieved an overwhelming majority in fresh elections, to a legislature with enhanced powers to change the constitution. He was the unchallenged master of the Greek arena, and he set about a hectic programme of social and economic reform, which included the break-up of large landed estates in Thessaly and the recognition of trade unions.

Another idea was much on his mind from winter 1910 onwards, and that involved a remaking of the entire geopolitical order in south-eastern Europe: the historically Christian powers, he thought, must bury their differences and unite to drive the Ottomans out of Europe. On this question, Venizelos had a useful interlocutor near at hand. That was his old friend Bourchier, *The Times* correspondent from County Limerick with whom he had established a useful connection in the Cretan mountains. In fact that connection had grown closer over the years. There was a time around 1905 when Venizelos as political leader of the Cretans found himself in opposition to Greece's Prince George, who was high commissioner of the island; Bourchier acted as trusted intermediary between the two men, although he could not bridge their differences and eventually annoyed the prince. While he stumbled as a peace-broker between two mighty Greeks, he would fare better in helping to seal bargains between the countries he knew best, Greece and Bulgaria.

Indeed, during at least one of Venizelos' triumphant appearances in Constitution Square, people noticed Bourchier standing beside him on the balcony. With characteristic grace, Venizelos would write of the journalist:

> When [he] was… devoting his energies and talent to… Cretan independence, I had the good fortune to come into close personal contact with him and appreciate his remarkable qualities. Chief among them was his ardent love of freedom, equal in strength to that of the great romantics of the early nineteenth century, but translated into the more sober and effective action of a great journalist of the twentieth.

In other words, Bourchier was seen by the politician as a more down-to-earth equivalent of Byron. Moreover, as the journalist himself recalled, interactions in Athens involved much more than mutual flattery.

> The conversations with Mr Venizelos which led to his proposal of an alliance with Bulgaria took place in the winter of 1910 and spring of 1911, mainly in my room at the Grande Bretagne Hotel. Venizelos' proposal, which was known only to King George and myself (the cabinet knew nothing of it) was entrusted to me in a sealed Packet.

The Bulgarians were hesitant to respond because they were under pressure from Russia to focus first on mending relations with their fellow Slavs in Serbia. But by February 1912, Bourchier received a signal from the highest level in Sofia that talks with Venizelos would be a welcome prospect. Bourchier was a happy witness at the signing of a Greco-Bulgarian treaty in Athens in May 1912. All was ready for a joint military operation to drive the Turks and their co-religionists from Europe. As Venizelos wired to Bourchier:

'I thank you and I clasp your hand as one of the principal artisans of this magnificent work that is the union between the Christian peoples of the Balkan peninsula.'

The strategy devised by Venizelos, with help from his Anglo-Irish messenger, worked brilliantly. It was based on a sound assessment of the balance of power in south-eastern Europe, which in early 1912 was shifting rapidly. The Ottoman empire was on the defensive on many fronts, ranging from rebellious Albania to the Aegean, which had been one of several theatres of a conflict with the Italians. This was an ideal moment for the Christian powers of the Balkans to set aside their bitter squabbles and unite against the sultan. They could always resume their own fights later.

Montenegro struck first, declaring war on 8 October. Within ten days, Greece, Serbia and Bulgaria followed suit. Greek armies did exactly what they had attempted, and miserably failed, to do in 1897. They struck north-west into Epirus and northward into Macedonia, and this time they were much more successful.

Meanwhile, the Greek navy, effectively led by Admiral Pavlos Koundouriotis, raised the Hellenic flag over one north Aegean island after another. By December he was able to choke off the entrance to the Bosphorus, a vital strategic point since the era of the Peloponnesian War. Common action by the Christian powers was producing impressive results, but this did not mean the old antagonism between Greece and Bulgaria had entirely vanished. In early November their respective armies were racing each other to Thessaloniki, to use the city's Greek name.

The Ottoman commander of the city, Hasan Tahsin Pasha, preferred to hand it over to the Greeks rather than the Bulgarians, perhaps because Muslim civilians were likely to fare slightly better under the Greeks. The Turkish official approached Greece's Prince Constantine with an offer of conditional surrender, to which the Prince replied that nothing but total surrender would suffice. But the sharp-eyed Venizelos rebuked the prince for his delaying tactic and cabled to him: 'You are requested to accept the surrender of

Thessaloniki which has been offered to you, and to enter [the city] without further delay. I will hold you responsible if there is even a moment's delay.' It was to be one of many sharp disagreements between the Cretan politician and the prince.

Cajoled by Venizelos to stop dithering, the prince made his entrance on 8 November, beating the Bulgarians by a day. This happened on the old-calendar feast of Saint Dimitrios, the patron saint of the city who looms large in the consciousness of all Balkan Christians. Four days later King George and Venizelos rode triumphantly through Thessaloniki, amid great rejoicing by the Greek community, about a quarter of the population, and a more cautious reception from other groups who included Spanish-speaking Jews (the largest element), Muslims and Slavs. As the most Europeanized and sophisticated of cities in Ottoman Europe, the city had at times been described as the co-capital of the sultan's dominion. Now it would be ranked with Athens as the co-capital (*symprotevousa*) of the Greek kingdom – and it could serve, where necessary, as an alternative power centre, as would soon become clear.

Venizelos was not merely an artful strategist, he was also an adept negotiator. With relish he accepted an invitation to London to deliberate with the European powers about how to reshape the map in the light of the Ottoman humiliation. He set out by train from Thessaloniki and arrived in Britain on 12 December. Negotiations proved more complex than expected, especially after 23 January 1913, when the Young Turk movement again seized power and instantly renounced a bargain deal which has just been made in London. But as Beaton observes, 'what [Venizelos] took back with him were not terms for peace, but something potentially even more enticing and more far-reaching' – in other words, an offer of war in alliance with Britain, whose leaders he had met and bonded with. Especially strong, fatefully so indeed, was the chemistry he established with David Lloyd George, who was then Chancellor of the Exchequer.

On his way back from London, Venizelos stopped in Thessaloniki to brief the king on the results of his British deliberations. It was the last time they would meet. On 18 March, a sinister and mysterious event took place. It was described accurately and succinctly in a US wire service report from the northern Greek city.

> George I, King of Greece, was assassinated here today. King George, who had taken personal command of his troops during the earlier period of the Balkan war, had been here since December, when the Turkish fortress was occupied by the Greeks after a short siege. The assassination occurred in the most thickly settled part of this city, whose normal population of 150,000 has been vastly increased by the presence of the soldiers. The assassin was a Greek of low mental type, who gave the name of Aleko Schinas. He shot the king through the heart and death followed almost immediately.

George died six months before completing a fifty-year reign, a period which – taken as a whole – was one of success and aggrandizement. Although the killer was described as a disturbed loner, many asked what motive might have existed. Conspiracy theorists wondered whether there was a plot to hasten the ascent to the throne of Crown Prince Constantine, who was perceived as pro-German. On the other hand, King George was already planning to abdicate in favour of his eldest son. The king's body lay in state for five days in the Athens cathedral and was finally interred at the royal estate in Tatoi north of the city.

Tragic as it was, neither the monarch's murder nor the ascent of King Constantine seemed to interrupt the run of successes which Venizelos was pulling off, by reacting nimbly to any development, diplomatic or military. The assassination came twelve days after the Greek army, commanded by Prince Constantine, had finally captured the strategic prize of Ioannina. Yet a treaty signed in London on 30 May 1913 looked inherently unstable, an invitation to further war, insofar as it created a Greater Bulgaria whose dimensions were provocatively large for all the neighbouring states. As things turned out, it was Bulgaria that hit out first, attacking the Greeks and Serbs, who fought back hard. The Turks took advantage of Bulgaria's preoccupation to seize back some of the territory they had recently lost, including the city of Edirne. Even Romania took a bite out of Bulgarian lands.

That fighting was over by the end of July, and on 10 August the region's powers agreed on a set of frontiers which are still broadly intact. The Ottoman empire would lose the great majority of its European lands, but it would keep the eastern part of Thrace, including the city of Edirne, which would henceforth be known as Turkey in Europe. Bulgaria was reduced in size.

As of early 1914, it seemed as though the change of monarch had made no fundamental difference to the political or geopolitical order in Greece. Venizelos was still riding high, having demonstrated with success that energetic networking and carefully picked alliances could be the path to expansion for the Greek kingdom – and that expansion was the answer to the kingdom's chronic problems of insolvency and underdevelopment.

For Greece, however, the Balkan Wars did leave a certain disconnect between borders and demography. In the newly won territories of Greek Macedonia and Thrace, Muslims were the largest single population group, exceeding the numbers of Greeks or Slavs. (The Serbian and Bulgarian armies had expelled many Muslims from the lands they took over, while the Greek army had provisionally allowed the Muslims to stay in the places it overran.) Ottoman Turkey, meanwhile, was in an angry and defensive mood and struggling to absorb an influx of perhaps 150,000 Balkan Muslim refugees. The Greek population of the western coast of Anatolia was under pressure to move aside, and in some places they were already being violently expelled.

A decade or so before a swap actually happened, that situation raised the spectre of a population exchange between Greece and Turkey, in which the Muslims of Greek Macedonia would be transferred to Turkey and the Greek communities of Asia Minor – in Hellenic parlance – would be shifted to the vacant lands of Greece. In summer 1914, Venizelos was on his way to Brussels to negotiate a Greek–Turkish settlement on exactly those lines, until it became clear that a much wider conflict was about to engulf Europe and the world.

How would the Venizelos prescription – diplomacy, alliance and expansion – work in conditions of general, global conflagration? Perfectly well, the Cretan statesman reasoned. As was almost always the case, he argued convincingly: being a coastal, seagoing nation, Greece must align with the maritime power of Britain and her French and Russian allies, and then reap the benefits of their expected victory. But right from the start of the war, it was clear that King Constantine felt differently. Having a German brother-in-law – the kaiser – did not automatically make him pro-German, but it did make him sensitive to German calculations. He could observe the looming alliance between Germany and the Ottoman empire, which was formally sealed in November 1914. The king feared that Greece would not fare well if it confronted two such powerful enemies. Venizelos saw things the other way round; he imagined the glorious prizes, including Constantinople, which might fall to Greece if the nation were party to a defeat of the Ottomans.

There is a paradox here. Logically, King Constantine should have been enticed by the idea that he might reign, as a new Byzantine emperor, in the city on the Bosphorus. He was, after all, called after the saintly emperor who founded the 'new Rome' in 330 CE, and he also shared a name with the sovereign (Constantine XI Palaiologos) who forfeited the city in 1453. Ordinary devout Greeks cherished the dream that the last Byzantine emperor, mysteriously frozen into a marble pillar, might come back to life and reclaim the city. Now a modern king named Constantine might actually turn that legend into reality – or so it seemed to humble Hellenes. Venizelos, by contrast, was at the pragmatic, modernizing end of the Greek spectrum, more interested in hard political and military reality than in folklore or superstitions.

Why then was the palace determined to keep Greece neutral and safe within her present boundaries – while Venizelos was formulating ambitious plans, whose ultimate end might be the replacement of Athens by Constantinople as the main centre of Hellenism? In truth, King Constantine himself may have been tempted at moments by dreams of a new Byzantium, but his German-trained advisers were not. A powerful restraining influence was exercised by Ioannis Metaxas, a decorated commander of the Balkan Wars who had spent four formative years at the Berlin War Academy. As for Venizelos, there was assuredly nothing mystical about his dream of capturing Ottoman territory, including the capital, with the help of Britain. Apart from its sentimental importance, the city was an enormous repository of Greek wealth and commercial energy whose addition to the Hellenic polity would mean a huge injection of strength. The Constantinople Organization had dreamed of a Greco-Turkish condominium on the Bosphorus; now it seemed possible that the Queen of Cities might be Greek pure and simple. For a practical type like Venizelos, the mystical allure of Constantinople probably mattered only insofar as it made ordinary Greeks even more willing to fight.

The palace's preference for caution may also reflect a deeper point about early modern Athens. The Greek royals, whether Greco-German or Greco-Danish, had ensconced themselves in a city that mixed northern European aesthetics, Balkan rusticity, breathtaking antiquities and a glorious physical environment. It was a combination that could by turns seem charming, promising or a little absurd. The imported dynasty and the neoclassical pretensions of Athens were somehow interconnected. It was far from obvious that this dynasty could ever be uprooted and transferred to another city, in the place where Asia began. If anybody was comfortable in Athens, it was the monarchs who presided over Constitution Square in their huge, gaunt fortress. It seemed natural for them to stay there.

As of early 1915, the capital of neutral Greece was awash with spies from the competing powers who were trying to build up networks of secret support. On 24 January, Britain offered 'significant territorial concessions in Asia Minor' if Greece would enter the war on the side of Serbia – but with an important catch. Greece was also asked to cede to Bulgaria some of its newly acquired territory, for example the port of Kavalla, as part of a bargain that would draw Bulgaria into the war on the British side. Venizelos was in favour of accepting, but on this and many other points he was overruled by the king and his cautious military advisers.

One of the British spies was Compton Mackenzie, a colourful Scot who would make a name for himself in popular fiction. In his Athenian memoirs, he conjures up an atmosphere of rambunctious intrigue, a world where the occasional discomfort was more than compensated by the throat-catching loveliness of the Attica landscape. He describes meeting an impassioned supporter of Venizelos who excoriates the faint-heartedness of the king and his Athens-centric vision, and insists that his nation can only find fulfilment in the *Megali Idea* – the Great Idea – of a Greece which recreates the Byzantine empire. The young man declares:

> The palace clique do not represent the country. They must pretend to be so patriotic but it is for the King they are thinking, not for Greece… They are afraid of Venizelos because they think he will sweep away the rottenness of Athens. For them the Megali Idea is a nothing.
>
> They are so happy in their little toy court, and they do not want to see a greater Greece in which they will be lost. They understand that the unredeemed Greeks of Asia Minor are bigger than they are. What is Kavalla if we may win Smyrna or perhaps even… Constantinople, the City. And Venizelos knows that with the help of Great Britain he can make a great Greece, because for Great Britain a great Greece will always be good.

In February, the Allies began their bombardments of Ottoman

positions at Gallipoli, and Venizelos was keener than ever to participate, using his capacity as prime minister to make a formal offer. Once again he was overruled by the palace, and he resigned on 6 March. His successor as prime minister, Dimitrios Gounaris,* renewed discussions with the Entente but tried to put strict conditions on Greek participation. The Allies baulked, convinced that Venizelos would soon return to power and offer unconditional support. His Liberal Party won elections on 12 June, and by August Venizelos had formed another government. The impasse with the king was deeper than ever. The Entente was still anxious for Greece to support Serbia and to do anything necessary to entice Bulgaria into the Entente. But in September, Bulgarian forces were mobilized in alliance with Germany and Turkey.

Every month of war exacerbated Greece's internal strains. By May 1916, Serbia had been overrun by the combined forces of Bulgaria and Austria and whatever was left of the Serbian army was brought to Thessaloniki, joining British and French troops who were already stationed there – all this with the blessing of Venizelos and in defiance of the king. In late May, Greece's national schism deepened further after the Germans induced the royal government to cede a frontier fortress to their ally, Bulgaria – prompting a furious reaction from the British and French, which embarrassed Venizelos and probably hardened the support of some Greeks for their king.

A fresh physical partition of Greece's recently expanded territory was ominously in prospect. In August 1916 Venizelos addressed a mass rally in Constitution Square, saying he still hoped for reconciliation with the king, but hinting darkly at other options if this failed. His military supporters in Thessaloniki showed what this meant by formally renouncing the authority of Athens. On 25 September, Venizelos returned to his native Crete, where he proclaimed a provisional government of Greece which would represent the true interests of the nation. Then he moved to Thessaloniki and

---

* Leader of the conservative and pro-monarchist People's Party.

took charge of a new administration, which declared war on the Central Powers led by Germany. The monarch remained in control of Athens, drawing on the support he still enjoyed in Old Greece, the longest-standing territories of the kingdom.

On 1 December 1916, the new-old city of Athens, with its dusty excitement, its brassy wealth, its giddy ambitions and its newly exposed antiquities, seemed to lose all innocence. For a few hours, it became a war zone, and that was enough. It all happened just over two decades after the beauty and romance of Attica had won the hearts of athletes and sports fans from many countries. Buildings and geographical features which had played an important role in the Olympics were suddenly turned into battlegrounds. The fighting pitted French and British troops against forces loyal to King Constantine, both the regular army and so-called reservists or armed volunteers.

To anyone who remembered the exuberance of 1896, this was an awful twist of fate. During that miraculous year, the modern and ancient sites of the city had formed a fine interconnecting landscape. The neoclassical exhibition hall known as the Zappeion Palace, with its neatly landscaped grounds, hosted the administration of the games and the fencing contests. The Royal Palace (today's parliament) with somewhat grander gardens was adjacent. A few minutes' walk in another direction was the marble splendour of the refurbished stadium, a site which – as many spectators noted – was neatly framed by two lowish, pine-covered knolls, both of which had powerful classical associations: the Agra and the Ardettos hills. Ardettos was the place where, in ancient Athens, jurors took their oaths. Not far from the stadium on the Ardettos slope is the probable burial site of Herodes Atticus, the Greco-Roman tycoon who – like George Averoff eighteen centuries later – had used his millions to beautify the stadium.

On 1 December* 1916, every single one of these places saw carnage. A French admiral in charge of a small detachment of British and French marines was trapped in the Zappeion as Greek gunners rained fire at them from the Ardettos hill. They had landed a few hours earlier in a calculated demonstration of limited force. But somehow the calculations had misfired. A decisive moment came when a French warship anchored off Phaleron harbour sent some carefully aimed shells towards the Royal Palace, damaging the king's kitchens and potholing his garden but avoiding any serious harm to the residence or its occupants. Princess Alice, the future mother-in-law of the British Queen, recalled sheltering in the basement of the palace while shells crashed down. An armistice was finally agreed, although the French would complain bitterly that pro-royal forces had reopened fire on the Zappeion after all sides had agreed to lay down their arms.

The city's day of terror was the culmination of a game of shadow-boxing between the Entente powers and the king. They were prepared to let him keep his throne, and remain neutral, on condition that he redeploy forces which might be of assistance to the German-led powers. Some units must be transferred from central Greece to the Peloponnese, while some Greek weaponry must be surrendered to the Entente.

To all appearances, King Constantine played a desperate double game. He told the Entente allies that he was willing in principle to yield to their demands but they must understand that he was under pressure from many quarters not to betray Greece's national honour. Whatever concessions he made, his own face must somehow be saved, or so he insisted.

Meanwhile, supporters of the king, and indeed agents of the kaiser, whipped up a kind of patriotic hysteria. To make up for the fact that Greece's regular army was being trimmed and partially stood down, they began recruiting 'reservists' who were prepared

---

* In Greece, these events are known as Noemvriana (November events) because the date was 18 November under the old calendar then in use.

to bear arms for the king – and, indirectly at least, for the kaiser. It is hard to believe that any of this was happening without the king's quiet encouragement.

According to Edouard Helsey, a French journalist who was in Athens and following the story closely, the king and France's Admiral Louis Dartige du Fournet either thought or pretended to think they had a subtle understanding. By bringing warships near Athens, and deploying a limited contingent on land, the Entente would make a discreet reminder of its power, without a shot being fired. That would make it much easier for the king to concede to the Entente demands, as everyone would see that he had no choice.

The Entente powers gave notice of the places in Athens where it intended to send its small force of marines, and the admiral – so Helsey recalled – gave a confident briefing on the eve of the operation. The French officer was no fool; he had already won a place in history for helping to evacuate embattled Armenians from south-eastern Anatolia in 1915. But on this occasion his mood was upbeat, even frivolous. Helsey writes:

> The little farce which had been planned seemed [to the admiral] like a pleasant prospect. He gathered the journalists who were in Athens and spelled out the plan.
>
> 'N'est-ce pas charmant? Isn't it charming?' he asked with an innocent smile, with his legs crossed, and trouser-bottoms exposing his pale-blue socks. 'Isn't it charming? I am occupying the Hill of the Nymphs!'

What happened was not charming. The exact course of events and above all the order in which they occurred is still unclear. What does seem certain is that in the small hours of 1 December 1916, a force of marines, perhaps 2,000 in total, landed and began fanning out to the agreed strategic points, which included the outcrops around the Acropolis, of which the Hill of the Nymphs – topped by a fine, Danish-designed observatory since the 1840s – happened to be one.

Meanwhile Greek forces were ordered by the royalist government to deploy in all those places, and to keep ammunition dumps and other military assets under careful guard. For several hours there was a silent standoff in the places where both Entente and Greek royalist troops had gathered. Things were particularly tense around the Philopappos hill near the Acropolis. Around 10 a.m., shots were fired from a Greek barracks at Rouf on the western side of the city. Fighting broke out around the Acropolis, near the observatory. A Greek unit guarding the Philopappos hill reported heavy losses. But the Entente forces had only limited ammunition, and by early afternoon a French unit near the observatory was forced to surrender. A small Italian unit was withdrawn from the fray.

The Zappeion, where the French admiral was holed up, was guarded by a Franco-British unit of 500 or so marines, who tried to break out and seize an ammunition dump near the First Cemetery. King Constantine contacted the French flagship and asked if he could talk terms with the commander – only to realize that the admiral was only a few hundred metres from the palace, pinned down in the Zappeion. There were bayonet clashes between Greek forces based on the Ardettos hill and the marines in the Zappeion. Both the monarch and the admiral began, through intermediaries, to look for a way out. King Constantine said he was willing to hand over six mountain-based artillery batteries, rather than the ten which the Entente were demanding; that offer seemed to provide a dignified exit. Then a huge battle erupted around the Zappeion, possibly between rival Greek camps. The commander of one battery, located on the Ardettos hill, gave orders for heavy shelling of the space in front of the Zappeion. The admiral, meanwhile, contacted his compatriots who were at anchor nearby and instructed them to make a limited but spectacular demonstration of their power by sending long-range shells into carefully chosen spots in the heart of the battle zone. Even as the French shells were landing in the vicinity, ambassadors from the Entente called on the king and secured his commitment to a ceasefire. Then, accompanied by senior Greek officers, they made a hazardous walk to the Zappeion and assured the admiral that the six batteries would be handed over in accordance with his wishes. By dawn the following day, the surviving Entente forces had been escorted to Piraeus by a Greek cavalry unit and seen onto their ships. The clashes had cost the lives of at least sixty French soldiers and thirty Greek ones. Dozens of wounded French and British servicemen had to be treated in Greek hospitals. The French admiral fell into disfavour in Paris because of the leniency of his response to the royalist Greeks.

The brief transformation of Athens into a battleground involving at least three European powers was traumatic enough. What followed in the city over the next few days was even worse in its consequences for the internal peace of Greece. The reservists and other supporters of the king went on a rampage against the backers of Venizelos, suspected (not absurdly) of abetting the Anglo-French incursion. One of the victims was Emmanuel Benakis, the mayor of Athens and patriarch of a super-rich family of traders in Egyptian cotton. A gang dragged him out of his opulent home – today's Benaki Museum – and it was feared that he might be taken to the Ilisos river and lynched, a fate which some other Venizelists had suffered. His daughter Penelope Delta, a novelist who wrote romantic accounts of the Greek–Bulgarian fighting in Macedonia, thought she might never see him again – though eventually she found him in the main city prison, from which he was duly released. Less well-connected Venizelists did not fare so well. At least thirty-five were killed and almost a thousand jailed, according to a French newspaper report. Mobs attacked the offices of pro-Venizelos newspapers and trashed their printing presses. Greece's political division also deepened, as the Allies formally recognized the government in Thessaloniki and imposed a blockade on Athens which put a strain on food supplies.

By June 1917, Venizelos had reasserted control over the whole of Greece. The Entente powers now insisted that King Constantine leave the country, and he along with most of the royal family were forced into exile. General Metaxas was among those deported to

Corsica, a punishment which reflected the strong French hand in Greek affairs. Constantine's second son, Alexander, took the throne. Venizelos once again addressed his supporters in Constitution Square. There had never ceased to a robust constituency of pro-Venizelos citizens in and around the Athens area, including the Cretans who were numerous in Piraeus, but it was a smaller and more subdued audience than he was used to. Royalists noted with dismay that he was backed up by colonial forces from France, which of all the Allied powers had been the most active in opposing the monarchy.

Venizelos spoke of 'national unity' as he prepared to make the offer of a final gesture of military support to the Entente while there was still a chance to win prizes for Greece. He ingeniously recalled the parliament which had been elected in June 1915 – ignoring the election in December 1915, which his Liberals had boycotted. By August 1917 he had secured a vote of confidence from the so-called Lazarus Parliament and prepared to send Greece into the European fray.

In practical terms, this meant assisting the Allies to fight with Serbia and against Bulgaria. Greece did make a respectable contribution, though its forces came mainly from the recently acquired parts of the kingdom, which were pro-Venizelos. In the old Greece, where loyalty to the king still ran high, some units mutinied and were severely disciplined.

By September 1918, an Entente force (about a third of it Greek) had broken Bulgaria's line and obliged it to sue for peace. The Ottoman empire signed an armistice on 30 October and Germany surrendered on 11 November. Entente forces including a small Greek contingent marched towards the Bosphorus. Likewise, some Greek ships were able to sail, with their allies, into the waters off Istanbul, although the Turkish negotiators had tried hard to avoid the humiliation of a Greek presence. For the next three years, Allied forces would remain in precarious occupation of the city, which they called Constantinople. This gave a kind of respite to the great conurbation's Greek and Armenian minorities, although many were apprehensive about what would happen when, as seemed inevitable, the Turkish authorities resumed control.

This was hardly the triumphant takeover of the city of cities of which some Venizelos supporters had dreamed, but it did give Greek forces some access to Constantinople in a way that warmed Hellenic hearts and disturbed Turkish ones. One little-known incident shows what the gamesmanship of Venizelos did, and did not, achieve.

In January 1919, a Greek naval ship passed through the straits carrying two Hellenic brigades on the way to Ukraine, where Venizelos, that endless maker of strategic bargains, had offered their services to the White Russian cause. The ship had a chaplain, Father Eleftherios Noufrakis, who shared the first name and the Cretan pride of the prime minister. He and four officers received permission to visit the Patriarch of their church, who still lived by the shores of the Golden Horn. Asking nobody's permission, they also took the opportunity to stop en route by the city's most important religious monument – Hagia Sophia, then in active use as a mosque, but before 1453, the most important temple in eastern Christendom.

Once inside they set about an act of worship which was as thrilling to some, and provocative to others, as a Jewish rite on the Temple Mount. One of the Greek officers knew how to chant the responses in an Orthodox service. The priest quietly put a stole around his neck and they celebrated a liturgy, symbolically completing the one that had been in progress when the conquest happened five centuries earlier. Standing under the light-filled circular dome, the five conducted the ancient rite with streaming tears. Some local people noticed what was happening and began protesting, but a Turkish officer mysteriously intervened and made sure the group had safe passage out of the building. The priest's diary is kept in a local museum in Crete – in spidery writing it describes how 'we sang hymns and thanksgiving for the wisdom of

God for His kindness to allow us to enter that legendary temple, with our weapons, and say our prayers'. The incident caused some embarrassment to the Anglo-French overlords of the city, and Venizelos felt obliged to reprimand the priest. But in private he sent a message of congratulations.

Among Greeks of a traditional bent, certain things hardly have to be said. The Metropolitan Cathedral of Athens, completed in 1862 with input from Theophil Hansen, is a decent but rather heavy building, a place of weddings and funeral services for kings and other grand people. It is said to contain marble from over seventy smaller churches that were pulled down when modern Athens was being landscaped. But few people would die for that monument. In fact, compared with the swirling majesty of Hagia Sophia, the main church in Athens seems, even to a loyal Athenian, like a gimcrack piece of kitsch.

# 17

# Of Loss and Consolidation
## 1919–36

*Huge influx of refugees arrives in Athens after Greek defeat
in Anatolia – humanitarian crisis, the Refugee Settlement
Commission – Venizelos escapes blame for the Anatolian
expedition, returns to power in 1928 – Venizelos builds schools,
opens food markets, completes new water system – political
crisis leads to the return of the monarchy – dictator Ioannis
Metaxas takes power in 1936 – literary movements as a creative
response to the Anatolian disaster – growth of Athens*

I n the autumn of 1922 and through the following year, a tide
of human misery swept over Greece, and its multiple effects
would remain palpable for the remainder of the twentieth
century. Among those effects was a dying down, indeed a virtual
disappearance, of the dream of a greater Greece whose territory
would span two continents. For much of its nine decades or so
of existence, the Hellenic state's masters had yearned to extend its
territory to all the places where Greeks lived, a process that would
have meant establishing a new capital in Constantinople. Now,
after a shattering military defeat, the small country of Greece had
to stop still and absorb a torrent of newcomers, many of them
destitute, that equalled at least a fifth of its population. Instead
of planning ambitious expeditions to the periphery of Hellenism,
politicians in Athens had to cope with feeding and housing the
tattered remainder of that periphery on their own doorstep. In the

course of that painful process, the role of Athens as a crucible of Hellenism would grow far more important.

The newcomers came in distinct waves. Many escaped from the flames that engulfed the great port of Smyrna on 13 September 1922. Others, generally in even worse physical shape, were evacuated from harbours on the Black Sea after being marched back and forth through the Turkish interior in conditions which only the hardiest endured. Others still were able to flee in a slightly more orderly way, in the sense that they could bring farm animals and a few possessions, from the European hinterland of Istanbul. A military adventure which began in May 1919, with the landing of Greek troops in Smyrna under an international mandate, had finally brought upon Greece the greatest disaster of its existence. Indeed, what happened must rank as one of the greatest misfortunes in the much longer history of Hellenism. On the fertile west coast of Anatolia, where the intellectual and commercial talents of Greek people had flourished for nearly 3,000 years – a greater claim of continuity, arguably, than could be made for Athens – the language of Homer and Heraclitus would no longer be heard. Such is the human capacity for denial that the effect on Athens of the Turkish army's victory was slightly delayed. A report in *The Times*, penned as the flames were engulfing Greek Smyrna, noted with surprise that

> externally [Athens] is calm and almost normal. The public services are in full swing, and at night the fashionable districts are crowded with people sitting in the open air, watching films, or listening to the band... Some people are inclined to regard the calm of the populace as being due to numbness engendered by the multitude of the disaster.

The numbness would soon wear off. Within a matter of weeks every available space in greater Athens was filled with desperate people: parks, municipal buildings, schools, churches. A well-known photograph shows refugee families occupying each of the boxes at the Municipal Theatre, one of the finest buildings designed by Ernst Ziller. The neoclassical grandeur of the Zappeion and its gardens was turned over to an orphanage. Tents were spread out in the grounds of the Temple of Olympian Zeus, and in the Agora around the Hephaisteion. Entire new suburbs of the city, planned and unplanned, were soon springing up.

One of the most vivid accounts of the humanitarian crisis came from Esther Lovejoy, a doctor from Oregon who was founder and president of American Women's Hospitals, a philanthropic agency set up by female pioneers of the medical profession. Having worked to relieve suffering all over the war zones of Anatolia, she had the odd experience in February 1923 of commuting between the luxury of the Grande-Bretagne Hotel in Constitution Square and the reception camp on the island of Makronisos, off the southern coast of Attica, where desperate folk from the Black Sea region were being offloaded. Given that most able-bodied men had been kept behind in Turkey as prisoners, there was a strong preponderance of women among the refugees. As the islet came into view, a vessel called the *Ionia* was bobbing up and down, unable to land because of a choppy sea. Several days earlier, it had sent a grim signal: 'Four thousand refugees. No water. No food. Smallpox and typhus aboard.'

Soon afterwards, Lovejoy observed a

tragic procession made up of women, children, the aged and a small proportion of able-bodied men, struggling through the sand with their bundles on their backs.

Many of the old people were exhausted, and had to be helped to the camp of the 'unclean' where all the newcomers were obliged to remain where they were deloused and their meagre belongings disinfected...

There were three hospital pavilions, one for non-contagious cases, another for typhus fever and a third for smallpox... A great many people died soon after landing, most of them from exhaustion due to lack of food and water, and other hardships incident to this terrible migration...

There were probably not more than eight thousand outcasts on the entire Island, including those landing from the *Ionia*... but the line waiting for food looked like twenty-thousand to me. Carrying all sorts of pots and pans in which to receive their portions, they moved slowly by our cauldrons, where they were given allotments of dark bread or mush or beans in accordance with the size of their families... Every woman was obliged to bring all of her children – [those] able to walk – in order to prove their number and prevent hoarding.

Shocked as she was, Lovejoy had no time for sentimentalism: she had to monitor the efficiency of the operation, start to plan for further fundraising and see to the welfare of her half-dozen associates who were managing the relief operation. What really flummoxed her was the experience of returning to the opulence of dinner-time at the Grande-Bretagne, where

Course after course was spread before the guests: hors d'oeuvres and cocktails to stimulate flagging appetites, followed by soup, fish, fowl, meat, desserts and all sorts of trimmings along the way, finished with coffee, cigarettes and liquor served in the lounge... Fresh from Makronisos, the spell of that horrible place was on my spirit. The room seemed full of hungry children.

Like many an Athenian visitor in search of balm for a confused soul, she joined a party of acquaintances for a night-time stroll around the Acropolis, but the solace was only partial. She could not get the hellish island out of her mind.

The wind was blowing... our tent cities were insecure. The exquisite Temple of Athena Nike proclaimed the eternal joy and truth of beauty – but ugliness and pain are also truths eternal.

The Caryatides are never more beautiful than in the pale light of the moon. For two thousand years they have been standing in the portico of the Erechtheion and there they will remain through coming generations in the midst of other woes than ours.

Taken as a whole, Greece's absorption of roughly 1.2 million refugees from Turkey is considered a success story. Over time, the resilience, the rich social capital and entrepreneurial energy of the former Ottoman Greeks entered the lifeblood of the Hellenic state. Most of the credit for the success goes, of course, to the refugees and their progeny. But nobody should forget the sheer hellishness of the conditions in which they entered Greece, or the mostly unsung heroines and heroes from various countries who eased their immediate plight and saved countless lives.

Glancing backwards at history, it might seem odd that the political after-effects of the Anatolian military disaster did not rebound against Eleftherios Venizelos. After all, he personified a policy of opportunistic diplomacy and expansion which had worked brilliantly until 1919 – and then started to go fatally wrong. But thanks in part to a weird set of circumstances, he and his supporters could plausibly claim – as of autumn 1922 – that all Greece's greatest military and geopolitical successes had been on their watch, while the greatest disasters were the responsibility of their monarchist opponents.

The immediate effect of the First World War, as we have seen, was to give the Greek state and its armed forces a tantalizing moment of access to the city on the Bosphorus, though nothing like the domination of Constantinople of which they dreamed. At the peace conference which started in Paris in January 1919 and culminated in the Treaty of Versailles in June, Venizelos turned in another masterly performance. In part by manipulating British and French fears of Italian opportunism, he persuaded the Allies to authorize a landing by the Greek army in May 1919 in the vibrant, multinational port of Smyrna, which was by far the most important commercial centre in the Aegean. It was a moment of internationally blessed glory for the Greeks and bitter disappointment and frustration for the Turks.

Having established themselves in Smyrna, the Greek forces fanned outwards to occupy a steadily increasing swathe of the Anatolian hinterland. The political master of the Smyrna-based Greek administration was a loyal follower of Venizelos who was under orders to insist on fair treatment for Greek and Turk alike. But it was not sufficient to stem the tide of anger that was filling the Turks, both humble and high-born, over the humiliation they had suffered at the hands of their historical rivals. A Turkish nationalist movement, determined to reassert control over Anatolia, began gathering pace rapidly.

In August 1920, Venizelos scored a fresh diplomatic triumph with the signing of the Treaty of Sèvres, which all but carved up Turkey and promised that the region now occupied by Greek forces could become Greek territory within five years. Venizelos could claim he had nearly fulfilled his dream of a Greece of two continents (Europe and Asia) and five seas: Ionian, Aegean, Mediterranean, Marmara and Black. In hard reality, though, the terms of the Sèvres accord were an unbearable provocation to the Turks and could only have been imposed by ruthless force. As Winston Churchill put it, the treaty amounted to 'peace with Turkey, and to ratify it, war with Turkey!'

The political masters of Greece seemed to have no difficulty recruiting and despatching the flower of the nation's youth, year after year, as long as glittering territorial prizes were in view. But in autumn 1920 a peculiar turn of events dimmed the prospects for the Greek cause. On 2 October, young King Alexander went for a stroll in the Tatoi estate. One of the few royals to have stayed in Greece when most of his family were expelled in 1917, he was an impulsive twenty-seven-year-old who had shocked old-timers by marrying a distinguished but non-royal lady, Aspasia Manou. A monkey of the Barbary macaque species got into a fight with the king's German Shepherd dog, and he tried to separate them, only to be attacked by another monkey which sank its teeth into his legs and chest. Just over three weeks later, Alexander died of sepsis. All this dramatically raised the stakes in the forthcoming elections. Alexander had reigned in name only over a country which Venizelos really controlled; now there was a possibility that the monarchy might return in a more full-blooded form. On 14 November, the nation voted and the monarchist party won; Venizelos went into exile and there was a referendum of dubious legitimacy which led to the restoration of King Constantine I.

A few years earlier, Constantine's name had been linked with caution and diplomatic neutrality – but having inherited an expeditionary war from Venizelos, he felt emboldened to pursue it. Meanwhile, for the Allies who had licensed Greece to march into Turkey, the calculus was changing. Increasingly they lacked the will or the capacity to impose terms on a 'defeated' Turkey whose determination to fight back was mounting. The return to Athens of a politically toxic king, whom they remembered as a devious friend of the kaiser, was the perfect excuse for queasy Allies to disengage from the Greek campaign. France and Italy hewed close to the Turkish nationalists led by Mustafa Kemal. Britain's prime minister Lloyd George was still wedded to the Greek cause, but the British establishment as a whole was more sceptical. This was a perfect recipe for a Greek disaster. In March 1921, the Greek army plunged deeper into the Turkish interior; by August their offensive had reached its furthest point, on the Sakarya river, not far from Ankara, and the army remained there for the winter. By the following spring, the military and diplomatic balance was clearly tilting towards Turkey. Athens accepted a British proposal for a League of Nations mandate over Greek-inhabited parts of Anatolia, but now the Turks led by Kemal were determined to impose a far more devastating punishment on the Hellenic army and their local kin. Kemal launched a huge offensive on 26 August 1922; the Greek army withdrew, torching several Turkish towns on the way, and sailed away from Smyrna on 8 September, leaving the city to a Turkish army bent on vengeance.

On 26 September, amid chaos and despondency in Athens, some pro-Venizelos officers based on the Aegean islands formed a 'revolutionary committee' and quickly secured the abdication and exile of King Constantine. His son took the throne, precariously, as George II, but it was the putschists who wielded effective power. Venizelos, still based abroad, kept aloof from the turmoil in Athens but agreed to represent the country diplomatically. Struggling with a humanitarian catastrophe and desperate for a scapegoat, the new regime staged a show trial in November of five politicians and one general, all in the monarchist camp. They were executed by firing squad at the Goudi hill, where the pro-Venizelos coup had been launched in 1909. Prince Andrew, whose son would marry Princess Elizabeth, the future British Queen,* was also put on trial (as a general in the ill-fated military campaign) and banished from Greece.

Meanwhile Venizelos did much more respectable work on the behalf of the new Greek administration, speaking for Athens at the Lausanne conference which started on 20 November and would eventually lead to a peace treaty between Turkey and her former adversaries the following July. Among the most pressing issues was the scope and nature of a widely expected population exchange between Greece and Turkey. This would formalize the departure of Orthodox Christians, who were already in flight from the former war zone, and provide for the departure of those not previously affected by war; it would also mandate the departure of hundreds of thousands of Muslims living in Greece. For the government in Athens, the biggest worry was that the prosperous Greek community of Istanbul, living under the fragile safety of a soon-to-end Allied occupation, would be uprooted en masse. There

---

* Philip, fifth and final child (and only son) of Prince Andrew of Greece and Denmark and Princess Alice of Battenberg, was born in Corfu in 1921, the year before his father's trial. Exiled from Greece at the age of just eighteen months, Philip lived in France, Germany and Britain, fought for the latter country in the Second World War and married Princess Elizabeth, whom he had first met in 1934, in 1947.

was a real fear that the Greek state, already strained to the limit, might collapse if this added influx took place. By January 1923, it was agreed that the Istanbul Greeks, defined rather narrowly, could remain in place, along with their spiritual leader, the Patriarch; in return the Muslim population of north-eastern Greece, adjacent to the border, was spared from expulsion.

As it staggered, and nearly foundered, under the impact of the refugees, the Greek state faced two separate challenges, neither of which it could shoulder alone. One was the immediate relief of suffering, food shortage and contagious disease; the other was the longer-term establishment of the refugees within the productive economy. In the first task, humanitarian agencies from the United States, especially the American Red Cross, played a decisive role which is little remembered now. If these agencies were made welcome, it was partly because America was not, at that time, tainted by the power games of European diplomacy which had paved the way for the enormous tragedy. In the longer-term challenge, a leading role was played by the League of Nations, in which Britain was the most powerful member. Huge help was also given by the government of the United States, which quietly supported the League even though isolationist sentiment in Congress had prevented the administration from joining.

Lobbied by Fridtjof Nansen, the Norwegian explorer turned troubleshooting philanthropist, the League established in Athens a powerful Refugee Settlement Commission which would operate almost as a state within a state. It was authorized to raise substantial sums of money and spend them on finding permanent homes, rural and urban, for the newcomers to Greece. It was agreed that its head would be American, his deputy British, while two other board members would be eminent Greeks. The first chairman was the American diplomat Henry Morgenthau, who as ambassador in Istanbul had been a friend and advocate of the Ottoman empire's Christian minorities. He soon became a player in Greek as well as international politics, shuttling between Athens and the corridors of financial power in London and New York. In 1923, Morgenthau formed the view that only a definite break with the monarchy would render Greece stable enough to be a credible recipient of international credit. In spring 1924, the Greeks voted in a plebiscite to a establish a republic, and this cleared the way for Morgenthau to secure a fresh advance of £1 million from the Bank of England, pending the loan of £10 million which the commission was able to clinch later that year. This was topped up by a credit of £7 million in 1928.

As international projects go, the money was spent effectively. The great majority of it was devoted to settling refugees in farms in northern Greece, occupying land that was freed up by the expulsion of the Muslim population. In a remarkable piece of social engineering, entire communities which had once existed in the remote parts of Anatolia were replanted in the newly drained lands of Greek Macedonia. But the commission also constructed new housing for refugees in Athens, Piraeus and other Greek towns. By the end of 1929, it had constructed over 27,000 makeshift houses in urban settings, and some new districts of greater Athens had been created: lively, hardscrabble places which saw more than their share of political passion, collective grievance and private strife.

In theory, the commission was aiming to provide each refugee family with one or two very simple rooms. But a hint of the real situation was given in 1929 by Sir John Hope Simpson, a British Liberal politician and international bureaucrat who, after overseeing the refugees in Greece, would go on to serve the British administration in Palestine as an advocate of Arab–Jewish partition.

In the cities of Athens and Piraeus, the Commission has built four large refugee quarters consisting in all of 11,150 habitations... some two-roomed, allowing for the accommodation of one family only; others are double houses, others again have accommodation for four, eight and sixteen families... Under the contracts signed by the occupants, a rent is charged that would result in the habitation becoming the property of the occupant... after fifteen years. In actual fact, however, when the houses were completed they were invaded by a number of families largely in excess of the accommodation, with the result that in certain... settlements many habitations contain one family in each room, and most of them contain more than one family... It is extraordinarily difficult to collect anything from the families so situated.

A further difficulty... has arisen from organised resistance to making any payment at all. All sorts of excuses are advanced – poverty, the existence of claims against the government, the inadequacy of the accommodation provided, allegations the houses have not cost what is being charged them, objections to any charge for public utility (roads, water, light) – in fact, any excuse of any kind which may afford an explanation for non-payment.

As Hope Simpson explained, the commission's remit did not include providing a livelihood for these strong-willed urban migrants, but it did what it could – by making land available for factories on favourable terms. One result was a thriving carpet-making industry, drawing on skills imported from Anatolia, which in 1927 earned £500,000 from exports to the United States. But this trade tumbled after the financial crash of 1929, which had made Greece insolvent by 1932.

The refugee quarters to which Hope Simpson refers are those of Virona (a variation on the name Byron), Nea Ionia and Kaisariani in Athens, and Kokkinia in Piraeus. On the southern edge of the city centre, Nea Smyrni (New Smyrna) hosted slightly more prosperous newcomers, and the existing district of Kallithea was swollen by refugees.

The refugee districts of Athens were tough places to live, but that did not mean they were chaotic. A fine piece of anthropological research by Renée Hirschon in the early 1970s described the communal life of Kokkinia – where in some respects, feelings of identity and social relations were remarkably unchanged since the district was first established in the 1920s. The frame-based houses were still largely intact, albeit cleverly expanded, mostly by digging basements. The provision of public utilities – paving, lighting, sewage and so on – was still very poor, but there again, people found creative solutions, including private sewage disposal systems. Since they were established, and even to this day, so-called refugee quarters of Athens have been distinguished by two seemingly contradictory traits: a high incidence of church-going and a strong left-wing vote. Both these attributes have something to do with the Ottoman experience, in which religious minorities were obliged to have well-developed systems for self-regulation. Strong churches and self-assertive politics were both responses to that challenge.

What Hirschon found was a robust and well-functioning community, where family and neighbourhood life was organized around the rituals and rhythms of the Orthodox calendar, with its elaborate obligations governing, for example, hospitality, marriage, death and mourning. The dowry system had been ingeniously adapted to the dire material conditions of Kokkinia. Elsewhere in the Greek world, a bride's parents might endow her with money or valuable trinkets or heirlooms. In the refugee quarter, the main asset a couple enjoyed was de facto possession of living space. When a daughter married, the house would be repartitioned and expanded to give the bride and her husband at least a tiny space of their own. Brides stayed under the family roof and imported husbands, after marriages that were mostly arranged by a match-maker. The whole community presented an extraordinary mixture of social conservatism and collective militancy.

The people of Kokkinia were intensely conscious of their roots in *Mikra Asia* (Asia Minor), and felt they were heirs to an urban culture, defined by manners, tastes and, above all, cuisine, that was superior to the host country of mainland Greece. Was that an accurate memory? In reality, the lives which they had abandoned were enormously varied: some had come from modest hamlets in the heart of Turkey; others had enjoyed prosperity on the Aegean coast. What all the 'refugees' had, and the host population lacked, was the experience of negotiating diversity: interacting with a multiplicity of ethnic groups and subcultures and calibrating relationships accordingly.

A century on, the impact of the huge incursion on attitudes, memories and tastes in greater Athens is still palpable. It helps to explain some deeply ambivalent attitudes towards Turkey and Turkish culture. Kokkinia's most famous son is probably the ballad singer George Dalaras, whose repertoire includes bitter laments for lost Greek communities and sentimental celebrations of Greek–Turkish friendship. Both genres can bring tears to the Athenian eye, often the very same eye.

As a more immediate effect of the influx that began in 1922, the conurbation of Athens grew, both demographically and spatially, to the point where it virtually slipped beyond the control of any public authority. The figures are impressive. The total population of greater Athens (including Piraeus and other immediately adjacent urban areas) had reached 1.1 million by 1940, up from 789,000 in 1928 and 451,000 in 1920. As of 1928, refugees made up 28 per cent of the 459,000 people who lived in the narrowly defined city of Athens, and 40 per cent of the 252,000 inhabitants of Piraeus. Motor transport, private and public, helped the urban area to remain coherent across long distances. Athens and Piraeus merged into a single built-up area connected by broad, fast-moving avenues. Syngrou Avenue, a thoroughfare linking central Athens with the refugee-dominated areas nearer the coast, was started in the 1890s but only completed in the late 1920s. This fusion of urban space did not deprive Piraeus of its salty character, with its football teams, its low-life sleaze, its dirty but delicious seafood restaurants located on rough alleys, its Oriental music, its pockets of bourgeois elegance. Athens did not take over Piraeus, but Piraeus blended with and began to influence Athens.

The whole city saw ever-greater extremes. It now included not just a handful of generous tycoons but a robust middle class, including some merchants or manufacturers who had once prospered in the Ottoman lands and were able to transfer their contacts and acumen to Athens. At one extreme the rich built garden suburbs well to the north of the city; at the other there were shanty towns where people lived in self-built shacks, far worse than the basic refugee houses of Kokkinia. It could be said that as a result of the Anatolian disaster, Athens acquired both a bourgeoisie and a proletariat.

Middle-class tastes in architecture became more experimental as the new fashions of western Europe began to replace neoclassicism. In April 1929 a new law made apartment buildings possible, simply by specifying that more than one owner could hold title in a single site. The regulations limited the height to seven storeys, but they did provide for bay windows, known by the German term *Erker*, which proliferated. Apartment blocks became a popular middle-class investment. During the 1930s, about 450 were built in central Athens. The mere fact that they had elevators and efficient plumbing and heating raised them to a level of comfort which most Athenians did not enjoy.

In 1928, after a series of rocky administrations including a military interlude (1925–6) under a bombastic Venizelist general, Theodoros Pangalos, Venizelos himself came back to Athens and formed an effective government. The Cretan's return heralded a series of well-publicized measures that improved both the appearance and the efficient functioning of the now-sprawling metropolis. One was an ambitious programme of high school construction in the modernist style, decreed by a liberal politician, George Papandreou, who was education minister. In 1933, the modernist architectural movement headed by Le Corbusier held its regular congress on a ship which made a stop in Piraeus. The great Swiss innovator visited a new school in central Athens and gave his approval by writing '*Compliments de Le Corbusier*' on the wall. But Greece's best architects also found plenty of private clients who were willing to try new styles. Although much of this architecture is lost or decaying, parts of its legacy can still be seen in ever-affluent areas of Athens like Kolonaki, in the anarchic bohemia of Exarcheia and once-respectable Kypseli.

One spectacular development was the completion of a new urban water supply which did much to boost public health. In 1929, the American company Ulen finished the construction of one of the world's most impressive dams, near Marathon. It was lined with marble from nearby Mount Pentelikon. It was the biggest of several jobs Ulen was contracted to carry out in the Athens area in 1924, as a desperate Greek administration struggled, with international assistance, to meet the sanitary needs of a suddenly expanded conurbation. The construction project, employing around 4,000 labourers of which many were refugees, was in itself a boost to the economy, and life in the purpose-built workers' accommodation seems to have been healthier than it was in refugee shanty towns. As well as making a beautiful reservoir, Ulen renewed part of the aqueduct built by Emperor Hadrian, which was still in use after seventeen centuries, and created a system to extract seawater from Phaleron bay which was used to flush out sewage and dampen roads, thus liberating precious fresh water for other purposes.

On 7 June 1931, there was a joyful ceremony to mark the dam water's arrival in Athens. Bands struck up the Greek and American national anthems as Venizelos turned on a fountain in the grounds of the Temple of Olympian Zeus. Henry Ulen, the entrepreneur who took a keen interest in his company's Athenian activities, would soon add to the general bonhomie by presenting the city with yet another fountain, still in existence: a hexagonal one located near the Zappeion, whose bilingual epigraph praises 'the service performed by more than 5,000 Greeks in constructing the water supply for Athens, Piraeus and its Environs'. Fanfare aside, the provision of ample clean water had an enormously benign effect in reducing the incidence of typhus.

Another well-publicized action was the creation of farmers' markets in five central districts of Athens, where an impressive range of locally grown fruit and vegetables was offered at reasonable prices. A grainy black-and-white publicity film shows Venizelos opening the market in Theseion Square in May 1929. He is seen making purchases from producers whose rich array includes currants, cheese, eggs, olive oil and oil-based soap. In-between the silent, jerky images a political message is flashed across the screen: the government is determined to cut out intermediaries who are profiting from the food chain and make cheap products available to every Athenian.

As the film explained, the market would help ordinary folk – as well as upmarket clients like Andromache Mela, the daughter of the archaeologically minded tycoon Heinrich Schliemann. To this day, the food markets of Athens, offering not only the usual fruit and vegetables but a huge range of herbs and spices, are one of the pleasures of life in the city.

The political climate darkened in autumn 1932, when the hitherto almost infallible political genius of Venizelos seemed to stumble. Several factors, including an ongoing global recession, had dented his popularity. In 1930, he had made a spectacular diplomatic rapprochement with Turkey, the price of which was a final financial settlement on terms which were favourable to Ankara – and dashed the hopes still harboured by many new arrivals that they might get decent compensation for properties left behind in Turkey. Refugees who had previously been firm supporters of Venizelos turned in a significant trickle towards a political movement that was gaining power across Europe: the communists.

The elections of September 1932 saw a virtual draw between the Liberals under Venizelos and his conservative opponents in the People's Party. A fresh ballot in March 1933 brought another stalemate but the People's Party under Panagis Tsaldaris commanded a majority thanks to the quirks of the electoral system. That prompted an intemperate reaction from a veteran of Venizelist republicanism. A military coup was launched by Nikolaos Plastiras – one of the officers who had masterminded the anti-monarchist 'revolution' eleven years earlier. Venizelos disowned the attempt but the whole atmosphere grew more volatile as the statesman and his wife had a close brush with assassination in June 1933, with gunmen chasing their car and raking it with bullets.

In March 1935, Plastiras made a new attempt, this time with the full support of Venizelos, who tried to use his still loyal supporters in Crete and northern Greece as a launching pad. The coup failed and Venizelos was forced into exile. Elections in June, boycotted by the Venizelist Liberals, showed a swing towards the right and, in particular, a lurch towards monarchism. A plebiscite in November produced an improbably high – 97 per cent – vote in favour of restoring the monarchy in the person of King George II, who had spent a decade in England. The monarch proved somewhat more moderate than the politicians and generals who had summoned him home; he insisted on a wide-ranging amnesty, including for Venizelos, who in turn was emollient enough to accept the re-establishment of the Crown and urge others to do so. It was his last public gesture before his death in 1936.

The result of all this good grace was an election in January 1936 in which pro- and anti-Venizelos forces took part on agreed terms. However, this produced yet another draw, with the communists holding the balance of power. That was the cue for General Ioannis Metaxas – the German-trained officer who had urged the royals to stay neutral during the First World War – to proclaim himself national leader for an indefinite period on 4 August 1936, the day before a general strike was due to be staged. The king remained on the throne, and did his best to keep Greece aligned with Britain, where he had strong family ties, even as the general and his advisers toyed with a version of the authoritarian nationalism that was sweeping continental Europe.

There were some obvious points of difference, and similarity, between the Metaxas regime and the fuller-blooded forms of fascism that were evolving elsewhere. Short, rotund and bespectacled, Metaxas did not look like a dictator. Unlike Mussolini, he did not command a mass movement or party. Indeed he repeatedly told Greek citizens that he would protect their interests both against the communists and the old political parties, which were all corrupt and self-serving. Where Mussolini lauded ancient Rome, Metaxas presented himself as the heir to a 'third Greek civilization' – after ancient Greece and Byzantium. But in the ancient Greek world it was the austere militarism and self-discipline of the Spartans, rather than the cerebral, freedom-loving Athenians that appealed to Metaxas most. He borrowed from general fascist repertoire by proclaiming himself 'First Farmer' and 'First Worker of the Nation' – a figure with whom all fellow toilers were supposed to identify.

The group which suffered most under Metaxas were the communists. His public security minister Konstantinos Maniadakis arrested, jailed and internally exiled thousands of them – as a result of which the Communist Party of Greece (KKE) probably gained in resilience. Likewise, in its attempt to impose a straightjacket on the turbulent world of Greek culture and letters, the regime achieved very mixed results, despite some quite vigorous efforts.

Two weeks after the general took power, a group of students proclaiming support for the Metaxas regime invited all comers to observe and participate in a book-burning ceremony in Pasalimani, one of the harbours of Piraeus. The range of authors targeted was wide and muddled. They included Gorky, Tolstoy, Goethe, Darwin, Freud and George Bernard Shaw, as well as some giants of modern Greek fiction. Along with the religiously dissident Nikos Kazantzakis, there were favourites of the Orthodox Church such as Dostoyevsky and Alexandros Papadiamantis, a pious, masterly teller of stories set in provincial Greece. In later book-burning events, the works targeted included classical works of genius such as Antigone and the Funeral Oration of Pericles as recounted by Thucydides. In November 1938, Maniadakis banned 445 books.

Karolos Koun was perhaps Greece's greatest theatre director of the twentieth century, one of the many cultural talents that emerged from the ashes of the Ottoman Greek world and found refuge in Athens. When Metaxas took power, Koun had already made his name by staging original productions at Athens College, the elite private school where he was a teacher. Later he founded his own theatre. As part of the witch-hunt launched by Maniadakis, he was called by the police and upbraided for staging 'communist' dramas. These turned out to include *Ploutos* (Wealth), the satire about material greed presented by Aristophanes in 408 BCE, and *Le malade imaginaire*, the great depiction of hypochondria by the seventeenth-century French comic dramatist Molière.

Still, especially in its overgrown, unmanageable form, life in Athens simply could not be subjected to the dreams of its eccentric, uniformed ideologues. At the highest and the lowest ends of Greek society there were new literary and artistic phenomena which no hot-headed security chief or blimpish officer ever dreamed of. And yet, nothing was completely unconnected with politics either. Some forms of culture could coexist with the new regime, or even serve it; others had to play a cat-and-mouse game.

With the establishment of the National Tourist Organization (EOT) in 1929, Greece became more conscious of her international image, almost playing up to northern Europe's romantic image of a country of dazzling antiquities, perpetual sunshine and pristine rustic simplicity. One offshoot of this development was the success of a photographer, Elli Seraidari, who was better known by her studio's artistic sobriquet of Nelly or Nelly's. Technically she was a refugee; born into the Greek minority in the vicinity of Smyrna, she escaped the catastrophe that befell her community because she was studying in Germany at the time. As a photographer in Athens, she produced striking images of marble pillars and limpid skies – and amazingly, she convinced famous ballerinas to pose almost naked amid the columns of the Parthenon. Her work had a nationalist edge which rather endeared it to the Metaxas regime, and in 1939, she designed the Greek pavilion at the World Fair in New York – a city where she decided to stay for the rest of her career.

Knowledge of ancient Athens and its physical legacy, in the form of artefacts and monuments, was increasing year by year, in part thanks to the excavation in the Agora which American archaeologists began in 1931. That project was the outcome of another, relatively happy chapter in Greek–American synergy. As of 1925, the pressure on every available piece of land in central Athens was intensifying, to the point where reserving the space around the Hephaisteion temple for archaeological work seemed almost impossible. With increasing impatience, owners of properties in that area were saying they must be bought out on fair terms or else permitted to consolidate and improve their buildings. Lacking funds for a buyout, the government agreed to the second option, but this drew strong protests from Greek archaeologists. So the government turned to the foreign archaeological schools, whose handsome offices were already a striking feature of the Athenian landscape. Only the American School of Classical Studies in Athens had any hope of raising the funds for the buyout plus the excavation. Even for that well-connected institution, there was some hesitation about taking on such a huge financial obligation, and the trustees initially refused.

In early 1928, there were tense negotiations in which the Greek side sought to insist on a full and rapid compensation of the affected owners, while the Americans wanted to spread the obligation over a period of up to thirty years. Finally, in August 1928, the Venizelos government found a solution by reducing the area of the concession to the American school: the eastern segment, including the Stoa of Attalos, would be overseen by the ASCSA, while an area to the west would remain under Greek responsibility. It was agreed that owners in the American zone would be bought out over a decade, with prices to be assessed by a committee of evaluation which would take into account documentary evidence, including tax returns. That triggered a fresh round of protests from owners, not on the principle of sacrificing their properties but on the procedure – which seemed likely to deliver low figures. Venizelos used all his charisma to insist on the passage of the relevant law, including clauses which the Americans had demanded to protect their interests. As a result, one of the world's most professional and productive archaeological endeavours got underway, and the understanding of ancient Athens grew from year to year.

Much less congenial for Greece's establishment was a powerful cultural wave that began not in the Athens intelligentsia but in the semi-criminal underworld of Piraeus with its hashish dens and hard-luck stories. It was music with an eastern twang that reflected the influence of the refugees but drew in musicians from all parts of Greece. The style was called *rembetika* and over time it would become one of Greece's greatest cultural exports. It veered between western scales and the very different intervals, known as *makam*, used in Middle Eastern melodies. One of its greatest exponents, Markos Vamvakaris, turned up in Piraeus from the island of Syros and did odd jobs in the docks before settling down to work in an abattoir. When he first heard the bouzouki he vowed that he would hack his own arm off if he could not master the instrument.

This music's defiantly indulgent, self-obsessed sensuality was the opposite of the austere image of Greece which the Metaxas regime wanted to project. Musicians were persecuted (an experience which they duly celebrated in song), instruments were confiscated and record companies were told to clean up their lyrics. But the music never stopped.

In the realm of high culture, too, the spirit of resistance proved stubborn. To gain a sense of that, it is worth reading, and then investigating a little more deeply, a news report from April 1937. According to *Kathimerini*, then and now a venerable daily, the 100th anniversary of the University of Athens was commemorated with an 'invocation of the goddess Athena' on the Parthenon. The show sounds spectacular if somewhat kitsch. It featured forty-six young members of Lyceum of Greek Women, an upmarket club with distinguished antecedents, founded in 1911 by a pioneering feminist magazine editor, Kalliroi Parren. As the daily describes the performance, the robed ladies processed to the sound of beating drums, while one of them played the role of Athena herself, emerging from the inner chamber of the Parthenon. A (male) law student addressed a prayer to the goddess in ancient Greek, on behalf of all Greek students, and the dancers laid flowers at her feet.

In another element of the centenary celebration, *Kathimerini* adds, the visiting French education minister Jean Zay made a speech in praise of the deep literary connections between his country and Greece; the visitor was given an honorary doctorate by the university's law faculty. What on earth does all that signify? Aged only thirty-three at the time, Zay was a promising member of the left-wing Popular Front government in France; he would soon be imprisoned and eventually killed under the collaborationist Vichy regime. Did his presence in Athens imply that he was tricked into lending legitimacy to a semi-fascist regime, perhaps through a sentimental respect for all things Greek? In fact the truth is more interesting. Zay was well aware of the nature of the Metaxas regime, and he took advantage of his visit to give heart to the liberal, Francophile segments of the Greek intelligentsia. On the occasion of the anniversary, a general invitation had gone out to European education ministers; among those who accepted, and took the chance to tour the country's archaeological sites, were Zay and his German Nazi counterpart Bernhard Rust.

Rust was received cordially by the Greek government, and less so by the educators and students. The German sulked in his hotel while Zay endeared himself to the Athenian intelligentsia by offering books and scholarships. When Zay promised to send 1,000 new books to the university library, Rust sent a message that his government would provide 10,000. Zay's biggest gesture was a doubling of the number of scholarships his country offered to Greek students; these would prove a boon to young Greeks fleeing a dictatorship forty years later. In conversation with Metaxas, Zay artfully secured the general's permission for him to address a gathering of Athenian students. Thousands came to hear him, and they greeted him with a spirited rendering of the *Marseillaise*. The student body sent signals of a more subtle sort to the august European visitors. The guests were treated to a performance in the Herodes Atticus theatre of *Antigone*, a play about principled defiance of authority, which had lost none of its power in the 2,377 years since it was first staged on that southern incline of the Acropolis. Reciting in ancient Greek but with modern pronunciation, a Cretan law student gave Antigone's lament, what a French professor (one of Zay's advisers) described as 'a note of sincerity which stirred the emotions'.

If there is one generalization to make about every single person who was trying, in the 1930s, to influence Athenian life – from boneheaded police chiefs to experimental writers, artists or architects – it might be this: they were all struggling to respond to the intractable reality created by the concentration, in a single urban space, of more than a million people who all represented, or aspired to represent, one variety or another of the Greek identity and experience. Previously Hellenism had been a scattered phenomenon, more numerous outside the Greek state than within in it; now it was much more densely packed, but not necessarily more coherent. Moreover, all these diverse forces, while ostensibly absorbed rather intensely with devising a new definition of Hellenism, were drawing on techniques and ideologies and experiences that came from other places. That was true of the communists and the semi-fascists, of the Francophone liberals, the modernist architects and the *rembetika* players.

It was also true of a new generation of Athenian writers, especially but not only poets, who were deeply concerned with exploring the meaning of Greekness while responding to intellectual impulses from elsewhere, ranging from surrealism to psychoanalysis. Several became writers of global importance. Many were struggling not only to adapt to a new city, Athens, but to process memories of the violent implosion of the wider Hellenism from which they had emerged.

One important breeding ground, or at least way station, for literary talent was the island of Lesbos, which absorbed some of the energy and flair of the Greek population in the adjacent Anatolian port of Ayvalik when that community came to a horrific end in 1922. For example, the writer known as Ilias Venezis, having narrowly escaped alive from Turkish captivity, spent the early years of his career as a civil servant in Mytilene, the capital of Lesbos. After vividly but not bitterly describing the tragedies attending the collapse of his childhood world, he moved to Athens in 1932 to work for the Bank of Greece. Although his writing was not of the kind that curries favour with any earthly power, he accepted a state literary prize from Metaxas in 1939.

Another literary giant who found himself working, reluctantly, for the Metaxas regime was George Seferiades, usually known as Seferis, who was one of several Athenian poets experimenting with surrealism. He too was a product of Ottoman Greek prosperity and refinement, born near Smyrna in 1900. His father was a successful lawyer, who later became a distinguished professor in Athens, where the family moved in 1914. The budding writer joined the Greek diplomatic service in 1927 and served the Metaxas administration in a capacity which involved dealing with foreign correspondents accredited in Athens. But his real passion was exploring, in verse, the threads of connection between the many layers of the Greek experience: from Homer's Troy to imperial Constantinople to the tragedies of his own era.

What Metaxas was attempting in a ridiculous way (by tracing links between ancient Sparta and the conquests of Alexander or the Byzantine emperors), Seferis was seeking to do with vastly greater learning, subtlety, irony and self-doubt. In a few deft words, he could fuse the travails of Odysseus returning from Troy and the recent, terrifying voyages experienced by his kin, fleeing the very same coastline. The stimulus to all this historical enquiry was the collapse of the *Megali Idea*, the fantasy of a territorially extensive neo-Byzantium that would gather in all Greeks. For all his philistinism, Metaxas could at least claim that he had seen the folly of the *Megali Idea* from the start – whether as an adviser to the palace in 1914, or as an opponent of the Smyrna landing in 1919. Only in 1930 had his political nemesis, Venizelos, fully accepted that Greek interests were best served by cordial relations with Turkey, based on respect for borders: a policy which Metaxas scrupulously continued.

Instead of a sprawling empire, Greeks found themselves faced with a sprawling metropolis, which was too big and diverse for anyone to master. It could at best be regulated (by, for example, limiting the number of floors in an apartment block) and sensibly administered, with water supplies and food markets. Its micro-communities could make ingenious compromises with the reality of a vast city by, for example, adapting old systems of match-making and dowry-giving without fundamentally changing them. But nobody could plan the future of this amorphous urban space with any confidence.

As Seferis could see, however, there was nothing more than an illusion of stability, of a final destination, in the great, confusing conurbation where his extended family had settled: in Kydathenaion Street in the heart of the Plaka district, to be precise. From that vantage point he records the superficially urban chatter of green-horns who wandered between the city's two main plazas – Syntagma or Constitution Square and Omonia, or Concord Square – even though it was painfully obvious that their unconscious mind was filled with entirely different images, from deserted quays to bare cliffs plunging into choppy waters.

> What are they up to, all these people who say
> they're from Athens or Piraeus?
> One comes in from Salamis, and he asks some fellow:
> 'I suppose you're on your way from Omonia?'
> 'Oh no,' the other one says, all pleased.
> 'From Syntagma. I ran into Yanni, he stood me an ice cream.'

Meanwhile Greece travels onwards
And we know nothing, we do not know that all of us
Are sailors high and dry
We have not grasped the bitterness of harbours
Where every ship has sailed.
And those who do sense it, we mock.

# 18

# The Darkest Decade
## 1940–50

*Manolis Glezos defies Nazi occupation by removing a swastika
from the Parthenon – famine takes hold in Athens – divisions
within Greece loom after Italian capitulation in 1943 – the
British liberate Athens in October 1944 – conflict erupts after
demonstrators are killed in December 1944 – a month-long
battle for Athens – the visit by Churchill at Christmas 1944 –
the poet Embeirikos recalls his abduction by communists – the
metallurgist George Varoufakis suffers in an anti-leftist witch-hunt*

Manolis Glezos was a magnificent-looking man, especially
in old age. He had a mane of white hair, and the look in
his glistening blue eyes could change teasingly. It oscillated
between mischievous schoolboy humour, shrewd interrogation of
those around him and righteous – but not pompous – indignation.
There was never any bitterness, although he was sentenced to death
four times and spent fifteen of his ninety-seven years in jail or
internal exile. Every one of his competing impulses seemed to come
from the heart, and this made for a personality of great charisma,
acknowledged even by those who felt that some of his political
choices were wrong.

When he died on 30 March 2020, people remembered one
main thing about his turbulent life. Eighty years earlier, he and
a fellow nineteen-year-old had carried out a uniquely spectacular
act of resistance against the Nazi masters of Athens, whose armour

rolled in on 27 April 1941. The deed gave heart to the city as it braced for a long night of occupation. If they had not noticed already, readers of the tightly controlled Greek press learned about it in a terse announcement which appeared in identical form in all newspapers: 'During the night of the 30th to the 31st of May the German military flag which was flying over the Acropolis was removed by persons unknown. Stringent investigations are being conducted. The perpetrators and their accomplices will be subjected to the penalty of death.'

Only in 1982, with the advent of a left-wing government, were Glezos and his friend Lakis Santas invited by Greek state television to tell the full story of what they did. One of the country's best-known journalists, Freddy Germanos, gave them more than an hour to describe that extraordinary night, with the aid of maps, old newsreels and brief appearances by others who were tangentially involved. In a country where broadcasting by the state monopoly was often pretty dreary, it made for an enthralling spectacle – not least because of the affectionate banter between two middle-aged men, recalling their wildest teenage jape. The two of them took turns to reminisce, in such perfect sync that it felt like a single narrative.

As they recalled, they were promising pupils at an Athens high school known for taking boys from rough districts and helping them succeed. They were full of young zeal, writing slogans against the 'fascism' of the Metaxas regime, and swearing to liberate Rhodes from the Italians, who had controlled the Dodecannese since 1912. Then, rather confusingly for the boys, on 28 October 1940 Metaxas suddenly became an anti-fascist hero as he led Greece into the Second World War. In what became known in the nation's annals as the great *Ochi* – No! – the general refused a demand from Benito Mussolini to let the Italian army, already in occupation of Albania, march into Greece. Glezos and his schoolfriends were slightly too young to join the heroic Greek campaign in the Albanian mountains which rallied the nation and at least briefly healed internal fissures between left and right, 'old Greeks' and Anatolian newcomers. Six months later, when the Nazis came to the aid of their beleaguered allies and pushed the Greek and British forces southwards, Glezos and his friends felt their hour had come. They and their parents had listened in anguish as Athens Radio gave its last free broadcast, culminating in the national anthem, hours before the city fell.

> The German invaders are at the gates of the city. Brothers and sisters, keep the spirit of the front firmly in your souls... Soon the radio station of Athens will no longer be Greek; it will be German, and it will broadcast lies. Greek people, do not listen! The war continues and it will continue, until the final victory. Long live the Greek nation!

As the radio had urged them, Athenians kept their doors and windows firmly shut as German tanks and goose-stepping soldiers took control of the city. But Glezos was soon having eager discussions with his gang, especially his close friend Lakis, about what resistance might be possible. 'The hard reality was that we had no weapons; we wanted to attack vehicles with Molotov cocktails but we didn't know how to make them... we were badly prepared.' Then one day Manolis and Lakis were walking in the Zappeion park and they glanced upwards and saw the German army banner – a swastika combined with older military symbols – flapping above the eastern end of the Acropolis. 'Do you see that?' Manolis asked his friend. '*En taxei* – Alright...' Lakis quietly replied, and their minds were made up.

Incredibly, they made a reconnaissance expedition on 9 May and established that the Sacred Rock, under cover of darkness, was accessible. A day later the Acropolis received a visit from Heinrich Himmler, one of many top Nazis who were fascinated by the ancient Greeks but despised the modern ones. On 20 May, the Germans launched an airborne invasion of Crete, and by the end of the month the island was in their hands and the whole of Greece was under Axis control. It was the fall of Crete that redoubled the determination of Manolis and Lakis to make a visible show of resistance. They met up at 8 p.m. on the appointed evening. Another friend of theirs, Antonis, also joined them, but when the mission was explained, he declined to take part, being more of an intellectual type than a commando. 'Very well, your job will be to write about us – because our mission may not succeed,' Glezos replied. He and Lakis then walked purposefully through the Psirri neighbourhood and into the upper reaches of the Plaka and Anafiotika districts till they reached the northern base of the Acropolis and entered the cavity which is now identified as the Mycenaean spring, a fissure in the rock that was first used as a water source 3,000 years earlier. American archaeologists had recently installed some very basic handles on the rock face. This made it possible for a fit person with steady nerves to move up or down the 40-metre funnel quite swiftly. Using only a pocket torch, they made their ascent – only to find that the final handle, which had been in place a few weeks earlier, was missing. They had to make a leap to reach the surface of the Acropolis, emerging just to the west of the Erechtheion. They were in a space which may in ancient times have been used by the Arrephoroi – the pairs of little girls who were chosen annually to weave a new robe for Athena, and feature in many other rituals on the Rock.

For Manolis and Lakis, simply standing on the citadel in the light of a quarter moon was an exhilarating experience. 'We felt we were worthy descendants of our [ancient] forebears,' recalled Lakis, with awe and amazement – not boastfulness – in his voice. As Glezos tells the story, they decided to throw a small stone to see if there would be any reaction from the German garrison which was concentrated near the Propylaea. There was none. In recent days, the sounds of a party had been heard from the western end of the Rock: apparently the Germans were celebrating the conquest of Crete. Perhaps that prompted them to let down their guard.

Glezos described how they crept along the northern wall of the citadel, passing the Erechtheion where, as he put it, 'Athena and

Poseidon had their contest over Athens', and finally reaching the raised, circular platform where the flagpole stood. Another pebble was thrown: again there was no reaction.

Leaping up to the pole, they tried dragging the hated banner down. It proved harder than expected. It was a big piece of cloth, over 6 metres wide. They realized that it was held in place by three wire ropes, and used Lakis' knife to break the binding that held them together. Surreally, Lakis borrowed Manolis' dark trousers (his own were conspicuously light) before bounding up again to the base of the pole and then tugging on one of the ropes. Suddenly the banner crashed down and enveloped them. 'We embraced each other and did a little dance,' Manolis would recall. They then folded the flag and returned to the cavity. Before leaving the pole, however, they pointedly covered it with their fingerprints, so that nobody would be falsely accused. The flag was far too big to bring away with them, so they cut a piece from the top left-hand corner, and threw the remainder down to the bottom of the defunct well which gave the Mycenaean spring its name.

By now it was well past midnight. Although they were breaking a curfew they did a small perambulation around the streets near Constitution Square and finally walked down Ermou Street as far as the Kapnikarea church, the lovely jewel of Byzantine architecture which stands in a small square in the eastern part of the street. At that point, a Greek policeman, guarding the nearby Savings Bank, stopped them and asked for their names and papers. Lakis showed his student ID, Manolis had none but gave his name accurately. They said they were coming home from a party. Not unkindly, the policeman said, 'You'd better get home quickly, don't let the Germans catch you.'

Over the following weeks, as a cry went up over the flag, the policeman realized he had met the perpetrators. But he was a good enough Greek patriot to keep the secret. Likewise, Greek prosecutors, tasked with investigating the flag's removal, apparently did what they could to distract the German authorities from the idea that it was an act of local resistance. It could, they said, have been a maverick Nazi soldier, perhaps an Austrian, perhaps the driver of a mysterious car which was seen driving up to the Acropolis around that time. At any rate, those are the desperate arguments which the Greek officials said they used, and Glezos was gracious enough to believe those officials. In those early days of the occupation, the national unity which had surged during the Albanian campaign returned, even (surreptitiously) among those servants of the Greek state who were working for the collaborationist government. Or so people very much want to believe.

In any case, Glezos and his friend would soon disappear into the underworld of the communist-led resistance movement, EAM (the National Liberation Front) and its military arm ELAS. Glezos' brother Nikos, three years his junior, followed suit, and his fate was different. In May 1944, a misspelled message – clearly scribbled in haste – arrived at the family home. It had been thrown from the back of a truck, complete with an address, in the hope that somebody would deliver it. It read: 'Beloved mother, I kiss you and send greetings. Today I am going to be executed. I am going… falling for the sake of the Greek people.' He was one of ninety-two people executed on 10 May.

To understand what Glezos and his family were about, it is important to remember that Manolis' earliest years were spent not in Athens but in the village of Apeiranthos on the island of Naxos, where his family came from. It was a place known even among Naxiots as a breeding ground for free and even criminal spirits. Life in Apeiranthos, where people made a decent but hard-earned living through stock-breeding and farming terraced hillsides, was both highly individualistic and also communal. As in many rural Greek settlements, households competed hard with each other but also felt and celebrated their common identity. The place had a rich tradition of oral poetry and storytelling: people would gather to tell fanciful tales, often with the playful first line: 'I went out thieving one day…' Well into his old age, Glezos would return with relish to the village which he had left at the age of ten: he would participate with gusto in the dancing and flirtation which a wedding celebration or feast-day could offer, sometimes for days on end. Like so many people who won distinction in the modern city of Athens, he arrived from elsewhere and he brought to the capital a mindset, and above all a sense of freedom, that came from a different place.

In Athens, the boost to morale created by the swastika's removal did not last for long, as food and other essentials ran short. The huge increase in the population of greater Athens, resulting from the Anatolian disaster, was suddenly a terrible liability. There were well over a million mouths to feed, the numbers swollen by destitute veterans of the Albanian campaign – unable to return to homes in other parts of Greece – and Axis troops. Both Greece as a whole and Athens in particular were desperately dependent on food supplies from elsewhere. An Allied blockade combined with a mixture of indifference, incompetence and malice from the Axis authorities. Even as the Germans and Italians vied to grab the assets of Greece, they competed to avoid responsibility for sending food to its population.

The winter of 1941–2 was perhaps the most nightmarish in the history of Athens since the late fifth century BCE, when the city suffered plague and then the economic hardships which went with military defeat. In the year following October 1941, deaths in the greater Athens area amounted to nearly 50,000, up from 15,000 the previous year. That conveys, at a bare minimum, the suffering which the conurbation endured, particularly during the depths of an icy winter when the population's health was devastated by vitamin deficiency and the sheer exhaustion of trying to stay alive. Suffering was particularly acute in Piraeus, and the refugee quarters whose inhabitants had barely recovered from the shock of expulsion from Anatolia. The industries which had provided some employment for refugee households largely collapsed. Frail bodies became frailer. People resorted to desperate measures, gathering wild grass and snails on the Attica hills, which became denuded as trees were chopped down for firewood.

The collaborationist government's attempts to procure more food from the countryside were unsuccessful, as the value of the currency printed to cover the costs of occupation plunged. Farmers simply withheld their produce, as the survival of their own communities took precedence. In an uncanny rerun of the anomie described by Thucydides, people ignored the elaborate church norms for the disposal of the dead and buried them wherever they could, or even dumped corpses for others to deal with.

Even if they were lucky enough to escape the worst, every Athenian who lived through that nightmare retains some dark memories. Maria Becket, a feisty campaigner for human rights and the environment, used to say that her life was changed by the experience of opening the door of her comfortable Athenian home to find the corpse of a starved girl who like her was around nine. Toula Michailidou, who grew up in another middle-class Athenian household, recalls that her parents' efforts to shield her from the worst horrors were not successful. On a walk near their house, they ran into a hanged man, and understood that he was a black marketeer. George Sfikas, a gentle octogenarian who devoted his life to mountaineering and botany, escaped starvation because his father was a baker; but when he, as a toddler, asked for something more than bread, his mother would take wool from the mattresses to sell in the market and raise a few extra pennies.

The food situation improved from mid-1942, as shipments of grain came via neutral states such as Sweden and Turkey, and as the Allies – under pressure from the Greek diaspora – eased the blockade. Grain from Canada, distributed by the Red Cross, proved to be a lifeline. But the near-breakdown of the country's internal food distribution had political as well as humanitarian consequences. Both in the countryside and in the rougher parts of Athens, the notional state authorities, operating as part of the collaborationist apparatus, lost legitimacy. Entirely new forms of authority, tough and resilient ones, began emerging to fill the vacuum. None was more effective than the communist-led National Liberation Front (EAM).

As in other Axis-held countries, a formally independent administration justified its existence by claiming that it was trying to mitigate the consequences of occupation for ordinary people; and at least in marginal ways, it did so. The Greek puppet government was headed initially by George Tsolakoglou, a general who had fought in the Albanian campaign. Other institutions, including the central bank, the police, the judiciary and the church, continued to function, with complex moral consequences. At the time of the German takeover, the head of the Athenian Church was Chrysanthos Philippides, an archbishop who had led the Greeks of Trebizond in north-eastern Turkey very resourcefully during the travails of the First World War. He refused to swear in a quisling government, and was replaced by another powerful cleric, Damaskinos Papandreou (no relation of the politicians of that name), who remained one of the few fixed points in the Greek firmament when the country plunged deeper into division and chaos. Both Damaskinos and the wartime police chief Angelos Evert were later recognized as 'righteous among the Gentiles' because they did what they could to protect the Athenian Jews from annihilation. As a result, that minority had a marginally better fate than the large, Spanish-speaking Jewish community of Thessaloniki, almost all of whom perished.

The Axis powers treated Greece as a source of bounty to be raided rather than as any kind of viable concern, with competition between Berlin and Rome for Greek assets becoming absurd and dysfunctional (for the Axis) at times. As historian Mark Mazower recounts in his vivid account of the occupation, executives from powerful German corporations were attached to the Werhmacht High Command and they used this position to requisition Greece's mining and metal output. It was not in the interests of either occupying power for Greece to starve – even a system of slave labour requires toilers to be alive and minimally healthy – but neither Axis power was prepared to make much effort to divert food to Athens.

Under the system of occupation, Germany was responsible for Athens, Thessaloniki and some Aegean islands, including most of Crete, while Bulgaria controlled swathes of Macedonia and Thrace and formally annexed them. That left Italy in charge of the remainder of the country, until its fascist government capitulated in 1943, with huge consequences for the balance of power inside Greece. The Germans took over the Italian zone, while ELAS fighters managed to capture a lot of Italian weapons and reinforced their de facto control of many rural areas of the country. It gradually became obvious that two very different forces were aspiring to control post-war Greece. On one hand, EAM was consolidating its authority over much of the country, with its own courts and local administration in which women were politically empowered for the first time. Outside Greece, mainly in Egypt, there were British-protected institutions: a monarch, a government-in-waiting and an army which did good service in the Allied cause despite having its own ideological fissures.

From late 1943, the collaborationist government became increasingly concerned with forestalling a left-wing takeover of Greece after the German withdrawal, which seemed increasingly likely. With the encouragement of the Germans it began to use the Greek gendarmes and a newly established force called the Security Battalions as a counterweight to ELAS. As Mazower observes, before the Italian capitulation, there was still some remnant of the proud, patriotic unity among the Greeks which had blossomed during the battle in Albania. After the capitulation, the war became more of a conflict among Greeks – in some respects a class war. Supporters of EAM coined the collective insult *germanotsoliades* – stooges of the Germans – to describe the various compatriots ranged against them, including a shadowy ultra-rightist group that was known by a single Greek letter: X or *Khi*. The term *germanotsoliades* was revived after 2010 to describe, rather unfairly, anybody who saw merit in the economic prescriptions being proposed by Angela Merkel as part of an emergency economic rescue.

Many of the most dramatic episodes of the occupation, especially in the months before it ended in October 1944, occurred in communities that were already used to suffering and strife: the poor but proud neighbourhoods dominated by Anatolian refugees, such as Kokkinia and – closer to the city centre – Kaisariani, which became known as little Stalingrad. These areas became military strongholds of ELAS and targets of the forces serving the collaborationist government. The labyrinths of rapidly constructed refugee housing proved to be favourable terrain for street fighters determined to keep the gendarmes and security battalions at bay. The Germans provided the collaborationist forces with logistical help but to an increasing extent this was a battle between Greeks, an ideological war in the making. Over five days in early March, the gendarmes and battalionists made repeated attacks on the heart of Kokkinia and were held at bay by a mixture of mass demonstrations and ELAS firepower. But the occupation forces did not leave quietly: they abducted 300 local men, and thirty-seven of them, including five refugees of Armenian origin, were executed. Over the following weeks and months, the authorities began a series of dawn round-ups or *bloccos* in which all able-bodied men would be ordered to appear in the nearest square. Homes would be searched for weapons, while hooded stool-pigeons picked out people who were alleged to be members or supporters of EAM.

Kokkinia suffered a notoriously brutal *blocco* in August 1944. The people fingered in such raids might be shot on the spot, or more likely hauled off to a detention centre, such as the one at Haidari. Even by the grisly standards of the time, this was a place of unspeakable horror, located near the road to Eleusis west of Athens. It was a place entirely without sanitation, or natural water supply; food and drink rations were minimal and beatings and whippings were frequent. It was from Haidari that 200 inmates were taken off to be executed at the Kaisariani firing range on 1 May

1944. In the nearby streets of Kaisariani – the refugee district under a hill that was associated in quieter times with a honey-making monastery – there had been a fierce battle in late April 1944: local ELAS units held at bay about 1,000 gendarmes and battalionists who were determined to wrest control of the district from them. As in Kokkinia, the fighters were not numerous, but they apparently enjoyed the support of a well-disciplined population.

Like their equivalents in west Belfast or Gaza, EAM and ELAS were ever more confident as masters of an unrecognized government, acting decisively and with greater consensus than any other authority could muster. Long before the Germans left, there were clear portents of an impending struggle for Greece: a struggle which had begun, in some people's eyes, during the Metaxas dictatorship of the 1930s. Others felt it had been brewing even longer, going back to the chaotic mixture of factions and interest groups which had waged the Greek war of independence of the 1820s.

Things came to a bloody climax at the end of 1944. It is worth recalling that in 1916, Athens had degenerated for just one day into a battleground involving foreign forces, mostly French and British, and rival Greek factions. Deaths and injuries probably totalled a few hundred. Three decades later, and nearly three months after the city's Nazi occupiers had withdrawn, the drama was re-enacted on a bloodier scale across an urban area whose size and population had vastly increased. The fighting raged for thirty-three days, left parts of the city in ruins and cost the lives of around 7,000 combatants, plus many more who were caught in crossfire, shelling or aerial bombing. This time the protagonists were EAM and its military arm ELAS on one side, and on the other the combined forces of a pro-Western Greek government, the British empire and Greek groups who were tainted in varying degrees by collaboration. Given that Britain was determined to prevail, and that Joseph Stalin had ceded influence over Greece to Winston Churchill, the outcome was never in doubt. By January the ELAS forces were in retreat, having endured and inflicted terrible suffering. The Athenian battle of late 1916 is known in Greek parlance as the Noemvriana; the much darker events which began in December 1944 are known as the Dekemvriana.

Older Athenians still wonder whether the capital stumbled into civil war or whether it was deliberately provoked by one side or the other. In theory, the fact that Churchill and Stalin were clear-eyed about the post-war future of Europe should have made everything very simple. The British leader met his counterpart in Moscow in October 1944, and as he recalled afterwards, he suggested that the Soviet Union should have 90 per cent of the influence in Romania and 75 per cent in Bulgaria, while in Hungary and Yugoslavia they would settle for 50 per cent each. In Greece, 90 per cent of the say would be British. (In further Anglo-Soviet talks a few days later, the Soviet share in Hungary and Bulgaria was raised to 80 per cent.) Stalin signalled his approval of the carve-up by making a large tick on Churchill's scribbled note.

Britain was already a powerful factor in Greece's future because of its role as host of exiled Hellenic politicians and troops in Egypt. Left-wing elements had been purged from these forces following pro-EAM mutinies in July 1943 and April 1944. The exiled army included a 'mountain brigade' which had fought well in Italy, and a special forces unit called the Sacred Band which had carried out sabotage operations in the Aegean islands.

On 18 October 1944, six days after the German pull-out, British forces marched into Athens, escorting the liberal politician George Papandreou who became prime minister. They received a tumultuous reception from crowds waving American, Soviet and British flags, and ELAS units were among the welcoming party. An agreement to merge the various Greek forces had already been brokered by the British at a meeting in Lebanon. Papandreou soon raised the Greek flag over the Acropolis and praised the heroic role played by local resistance forces in defeating Nazism. He formed a cabinet which included six ministers from EAM. But with every November day, the omens looked more sinister. ELAS refused to disarm and dissolve itself unless the mountain brigade suffered the same fate, and unless collaborationist forces like the Security Battalions were disbanded and held to account.

Watching events in Greece, Churchill opined that a clash with EAM was inevitable, and he warned Papandreou against dissolving the mountain brigade. EAM's leaders also braced for a confrontation. They were prepared, under Soviet pressure, to share power but not to be squeezed into non-existence. At least that is the best guess anyone can make. Doubtless there were tensions within the communist camp between the soft line which Moscow was imposing and the militancy of the commanders who had fought hard to achieve control of Greece.

On 1 December, the British commander General Ronald Scobie issued an order for the disarmament of resistance forces, in practice mainly ELAS, and said there would be dire consequences if this was not obeyed. The EAM ministers withdrew from government, and called a general strike for Monday 4 December. They also called supporters to a demonstration on 3 December in Constitution Square, which the government after some hesitation forbad. News of the ban was carried in all newspapers except the communist one, *Rizospastis*, which claimed to have received it too late. On Sunday morning, tens of thousands of people converged on the square. The flags they brandished were carefully chosen: many American ones, a few Soviet, hardly any British. (At that time, America was critical of Britain's anti-EAM line, while the Soviet position was tolerant, as promised, of British-guided policy.) The huge square, including the pale fortress known as the Old Palace, was ringed by police and other forces who were watching from upper floors and wished the communists every possible harm. These included the communist-hunters of *Khi* – whose leader Colonel George Grivas would later wage war in Cyprus.

Shots came from somewhere, or more likely from several places, and around thirty people were killed. Arguments about the incident have long raged, but it seems clear that the bullets came from Greek police and other forces who were ranged with the government, including perhaps *Khi*. One important testimony came from Nikos Farmakis, a right-wing politician, businessman and *Khi* veteran. He and his armed comrades were observing the demonstration from an upper floor of the palace (the current parliament). As Farmakis recalled much later, the police had told their own men and armed supporters to hold fire until the demonstrators reached the Tomb of the Unknown Soldier, below the palace; then they could 'fire freely' at the demonstrators. The resulting horror felt, to any ordinary Athenians who leaned towards EAM, like a declaration of war. The next day a general strike began, and Sunday's victims were buried in an impressive public demonstration, in which three women carried a newly made banner with a message: 'When the people face the danger of tyranny, they must choose between tyranny and weapons – EAM.'

EAM had clearly opted for weapons, but at first it chose its targets carefully. Initially it avoided attacking British forces but focused on the police targets associated with right-wing and collaborator forces, including prisons where notorious collaborators were held. It suspected the pro-British forces of preparing to release the collaborators, and it wanted to mete out its own punishment. An early flashpoint was the headquarters of *Khi*, in the Theseion district near the ancient Agora; ironically British soldiers had to rescue Grivas, who would later be responsible for killing many of Her Majesty's forces in Cyprus.

Although he was responsible for many other fronts in a global contest, Churchill was following events in Athens hour by hour. It was on 5 December that he issued two memorable communications. One was to General Ronald Scobie:

> You are responsible for maintaining order in Athens and for neutralizing all EAM-ELAS hands approaching the city. You may make any regulations you like for the strict control of the streets or for the rounding-up of any number of truculent

persons. Naturally ELAS will try to put women and children in the van whenever shooting may occur. You must be clever about this and avoid mistakes. But do not hesitate to fire at any armed male in Athens who assails the British authority or the Greek authority with which we are working... Do not... hesitate to act as if you were in a conquered city where a local rebellion is in progress.

The other, equally blunt message was to Rex Leeper, the British ambassador:

You must force Papandreou to stand to his duty and assure him that he will be supported by all our forces if he does so. Should he resign, he should be locked up till he comes to his senses, when the fighting will probably be over. It might well be that he should be in bed and inaccessible. The day has long gone past when any particular group of Greek politicians can influence this mob rising.

I have put the whole question of the defence of Athens and the maintenance of law and order in the hands of General Scobie and assured him that he will be supported in the use of whatever force is necessary... You [and Papandreou] should both support Scobie in every possible way and you should suggest to him any means which occur to you of making his action more vigorous and decisive.

ELAS escalated its attacks on government targets, especially the police. Its commanders must have been taken aback by the firmness with which Britain was prepared to back up its Athenian partners. Where ELAS commanders in the field longed to hit even harder, they were held back by their political leaders, presumably under the ultimate influence of Moscow. ELAS could have made devastating attacks on the British forces that were deployed across Greece in small numbers, but the political guidance was to avoid doing so.

With regard to the Acropolis, the military calculus was, if anything, more complicated. ELAS veterans said afterwards that they asserted control of the citadel as soon as the fighting erupted, only to withdraw after talks mediated by the Red Cross, on the understanding that the citadel would be treated as a neutral, sacred space. Whatever the understanding, British paratroopers took control of the Rock on 6 December. In a remarkable set of photographs of the period taken by the Ukrainian photographer Dimitri Kessel, they are seen firing mortars and machine-gun fire into the nearby districts of Athens. Returning fire caused damage to the monuments of the Acropolis, but it was relatively minor compared with previous battles over the Rock. However, there is one murky story that emerges in an official military history of Greece, which in turn cites various Communist Party of Greece (KKE) documents. It says the leadership of the KKE gave orders for the British-occupied Acropolis to be blown up. However, the ELAS commander who received the order refused to carry it out, and he later alleged that the person who gave the instruction, a member of the KKE politburo, must have been serving dubious foreign interests if he issued such an outrageous order. He was then assured that the order had been approved by the entire party leadership. Is that story true? It could be black propaganda.

It was widely alleged, at the time and long afterwards, that Churchill made the situation worse by insisting unconditionally on the return to Greece, at some early date, of King George II. Many people, including Ambassador Leeper and his American counterpart in Athens, Lincoln McVeigh, thought the imposition of an unpopular monarch was a counterproductive policy, which would alienate many middle-of-the-road Greeks. In reality, Churchill was not only ruthlessly bent on prevailing in Greece, he was ruthless enough to be flexible as expediencies shifted. By 11 December or thereabouts, he and others had concluded that Scobie was not up to the job and needed replacing as commander. But removing him openly would be a sign of weakness, so two new commanders were brought in, along with ample reinforcements, while formally leaving Scobie in place but with diminished authority. On the question of Greece's future head of state, Churchill likewise changed his mind: he came round to the view that installing the Archbishop of Athens, Damaskinos, as regent would be a better solution. This was a change from his earlier assessment that the cleric was a 'pestilential priest, a survival from the Middle Ages'.

Over Christmas 1944, Churchill and his foreign secretary Anthony Eden did something astonishing: they paid a flying visit to Athens, or rather to the still encircled city centre which remained under British and government control. The British embassy, a former residence of prime minister Venizelos, was a large, exposed mansion on Vasilissis Sofias Avenue, where the entire diplomatic staff was camping out in freezing conditions as sniper fire crackled outside and bullets dented the walls. Much of the fire was coming from Kaisariani, the communist bastion a couple of kilometres to the east. Churchill seemed to relish the dramatic environment as he gave a press conference for British and American journalists who were dubious about his policies. Having expressed a wish to 'meet this scheming little Greek cleric' who was now a contender for supreme political power, he rapidly established good personal chemistry with Archbishop Damaskinos, who at six foot six was lofty, not little.

On Christmas Day, the prelate was invited to board HMS *Ajax*, the ship which was escorting Churchill. The visit took a surreal turn because the sailors were in the midst of a Yuletide fancy-dress party, and they assumed on seeing the robed prelate that he was simply one of the costumed revellers. On the evening of 26 December, some more serious business was done. Churchill and his new clerical friend co-presided at a conference in the Greek foreign ministry. As Churchill recalled later, 'We took our seats in a large, bleak room after darkness fell. The winter is cold in Athens. There was no heating, and a few hurricane lamps cast a dim light upon the scene.' They were joined by the American and French ambassadors, the Soviet military representative Mr Popov… and three communist representatives who were invited at Churchill's suggestion. 'The three communist leaders were late. It was not their fault. There had been prolonged bickering at the outposts… I was already speaking when they entered the room. They were presentable figures in British battle dress.'

Over the next two days, more serious political negotiations took place. Crucially, it was established that the archbishop was a legitimate and credible figure in the eyes of most non-communist Greeks. Churchill had to use all his personal authority to persuade the king to agree to a regency on 30 December. Papandreou was replaced as prime minister by Nikolaos Plastiras, the republican general who had staged a liberal anti-monarchist coup in 1922. But the prime minister's willingness to engage in jaw-jaw with Greek politicians and clerics did not imply any let-up in war-war. On 27 December British forces launched fresh attacks on ELAS throughout the area of greater Athens, with Spitfires strafing the neighbourhoods where the leftists were strongest, and their final expulsion from the capital became inevitable.

ELAS was not letting up either. During Churchill's stay, a plot was discovered to bomb the Grande-Bretagne Hotel where he was staying. As he said in a message to his wife, 'You will have read about the plan to blow up our headquarters at the Hotel Grande Bretagne. I do not think that was to my advantage. Nevertheless, a ton of dynamite was placed in sewers by extremely skilful hands.' Among those hands were those of Manolis Glezos, who told the *Observer* in 2014: 'I myself was holding the wire with the cord and had to unwrap it' after spending hours crawling about, along with a team of thirty, through the sewage. As Glezos and many others recount the story, the operation was called off at the last moment when it was learned that Churchill was in the hotel; blowing up General Scobie would have been, for ELAS, a legitimate act – but eliminating one of the Big Three leaders of the anti-Hitler coalition would have been a step too far. Questions remain, though, about whether the dynamite (which would have killed the Soviet envoy to Athens and hundreds of ordinary Greeks) was ever meant to go off. Possibly the whole operation was just a warning.

Whichever side they were on, elderly Athenians still ponder that and many other questions which arise out of the December events. Sfikas the botanist, whose family included several ELAS fighters, recalls the bitterness people felt when, from their viewpoint, the British ceased to be friends. 'Literally from one day to another, they went from being allies to terrible enemies.' He remembers a rude little street song among boys of his age: 'The girls who used to go with Germans, the girls who used to go with Wops, now they've got little English boys in shorts...' Two of his uncles were detained – one sent to an island prison, the other to a camp in Egypt which had been built for Italian prisoners. 'They were idealists; they didn't realize that the big powers had already sorted things out over their heads...' His cousin Nestor, later a famous iconographer turned digital artist, was old enough at sixteen to help the ELAS fighters, albeit not with weapons, in their four-day assault on the gendarmerie building in Makriyanni, south of the Acropolis, which was routed with the help of British armour. Nestor remembers making a frantic dash back to the Nea Smyrni district, where rebels were still safe. 'The Russians had taken Romania... and Greece fell into the hands of the English; they had made an agreement with Stalin. The English were free to do anything they wanted,' he recalled, interviewed at the age of ninety-one.

A different perspective on the same events was offered by Andreas Embeirikos. He was one of the most brilliant, original figures to emerge from the literary and intellectual world of Greece in the twentieth century. Like his friend George Seferis, he wrote poetry and prose that mixed a Greek sensibility with styles and techniques which had emerged far from the Aegean. Both were pioneers of modernism in Greek literature. Of the two, Embeirikos was more innovative; he interrogated every aspect of his background as the son of a wealthy and influential Greek shipowner. Born in Romania in 1901, he had studied in London, and then in Paris, where he qualified as a psychoanalyst. By the early 1930s, he had embraced Marxism and saw some merit in the Soviet Union. He renounced all involvement with his father's business, and was horrified by the repression of a strike at a mine in Euboea which his father controlled. But he was too free a spirit to conform to any Marxist orthodoxy, preferring the eclectic approach of French friends like André Breton, who combined anti-fascism with surrealism. He was close to Marguerite Yourcenar, who dedicated a book to him.

But the most decisive episode in his colourful life was not in a Parisian salon. It was the week he spent as one of the 15,000 or so people who were taken hostage by ELAS in the midst of their losing the battle for control of Athens against the combined forces of the British empire and the Greek government. His nightmare started on 31 January 1944, by which time the communists had seen many of their real or perceived supporters deported to Egypt by the British, a process that might now be called rendition.

Three men came to the poet's apartment in the Patision district of Athens, which was inside the rebel-controlled sector, and not far from the line where gun battles were sputtering. The trio searched the place for weapons, saying they were from the Civil Guard – *politikofylaki* – a secretive unit that was answerable to EAM. He was told that he must come for 'a little questioning' about his life and views. His captors seemed to have no idea that he had been a Marxist, or a poet: they simply saw him as a shipowner's son and a presumed class enemy. His mother, living in the same building, saw him off with a deep foreboding.

Over the next seven days, the poet was marched with hundreds of other people between many places of confinement, first in Athens and then in the mountains of Attica and Boeotia. Each place of captivity was more horrible, crowded and ominous than the next. First he was held in a building not far from his home, where he recalls one of the guards sneering at him: 'Do you have a mother, a father? Well, they will cry for you soon...' Embeirikos had a strong sense that his death was imminent, and felt his life flash before him: his joys, sorrows, love affairs and above all memories of his half-Russian mother.

Then he was taken to a north-western suburb of Athens, Peristeri, where the basement of the Phoibos cinema had been turned into an internment centre for hundreds of people, of every age, ideology, class and gender. He was questioned there by a notorious interrogator called Panagopoulos who sent many people to their death. The most persistent query was 'why did you never join EAM?' – and when he tried saying that he believed in a more liberal kind of socialism, the questioner would reply with contempt. Ironically it was his Russian blood which had given him a certain, initially sympathetic interest in the Soviet Union. Embeirikos recalled feeling a surge of bitterness over the fact that he had renounced the privileges that went with his background, and supported workers' rights, only to be persecuted as a so-called enemy of the people.

Then he and his fellow captives were marched through the countryside. The weather was freezing, and the captives were poorly clad; with every kilometre their stamina and health deteriorated. But if they fell behind, they were at risk of being summarily shot. At one stopping point, he chatted to a lady called Goulandris: not one of the shipowners of that name but an ordinary member of a family well-known, like his own, on the island of Andros. She was then marched off in a different column, and he heard afterwards that she had been shot because, being stout and breathless, she could not keep up. At times, British aircraft were looming overhead – and the poet felt astonished at the coolness and bravery of his guards.

Another place of captivity was a church in the village of Krora which had been a stronghold of the resistance. It was a wrecked, eerie place. Many buildings in and around the village had been burned by the Germans in retaliatory raids. The interior of the church, which had contained some beautiful icons, was half-ruined and the *ieron*, the sacred space around the altar, was packed out with desperate people and their jailers. Here too he saw and heard terrible things: every so often a list of names would be read out, the individuals would be hauled away and they would not return. He overheard his guards discussing a particularly horrible event that had taken place on the north side of Athens. The installations of the Ulen company, where water from the Marathon dam was directed towards various districts of Athens, had become an ELAS stronghold where 'enemies' were executed. Among the victims were around thirty ordinary policemen and a star of the Athenian stage, Eleni Papadaki. Many of the killings (though not Papadaki's) were carried out with an axe. As Embeirikos remembers thinking, there was plenty of water to wash away the blood.

On yet another march northward, as far as a village near Thebes, Embeirikos caught some sleep under a tree, and woke up with a sense that he must rush to rejoin his column or risk being shot. But he saw members of his column running towards him – they said the march had been broken up by a heavy attack with British Spitfires. He was sick and dazed, but free. He staggered as far as a simple farmer's house near the town of Avlona, and won a promise of shelter by addressing his host in Arvanitika, the Albanian-based dialect which was widely spoken in the environs of Athens. By a fluke he had a basic knowledge of the language. In a spirit of Tolstoyan self-abasement, he had once laboured alongside the farm workers on an estate near Athens which his father owned – and picked up some of their Arvanitika. The farmer not only took him in but gave him fresh clothes and helped him to present himself as a member of the local community. Then three more people sought and received shelter in the same house – two men who were fighters with ELAS and their female comrade who was terribly wounded.

The trio were stoical, and generally he was astonished by the bravery of the communist forces. At one point he crouched in a safe place while watching a battle raging between tenacious ELAS foot soldiers and British Sherman tanks. It was obvious that the people who had so nearly killed him believed passionately in what they were doing, and this was driving them to extremes of courage as well as cruelty.

Finally he had the good luck to be picked up by a Red Cross vehicle and taken back to Athens: exhausted and in a high fever. He remained gravely ill for more than a week before recovering and attempting, over the remainder of his life, to make sense of what he had experienced. All his later writings, including an erotic novel entitled *Megas Anatolikos* (The Great Eastern) set on a passenger ship, were in one way or another a response to his week-long brush with death. He confided every detail of the experience to his son, Leonidas, who was born in 1957, and it was a frequent topic of conversation right up to the poet's death in 1975.

As the poet's story shows, certain places in Athens had, by the start of 1945, become lethally dangerous for anybody who was perceived as a right-winger or even the wrong kind of leftist. From spring 1945 and especially from 1946 onwards, it was the other way round. Athens and Greece in general became a perilous place to profess any kind of socialist belief, or any utterance or behaviour that could be construed as close to communism. Even after tensions died down a little, simply being perceived as a fellow traveller – *synodoiporos* – with leftism could affect a person's life chances in all manner of ways. From 1946, the locus of left–right fighting moved to the northern border of Greece, and to some extent the Peloponnese, as a communist-led army drew on Yugoslav and Albanian help to challenge a Greek government whose main international protector, as of early 1947, was the United States. The atmosphere amid the ruins and exhaustion in Athens was somewhat calmer, superficially, but it was still a very unhealthy place to be seen as any kind of leftist. One person who experienced that atmosphere was a gifted budding metallurgist who had grown up in the large Greek community in Egypt and was asked, while in Athens in 1946, to sign a statement eschewing communism. He refused, saying with the truculence of youth that although he was not a Buddhist, he would not sign a paper against Buddhism. George Varoufakis was rewarded by three years of incarceration, some of it in the dreadful conditions of Makronisos, the islet off Attica which had hosted Anatolian refugees in 1923 and had since become a huge prison camp where real and suspected communists were re-educated and encouraged to confess their errors.

Even after his release, the perception that Varoufakis was politically suspect continued to affect his life. A fellow student, a young woman called Eleni from a conservative background, was delegated by a group of far-rightists to keep an eye on him and see whether he showed any sign of subversive behaviour. Inconveniently for the rightists, the two students fell in love and eventually settled down as a couple, both active on the centre-left when circumstances allowed. Then Varoufakis embarked on a career, and its early evolution says a lot about Greece in the immediate aftermath of the 1946–9 civil war. He had an excellent degree, and like many of the energetic Hellenes who had lived in Egypt, was fluent in English and French. Greece was industrializing as Marshall Aid flowed in from the United States. Getting a job should have been easy, and he received plenty of offers. Yet the day after he started work, the police would come to his boss and demand his dismissal as a 'communist'; Varoufakis was then sent away.

Finally he was hired by Greece's best-known steel magnate, the owner of a mill in Eleusis. Panagiotis Angelopoulos was a feisty, self-made man who was powerful enough to ignore the security police's order to fire the new recruit. (He did take the chance to cut his employee's pay.) Varoufakis became the tycoon's inseparable companion as they inspected steel-making technology all over the world. Varoufakis also found time to study the metallurgists of ancient Athens. As he discovered, they knew far more about iron and its compounds than did any of the ham-fisted restorers who made an incompetent effort at conservation around 1900, damaging the columns of the Parthenon with rust-prone clamps. The story of Varoufakis and his career is worth telling, because it highlights both the devastating effects of left–right divisions in post-war Greece and the way people, at an everyday human level, got round this problem.

After Greece fell under military rule in 1967, Varoufakis feared his progressive political ideas might once again get the family into trouble. When his son graduated from one of the top private schools in Athens, he urged the boy to study in some safer country like England, and the advice was taken. Forty years later, Yanis Varoufakis became one of the world's best-known Greeks, first as finance minister for a stormy six months in 2015, and then as a radical guru on global economics.

# 19

# A Wedding and Four Funerals
## 1960–2000

*Change and continuity in an expanding Athens – apartment
buildings as an instrument of urban growth – rites of passage
as historical markers – the burial of Andreas Papandreou in
1996 – the wedding of King Constantine in 1964 – the funeral
of George Seferis in 1971 – the funerals of Mayor Antonis Tritsis
and Melina Mercouri, Socialist colleagues whose paths divided*

How much really changed in Athens in the late twentieth
century, apart from the obvious fact that the city grew much
bigger? The question might seem almost absurd. This was,
after all, the epicentre of a country which lurched from rocky
democracy to a brutal dictatorship, lasting from 1967 to 1974; and
from the right-wing hegemony which prevailed after the civil war
to the radical leftist mood which took hold after 1981.

To anyone who was directly affected by the tragedy of the
dictatorship – for example, through the captivity or torture of
a family member – it is provocative even to pose that question.
The death and revival of democracy were not trivial events, and
no Athenian was untouched by them. Almost the entire public
discourse of Greece since 1974 has been, in one way or another,
a reaction to military rule, a cry of determination to make sure it
will never come back.

But then try a thought experiment. Imagine how greater Athens
would look to an observer who was studying the city intently, but

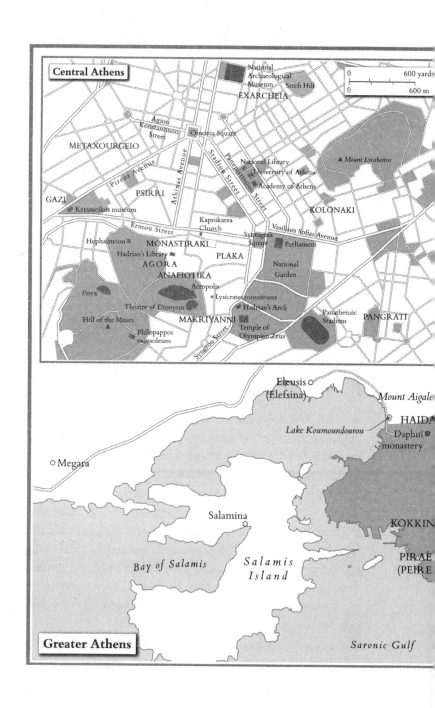

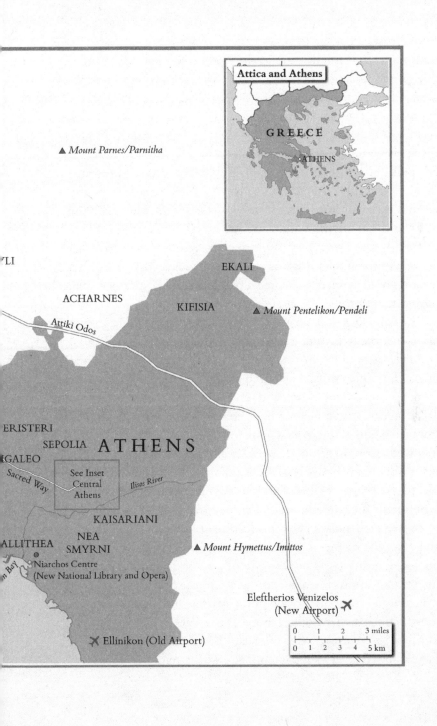

▲ Mount Parnes/Parnitha

Attica and Athens

GREECE

ATHENS

EKALI

ACHARNES

KIFISIA

▲ Mount Pentelikon/Pendeli

Attiki Odos

ˈLI

ERISTERI

SEPOLIA    ATHENS

GALEO

Sacred Way

See Inset
Central
Athens

Ilisos River

KAISARIANI

NEA
SMYRNI

ALLITHEA

▲ Mount Hymettus/Imittos

Niarchos Centre
(New National Library and Opera)

Eleftherios Venizelos
(New Airport) ✈

n Bay

✈ Ellinikon (Old Airport)

| 0 | 1 | | 2 | | 3 miles |
|---|---|---|---|---|---|
| 0 | 1 | 2 | 3 | 4 | 5 km |

from a distance – say from a satellite with powerful sensors. To that observer, it might seem as though the city had experienced one simple, linear trend – not a zigzag. To put it plainly, the urban area endlessly grew, as families and individuals flowed in from the countryside; the model and patterns of growth, and the resulting sociology of the city, did not change all that much. It started in the 1950s, when much of provincial Greece was wrecked by civil war and political contention. The rapid economic expansion stimulated by American aid was concentrated in the capital. Also, for a person tainted by leftist associations, there was more chance of finding work in the anonymity of greater Athens than in a village where everybody knew everybody. One perverse result of the anti-leftist bias in Greece of the 1950s was that many people of mildly socialist leanings became small entrepreneurs, starting shops or other small businesses in Athens.

The emptying of the countryside and the hypertrophic growth of the metropolis became a self-compounding process. Small towns and villages became unsustainable (with migration to Germany or Anglophone countries as well as Athens) and the Athenian monopoly on decent schools and services became more entrenched. To be precise, the population of greater Athens more than doubled from 1,379,000 in 1951 to 3,027,000 in 1981. Much of this expansion followed a certain template which was endlessly reproduced. In 1930s Athens, the newly legalized *polykatoikia* – multiple dwelling-place – had flourished as a middle-class indulgence and field of experiment for contemporary architectural styles. But from the 1950s, the *polykatoikia* became a feature of humbler Athenian life and a flexible way to accommodate urban growth. Anybody who possessed a tiny piece of property or land in greater Athens felt the temptation to invite a contractor to tear down any existing structure and erect a five- or six-storey apartment building, in return for which the owner would get one or two flats in the new edifice. The new *polykatoikies* were not usually designed by architects, and they followed a very simple template, with a reinforced concrete frame, lift and staircase – and sometimes, an agreeable balcony which could be decked out with plants and used as a dining space in summer. With little regard for aesthetics or public amenities, every available Athenian space was covered in these multistorey blocks. Neoclassical and modernist dwellings were pulled down, waterways and green spaces were covered up, and the city gained the appearance of an uninviting concrete jungle.

At the same time, this system had real merits. It helped turn a nation of small farmers into small urban property owners. The new buildings were places of social mixing: more expensive apartments on the upper floors, cheaper ones lower down and, very often, professional premises, from clinics to law offices to workshops, all under the same roof. Expanding Athens did not acquire any horrible, jerry-built tower blocks or high-rise slums. It found a way of developing that empowered many ordinary people, even as it blighted the city's appearance. True enough, building contractors, some of them very big, became a powerful lobby in post-war Athens, and they have never lost that power. But many of the new *polykatoikies* were erected by very small-scale operators, who did some of the work with their own hands. It was a system that enabled social change – a massive shift from the countryside to the city – but also set limits to that change by providing an environment where small property owners could abound and family structures could remain intact. In the refugee quarters of Piraeus, parents had created dowries for the younger generation by digging basements or adding makeshift rooms. Now, among slightly better-off Athenians, five-storey buildings provided a perfect setting for several branches of an extended family to coexist.

Wherever the political wind was blowing, these trends continued. Athens simply got bigger and bigger, creating a mix of modest private affluence and public degradation. Governments of all stripes, including the military one, fostered the system through tax breaks and the issuance of building permits in a spirit that was lax, corrupt or both. It is true that the military government had a soft spot for high-rise office buildings, and the few that exist in Athens, such as the Athens Tower, mostly date from that period. But this did not fundamentally change the urban landscape. Whoever held power, the vast, unwieldy bureaucracy never played much of an active role in providing houses for the families who were cascading into Athens; but in various healthy and unhealthy ways it helped people to help themselves. Perhaps the one important thing the state did was to employ people in huge numbers, often without requiring them to do very much except sporadically enforce bureaucratic rules, which created opportunities for petty corruption. The state payroll lubricated the system whereby countless new Athenians were accommodated, but the state was not directly involved in building.

Now consider another, similarly contrarian method of studying long-term change – and continuity – in the recent life of the Athenians. As in ancient Athens, outdoor gatherings, whether rehearsed or spontaneous, solemn or frivolous, pious or secular, have always played a fundamental part in city life. In modern Athens, where the state religion is Orthodox Christianity, public and semi-official ceremonies take place at all the great landmarks in the ecclesiastical calendar – Easter, the Dormition of the Virgin Mary, the Baptism of Jesus Christ. The latter feast, on 6 January, involves a bishop tossing a cross into a pond, lake or harbour, with hardy swimmers competing to retrieve it: politicians, mayors and officers of the army and police are in proud attendance. In the greater Athens area, the handiest available stretch of water is the murky harbour of Piraeus. Such rites are a devotional event for some, and a moment of civic religion for almost all; the two things are closely interwoven. Earthly politicians and bureaucrats relish the glow of sanctity and community spirit. On one date, the religious element is almost eclipsed by the secular. The Feast of the Annunciation (the angel Gabriel telling the Virgin Mary of her pregnancy) on 25 March is melded with a celebration of Greek national independence, involving marching soldiers and the display of new weapons. There is little room for improvisation in these rituals, and attending them is part of the socialization of any Greek child. Through elected governments of the right and left, and under the dictators, none of these rituals changed.

Mass political rallies are another open-air ritual – sometimes just a show of force through numbers, sometimes a courageous act of defiance which can culminate in physical fighting or repression. But they are never exactly spontaneous; supporters are bussed in, galvanized, disciplined – even if they can sometimes spin out of control. Even the burst of popular jubilation which greeted British forces entering Athens in October 1944 was not quite so impulsive an outburst as it appeared to be. Most of the placards and Allied flags were supplied by the resistance movement, EAM, and they sent a signal to London: we control the streets and you will have to reckon with us if we are going to coexist in this place.

In some ways, the most sensitive bellwether of the Athenian public mood comes with rites of passage involving important public figures – baptisms, weddings, but above all, funerals. Public participation in these events is never compulsory – Greece is not North Korea – and sentiment does not have to be faked. Of course, rites of passage for the great and good do need to be choreographed, for the people most intimately involved. But the presence, or absence, of the general public is a less predictable business. This has long been one of the ways – at least as important as political rallies, or the rituals of civil religion – in which the Athenian citizenry have made their feelings known. So as a prism for examining the story of the city in the latter part of the twentieth century, these enormous, impassioned, private–public occasions will do as well as any. Let us start, then, at the conclusion, with the city's collective farewell to a personality who loomed powerfully over the life of Greece and its capital for longer than anybody else in modern times.

In politics he had been associated with renewal, radical change, the destruction of old establishments, entrenched privileges, old geopolitical and social orders. Yet the funeral of Andreas Papandreou, on 26 June 1996, was a remarkably old-fashioned affair. He had been at the helm of national politics for all but three of the previous fifteen years, and a wild card in Athenian affairs (albeit sometimes from abroad) since the early 1960s. Only five months had elapsed since he was forced to quit as prime minister by failing health, and by the perception that a shadowy entourage, including his second wife Dimitra, were exploiting his enfeeblement. In earlier phases of life he had been a liberal American academic, running the economics faculty at Berkeley; it was in that role that he returned to his homeland in 1959, offering technocratic advice on how the brisk pace of GDP growth could be maintained.

Later, as Greece's travails pushed him much further to the left, he had adopted the style of a roving Marxist intellectual, eschewing the suit and tie for leather jackets and roll-neck jerseys. In his final years he looked more like what he ultimately was: a traditional Greek power broker and patronage dispenser who knew how to articulate grievance and aspiration while shoring up some of the traditional features of Greek society. He had thousands of godchildren. Correspondingly, the funeral in the Metropolitan Cathedral was a very traditional one. It must have been rather bewildering for the ill-assorted array of foreign dignitaries who were present – from Britain's defence minister Michael Portillo to Slobodan Milošević, the strongman of Serbia.

During his first two terms as prime minister, from 1981 to 1989, Papandreou had at times challenged the power and wealth of the church, but his final obsequies were thoroughly religious. It was rumoured that Andreas himself had a kind of conversion experience when, during a close brush with death in 1991, he had shared a hospital ward with Father Iakovos Tsalikis, one of the revered monastic saints of modern times, and received a blessing from the sage – along with a clairvoyant prediction that he would recover, regain power and serve the good of the country.

The Orthodox funeral is long, elaborate and, for those who can follow it, full of beautiful imagery. It has a good deal to say about the finitude and fallibility of every human being – 'there is no man living who does not sin' – and about the inexorable tragedy of physical decay, leavened by the hope that whatever is divine within us will live on. 'I am the image of God's ineffable glory, even though I bear the wounds of sin.'

From the funeral service's high theology, Greek culture distils at least the following impulses: death should be a time for mutual forgiveness, reconciliation, a setting aside of minor grievances and personal injuries. In that spirit, Papandreou was lauded by his sons – who had not taken easily to his remarriage to a much younger woman – and by politicians of more than one ideological hue. The casket was mounted on a gun carriage and escorted by soldiers: in other words, this was a state funeral of a grandeur which had not been seen in Athens since the obsequies in March 1964 of King Paul (the brother and successor of George II whose return to Greece had been so contentiously advocated by Churchill). Followed by perhaps 200,000 people from all over Greece, Papandreou's funeral cortège snaked past Hadrian's Arch and the Temple of Olympian Zeus to the First Cemetery, where Andreas was laid to rest just a few metres from his father, George Papandreou, a national leader with whom his relations had been complex and tempestuous. Not much further away were the graves of many companions on the tortuous political march of Greek socialism; some had remained faithful to the end, while others had disappointed him by taking a different route.

Apostolos Kaklamanis, a political ally who remained alive and loyal, was careful in his funeral oration to laud the unbroken tradition connecting the Papandreous senior and junior. This was not a time to mention awkward filial differences. Kaklamanis recalled the surging passion which had attended the funeral of George Papandreou, 'the grand old man of the democracy', back in 1968 – a time when democratic liberty had just been snuffed out.

Meanwhile, a humbler, anonymous participant in the final journey of Andreas explained to a visiting foreign correspondent why people had come. More than anyone, the *younger* Papandreou had personified the joyful restoration of Greek democracy which came about in 1974, followed by the victory of his Socialist party in 1981. He had embodied the hope of a Greece which could walk tall in the world, unencumbered by humiliating dependence on any foreign power. 'It may all have been an illusion, but it was a beautiful illusion.' That was a very accurate expression of the collective feeling.

The interment was heart-rending. The last Mrs Papandreou, Dimitra – a former air hostess with whom he began a controversial liaison in 1986 – wept profusely as the coffin was lowered into the grave. Minnesota-born Margaret Papandreou, who had been his spouse for thirty-eight years, stood further back with her four children, one a rising politician and future prime minister. Dimitra retreated to the so-called 'pink palace' in the elite suburb of Ekali where she and Andreas had lived. Margaret and her children went back to the Papandreou dynasty's old home in another northern suburb, Kastri. It was a comfortable but not ostentatious villa, in the shade of pine trees: a place where much of the modern history of Greece had played out, including the events that transformed Andreas from a Californian technocrat to the maverick of Athenian politics.

As of March 1961, a centre-right government under Constantine Karamanlis won re-election. This confirmed the status of Greece as a loyal NATO partner and bulwark of the American-led alliance against communism. Relations with the United States had been particularly close since American military aid led to the final defeat of communist forces in the war on the northern Greek border of 1947–9. Things reached the point where American diplomats virtually dictated which electoral system the country should adopt; and they were instrumental in choosing Karamanlis as prime minister in 1955.

But in 1961 there are clouds in the Greek–American sky. The result is challenged by George Papandreou, the opposition leader, who insists the ballot was marred by fraud and violence, practised by a dark state-within-a-state which has a licence to act freely and illegally in ways that kept the country nailed to the West.

At this stage, Papandreou remains a dutiful anti-communist (as he was during his time as prime minister under British protection) but he and his supporters increasingly insist that Greece must be 'an ally not a satellite' of the United States. The atmosphere is inflamed by the still-keen desire in both countries for the union of Cyprus and Greece. Both on the far-right and among Papandreou's centrists, there is a feeling that Karamanlis should not have accepted a British-brokered compromise under which Cyprus became an independent, bicommunal (i.e. Greek–Turkish) state.

In November 1963, George Papandreou achieves a narrow electoral victory; he scores a more convincing win the following January, and Andreas joins him in parliament. In July 1965 there is a deep political crisis as young King Constantine refuses to let George Papandreou, already prime minister, add the defence portfolio to his duties. One of the king's arguments is that Andreas Papandreou is under investigation on suspicion of fomenting a leftist republican coup in the officer corps. George Papandreou is forced to step down after some members of his Centre Union party abandon him. Andreas Papandreou blames this 'apostasy' on American meddling, and on the machinations of a Cretan politician called Constantine Mitsotakis. This creates a feud between the Papandreou and Mitsotakis families that (on the Papandreou side, anyway) will cascade down the generations. Some compare it to the family quarrels which surfaced in the first Athenian democracy, where Kimon and Pericles were divided not just by ideological differences but by old sores: Pericles' father Xanthippos had prosecuted and ruined Kimon's father, the great commander Miltiades.

As the political impasse deepens, Andreas Papandreou takes a more radical line than his father, hinting that Greece should break free from American tutelage. Andreas also takes a bolder position than the prime minister on the question of Cyprus. George

Papandreou is willing to consider an American plan for uniting most of Cyprus with Greece, with some sweeteners for Turkey. Andreas, like the Cypriot leader Archbishop Makarios, insists that the island must remain undivided whatever happens.

Elections are set for May 1967, in which the Papandreous are expected to do well. On the political right, there are open fears that Greece might soon break away from NATO and join the non-aligned movement. It is to pre-empt this, apparently, that a small group of middle-ranking officers – 'the colonels' – stage a coup d'état and suspend all democratic and civil freedoms, ushering in a dark political night that will last seven years. George Papandreou is placed under house arrest at his home in Kastri, while his son Andreas is imprisoned. Only after strong pressure from his erstwhile colleagues in American academia is he released and, in January 1968, allowed to head for exile in Sweden. His children grow up in Scandinavia and North America, absorbing the culture of those places. Those are some of the memories the Papandreou family pondered in the hours after they, and hundreds of thousands of others, buried Andreas.

Some older Athenians may not care to be reminded of this, but they came out in their hundreds of thousands to cheer the union of their young king and queen. And for anyone who has a soft spot for tinsel and glamour, the ceremony on 18 September 1964 was a delightful fairy tale. Constantine was just twenty-four, and looked even younger, grinning bashfully in a white military uniform, decked out with braid and badges. Four years earlier he had made his country, and his royal father, Paul, very proud by winning a gold medal for sailing at the Rome Olympics. Then in March 1964, the monarch – who was relatively popular, as Greek kings go – succumbed to cancer, leaving his yachtsman son to reign and marry at a tender age. The new queen was an eighteen-year-old princess of Denmark and consequently a distant relation of her fiancé, whose family are of Danish and German origin. She looked a bit overwhelmed by the rich Greek chanting, as – in all likelihood – were many of the royal personages from across Europe who had crowded into the cathedral.

The Orthodox wedding is a swirling combination of choreography, poetry and song, much of it derived from rites in the religion of ancient Israel, in which the figures of priest, king and the Lord seem to merge. In Orthodoxy, all married couples become temporarily royal when their union is sealed. Regardless of the couple's earthly rank, there is a key moment in the Byzantine practice when the chief witness holds 'crowns' over their heads and then swaps them backward and forward. For most Greeks, a pair of simple white rings does the job, but in this case they were real-looking crowns, and they were held not by the groom's best male friend, but by his mother, the formidable German-born Queen Frederica. It was one of those weddings where the two ladies in the groom's life seemed to be vying for his and the world's attention. For the gossip columnists, that only added to the fun.

The night before, the new queen was more clearly at the centre of things as she and Constantine attended a pageant in the Herodes Atticus theatre that recalled the city's ancient glories. Maidens in white re-enacted the ritual in which a freshly woven piece of cloth was brought to the Acropolis on a replica ship and then offered to Athena. In the absence of the goddess of wisdom, it was Anne-Marie who got the fabric. For a moment at least, this shy young Scandinavian was cast not as queen of the Greeks but the divine guardian of the Parthenon. If it all sounds a bit over the top, remember that there is something about the night air of Athens, in the vicinity of the Parthenon, which – as many visitors have attested – can make the craziest of things seem plausible. 'The city smelled so fragrant in those days,' insists Toula Michailidou, one of the genteel Athenian ladies who cheered on the newlyweds. With the passage of nearly six decades, the past is not merely rose-tinted but blossom-scented.

Also, remember that those nuptials were not the only piece of frothy entertainment that Athens was exporting to the world in the early 1960s. Greeks were discovering the cinema, and the global cinema was discovering Greece as a place to make films and present a feel-good version of the country's landscape and heritage. As young Constantine was winning his sailing medal in Rome, a rising film star called Melina Mercouri had gained an accolade at the Cannes film festival for acting – in the part of a happy-go-lucky Piraeus prostitute who charms a pompous American classics professor. That film, *Never on Sunday*, made Manos Hatzidakis into one of the world's favourite composers of toe-tapping Greek music. By 1964, the promotion of Greece as a place where stuffy northern Europeans could shed their inhibitions saw another brilliant success in *Zorba the Greek*. What captivated the world was not only the story of a young Englishman being livened up, and taught to move with the beat, by a wizened Greek; it was the simple, hypnotic, accelerating dance music – which would soon be enjoyed by moussaka-munching customers in Greek tavernas from New Jersey to north London. Mikis Theodorakis, who wrote the music for *Zorba the Greek*, became a new personification of Greek sun and fun – even though his own life, as a communist who had been detained and badly tortured on Makronisos island, had been far from a walk on the beach.

Observing the Camelot scene of the Athenian wedding, was there any sign that the plot might turn sour? At the age of seventy-six, Prime Minister George Papandreou seemed content at first to play the role of kindly mentor to a monarch who could have been his grandson. But neither Andreas Papandreou nor his American wife Margaret, both products of progressive American academia, look happy amid the elaborate formalities of the royal receptions. Another straw in the wind: of the various foreign dignitaries who came to the wedding, none got a warmer reception from the Athenian crowd than Archbishop Makarios, prime mover of the Greek-Cypriot struggle against the British. In the eyes of his admirers, he was the real moral champion of Hellenism.

Tension was already brewing between the different factions in the leadership of the Greek world, and because of the Cold War, this was more than a family quarrel. The United States feared that Greek–Turkish war over Cyprus might blow apart the south-eastern wing of NATO, of which Greece and Turkey were supposed to be bulwarks. America had floated the idea of dividing Cyprus between the two NATO members, on terms that were pretty generous to the Greeks. That would have brought the island into the western sphere of influence and stopped it becoming a wild card in strategic affairs. But Archbishop Makarios rejected the American plan or any proposal that would have involved partitioning his island. If it could not be joined in its entirety to Greece, then it should retain its status as an independent island with ties to the non-aligned movement and cordial relations with the Soviet Union. To many Athenians, not excluding George Papandreou, the American proposal was a tempting one. However, Andreas Papandreou sided with Archbishop Makarios in insisting that on principle, the island must be spared partition, and free to chart its own course in world affairs. That might seem like humane common sense, but at that particular time, it was provocative to America and NATO.

That created an ominous convergence of interest between American strategists and the Greek far right, who saw the elimination of Archbishop Makarios and the union of most of Cyprus with Athens as a doubly desirable turn of events. At a stroke, Hellenism could be liberated from a cleric (Makarios) who dallied with international atheism, and the influence of a former American (Andreas) who was ever more anti-American.

This was a confusing state of affairs for the young king to absorb and handle, and a crisis in his relations with other poles of Greek authority was not long in coming. In the summer of 1965, George Papandreou resigned rather than accept the king's superior authority in matters of cabinet appointments. Constantine accepted the resignation and began looking for an alternative, leaving old man Papandreou, along with his centrist and centre-left supporters, enraged by the palace's apparent abuse of power. Andreas Papandreou was a lightning conductor for that rage. He was indignant over what he saw as a conspiracy between the military, the political right and the crown to subvert the will of the people, and furious in particular with his political rival Mitsotakis for engineering a political revolt which deprived the Centre Union of its parliamentary majority.

Tens of thousands of Athenians from the political left and centre-left took to the streets to chant their rage. Sometimes the anti-royal slogans got very personal: 'Alexia, *pare thesi* – state your position,' they would shout, taunting the king's newborn daughter. In a more calculating and cerebral way, Andreas Papandreou directed his ire against a right-wing clique which he saw clustered round the palace. He was also dismayed with his father's relative emollience in the face of these threats, and the older Papandreou in turn became exasperated at times with his firebrand son. But Papandreou senior was nearly eighty, and by dint of biology alone it seemed to many that the more radical line of Andreas was the way of the future. In March 1967, two American diplomats walked out of a press luncheon minutes before Andreas delivered a blistering attack on the United States, a country whose passport he had once held.

By early 1967, there were fears on the far right that Andreas Papandreou was determined not only to keep Cyprus out of NATO's orbit but to remove Greece itself from that military alliance. Elections were scheduled for 28 May 1967 and it was anticipated that the Centre Union, including Andreas as leader of its radical wing, would do well. Rumours swirled around Athens that the army leadership, perhaps in collusion with the king and the American embassy, would nip matters in the bud by seizing power.

In the end, a different, even darker coup took place. In the small hours of 21 April 1967, the king found that army tanks had come to disturb the tranquillity of his summer residence in Tatoi – a rambling stone mansion with Gothic features, deep in a forest of cypress and pine trees. He was in the habit of travelling daily by helicopter between his palace in the city centre and the more peaceful atmosphere of Tatoi, about 25 kilometres north of the city: a halcyon existence which may have lulled him into an utterly mistaken perception of how close to violent implosion the Greek polity was.

Tanks were also patrolling the centre of Athens, and 10,000 people, including leading politicians from across a wide ideological spectrum, had been arrested. After a visit to military headquarters, the king agreed to swear in a new army-dominated government on condition that it included at least some civilians. He insisted that what he did was the only way to prevent civil war. History did not forgive him. He lent further legitimacy to the new order by joining the Easter celebrations a few days later: this meant not only attending grand services but visiting military barracks and heartily cracking hard-boiled eggs with awe-struck soldiers. It was a propaganda boost for the colonels. The following November, the king attempted a clumsy counter-coup by flying to northern Greece and rallying units of the armed forces, including the navy and air force, who were still loyal to him. But he was outwitted by pro-junta army generals and he had to flee, with his mother and young family, to exile in Rome. This curtain had well and truly crashed down on this production of Camelot.

The Nobel Prize winner was an unlikely popular hero, yet his funeral on 22 September 1971 became a great and solemn milestone in the history of Athens. George Seferis was no firebrand, no political agitator or crowd-pleaser. For most of his career, he was a dutiful, discreet servant of the state (including the Greek government-in-exile during the Second World War) while working as an increasingly senior diplomat, with postings in London and Ankara. In retirement, he had lived quietly in the central but relatively modest neighbourhood of Pangrati, relishing the seashell collection which he and his wife had built up. His appearance was not charismatic. In middle life, he was a bald, portly and benign figure, whose polite but shy smile concealed a vast poetic imagination. Humdrum as his everyday life sometimes was, his writing could roam through the aeons, probing the breaks and continuities in the story of Hellenism. He had put down some deep roots in Athens but his soul was in exile from the fertile lands of Asia Minor – Greek Anatolia – where he grew up, and he had an intuitive feeling for remote coasts, for voyages made in desperation and longing. In the speech he gave on accepting the Nobel Prize in 1963, he put forward a humane manifesto for modern Hellenism, based on landscape and language rather than genetics, on which nobody has improved.

> I belong to a small country. A rocky promontory in the Mediterranean; it has nothing to distinguish it but the efforts of its people, the sea, and the light of the sun. It is a small country, but its tradition is immense and has been handed down through the centuries without interruption. The Greek language has never ceased to be spoken... When I read in Homer the simple words *phaos eelioio* [light of the sun] – today I would say *phos tou eliou* – I experience a familiarity that stems from a collective soul rather than from an intellectual effort...

Seferis' aversion to modern political struggles rendered all the more moving his pronouncement against the military dictatorship on 28 March 1968. A little earlier, he had disappointed some people, during a visit to New York, by refusing to comment on his country's domestic affairs while 'safely outside the boundaries of his government's displeasure'. Only on returning to his home city did he issue a statement which read in part:

> Everyone has been taught, and knows by now, that in the case of dictatorial regimes the beginning may seem easy, but tragedy awaits, inevitably, in the end... I am a man without any political affiliation, and I can therefore speak without fear or passion.

I see ahead of me the precipice towards which the oppression that has shrouded the country is leading us. This anomaly must stop. It is a national imperative.

The grave, prophetic declaration was picked up by Greek-language broadcasters all over the world, including the BBC, and gave heart to people inside and outside Greece who longed for the return of democracy. Three years later, Seferis died. The military rulers had grumpily stripped him of various privileges but they could not deny him a decent funeral. His obsequies were held not in the cathedral but in a smaller church in the Plaka, close to the home where his parents had settled on moving to Athens, near the place where he had watched the bullets fly in December 1944 – and contemplated the beginning of the Cold War. But like all great Athenian funerals, it included a walk down Amalias Avenue, on the way to the First Cemetery. Unevenly, a little off tune, the crowd began singing what became his most famous lines, a favourite song of Greece: lines that mixed a scene of beauty and desolation with deeper intimations of the fickleness of human life, love and passion:

On the secret shore
Pale as a pigeon
We thirsted at noon
No water to drink.

There on the golden sand
We inscribed her name
It's as well the sea-breeze blew
and wiped out the letters.

With so much heart, such spirit,
So much passion and desire,
We'd taken up that life of ours.
All wrong!
Time for us to change that life.

What made the moment unforgettable was the musical setting. The mourners were not great singers but the melody was deeply haunting. It was a perfect fusion of sound and sense, achieved by Mikis Theodorakis, familiar to the world for the feel-good twangs of Zorba, but known in Greece as a turbulent communist who had suffered horribly during the civil war, experiencing captivity in at least four different prison islands. Trained at the Paris Conservatoire, Theodorakis crafted a musical style which drew on many layers of Greek experience: the chants of the Orthodox Church, folk music – and the low-life *rembetika* blues which was initially disapproved in equal measure by conservatives and orthodox communists. Perhaps the greatest achievement of Theodorakis lay in bridging triumphantly the gap between high culture and the popular sort.

In some ways, Seferis the poet and Theodorakis the composer were an unlikely mixture. In 1944, while Seferis was loyal to the British-protected government, Theodorakis was leading a unit of ELAS in Athenian street battles. A couple of years later, while Seferis was mentoring British-sponsored scholars and cultural grandees in Athenian tavernas, Theodorakis was being hauled off to one island prison after another. Seferis had no particular interest in worldly wealth or glamour but he was an obedient officer of the royal Greek government. Theodorakis, in the early 1960s, joined many leftist Greeks in protesting over the wealth and darkly conservative influence that was wielded, in their view, by the palace. One thing they had in common: both had origins on the eastern side of the Aegean (Theodorakis' mother came from Çesme in Turkey, Seferis hailed from Vourla near Smyrna). In other words, both had intimations of a place where Hellenism really existed in a vibrant and self-confident form for nearly three millennia. They brought that sensibility to Athens. Neither was viscerally anti-Turkish; they carried memories of a time when Greeks and Turks coexisted fruitfully.

And in that spontaneous funeral song, the radical Mikis and cautious Seferis came together. As of June 1967, the music of Mikis had been forbidden: it could not be recorded, played in public or even whistled. The composer himself was finally packed off to France after being incarcerated or internally exiled in many different parts of Greece, although by that stage (in contrast to his civil war travails) he was too old and famous to be tortured. He left for Paris on 13 April 1970, and was met on arrival by Melina Mercouri and her husband, the film director Jules Dassin, joining an array of Greek luminaries who were campaigning against the colonels from abroad.

With Andreas Papandreou, a contender for the moral leadership of the exiled Greek left, Theodorakis did not enjoy so much personal warmth. But all the expatriate activists were united by their acute concern over what was happening in Greece. They all took great encouragement from news that the funeral of an intensely cerebral poet, a man who was a prophet rather than a street fighter, had turned into a show of principled opposition by many tens of thousands of people. Not only did the crowd sing the famous verses. They also hailed Seferis as '*Athanatos!* – Immortal! – as well as chanting '*Dimokratia! Eleftheria!* – Democracy! Freedom! In September 1971, those were dangerous words to utter on Amalias Avenue.

In the end it would take more than bold chants to bring the junta down. Two years later, on 14 November 1973, students at the Polytechnic (a historic place of learning in central Athens, located next to the National Archaeological Museum) began a sit-in, using the slogan, '*Psomi, Paideia, Eleftheria!*' 'Bread, Education, Liberty!' Thousands of people, including construction workers and some Attica farmers who had grievances of their own, came out in their support. By 16 November, there was an escalating confrontation in and around the Polytechnic with Molotov cocktails being thrown, a student radio station galvanizing the revolt and army snipers taking a cruel toll from adjacent buildings. In the small hours of 17 November, a tank crashed through the gates of the Polytechnic and the radio fell silent. At least twenty-four people were killed in the vicinity.

In the short term, this led to an even harsher military regime. Supreme power was grabbed by Brigadier Dimitrios Ioannides, commander of the military police, which on his watch had become a ruthless force for the repression of dissent. But the fanaticism of the new order proved self-destructive. In July 1974, the Ioannides regime finally carried out the move which hard-line forces in Athens had been contemplating, with some quiet encouragement from shadowy Americans, for many years. That move was the overthrow of Archbishop Makarios as leader of Cyprus and his replacement by an ultra-nationalist rival on whom they counted to proclaim the union of all or most of the island with Greece. The action backfired in multiple ways: it failed to topple Makarios and it provoked an invasion by Turkey, which eventually seized about a third of the island. In an atmosphere of chaos and national disaster, the military regime in Athens collapsed and Constantine Karamanlis returned to Athens from his self-exile in Paris to restore Greek democracy. The freedom of Greece had come at the price of catastrophe in Cyprus. It was exactly as Seferis, in his dreamily intuitive way, had foreseen: the dictatorial regime had embarked on a course which 'seemed easy at first', only to find that 'tragedy awaits in the end'.

Most political leaders are said to campaign in poetry and govern in prose. With Andreas Papandreou, it was different. Both before and *after* he was elected, he did everything he could to preserve an atmosphere of high melodrama in Athens. His victory at the ballot box came on 18 October 1981, when his Panhellenic Socialist Movement (PASOK), claiming to represent an entirely new brand of leftist politics, triumphed over the tired old centre-right. For nine months prior to that sweet success, he filled Constitution Square and other public spaces in Greece with his own style of gathering: fireworks, bunting, booming loudspeakers and a few well-chosen pieces of music. Carl Orff's *Carmina Burana* was one favourite; another was a happy Greek melody with a revolutionary edge,

*'Kalimera Ilie'* – Good Morning, Sun – penned in 1973 by Manos Loizos as hopes were rising of a return to democracy. After he won power, regardless of whether new electoral tests were looming, the rallies continued. 'Greece belongs to the Greeks' was one of his most resonant slogans.

He pledged, albeit with increasing vagueness, to leave NATO and expel American defence facilities. The economy would be transformed by the 'socialization' of large enterprises, giving workers and local government a stake in their administration. Like many a populist leader who takes up the cause of anti-imperialism, he cultivated the image of a brave warrior waging a courageous but unequal war against an unjust world. If the struggle faltered, it was hardly his fault. Fiery rhetoric and gestures served as a smokescreen for deep compromise. After taking power, Papandreou bargained successfully with the European Community's paymasters while disrupting foreign policy discussions by refusing to condemn Soviet and pro-Soviet regimes in eastern Europe over, for example, martial law in Poland. But in the end, after raising anti-American rhetoric to a crescendo, he gave the Reagan administration what it most wanted, which was a firm legal agreement to preserve the main American bases in Greece: one at Ellinikon airport, a listening post at Nea Makri on the other side of Attica and two facilities in Crete. Incredibly, he persuaded the Reagan administration to support his case for a somewhat better financial deal from the European Community, whose subsidies rapidly delivered a cascade of funds to the Greek provinces.

Some of his chosen political associates were people of limited education and little refinement whose principal quality was unwavering loyalty. But among his governing team, two personalities were well-known as radical luminaries in their own right. One was Melina Mercouri, who during the junta years had transformed her image from glamorous film star to fiery political warrior, though she could still use the first persona when it suited. Now she was culture minister, in charge of Greece's antiquities. The other figure, less well known internationally, was a city planner and economist who stood out for his serious-mindedness. A former athletics champion, his physical fitness was an unusual feature in a cabinet where chain-smoking and whisky-guzzling was the norm. Antonis Tritsis was part of a group of anti-junta activists who planted a small bomb in the National Gardens in 1970 when America's defence secretary was meeting the Greek leadership. Most of his comrades were arrested, but Tritsis managed to escape to Italy. By the time he took office in 1981 as minister for public works and the environment, he was one of the better qualified, in technical terms, for his job: he was an alumnus of the Illinois Institute of Technology, and he was deeply influenced by the globally renowned Greek city planner, Constantinos Doxiadis.

Melina Mercouri's term as minister of culture was long on gestures and theatrics. Entry to museums and archaeological parks was made free for Greeks. Above all she raised the temperature in Greece's campaign for the return of the Parthenon marbles – challenging and embarrassing the director of the British Museum. Visiting London in 1983, she had a brief, unplanned meeting with Sir David Wilson and, with cameras rolling, took him to task over the sculptures. The film clip still makes for a compelling watch. 'You will ruin the British Museum,' he says, scoldingly. 'I don't want to ruin the British Museum, I want my marbles back,' she retorts, in a voice that is rasping but also a bit playful. 'You want your marbles but other people want theirs,' Wilson replies, in a condescending tone. 'They are part of the monument... it's a unique monument,' Mercouri insists. 'There are many unique monuments,' her British interlocutor hits back. The scene could have been extracted from any of the films along the theme of stuffy-northerner-meets-lively-Greek.

Tritsis, meanwhile, focused on substance. Papandreou had told the Athenians that the city's pollution cloud or *nefos* was the fault of greedy industrialists in league with a corrupt conservative government. In truth things were never that simple. The *nefos* certainly existed: a report from the European Parliament in 1983 found that Athens had the dirtiest air of any major city in the European Community. On windless days, warm pollutants would rise from the ground until they met cooler air and formed a noxious photochemical mixture. The storeyed mountains of Attica were trapping the poison. Tritsis could see that there was no magical or populist solution: the problem would have to be tackled with a mixture of better public transport, restrictions on private car use, greener fuel for cars and heating, and fewer permits for industrial facilities. He did what he could. Some people were exasperated by the way he changed his mind: he went from being an enthusiast for a big metro system to a sceptic who proposed a new tram network instead. But at least he focused on the problem, not on promoting himself. As he saw it, ordinary people would have to play their part in decongesting the city, and getting its clogged traffic under control – thereby improving the quality of life for everyone.

In early 1983, he pushed through a law which marked a serious attempt to deal with the problem of illegal building in greater Athens. It offered procedures and incentives for fixing illegal features in a building, but it also made clear that ultimately, after every chance had been given, the state would demolish illegal structures. For some categories of illegal dwelling, it would be the owner's responsibility to tear them down. In a spirit of egalitarianism, he made it illegal to fence off land any closer than 500 metres from the sea. In 1984, he sent bulldozers to carry out one exemplary piece of demolition: tearing down an illegal seafront villa on the east coast of Attica which had once belonged to George Papadopoulos, the jailed leader of the military dictatorship.

Nearly forty years on, the Tritsis law is still a reference point for any government proposal which aims to regulate building in Athens. But most provisions of the law, including the call for demolition, were soon overridden by waivers of indefinite duration. In the end, it was not buildings that were removed, it was Tritsis himself – he was forced out of office in 1984 amid strong rumours that the real estate lobby, and some ordinary property owners, felt he was treading on their toes. By then, however, he had already achieved some good things during his term as minister: for example, the Plaka neighbourhood was partially pedestrianized, and was cleared of the sleazy nightclubs which had flourished there since the colonels' time. It became a vastly pleasanter place to visit, work or live.

In 1986, he was given another chance to make radical change as minister of education and religious affairs. This was a portfolio whose name was revealing. It reflects the deep interconnection between the Orthodox Church and an educational system where religious instruction was compulsory. In this job, the self-appointed mission of Tritsis was to negotiate a transfer to the state of the majority of church land. This was not undertaken in a spirit of zealous anti-clericalism. Church and state are for better or worse intertwined in Greece, with the state paying the salaries of priests and even chanters. The church's land holdings – like many Greek land holdings – were huge and poorly managed. Any plan for rational land use in Greece (including the protection of land from dysfunctional uses) had to involve the transfer of church property to agencies who could manage it more competently; or at least so the argument went. Tritsis did the necessary bureaucratic work, drew up a law – and was finally let down by Papandreou when it became clear that the political cost was too high. 'Antonis, you have made history,' Papandreou memorably said – while sacking him.

In 1989, Greek politics dived into turmoil, as concerns mounted over Papandreou's health and a tangle of bizarre corruption scandals. Controversy swirled around a Greek-American, George Koskotas, who had built up a huge financial empire, including the mysteriously expanding Bank of Crete, with which state agencies were encouraged to deposit their cash at low rates of interest. It was alleged that senior members of PASOK had prevented any real examination of these malpractices, and one was apparently rewarded for this with a stack of banknotes delivered in a cardboard box that had once contained disposable nappies. There were separate scandals concerning defence contracts and fraudulent grain subsidies obtained from the European Union.

Many of Papandreou's long-standing allies, including those on the left, deserted him. Elections in June 1989 produced an inconclusive result, with a communist-dominated coalition holding the balance of power. Kharilaos Florakis, veteran leader of the pro-Soviet communists, refused to share power with the scandal-ridden PASOK and, in an amazing historical development, formed a short-term coalition with New Democracy, the centre-right party, with the sole task of cleaning up public life and putting an end to scandals. Fresh elections were called for November 1989, and the results were another stalemate; an eighty-five-year-old former central bank governor, Xenophon Zolotas, formed a caretaker government. Only in April 1990 did an election deliver a clear outcome: a victory for New Democracy, now headed by Constantine Mitsotakis. This was bitterly galling for Andreas Papandreou, who still blamed the Cretan for bringing down the centrist government, headed by his father, in 1965.

Amid all this peculiar political churning, there were some dramatic changes of allegiance. In November 1989, the veteran communist Mikis Theodorakis showed his disappointment with the PASOK-dominated left by joining the New Democracy ticket. Tritsis was another politician who changed sides. In spring 1989 he abstained in a parliamentary confidence vote and was expelled from PASOK; he then founded his own small party which never got very far. The following year he decided to stand as an independent for mayor of Athens, and wrote to the leaders of all the main parties to seek their moral support. It was Mitsotakis, by this time prime minister, who took up the offer. So in October 1990 Tritsis found himself running for mayor against his old Socialist colleague – Melina Mercouri.

In a sign that politics were changing, the outcome was shaped less by huge street rallies, and more by television slots. Mercouri's were theatrical, featuring her impassioned declaration that 'Athens is the responsibility of us all...', while those of Tritsis were more down-to-earth, presenting a candidate 'who knows Athens' and could be trusted. Voters in the municipality (which only covers the city centre, not Piraeus or the suburbs) preferred low-key pragmatism to theatrics. Tritsis prevailed with 50 per cent of the vote (against 46 per cent for Mercouri) and set to work enthusiastically, without losing any of his penchant for the unexpected. Days before taking up his job in February 1991, he visited Baghdad in the aftermath of Iraq's defeat by an American-led coalition, and said the city had been randomly – not surgically – bombed. As in his previous jobs, Tritsis was popular with his subordinates, including the garbage collectors with whom he used to travel on their dawn collections. But his stewardship of Athens lasted little more than a year. In April 1992, at the age of just fifty-five, he suffered a stroke while at work in his office and died a few days later.

As historic Athenian funerals go, the mayor's was one of the most poignant. His death had been so sudden and unexpected, cutting off a conscientious and well-liked politician in his prime, that the grief was real. There was none of the discreet sense of relief over the passing of someone who, politically or biologically, seems to have lived a bit too long. As always, the Metropolitan Cathedral was uncomfortably packed. There were soldiers, bands and many priests. Although Tritsis had been an adversary of the Orthodox episcopate, and he was threatened with excommunication, his final obsequies were affectionately overseen by the bishop of his home island of Cephalonia. The entire political class of a troubled polity seemed to have gathered around the coffin, with their quarrels temporarily silenced. The mourner in chief was the prime minister, Constantine Mitsotakis, whose giant Cretan frame was standing up well to old age. Close to the coffin was the hatchet-faced Andreas Papandreou, himself now in frailer health – looking less like a roving revolutionary and more like a crusty old Balkan paterfamilias.

But it was Mercouri who spoke for PASOK, memorably. By now she herself was far from well, as a life of heavy smoking took its toll. But she could still perform, using her fragility, her near-inability to complete a sentence in a single breath, to good effect.

Dear friend Antonis, it is with real sorrow that Pasok and its president Andreas Papandreou bid you farewell as you leave for your final journey. It is hard to believe that Antonis Tritsis, as mayor of Athens, will no long be with us as we continue our struggle over the causes that unite us, overcoming the things that have sometimes divided us.

Tellingly, she hailed Tritsis as a battler against mediocrity, against conventional wisdom and passivity. That was a well-made point. With him or without him, the era of political passion which he, Andreas and Mercouri all personified was ebbing away. Concluding her short statement, she channelled Shakespeare as well as Thucydides.

As you leave, dear friend Antonis, the love of us – and the love of the city of Athens – will accompany you on your last wandering. The soil of Attica now opens its arms to receive you – and it will receive from you the strength to turn our visions into reality. Good Night, Sweet Prince.

Then, about two years later, it was Mercouri's turn to leave the stage. By this time, she and Papandreou were back in office, having returned to power in October 1993: they had reoccupied their old offices as culture minister and prime minister. They were both vulnerable, elderly people. Melina could work only a few hours a day. She had been diagnosed with lung cancer and there were days when she had to combine work with chemotherapy sessions. She found her ministry's powers were being trimmed and she lacked the strength to fight back. In February 1994 she cut a sad, anxious figure as she announced she was going to New York for what she gallantly described as a check-up. Wearing a filmy outfit of pale blue, she joked that she had chosen the colours of Greece to give her courage; but perhaps for the first time in her life she showed a frightened face to the public. She died on 6 March 1994 at the Memorial Sloan Kettering Hospital in Manhattan.

The return to Greece of her earthly remains was magnificent. As the Olympic Airways jumbo carrying her coffin entered Greek air space, it was guided to the ground by air force fighters. Then a cortège led by thirty outriders drove along the Attic seashore and up Syngrou Avenue, the crowds getting thicker as it approached the city centre. She lay in state for two days, not in the brass heaviness of the cathedral but in the beautiful, much older chapel beside it, whose name, origins and structure are both polytheistic and Christian – and deeply Athenian. (It was once called the Chapel of She-Who-Is-Quick-To-Hear, which was one of the many titles of the Virgin Mary.) A tonne of flower petals were provided by the city hall for people to rain on the coffin as it made its way, on 10 March, to the First Cemetery.

After the service, the body was brought into the cathedral square and a ten-gun salute boomed out from Mount Lycabettus. High military and religious honours were accorded to a woman who never professed to be a saint – and who once expressed the hope that modern wars and military spending could be stopped by the methods used in *Lysistrata*, the ancient Athenian farce by Aristophanes. In other words, there should be a sex strike by the wives of powerful men, forcing 'every John, Jean and Ivan' who had weapons or missiles at his command to opt for peace.

It was undoubtedly the most passionate send-off which modern Greece had ever given a woman. The simple thing that many Greeks understood about Mercouri was this: she had won international fame by promoting their country's heritage in a form that was not high-falutin or refined but bold, confident and funny. On behalf of a country that felt misunderstood by the world, she had sallied forth and compelled powerful men to take her seriously. As a challenge to scholars and curators in distant lands who purported to be the gatekeepers of Hellenic culture, she had proposed a different version of Greekness, and done so with passion, flirtatious charm and an unmistakable throaty laugh.

Rites of passage, by definition, are a time to look backwards and forwards, and they can also bring to the surface some deep, paradoxical truths. The grand wedding of 1964, endowing Greece with the world's youngest king and queen, was accompanied by much breezy rhetoric about the long and happy reign that lay in prospect: it might even match the half-century chalked up by King George I, who had founded the dynasty a century earlier. But for those who knew how to read the omens, there was plenty of reason to fear a much darker outcome. Constitutional monarchy can work well enough in a country like Denmark where there is a tradition of political consensus and competent administration; neither of those conditions applied to Greece.

The funerals of Melina Mercouri and Andreas Papandreou set the seal on vanishing eras. For all their radicalism, they both came from old political dynasties whose days were numbered. Melina represented a style of feminism that would have little traction in the twenty-first century, one that implicitly acknowledged the decision-making role of men while trying to subvert it through seductive wiles. In his ideological trajectory, Andreas Papandreou had often seemed behind the international curve: he was still building a centralized, hypertrophic state at a time when, even on the left, the failure of state-socialist bureaucracies was increasingly accepted. He courted the elderly tyrants of the Warsaw Pact precisely when they were about to disappear forever from the international stage. His message was better adapted to his Greek supporters, who were not revolutionary proletarians but small business owners, small farmers, the builders and owners of *polykatoikies*. Through a mixture of borrowing and European aid, he found the money not to destroy but to shore up the old structures of Greek society, with guild-like arrangements that protected small interest groups while serving the general interest rather badly. But in a ruthlessly globalizing world, there was a limit to the duration of this political trick.

Yet there are some funerals that look forward, and this is not necessarily connected with the age of the deceased. The crowd who said farewell to Seferis could not have known that by singing his poetry, they were endowing Greece with a new national anthem. But by calling him 'athanatos' – immortal – they were touching on a deep truth: Seferis had a vision which transcended the boundaries of time, and could see that the nightmare of the colonels would eventually end, albeit at a heavy price.

Mayor Tritsis did not consider or present himself as infallible, and therein lay his virtue. He was genuinely committed to improving the quality of life in Athens, and ready to try one thing after another to achieve that end. The very fact that he was cut off in the middle of his working life meant that funeral rhetoric about a man 'pursuing his vision' or 'fulfilling his dream' seemed movingly appropriate, and likely to inspire imitators. The fact that he had grown up in a vastly more benign environment – the island of Cephalonia – had probably redoubled his determination to free Athens from the worst extremes of urban degradation. To this day anyone with a proposal for making Athens a more liveable place is happy to invoke his memory.

20

# Pride, a Fall and an Open Future
## 2000–18

*The August 2004 Olympics as a moment of triumph – Dimitris
Papaioannou choreographs the ceremonies – euphoria over
the games and euro membership – riots in December 2008
foreshadow an economic crash which becomes acute in 2010 –
a suicide in Constitution Square articulates despair – George
Papandreou's failed referendum proposal – amid successive
bailouts, the leftists of Syriza take power in 2015 – a July
2015 referendum becomes a 'no' to Greece's creditors – Syriza
compromises but its economic pundit Varoufakis remains defiant*

It was alright on the night – far better than alright. As a giant
sporting festival, as a kind of ritual in a new global religion, as
an offering from Greece to the world, the homecoming of the
Olympics was a sensation.

'These have been unforgettable, dream games,' declared Jacques
Rogge, the president of the International Olympic Committee
after the seventeen-day extravaganza involving 10,000 athletes
from nearly 200 countries. Before the Athens games opened on 13
August there had been several years of sceptical predictions, and a
last-minute scramble to complete venues, plant trees, pave roads,
iron out computer glitches, welcome 30,000 journalists and give the
holders of 4 million or so tickets decent value for money. Memories
of the September 2001 terrorist attacks were fresh in people's minds,
as was the 2003 war against Saddam Hussein's Iraq – which had

stoked anti-American sentiment in many countries, including Greece. Anti-American terrorism had a dark history in Athens, although the best-known urban guerrilla group, 17 November, had recently been wound up. Many newspapers, including *The Times* of London, fretted over the safety of the event. At the insistence of America, Britain and Israel, the Greek games organizers had spent over $1 billion on security alone, calling in NATO surveillance aircraft to patrol the Attic skies.

Yet it was a message of humour, lightness and peace that the Hellenic hosts sent the planet, through opening and closing ceremonies that mixed space age phantasmagoria with intimations of antiquity. In a country without much tradition of volunteering, about 45,000 Athenians of all ages and walks of life gave up time to act as guides at thirty-seven athletics venues and twenty-seven other sites. Veterans of this titanic effort still become emotional when they look back on it. 'We were driven by feelings of pride and joy which set aside all the worries about extravagance and over-spending,' recalls Catherina Mytilineou, who looked after 1,200 volunteers at the press centre in the main stadium. 'It felt as though some female divinity had cast a spell on us and filled us with a collective determination to look after every visitor.' A fellow volunteer who worked in the centre of Athens recalls how

> the city was glowing with pride, showcasing the ancient monuments, the brand-new stadiums with their cutting-edge designs… we were so happy to be showing athletes from around the world where the Olympic spirit had come from. The whole city was dressed in its finest attire to host the most important party of its modern history.

Above all, it was a sweet moment of vindication for a forty-year-old Greek choreographer, Dimitris Papaioannou, whose rich and playful fantasies opened and closed the proceedings. Setting forth the glories of Greek history to an excited, sympathetic audience,

with an ample budget, might sound like an enjoyable assignment, almost an easy one. But in truth there were many potential pitfalls, and in the view of people who studied the show carefully, they were neatly avoided.

Where did the traps lie? The awkward truth was that in modern Greece, there had been many efforts to present the Hellenic story as a single, almost linear progression. In the 1930s, General Metaxas claimed to be the guide of the 'third Greek civilization' – after classical Hellas and Byzantium – and he encouraged kitsch ceremonies which delivered that message. The army officers who took power in 1967 described their country as 'Greece of the Christian Greeks' – another formula that was supposed to encapsulate the classical world and Christian Byzantium. The colonels were given to organizing garish processions in the new-old Olympic stadium, combining *faux* ancient costumes and the multiple pleats of the foustanella skirt, sported in more modern times by Greek men, especially soldiers. All those clichés had to be avoided. Then recall the fact that the whole neo-Olympic movement, including its Greek part, had some dark connections with nationalism, even national socialism. The kindling of a flame by classically attired maidens in ancient Olympia, and the transport of that flame to the modern Olympic venue, was largely dreamed up by Joseph Goebbels for the 1936 Berlin games. For the Athens games of 2004, these were ghosts which needed to be well and truly exorcised.

Papaioannou's show, by general agreement, managed this with subtlety. The Greek flag was not introduced to the crowd by soldiers or even robed goddesses. Instead the stadium floor was turned into a huge shallow pool of water, on which a little boy was scudding along in a paper boat, shyly holding his country's banner. He hopped out and presented it to the bigwigs who were in charge of the games. Then, in one scene after another, high-tech and history were artfully mixed. First Lydia Koniordou, a formidable interpreter of ancient drama, used her commanding presence to deliver some famous lines from Seferis: a reflection on the ancient artefacts which inescapably haunt the modern Greek imagination, in their beauty and brokenness.

> I woke with this marble head in my hands;
> it exhausts my elbow,
> I don't know where to put it down.
> It was falling into the dream
> as I was coming out of the dream
> so our life became one...

Then electronics seem to take over. A digital human head in Cycladic style – 3,000 years old yet weirdly modern – appears in the air; it disintegrates to reveal a kouros statue from a later period, and then a sculpture from the golden age of Athens, celebrating the human body as a lifelike individual. Then come digital images of men and women of many ages and ethnicities, and finally fragments of disintegrating sculpture are seen descending into the water.

In a later sequence, a winged, blue-tinted actor, representing Eros, floats in the air while a young man and woman play about in the pool of water; shortly after that Eros flutters no less benignly over a pregnant woman whose belly is glowing: a scene which has been anticipated, moments earlier, by a sparky parade of actors in the bright colours of Minoan art, including a fertility goddess with conspicuous breasts. Stars appear as the pregnant woman descends into the pool, and the sparkles float upwards to form a double helix, the structure from which all life originates. Soon all the actors are wandering through and around the shallow pool, and an olive tree emerges from the water: the gift of the goddess Athena to her city. As with all Papaioannou's work, it presents the human story as a journey of self-discovery through experience and experiment. Neither war nor authority nor religion in the conventional sense play much part in his world.

Papaioannou's own story is one of vulnerability, not privilege. Growing up in a household 'without art' in the modest Athenian district of Kallithea, he was discovered by Yannis Tsarouchis, the greatest Greek painter of his generation. Although his first artistic medium was illustration and cartoons, Dimitris was overwhelmed at the age of nineteen by the work of the German choreographer Pina Bausch and started a dance theatre of his own on a shoestring budget.

In contrast with the religious imagery of the London Olympic opening in 2012, designed by two Liverpudlians of Catholic Irish heritage, Christianity played relatively little part in the Athens show. For better or worse, Papaioannou chose to focus on the humanist side of the Greek heritage, not the monotheistic part. This at least had the merit of avoiding the over-simplified bombast of the Metaxas era and the colonels' regime, when Greek chauvinists liked to pretend that all aspects of the Hellenic heritage were essentially the same.

As Athenians pondered that glorious Olympic show, it was viewed by many as a high point in a period of several intoxicating years when everything seemed to be pointing in the right direction for their city and their country. The turn of the twenty-first century was Greece's time of laughter and forgetting. For most people, though by no means everybody, living standards were rising impressively. As of January 2002, Greeks said goodbye to the drachma, with its cute coins featuring the Athenian owl and its banknotes celebrating modern Greek heroes as well as Athena, Poseidon and Apollo. In their place came the euro, inscribed in Greek as well as Latin letters in deference to the monetary system's newest member. Whatever its long-term effects, the immediate consequence was to make many people feel somewhat better off. Both the Greek state and individual Greeks felt they could borrow more easily. In fact, the state could borrow on the same terms as Germany, given that the financial markets – however mistakenly – viewed the eurozone as a single economic space. But the biggest change, very much related to the Olympics, was the improvement in the general quality of life in and around Athens, thanks to better roads, hugely upgraded public transport and cleaner air. In the run-up to the games, several interconnected projects, which had been held up for many years by squabbling, dithering and self-serving politicians, finally came to fruition. The most important included a new metro system, plus a suburban railway; a new airport; and a network of toll roads which could bring people arriving by air into the centre of Athens, or anywhere else in Attica. These projects recognized Attica for what it was: a gigantic concrete sprawl of nearly 4,000 square kilometres – easily the biggest in the Balkans – and a natural linchpin for trade, shipping and tourism, which could only serve those purposes if it had the necessary infrastructure.

The brand-new metro interlocked neatly with a creaky old underground system, dating from the nineteenth century, which ran between Kifisia and Piraeus. The freshly built network was – and remains – clean and efficient and inexpensive. It was designed to take 450,000 people into the city centre every day, and reduce the number of noxious car journeys by at least half that amount. Air quality improved at a stroke. The metro's creation also brought a treasure trove of archaeological discoveries, including Roman baths and aqueducts and houses and artefacts from all eras of the city's history. It helped that William Stead, the engineer who monitored the project for America's Bechtel corporation, had a degree in archaeology as well as transport engineering. The finds under Constitution Square were so rich and varied that it was frustrating, archaeologists complained, to have to cover the space over again. But as an American life coach might say, that problem was turned into an opportunity. Syntagma was one of several metro stations that became a micro-museum, complete with artefacts and segments of soil containing many layers of history. Thus one slice of earth in the Syntagma dig was found to contain a cistern from Ottoman times; an early Christian grave; a road leading due east to the Attic plains; part of an aqueduct dating from the sixth century BCE; and part of the Eridanos riverbed.

The new airport was named after Eleftherios Venizelos, who among his many achievements was the prime mover of Greek aviation, civil and military, in the 1930s. Located about 30 kilometres to the east of central Athens, it was big enough to accommodate not merely the Olympic traffic but the expansion in air traffic that was expected over the next couple of decades. Despite all Greece's travails, that expansion did materialize – from 12 million passengers in the airport's first full year of operation, 2002, to 25 million in 2019. Closely connected was the Attiki Odos (literally Attic Way), a 70-kilometre matrix of highways that allowed people arriving at Venizelos not only to head downtown but to make for the shipping terminal in Piraeus, skirt round Athens to the industrial areas west of the city, around Eleusis, or head northwards to Thessaloniki. It was one of the biggest co-financed (private/public) road projects in Europe.

For pilots the new terminal was a merciful improvement on the short runways at the old Ellinikon airport, where it was hard to land on windy days. Anybody coming to Athens by air had the sense of arriving in a country that was firmly located in the prosperous European mainstream. Ellinikon, by contrast, had felt somewhere between Balkan and Middle Eastern, with its scent of melon rind, Oriental tobacco and old-fashioned floor polish. A nostalgic memory, but ill-suited to Greece in the twenty-first century. A clean, silent suburban railway was another link between the airport, the city centre and the remainder of Attica; soon the metro would also reach the Venizelos terminals.

One thing connects all these projects, although it is rarely mentioned. They were set in motion by a pragmatic self-effacing politician called Stefanos Manos – only to be sabotaged, delayed or debated by others. A graduate of Harvard Business School who ran a food company before entering politics, Manos held a series of economic positions in centre-right governments between 1977 and 1981, and then between 1992 and 1993. But he is no zealous ideologue; he has twice founded small parties of his own and finally, in 2004, entered parliament on the centre-left ticket of PASOK. Almost all the projects he began have turned out well;

nor, contrary to perceptions, were they unnecessarily extravagant. They were properly costed, with the financial estimates based on the assumption that the projects would be managed competently. Even the 2004 Olympic Games in Athens can be assessed positively from the perspective of financial good practice allied to organizational competence; the games brought huge tangible and intangible benefits to Greece, and their costs, colossal as they were, could have been absorbed over time, especially if the newly built sports facilities had been well managed instead of being allowed to rot. In his early eighties, Manos takes a philosophical attitude to Greek affairs and describes himself as 'somewhat detached from urban development these days', with little desire to taunt others over their mistakes.

In truth, all the Greek political parties have had their intelligent pragmatists, their ideologues, their crowd-pleasers and, to put it bluntly, their thieves. Greece's membership of the euro, which could have been turned to great advantage, was in large part engineered by Kostas Simitis. He was a German-trained super-pragmatist who, as prime minister from 1996 to 2004, nursed the Greek body politic back to partial health after the scandals that overshadowed the final, ailing years of Andreas Papandreou. It was widely asserted, afterwards, that Greece should never have been allowed into the eurozone because it 'lied its way in' by presenting false economic statistics. That was not quite true. When the decision was taken in 2000 to admit Greece to the euro club, the country had in fact made a big improvement in its general economic performance, as compared with the early 1990s. If any massaging of the figures occurred, it was no worse than any other eurozone players had engaged in. The improvement could, in theory, have continued if the politics had been right. Alas, they were not.

Eurozone membership immediately made Greece a much more attractive proposition for investors, and it could have been used to stabilize the country's public finances, but there was no electoral constituency whatever for responsible behaviour – and a huge perceived political advantage from a policy of 'spend spend spend'.

That electoral advantage was reaped by the notionally centre-right government under Kostas Karamanlis, which took power in 2004 – just in time to bask in the glow of the Olympic Games and foster a euro-driven boom.

Nor was there much appetite for prudent private behaviour, as loans became available for consumer purchases, from cars to television sets to holidays. This was a time when Athenian students treated themselves to weekends in London on a whim, and taxi drivers told stories of their excursions to Las Vegas. Real-estate prices were rising all over Athens, and in a nation of small property owners, this created a powerful feel-good factor.

At the other end of the economic scale, euro membership had one ominous consequence. As long as Greece used the drachma, even a perpetually devaluing drachma, it was possible for some to live very cheaply indeed – almost outside the money-based economy – by consuming only local products (olives, feta cheese, fruit and vegetables in season) and buying no fancy imported consumer goods. With the advent of the euro, the most basic of staples jumped in price rather steeply. A thousand-drachma note, with its lovely scenes of Olympia and Delphi, felt like a meaningful piece of paper; now it turned out to be worth less than three euros, hardly enough to bother picking up off the floor.

Perhaps the broadest social change was not the bursts of foolish private extravagance, nor the cries of bewilderment from the poorest, but the availability of middle-range consumer goods, including clothing and furniture from big European franchises. The spanking-new motorway and railway did not merely connect Athenians with the airport; it also led the way to a vast IKEA outlet selling beds and cupboards which met the needs of middle-class couples and hard-working immigrants alike. Suburban shopping also led to more suburban living, as the northern edges of Athens expanded and offered a lifestyle not dissimilar to Florida. In a sclerotic society, technology gave a kickstart – sometimes a healthy kickstart – to social and generational change. Most professions were rigidly organized in ways that protected the interests of the middle-aged and elderly. But mobile phone and computer technology, and the need for quick-minded and digitally literate youngsters to sell and fix new devices, led to the opening up of new sectors where youth and energy could find an outlet.

Athens had suddenly become ethnically diverse, with the arrival of Albanians, then people from other Eastern European countries, including Ukraine, Poland, Romania and Bulgaria – and also newcomers from Pakistan, the Middle East, China and Africa. As long as there was plenty of money flowing through the system, this change seemed manageable. Immigrants did jobs that Greeks no longer cared for. As intergenerational ties weakened a little, home helps and carers for the genteel and elderly, living quietly in their Athenian apartments, almost invariably came from countries like Albania, Georgia or the Philippines. For the Greek parties to this transaction, it was a boon.

The end of war in the Balkans also brought its dividends. With their instinctively pro-Serb sympathies, most Greeks had little liking for the Western military intervention in the Balkans which eventually cauterized the conflicts occasioned by Yugoslavia's break-up. Still, whatever they thought of NATO's methods, people in Greece undoubtedly benefited from the advent of regional peace which left their country as the only comparatively prosperous EU member in a corner of Europe battered by war and dislocation. Yet another bonus was the rapid improvement of relations with Turkey, which had come close to explosion in spring 1999 when it looked as though the Aegean rivals might enter a land war in the southern Balkans on opposite sides. By a weird turn of events, earthquakes in both countries changed the atmosphere: a huge quake near Istanbul and a lesser one, near Mount Parnitha north of Athens, which claimed 143 lives on 7 September 1999. This led to amazing scenes. Antagonism between the Turkish football club Galatasaray, based in the European side of Istanbul, and Greece's PAOK of Thessaloniki normally runs quite high, not least because they trace their origins to rival communities (Turkish Muslims and Greek Christians) in the same city. But during a match shortly after the Turkish quake, which claimed over 17,000 lives, the Galatasaray players drew tears and cheers by unfurling a banner in Greek that read: 'We thank the brotherly Greek people because they share our pain.' Helped by this benign climate, the Greek and Turkish foreign ministers hammered out an agreement under which Athens would approve and encourage Turkey's application to join the European Union, instead of blocking it as before.

Fragile as it was, the upturn in Greek–Turkish ties was a help to Greek investors, to tour operators in both countries, and to concertgoers, who were able to enjoy the thrill that attends any event in which Greek and Turkish musicians improvise on stage. When Simitis transferred the reins of government to Kostas Karamanlis on 10 March 2004 – about five months before the Olympics – he was handing over a country which was full of optimism, for some good reasons and some foolish ones. In theory this was an electoral victory by moderate conservatives over moderate social democrats (which PASOK had by now become). In practice, the reins of fiscal control were about to be loosened, with terrible results.

There were many tragic deaths in Athens around that time, and Constitution Square was the setting for many extremes of human emotion. But the suicide of Dimitris Christoulas, a retired pharmacist aged seventy-seven, touched the stoniest of hearts. It was meticulously planned. He made sure that he had paid his share of the common expenses in the apartment building where he lived. On the previous evening, neighbours had spotted him sitting quietly on his balcony. It was in keeping with his local reputation as a soft-spoken but stubbornly high-principled figure. He had taken part the previous year in a protest by 'aggrieved citizens' – as they called themselves – who camped out in the city's central expanse to protest against the ravages of austerity. Then on the morning of 4 April 2012, Christoulas headed for a tree – the tree where he had pitched his tent the previous year – and shot himself in the head, leaving a note which compared the government to the collaborationist administration which took power in 1941, headed by General George Tsolakoglou. 'Today's neo-quislings', he wrote,

> had annihilated all traces [of hope] for my survival, which had rested on a very decent pension for which I paid over thirty-five years with no help from the state. My advanced age does not allow me to react in a dynamic way – although if a fellow Greek were to grab a Kalashnikov, I would be right behind him. I see no solution other than this dignified end to my life, so I won't find myself delving in garbage cans for my sustenance. I believe that young people with no future will one day take up arms and hang the betrayers of this country in Constitution Square, just as the Italians did to Mussolini.

Soon the tree became a shrine, with wreaths, flags and scribbled denunciations of the 'murderers' who were responsible for the old man's death. His final message had been dark but in some ways well-aimed. The country was now sliding deeper into a morass of bailouts, stinging austerity and protest. The intensity of Greece's financial woes had become obvious soon after October 2009, when George Papandreou – son of Andreas – led PASOK to an election victory. Having grown up (during the family's exile) in Sweden and North America, George was an altogether gentler soul than his father, committed to social democracy and environmentalism and a comfortable partner for centre-leftists in Europe and the United States. But he had done one thing whose rashness soon looked clear, at least to his foes. He had campaigned on a promise of more state handouts. He even declared that 'the money is there, *lefta yparchoun*': all he meant, he insisted, was that cutting sleaze could free up cash. But soon after he took power, it became painfully clear that it hardly mattered what his ideological leanings were or what electoral pledges he had made.

The coffers were all but empty and the debt mountain was unmanageable. Not for the first time in Athenian political history, governing Greece would at best be a matter of crisis control in uneasy co-operation with the country's lenders. In the wider Western world, an implosion which began in American financial markets had thrown the capitalist economies into recession and brought the entire global monetary system close to collapse. It was a climate that spelled doom for the vulnerable and imprudent, and Greece was perceived by the markets as both those things. It took some time for the full effects of the global financial crisis to be felt in Greece, but in certain respects, the streets of Athens had proved a rather sensitive barometer for measuring the state of the world.

On 6 December 2008, the streets of the capital erupted after police shot dead a fifteen-year-old boy, Alexis Grigoropoulos. Rioting continued for a month and spread to many other countries. Among the worst-affected parts of Athens were the student district of Exarcheia, where the police had never had much control, and Ermou Street, running west from Constitution Square, whose smart new shops became a target for arson and looting. It was hard to pinpoint the cause of the malaise; the economy was slowing down but not yet in crisis. The boy who died was not at the margins of Athenian society, but a pupil at an expensive private school. What the riots brought home was the way in which the Olympics and euro-fuelled consumerism had papered over but not solved some deep-rooted problems in society.

In some ways, consumerist euphoria had simply made things worse by creating rising expectations. Thanks to its inefficiency and sporadic brutality, the state had never been fully legitimate in the eyes of many Athenians. Memories of street war in December 1944, of brutal repression under the colonels, and of the student uprising of November 1973, all helped to ensure that. At a more practical level, family solidarity was slackening and a rising generation of both sexes yearned for financial independence but saw little chance of achieving it. Even as early as 2008, people felt some intimation that a massively expensive pension system, in which countless interest groups had carved out special privileges, was nearing collapse. The rising cohort would not simply have to work harder than their parents, they would have to work much longer. The shock-absorbers of Greek society, including decent pensions and ample opportunity to acquire property, might soon cease to exist.

By spring 2010, the country could no longer carry out its everyday business, because it was impossible to borrow at affordable rates. Papandreou sought a bailout from a 'troika' of agencies – the European Central Bank, the European Commission and the International Monetary Fund – which would haunt the Greek horizon for almost a decade. The following month, the government secured a loan of €110 billion, on the understanding that public spending (including on wages and pensions) would be slashed and the economy reorganized. A wave of protests quickly turned violent, and tear gas billowed around the luxury hotels on Constitution Square, where guests paying hundreds of dollars a night had to be kept indoors or discreetly evacuated. All this was happening only six years after the hoteliers of Athens had splashed out on a pre-Olympic refurbishment and raised their prices accordingly. On 5 May 2010, two women – one of them pregnant – and a man were burned to death in their workplace, the Marfin Bank, just a few minutes' walk from the city centre, after hooded rioters ignited the place with Molotov cocktails. This prompted Greece's state president, Karolos Papoulias, to describe the country as being 'on the edge of the abyss'. In a more benign form of protest, a group of 200 communists went up to the Acropolis and rolled out banners declaring: 'Peoples of Europe, Rise Up'.

For its well-wishers and its adversaries alike, it was now clear that the whole European project, and the eurozone in particular, was being shaken to its foundations. The woes of the comparatively

**19.** The Zappeion, a splendid neoclassical building endowed by the wealthy Evangelos Zappas, hosted fencing contests during the first modern Olympics of 1896, a landmark event for the young Hellenic kingdom.

**20.** A Cretan revolutionary, intellectual and master statesman, Eleftherios Venizelos became the dominant personality in the Greek world when he arrived in Athens in 1910.

**21.** Orthodox Christian refugees poured into Athens following Greece's defeat in Anatolia in 1922. They occupied every available space, including the grounds of ancient monuments like the Hephaisteion temple.

**22.** After taking power in 1936, General Ioannis Metaxas mimicked the style of Europe's fascist powers while remaining firmly pro-British in foreign policy.

**23.** For Athenians, the Nazi military banner symbolized a brutal occupation which lasted from April 1941 until October 1944, a time of hunger, humiliation and harsh punitive measures.

**24.** Having won youthful fame for tearing down the swastika from the Acropolis in May 1941, Manolis Glezos remained an impassioned political activist until his death in 2020 aged ninety-seven.

**25.** By paying a surprise Christmas visit to Athens in 1944, Winston Churchill signalled his determination to defeat the communist-led resistance movement that controlled much of the city.

**26.** When King Constantine of Greece married Princess Anne-Marie of Denmark, his third cousin, in September 1964, there was much optimistic talk about a long and happy reign. But dark political clouds were on the horizon.

**27.** In June 1996, the funeral of Andreas Papandreou, a strong-willed socialist who demanded absolute loyalty from his followers, marked the end of a political era in Greece.

**28.** With spectacular opening and closing ceremonies, the 2004 Athens Olympics delivered a message of optimism, lightness and humour to the world.

**29.** As Greece succumbed to a deep economic crisis, with unmanageable debts and humiliating bailout terms, parts of Athens became riot-scarred zones of social conflict and depression.

**30.** As a sharp critic of Europe's monetary establishment, Yanis Varoufakis became a global celebrity during six turbulent months as Greek finance minister, culminating in an impassioned popular vote in July 2015.

**31.** Known in the United States as the 'Greek freak', Giannis Antetokounmpo is one of the world's top basketball players – and a proud son of Athens, where he was born to Nigerian parents.

**32.** The downtown district of Metaxourgeio sums up the contradictions of modern Athens: developers aspire to gentrify it, painters and performers call it an artistic hub and archaeologists want to dig.

**33.** In multicultural greater Athens, many rites and religions co-exist: Shia Muslims, commemorating the battle of Karbala in 680 CE perform their annual ceremony of Ashura in Piraeus.

tiny Greek economy might be the spark that ignited the entire building. This anxiety created huge tension in all transactions between Greece and its partners. In multiple ways, Papandreou was forced to unravel the rudimentary welfare state, and the multiple networks of protections and privileges which had been built up by his father and PASOK. He put as brave a face on things as he could, insisting that his highest priority was not to make cuts everywhere but rather to fight dysfunctional forms of corruption – which would be a desirable aim even if Greece were not in the throes of a rescue from an acute crisis. By early 2011 it was clear that Greece would soon need yet another bailout, accompanied by another round of agonizing austerity. Papandreou was walking a tightrope, and he fell off. In October, after being presented with his partners' latest terms, he said there was no choice but to call a referendum. He wanted to share the responsibility for imposing even greater pain on the country. This caused loud cries of alarm from the leaders of the Western world, not least because their own relations with one another were in crisis. Barack Obama and France's Nicolas Sarkozy wanted to create a vast fighting fund to stave off any attacks by speculators on the credibility of the international monetary system and the eurozone in particular. Chancellor Angela Merkel retorted that under the constitution imposed on Germany by the victorious Allies in 1945, there were limits to her legal power to participate in this exercise. At a time when the planet's political and economic titans were arguing about how to stop the house falling down, a cry of stubborn resistance from turbulent Greece was the last thing they wanted to hear. But to people on the streets of Athens, it seemed as though the masters of the world had shown their true feeling: one of utter indifference to the opinion of the Greek voters or their elected leaders.

Papandreou was summoned to a meeting in Cannes of the Group of Twenty leading world economies – and given a roasting by his fellow Europeans, especially Sarkozy. Greece should expect no more aid unless it ratified the latest rescue proposals, the prime minister was told. His predicament grew worse, as his own finance minister (and rival) Evangelos Venizelos turned on him. They spent an exhausting day together in Cannes. On the flight back, Papandreou dozed off. Literally behind his leader's back, Venizelos prepared a statement, which he issued from the VIP lounge of Athens airport as soon as they arrived. It said that membership of the eurozone was 'an achievement by the Greek people' and they should not be allowed to overturn that achievement by voting themselves out.

From the viewpoint of cold logic, there was some force in this argument. A crash out of the eurozone would have dire short-term implications for the whole Greek population, consequences which the voters in a referendum probably did not fully realize: should they be helped to commit such an act of self-harm? But to citizens like the elderly Mr Christoulas, the situation looked eerily familiar. Their own government was colluding in a externally mandated programme to slash the wages and pensions of ordinary Greek people. For anyone with a long memory, comparison with governments that had served at the behest of the Nazis (essentially implementing a programme to sequester Greece's resources) did not seem exaggerated. There were, of course, vast differences. The leaders of northern Europe were not subjecting Greece to military occupation, they were paying a price for what they now saw as a rash act of political goodwill towards Athens.

Those leaders and their voters had come to regard admitting Greece to the eurozone as a gesture of risky generosity on the part of Europe's richer members. Now they were being asked to spend precious capital, literally and metaphorically, on keeping the Greeks in the eurozone, even though all economic logic suggested that they had failed to meet the demands of membership and should simply be allowed to crash out. The 'terms' they were imposing on Greece were the bare minimum needed to make sure the economy stabilized and did not turn into a bottomless hole. In Athens, by contrast, it seemed that the near-destitution of many hitherto solvent and respectable Greek citizens was a matter of utter indifference in places further north.

One thing was well understood by most people on the inside of this debate. For Greece to crash out of the eurozone could be agonizing, at least in the immediate future, for both Greece and the zone. But in the medium term, it might well be argued, it could be exactly the right thing for Greece. The country would revert to the drachma, whose value would plunge and plunge, rendering all Greek banks and most Greek firms insolvent and wiping out the country's ability to pay for food, fuel and other imports on which it was heavily dependent. But once the drachma stabilized, the Greek tourist product and other Greek products would rapidly become attractive and competitive, as those of Turkey were. The trouble was that Greek democracy might not survive the process; the upheaval and human suffering would be so massive that it might precipitate a return to dictatorship.

Indeed, there seemed to be a real risk that whatever the Greek leadership did, democracy might wobble. If the country's masters simply signed up to Europe's demands for seemingly endless austerity, many Greek voters would draw the conclusion that voting was a waste of time. On the other hand, if they took the chance to defy Europe's bosses, they would condemn themselves to a period of chaos and shock, arguably beyond any elected government's capacity to bring under control. A similar sense of despondency seems to have gripped the ancient Athenian democracy at moments – such as the defeat by Sparta in 401 BCE or by Macedonia in 322 BCE – when the city lacked all agency. But the democratic spirit generally came back.

As Papandreou could see, as of late 2011, even if Greece and the European partners stitched together a fresh deal, perhaps with a sweetener or two for Athens, the politics would still not be easy to manage. He could not bear the political weight alone, and indeed he might not be able to bear it even with the help of other politicians. On 3 November, Papandreou finally scrapped his idea of a referendum, and within days he was trying to put together a government of national unity, mandated to handle the crisis, on the understanding that he would not be part of it. Eventually a technocrat called Loukas Papademos, a former vice-president of the European Central Bank, formed a caretaker government drawn from all parties, and Papandreou bowed out. While he would still enjoy some standing in the world as president of the Socialist International, it looked as though neither he nor any other member of the Papandreou family would again occupy centre stage in Greek affairs. In the end, the politics of consensus-building – which was his natural style – and the expediencies of emergency management could not coexist, or so he found. So by the time Christos Dimoulas made his complaint about the return of a 'quisling' government, the quiet banker was the recipient of his desperate cry. Papademos was of course no quisling: he was a competent and discreet functionary, who probably helped to keep the spectre of total collapse at bay. But the idea of central bankers running the country made Athenians nervous. After all, the central bank had been one of the institutions that never stopped functioning during the occupation.

The Papandreou dynasty might be fading into the past, but in some degree, the style of Andreas Papandreou – at his most tub-thumping and mercurial – lived on. To observe this, let us remain in Constitution Square, and fast forward four years. On the evening of Sunday 5 July 2015, the city's central expanse was filled not with tear gas, petrol bombs or even angry chants, but rejoicing. Greek flags were fluttering, and there were spontaneous displays of dancing to familiar tunes, as though a happy family wedding was in progress. '*Tipota to idio, apo 'do kai bros!*' was one of the slogans being joyfully repeated. 'From now on, nothing will be the same!' Greeks had voted in a snap referendum on the latest, complex set of terms handed down by the country's European creditors in exchange for fresh assistance; and the result showed a bigger-than-expected 61 per cent in the 'No' camp, even though the question on the ballot paper, referring to two highly arcane documents, was pretty hard to comprehend. For the revellers, that hardly mattered: the meaning of the word 'No' – associated with some legendary moments in the country's history – could not be clearer.

Where George Papandreou had feared to tread, another leftist leader had rushed in. He was Alexis Tsipras, a handsome and eloquent political operator born in 1974 who had learned the skills of gamesmanship and oratory in a communist youth movement. Like Andreas Papandreou in 1981, he had ridden to power on a promise that his brand of leftism would be of the revolutionary sort, utterly overturning all the conventions of bourgeois politics. His party – the Coalition of the Radical Left, Syriza – was presented as a popular movement, not a party in the old sense. It would tear up the memorandum stipulating painful cuts and reforms which the country's creditors had imposed. And those creditors, however scheming and malicious, would have to reckon with the firmly expressed will of the Greek people. That was the rhetoric, and it proved attractive to a deeply depressed electorate: attractive enough to secure Tsipras a handsome election victory on 25 January 2015 over the centre-right incumbent, Antonis Samaras of the New Democracy party. Samaras had achieved a modest easing of Greece's financial travails, but for one reason or another the country's European partners pointedly declined to offer him any of the concessions which might have secured him a fresh term of office. Afterwards, many wondered whether Samaras, seeing the fresh crisis that was looming, surrendered office to Tsipras with a degree of relief.

High European politics suddenly turned into a rather gripping kind of public theatre. In the Athenian camp were two contrasting figures. There was Tsipras: smiling, agreeably comfortable with himself and monoglot in Greek, like a rambunctious but good-hearted schoolboy who was difficult to dislike. At his side was Europe's most unconventional finance minister, Yanis Varoufakis – a supremely articulate, bilingual economist and game-theory specialist with experience of left-wing academia in Britain, America and Australia. Neither politician ever wore a tie. Varoufakis spoke perfect, rather posh English with that slight hint of foreignness which is typical among alumni of the smartest private schools in Athens. (He had attended one thanks to a scholarship.) In other respects he was far from typical. A trim fifty-three-year-old, he was much given to motorbikes, collarless shirts and leather jackets. His critique of the European financial establishment won him admiration among left-leaning youngsters in many countries, as well as crusty English Tories.

Varoufakis was given to warning his German interlocutors about the need to avoid any resurgence in Europe of fascism, born out of social discontent – of which there were already signs in rough parts of Athens, as the far-right Golden Dawn movement turned economic misery and racial tension to its advantage. Meanwhile, one of Tsipras' first acts on taking office was to lay a wreath in memory of the 200 resistance fighters who had been executed in the red Athenian neighbourhood of Kaisariani on 1 May 1944. For people of a leftist family background, this gesture had vast resonance. Settling into power, his colourful team quickly understood the dilemma they faced. They had been elected on a promise to put an end to the country's financial tutelage by hard-hearted outsiders, exercised through a 'memoranda' of measures that the Greek parliament was expected to adopt with few questions asked. The money from a second rescue package was running out and they did not want to pay the political price for a third one. Instead they were looking for a renegotiation of the entire debt mountain, including some debt forgiveness which would put Greece on a more sustainable path. The International Monetary Fund agreed with the idea of forgiveness, but the Europeans – Germany in particular – were adamant that this was not possible as long as Greece remained in the eurozone. Longer payment schedules were always negotiable, but not the actual cancelling of debt. Varoufakis poured scorn on this stance as a dishonest exercise in 'extending and pretending' that the problem was merely one of liquidity rather than plain insolvency.

His intellectual arguments were often well-grounded, but grumpy German politicians complained that patronizing lectures were hardly the right tone for a country that was being helped off its knees by a considerable, costly act of European forbearance. By late February 2015, the government had secured an extension of existing loan arrangements, on the understanding that there would be fresh negotiations, about both Greek economic policy and further credits by early summer. A crunch was approaching.

On 25 June, there was a hard day of negotiating among the eurozone's finance ministers. Tsipras concluded that discussions about a third bailout were moving backwards. The creditors were demanding more cuts to pensions, and higher taxes on sensitive groups, like island hoteliers: he could not sell this to the Greek parliament. He announced a referendum on Sunday 5 July. Within days, financial meltdown seemed to be looming, as the markets sensed that Greece's days in the eurozone might be numbered, and the European financial authorities stopped helping Greece with emergency liquidity. All Greek banks were closed and a daily limit of €60 was placed on withdrawals from cash machines, many of which turned out to be empty. In the tourist business, there were loud complaints that an entire season would be lost amid the chaos – though foreigners' credit cards continued to work quite well. The Greek leadership kept its nerve. On 3 July, Tsipras told a crowd of perhaps 250,000 in Constitution Square that a 'no' vote would enable the country to remain in the euro club, with dignity. New Democracy, under Samaras, spoke for the pro-European camp, who reckoned that having it both ways was simply impossible: voting 'no' would mean forcing the country into isolation and hunger, far worse than the hardships (including 25 per cent unemployment) that were already being endured.

In several respects, the referendum results were utterly different from what anybody imagined. First the 'no' margin was unexpectedly large, and one fairly rapid result was that Samaras stood down as leader of New Democracy. More surprisingly, within hours of the news, there was a split between Tsipras and Varoufakis. Varoufakis believed that Greece should be prepared to survive outside the eurozone rather than capitulate endlessly to the creditors' demands. He had started making secret preparations for the issuance of a parallel currency. Tsipras, on the other hand, saw the vote as a licence to go on negotiating more or less as before, seeking a few concessions at the margins but accepting the principle of credits in return for austerity and liberalizing reform. Having given the electorate a chance to let off steam, he went to Brussels a few days later and broadly gave in to the lenders' demands, after a marathon negotiating session.

Varoufakis retired from the political front line to become a bestselling author, exposing the iniquities of the international monetary system, and denouncing the masters of the European currency. He founded a transnational political party, DiEM25,* with the aim of harnessing leftist thinkers in many democracies to the cause of remaking Europe. Tsipras, meanwhile, found that, in narrow political terms, his gamble had paid off. The revellers' slogan that 'nothing will ever be the same again' turned out to be pathetically mistaken, but perhaps that did not really matter. Having emitted a primal scream, voters might now be prepared to return to the hard grind of satisfying the country's creditors in return for a fresh financial lifeline. Within a couple of months Tsipras had secured a third bailout of €86 billion (on top of two previous ones worth €240 billion in total), and it was clear that Greece would remain under international tutelage for several more years. Something comparable had happened before. In the 1980s, Andreas Papandreou had articulated the country's desire to expel all American bases by organizing noisy demonstrations in favour of that (strategically perilous) course; he then put the bases on a firmer legal footing than they had even been, while claiming not to have changed his mind. Tsipras had done something similar,

---

* The Democracy in Europe Movement 2025.

with a breathtaking mixture of chutzpah, chicanery and political calculation, for which the electorate somehow forgave him, because they liked him and accepted his claim that he had no other choice.

Interviewed by the author three years later, in the modest central Athens apartment where he lives with his wife Danae Stratou, an installation artist, Varoufakis remained utterly convinced that his line was the right one. If Greece had been pushed out of the euro, as a result of holding firm against externally imposed policies, there could in his view have been turmoil for ten to twelve months, wiping out 'anything between 9 and 13 per cent of GDP, which would be tragic'. However, the country would have bounced back, and by 2018 its GDP might have been growing at up to 10 per cent per year. And what about the view, later adopted by many Greeks, that the crisis of summer 2015 was a pointless waste of hundreds of millions of euros which changed nothing in the end? Whatever damage Greece did suffer, and whatever it might have suffered from continuing to hold firm, should be blamed on the mandarins of Brussels and Frankfurt, Varoufakis insists.

> If the European Central Bank and the powers that be in Europe decided to crush our banks and asphyxiate us – and that caused some damage to the Greek economy – I believe that all the slings and arrows [of blame] should be sent to them. To people who say, 'ah, but you caused a lot of damage,' I reply, 'ask yourselves who caused that damage'… It's a bit like arguing that saying 'no' to Mussolini in October 1940 was responsible for the occupation of Greece.

Many of Varoufakis' compatriots see something exasperating about his blithe self-confidence, and find it hard to understand why he has such a widespread international following. Encountered at home, he is a more vulnerable and human figure than his TV image might suggest. He speaks with humour about his daily Skype conversations with his adolescent daughter in

Australia; about his parents' dismay – many years ago – over his own teenage laziness; about the Labrador which he and Danae compete to overfeed and spoil; about the snazzy cocktail bars in nearby Mavili Square, a pleasure of his youth that he still occasionally indulges. He is more fun to be around, and to spar with, than one might guess from afar. From his father, who analysed the metallurgical skills of the Parthenon's constructors, he has inherited a keen interest in ancient Greece. Through the prism of game theory, he has reflected on the Melian Dialogue, a grisly passage by Thucydides in which the Athenians warn the inhabitants of Melos, a tiny island, that they will be destroyed unless they join Athens in its standoff against Sparta. It was a rule of life, the Athenians said, that 'the strong do what they can and the weak suffer what they must'. Varoufakis used that line as the title for one of his books on international economics.

Both ancient Athens and modern Athens are places where passionate, ingenious arguments – often delivered in the open air – can sway people's feelings and determine what actually happens, in unpredictable ways. But perhaps the biggest difference is that the policy dilemmas of ancient Athens, like those of Victorian Britain and modern America, were those of a powerful state, wondering how precisely it should use that power. In modern Athens, by contrast, there have, of necessity, been tortuous discussions about how to conduct oneself from a position of weakness: when to capitulate to overwhelming power, when to stand firm, how and when to seek some advantage at the margins.

In August 2018, it was announced that Greece had emerged successfully from its final bailout. 'Today we can safely conclude the programme with no more follow-up rescue programmes, as for the first time since early 2010, Greece can stand on its own feet,' declared Mario Centeno, one of Europe's senior financial mandarins. 'This was possible thanks to the extraordinary effort of the Greek people, the good co-operation with the current Greek government and the support of European partners through loans and debt relief,' he added.

This time there was neither rejoicing, nor rioting, nor any act of self-destructive protest in Constitution Square. Perhaps people were too exhausted for that. However, there were palpable signs of economic recovery, as boutique hotels, fusion restaurants and adventurous art galleries brought new life to the surrounding streets.

# 21

# And Greece Travels Onwards

*The volatility of Athens – recovery in 2018 – Mitsotakis
succeeds Tsipras – the refugee crisis – Athens becomes more
cosmopolitan – tourist product improves – conflicting
pressures on Athens – contested Metaxourgeio as a microcosm
of the city – proposals for an Athenian Riviera – ecological
blight in the west of the city – the challenge of symbiosis in
a city of four million, stopped in its tracks by Covid*

Great cities can decline very rapidly, and rebound very quickly too. Sometimes, decline is triggered by some easily identifiable event – an invasion, a severing in vital supplies, a natural disaster. Sometimes there is an unexpected collapse in the terms on which the city's various classes and communities coexist. Sometimes cities grow too large, sometimes they become unsustainably small. But recovery can start as soon as the factors which fostered a flourishing community in the first place start to reassert themselves. That cycle has often recurred in the history of Athens.

In 401 BCE, when the Spartans ordered the destruction – to the sound of flutes – of their enemies' walls, the decline of Athens from its imperial prowess must have looked irreversible. The city's menfolk had been decimated, the fleet which once commanded the Aegean had been destroyed, the city's capacity to procure foodstuffs and other vital commodities from distant lands had been reduced to zero. Yet within a couple of decades, Athens was once again a moderately successful, extrovert polity – practising democracy, fostering excellent art and philosophy, building ships and establishing maritime alliances. Then consider some of the extraordinary twists in the city's modern story.

As of 1945, the city had been brought to its knees by the combined effects of Nazi occupation and fighting between the communist-led resistance and the British-backed government. And yet, with the very important exception of those directly affected by anti-leftist persecution, the 1950s are remembered fondly by many older Athenians as a time when living standards were soaring, new films and songs were proliferating and the charms of the city were discovered by the world. Even among some who were directly affected by ideologically based persecution, there are memories of the ingenious ways they got round this problem, for example by starting businesses of their own. As one would say in modern Greek, this is a country in which *ola katastratigountai*, everything is challenged. Almost all laws, norms, policies and barriers can be overcome, circumvented, undermined – usually in ways that involve human emotions, relationships and mini-stratagems prevailing over formal rules.

Within a year or two of Greece's emergence, in 2018, from lender-imposed austerity, the feeling of recovery on the streets of central Athens was discernible and exciting, though by no means were all residents benefiting. At the low ebb of the crisis, many downtown districts had become nasty places: boarded up, malodorous and menacing. Suddenly that changed. Jeremy Downward, a Hellenized Englishman who has lived in central Athens for thirty years, recalls it like this:

The city in crisis had a forlorn, unloved and drab feeling. Then slowly but surely something happened, almost imperceptibly at first. Increased visitor numbers and cheap flights played a role. Perhaps it was the realization among the Athenian young that the only way they would find employment was to create it themselves. A couple of years later the city became quite lovely – vibrant, hip, fun, upbeat, a real flowering of creative energy.

Imaginative restaurants, experimental art galleries and lively cafés and bars started to appear in the midst of the wreckage. The crisis became a kind of selling point as Athens started to present itself as a new Berlin, where unconventional art could flourish in rough, inexpensive physical environments. The really adventurous could sample a taverna meal in the anarchic streets of the Exarcheia district in the knowledge that Molotov cocktails and tear gas might at some point disrupt the taramasalata.

In mid-2019 there was a change of political guard. Kostas Bakoyannis, at forty-four the youngest scion of the Mitsotakis dynasty, was elected mayor of Athens on a centre-right ticket on 2 June; he took over from the centre-leftist municipal team of George Kaminis. A month later, his uncle Kyriakos Mitsotakis trounced the leftists of Syriza and became prime minister, at the age of fifty-three. If Greek politics over the past half-century were conceived as a feud between the Papandreou and Mitsotakis families, then the latter had emphatically prevailed. No less than the Papandreous, the younger generations of the Mitsotakis family had strong connections with American academia, but the connections were different. Where Andreas Papandreou emerged from the old campus left, the new prime minister was a product of Harvard Business School and McKinsey, the management consultancy. His nephew, a lanky, grinning, dishevelled figure who recalled Boris Johnson in his city hall days, had been to Harvard's Kennedy School of Government and picked up its vocabulary. *Pace* his uncle, he had concluded that 'anything really interesting in public policy is happening in cities… cities are the true laboratories of change, the engines of growth… while nation-states are failing because of partisanship, a toxic environment, bureaucracy'.

Even if the language changed, the most powerful trends at work in Athens and Greece showed some continuity between Syriza and New Democracy. Syriza, in its latter days, had become broadly friendly to foreign investment in business and real estate, and it had won the admiration of northern Europeans, including Angela

Merkel, for steering the country through the rigours of austerity. In a very strange geopolitical twist, for anybody who remembered the post-junta years, a radical turn in Turkey's foreign policy stimulated a rapprochement between Greece, America and Israel. Israelis, Greeks and Greek-Cypriots entered agreements to exploit and transport the energy resources of the eastern Mediterranean, and put a stop to what they saw as Turkish expansionism. With a nonchalance that would have shocked earlier generations of Greek leftists, Tsipras seemed to enjoy hobnobbing with Donald Trump and Binyamin Netanyahu. As he handed over power to Mitsotakis, the biggest worry in the Athenian corridors of power was no longer about economics, but rather about the perceived risk of a 'hot incident' in the Aegean between Greek and Turkish forces, triggered by differences over energy rights. Barely a month after taking power, the Mitsotakis government caused a shock in progressive circles by sending the police to evict refugees and migrants from properties in and around Exarcheia, where several thousand newcomers had been squatting, in quite well-organized communities. But these evictions had begun under the Syriza government, with the approval of the centre-left mayor Kaminis. They all agreed that asylum seekers should be directed to the government's own facilities, in the Aegean islands or in Athens – where the authorities could watch them and, to a very limited degree, look after them.

Even as earlier cohorts of (mostly economic) migrants settled down in Athens, raised families and became part of the urban scene, Greek authorities from 2015 onwards had faced an acute problem in the form of mass, uncontrollable migration to the Aegean islands. In the eyes of Athenian officialdom, the problem was much exacerbated by Turkey's desire to pressurize the European Union, by turning on and off the flow of desperate folk (mostly Afghans and Syrians) on the move. In autumn 2015, the situation in Greece became acute as countries to the north sealed their borders, disrupting a trek northwards towards Germany. It eased considerably the following spring after a deal involving generous EU aid to Turkey, and the return of failed asylum seekers. From that time on both Greek and European authorities seemed bent, in the view of humanitarian agencies, on keeping conditions fairly grim in the island camps, where thousands of refugees were still holed up – as one of many disincentives to anyone who was thinking of making the journey. In the early months of 2020, tension on Greece's borders surged as Turkey appeared to be pushing migrants into Greek territory by land and sea – only to encounter some very forceful pushbacks from the Hellenic authorities, a policy which Mitsotakis defended. As of 2021, several thousand migrants and asylum seekers were living in three government-run centres in greater Athens – a little physically safer than they had been on the island camps, but desperately short of money and even food. By this time, the attention of Greece and the world had moved on.

The confusing thing about Greece in the crisis and post-crisis years is that it was simultaneously coping with an almost unmanageable influx of people and an exodus of its own sons and daughters in search of employment or professional training. Every downturn in Greek fortunes had triggered waves of temporary or permanent migration. Think of the financial crises of the 1890s, which propelled people to the New World or the flourishing ports of the Ottoman empire; or the doldrums of provincial Greek life in the 1950s, when those who did not crowd into fast-expanding Athens headed instead for German factories, Belgian coal mines or Australian fish restaurants. The crash which began around 2009 was certainly no exception. The Athens of the Olympic Games had been a thrilling place to be young; now parents reluctantly told their school-leaving offspring to go abroad and stay abroad. Of those who remained in Greece, more than half were unemployed. It was not only the young who left. Hard-working, middle-aged people who had expected to live out the remainder of their years close to home, in the company of their extended families, found themselves digging roads in Scandinavia or driving trucks in Bavaria.

A decade later, as recovery started, it felt as though this agonizing exodus was having some oddly beneficial side effects, at least for a minority. As some of these footloose young Greeks trickled back, the face which Athens presented the world became much more stylish, polyglot and self-confident. The most tangible sign of this was the profusion of sophisticated eateries, boutique accommodation and music based on gloriously unlikely combinations. Whether this came from the poor migrants who had settled in the city, or from Greeks returning after long sojourns abroad, Athens suddenly seemed to enjoy being cosmopolitan – and shedding some of the profound cultural conservatism and defensiveness which had been a feature, and a survival strategy, of modern Greece. The old clichés of Greek tourism – sun-burned, tipsy northern Europeans eating warm moussaka and moving awkwardly to the bouzouki – gave way to some far more sophisticated interactions between Athenians and outsiders, with the boundary between the two becoming ever more blurry.

Greekness did not disappear in the process, as many remarkable stories make clear. Dining out in Athens used to involve a search for very simple food, in which the excellent local ingredients were tampered with as little as possible and the atmosphere unselfconsciously reflected the islet or village where the owner or *taverniaris* originated. Such tavernas still exist. Yet today, the most celebrated chef and restaurateur in Athens may well be Sotiris Kontizas, a business studies graduate with a Greek father and Japanese mother – and a talented inspirational speaker, in down-to-earth Greek, about ways to find balance and serenity in life. His establishment, called Nolan, in a street parallel to Constitution Square, aims to combine the healthiness of two culinary traditions. For a purer Japanese experience, delivered by the Greekest of hands, gourmets can head down the coast to sample the wares of Tony Vratsanos, a prize pupil of the global king of sushi, who has used this learning to run a franchise in a posh seaside hotel in Vouliagmeni.

Such tastes may be rarefied. But Athenian accommodation has come a long way from the concrete shells which proliferated under the colonels, with noisy air-conditioning and a morning offering of staleish sponge cake and tinned orange juice. Now small independent inns, some in quite edgy neighbourhoods, serve up the healthiest of local produce, from olives to honey. The business of supplying organic foods and herbs to demanding customers, whether in Athens or further afield, has brought new life to parts of rural Greece. For at least a trickle of entrepreneurial young Athenians, producing food or other traditional items in their family villages seemed to promise a richer life than anything the city could offer. Reversing a historic trend, they have left Athens not for London or Amsterdam, but for a terraced mountainside or coastal olive plantation. And then there is Airbnb – which in good ways and bad has upended the Athenian landscape, enabling anybody who owns property across most of the conurbation to monetize it easily. The most dramatic effects have been in the Koukaki and Makriyanni neighbourhoods on the south side of the Acropolis, where a majority of the living space is now available for short-term rent, and there are laundrettes and cafés which are designed with those renters in mind. The losers, of course, include people of modest incomes – teachers, low-ranking state employees and even students – who used to be able to live affordably in these districts. In the gimmicky bars and cafés of Monastiraki on the other side of the Acropolis, the young servers have broad smiles and speak excellent English, but they are probably commuting to work from very distant places, because staying in the centre, even modestly, has become unaffordable.

As for the sale-and-purchase property market, the scene has been transformed by 'golden visas' under which investors from outside the European Union could buy themselves a five-year right of residency if they were prepared to spend at least €250,000 on a home, or else invest in a business. Other EU countries like Spain and Portugal make similar offers but Greece had the lowest threshold. About 10,000 took up the offer in 2018, up from 3,700 in 2016. The majority of investors were Chinese; then came Russians and Turks. (Turkish arrivals in Athens included both liberals who dislike their country's Islamizing authoritarianism and followers of the Islamic preacher Fethullah Gülen, whose once-influential movement became a public enemy after the coup attempt of 2016.)

Chinese interest in greater Athens, be it micro- or macroeconomic, has been growing on many different fronts. The beginnings of a new Sino-Hellenic amity can be traced to a halcyon period after 2000, when the Chinese economy was booming and Greek shipowners made new fortunes delivering commodities to the emerging superpower. The euro crisis brought new factors into play. It rendered Greece desperate for investment, while its European partners were equally keen for Greece to privatize state assets. China has been one of the great beneficiaries. In 2016, China's biggest shipping company, Cosco, obtained a majority stake in the port of Piraeus, where it had already invested heavily in improving container facilities. The Chinese presence has transformed the atmosphere in a commercial port which was plagued by strikes, inefficiency and corruption. In April 2019 there was an unexpected setback for China as the Central Archaeological Council blocked Cosco's plans for further investment – including a shopping mall and hotel complex. This immediately prompted suspicions that the Syriza government was yielding to pressure from other quarters, including unions or local business owners. But in November 2019, with a centre-right government in power, China seemed to receive a fresh green light, as President Xi Jinping visited Athens and signed a pledge, along with Prime Minister Mitsotakis, to 'overcome any obstacles' to the implementation of China's plans for the 30-kilometre strip of coastline. Under Chinese tutelage, Piraeus has already become one of the two biggest commercial ports in the Mediterranean, vying with Valencia in Spain.

Protected by the strategic relationship between the two countries, tens of thousands of ordinary Chinese people – most of them from the southern coastal regions of Fujian and Wenzhou – have migrated to Greece, opening small shops in the rougher sections of Athens as well as some remote parts of Crete and the Cyclades. When the recession was at its deepest, Greek consumers were glad of the cut-price clothes offered by these stores.

Greece and its capital are changing even faster than the headline numbers suggest. Defined at its broadest, the Athens metropolitan area now comprises about 3.7 million people, nearly 40 per cent of Greece's shrinking population. That number has been roughly stable over the last decade, but only because of immigration, or the fact that unregistered residents are acquiring legal existence. Among Greek-born people, deaths far exceed live births. The central area making up the municipality of Athens – *demos Athenaion* – has been losing population rapidly, to the suburbs, since at least 1981, when it peaked at around 900,000 inhabitants. Of the 600,000 or so people who live in the *demos* today, around 200,000 are foreign-born.

Among the 4 million people who somehow coexist in the urban sprawl of Attica, there have been some extraordinary interactions, things no sociologist or nativist ideologue ever dreamed of. Sepolia is one of several neighbourhoods north of Omonia Square where poor migrants congregated in large numbers from the 1990s. If it is famous for anything, it is a strong sporting tradition. As the atmosphere in Athens was soured by economic downturn, it was a perfect recruiting ground for the bully boys of the Golden Dawn party, who would offer to protect and look after vulnerable and elderly Hellenes. Golden Dawn also claimed to have powerful friends in the church.

But there were some happy exceptions to this trend. The priest in charge of the Sepolia parish, Evangelos Ganas, was a popular, articulate and discreetly helpful figure who was liked by local people of all races. They included a Nigerian couple who had given their sons Greek names after settling in Athens in 1992. The middle one,

Giannis, was a keen member of the Sunday school, exceptionally tall and outstanding in other ways: 'There was an innocence, and a hopefulness, about his eyes,' the priest would recall long afterwards. On 28 October 2012, Father Evangelos baptized eight-year-old Giannis and his brother Alexandros. Things moved rapidly. As a 2-metre-tall teenager, Giannis was out on the street, helping his family by hawking handbags and sunglasses. Soon after that, he become one of the world's most famous basketball players and an adored national hero of Greece. The story of his discovery is surreal. A successful Athenian basketball coach was bicycling through the rough streets of Sepolia when he spotted Giannis and one of his brothers training in a makeshift court. Since 2013, Giannis has lived mainly in the United States and played for the Milwaukee Bucks, but the 'Greek freak' – his American nickname – still professes to be a proud citizen of the Hellenic republic and slips easily into working-class Athenian patter. Nobody has done more than Giannis Antetokounmpo to give younger Greeks a broader understanding of nationality.

On the western edge of Athens, the heavily polluted district of Aigaleo has lost some of its sheen since King Xerxes planted his throne there to observe the battle of Salamis. But for Pakistani migrants who love to play cricket, it has some happy associations. Whenever the municipal football ground was not in use (especially at Greek Christian holidays like Easter and Christmas), an Athenian-Pakistani called Mehdi Khan Choudry found he could borrow the ground and organize two-day cricket tournaments involving a dozen local teams, all South Asian. As a result, the industrial slums of Attica have begun to rival the genteel, once-British island of Corfu as the epicentre of Greek cricket.

The practice of Islam in greater Athens is one of many areas where theory and practice have often diverged. Only in late 2020 did the Muslims of Athens see the opening for regular worship (subject to Covid restrictions) of a so-called official mosque, a converted building in a former naval base, off the old Sacred Way running westwards from Athens. This followed decades of tense negotiation involving Islamic governments and politicians and religious authorities in Greece, including the Orthodox Church, which has enjoyed something close to a veto on the opening of new places of worship. But in fact, there had long been dozens of informal places of Islamic worship across the city, catering to perhaps 250,000 Muslim residents. Many of them operated in tiny apartments, basements or converted garages. Their day-to-day relationship with the authorities was generally good. The police relied on prayer leaders to keep an eye out for Islamist hotheads, and the police kept the worshippers minimally safe from Greek extremists. For the Arab business executives or sports players who were staying in the posh hotels of Syngrou Avenue, there were handy and well-organized premises in the basement of respectable buildings. In the rougher parts of town, around Viktoria Square, there were somewhat more basic prayer spaces, in tumbledown flats, where the language of the sermon was often Urdu rather than Arabic.

For Shia Muslims, Piraeus became a stronghold. They fitted out for prayer a spacious, deep basement in a row of warehouses on a backstreet just a few minutes' walk from the harbour. And on the festival of Ashura the Shia practice of public self-flagellation to mark the martyrdom of Hussein, the Prophet Mohammed's grandson, is vigorously conducted near the quayside immortalized by Melina Mercouri. In 2018, the authorities started encouraging de facto Muslim prayer spaces to seek a licence and undergo safety and fire regulation checks. About a dozen entered this bureaucratic labyrinth. But this is one of many areas of greater Athenian life where official procedures follow social reality rather than moulding it.

Urban spaces are, by their very nature, places of pragmatism and plasticity, often with intriguing results. In Ottoman cities, the various ethnic and religious communities were carefully kept apart by their leaders, but that did not prevent individuals from falling in love, doing business together or creating and enjoying entertainment, even if subterfuge was sometimes necessary. In the smallish town of Ottoman Athens, where segregation was rigorously enforced, barriers came tumbling down in the mêlée of the pre-Lenten carnival, as Byron observed. But there is never any guarantee that social or inter-communal peace, however ingeniously negotiated, will persist. The 2008 riots in Athens were not, in any sense, race riots – but they were probably made worse by the fact that the police had all but lost control of some ethnically diverse neighbourhoods of Athens.

Even in parts of Athens which are generally agreed to be a success story, there is a sense that things could turn sour unless the residents and stakeholders remain alert. Take two districts, one thriving and the other much more edgy. The winding thoroughfares of Plaka and the steep lanes that connect them are glorious places to stay, visit or live. This is the oldest continuously inhabited part of Athens, and therefore one of the oldest continuously inhabited places in the world. Whether the city was a great Aegean power, a Roman or Macedonian outpost, a Catalonian or Frankish-run hamlet or an Ottoman town, people always lived on the northern slope of the Acropolis. Yet as of the early 1970s, the place was becoming a red-light district and a den of noisy, low-grade nightclubs. Only in the later part of that decade did a coalition – ranging from residents to cultural figures and important players in the travel business – manage to make the case that the district's decline must be stopped. Thanks to a brave handful of politicians on the centre-right and left, facing down colleagues who had different ideas, land-use regulations were changed and bars and discos closed down. The residents who confronted the nightclub owners faced harassment and threats, but they prevailed. Plaka became a mixed neighbourhood of shops, hotels, residents of different income brackets and beautifully restored historic buildings. In the footsteps of travellers like Byron, Stuart and Revett, Spon and Wheler or Ciriacus of Ancona, it is possible to walk enjoyably between the area's two classical treasures: the Lysicrates monument commemorating a prize won for a musical performance around 335 BCE and the Tower of the Winds, probably built about four centuries later. Along the route there are reminders of just about every other phase in the town's history, including early medieval churches and a former hammam. But this state of affairs is fragile, according to the country's most venerable conservation movement, Elliniki Etaireia*, which is located in the heart of Plaka. Both in the mid-1990s and again in 2014, there were moves to change the regulations in ways that might have brought noisy entertainment back, and made life unbearable for long-standing residents. As of 2021, there are worrying signs that shadowy commercial forces are once again trying to concentrate ownership in a few hands, while allowing existing proprietors to retain small equity stakes so it appears that little has changed. 'The only way of conserving Plaka is perpetual vigilance,' says Lydia Carras, a co-founder with her husband Costa of Elliniki Etaireia.

Then move about a kilometre away, to a location which has often been liminal, contested and perceived in wildly conflicting ways, even in ancient times. The multiple gates on the western side of Athens were ingeniously built into the Themistoclean wall that went up in the aftermath of the battle of Salamis. For centuries this cluster of entrances and fortifications must have been an imposing sight. The Sacred Gate, with the Eridanos river running alongside it, led due west to the psychic wonderland of Eleusis. Only a few metres to the north was the Dipylon or Double Gate, set back from the wall, which led to Plato's Academy, with important graves and monuments flanking the route. A soldier entering the city by this portal found himself in a quadrangle surrounded by crenellated turrets; this must have been a powerful deterrent.

But was the area on either side of these gates pleasant and dignified, or sordid? Ancient writers cannot agree. Thucydides

---

* Greek Association for the Protection of the Environment.

describes the *Dimosion Sema* or Public Cemetery (apparently just outside the Double Gate, on the way to the Academy) where Pericles gave his oration as 'the most beautiful suburb' of the city, and a dignified place to inter and honour the war dead. But in the very same neighbourhood, the satirist Aristophanes sets a vignette in which a seller of dubious sausages, made of dog and donkey, exchanges bawdy insults with a tired old prostitute. Then Pausanias, writing half a century later, waxes even more lyrical about the roadside cemetery, describing it as the burial place not only of the war dead, but of almost all the city's democratic heroes – Pericles; the constitution-writer Kleisthenes; the tyrant-slayers Harmodius and Aristogeiton; and Thrasyboulos, who fought to restore democracy in the twilight of the golden age. All these people, we assume, had fine graves – which might be found if only we knew exactly where to look.

In the present day, this is still a contentious patch of urban space. The gates themselves and a small part of the routes leading out of them have been uncovered and form part of the lovely archaeological site of Kerameikos. But that site comes to an abrupt end on the bustling highway of Pireos Avenue, and on the other side, there is an area called Metaxourgeio, about which guidebooks, sociologists and developers have sharply conflicting things to say. It is a lamentably neglected, drug-infested slum, where elderly Greeks and vulnerable newcomers – united by poverty – eke out a desperate existence, made worse by voracious developers in search of quick profits. Or, from another perspective, it is an exciting artistic hub, where at least some neoclassical buildings have been beautifully restored, and rusty old warehouses turned into lofts for alternative urban living. The district takes its name from an important silk factory (*metaxi* is modern Greek for silk) which made it into a working-class stronghold; it is now a municipal art gallery. Nearby is the National Theatre, a marvellously florid piece of design by Ernst Ziller, standing on the edge of Metaxourgeio and stubbornly proclaiming the value of high culture.

Many different parties are contesting the future of this grimy piece of urban real estate. Among them are brothel owners and drug dealers; an artistic community including jugglers and musicians as well as painters and sculptors; developers who have refurbished some decaying structures and turned them into miniature 'gated communities', where life can be comfortable and secure. One resident is Katerina Sakellaropoulou, the eminent judge who became president of Greece (a ceremonial but important post) in 2019. Another party to discussions on Metaxourgeio's future consists of social geographers on the Greek left who, taking their cue from counterparts in Britain and America, have a strong antipathy towards gentrification in virtually all its forms. Scholars such as Georgia Alexandri have researched and written extensively and passionately about Metaxourgeio and the neighbouring district of Gazi, named after the highly polluting gasworks which operated there until the 1980s. And finally, with the potential in the medium term to trump all the other claimants, there are the archaeologists. Given that such extraordinary finds were made on one side of Pireos Avenue, should we not expect similar treasures to emerge on the other side, just a little further north and west? That is their argument. A multiple male grave, dating from the time of the Peloponnesian War, was discovered under one of the district's decaying structures in 1997. Even if these were not the actual fallen heroes that Pericles lamented, it was clearly a similar kind of warriors' tomb. Nothing much happened until spring 2021, when the culture minister, Lina Mendoni, announced that the immediate area of the find would be thoroughly excavated, in the expectation of uncovering the 'most important cemetery of the ancient world...' Now was the time, she said, to discover what Thucydides meant when describing this location as the loveliest of suburbs. In the immediate future, Aristophanes' portrayal of cheap sausage sellers and tired sex workers may have more verisimilitude.

Metaxourgeio, says the Greek-Nigerian rapper and songwriter Manolis Yinka, is a place 'full of contradictions' – which he thoroughly enjoyed negotiating during the decade or so when he lived in the district. His own career has many well-handled contradictions, epitomizing today's Athens. His Nigerian parents were among the first Africans to settle in the Patisia district in the 1980s. One of the grimmer memories of his youth is of going to pay a household utility bill, when he was around twenty, and finding himself thrown in a police cell for eight hours until he could prove he had grown up in Greece and possessed a birth certificate. His musical career took off when he joined a band called Imam Bayildi, which combined *rembetika*, Greek folk music, hip-hop and reggae – to the delight of audiences in London, Edinburgh and Montreal. In due course he would become the most senior member of a cluster of Greek-African rappers, wittily manipulating Greek and transatlantic themes. The other members of the band, including players of the saxophone, guitar and bouzouki, were no slum-kids; some had been to private schools. And the admirers of Yinka's verbal pyrotechnics, flipping between Greek and English, include many youngsters from prosperous homes. Even the name of his old band – a Turkish expression meaning 'the imam fainted' which is also the pan-Aegean word for stuffed aubergines – reflects a rather middle-class or intelligentsia style of humour. Life has given Yinka the ability to move between cultural spaces.

In a sense, the contest over the future of that small, crumbling patch of ground in the heart of Athens is a microcosm of a vastly bigger contest over the future of the whole urban area. It is almost literally being pulled in different directions. The Olympic Games, the Venizelos airport and the new retail network drew the conurbation eastwards and northwards. The world-famous city planner Constantinos Doxiadis – best known for conurbations in Pakistan and the United States – had a vision for his native Athens which would have involved moving some of the country's administration to the northern suburbs of the city so as to let the area around the Acropolis breathe more easily. In a very partial way, that vision has come to pass. Despite the ever-increasing number of visitors, the antiquities of Athens – starting with the Acropolis and the Agora – have never been so attractively presented to visitors. The pedestrianization of Dionysiou Areopagitou (the avenue running south of the Acropolis) and of the connecting thoroughfare of Apostolou Pavlou makes possible a long, enjoyable walk through monuments and vegetation that bring the ancient city to life. Such a stroll can either end or begin with a visit to the Acropolis Museum, opened in 2009, whose glass gallery gives an idea of how the Parthenon sculptures would look if they were repatriated from foreign places and displayed against the brilliant Attic light. A cleverly built walkway also allows visitors to gaze down at the streets and homes from late antiquity which were discovered while making the museum. So it might be argued that in recent years the primacy of the Acropolis as the spiritual centre of Athens has been more clearly affirmed than ever, while the move northwards of residents and shops has decongested the centre in a benign way.

But for better or worse, the centre of gravity of greater Athens is also being pulled southwards. To understand this story, it may be helpful to recall the competition of the late nineteenth century among wealthy Greeks of the diaspora to adorn Athens with magnificent buildings, both private and public. That competition continues, and (as was the case 150 years ago) it can long outlast the particular tycoon whose fortune is being dished out. The foundation established by Aristotle Onassis (along with his many other bequests to Greece, including a cardiac hospital) established a cultural centre in a shimmering glass cube called Stegi (Roof) on Syngrou Avenue in 2010; part of its self-imposed mission was to explore the boundaries of art, technology and gender. Then in 2017, also near Syngrou, the Stavros Niarchos Foundation unveiled another, even more dazzling piece of contemporary architecture and landscaping: a new home for the Greek National Library and the Opera, complete with a seawater canal and showpiece Mediterranean garden. Work on this project – costing nearly $1 billion, designed by Renzo Piano – had rumbled on while the city was in the depth of its economic crisis.

Its opening seemed to be a signal that better times might be in store for Athens.

But the scale of those two projects is vastly exceeded by a plan to create a new Athenian Riviera in the space once occupied by Ellinikon airport. The area had served as an Olympic site before sliding into decay. Priced at $8 billion, the project aspires to create 'the large urban park in Europe' as well as erecting luxury residences, hotels, a yachting marina and a casino. It would make that part of Athens feel more like Monaco, Miami or Dubai. Lambda, the consortium leading the development, is headed by Spyros Latsis, master of an oil and shipping empire and close friend of the British (and Greek) royals. Will the plan come to pass? Lambda accused the Syriza government of causing needless delays by haggling over the share of the land that would be given over to green space; prime minister Mitsotakis has promised to accelerate the project, and met Latsis soon after taking office, though things have not progressed quite as fast as either party initially promised. Lambda has had to buy out partners based in China and Abu Dhabi who seemingly lost enthusiasm for the development. One way or another, a kilometre-long stretch of seaside space that lapsed into rusty desuetude over a couple of decades will surely be exploited and attract visitors and investors. That will bring more money to Athens, but also consume more water and energy and produce more waste.

Apart from its north–south tug-of-war, the Athens urban area has long felt tension between an impoverished, environmentally degraded west and a far more prosperous and better planned eastern side, abutting Mount Hymettus. The greatest blight on the western landscape, literally and metaphorically, is the Fyli landfill, the county's largest dump. In antiquity this was a place with noble associations, as the hideout where Thrasyboulos prepared to fight for Athenian democracy. But today's Fyli is ghastly. It exudes an unspeakable odour of methane and stale waste and is perpetually on the verge of saturation. There is a small recycling plant, but the great majority of the waste is buried – a microcosm of the situation in

Greece as a whole. In many surrounding neighbourhoods, the stench is so unpleasant and unhealthy that people cannot sit outdoors and enjoy their balconies. It is contributing to the pollution of Lake Koumoundourou, a biodiversity haven that was sacred in ancient times to Persephone. Another lingering worry is the fact that the channels carrying water to Athens from the Mornos reservoir, in the heart of the mountains 200 kilometres to the west, might be affected; this is a fine piece of engineering and sufficient, for the time being, to meet the conurbation's water needs. But it passes only 300 metres from the dreadfulness of Fyli.

Kriton Arsenis, a passionate environmentalist who represents that side of Athens in parliament, imagines the day when the Sacred Way leading west out of the city could once again be an inspiring route to travel as opposed to an endangered blackspot. The coastal road to Eleusis was at the heart of ancient Athenian spirituality. At and around the monastery of Daphni, people could enjoy the superb Christian art, the remains (built into the monastery) of a temple to Apollo, the nearby sanctuary to Aphrodite – and Persephone's lake. 'They would feel the entire sacred landscape,' he thinks. That is not impossible now. But it would help if the two ends of the journey – western Athens and Eleusis – were not so ravaged by the worst of modern civilization.

Apart from being exceptionally polluted by steel mills, cement factories and oil refineries, Eleusis is already affected by what may be one of Greece's most serious problems in a warming world: the vicious circle of soil erosion and flash flooding on mountainsides which have been denuded of their traditional vegetation. At least fifteen people were killed by inundations in nearby locations in 2017. It says something of the site's extraordinary numinosity that people can still feel it, even after all the damage to the local landscape. Flash flooding is likely to be an increasing problem in the heart of Athens – despite the sensible efforts now in progress to reforest Mount Lycabettus and replace its hard roads with water-permeable ones. Mayor Bakoyannis and his team of city planners have mooted the idea of uncovering part of the Ilisos river; that would bring badly needed release to the city's natural waterways and refreshment to a thirsty city. Hadrian's aqueduct, in use until a century ago, is being refurbished to the point where it can deliver water for non-drinking purposes. All this will help, at the margin.

For Athens and Attica to flourish in the remainder of the twenty-first century, a different trade-off between private affluence and public squalor will be needed. Since the time of King Otho, modern Athens has always been a place where a few individuals enjoyed ostentatious prosperity, and sometimes a place where a remarkable number of people could acquire modest wealth in the form of small businesses or homes. It hosted micro-communities – from the builders of Anafiotika to the Anatolian refugees of Kokkinia to the artists and rappers of Metaxourgeio – who had a strong sense, often imported from elsewhere, of the common good within their small social world. But a sense of loyalty to the city as a whole has been lacking. That could be because so many people who dwell in Athens are really, in their hearts, living elsewhere – in the island or remote village where they grew up, spend summers and holidays if possible, and retain their voting rights. For Athens to be sustainable at 4 million people, it will need some kind of all-encompassing civic sense, one that embraces the tour guides of the Acropolis, the fusion chefs of Monastiraki, the rappers of Metaxourgeio, the parish priests of Sepolia, the dump-truckers of Fyli, the croupiers of Ellinikon, the dock workers of Chinese-run Piraeus. At a certain level, the consolidation of modern Athens has been helped by the common experience of the mysteries, challenges and joys of Greekness, the feeling that comes from reading an inscription from 2,000 years ago and understanding its meaning without effort. That can still work, as long as people understand that Greekness comes in many varieties and compounds, as it always has.

And then there is the unexpected. Almost every single develop-ment described in this chapter – the new cosmopolitanism of Athens, the multicultural music scene, the enjoyment of magnificent modern buildings – has been stopped in its tracks by Covid. The onset of the pandemic in spring 2020 was handled remarkably well, with a disciplined lockdown and very low case numbers. Quarrels over whether churches should open led to some nasty squabbles between religious and secular Greeks. Then they were silenced, to some extent, by the nation's universal admiration for Sotiris Tsiodras, a chief medical officer who was a Harvard-trained epidemiologist – and therefore clear-eyed about the virus – and also, in private life, a devout Orthodox Christian who was seen practising Byzantine chanting in a prudently locked church.

By spring 2021, the country was almost overwhelmed by a second wave and tempers were frayed. The fusion eateries, the operas in the Niarchos complex and the Greek-African rap sessions were silenced as people waited grumpily at home. In a thoroughly nasty scene, young people held a rowdy Covid party in a square in one of the poorer parts of Athens; when an elderly resident complained of the licentious things that were happening in the entrance of her apartment, her words were mockingly shared as a video clip on social media. This was not Athens at its best; it was a bad omen for the city's ability to preserve social cohesion in a time of extreme stress.

The explanation of Thucydides for the success of Athens and Attica seems, to a twenty-first-century reader, both naïve and sophisticated. He believed that the city-state flourished precisely because of the relative poverty of the soil, which forced people to co-operate, innovate and in due course move outwards. More fertile places lent themselves to tyranny and to frequent battles for control of resources. The negative part of his theory is certainly well-founded, and modern. Today's political scientists have written much about the resources curse, the tendency of petro-states to spawn tyrannical regimes who can simply buy off dissent. But what about the other side of the coin? Necessity *can* be the mother of social and political invention, and in Athens it often has been. One of the uncanny similarities between modern and ancient Athenian public affairs is an obsession with procedures, constitutional niceties, electoral rules – all of which are supposed to serve the ultimate purpose of channelling conflict and disagreement and avoiding outright violence. That propensity, combined with quick wits, eloquence and flair, has often served Athenians well – and it has often dramatically failed, sometimes because the egos of the individuals involved were too big to consider compromise. Whenever the conflicting external pressures on Greece have meshed with the private agendas of Athenian power brokers, the result has been disaster, as happened in 1916 and 1944.

For much of its 200-year life, modern Greece has been in the eye of geopolitical storms: torn between cultural and religious ties with Russia, and strategic links with the Anglo-Saxon powers that dominated the sea. In the twenty-first century, the magnetic forces may be quite different. There will be commercial pressures – and opportunities – from China and demographic and humanitarian pressures from the greater Middle East and Africa.

Greece and its capital will also face challenges of a more immediate, physical kind, as became ominously clear in August 2021. Along with several other Mediterranean places, the country was struck by a wave of fires. About 100,000 hectares of Greek woodland were destroyed in a few days; the worst-hit areas were the island of Euboea and the north-western side of Athens, where thousands of people had to flee their homes. The area of Varybobi, on the lower slopes of Mount Parnes, suddenly ceased to be an agreeably cool summer refuge, with children's summer camps and posh riding schools, and became a nightmarish inferno instead. High, shifting winds made the flames horribly hard to extinguish, and the whole of Athens was shrouded in smoke.

This was the first Greek disaster that was widely blamed on climate change, and it will not be the last. Athens and its masters will need all the city's millennial wisdom to stand in the middle of these storms – be they geopolitical, economic or physical – and somehow survive.

# Notes on Sources

**Introduction: Rocks That Matter**

The words from Homer on page 14 are quoted from *The Iliad with an English Translation* by A. T. Murray, London: William Heinemann, 1924.

**1 The Beginnings of Greatness**

Piecing together the story of Athens in the sixth and seventh centuries BCE requires detective work and imagination. The written sources are rich but late. Plutarch, a prolific essayist, philosopher and priest at the temple of Apollo in Delphi, penned brief but densely packed lives of prominent figures in Greek and Roman history. He lived long after most of his subjects, from about 46 to 119 CE, but we can assume that he had access to many earlier sources that have long since been lost. After the mythical hero Theseus, the first historical personality he tackles is Solon. For anyone trying to understand the achievements of that ruler, as well as what went before and immediately after, Plutarch's account of Solon is a first port of call. It is to Plutarch's Life of Solon (Chapter 12) that we owe the story of Kylon's men and their cruel treatment by Megakles. Plutarch also describes (Chapter 17) the division of the Athenians into four classes, based on property.

Equally enjoyable and colourful, and closer in time to the relevant events, are the accounts of Herodotus, who was born in Halicarnassus (the modern Turkish port of Bodrum) around 484 BCE and later migrated to Athens and then to an Athenian-led colony in Italy. He is an advocate for his adopted Athenian homeland and its noble origins, but is equally fascinated by the other cultures of the greater Middle East, including Persia and Egypt. We have the *Histories* of Herodotus to thank for a vivid account (Book 1, Chapter 30 onwards) of the debates between the Athenian traveller Solon and the super-wealthy Croesus on the nature of happiness: hardly a verbatim account, but a revealing clue as to how the Athenians understood themselves.

The translation of Herodotus' description of Solon's wanderings on page 23 is my own. Solon's poetry survives because it is mentioned in a speech by Demosthenes, *On the False Embassy*, section 255, available at perseus.tufts.edu, first published in *Demosthenes with an English Translation* by C. A. Vince M.A., and J. M. Vince M.A., Cambridge, MA, Harvard University Press; London, William Heinemann Ltd., 1926.

Another vital text for people trying to understand Solon and his successors is the *Constitution of the Athenians* which was written in the 320s BCE, either by Aristotle or by one of his pupils. This text was rediscovered by chance in the late nineteenth century on pieces of Egyptian papyrus, and it sets out to trace the evolution of the Athenian democracy, and its elaborate institutions, in extraordinary detail. It portrays Solon (in Chapter 6) as a statesman who was unfairly maligned for his handling of the debt crisis, when in fact he had steered a careful middle course between debtors and creditors.

With regard to his successor Peisistratus and his two sons, the ancient texts are remarkably unanimous in their positive assessment of the tyrant and very divided in their description of his two sons and their unhappy story. The Aristotelian *Constitution* speaks of Hippias and Hipparchus ruling jointly until the latter's death, while other sources, and most modern scholars, doubt whether

Hipparchus ever wielded much power. On the other hand, the other great philosopher, Plato, devotes an entire dialogue to the story of Hipparchus and suggests that he, as long as he remained alive, was the main authority in Athens.

Herodotus describes the killing of Hipparchus (Book 5, Chapter 55 onwards) and notes that as a result the Athenians 'lived under an even harsher tyranny than before'. An alternative account is given by Thucydides, the great Athenian father of objective, analytical history, starting at Book 6, Chapter 54 of his magnum opus, *The History of the Peloponnesian War*. Although is he is best known for describing the conflicts of his own lifetime (*c.* 460 to *c.* 400 BCE), Thucydides finds it worthwhile to jump backwards in time and offer his own cynical interpretation of the killing of Hipparchus, insisting that sexual jealousy rather than idealistic opposition to tyranny was the main motive (Book 6, Chapters 53–9). The fact that Thucydides is generally so icily detached in his assessment of human motivations, and has no particular leaning towards the salacious, lends plausibility to that view.

## 2 Victories of Brilliance

There is an abiding fascination about the great battles in which the emerging democracy proved itself against numerically superior Persian invaders. Both the heart-stopping tension and cunning use of terrain and human psychology are well brought out in the ancient sources: first and foremost Herodotus for Marathon, while for Salamis, Herodotus and Aeschylus are the twin starting points. The Roman writer Cornelius Nepos adds nuance to the basic story of Marathon. Although the Persians realized that the narrow strip of land would not suit their cavalry, they wanted to attack before the Athenians got help from Sparta, he plausibly notes. Not much archaeological evidence has emerged to challenge or supplement those accounts, with one significant exception.

The 'decree of Themistocles' is an inscription on stone, discovered in 1959, which purports to spell out the details of the evacuation of Athens that was successfully proposed by the great naval strategist. If the stone is authentic, it suggests that the exodus was not a last-minute expediency, as Herodotus implies, but a carefully planned operation which may have unfolded several months before Salamis.

With regard to Marathon, the legendary runs ascribed to Pheidippides (which may be a corruption of Philippides) are a confusing aspect of the written sources. Lucian was a popular satirical writer who lived in Roman Syria in the second century CE. He asserts in a throwaway line (*De Lapsu, 3*) in an essay on forms of greeting that the runner Philippides [*sic*] dropped dead after dashing to Athens and declaring, 'Rejoice, we are winning…' Plutarch, in another passing allusion, tells a similar story but says the name of the expiring runner is generally thought to be Eucles (*De Gloria Atheniensium 3*).

Both battle terrains are within easy reach of Athens (although relatively few tourists make the effort), and careful interrogation of the landscape had become an almost obsessive pastime for many a military historian and classicist. The seminal essay on Salamis by Nicholas Hammond, the British scholar, wartime resistance operative and connoisseur of Greece, is one fruit of this study.

At least since the nineteenth century, scholars have been arguing over whether the Persians entered the Salamis straits during the night before the battle or merely stood guard at the southern entrance. Up to a dozen eminent authorities can be found on each side of that debate, as was explained to me by Colonel Athanasios Athanasiades, a military history buff who has studied them all. I was blessed to have the colonel, as well as the excellent drivers Takis Koumoutsakos and Nikitas Arvanitis, as my own escorts on trips to Marathon and Salamis. Evi Mikromastora, who runs the museum on Salamis, and George Panagopoulos, the mayor, were equally helpful.

Johan Henrik Schreiner, a Norwegian scholar, argues that there were two separate Greek–Persian fights at Marathon, only one commanded by Miltiades. Peter Krentz is a modern scholar of Marathon who concludes that Herodotus was mostly right, even if the weight of the Athenian armour has been exaggerated. Barry Strauss, a history professor who is also a successful storyteller, likewise vindicates the contemporary accounts of Salamis, and argues that the battle's historical significance is clearer than ever now.

Gonda van Steen, a professor at King's College, London, has shown how the Salamis battle cry was reinterpreted and exploited at different times in modern Greek history, mostly famously by General Metaxas as the Greek army was about to fight the Italians in Albania.

The replica trireme *Olympias*, built by British and Greek enthusiasts and later an exhibit at the Averof naval museum, is a perpetual and rich source of interest for those interested in ancient sea battles (https://averof.mil.gr). So too is the Zea Harbour Project, directed by Bjorn Loven, which discovered the shipsheds of Piraeus and much else besides: see www.carlsbergfondet.dk.

Sources for Marathon include the following:

Chrestos Dionysopoulos, *I Machi tou Marathona, Istorike kai Topografike Proseggisi*, Athens: Kapon Press, 2012
Herodotus, *The Histories*, Book 6, especially lines 109–17
Peter Krentz, *The Battle of Marathon*, New Haven and London: Yale University Press, 2010
Cornelius Nepos, *Miltiades*, Book 4
Johan Henrik Schreiner, *Two Battles and Two Bills: Marathon and The Athenian Fleet*, Oslo: Norwegian Institute at Athens, 2004

Sources for Salamis and maritime warfare include the following:

Aeschylus, *The Persians*, especially lines 380–430; on pages 52, 53 and 54, the lines quoted are from Peter Levi's translation and are used with the permission of the estate of Peter Levi

Robert Garland, *Athens Burning: The Persian Invasion of Greece and the Evacuation of Attica*, Baltimore: Johns Hopkins University Press, 2017

N. G. L. Hammond, 'The Battle of Salamis', *Journal of Hellenic Studies*, vol. 76, pp. 32–54, 1956

Herodotus, *The Histories*, Book 8, lines 40–96

Bjorn Loven and others, *Ancient Harbours of the Piraeus: The Zea Shipsheds and Slipways*, Aarhus University Press, 2012

John Morrison, John Coates and Boris Rankov, *The Athenian Trireme: The History and Reconstruction of an Ancient Greek Warship*, Cambridge University Press, 1986

Johan Henrik Schreiner, *Two Battles and Two Bills: Marathon and The Athenian Fleet*, Oslo: Norwegian Institute at Athens, 2004

Gonda van Steen, 'Now the Struggle is for All', *Comparative Drama*, 2010, vol. 44–5, no. 1

Barry Strauss, *The Battle of Salamis: The Naval Encounter that saved Greece and Western Civilization*, New York: Simon and Schuster, 2004

## 3  Golden Years

For anyone trying to understand the highly complex political and military developments that unfolded in Greece during the half-century between Salamis and the great Peloponnesian War, the ancient (if not contemporary) texts are the essential basis of all enquiry.

Thucydides (Book 1, 89–117) gives his own terse and densely packed summary of those years, including the story of the Athenian defences masterminded by Themistocles in cunning defiance of the Spartans. Plutarch's life of Kimon is an enjoyable and convincing description of a flesh-and-blood human being, described as 'tall and stately with a thick, curly head of hair' and 'engaging and attractive to the common folk' who were fed up with the brainy arrogance of Themistocles. Plutarch presents a soldier's soldier who was a populist but not a democrat and never wavered in his loyalty to Athens, even when ostracized. It is to Plutarch that we owe a frank but not salacious account of the rumours about Kimon's possibly incestuous relationship with his sister Elpinike. On the other hand, Plutarch's account of Pericles as an austere and reserved figure of iron self-discipline is a tad too hagiographic to be entirely trusted. The run of shrewd military judgements – which fights to pick and which to avoid – are a better guide to Periclean brainpower.

As the chapter explains, the written sources have been fleshed out, in a most fascinating way, by the careful study of the *ostraka* or pottery sherds which were used to expel undesirable characters from the Athenian political arena. Two immensely diligent scholars, working far from the limelight, have spent years scrutinizing these objects, studying the handwriting, the private jokes and obscenities, and the variety of broken household objects that were used. They are Stefan Brenne of Germany's Giessen University and James Sickinger of Florida State University. Brenne has devoted an academic lifetime to studying and cataloguing the *ostraka* found in the Kerameikos cemetery half a century ago, while Sickinger has focused on finds in the Ancient Agora. Brenne has published a catalogue of his finds in a door-stopping volume in his native Germany, while Sickinger has presented his latest work in the journal of the American School of Classical Studies in Athens, and in a lecture to the school.

Among secondary sources of a more conventional kind, the works of Yale University's emeritus Professor Donald Kagan (about the Peloponnesian War and what went before) are considered an essential starting point, as are those of Cambridge University's Professor Paul Cartledge. The latter was kind enough to share some important personal insights, though he bears absolutely no responsibility for my conclusions.

Having overseen the conservation works at the Acropolis over three decades, Manolis Korres is generally agreed to be the greatest living expert on the Parthenon and the other Periclean monuments. He has written with particular insight on the engineering and logistical challenges of bringing so much marble to the citadel and deploying it so efficiently and beautifully. I was privileged to have an hour's conversation with him in April 2019, although it focused mainly on the use of the Acropolis in subsequent eras, including the modern one.

As the chapter mentions, Joan Breton Connelly has made one of the most dazzling and original contributions to scholarly debate over the Parthenon sculptures, constructing a careful argument over the subject matter of the frieze which comes to a head in Chapters 4 and 5 of her book. I feel unqualified to judge whether her conclusion is ultimately well-founded, but it is almost universally agreed that she sets a new standard in explaining the context in which these superb artefacts were produced.

From the thousands of books and essays written about this period, my personal and highly select bibliography would therefore include:

Stefan Brenne, *Die Ostraka vom Kerameikos*, Wiesbaden: Reichert Verlag, 2018

Paul Cartledge, *Democracy: A Life*, Oxford University Press, 2018

Joan Breton Connelly, *The Parthenon Enigma*, first published in New York by Random House, and in the United Kingdom by Head of Zeus, both in 2014

Ian Jenkins, *The Parthenon Frieze*, London: British Museum Press, 1994

Donald Kagan, *Pericles of Athens and the Birth of Democracy*, New York: Free Press, 1991

Manolis Korres, *From Pentelicon to the Parthenon*, Athens: Melissa Publishers, 2003

James Sickinger, 'New Ostraka from the Athenian Agora', *Hesperia* (journal of the American School of Classical Studies in Athens), no. 86, pp. 443–508, 2017

## 4  Pride and a Fall

The texts which form the basis of this chapter are very familiar. The funeral speech of Pericles is to be found in Book 2 of Thucydides, sections 34–46, and the historian's account of the plague comes immediately afterwards in sections 47–55.

For Thucydides' account of the great Periclean oration, and the plague, I have made my own translation, taking into account those of Benjamin Jowett (1817–93) and Charles Forster Smith (1852–1951).

The so-called reception of these texts, especially the funeral oration, is a gigantic field of study, stimulating hundreds of books, scholarly essays and theses. The interpretation of Thucydides in general has become a contentious and intensely topical issue, mainly thanks to the theory of Professor Graham Allison that America and China are at risk of falling into the 'Thucydides trap': the high probability that a well-established power will clash with a rapidly rising one. The entire 'trap' hypothesis, which has been roundly criticized by Chinese officials, focuses on one line in the great work by Thucydides (Book 1, Section 23), which asserts, 'what made war unavoidable was the growth of Athenian power and the fear which this caused in Sparta'. In a summary of the debate in *The World Today*, journal of the Royal Institute of International Affairs, published in December 2019, I argue that fixating on one sentence does an injustice to the great historian's analysis.

Regardless of the Greek chronicler's impact on Sino-American relations, the funeral oration's hymn to liberal democracy has been a source of fascination for Anglo-Saxon readers since it was translated by the political philosopher Thomas Hobbes (1588–1679). Both for Britons at the height of their empire, and American strategists at the peak of the Cold War, Thucydides has been read as a kind of manifesto for liberal imperialism, describing a state which is democratic, pluralist and law-governed in its domestic governance but prepared to act decisively and ruthlessly in far-flung places. This has generated an enormous literature about Thucydides and his interpretation. Bristol University has served as a hub for a wide-ranging study of this literature.

The egregious sexism of one passage in the funeral oration has also generated a huge body of academic writing, as has the shadowy role which may have been played by Aspasia, the lover of Pericles. Bettany Hughes, a classical scholar as well as a skilled popularizer of classical lore, has led the field in efforts to discover the real Aspasia.

An outstanding and at times provocative figure in the interpretation of Athenian democracy and its merits (including wartime resilience) is Stanford University's Professor Josiah Ober, advocate of the view that Athens, like modern democracies, drew strength from its practice of noisy, pluralist debate in which truth has a chance to drive out lies. In collaboration with his colleague Federica Carugati, he has developed the idea that far from collapsing under the shock of the Athenian plague, the city's democracy mutated: in some ways, they argue, the fourth-century democracy, with its judicial constraints on the actions of the citizens' assembly, was a more sophisticated system than its Periclean predecessor.

My own reflections on the Periclean oration were stimulated by repeated visits to the Kerameikos cemetery, several under the direction of Maria Fotouchou, an outstanding professional guide. The two archaeologists who confided to Euphrosyne Doxiadis their ideas about the site of Pericles' grave were Stephanos Koumanoudis and Spyros Iakovidis.

My own particular pathways into this enormous field of knowledge have included:

Peter Adamson, 'Why is Aspasia a Woman? Reflections on Plato's Menexenus', chapter in *Natur – Geschlecht – Politik*, Munich: Wilhelm Fink, 2020

Graham Allison, *Destined for War: Can America and China Escape the Thucydides Trap?*, New York: Houghton Mifflin Harcourt, 2017

Federica Carugati, (chapter in) *Rethinking Mass and Elite: Decision-Making in the Athenian Law-Courts*, Edinburgh University Press 2018, with Barry Weingast

Edith Hall, lecture, *The Greatest Speech of All Time*, delivered at Gresham College in March 2019. See: https://www.gresham.ac.uk/lectures-and-events/pericles-funeral-oration-cemetery

Bettany Hughes, *The Hemlock Cup: Socrates, Athens and the Search for the Good Life*, London: Vintage Books, 2011 (especially Chapter 17, on Aspasia)

Christine Lee and Neville Morley (eds), *Handbook to the Reception of Thucydides*, New Jersey: John Wiley and Sons, 2014

Josiah Ober, *Democracy and Knowledge: Innovation and Learning in Classical Athens*, Princeton University Press, 2014

Jennifer T. Roberts, *The Plague of War: Athens, Sparta and the Struggle for Ancient Greece*, New York: Oxford University Press 2017

## 5  A Blazing Twilight

The *Symposium*, written by Plato sometime after 385 BCE, is a relatively short, enjoyable text which in many ways speaks for itself. It cannot be a verbatim or even an approximate description of an actual conversation, but it is an absorbing, compelling portrayal of a scene in which decadence and camp flirtation alternate with flashes of real wisdom.

One of the scholarly puzzles over the *Symposium* is the origin of the mysterious feminine figure of Diotima, introduced by Socrates as a shadowy source of mystical knowledge. She (for example in a paper by Nancy Evans) has been convincingly linked with Demeter, the cereal-goddess worshipped at Eleusis who likewise served as a guide and gateway to alternative spheres of reality.

To reconstruct the domestic scene described in the *Symposium*, archaeology provides remarkably little help: a dwelling place found in 1966 at Menander Street (these days a rather edgy part of central Athens) is one of the few known remains of private abodes from classical Athens. Plenty of houses were found during the digging of the Athens metro and the Acropolis Museum, but they mostly date from later centuries. That leaves vase-painting as the principal source of images of classical Athenian life and pleasure. My eyes were opened to the richness of this material by Dr Christina Avronidaki of the National Archaeological Museum and Dr Ted Papakostas, a rambunctious propagator of classical knowledge through social media and high-tech graphics.

The life of Alcibiades by Plutarch is one of the most enjoyable, densely packed and confidently written of that writer's mini-biographies. Especially when this material is cross-checked with Thucydides, it becomes possible to build up a relatively full picture of this restless, gifted and narcissistic character who blazed across the Athenian sky during the final years of the fifth century BCE.

Thucydides introduces Alcibiades (see Book 5, Section 43 onwards) as the leader of the war party in 420 BCE who for cynical reasons wanted to stir up Argos against Sparta and undermine the peace with that city. Thucydides goes on in Book 6 to provide a formidably detailed account of the Sicilian expedition, including the debates which preceded the armada's despatch and the mysterious episode of the mutilation of the Herms and other blasphemies for which Alcibiades was blamed. Every twist and turn of the war is covered until the oligarchic coup of 411 BCE, at which point the story abruptly breaks off. Although Thucydides lived until around 400 BCE, the rupture in the narrative suggests that he either died or became incapacitated before fulfilling his declared aim, proclaimed in the opening lines: of chronicling the most important war in human history, for the benefit of every future generation.

After 411 BCE the narrative is taken up by the *Hellenica*, one of the works of Xenophon, a roving general with a literary bent for whose simple prose generations of Greek-learners have been grateful. He lacks the intellectual sophistication of Thucydides but recounts the series of disasters which befell Athens with impressive detachment. It is possible that Xenophon edited at least the final section of Thucydides' work; that would explain why there is such a neat chronological join between the two histories.

The *Hellenica* tells the story of the inter-Greek wars from 411 to 362 BCE. It seems that the first two sections or 'books' were written while he was living in Athens and the remaining five while he was in exile in Sparta. Book 2 recounts the great naval clashes which brought the Peloponnesian War to an end and the installation of a pro-Spartan dictatorship, as well as its overthrow.

My own interest in Alcibiades had an unexpected early stimulus in a remarkably rigorous undergraduate thesis written at Middlebury College by a budding classics scholar, Filippos Papageorgiou, who would later pursue his studies at Yale. It is in the public domain on academia.edu under the title *Loyalty, Leadership and Empire in the Peloponnesian War*. Only after reading it did I realize he was the son of a respected Athenian cultural figure and friend, Nilufer Caglar.

Some aspects of Alcibiades and his era remain irreducibly elusive and intriguing. Among them is the mutilation of the Herms and the blasphemy against the Eleusinian mysteries. In a wonderful book, the German-Romanian professor Alexander Rubel minutely dissects the conflicting and converging evidence, which includes Thucydides, Plutarch and a speech by Andokides, an orator who was accused of complicity in the blasphemous acts. Analysing this and other episodes of religious politics at the turn of the fourth century BCE, he makes the case that Athenians took their religion more seriously than most modern readers can easily grasp. Rubel's doctoral thesis was examined by Robert Parker, Oxford University's doyen of the study of ancient Athenian religious practice.

My own study of the arcane humour of *The Frogs* began when I was a fifteen-year-old pupil at Shrewsbury School, where Richard

Raven tried with mixed results to convince a sceptical adolescent that 2,500-year-old jokes should still raise a laugh. The fact that we used the edition of W. B. Stanford, whose name I knew as a respected figure in Irish academia, helped a little. The foundations laid in my teenage years, however shaky, were enough for me to resume my reading more than forty years later. Hence my concise personal bibliography would include:

Aristophanes, *The Frogs, as edited by W. B. Stanford*, London: Macmillan and Co., 1958

Alexander Rubel, *Fear and Loathing in Ancient Athens: Religion and Politics during the Peloponnesian War*, published in English translation (by Michael Vickers) by Acumen Publishing, Durham, 2014

I also drew on these academic essays, dealing with Diotima; the banter over Alcibiades in *The Frogs*; and on the scanty information about domestic architecture in fifth-century Athens:

Nancy Evans, *Diotima and Demeter as Mystagogues in Plato's Symposium, Hypatia Journal* (2), 2006

J. Walter Graham, 'Houses of Classical Athens', *Phoenix: Journal of the Classical Association of Canada*, Spring 1974

J. L. Marr, 'Who Said What about Alcibiades?', essay in *The Classical Quarterly*, May 1970

## 6  A Chastened Democracy

Our main evidence for the trial and execution of Socrates comes from two writers, Plato and Xenophon. Both are concerned to protect Socrates, posthumously, from the charge that he was an enemy of the democratic state who culpably reared monsters. Both writers are themselves sceptical of democracy, and that makes it harder for them to construct their arguments. Nonetheless, the two authors bring great passion to their task, and the resulting texts, especially those of Plato, are thrilling to read.

Plato's account of his master's trial and death is laid out in four shortish self-explanatory texts. *Euthyphro* describes how Socrates, on the verge of being indicted, engages a fellow citizen in a debate about the nature of piety. *The Apology* presents Socrates' self-defence and exchanges with his accusers. In *Crito*, Socrates explains to a friend why he thinks it would be wrong to try escaping. *Phaedo* combines an account of the sage's dignified passing with debates about the immortality of the soul.

Xenophon's account is of lesser literary stature, but provides an important counterpoint. It puts more emphasis on the divine intuition which the sage claimed to feel, and faces more bluntly the hard truth that some pupils of Socrates turned out bad. In Xenophon's *Memorabilia* (Book 1, 1–2) we hear a prosecutor insisting with devastating force that the thinker must bear responsibility for two notorious pupils, the tyrant Kritias and the wildly irresponsible Alcibiades.

Xenophon also presents the character of Socrates in his own version of the *Symposium*, a maudlin drinking party featuring different characters but a similar scene to that of Plato's masterpiece. In contrast with Plato's subtlety, Xenophon's writing was described with the Greek word *apheleia*. In modern Greek that means naïveté. Thanks to an edition of Xenophon's *Symposium* produced by Anthony Bowen, a Cambridge classicist who was my childhood teacher, I understand that in ancient Greek *apheleia* meant something more flattering: literally a 'lack of pebbles', an absence of lumps and bumps. That is why Xenophon is so refreshingly easy to read.

Among modern writers on these texts, an extraordinary figure is the American journalist I. F. Stone, who in his sixties became fascinated with the trial of Socrates, which he describes as a 'black eye for everything I believe in, for democracy and free speech'. He concludes that Plato's account is a masterly piece of propaganda, whose secret, unstated purpose is to discredit democracy by showing the capriciousness of which ordinary people are capable. Stone also draws attention to lesser-known nuggets of evidence. For example, a speech by the orator Aeschines in the year 345 BCE which asserts, as though it were commonly known, that Socrates was executed mainly because he was the teacher of the dictator Kritias. Generally, Stone shows that the charge of being complicit with dictatorship was a very dark cloud hanging over Socrates, not completely without reason. (See I. F. Stone, *The Trial of Socrates*, New York: Anchor Books, 1989.)

Through Alexander Rubel's already-mentioned work, *Fear and Loathing in Ancient Athens*, and also through conversation with Professor Paul Cartledge, I came to see that the purely religious charges against Socrates were serious in themselves, not just a pretext.

Anybody can study the bare facts of Athenian history in the early fourth century BCE and observe that, after the philosopher's execution, the spectre of civil war seemed to disappear. But it is the British classicist Robin Waterfield who develops, in a sophisticated way, the argument that Socrates' death was a conscious act of self-sacrifice which served to mend the internal injuries of the city. It follows that the sage's mysterious reference to offering a cock to the healing god Asclepius was an oblique allusion to his own act of healing sacrifice. (See Robin Waterfield, *Dispelling the Myth: Why Socrates Died*, New York: W. W. Norton, 2009.)

My understanding of the sculpture of Dexileos the cavalryman was developed in visits to the Kerameikos cemetery and in conversation with Dr Robert Pitt, formerly on the staff of the British School at Athens and now a lively lecturer with College Year at Athens.

Our knowledge of the wars in which Thebes emerged as a dominant power in Greek affairs rests in the first instance on Xenophon, who writes in praise of the Theban general Epaminondas in Book 7 of his *Hellenica*. Plutarch's life of that general has been lost, but we do possess his life of the other great Theban commander, Pelopidas.

The story of Thebes, and the Theban spring, found a modern chronicler in Paul Cartledge, who in 2020 presented an exuberant account of that city as part of his ongoing efforts to counter an excessively Athens-centric view of Greek history. Any such effort has the happy side effect of throwing fresh light on Athens, and the ways it responded to its neighbour's resurgence. (See Paul Cartledge, *Thebes: The Forgotten City of Ancient Greece*, London: Picador, 2020.) He is also an authoritative writer on the evolution of Athenian democracy, wrestling with the paradoxical fact that we have more detailed evidence about fourth-century BCE politics than of the preceding era, so we have to work our way backwards into the golden era.

Josiah Ober and his Stanford colleague Federica Carugati shared with me an unpublished paper which develops the idea that the *graphe paranomon* (judicial sanctions against those who proposed misleading or bad laws in the assembly) represented a mutation, arguably a healthy mutation, in response to the unbridled power of the assembly in the fifth century BCE.

The anecdote about shipping fraud, designed to illustrate the flavour of commercial and legal life, is taken from the oration of Demosthenes, *Against Zenothemis*. Much more is said about Demosthenes in Chapter 7.

## 7 A Dance of Death with Macedonia

Our knowledge of the wars between the Greek states from the mid-fourth century BCE onwards becomes quite shadowy. In the absence of a master historian like Thucydides or a diligent one like Xenophon, some ingenious piecing together is needed. For example, although the Crocus Field battle is often described as the most sanguinary clash in Greek history, relatively little is known for sure about how it unfolded, and the date is not quite certain, though most estimates suggest either 353 or 352 BCE. The main written source for this episode is Diodorus of Sicily, the Greek historian of the first century BCE who wrote a monumental history called *Bibliotheca Hellenica*, comprising forty volumes, of which fifteen survive.

I was privileged to pay two visits to Aiges and the nearby village of Vergina in late 2018, both as a guest of Dr Angeliki Kottaridi, who has assumed the mantle of her famous teacher Manolis Andronikos as the prime mover of Macedonian archaeology in Greece. The second visit was made as a lucky participant in a wonderful gathering of Greek, Turkish and west European scholars, all reflective of Dr Kottaridi's belief that the legacy of Philip and Alexander must be viewed as a palimpsest of overlapping and interlocking eras and cultures. She has made the case that Philip is no less worthy of study than his son Alexander, and has designed the expanding Aiges exhibits in a way that showcases the father-and-son drama, as well as the amazing global legacy of Macedonian conquest. Precisely that view is implied in the monumental new work by Adrian Goldsworthy: *Philip and Alexander: Kings and Conquerors* (London: Head of Zeus, 2020). Goldsworthy's third chapter gives an objective view of the emerging relations between Macedonia, Athens and other Greek city-states.

No such objectivity has ever been ascribed to Demosthenes, another object of study for Plutarch and a man generally agreed to have been one of history's most persuasive orators. Much of what is known about the looming clash between Macedonia and Athens emerges from his attacks on Philip (and on his fellow Athenians for their cowardice) in three great orations known as Philippics. The speeches of Demosthenes are also a vital source for the domestic policy concerns of Athens in the late fourth century BCE, including debates over naval spending and public welfare.

For modern Greek chroniclers of the long Hellenic story, such as Constantine Paparrigopoulos, Demosthenes poses a problem.

The orator is a supreme case of Athenian resolution and patriotism, but he presents the Macedonians as 'barbarians' and therefore outside the Greek family. Paparrigopoulos, author of an august encyclopedia, is among those who see Demosthenes as unrealistic in his response to Macedonia's rising power. Donald Kagan, doyen of American classical historians, is at the other end of the spectrum in his view of Demosthenes as the Churchill of ancient Greece.

In imagining the way in which Athenian refinement was propelled east by Macedonian arms, I was helped by the writings of Yaamir Badhe, a proud South Asian Hellenist and budding journalist. He is the only Oxford classics student in recent memory to turn in his undergraduate essays in ancient languages.

Plutarch helps us with a portrait of Alexander, although his style of succinct sketch is hardly adequate to deal with such a towering, enigmatic personality. Possibly more vital, in that otherwise we might know little else, is Plutarch's portrait of Demetrius Poliorketes, the Besieger, who with his father Antigonus was one of the contenders for a slice of Alexander's empire. Plutarch is indulgent in his treatment of the Besieger, describing him as handsome, touchingly devoted to his father, a valiant soldier – and also dissolute and self-indulgent, but in a way that did not cancel out his virtues. Plutarch implies that the Athenians spoiled him by piling on his head a plethora of honours, including a semi-divine status.

There is a modern piece of research that provides a counterpoint to this picture: *Religion in Hellenistic Athens*, by the US classicist Jon D. Mikalson (University of California Press, 1998). With very meticulous use of epigraphic as well as literary evidence, he shows that whatever the honours they poured, in the heat of the moment, on Macedonian conquerors, the Athenians remained attached to their old religious ways, centred on the worship of twelve Olympian gods, which resurfaced in a fairly pure form whenever Macedonian pressure slackened.

The writings of Zeno of Kition have not survived. Tantalizingly, we know the titles of many of his works: *On Life According to Nature*,

*On Passions*, *On Duty*, and so on. Diogenes Laërtius, a Greek writer of the third century CE, has quite a lot to say about him, including his relationship with the Macedonian monarch Antigonus.

## 8  Other People's Empires

My own understanding of the way Hellenistic and Roman benefactors transformed the Athenian skyline grew, in the first instance, from the experience of staying for several months in 2018 and 2019 in the heart of Monastiraki, a few minutes away from the Roman Agora and Hadrian's library.

I used an unlikely variety of routes to deepen my knowledge of the process by which wealthy and powerful outsiders transformed the Agora, endowing an undemocratic Athens with ever-grander renderings of the architectural styles that had emerged in the democratic era. One eye-opener was a fine master's thesis penned at the architecture school of MIT by John Vandenburgh Lewis in 1992, which has recently become available on ResearchGate: *Rhetoric and the Architecture of Empire in the Athenian Agora*.

To grasp the very latest knowledge about the Stoa of Attalos, as constructed around 150 BCE and rebuilt in the 1950s, I benefited from the Zoom lecture delivered on the spot on 5 November 2020 by John Camp, long-time director of excavations at the Agora and doyen of one of the world's most professional archaeological operations. I was privileged to meet him at his office on the upper story of the Stoa, home of the archaeological dig, in May 2019. This was a renewal of an acquaintance which began when, as a naïve seventeen-year-old, I was introduced by a kind mentor to some promising classical scholars, including both John and his sister Margot, who was lecturing at College Year in Athens. In our 2019 meeting, John took me down the corridor to meet James Sickinger, expert on *ostraka*, with profitable results.

Both the November 2020 lecture and an equally illuminating one delivered by John Camp at the Royal Stoa in September 2020, plus a treasure trove of fascinating talks and seminars on every aspect of Greek history, can be found on the website of the American School of Classical Studies in Athens (ASCSA), by searching under video archive: https://www.ascsa.edu.gr/.

In the journal of the ASCSA, the historic background to the Stoa of Attalos and kings of Pergamon who adorned Athens has been laid out by Christian Habicht (see 'Athens and the Attalids in the Second Century BC', *Hesperia*, July–September 1990, vol. 59, no. 3). The story of the Attalids and the eventual cession of the kingdom to Rome has also resonated on the Greek left since Kostas Varnalis wrote his Brechtian play, *Attalos III*, in 1968.

Dylan Rogers, formerly assistant director of the ASCSA and now lecturer at the University of Virginia, generously let me see an early iteration of his research on the siege of Athens in 86 BCE which weighs the conflicting evidence. 'Sulla and the Siege of Athens: Reconsidering Crisis, Survival and Recovery in the First Century BC' is due for inclusion in *The Destruction of Cities in the Ancient Greek World*, edited by E. M. Harris and S. Fachard, which is to be published by Cambridge University Press in 2021.

The textual analysis of Saint Paul's sermon on the Areopagus and its classical Greek references was pioneered by J. Rendel Harris, an English Biblical scholar who died in 1941. In the midst of the First World War and the struggle for Irish independence, a certain H. J. Lawlor found time to elaborate on Harris' research. See 'Saint Paul's Quotations from Epimenides', *Irish Church Quarterly*, July 1916.

Many a scholar has tried to situate the Athenian discourse of the apostle in the trends and fashions of the Greco-Roman world. But none has done that as originally as Yale Professor Laura Nasrallah, mentioned at the end of the chapter, who sees a close parallel between Hadrian's Greek commonwealth, based in Athens, and the spiritual commonwealth of Roman cities presented in the New Testament. See 'The Acts of the Apostles, Greek Cities and Hadrian's Panhellenion', *Journal of Biblical Literature*, September 2008. In quoting Acts 17:16–32, I used the King James Version.

To understand the impact on Athens of the Roman emperors Augustus and Hadrian, I turned to the research and teaching of Diane Kleiner, Dunham Professor of History of Art and Classics at Yale University. Specializing on the effect of Roman power on Athens and Greek taste on Rome, she has not only written scholarly works but has pioneered online public education. Anybody can follow her open lectures, which are easily findable on https://oyc.yale/edu. They cover not only the emperors' Greek building projects but her own research on Athens' Philopappos monument.

Whether as an aesthete, philhellene, builder or ruthless commander, Hadrian has impressed many a biographer and historian, from the peevish genius of Georgian England, Edward Gibbon, to Marguerite Yourcenar, the prize-winning Franco-American woman of letters who published her *Memoirs of Hadrian* in French in 1951. She felt she knew Hadrian better than a member of her own family, and had seen past the banalities of contemporary biographers.

For a rigorous approach to the ways in which Hadrianic Rome tried to appropriate Athens and Attica, and make a theme park of old Greek glory, I turned to an excellent PhD thesis, submitted at Oxford in 2017 by Sarah McHugh: *Renewing Athens: The Ideology of the Past in Roman Greece.* Among many insights, she pinpoints the real significance of Hadrian's Arch. Far from dividing the city between the old realm of Theseus and a new one established by Hadrian, as many assume, it asserts both the rule of Hadrian *and* the ancient genius of Theseus in all parts of Athens, old and new.

In my case, a visit to Eleusis in late February 2020, under the guidance of archaeologist Popi Papangeli, who has devoted a lifetime to stewarding that numinous site, helped a lot. It brought home the reasons why Hadrian and his successors were fascinated by the region's spookiest place and wanted to beautify it. The experience was sharpened by spring flowers emerging in a crisp winter breeze, and an (accurate) intimation that life as we knew it was ending.

## 9 Polytheists and Barbarians

As the text makes clear, I continued when researching this chapter to delve deeply into the doctoral thesis of Sarah McHugh. While others have written about the grand, Athens-centred cultural initiatives of the second century CE, she stands out by demonstrating how the whole of Attica was transformed into a classical theme park for Roman benefit.

Entering the period of late antiquity, two big challenges face the writer: imagining Athens as a rowdy, chaotic centre of high scholarship, including philosophy, and documenting the ravages of the barbarians.

In this and many fields, Garth Fowden, Emeritus Professor of Divinity at Cambridge, has been a discreet and patient guide as long as I can remember, starting with a helpful telephone call when he was an Oxford post-graduate and I was a Greece-bound school-leaver. In recent months he has very generously put much of his lifetime's work as a scholar of late antiquity in the public domain on academia.edu. (See https://cambridge.academia.edu/GarthFowden/Books.) The offering includes his 1979 doctoral thesis on neo-Platonism. It also includes work that was accomplished jointly with his wife Elizabeth Key Fowden, an American-Athenian scholar of late antiquity and religious transition, such as their co-authored book *Contextualizing Late Greek Philosophy* (Athens: National Hellenic Research Foundation, 2008). As will become clear, a couple of my later chapters were helped decisively by Elizabeth Key Fowden's entirely separate work on aspects of the Ottoman era, including travel writing on Athens. While I was aware of Garth's expertise on late antiquity and early monotheism, only while researching this book did I realize his hard-won knowledge of Attic topography and military history, acquired during arduous hikes. This is exemplified in his paper 'City and Mountain in Late Roman Attica', *Journal of Hellenic Studies*, vol. 108, 1988.

Before piecing together the story of Gregory, Basil and Julian during their studies, I had the illusion of being quite well-read in secondary accounts of this intriguing period. It was important and illuminating to read the primary sources, including Gregory's Oration 5 which excoriates Julian, and Oration 43 in which he recalls the student friendship with the newly deceased Basil. An essay by an old-fashioned American classicist helped me to see why Gregory of Nazianzus is not considered a very approachable figure even by those who admire him as a thinker and writer (Brooks Otis, 'The Throne and the Mountain: An Essay on St Gregory Nazianzus', *The Classical Journal*, January 1961). And yet even the most ethereal of figures in sacred history can appear on the horizon in surreal ways. In 2004, as an *Economist* reporter whose beat included religion, I learned of a Vatican initiative to repatriate the relics of theologian Gregory and another church father to the Orthodox Patriarchate in Istanbul. I felt at first that this was far too arcane to propose reporting on. To my shock, I then got a call at my London desk from my (staunchly secular) editor Bill Emmott, who happened to be in Istanbul: 'I've just heard about these relics; please write about them.'

In imagining the campus camaraderie between Gregory and Basil, I could not help recalling a very rough modern parallel. Anybody who frequented the arts faculties or certain cafés in Oxford in the 1990s might have picked out a duo of conservatively, but not clerically, dressed doctoral students, exchanging private Slavic witticisms in-between diligently followed lectures. One is now a leader of the eastern church, and a figure of global influence, the other a monk and theologian in a rival branch of the church. Life has to some degree separated these brainy Russians, but student memories, presumably, remain a bond.

Emperor Julian, like Emperor Hadrian, is a figure who generates huge literary as well as scholarly interest. Gore Vidal's novel *Julian* (first published in the United States in 1964) did more than most academic scholars could ever dream of to make the general public aware of the fourth-century culture wars. A vastly more rigorous, but equally page-turning, treatment is that of Polymnia Athanassiadi in *Julian: An Intellectual Biography*, first published as *Julian and Hellenism* by Oxford University Press in 1981.

In exploring the physical history of Athens in the late Roman times, I was vividly aware of the benign spirit of Alison Frantz (1903–95), an American scholar who devoted an academic lifetime to Athenian archaeology. Her book *Late Antiquity AD 367–700*, published by the American School of Classical Studies in 1988, was an expensive but indispensable acquisition. Assisted by her colleague John Travlos, a Greek with roots in Naxos and Russia, she brought commanding expertise to questions like the barbarian raids on Athens and the presumed 'House of Proclus', a luxurious philosopher's residence discovered in the 1950s.

If I have a soft spot for any archaeological discoveries in the vicinity of Dionysiou Areopagitou Street, it is because I was lucky enough (much luckier than I then knew) to stay in one of those marble-fronted mansions, as a guest of the distinguished philhellene John Leatham, for several formative weeks in 1976.

I am particularly grateful to Lambrini Chioti, author of an excellent doctoral work on the Herulian raid and its aftermath, for taking time to answer my questions quite shortly after becoming a mother. Her thesis, in Greek with a summary in English, is accessible on the Internet, via https://thesis.ekt.gr/thesisBookReader/. Her paper on the same subject is due for inclusion in an edited volume, *The Destruction of Cities in the Ancient Greek World*, edited by S. Fachard and E. M. Harris, whose publication is planned by Cambridge University Press.

The question of when the Parthenon was burned (and whether the metopes were destroyed simultaneously) is one of those historical riddles that may never be solved. In a succinct essay, the late Charalambos Bouras explains why he tends (like Alison Frantz) to blame Alaric; the case for holding the Heruli responsible is equally respectable, as argued by John Travlos, Manolis Korres and, on balance, by Dr Chioti. Professor Bouras' essay can be found at https://ejournals.epublishing.ekt.gr/index.php/deltion/article/viewFile/4810/4586.

Arguments about how and when the Athenian philosophical tradition was ended (was it 529 or a bit later?) tend to be tetchy and arcane. The following paper helped me to navigate my way through the evidence: Edward Watts, 'Justinian, Malalas and the End of Athenian Philosophical Teaching in AD 529', *Journal of Roman Studies*, vol. 94, 2004.

## 10 A Christian Millennium

The story of transition from polytheism to Christianity – whether we trace it through the shifting use of monuments or in the realm of ideas and feelings – is an emotionally charged business, and in the case of Athens it passes through thick clouds of obscurity. As the chapter makes clear, the emergence of early Christian Athens receives only a tiny fragment of the scholarly attention that is perpetually focused on the classical city.

The scholars who do focus on Christian transition are a small, intimate and contentious community, and I have reasons to be grateful to many of its members. Anthony Kaldellis showed great generosity in sharing with me without hesitation the text of his book *The Christian Parthenon: Classicism and Pilgrimage in Byzantine Athens* (Cambridge University Press, 2009). It was Nun Nectaria McLees, a grateful reader of the professor's writing, who pointed out to me that standard tourist guides devote only a couple of lines, one for each 500 years, to the Parthenon's Christian millennium. More in the realm of ideas, Dr Arthur Urbano of Providence University showed similar generosity in sharing with me two key chapters from his book *The Philosophical Life: Biography and the Crafting of Intellectual Identity in Late Antiquity* (Patristic Monograph Series, 2013).

However strong their personal beliefs, scholars who operate in this contested area have not let them stand in the way of academic rigour. John Pollini makes no secret of his conviction that Christian misbehaviour in Athens was part of a pattern reproduced across the eastern Mediterranean. As he bluntly puts it, 'Christians in general had a history of destructive rampages, especially when instigated by overly zealous bishops and other clergy who wanted to wipe out polytheism by any means possible.' But his argument about Athens is based on research, not essentialism. His paper, 'Christian Destruction and Mutilation of the Parthenon' is available on academia.edu.

Michael Choniates may be a sympathetic figure, but the study of life and extensive writings is a recondite business. His works were edited by Spyridon Lambros, a Greek history professor who served briefly as prime minister in 1916. For those who can read Byzantine Greek, the text is easily available as a free e-book, via https:/books.google.co.uk. For those who happen to read Russian more easily, the key texts are presented and analysed by Alexei Kryukov in a doctoral thesis at Moscow State University, with the aptly Chekhovian title (my translation): *Scholarly Tradition and Provincial Realities in the Homilies of Mikhail Choniates 1182–1205* – and it is easily available on academia.edu. (Original title: Ученая традиция и провинциальные реалии в гомилиях митрополита Афинского Михаила Хониата (1182–1205 гг.))

As I gratefully discovered, the multilayered metaphors of light used by Choniates in his maiden homily to the Athenians are carefully dissected by Stephanos Efthymiades, in his paper 'Michael Choniates' Inaugural Address at Athens: Enkomion of a City and a Two-fold Spiritual Ascent', which is likewise available on academia.edu.

An even more specialized, but exciting, piece of research is that of a young American scholar, Byron David McDougall, who looked at Choniates' use of metaphorical language from Plato, specifically a description of a festive torch-race. It is entitled 'Michael Choniates at the Christian Parthenon and the Bendideia Festival', and can be found at https://grbs.library.duke.edu/article/view/15131.

The monastic document which describes economic activities in Athens around 1100 came to my attention through Professor Kaldellis' book. He in turn acknowledges the work of Eugenie Granstrem and two other scholars whose primary research is published as *Fragment d'un praktikon de la région d'Athènes avant 1204* and available, for those with patience and good broadband, via the website www.persee.fr.

A much broader looker at Athens during that period, and earlier, can be found in a doctoral thesis for the University of Birmingham by Elisavet Tzavella, which extracts everything possible from the limited evidence. It is entitled *Urban and Rural Landscapes in Early and Middle Byzantine Athens*, and can be found at https://core.ac.uk/download/pdf/16292781.pdf.

The so-called Annunciation Metope is in the Acropolis Museum, which in the course of conservation has identified the sculpture as a work of extremely high quality, depicting Hera and her daughter Hebe. The respectful counterarguments against the Annunciation thesis (or at least against its certainty) are put forward by Benjamin Anderson, assistant professor at Cornell University, in a paper called 'The Defacement of the Parthenon Metopes: Dating and Interpretation', *Greek, Roman and Byzantine Studies*, 57 (2017), pp. 248–60.

The Shroud of Turin's link with Athens is laid out in an essay by Alessandro Piana, easily findable on academia.edu: 'Othon de la Roche and the Shroud: An Hypothesis between History and Historiography'.

## 11 Latin and Greek: the Late Middle Ages

The study of Athens under Latin rule is, to put it mildly, a recondite business. But the handful of historians who have explored this period brought great passion to their work. One was William Miller (1864–1945), who ranks among the best writers in English about Greece. As a print journalist who also enjoys delving into history,

I have a soft spot for this undervalued figure. A classics graduate who studied for the London bar but never practised, Miller moved to Rome in 1903 and to Athens in 1923, staying in Greece till the eve of the German invasion in 1941. He and his wife Ada lived out their final years in South Africa.

Greece and the Balkans were always his strongest academic interests, but his Italian spell gave him a feel for Romance languages and Latin culture which informed his deep research into the medieval era. As a correspondent for over thirty years for the London *Morning Post*, he considered himself primarily a journalist. In his early fifties, he resisted pressure for him to seek a newly established London professorship on grounds that it was too late to change profession. But his best historical writing matches the highest academic standards.

In 1908 he produced *The Latins in the Levant: A History of Frankish Greece* (London and New York: E. P. Dutton), which is still a vital starting point, although the detail is a little too densely packed to make for easy reading – in contrast with the delightful fluency of everything else he wrote. As he declares in the preface, 'I can conscientiously say that I have consulted all the books known to me in Greek, Italian, Spanish, French, German, English and Latin'. He had also looked at archives in Rome and Venice and visited every Frankish site in Greece.

On a personal note, I feel a tingle of pride in claiming a tenuous chain of connection with Miller. Arriving in Athens in 1976, I had the good fortune to be entertained by Peter Megaw, a fellow Ulsterman and doyen of archaeology in Greece and Cyprus. He remembered Miller and his wife Ada as venerable and hospitable figures in the 1930s who frequented the garden of the British School of Archaeology. In that decade, the Millers were known as a devoted couple with no children of their own who showed great generosity towards incoming students, exactly as Peter and Electra Megaw (an accomplished artist) had become by the 1970s.

An outwardly more conventional and even more rigorous scholar was Kenneth Meyer Setton (1914–95), ultimately a Princeton professor and editor of a five-volume history of the Crusades. His 1948 book, *Catalan Domination of Athens, 1311–1388* – beginning with the laconic words, 'No chapter in the history of Athens is without importance' – is still considered an authoritative work on the subject. To the list of languages studied and used by Miller he crucially added Catalan, and he was a corresponding member of the Institute of Catalan Studies in Barcelona. This meant that he was able to consult modern and medieval Catalan authorities. These included the writings of Antoni Rubio i Lluch (1856–1937), a Catalan Hellenist; also, along with other primary sources, the memoir of the medieval Catalan soldier and chronicler Ramon Muntaner. (That work has been translated into English by Robert D. Hughes, and was published in 2006 by Boydell and Brewer in association with Barcino of Barcelona.)

For the early part of the Catalan period, I drew on Setton's paper 'The Avignon Papacy and the Catalan Duchy of Athens', *Byzantion*, 1944–5, vol. 17.

A new generation of scholars has built on the insights of Miller and Setton. One is David Jacoby, who established the location of the 1311 battle in which the Catalans overthrew the Franks. He was co-editor of a volume entitled *Latins and Greeks in the Eastern Mediterranean after 1204* (London: Frank Cass, 1989).

Other important works include *The Franks in the Aegean, 1204–1500* by Peter Lock (London and New York: Longman, 1995) and *Contact and Conflict in Frankish Greece and the Aegean 1204–1453*, edited by Nikolaos Chrissis and Mike Carr, published by Ashgate in 2014 and Routledge in 2016.

A breath of fresh air in the study of Frankish Greece has come from Dionysios Stathakopoulos, who recently moved from King's College London to take up a professorship at the University of Cyprus. His perceptive and witty account of a quartet of Italian and semi-Hellenized noblewomen of the Latin era brings the subject alive in an entirely new way. It is contained in a paper entitled 'Sister, Widow, Consort, Bride: Four Latin Ladies in Greece', published in the edited volume *Cross-Cultural Interaction between Byzantium and the West 1204–1669*, by Routledge in 2018. He also questions conventional wisdom about the origins of Antonio Acciaiuoli, who was master of Athens from 1405 until 1435.

Study of the Catalan period in Greek history is very much alive in Barcelona, as was shown by the publication in 2020 of a rich historical essay by Professor Eusebi Ayensa i Prat in the Catalan Historical Review: *Catalan Domination in Greece during the 14th Century: History, Archaeology, Memory and Myth*. See http://revistes.iec.cat/index.php/CHR.

All such research treads in the footsteps of Ramon Muntaner, a medieval pioneer of the Catalan language who dreamed of Iberian unity. On a personal note, this chapter in particular is an unworthy homage to my late friend Cristián Carandell, who translated modern Greek poetry into Castilian and Aristophanes into Catalan.

## 12 Before and After the Bombardment

The fact that early Ottoman Athens experienced a spurt of economic and demographic growth, as well as church-building (all of this in contrast to the misery of the later Ottoman years), is not widely discussed, either in academic work or in textbooks. One honourable exception is the work of Dimitris N. Karidis, Professor of Urban History at the National Technical University of Greece. His wonderfully comprehensive work, *Athens from 1456 to 1920: The Town under Ottoman Rule and the 19th Century Capital City*, was published in Oxford by Archaeopress in 2014.

It is to the credit of both scholars, and to the benefit of readers, that he has collaborated with Professor Machiel Kiel, a forthright Dutchman who has devoted an academic lifetime to Ottoman architecture in the Balkans, and to campaigning against its disappearance. One of his seminal articles, published in 2002, is a densely packed argument about the date of one of Athens' two surviving mosque buildings, which delivers many broader insights into the Ottoman town: 'The Quatrefoil Plan in Ottoman Architecture Reconsidered in Light of the "Fethiye Mosque" of Athens', *Muqarnas: An Annual on the Visual Culture of the Islamic World*, XIX, 109–22.

An unusual (in Greece, anyway) account of church construction in early Ottoman Athens was given by the great Professor Charalambos Bouras at a symposium on Ottoman Athens organized at the Gennadius Library in April 2015. Every single contribution to that symposium was a rich feast, and they can all be viewed in their entirety on the 'video archive' of the website of the American School of Classical Studies in Athens. The intervention of Professor Bouras, who died just over a year later, is in Greek, but most of the others are in English: https://www.ascsa.edu.gr/News/newsDetails/videocast-the-topography-of-ottoman-athens.-archaeology-travel-symposium.

Another contributor to that symposium, besides being a long-standing friend, was of invaluable help in putting together this chapter. As part of her ongoing work on the Parthenon's Islamic period, Elizabeth Key Fowden laid out a compelling argument that Ottoman travellers' tales of Athens of the seventeenth and eighteenth century need to be taken just as seriously as the better-known western adventurers' accounts. It is thanks to her that I was prompted to juxtapose the testimonies of Evliya Çelebi, George Wheler and Jacob Spon – although I made a slightly different choice of material from the writings of that colourful trio. The 2015 symposium was the basis for an excellent edited volume, co-published in 2019 by the Aikaterini Laskaridis Foundation: *Ottoman Athens: Archaeology, Topography, History*. Apart from her contribution to the conference and to that book, a version of Elizabeth Key Fowden's rich comparison can be found here: 'The Parthenon, Pericles and King Solomon: A Case Study of Ottoman Archaeological Imagination in Greece', *Byzantine and Modern Greek Studies*, 2018, 42, pp. 261–74.

Even more recently, the ASCSA and the Gennadius Library

have made a powerful contribution to the study of the 1687 siege of Athens and more generally the campaign against the Ottomans waged by Francesco Morosini. This took the form of a conference on 23–4 January 2020, whose proceedings are available on the video archive, and an exhibition on the subject which ran from November 2019 to February 2020, the last time when such things were still possible. A very helpful summary of the various strands of evidence concerning the 1687 bombardment (and the events before and after) was given by Cornilia Hajdiaslani, both at the conference and in several other contexts. An earlier version of her writing on the subject is available here: https://www.openbook. gr/o-morozini-oi-venetoi-kai-i-akropoli/.

For a real-life biography of the saintly patroness of Athens, aka Revoula Benizelou, there is an excellent essay by Youli Evangelou of the Institute of Historical Research in Athens: *Saint Philotei: An Athenian Noblewoman – a Bold Nun.* See https://archontiko-mpenizelon.gr/wp-content/uploads/2016/02/Saint-Philothei.pdf.

For more about Martin Kraus (or Crusius), the Tübingen scholar who studied Athens at a distance, see Richard Calis, 'Reconstructing the Ottoman Greek World: Early Modern Ethnography in the Household of Martin Crusius', *Renaissance Quarterly*, vol. 72, Spring 2019.

When looking at the arguments which have raged over the 1687 bombardment, it was inspiring to find that this matter was being mulled over at a time when Athens was experiencing modern travails that were no less severe. See 'The Venetians in Athens and the Destruction of the Parthenon in 1687' by Theodor E. Mommsen in the *American Journal of Archaeology*, vol. 45, October to December 1941.

The story of Anna Akerhjelm and her unique perspective on the Morosini siege is told by John J. Gahan in 'A Woman Visitor to Athens in 1687', *Balkan Studies*, vol. 37, no. 2, 1996. As Gahan points out, this Swedish lady, no less than Spon or Wheler, was a witness to the city on the eve of catastrophic events.

The tragic saga of Spon and Wheler's sometime companion,

murdered in Persia, is told by Matthew Walker in 'Francis Vernon, the Early Royal Society and the First English Encounter with Ancient Greek Architecture', *Architectural History*, vol. 56 (2013), pp. 29–61.

The writings of Dr Spon were republished in Paris in 2004 by Éditions Honoré Champion: *Voyage d'Italie, de Grèce est du Levant 1678: Textes présentes et édités sous la direction de R. Etienne.*

I am particularly grateful to Dr Fiona McIntosh-Varjabedian of the University of Lille for sharing with me her paper: *Jacob Spon et George Wheler: Redécouvrir un Monde Devenu Inconnu.* It features in a collection entitled *Des Voyages vers l'Inconnu entre 1630 et 1880*, edited by Florence d'Souza and published by EME editions.

The Athenian travelogue of George Wheler is available through the website of the University of Michigan. See https://quod.lib.umich.edu/.

Evliya Çelebi's Athenian impressions are included, in a well-translated form, in *An Ottoman Traveller, a Selection from the Seyahatname*, published by Eland Books in 2010. The translators are Robert Dankoff and Sooyong Kim.

## 13  Stones of Contention

There is a huge and prolix range of sources which can be consulted to illuminate the history of Athens in its final Ottoman years, yet they do not add up to a complete or coherent picture. As a result, many questions about that period, including the details of the town's administrative system, remain shadowy. For insights into the honey-making monks of Attica, I have drawn on an excellent paper by Giorgios Pallis of the History and Archaeology Faculty of Athens University: *Beekeeping in Attica during the Ottoman Period: A Monastic Affair.* It is one of the many nutritious offerings on his page: https://uoa.academia.edu/GeorgiosPallis.

I am grateful both to Elizabeth Key Fowden and to Hasan Çolak for guiding me to the work of Gülçin Tunali and in particular her doctoral thesis, examining the account of Athens by Mahmud Efendi. The thesis was presented at the University of Bochum in 2013, under the stimulating title *Another Kind of Hellenism?* See: Scribd.com/document/334328999/Gulcin-TUNALI-pdf.

In *Ottoman Athens: Archaeology, Topography, History*, the 2019 compendium edited by Maria Georgopoulou and Konstantinos Thanasakis, there is a contribution by Tunali as well as one by Fowden: both argue for the importance and legitimacy of comparing Mahmud Efendi with other chroniclers of Ottoman Athens, including Spon, Wheler and Evliya Çelebi. Elsewhere in that superbly presented volume, there is a joint contribution from Eleni Korka (honorary director-general of antiquities at the Greek culture ministry) and Seyyed Mohammad Taghi Shariat-Panahi which looks in detail at documents in the Ottoman archives relating to the permits granted in 1809 for the export of the remaining portion of Lord Elgin's collection of antiquities. It also sets the scene for the Franco-British competition in Athens against the background of the Napoleonic wars. The authors' analysis of Ottoman documents builds on and acknowledges earlier research by Edhem Eldem, including his paper: 'From Blissful Indifference to Anguished Concern: Ottoman Perceptions of Antiquities, 1799–1869', in Zainab Bahrani, Zeynep Çelik and Edhem Eldem (eds), *Scramble for the Past: A Story of Archaeology in the Ottoman Empire, 1753–1914* (Istanbul: SALT, 2011).

By way of a general introduction to Ottoman Athens, I was grateful to my e-friend Markos Kominis for sharing with me his thesis, presented at the Aristotle University of Thessaloniki in 2008. *I Athina kata ta Teleutaia Chronia tis Othomanikis Dioikisis* (Athens in the Last Years of Ottoman Administration), which distils the available sources, in Greek and other languages, with perfect clarity and commendable agnosticism about the many aspects of that period which must remain an open academic question. That in turn led me to one of the most colourful contemporary sources, the Athenian merchant Panagis Skouzes (*c.* 1776–1847). His memoir

*Chronika tis Sklavomenis Athenas* (Chronicle of Enslaved Athens) was published Athens in 1948 and remains a popular feature on the history curriculum of Greek high schools.

Copies of *Antiquities of Athens* by James Stuart change hands for fabulous sums in the antiquarian book trade. Fortunately the text of his writing, being long out of copyright, is easily available through Internet resources such as: https://archive.org/details/antiqvitiesAtheIStua/. While searching for a version in book form, I found it easier to procure a French translation, printable on demand from Hachette Livre under a project funded by the Bibliothèque Nationale de France (see http://gallica/bnf.fr/ark:/12148/). Interest in Stuart and Revett, always lively among historians of British architecture and taste, was further stimulated by an exhibition in 2008 at the Victoria and Albert Museum. See: https://www.vam.ac.uk/articles/james-athenian-stuart. The many academic studies of their work include 'Stuart and Revett: Their Literary and Architectural Careers', by Lesley Lawrence, *Journal of the Warburg Institute* (vol. 2, no. 2, October 1938), and 'Athenian Stuart' by Charles Harris Whitaker, *The American Magazine of Art*, vol. 24, May 1932. The account of Stuart's narrow escape as told by Dr Thomas Percy was published in the *European Magazine* in November 1804.

The spectre of Lord Elgin haunts anybody who has worked in Athens for a British or British-based news organ. I was in the audience on 12 June 1986 when a classics student called Boris Johnson chaired a debate on the marbles at the Oxford Union. This featured a strong speech by Melina Mercouri as Greek arts minister. See: https://melinamercourifoundation.com/en/oxford-union-june-12-1986/. At least as convincing was the Demosthenic argument expounded by an Oxford philosopher, Michael Dummett, who proposed a thought experiment. If the sculptures had simply remained in Athens, would any visitor now look at them and say, 'Why aren't they in London?'

In 2003, I had the sensitive task of chairing a conference in

Athens on the marbles which was convened by the local conference arm of the *Economist*, but not strictly under the *Economist* franchise. Some impressive contributions were made by Professors Anthony Snodgrass, Paul Cartledge and (in his capacity as director of the new Acropolis museum) Dimitris Pandermalis. The former British foreign secretary, David Owen, also contributed interesting ideas over how arguments over legal title could be finessed to everybody's benefit. Much later I also had the privilege of sitting in on an informal discussion in which Neil MacGregor, as director of the British Museum, laid out to a group of journalists his argument that retaining the sculptures served the purpose of presenting the entire pageant of human civilization under a single roof.

At the coalface of art-historical and archaeological research, it is gratifying to discover that professional Greco-British relationships are more cordial than might be imagined. The late Ian Jenkins, keeper of the sculptures, and author of *The Parthenon Sculptures in the British Museum* (British Museum Press, 2007), was respected by many Greek colleagues. The main documents relating to the marbles saga are laid out in a research paper that was issued in 1916 on the hundredth anniversary of the decision to acquire the artefacts for the British state. *Lord Elgin and his Collection*, by Philip Hunt (not the cleric) and A. H. Smith, was published in vol. 36 of the *Journal of Hellenic Studies*, and runs to 210 pages. The story is fleshed out in a 2002 paper by Dyfri Williams: '"Of Publick Utility and Publick Property": Lord Elgin and the Parthenon Sculptures', in A. Tsingarida and D. Kurtz (eds), *Appropriating Antiquity: Saisir l'Antique* (Brussels), pp. 103–64. The authoritative English-language book on the subject is *Lord Elgin and the Marbles* by William St Clair, first published by OUP in London in 1967. In the wonderfully peppery work by Christopher Hitchens, *The Elgin Marbles: Should They Be Returned to Greece?*, first published by Chatto and Windus in 1987, I find my name among a shortish list of Athens-based people, along with Melina Mercouri, who are thanked. I cannot claim to have made much intellectual contribution, but for the record, I did accommodate Christopher in Athens for a disorderly week in 1985 which did much to improve the mind and nothing whatever to improve the metabolism. It is touching to find the book dedicated to his then infant son Alexander Meleagrou-Hitchens, who went on to study classics and become an eminent authority on violent extremism.

### 14  A Poet Dreams on a Rock

The memoirs of Edward Daniel Clarke, published between 1810 and 1824, under the title *Travels in Various Countries of Europe, Asia and Africa*, are of course long out of print, but they can be found online via the Hathi Trust digital library (see: https://catalog.hathitrust.org/Record/008588312).

A description of the removal of a statue from Eleusis, and of local reaction, is given on pages 79–80 of *Modern Greek Folklore and Ancient Greek Religion* by John Cuthbert Lawson, published by Cambridge University Press in 1910. For a different perspective on Clarke, see 'Edward Daniel Clarke: The First Professor of Mineralogy at Cambridge', an article written by Duane W. Roller in *Earth Sciences History*, 1988 vol. 7, no. 2. I am not, incidentally, related to that Clarke – though I do claim kinship with another protagonist in the Elgin drama, the Anglo-Irish politician Sir John Newport, who felt the diplomat was guilty of 'the most flagrant Pillages' and had made unfair use of his public office. Lord Byron was extremely prolific, writing 3,000 or more letters as well as his long pieces of narrative verse. A huge amount of this material, including letters the poet wrote from Athens and the reminiscences of his friend Hobhouse, can be found on the website assembled by the passionate Byron scholar Peter Cochran, who died in 2015. See http://petercochran.wordpress.com. It is to Hobhouse rather than Byron that we owe several important anecdotes about their stay in Athens, including the cheeky Spaniard who was so severely punished and the encounter with the young Greek patriot Andreas

Londos. Of the many biographies of Byron, some franker than others, the outstanding one is by Fiona McCarthy, *Byron, Life and Legend*, published by John Murray in 2002. Similarly indispensable, though with a narrower focus on Byron's role in the independence struggle, is *Byron's War: Romantic Revolutionary* by Roderick Beaton, published by Cambridge University Press in 2013. For a comparison between Byron and other figures who provided intellectual support for the Greek revolution, see Professor Beaton's article 'Imagining a Hellenic Republic, 1797–1824: Rigas, Korais, Byron' in *Comparative Critical Studies*, June 2018. For a broader perspective, see his *Greece: Biography of a Modern Nation*, published by Allen Lane in 2019, a work in whose launch I was honoured to play a role at the London Hellenic Centre on 14 March 2019. This book has been a huge stimulus to my endeavours in this chapter and all subsequent ones. Almost all Byron's literary oeuvre can be found in *Lord Byron: The Major Works*, which was first published by Oxford University Press in 1986 and edited by Jerome McGann.

One of the best overviews in English of the Greek revolution, including its Athenian dimension and the poignant story of Odysseas Androutsos, is *The Greek War of Independence* by David Brewer, published by Overlook Press in 2001. The memoirs of General Makriyannis can be found online in Greek at http://el.wikisource. org/wiki/Απομνημευματα_Μακρυγιαννη. An English translation was made by H. A. Lidderdale and published by Oxford University Press in 1966. The general's song to Gouras is discussed in the essay 'The Warrior as Oral Poet: A Case History' by J. A. Notopoulos, published by *The Classical Weekly* in November 1952.

The remarkable doctoral thesis by Şükrü Ilicak, looking at the independence war in the light of the Ottoman archives, can be found here: https://cmes.fas.harvard.edu/publications/radical-rethinking-empire-ottoman-state-and-society-during-greek-war-independence. The edited volume *Ottoman Athens: Archaeology, Topography, History* includes Ilıcak's paper, 'Revolutionary Athens through Ottoman Eyes, 1820–28'. Among the many sources, from the familiar to the previously unknown, which this paper cites, is George Finlay's tragicomic description of the final Ottoman departure from the Acropolis. The memoirs of George Waddington, *Visits to Greece in 1823 and 1824*, were first published in 1825 by John Murray. These days they can be found online at: https://books.google.co.uk/books?id=SX82. I found it very easy to order a print-on-demand copy of Waddington's book made available through an arrangement by the British Library.

## 15  Hellenism and Its Expanding Hub

Among contemporary historians of early modern Athens, an outstanding figure was Eleni Bastea, who was Professor of Architecture at the University of New Mexico and author of an authoritative work, *The Creation of Modern Athens: Planning the Myth* (Cambridge University Press, 2000). Born in Thessaloniki, she spent most of her academic career in the United States after completing a doctoral thesis at Berkeley. Details of her many academic articles can be found on her page on academia.edu. Her work has been of enormous help to all those who have approached the same subject matter in a less academic way: for example, the film-maker Maria Iliou, who launched her documentary, *Athens from East to West 1821–96*, at the Benaki Museum in February 2020.

Very poignantly, Eleni Bastea died in mid-career after a struggle with cancer just weeks before the presentation of a film whose scholarly foundations she had helped to lay. Another chronicler of Athens who freely acknowledges a debt to Professor Bastea is Sir Michael Llewellyn-Smith, former ambassador and eminent scholar of the Greek–Turkish war of 1919–22. His book *Athens: A Cultural and Literary History*, was published by Signal Books of Oxford in 2004 and has been at my side, along with that of Eleni Bastea, as I wrote this and all subsequent chapters. In an earlier generation of Greek scholars, a distinguished authority on Athens and its urban development was Kostas Biris (1899–1980), whose work *Ai Athinai, apo tou 19ou eis tou 20ou Aiona* (Athens from the 19th to the 20th Century) was published in 1966 and reissued by Melissa Publications in 1995. With its fine illustrations it remains an indispensable work for those who can read Greek – in its old-fashioned *katharevouza* form.

A unique perspective on the German contribution to the planning and architecture of Athens is provided in the formidable oeuvre of Professor Alexander Papageorgiou-Venetas, an architect, architectural historian and city planner whose career has been divided between Greece and Germany. He is the author of 33 books and 105 articles in Greek, German, English and French. His books include *Athens: The Ancient Heritage and Historic Cityscape in a Modern Metropolis*, first published in 1970 and republished by the Archaeological Society of Athens in 1994; and *I Nea Athena, Protevousa tou Ellinismou* (The New Athens, Capital of Hellenism), published by the Historical and Ethnological Association of Greece in 2017. Details of the professor's prodigious output can be found on his website: http://papageorgiou-venetas.com. For access, in fairly concentrated form, to his view of the inter-German debates about the location of the royal palace, see his article 'Bauen in Athen: Neue Wege des Klassizismus' (Building in Athens: New Ways of Classicism) available on the website.

Another way to gain a feeling for the lives of Kleanthes and Schaubert is to visit the house in Plaka which they bought in 1831. It is now a museum devoted to the earliest years of the University of Athens, which was initially accommodated in that same modest building on Tholou Street. A website, www.anafiotika.gr, tells the story of Anafiotika, whose steeps hills were a favourite, if somewhat physically taxing, place to wander during my recent sojourns in Athens. Some basic information about the history of the Greek parliament building, which was initially King Otho's palace, can be found on the parliamentary website (see: https://www.hellenicparliament.gr/en/Vouli-ton-Ellinon/ToKtirio/Istoria-Ktiriou/). More information about the immediate effects of the independence war on the townscape of Athens can be found in an essay by John Travlos (originally a lecture in Greek) that is available on the website of the American School of Classical Studies, 'Planning the New City and Exploring the Old' (see: https://www. ascsa.edu.gr/uploads/media/hesperia/147880.pdf).

The pre-eminent scholarly authority on the life and works of Florence Nightingale is Lynn McDonald, professor emerita at the University of Guelph in Canada, and editor of a multivolume series of the philanthropist's letters and reflections. Nightingale's reminiscences of Athens are contained in vol. 7, published in 2004 by Wilfrid Laurier University Press, entitled *Florence Nightingale: European Travels*. William Thackeray's caustic account of Athens features in his *Notes of a Journey from Cornhill to Grand Cairo, by Way of Lisbon, Athens, Constantinople and Jerusalem*, first published in 1846. It can be accessed in digital form via the Hathi Trust (see: https://catalog.hathitrust.org/Record/008586279). Aubrey de Vere's *Picturesque Sketches in Greece and Turkey* is likewise available digitally (see: https://books.google.td/books?id). For a detailed look at the story of David Pacifico and its complex diplomatic fallout, see an article by Dolphus Whitten, Jr: 'The Don Pacifico Affair', *The Historian*, vol. 48, February 1986.

## 16  Racing to War

The definitive account of the first modern Olympiad is the book penned on the occasion of the 2004 games by Sir Michael Llewellyn-Smith: *Olympics in Athens 1896: The Invention of the Modern Olympic Games*, published in London by Profile Books. He also describes the American team's memorable contribution to the contest in an academic paper, 'The Olympic Games at Athens and the Princeton Connection', *Princeton University Library Chronicle*, vol. 64, Spring 2003. During the time he was researching and producing all this work, the author was extremely generous and open with me (as a pesky e-mail correspondent who had only begun dabbling in neo-Hellenic history) about his lines of enquiry. One benign result of this generosity was to convince me that I would never be able to engage with this subject matter with anything like his level of detail.

However, as a former reporter for *The Times* I have always remained intrigued by the despatches from Athens, during the Olympics and many other historical episodes, by *The Times* correspondent James David Bourchier. Substantial articles on the Olympics were published in *The Times* on 1 April, 6 April, 11 April and 13 April 1896. Bourchier (revered in Bulgaria, where he is often pronounced Bow-cher to rhyme with voucher) is a remarkable and significant figure in early twentieth-century Balkan history, and this chapter provided an opportunity to highlight some of his activities. The Anglo-Irish reporter was a latecomer to journalism, settling into his job as Balkans correspondent for *The Times* around 1890, his fortieth year. The only full-length book about him, *The Life of J. D. Bourchier* (London: Hurst and Blackett), was written by Lady Ellinor Grogan in 1926, six years after his death, and is now hard to obtain. Scholarly articles include one by Frederick C. Griffin, 'James David Bourchier', published in *The Historian* in November 1964. There are also two more Irish-focused assessments: Christine Morris, 'An Ardent Lover of Cretan Freedom: J. D. Bourchier, 1850–1920', in J. V. Luce, Christine Morris and Christina Souyoudzoglou-Haywood (eds), *The Lure of Greece; Irish Involvement in Greek Culture, Literature, History and Politics* (Dublin, 2007); and 'J. D. Bourchier: An Irish Journalist in the Balkans' by Michael Foley, *Irish Communication Review*, vol. 10, issue 1, article 6, 2007, available at: https://arrow.tudublin.ie/icr/vol10/iss1/6. Despite the vast differences between us (I have never brokered a military alliance between Balkan states) I have sometimes felt a sneaking affinity with Bourchier, who like me was a roving foreign correspondent of Irish Anglican background, whose professional haunts included the corridors of diplomatic power and some wild war zones, even though mine were more in the Caucasus than in the Balkans. In 1917, he found himself in Petrograd, fearful of drinking the poisonous tap water and struggling to satisfy the foreign desk of *The Times*: experiences I have also tasted, although the city had undergone many changes of name and fortune by 1990.

While Bourchier is (except in Bulgaria) an undeservedly obscure historical figure, his friend Eleftherios Venizelos is of course a towering personality in the annals of Greek and European history, and he looms large in all accounts of Greece and the Balkans from the turn of the twentieth century onwards. The story of his transition from Cretan to Athenian to pan-European politics is complex enough, but the main facts are well laid out in all accounts of modern Greece. For anyone studying his life (including many of the episodes mentioned in this chapter), a vital resource is the edited volume assembled by Paschalis Kitromilides: *Eleftherios Venizelos: The Trials of Statesmanship* (Edinburgh University Press, 2006). At the time of writing, a new book by Llewellyn-Smith on the first half of the Cretan's career has just appeared: *Venizelos: The Making of a Greek Statesman, 1864–1914*, published in London by C. Hurst.

As an invaluable guide to the Greco-German public architecture of Athens at the turn of the twentieth century, Dr Marilena Casimati was kind enough to share with me her magnum opus on Ernst Ziller, consisting of a bilingual (Greek and German) edition of his autobiographical writing with commentary and illustration: *Anamniseis tou Ernst Tsiller* (Memoirs of Ernst Ziller) (Athens: Politeia, 2020).

Compton Mackenzie's memoir of his activities in Athens during the First World War, *First Athenian Memories* (London: Cassell, 1931), became the subject of a colourful court case in which he was accused of breaking the Official Secrets Act and fined £100. A new version was eventually published in 1939, and Biteback of London published the full text in 2011.

A detailed account of the gun battles of 1 December 1916 from a French perspective is provided in 'Le Guet-Apens d'Athènes' (The Ambush of Athens) by Edouard Helsey, in the *Revue des Deux*

*Mondes*, April 1955, and now available via JSTOR. The battle was also written up in the British press, for example by G. J. Stevens, a *Daily Telegraph* correspondent who was inside the Zappeion at the time of the shootout and filed a series of despatches in early December 1916. Admiral Louis Dartige du Fournet, the Breton mariner at the centre of those events, is a considerable figure in his country's naval history, although he was removed on 12 December 1916 from his post as Allied commander in the Mediterranean. This was because of his perceived leniency in ordering only a light shelling of the environs of the Greek royal palace. Armenians consider him a hero because he rescued 4,000 of them from Musa Dagh in Anatolia in 1915. He produced several volumes of memoirs, but his account of the First World War, *Souvenirs de Guerre d'un Amiral, 1914–1916* (War Memories of an Admiral) (Paris: Plon-Nourrit, 1920), is now hard to obtain.

The story of the Orthodox liturgy in Hagia Sophia in January 1919 is told in a newish biography, *Archimandritis Eleftherios Noufrakis: Mia Emvlimatiki Morphi tou Ellenismou* (Archimandrite Eleftherios Noufrakis, an Exemplary Representative of Hellenism) by Antonis Stivaktakis, published by the Kryoneritis Cultural Association in 2015. The priest's diary, recounting the incident, is on display in the museum in the Cretan village of Alones near Rethymnon.

For this and all subsequent chapters, my starting points included some well-established histories of modern Greece, including:

Roderick Beaton, *Greece: Biography of a Modern Nation*, London: Allen Lane, 2019

Richard Clogg, *A Concise History of Modern Greece*, 3rd edition, Cambridge University Press, 2013

John S. Koliopoulos and Thanos M. Veremis, *Modern Greece: A History Since 1821*, Oxford: Wiley-Blackwell, 2010

C. M. Woodhouse, *Modern Greece: A Short History*, first published by Faber and Faber, 1968

## 17 Of Loss and Consolidation

The influx of Greek Orthodox refugees from Anatolia and Thrace, which hugely changed Athens and other parts of Greece, is the subject of my own book, *Twice a Stranger: How Mass Expulsion Forged Modern Greece and Turkey*, published by Granta of London in 2006, and then by Harvard University Press. It was later published in Greek translation by Potamos and in Turkish by Bilge University Press.

My return to this topic prompted me to reread some parts of the basic bibliography, including:

Renée Hirschon, *Heirs of the Greek Catastrophe: The Social Life of Asia Minor Refugees in Piraeus*, first published Oxford: Clarendon Press, 1989, republished Oxford and New York: Berghahn Books, 1998

Renée Hirschon (ed.), *Crossing the Aegean: An Appraisal of the Compulsory Population Exchange between Greece and Turkey*, New York and Oxford: Berghahn Books, 2003

*Lausanne Conference on Near Eastern Affairs 1922–1923. Records of Proceedings and Draft Terms of Peace*, available from Book Depository, US

Esther Pohl Lovejoy, *Certain Samaritans*, New York: Macmillan, 1927

George Mavrogordatos, *Stillborn Republic: Social Coalitions and Party Strategies in Greece, 1922–1936*, University of California Press, 1983

Henry Morgenthau, *I Was Sent to Athens*, Garden City, NY: Doubleday, 1929. (Substantial extracts can be found on ww.hri.org.)

Dimitri Pentzopoulos, *The Balkan Exchange of Minorities and its Impact on Greece*, first published by Mouton of Paris in 1962, then published by C. Hurst of London in 2002

The internationally assisted effort to build houses for newcomers in the greater Athens area and elsewhere in Greece was presented with frankness by Sir John Hope Simpson in a speech in June 1929 which was published a few months later. See: 'The Work of the Greek Refugee Settlement Commission', *The Journal of the Royal Institute of International Affairs*, vol. 8, no. 6, November 1929, pp. 583–604.

To trace the broad population trends in the Athens conurbation I turned to a study by Viron Kotzamanis, professor of demography at the University of Thessaly, 'Athina, 1848–1995, i Dimografiki Anadysi mias Metropolis' (Athens, 1848–1995, the Demographic Emergence of a Metropolis), in *Epitheorisi Koinonikon Erevnon* (Review of Social Research), 1997.

Renée Hirschon, a retired professor of social anthropology who worked at the University of the Aegean before joining St Peter's College, Oxford, has been exceptionally generous in sharing her insights. She offered invaluable help both with the current book and my previous one. It is now clearer than ever that her research in the Kokkinia district of Piraeus was a landmark in social science, showing that many features of 'traditional' culture could have a robust and enduring existence in an urban setting. Far from being 'holdovers' from rural culture, the marriage and dowry customs of the Kokkinia refugees were – as she demonstrates – a sophisticated adaptation to the realities of metropolitan life. For a more detailed presentation of her fascinating observations on the way 'refugee houses' in Piraeus were physically expanded to create dowries, I turned to her paper, 'Under One Roof' in *Urban Life in Mediterranean Europe*, edited by M. Kenny and D. Kertzer, University of Illinois Press, 1983.

As I considered the Venizelos government of 1928–32, a wide range of academic resources were of assistance. For the activities of the Ulen company and its role in transforming the Athenian water supply, this article by Betsey A. Robinson is authoritative: 'Hydraulic Euergetism: American Archaeology and Waterworks in Early 20th Century Greece', *Hesperia*, vol. 82, no. 1, January to March 2013.

For the negotiations with the American School of Classical Studies that led to the Agora excavation, the following article by Nikki Sakka is a definitive account: 'The Excavations of the Ancient Agora of Athens: The Politics of Commissioning and Managing the Project'. It was published in an edited volume produced by the Benaki Museum (*Archaeology and Hellenic Identity, 1896–2004: The Frustrated Vision*, edited by D. Plantzos, 2008), and it can be found here: https://ejournals.epublishing.ekt.gr/index.php/benaki/article/viewFile/17981/15983.

The 1933 gathering of the Congrès International d'Architecture Moderne (CIAM 4), which took place on a Mediterranean voyage that docked in Piraeus, has been described in an expensive tome: *Atlas of the Functional City – CIAM 4 and Comparative Urban Analysis*, edited by Evelien van Es and others (Bossum, Netherlands: Thoth Publishers, 2014).

The initiative by Venizelos to launch open-air food markets in various parts of Athens is presented in a piece of newsreel that was re-conditioned by the Greek state broadcaster ERT and can be seen here: https://www.ert.gr/ert-arxeio/diethnis-imera-archeion-9-iouniou/.

For a basic account of the authoritarian administration of Greece under General Ioannis Metaxas, I turned to *To Kathestos Metaxa, 1936–40* (The Metaxas Regime 1936–40), by Spyridon Ploumides, published in 2016 as part of the series *Vasiki Istoriki Vivliothiki* in Athens.

The story of the visit to Athens by Jean Zay, the French education minister, in 1937 is told in an article by Hubert Pernot, a French scholar of modern Greek, 'Les Fêtes du Centenaire de l'Université d'Athènes', in the *Bulletin de l'Association Guillaume Bude*, vol. 56, pp. 7–14, 1937, which can be found on the website www.persee.fr.

The lines by George Seferis, quoted at the end of the chapter, are extracted from one of the Nobel laureate's best-loved poems, often known by its first line, 'Wherever I travel, Greece is wounding me…' Its formal title is an enigmatic one: 'In the manner of G. S.' I have made my own translation. I am grateful to Euphrosyne Doxiadis for telling me how she and her school friends visited Seferis at his home (in the Pangrati district of Athens) and treated him to a performance of this poem, of which he approved.

## 18 The Darkest Decade

I had the good fortune to meet Manolis Glezos at least three times during the years (1982–6) when I was a young Reuters correspondent in Athens and he was a politician who had nailed his colours to the ruling PASOK movement headed by Andreas Papandreou. One memorable meeting took place during a commemorative voyage to the eerie, deserted island of Yiaros, which had been used as a place of captivity during the military rule of 1967–74. Glezos was instantly likeable as a person of integrity and charm – an unusual mix – although his political judgements were not infallible.

In one of our conversations he had recently returned from Albania with a moderately favourable impression of that country's dictator, Enver Hoxha – under whose iron fist a free spirit like his would not have survived very long. Against a background of strong concern in Greece about the fate of Albania's Greek community, Hoxha had assured Glezos that his country and the Greek minority were linked 'like fingernail and flesh' – *san to nychi me tin sarka* – a metaphor which I did not find reassuring. I am very grateful to my friend Emmanuel Hatzipetros, a Greek-Canadian journalist and latterly entrepreneur, for some insights into the Cycladic village from which he and Glezos originate. Glezos and Lakis Santas describe the seizure of the swastika from the Acropolis in an interview with Freddy Germanos that was also broadcast by ERT (Greek state television) in early 1982 and can easily be found online. Here is one link: https://www.documentonews.gr/article/o-manwlhs-glezos-sthn-ekpomph-toy-frenty-germanoy-video/.

Glezos discussed his role in preparing a bomb attack on the

Grande-Bretagne Hotel in an interview for the *Observer* with Helena Smith and Ed Vulliamy, published on 30 November 2014. The interview was extensively republished, sometimes with the misleading implication that Glezos and his friends 'nearly' assassinated Churchill. In fact it was precisely because of Churchill's presence that the bomb plot was called off.

Both the German occupation of Athens and the tragic conflict which broke out in the city afterwards have been widely written about and, in a sense, widely covered up. Almost anybody with direct experience of these horrific events was, almost by definition, viewing only one side of the looking glass. As of mid-December 1944 some Athenians saw British tanks and aircraft as protectors against a ruthless communist enemy; others saw the British as imperialist meddlers who were inflicting at least as much damage as the Germans ever had. To some extent, it was a question of where you lived: inside the enclave controlled by British and government forces (sometimes called Skobya after the British commander General Scobie) – or in the poorer areas where communist-guided resistance forces were entrenched. Athenians who witnessed these events, even as children, are becoming rarer as of 2021, but I did my best to speak to a representative sample. With the indispensable help of Manos Tzafalias, and of the magic world of Zoom, those who shared memories included George Sfikas, Philippos Dragoumis, Nestor Papanikolopoulos, Toula Michailidou and others I will not name. None of the individuals mentioned bears the slightest responsibility for what was eventually written.

Among English-language books on the Axis occupation of Greece, the outstanding one – based *inter alia* on German, British and American archives – is that of Mark Mazower, a Columbia history professor: *Inside Hitler's Greece: The Experience of Occupation 1941–44* (Yale University Press: 2001). The emergence of the resistance movement in the poor quarters, especially the refugee quarters, of greater Athens is an amazing story that has not been recounted to an adequate degree in the English language, although it is very well adumbrated by Mazower. A lot of video material, including many first-person accounts, has become available recently in the form of either documentaries or locally made films that focus on a particular event. As of now much of this material is accessible only to Greek-speakers, but that will change. These startling stories deserve their place in the modern history of Europe, and it is very much to be hoped that they will be subtitled for the benefit of speakers of other languages.

A documentary about the 200 executions on 1 May 1944 (including testimony from those who narrowly escaped) was made by Giorgos Tsiokos and first shown in 2019. It can be found at https://www.ert.gr/arxeio-afierwmata/protomagia-1944-2. Another documentary, *Oi Partizanoi ton Athinon* (The Partisans of Athens), by Yiannis Xydas and Xenofon Vardaros, describes among other things the strikes, protests and security systems which the resistance was able to organize as it gained de facto authority in parts of the city. It has been subtitled in English, Italian and Hungarian, and can be found here: https://player.vimeo/com/269394467. A film on the round-up or *blocco* in Kokkinia of August 1944 can be found at https://archive.ert.gr/7475/.

The extraordinary events of December 1944, including Churchill's Christmas visit to Athens, have been described from a British perspective in many memoirs, including these:

Lord Avon, *The Eden Memoirs: The Reckoning*, London: Cassell, 1955

Sir John Colville, *The Fringes of Power: Downing Street Diaries 1939–1955*, London: Weidenfeld & Nicolson, 2004

Piers Dixon, *Double Diploma, Sir Pierson Dixon*, London: Hutchinson, 1968

Osbert Lancaster, *Classical Landscapes with Figures*, London: John Murray, 1954

Reginald Leeper, *When Greek meets Greek*, London: Chatto and Windus, 1950

All Churchill's communications during the Athens crisis, and many other relevant nuggets of information, can be found in vol. 20 of *The Churchill Documents*, edited by Martin Gilbert and Larry P. Arnn (Michigan: Hillsdale College Press, 2018).

Among Britons who were both chroniclers and protagonists of those events, an outstanding figure is C. M. 'Monty' Woodhouse, later Lord Terrington, and it is worth paying careful attention to the fine-grained analysis he offers in *The Struggle for Greece 1941–1949* (republished in London by C. M. Hurst in 2018). What makes Woodhouse's narrative stand out is the way he shows how many different agendas were at work on both the Greek and British sides. He is a shrewd and well-placed observer of all the leading players, and can be sharply critical of his compatriots.

For an even more detailed but ideologically different perspective, the left-wing German historian Heinz Richter presents an intricate analysis of British policy in Greece. His focus is not on the December events but on February 1945 (the Varkiza peace agreement) onwards: *British Intervention in Greece: From Varkiza to Civil War* (London: Merlin Press, 1985). Andreas Embeirikos was less well-known in the Anglophone world than his two close friends and fellow poets, the Nobel laureates George Seferis and Odysseas Elytis. However, Embeirikos' friendship with Marguerite Yourcenar guaranteed him a place in French literary history. His life and work are described in Georgis Yatromanolakis, *Andreas Embeirikos: O poihths tou Erota kai tou Nostou* (Andreas Embeirikos: The Poet of Eros and Return) (Athens: Kedros Press, 2003).

I have known the poet's son Leonidas – an exceptionally wise observer of the culture, history, diversity and musicology of modern Greece – for many years. Only recently did Leonidas share with me the story of his father's terrible, but alas not unusual, travails. I interviewed Yanis Varoufakis about his life and family memories for the *Financial Times* in March 2018: the story of his father George's career comes from that interview.

## 19  A Wedding and Four Funerals

More than any previous chapter, this one reflects my own lived experience, as a young Reuters correspondent in Athens between July 1982 and April 1986, and then a frequent visitor on journalistic assignments for various news organizations after that. My Reuters work involved following the minutiae of Greek politics and national affairs, when Andreas Papandreou was newly in office and the flame of socialist zeal was burning bright.

Like other foreign correspondents, I covered many rallies in Constitution Square at which Papandreou and other politicians addressed huge, excited crowds. Much as J. D. Bourchier did during the speeches of Venizelos in 1910, we correspondents stood on the same upper floor as Papandreou and observed the electrifying effect he was having on his banner-wielding supporters. This was also a time when Greek politicians and public intellectuals were much preoccupied with raking over the recentish past: both the military dictatorship of 1967–74 and the events immediately prior to that, including the constitutional crisis involving Prime Minister George Papandreou and young King Constantine in 1965. Two decades on, Andreas Papandreou still seemed obsessed at times with those events, especially the 'apostasy' from the Centre Union parliamentary bloc which fatally undermined his father's power base. So it was necessary to have a decent knowledge of Greek affairs in the mid-1960s in order to interpret some of the later pronouncements of the Socialist leader as head of government. 'This is no longer 1965,' he would say, by way of making clear that he would not tolerate any dissent from the PASOK party line, and that anybody who showed even mildly rebellious tendencies would be expelled. At a more humdrum level, memories of key moments in the dictatorship (including the Seferis funeral and the Polytechnic revolt) were still vivid in the early 1980s: many colleagues in the foreign press corps had been involved in covering them, and I met some protagonists of the Polytechnic tragedy. People who admitted feeling any nostalgia for the Greek monarchy – as of the 1980s, a deeply unpopular cause – were harder to find, but they did exist, and still do exist.

Covering Greek politics, even as a young reporter, involved entering a small, gossipy circle and getting a feel for the personalities involved. I had plenty of chances to observe Andreas Papandreou at close quarters, without ever developing any personal connection. Later I did get to know his three sons: George, who would follow the family tradition and become prime minister; Nikos, who is an economist and a remarkably talented writer; and Andreas junior, who is an academic environmentalist. The basic facts of the Papandreou family story are all in the public domain, and they have been well described by Stan Draenos. None of the above-mentioned people bears the slightest responsibility for anything I have written.

I interviewed Antonis Tritsis in September 1984, shortly before his resignation as environment minister. I followed Melina Mercouri's activities at the culture ministry, not only as a campaigner for the Parthenon marbles but as a promoter of cultural life in many other genres. For example, I recall watching a play with her at the small municipal theatre in Kalamata – and her insistence that the performance was fully up to Broadway standards.

Both she and Tritsis were charming, impulsive and bent on radical change, but Tritsis seemed more engaged with hard reality, with negative consequences for his career. Among Melina's more flamboyant gestures was this one, witnessed by a close friend. One evening, she was taken to task by Vangelis, composer of the music for the film *Chariots of Fire*. He wanted to know why the gates of the Acropolis were always closed after dark, thereby denying people the near-transcendental experience of exploring the citadel in the moonlight. 'Vangelis, I will open the gates for you!' she exclaimed, and promptly whisked the composer off to the Acropolis entrance and instructed a bewildered guard to let him in.

Here are some of the books that I used most, back then or more recently, to build up my knowledge – without ever assuming that any of them gave a complete or objective picture:

Richard Clogg and George Yannopoulos (eds), *Greece under Military Rule*, London: Secker & Warburg, 1972

Stan Draenos, *Andreas Papandreou: The Making of a Greek Democrat and Political Maverick*, London: I. B. Tauris, 2012

Stelios Kouloglou, *Sta Ikhni tou Tritou Dromou* (Tracking the Third Way), Athens: Odysseas, 1986

Melina Mercouri, *I Was Born Greek*, Garden City, NY: Doubleday, 1971

Alexis Papahelas, *O Viasmos tis Ellinikis Demokratias* (The Rape of Greek Democracy), Athens: Estia, 1997

Andreas Papandreou, *Democracy at Gunpoint: The Greek Front*, Garden City, NY: Doubleday, 1970

Margaret Papandreou, *Nightmare in Athens*, Englewood Cliffs, NJ: Prentice Hall, 1970

Nick Papandreou, *Father Dancing: An Invented Memoir*, London: Viking, 1996

Stephen Rousseas, *The Death of a Democracy: Greece and the American Conscience*, New York: Grove Press, 1967

Laurence Stern, *The Wrong Horse: The Politics of Intervention and the Failure of American Diplomacy*, New York: Times Books, 1977

C. M. Woodhouse, *The Rise and Fall of the Greek Colonels*, London: HarperCollins, 1985

The observations I make about the *polykatoikia* – apartment building – are more or less familiar to anybody who has lived in or frequently visited Athens for the last several decades. The foremost academic expert on this model of urban development is Panos Dragonas, Professor of Architecture at the University of Patras, one of whose scholarly articles on the subject can be read in the following tome: 'Polykatoikia' (Apartment building) in Joachim Fischer and Chris van Uffelen (eds), *1000X European Architecture*

(Berlin: Verlagshaus Braun, 2007). Professor Dragonas' insights have been taken up by Feargus O'Sullivan, a London-based pundit on urban planning, whose writings can be found at www.bloomberg. com/citylab.

## 20  Pride, a Fall and an Open Future

In this chapter, even more than the previous one, I drew on my own experiences as a journalist and the broad range of personal acquaintances which I was able to build up during a professional lifetime of periodic involvement with Greece.

As it happens, I met the Olympic choreographer Dimitris Papaioannou in the 1980s, when he was a budding artist and illustrator. However, I enjoyed his opening and closing ceremonies for the 2004 Olympic Games in the same way as hundreds of millions of others did, as an awestruck electronic spectator. To understand the deeper semiotics and the pitfalls he artfully avoided, I drew on the brilliant doctoral thesis presented at the University of Surrey in 2007 by Ioanna Tzartzani: *Interplays of Ethnicity, Nationalism and Globalization Within the Greek Contemporary Dance Scene: Choreographic Choices and the Construction of National Identity.*

Athenian politics used to be a familiar, known quantity until the whole picture was upended by the advent of Syriza. So a confession is in order: I had some personal acquaintance with many of the senior players in the two parties which dominated the country before 2015, PASOK and New Democracy. However, the leadership of Syriza felt like an entirely new world, with the exception of Yanis Varoufakis, with whom I had spent an evening in 2002: he had recently returned to Greece from Australia and was informally advising George Papandreou, then foreign minister. I had a longer conversation with Yanis on 2 March 2018 on which this chapter, like the previous one, draws.

I had known George Papandreou since the early 1980s, when as an idealistic junior member of his father's administration, he was pioneering the cause of adult education in the Greek provinces. In autumn 2002, I became aware of the prescient work that he was doing, as foreign minister, to pioneer intelligent thinking about economic migration from the poor to the rich world – and followed several of his brainstorming sessions involving policymakers and academics from all over the Western world. Many of the results of that labour can be seen on the website of the Migration Policy Institute based in Washington, DC – http://www.mpi.org. In July 2009 I had the stimulating experience of sitting in on a talkfest he organized about the future of the global centre-left, about which I wrote in the *Economist* of 30 July 2009 under the headline, 'The challenge of turning malcontents into (sensible) militants'.

All the deliberations of that decade can seem rather Pollyannaish when set against the storms that were to break over Greece, and the world, in the years that followed. In fairness to George Papandreou and his fellow symposiasts, there were plenty of people back then who had clear intimations of what was coming. I happened to be in Athens on 5 May 2010, the day when protests against creditor-imposed austerity turned violent and claimed the lives of three bank workers, including a pregnant woman, whose workplace was set on fire. It was a frightening time. Life took me back to Constitution Square a year later, at a moment when protests and agitation of a more peaceful kind were in progress. For the *Economist* edition of 30 June 2011 I filed a report which began: 'In the middle of Syntagma Square in central Athens, flanked on one side by parliament and on another by luxury hotels, would-be revolutionaries jostle for space with phlegmatic African street-traders selling handbags. On June 22nd one group of youngsters conducted a spontaneous "economics lesson" in which terms such as "credit event" and "haircut" were explained and deconstructed. Petrograd 1917, or even Paris 1968, it was not. Nonetheless, the stakes are very high. It is entirely possible that in the weeks to come the situation in Athens could go from being strained, angry and confused to plain catastrophic.' Then in July 2015, as the Syriza referendum conjured up the spectre of a dramatic Grexit, I found myself professionally involved in Greek affairs in a different way, as acting editor of the *Economist*'s European pages. Along with colleagues based in Greece, including Kerin Hope, Sacha Nauta and Matt Steinglass, I had to keep abreast of a situation that was changing by the hour and had the potential to bring chaos not just to Greece but to the European monetary system. One of the snapshots I helped put together, 'Angry in Athens, livid in Lesbos', was published on 16 July 2015.

Whatever the insights I derived from these experiences, it would be silly to compare my own sporadic involvement with that of colleagues who faced the testing and at times frightening experience of following the Greek crisis day in and day out. Those colleagues whose work is well known to me include Kerin Hope, Derek Gatopoulos, Marcus Walker, Helena Smith, Tasos Telloglou, Nektaria Stamouli, Dan Howden and Tom Nuttall. Among the best books written by journalists who did follow the entire extraordinary saga are *The 13th Labour of Hercules: Inside the Greek Crisis*, by Yannis Palaiologos (London: Granta Books, 2014), and *The Last Bluff: How Greece Came Face-to-Face with Financial Catastrophe and the Secret Plan for Its Euro Exit*, by Viktoria Dendrinou and Eleni Varvitsioti (Athens: Papadopoulos Publishing, 2019). Both these books show the ability of a rising generation of Greek journalists, writing in witty, perfect English, to expound the affairs of their country to an intelligent, cosmopolitan audience.

It was a memorable experience to attend the launch, on 14 October 2019, of the Greek translation of *The Last Bluff* – at which Alexis Papahelas, the editor of *Kathimerini*, led an immensely intricate and fine-grained discussion with the co-authors as well as a panel of European financial pundits. About 400 people, packed into the auditorium of the Pireos branch of the Benaki Museum, were manifestly transfixed. I do not think I have ever attended a discussion that was so arcane and cerebral and yet so gripping for a huge audience. It suggested that the 2,500-year-old Athenian tradition of vigorous, sophisticated and open-ended debate was alive and well.

Then, of course, there are the globally bestselling books of Yanis Varoufakis, who was laughingly described as the 'ghost at the feast' of that Benaki discussion, although there was a rich and festive enough conversation among those who were physically present. His account of the Grexit crisis, described in the *Guardian* as 'one of the greatest political memoirs of all time', is *Adults in the Room: My Battle with Europe's Deep Establishment* (London: Bodley Head, 2017). As mentioned in the chapter, Varoufakis explores a Thucydidean theme in *And the Weak Must Suffer What They Must: Europe, Austerity and the Threat to Global Stability* (London: Bodley Head, 2016). From his perspective, the crisis in which he was intimately caught up had been accurately foreshadowed in *The Global Minotaur: America, Europe and the Future of the Global Economy* (London: Zed Books, 2011).

To judge by their Twitter profiles, the two most famous Athenian-born people are Varoufakis (1 million followers) and the basketball player Giannis Antetokounmpo (1.5 million). My concluding chapter has more about the second Giannis, who spells his first name in the more usual way.

## 21  And Greece Travels Onwards

The previous two chapters reflected my life as a journalist. This one is based more on the everyday experience I gained in the course of some extended stays in Athens through 2018 and 2019, ending abruptly on 2 March 2020. These stays were a chance to experience the texture of life in a city that was changing by the day, becoming more cosmopolitan, more stimulating and, in certain ways, more ruthless. The cultural experiences I tasted ranged from opera at the Niarchos Centre to hip-hop at the Afrikana jazz club in Gazi. The culinary experiences were, as the chapter makes clear, equally diverse and at times surreal.

I was able to gain some insights into the world of Islam in Athens by collaborating with Demetrios Ioannou, a talented young photo-reporter, and the fruits of our labours were published on the *Economist* website here: https://www.economist.com/erasmus/2018/05/27/where-islam-flourishes-despite-being-half-underground.

In the course of this research we interviewed Naim al-Ghandour and Ashif Haidar, who in turn introduced me to Mehdi Khan Choudry, the cricket king of Aigaleo. That in turn helped me to collaborate with my colleague Alex Sakalis on an article about cricket in Greece – 'How cricket thrives in Greece' – published in the *Economist* on 13 September 2018. The involvement, albeit indirect, of Alex with this book goes much further than that. As a passionate aficionado of the lost urban landscapes of Athens, including the neoclassical and modernist heritage, he greatly enhanced my feel for that subject. His writing can be found on www.alexsakalis.wordpress.com.

My interest in the Chinese community of Athens, and the strategic link between China and Greece, goes back to 2008. I co-authored, with Kerin Hope and Tracey Rosen, a piece about the micro- and macroeconomic connections that make up Sino-Hellenic friendship. It was published in the printed *Economist* on 21 August 2018: 'Doing business for aeons'. Rosen was at that time researching a doctoral thesis at the University of Chicago on the Chinese in Greece; she is now a lecturer at the social studies faculty of Harvard: https://socialstudies.fas.harvard.edu/people/tracey-rosen.

Thanks to Manos Tzafalias, an ever-faithful helper and friend, I met Manolis Yinka, who generously shared some of his experience as a Greek-African musician. Manolis described the African-Athenian scene of his youth, of which the Antetokounmpo family were part. Manolis' chosen meeting place was the Blue Parrot, a café-bar in the heart of Metaxourgeio. In trying to get some sense of the dynamics of that contradictory neighbourhood, I was greatly stimulated by the work of the urban geographer Dr Georgia Alexandri, currently a post-doctoral fellow at the University of Leeds. Her doctoral thesis at the Harokopeio University of Athens can be found here: https://www.didaktorika.gr/eadd/handle/10442/37340. Other parts of her prolific output, including many contributions to academic journals, can be found on her page on academia.edu: https://leeds.academia.edu/GeorgiaAlexandri. Some of her writing is co-authored with the architect and activist Eleni Tzirtzilaki, whose theory of nomadic architecture is developed here: www.nomadikiarxitektoniki.net. Although I have learned a lot from writers of this school about Metaxourgeio and neighbouring Gazi, I cannot entirely share the ideological perspective, one which views with *a priori* suspicion all application of private funds to the regeneration of neighbourhoods and buildings. Nor, with the deepest respect, can I concur with Dr Alexandri's negative assessment of the evolution of the Plaka neighbourhood. The story of Plaka and the struggle to save it, spearheaded by the NGO Elliniki Etaireia, can be found in part on the website www.ellet.gr.

For a critique of the development of Metaxourgeio, in a somewhat different vein, see this lively article by Euphrosyne Doxiadis which expresses disappointment over the apparent fact that potentially important archaeological knowledge is being sacrificed in the cause of building 'basements with swimming pools' for the enjoyment of modern seekers of new urban experiences: https://popaganda.gr/stories/diplo-ipogio-pisina-ke-telika-sotirio-odostroma-tis-pireos/.

I have known Kriton Arsenis, one of the most passionate environmental voices in Greece and indeed Europe, since 2007 and our paths have crossed in the Cyclades, in London as well as New Orleans, where we both took part in a symposium on the environment convened by HAH the Ecumenical Patriarch in 2009. In the final stages of the preparation of this book, he was willing to take an hour of his busy life, as a parliamentarian and young father, to speak in a broad way about the ecological and sustainability challenges confronting greater Athens, especially the western side facing Eleusis, to which he feels a deep personal commitment. While bearing no responsibility for my conclusions, some of which he would dispute, his input and patience were of decisive help. Another provider of last-minute help (as well as assistance at much earlier stages) was Dylan Rogers of the University of Virginia, co-editor of the *Cambridge Companion to Ancient Athens*, published by CUP in 2021. From a different ideological corner, Stefanos Manos was a wonderfully illuminating informant. He was able to confirm that for scholars, the location of the *Dimosion Sema* or Public Cemetery of ancient Athens is far from a settled matter.

# Acknowledgements

As with major personal endeavour, the researching and writing of this book was made possible by the support and disinterested kindness of many new and old friends; some provided vital insights, others practical help, others pleasant companionship, many offered all of the above.

Among friends who live or have lived in Athens, the list (by no means exhaustive) would include: Lydia and Costa Carras, Euphrosyne Doxiadis, Panos Georgakopoulos, Ieromonachos David; Leonidas Embeirikos; Eleni and Daniel Howden; Maria Iliou; Giovanna Kampouri; Paschalis Kitromilidis; Kalliopi Kontozoglou; all branches and generations of the Kourkoulas family; Maria Kopanitsa; Ioanna Kopsiafti; Marianna Koromila; Spyros Kosteletos; the late George Kourias; Yorgos Kyriakopoulos; Yannis, Anna and Dimitris Livanios, Emmanuelle and Antonis Lionis; Sophia and Panos Loulias; Rafael Mahdavi; Alex Massavetas; Despoina and Vanya Masteropoulos; Catherina Mytilineou and her mother Smaro; Aliki and Yannis Palaiologos; Ritsa Panayotou; Vasilis Papadimitriou and his family; Thanasis Papatheodorou; Kostas Paschalidis; Christos Sclavounis: Eleni and Simos Sichiaridis, Kate Smith; Yannis Stavrou; Tasos Telloglou; Ioulia Tsakiri; Andrew Watson.

Among friends, Greek and otherwise, who live elsewhere, I must acknowledge the help – moral and practical – of Mando Meleagrou, Olivia Musgrave and her extended family, Nicky and Jenny Richardson, Martin Kisch and Lady Marina Marks, Natasha and George Lemos, Irene Lemos, Renee Hirschon and Paul Cartledge.

The practical challenges of writing in the era of Covid, which were acute at times, were eased by the friendship and solidarity of, inter alios, Rab Booth, Anne Fleming, Margaret Barker, Tommy, Catherine and Fionan Sands, Jonny Clark and his family,  the McGrath family,  the Carson family, Marian and Pablito Clark and all their kin, Hermann and Marion Baur, Fergus and Angelique Bell, Maddie Stewart, Yana Stajno, Father George Zavershinsky and others living further afield – in places like New Jersey, Istanbul, British Columbia and various parts of Australia and New Zealand – who hardly knew how much they were helping.

Two intellectual debts, to scholars I have not yet met, need to be acknowledged: to Nassia Yakovaki for her insights in the concept of modern Greece, and to Gioula Koutsopanagou for sharing her deep research on the Greek civil war and its reception in Britain.

Finally I would like to express profound gratitude to Richard Milbank who conceived this book and skilfully nursed it into existence; and to Matilda Singer who patiently filtered the manuscript and saw to many practical details.

# Image Credits

1. Martin von Wagner Museum/Daderot/ Wikimedia.

2. yiannisscheidt/ Shutterstock.

3. Heritage Images/CM Dixon/akg-images.

4. Jastrow/Wikimedia.

5. Erin Babnik/Alamy.

6. Jastrow/Wikimedia.

7. Roseanne Tackaberry/ Alamy.

8. Erin Babnik/Alamy.

9. *Alcibiade recevant les leçons de Socrate*, by François-André Vincent/Fulvio314/ Wikimedia.

10. Dorieo/Wikimedia.

11. isadoros andronos/ Shutterstock.

12. *St Paul Preaching in Athens*, by George Baxter, after Raphael. Print by Bradshaw & Blacklock. Artokoloro/Alamy.

13. Jeanhousen/ Wikimedia.

14. akg-images/Pirozzi.

15. INTERFOTO/ Alamy. Contemporary Italian engraving.

16. *Athens from the Foot of Mount Anchesmus* (1821) by Edward Dodwell/The Picture Art Collection/Alamy.

17. Charles Meryon/ Heritage Arts/Getty Images.

18. *Illustrated London News*/Antiqua Print Gallery/Alamy.

19. Bob Thomas/ Popperfoto/Getty Images.

20. Photo12/Universal Images Group/Getty Images.

21. Library of Congress (loc.gov/ item/2010650546).

22. akg-images/ Sammlung Berliner Verlag/Archiv.

23. Photo12/Universal Images Group/Getty Images.

24. Vangelis Evangeliou/ SOPA Images/ LightRocket/Getty Images.

25. Fremantle/Alamy.

26. Rolls Press/ Popperfoto/Getty Images.

27. Papadopoulos Charalambos/Getty Images.

28. Chris Ivin/Getty Images.

29. Pigi Cipelli/ Mondadori/Getty Images.

30. Milos Bicanski/Getty Images.

31. Mike Stobe/Getty Images.

32. Martin Leitch/Alamy.

33. dpa picture alliance/ Alamy.

# Index

Abydos, Battle of 118
Academy of Athens 360–1
  see also under Plato
Acarnania 176
Acciaiuoli, Antonio 259–60
Acciaiuoli, Antonio II 261
Acciaiuoli, Francesca 256–7
Acciaiuoli, Franco 264–5,
  266–7
Acciaiuoli, Nerio 253,
  254–6, 257
Acciaiuoli, Nerio II 260–1,
  264
Acciaiuoli, Niccolò 252–3
Achaemenid dynasty 24–5
*The Acharnians*
  (Aristophanes) 94,
  100–1
Acropolis 1–2, 2–5
  and barbarian raids 205–6
  Byron's visit 322–3, 370
  caves 4, 6–7
  Cyclopean walls 5
  Elgin's removal of
    sculptures 313–19,
    367–8
  Florence Nightingale's
    visit 369–70
  Frankish Tower 340, 357
  and the Greek War of
    Independence 332–6,
    338–9, 340–3
  Hill of the Nymphs 399
  inscriptions in the
    Christian era 227–8
  and the Latin Empire
    254–5
  the Mycenaean spring 6

nineteenth-century
  transformation of
  356–60
and Ottoman Athens 268
Persian destruction of
  49–50, 76
the Rock 3–7, 14, 19, 49
shrine of Athena 19,
  28, 35
Roman monuments
  187–8
temples
  Dionysus 30
  the Erechtheion 119,
  120
  Poseidon 163
theatre of Dionysus 162
wartime British
  occupation 447
see also the Parthenon
Acropolis Museum, Athens
  80
Adair, Sir Robert 318
Aegean Sea 8, 10, 272
Aegeus, mythical king 8–9,
  290
Aegina 48, 72
Aegospotami, Battle of
  122, 140
Aelius Aristides 204–5
Aeschylus 123–4, 146, 162–3
  *The Persians* 52–3, 54
Africa 535
Agamemnon 141
Agathias 220–1
Agesiliaus, king of Sparta
  141, 143, 146
Agis, king of Sparta 116
Aglaurus 7

Agora
  Church of the Holy
    Apostles 228–30
  Roman era 361
  temple of Hephaestus 229
Agora of Athens 173–4,
  178, 182
  Roman 187
Agrippa, Marcus 187
Aigaleo (district) 523, 594
Aigaleo, Mount 52, 207,
Aiges 150–1, 152, 157
  palace of 348
airport 494–5, 497, 529
Akathist (Orthodox hymn)
  236
Akerhjelm, Anna 282–3
Alans 248
Alaric, Gothic warrior
  214–16, 232, 329
Albania 252, 432, 436, 440
Alcibiades 104–6, 107, 109,
  111–13, 114–15, 116–19,
  120–1, 122–4
  accusations of blasphemy
    114–15, 120, 130
  in Aristophanes' *The Frogs*
    123–4
  and Byron 325
  death 122
  personality 104–5
  in Plato's *Symposium*
    110–11
  and Socrates 132, 134–5,
    212
Alexander the Great 150,
  158, 159, 160–1, 166,
  167, 173, 178, 183, 185,
  202, 290

Alexander, king of Greece 402, 410–11
Alexandri, Georgia 528
Alfred, Prince 371
Ali Pasha 321, 331, 333, 338, 339, 350, 373
Alice, Princess 398
Alkmeonid clan 19, 27, 32, 34–5, 104
Amalia, Queen of Greece 348
Amazons 164
American Civil War 87
American Revolution 84
American School of Classical Studies 424–5
Amphictyonic League 155
Amphipolis 99, 154, 157
Ampurias 250
Anafi islet 346, 349
Anafiotika neighbourhood 346–8, 349
Anatolia 34, 38, 46, 411
refugees from 405–9, 413, 414–18, 441, 533
Anaxagoras 70
Andrew, Prince of Greece 412
Andronikos II, Byzantine emperor 248
Androutsos, Odysseas 338–40, 341
Angelopoulos, Panagiotis 455
Anne-Marie of Denmark, Queen of Greece 466–7
Antetokounmpo, Giannis 523
anti-Semitism 364
Antigonids 171
Antigonus Gonatas 171–2
Antigonus *Monophthalmos* 166, 168, 169, 170, 171
Antiochus of Ashkelon 182, 184, 195
Antiochus Epiphanes 195
Antipater 162
antiquarians 300–3
*The Antiquities of Athens* (Stuart and Revett) 303
Antoninus, Emperor 204
Antoninus Pius 201

Antony, Mark 185–6
Anytus 135
Aphrodite, goddess 7
Apollo, god 6, 40, 95, 156, 158
Apostolou Pavlou 530
Appian 179–80
Apsines 210
aqueduct 194, 419, 533
Aragon, kingdom of 244–5, 253–4
Aratus 191–2
Arcadian League 145
archaeological excavations 424–5
archaeological finds
drinking cup of Pericles 71–2
the 'Hockey Players' 61
mass burials 20
*ostraka* 64–5
the Royal Stoa 128–30
shipsheds 47–8
Syntagma 494
warriors' grave 528
Archelaus 180, 181
Archidamian War 92
architecture
nineteenth-century 348–9, 352–4, 355, 377–9
twentieth-century 418–19
archons 18–19, 180
'king archon' 129, 174
Solon 20–7
'war archon' 42
Ardettos 397
Areopagus 18, 49, 189, 190, 219, 269, 281, 369
Ares, god 12
Arginusai islands 121
Argos 111, 240
Arianism 211
Ariphron 72
Aristagoras 39
Aristides 65, 66
Aristides, Aelius 202
Aristion 180–1
Aristogeiton 30–1, 350, 527
Ariston 184
Aristophanes 94, 129, 132, 146, 423, 527, 528
*The Acharnians* 94, 100–1
*The Clouds* 108–9, 131
*The Frogs* 123–4

*Lysistrata* 123, 486
Aristotle 29, 158, 258
Arrephoroi 434
Arsenis, Kriton 532
Artabazus 154
Artaphernes 40
Artaxerxes II of Persia 139, 140, 142, 154
Artemis (goddess) 40, 45, 306
Artemisia, queen of Halicarnassus 54–5
Artemisium, Battle of 46–7, 48
artists 26–7
Aspasia 91, 100–1
asylum seekers 517–18
Athena, goddess 11–16, 19, 28, 49, 170, 187, 235
and Athenian democracy 86
and King Otho 351–2
Nike temple 119
olive tree 12–13, 49, 119, 492
olive-wood effigy of (the *xoana*) 119
Panathenaic festival in honour of 29, 80–1, 84, 163, 170, 376
and the Parthenon 78, 86, 262
statues of 76, 162, 179, 188, 232
temples 45, 76, 232, 280, 281, 283, 318, 319, 357, 360
Athenian League *see* Delian League; Second Athenian League
Athenion 180
Athens International Airport (Eleftherios Venizelos) 494, 495, 529
Athens Tower 460
Athinas Avenue 353
Atlantis 23–4
atoms 166
Atossa, Persian queen 52
Attalid dynasty 175
Attalos I, king of Pergamon 176
Attalos II, king of Pergamon 175

Attica 6, 10, 29, 35, 102
  Solon's rule 20–7
Atticus (Titus Pomponius)
  183
Augustus, Roman Emperor
  185–8, 192
Aulis 141
Aulus Gellius 203
austerity crisis 499–513
Averoff, George 372–3, 377,
  381, 397

*The Babylonians*
  (Aristophanes) 94
Bakoyannis, Kostas 516,
  532–3
Baldwin, Count 241
Balkan Wars (1912–13)
  388–93, 394
Balkan wars (1990s) 331,
  498
Bank of Crete 482
Baptista Vretos 307
barbarian raids 203–7,
  214–16, 232
Basil of Caesarea 210–11,
  212, 213, 222
Basil II, Byzantine emperor
  230–1
Bausch, Pina 493
Beaton, Roderick 376, 390
Becket, Maria 438
beekeeping 289, 295
Bekir 307
Bellos 307
Benakis, Emmanuel 401
Benizelos, Ionnes 299
Black Death 93, 95,
Blake, Arthur 375
Boeotia 30, 75, 105–6, 141,
  143, 207, 253
book-burning 422
Bouras, Charalambos 216
Bourchier, James David
  380–1, 387–9
bouzouki 425, 519, 529
Brasidas 99
Brenne, Stefan 66–7
Breton, André 451
Britain
  and the Acropolis
    monuments 318
  and the Balkan Wars
    390–1

British politics and
    Kleisthenic
    democracy 36
  and the Crimean War
    366, 368–9
  and the First World War
    393, 395, 397
  and the Greek War of
    Independence 344
  and the kingdom of
    Greece 361, 363,
    364–6
  liberation of Athens
    (1944) 442, 443–50,
    461
  and the United States 183
British Commonwealth 198
British Empire 113
Bronze Age 5
Brutus, Marcus Iunius 184,
  185, 186
building works
  illegal building in greater
    Athens 481–2
  nineteenth-century
    transformation of the
    Acropolis 356–60
  Pericles' building of the
    Parthenon 119–20
  *polykatoikia* 458–60
  Roman Athens 194–7,
    200, 201, 217
  *see also* houses
Bulgaria 384, 385, 388–9,
  392, 395, 402
Burns, A. R. 145
Bush, George W. 11, 88
Byron, George Gordon,
  Lord 321–5, 326–30,
  338, 363, 368, 370, 525
Byzantine Athens
  and the Catalan Company
    248
  Christianity 224–43
Byzantium 154, 158, 208,
  395

Caesar, Julius 184, 185,
  186, 187
Callimachus 42
Caltabellotta, Peace of 245
Cambyses 40
capital city, Athens as choice
  of 350–1
Carlyle, Joseph 315

Carras, Lydia 526
Carrey, Jacques 287
Carthage 176
the Caryatids 119, 187, 188
Cassius Dio 188
Catalan Company 245–52,
  253–4
Catholicism
  the Church and the Latin
    Empire 250–1, 254–5,
    255–6
  Frankish rule in Athens
    242–3
  and the Parthenon 293
Çelebi, Evliya 291–4, 297,
  319
Centeno, Mario 512–13
Cephalonia 256–7, 328,
  484, 488
ceramics 23, 240
Chaeronea, Battle of 150,
  158, 160, 162
Chaerophon 132
Chalkidike peninsula 156
Chalkis 158, 177, 269
  Ottoman rule in 269, 272
Chalkokondyles, George
  260
Chares 154
Charlemagne, king of the
  Franks 226
Charles
  king of Sicily 244
China 521–2, 535
Chios 154, 332
Chioti, Lambrini 205,
  206, 216
Choiseul-Gouffier, Comte
  de 309–11
Choniates, Michael, Greek
  archbishop of Athens
  234–6, 238–9, 240,
  241–2, 293, 295, 359
Choniates, Nikitas 241–2
Chosroes, king of Persia
  220–1
Christian Bible
  Acts of the Apostles
    188–91, 198–9
  and the Christian
    Parthenon 236
Christianity 207, 210–14,
  217
  Arianism 211, 216
  Byzantine Athens 224–43

and Constantinople
208–9
and Frankish Athens
241–2
Greek Christians and the
War of Independence
333, 335, 337
and Greek mythology 15
the Holy Shroud 242–3
iconoclasts 225
and neo-Platonism
219–23
the Orthodox Church and
the Greek state 482
Orthodox festivals 460–1
Orthodox funerals 462–3
in Ottoman Athens 268,
269
and the Parthenon 226–8,
229, 231–6, 237, 238,
241, 254, 258, 262, 359
Paul the Apostle in Athens
188–92
and Roman Athens
188–92, 207, 208–14
see also Virgin Mary
Christoulas, Dimitris
499–500
Church of the Holy
Apostles 228–30
Church, Sir Richard 344
Churchill, Winston 87–8,
410, 442, 443, 444,
447–50, 463
Cicero 182–4, 186
cinema 470
citizens
in ancient Athens 22
city walls 61–2, 66, 122–3,
239, 305–6
city-states 9–11
civil war (1946–9) 340,
455, 458
Clarke, Edward 315, 317
Clarke, Edward Daniel
320–1
Cleombrotus, king of Sparta
144
Cleopatra 185–6
climate change 535
The Clouds (Aristophanes)
108–9, 131
Cold War 60, 471

the colonels 466, 473, 477,
482, 488, 491, 493,
501, 520
communism see EAM
(National Liberation
Front)
Connelly, Joan Breton 81,
232, 289, 292
Constans II, Byzantine
emperor 225
Constantine the Great,
Emperor 208–9,
212, 290
Constantine I, king of
Greece 391–2, 411, 412
as Crown Prince 375, 380,
383, 389–90
and the First World War
393–4, 396, 397,
398–9, 400–1
Constantine II, king of
Greece 70, 470,
471–2, 472–3
wedding 466–7, 487
Constantine IV, Byzantine
emperor 225–6
Constantinople 205, 208–9,
224, 226
and the First World War
402–4
Frankish invasion of 241,
243
and Greek independence
355
Hagia Sophia 227, 228,
298, 403–4
Ottoman conquest of
242, 264–6
see also Istanbul
Constantinople
Organization 385–6,
394
constitution 354, 371
Constitution Square see
Syntagma Square
consumerism 495, 501
Contarini, Bartolommeo
264–5
Corfu 144, 371
Corinth 27, 29, 72, 140,
172, 240, 260
Paul the Apostle in 192
Corinthian war 141
Corsica 38
Coubertin, Pierre de 379

coup d'état of April 1967
466
see also the colonels
Covid pandemic 95, 534
Crete 9, 12, 24, 278, 364,
382–3, 385, 386–7,
396–7
German invasion of
433–4, 440
cricket 523
Crimean War 366, 368–9,
370, 378
Crito 126
Croesus, king of Lydia
24–5, 38
Cromwell, Oliver 156
Crosus Field, Battle of the
156, 157
Crusaders 260–1
Crusius, Martin 273–4
Cunaxa, Battle of 139
Cynics 164
Cynoscephalae, Battle
of 177
Cyprus 24, 74, 117, 140,
465–6, 470–1, 478
Cyriacus of Ancona 261–3,
266
Cyrus the Great, Persian
king 25, 37, 38
Cyzicus, Battle of 118

da Martoni, Niccolò 256–8,
262, 263
Dalaras, George 417
Damaskinos, Archbishop
448–9
Damaskios 219, 223
Daphni monastery 230–1,
248, 380, 532
Darius, Persian king 39–40,
41, 42, 139
Dark Age 6
Dartige du Fournet,
Admiral Louis 399
Dassin, Jules 477
Datis 40
de Botton, Alain 165
de la Roche, Guy 248
de la Roche, Otho 241, 243
de Vere, Aubrey 367–8
deities 4, 5, 6–7
Dekemvriana 443–50
Delacroix, Eugène 332
Deleon 105–6

Delian League 74, 144
Deliyannakis, George 209
Deliyannis, Theodoros 361
Delos 40, 66, 68, 74, 180, 185
Delphic oracle 32, 33–4, 48
  and Philip of Macedon 150, 155–6, 157, 158
  sanctuary of Apollo 156
  and Socrates 131, 132
  and Sparta 155–6
Delta, Penelope 401
Demeter, goddess 320
Demetrius the Besieger 167–70, 171, 306
Demetrius of Phaleron 166–7, 168, 169
democracy in ancient Athens 2, 69–70, 103, 135–7, 166, 505
  changing the law 136
  degeneration of 180
  and foreign domination 174
  Kleisthenic 35–6
  and Macedonia 162
  ostracism 63–8, 70–1, 72, 74, 87, 127, 130
  and Pericles 84–8, 90–1
  and Socrates 127, 130, 132, 133
Democritus 165
Demosthenes, Athenian orator and politician 159–63
Demosthenes, naval commander 98, 99
Dexileos 141
  memorial to 137–8
Dexippus, historian 206–7
diaspora 371–3, 380–1, 530
DiEM25 party 510
Dikaiopolis 95
Dimoulas, Christos 506
Diodotus 93
Diogenes of Babylon 179
Dionysios (Denis the Areopagite) 258, 269
Dionysios, Sicilian tyrant 148
Dionysiou Areopagitou 530
Dionysus, god 30, 123, 170, 194, 196
  Theatre of 162, 178, 218

Disraeli, Benjamin 36, 93, 113, 365–6
Doolittle, Hilda 15
Downward, Jeremy 515–16
Doxiadis, Euphrosyne 97
Doxiadis, Constantinos 480, 529
Dragouomis, Ion 385
Dramiton 72
Drury, Henry 324–5
Duris of Samos 171

EAM (National Liberation Front) 436, 439, 441, 442, 443, 444, 445, 461
earthquakes 498–9
Eastcourt, Sir Giles 287–8
economic development 361–2
economic recovery 513, 514–16, 519–22
Eden, Anthony 448
Egypt 23, 40, 72, 73–4, 177, 185
  Florence Nightingale in 369
  Ottoman 312, 314, 317, 344–5
Ekali 464
ELAS (communist resistance movement) 436, 440, 442–3, 443–4, 446–7, 449–50, 451–4, 476
Eleusian mysteries 114, 176, 198, 212
Eleusis 84, 114, 129, 143, 532
  barbarian raid on 203–5, 216
Elgin, Thomas Bruce, seventh Earl of 312–18, 323, 327, 367–8
  Byron on 329–30
  See also under Parthenon
Elizabeth II, Queen (Princess Elizabeth) 412
Elliniki Eraireia conservation movement 526
Ellinikon airport 479, 496, 531
Embeirikos, Andreas 450–4

England 233, 303, 314, 318, 319, 327, 328, 369, 421, 456
Enver Bey 385
Epaminondas of Thebes 143, 145–6
Ephesus 38
Ephialtes 70
Epicureans 179, 189, 191
Epicurus 165–6
Epimenides 191
equality before the law in ancient Athens 22–3
Erechtheion 119, 120, 187, 238, 310–11, 313, 318, 342, 434–5
  repairs to 357
Erechtheus, mythological king 6, 7, 13–14, 81, 163, 232
Eretria 40, 41
Ergotimos, artist 26
Eridanos river 84
Eros, god 7
Esma Sultan 305, 307
Español, Berenguer 250
ethnic diversity 498
Euboea 17, 40–1, 47, 75, 158, 249, 269, 333, 334, 339, 348, 451
Euboulos 154
Eumenes I, king of Pergamon 176
Eumenes II, king of Pergamon 177–8, 187
the Eumenides (furies) 369
Eunapius 216
Euripides 81, 123, 129, 146, 162–3
euro crisis 492, 496–7, 502–7, 521
  see also financial crisis (from 2009)
European Union 383, 479, 481, 483, 499
  and asylum seekers 517–18
  bailouts 500, 502, 503, 509, 510, 512
  'golden visas' 520–1
Euthyphro (Plato) 128
Evagoras, king of Cyprus 140
Evert, Angelos 439
Exarcheia 419, 501, 516, 517

expatriate Greeks 371–3,
    380–1
  in the Ottoman Empire
    383–4

famine 437–8
Farmakis, Nikos 445
fascism 421–3
Fauvel, Louis-Francois-
    Sebastien 310–11, 313,
    318, 323
fifth-century BCE Athens
    56–124
  see also Pericles
Filothei, Saint 274–7
financial crisis (1843) 354–5
financial crisis (from 2009)
    499–513, 521
  see also euro crisis
Finlay, George 345
fires 535
First Peloponnesian War 75
First World War 393–403,
    409
Flack, Edwin 375
Flamininus, Titus Quinctius
    177
flash flooding 532–3
Flodden Field, Battle of 145
Flor, Roger de 245–8
Florakis, Kharilaos 483
Florence
  Acciaiuoli dynasty 252–3,
    254–6, 259–61, 264–5
food markets 419–20
foustanella 380, 491
Fowden, Elizabeth Key 299
Fowden, Garth 207
France
  and the First World War
    393, 397, 400–1
  French rule in Sicily 244
  and the Greek War of
    Independence 344
  and the kingdom of
    Greece 361, 363–4,
    366
  and Ottoman Athens
    309–12
Frankish invaders 240–2,
    248–9
Frantz, Alison 216, 218,
    219, 225
Frederica, Queen of Greece
    70, 467

Frederick, king of Sicily
    245, 249–50
French Revolution 84,
    311, 325
French visitors to Athens
    287–91
Freud, Sigmund 15
The Frogs (Aristophanes)
    123–4
Froissart, Jean 256–7
funerals 461–6, 475–7,
    484–5, 485–8
funerary monuments 97
Fyli 321
Fyli landfill 531–2

Gaius Acilius 179
Galatians 172
Gallipoli peninsula 42,
    46, 396
Ganas, Evangelos 522–3
Gärtner, Friedrich von
    348–9
Gaspari, Monsieur 310
Gazi district 528
geography of Greece 9
George I, king of the
    Hellenes 370, 371,
    379, 380, 390, 487
  assassination 370, 391
  and the Ottoman war 383
George II, king of Greece
    412, 421, 447, 463
  as Prince George 375,
    382, 387
George IV, British king 333
Germanos, Freddy 432
Gibbon, Edward 193
Giraud, Jean 282–3
Giraud, Nicolo 324, 327–8
Gladstone, William 93
Glezos, Manolis 431–9, 449
Glezos, Nikos 436
Goebbels, Joseph 491
Golden Age of Athens see
    fifth-century BCE
    Athens
Golden Dawn movement
    508, 522
'golden visas' 520–1
Gounaris, Dimitrios 396
Gouras, Asimo 342–3
Gouras, Ioannis 341–2,
    343, 357

Greco-Turkish war (1919–22)
    405–6, 410, 411
Greek Church see Orthodox
    Church
Greek Enlightenment 325
Greek language 9, 10, 222,
    362–3
  Attic dialect 202
Greek Revolution/War
    of Independence
    330–45, 350
  and Byron 328–9
Gregory of Nazianzus (the
    Theologian) 210–12,
    213, 222
Grigoropoulos, Alexis 501
Grivas, Colonel George
    444, 445
Gülen, Fethullah 521

Hadji Ibrahim Effendi 317
Hadrian, Emperor 192–9,
    200, 201, 203, 206,
    258, 290, 359
  Arch of 197, 263, 351
  Library 194, 296
Haidari detention centre
    441
Hall, Edith 96
Halmyros, Battle of 249
Hansen, Christian 360
Hansen, Theophil 379, 404
Harmodius 30–2, 350, 527
Hasan Tahsin Pasha 389
Haseki, Hadji Ali 305–9
Hassan Aga 302
Hatzidakis, Manos 470
Hegeso monument 97
Helen, Saint 258
Hellenism 159, 202, 427
  and Christianity 235
  and Constantinople 394
  in European countries
    362
  and the Greek diaspora
    371–2
  and nineteenth-century
    Athens 349, 359,
    362–3
  and the Olympic Games
    491
  philhellenism 192–3, 333
  and Seferis 474, 476
Helsey, Edouard 399

the Hephaesteion 229–30,
    262–3, 288, 322, 352
Hephaestus, god 11, 13, 15
Heracles 229
Herculius 216
Herms, desecration of the
    113–14
Herodes Atticus 200–2,
    203, 205, 376, 397
Herodotus
  on the Persian wars 41,
    43, 44, 48–9, 49–50,
    54
  on Solon 23, 24–5
Herulian raid 205–7, 209,
    215, 216
Himmler, Heinrich 433
Hipparchus 30, 31–2
Hippias 30–1, 32, 34, 41, 44
Hirshon, Renée 415–16
historical writings
  in Ottoman Greece
    296–9
Hobhouse, John 321–2, 323,
    325, 326, 338, 370
Homer 5, 10, 99, 151, 167,
    342
  and Athena 11–12, 14, 15
  on Peisistratus 29
honey-making monasteries
    295–6, 309, 328
Hope Simpson, Sir John
    415–16
houses 418
  ancient Athens 107
  Byzantine era 239–40
  Ottoman Athens 268–9
  polykatoikia 460–2
  refugees 414–16, 418
  Roman Athens 217–19
  twentieth-century 377,
    418–19
humanism 165
Hume, David 85
Hunt, Philip 313, 315–17
Hymettus, Mount 295
Hyperbolos 112

Iakovos, Metropolitan 280
Iamblichus 213
Ibrahim Pasha 344
Iliad (Homer) 11, 14, 15
Illcak, Şükrü 333
Illyrians 152
immigrant labour 498

Innocent III, Pope 243
International Monetary
    Fund 508
Ioannides, Dimitrios 478
Ion 6–7
Ionian Greeks 6–7
  and the Persian wars
    38–9, 44, 53, 55
Iraq 289–90, 486
Irene, Byzantine Empress
    225–6
Isagoras 34–5
Islam 291, 293, 294
  Muslims and the Balkan
    Wars 392–3
  Muslims and the Greek
    War of Independence
    332–3, 336, 337
  and Paul the Apostle 191
  practice of in greater
    Athens 523–4
  see also Ottoman Athens
Isocrates 147
Istanbul 272, 273, 276, 286,
    287, 296, 297, 299,
    302, 304, 309, 310,
    312, 313, 315, 318, 322,
    331, 338, 340, 384,
    385, 402
  compared with Athens
    372
  earthquake near 498
  European hinterland
    of 406
  Greek-speaking
    population of in early
    twentieth century
    383, 412, 413
  Orthodox Christian
    Patriarch in 273,
    299, 332
  see also Constantinople

Jan Sobieski, king of Poland
    278–9
Jerusalem
  Solomon's Temple 298
  Temple Mount 1, 15, 193
Jesus Christ 191
Jews
  and the Nazi occupation
    439
  Pacifico affair 364–5, 366,
    368, 369

and Paul the Apostle 189,
    190–1
and Roman emperors
    192–3, 213
of Thessaloniki 439
Joanna of Châtillon 249
John XXII, Pope 250
judicial system
  in ancient Athens 62, 72
Julian of Cappadocia
    209–10
Julian, Emperor 207,
    212–14, 215
jurors 126, 136
Justinian, Emperor 219,
    220, 221, 224, 290

Kagan, Donald 74
Kaisariani (district) 415, 441,
    442, 448, 508
Kaisariani monastery 295,
    296, 297, 309
Kaklamanis, Apostolos 463
Kaldellis, Anthony 227,
    234, 238
Kallias 74
Kallithea 415, 493
Kaminis, George 516
Kanaris, Constantine 371
Kapnikarea church 358
Kapodistrias, Ioannis 350
Karamanlis, Constantine
    464, 465, 478
Karamanlis, Kostas 497,
    499
Karneades 179
Kassander 166
Kavallares, Theophanes 296
Kazantzakis, Nikos 422
Kea 241–2
Kekrops, mythical king 7,
    12–13
Kellner, Gyula 375
Kemal, Mustafa 411
Kennedy, John F. 183
Kerameikos cemetery 61,
    66, 84, 97, 182, 354,
    527
Khi 444, 445
Khremonides 171
Kifisia 74, 203, 494
Kimon 68–70, 72, 73, 74,
    142, 149
King's Peace 142

Kleanthes, Stamatis 352–3,
    354, 360
Kleinias 104
Kleisthenes 32, 34, 35, 147,
    527
Kleisthenic democracy 35–6
Kleitias, artist 26
Klenze, Leo von 352, 353–4,
    358
Kleomenes, Spartan king
    33–4, 34–5
Kleon 92, 94, 99, 109
Knidos 141
Kokkinia 415, 416–17,
    441, 533
Kolonaki 419
Königsmarck, Count Otto
    Wilhelm von 279,
    282, 283
Koniordou, Lydia 491–2
Konon 121, 139–40, 141–2
Konon Walls 142
Kontares, George 297
Korka, Eleni 319
Korres, Manolis 216, 232
Kos 154
Koskotas, George 482–3
Koukaki 520
Koumoundourou, Lake 532
Koun, Karolos 423
Koundouriotis, Admiral
    Pavlos 389
Krannon 162
Kreousa 6
Kritias 132, 133, 134, 135,
    166–7
Kritolaus 179
Kritovoulos, Mikhail 265–6
Ktesiphon 161
Kylonian affair 19–20, 27
Kythera 318

Lakhares 169, 170
Lamarchus 113
Lambda 531
Lambros, Spyridon 381
Lamian War 162
Latin Empire 244–67
    the Catalan Company
        245–52
law courts
    in ancient Athens 22–3,
        28–9, 73, 136, 147
    shipping fraud 147–8, 160
Lazarus Parliament 402

Le Corbusier 418
Le Roy, Julien-David 304
League of Nations 413
Leeper, Rex 446, 447
Leo III, Pope 226
Leo IV, Byzantine Emperor
    225
Leonidas, king of Sparta 46
Lepanto, Battle of (1571)
    273
Lermusiaux, Albin 375
Lesbos 17, 121, 428
    revolt against Athens
        92–3
Lesk, Alexandra 311
Leuctra, Battle of 144–5
Licinius 208, 209
Lincoln, Abraham 87
Linear B script 12
living standards 493–4, 515
Lloyd George, David 390,
    411
Lluria, Roger de 251–2
Loizos, Manos 479
Londos, Andreas 325, 326
Louis, Spyridon 375–6,
    379–80
Louis XIV, king of France
    287
Lovejoy, Esther 407–9
Ludwig I, king of Bavaria
    348–9, 350, 353, 354,
    358
Lusieri, Giovanni Battista
    313, 314, 315, 316,
    317–18, 321, 324, 327
Lycabettus, Mount 194,
    258, 296, 486, 532
Lyceum 181
Lydia 24, 38
Lykourgos 162–3, 376
Lysander 120–1, 121–2, 132
Lysicrates monument 526

Macedonia 40, 149, 150–72,
    175
    Aiges 150–1, 152, 157
    army 153, 177
    and the Balkan Wars
        392, 393
    Lamian War 162
    Macedonians compared
        with Athenians 151–2
    Olynthos 156
    Ottoman 382, 384

refugee resettlement
    in 414
    and the Roman Republic
        176–7, 178
    Seleucid dynasty 178
    see also Alexander the
        Great; Philip of
        Macedon
McHugh, Sarah 202, 203
Mackenzie, Compton 395
Macmillan, Harold 183
McVeigh, Lincoln 447
Mahmud Efendi 297–9, 319
Makarios, Archbishop 466,
    470–1, 478
Makfi 306–7
Makri, Theodora 322
Makriyanni 520
Makriyannis, Ioannis
    341–2, 343
Makronisos, refugees on
    407–8
Malalas, John 220
Maniadakis, Konstantinos
    422, 423
Manos, Stefanos 494–6
Manou, Aspasia 410
Mantinea 112
    Battle of 145–6, 152
Marathon, Battle of 41,
    42–6, 50–1, 57, 60, 68,
    164, 171, 375
Marcus Aurelius, Emperor
    201, 204
Mardonius 40, 57
maritime fraud 147–8
maritime power 47–8,
    56, 57
Massilia 38, 148
Mavrokordatos, Alexander
    328–9
Mavromichalis, Petrobey
    350
Mazower, Mark 439, 440
Medes 37
Medici family 255
Megakles 19–20, 27, 28,
    66, 67
Megali Idea 428–9
Megara 21, 72, 75, 101, 340
Mehmet, Sultan 264, 265–6
Mela, Andromache 420
Melian Dialogue 512
Mendoni, Lina 528
Menexenus (Plato) 101

Mercouri, Melina 470, 477, 479–80, 483–4, 524
funeral 485–7
Merkel, Angela 441, 503, 516–17
Metaxas, General Ioannis 53, 394, 401–2, 421–2, 423, 425, 426, 428, 432, 442, 491
Metaxourgeio 527–9, 533
Metis, nymph 11
metro system 494
Metropolitan Cathedral of Athens 404, 484
Michael IX, Byzantine emperor 248
Michailidou, Toula 438, 467
Middle East 535
migration 517–18, 522–3
asylum seekers 517–18
Chinese 521–2
'golden visas' 520–1
Greek-Nigerians 522–3, 528–9
Miletus 38–9, 100
military dictatorship 457, 466, 473, 474–5, 477–8, 481
Mill, John Stuart 85
Miller, William 255, 377–8
Milošević, Slobodan 462
Miltiades 42, 43, 46, 465
Minotaur 26
Missolonghi 328
Mithridates VI of Pontus 179–80, 182, 184
Mitriades 68
Mitsotakis, Constantine 467, 483, 484
Mitsotakis, Kyriakos 516, 517, 521, 531
monasteries, honey-making 295–6, 309, 328
Monastiraki 520, 533
Montona, Matteo de 257
Morgenthau, Henry 413–14
Morosini, Francesco 278–9, 280, 281, 284–5, 293
mosques 358
Mounichia 168
Murad, Turkish sultan 261
Muses, Hill of the 170, 263, 280
museums

Acropolis Museum 232, 233, 530
Benaki Museum 353, 401
Epigraphical Museum of Athens 144
Greek Numismatic Museum 378
Museum of the City of Athens 287
National Archaeological Museum 144
music 425, 476–7, 478–9, 519, 529
Mussolini, Benito 422, 432
Mycenaean civilization 5–6
Mycenaean spring 434, 435
mythology of ancient Athens 6–9, 11–16, 29–30
Mytilineou, Catherina 490

Nansen, Fridtjof 413
Naples 255–6
Napoleon Bonaparte 325
National Gardens 206
National Library of Greece 360–1, 530–1
National Society 381–2
National Theatre 527
NATO 75, 472, 479, 498
Nauplion 255
and Greek independence 339, 345, 350–1
naval power and warfare 47–8, 90, 92, 98, 118, 140, 141–2, 158–9
Navarre, Company of 252, 253
Naxos 39
Nea Smyrni 415, 450
Neezer, Christopher 356
Nemea river, Battle of the 137
neo-Platonism 219–23
neoclassical architecture 378–9
Neolithic era 5
Nestorios 212
Netanyahu, Binyamin 517
Never on Sunday (film) 470
New Democracy Party 482, 507, 509–10, 516–17
Niarchos complex see Stavros Niarchos Foundation

Nightingale, Florence 368–70
Nikias 99, 111, 112, 113
Nikochares 129
Noemvriana events 398, 443

Obama, Barack 2, 503
Ober, Joseph 98
Octavian (later Augustus) 185–7
Odeion 184, 205
Odysseus 428
Odyssey (Homer) 11–12, 15
Oedipus Rex (Sophocles) 93–4
Olier, Charles-François, Marquis de Nointel 287
olive oil 13, 23, 29
Olympia 77
Olympic Games
ancient Greece 10, 19, 201, 376
(1896) 374–7, 379–81
(2004) 194, 289–93, 497, 529
Olympiodorus 221
Olynthos 156
Omar, son of Tourakhan 265
Omer Bey of Euboea 333, 334, 339, 340
Omer Vrioni 333–4, 339
Omonia Square 353, 429, 522
Onassis, Aristotle 530
Onesippus 129
opera 534
Orthodox Church 248, 249, 250, 253, 255, 261, 264, 265, 369, 422, 482, 524
calendar 416, 460
development of worship 227–8
festivals 460–1
funerals 462–3
and the Greek state 482
monasteries 295
music 476
and the Parthenon 266, 293, 367
Patriarchate/Patriarchs 255, 273, 275, 276, 286, 298, 308, 332, 403, 413

and Russia 363
in sixteenth-century
    Athens 268–9, 273,
    279, 286, 289, 291
Orwell, George 85
ostracism 63–8, 70–1, 72,
    74, 87, 127, 130
*ostraka* 64–8, 70, 71
Otho, king of Greece 348,
    350, 351–2, 354–5, 364,
    365, 533
    manifesto 358–9
    removal from power
        370–1
Ottoman Athens 265–7,
    268–319
    antiquarians in 300–2
    and Byron 326–7
    government of 269–72,
        304
    Greek Christians in 268,
        269, 272, 274–7, 279,
        290–1
    Haseki's rule 305–9
    honey-making
        monasteries 296
    segregation of
        communities 524–5
    seventeenth-century
        visitors to 286–94
    Venetian–Ottoman War
        277–86, 296, 357
Ottoman Empire
    and the Balkan Wars
        388–92, 392–3
    conquest of
        Constantinople 242,
        264
    and Crete 382–3
    and the First World War
        393, 402–4
    Greco-Turkish war (1897)
        382–3
    Greek community 372,
        383–6, 412–13
    and the Greek War of
        Independence 328–9,
        330–45
    and nineteenth-century
        Greece 363–4
    Orlov revolt 309–10
    the Sublime Porte 312, 313
    Young Turks 385–6, 390
    *see also* Turkey

Pacifico, David 364–5, 366,
    368, 369
Painted Stoa (*Stoa Poikile*)
    163–4, 239
Paleologos, Constantine
    260
Palmerston, Lord 365–6
Pan (god) 7, 44, 45
Panathenaic festival 29,
    80–1, 84, 170, 182, 376
    stadium 162
Pangalos, Seraphim 275
Pangalos, Theodoros 418
Pangrati 473
Panhellenism 149, 196–8
papacy
    and the Catalan Company
        250–1
Papadiamantis, Alexandros
    422
Papadopoulos, George 481
Papaioannou, Dmitris
    490–1, 492–3
Papandreou, Andreas 470,
    472, 477, 484, 503,
    510–11, 516
    funeral of 462–6
    as prime minister 478–81,
        482, 485, 496
Papandreou, Dimitra 462,
    464
Papandreou, George
    (senior) 418, 449,
    463, 464–5
    as prime minister 443–4,
        446, 465–6, 470, 471
Papandreou, George (son of
    Andreas) 500–1, 502,
    503–4, 505–7
Papandreou, Margaret 464
Papdemos, Loukas 506
Papoulias, Karolos 502
Paris Peace Conference
    409–10
Paros 68
Parren, Kalliroi 426
Parthenon 3, 119–20, 298
    and barbarian raids
        215–16
    bombardment of (1687)
        277–84, 285
    Christian 226–8, 229,
        231–6, 237, 238, 241,
        254, 258, 262, 359

current restoration project
    79
Elgin's removal of
    sculptures 313–19, 323
Florence Nightingale's
    visit 370
frieze 79, 80–1, 232–4,
    262, 289, 311, 368
and the 'golden' mean 86
and the Latin Empire
    255, 256
marbles 319, 356, 480
mosque 358
and Ottoman rule 266
pediments 234
presentation of Athena
    and Poseidon 86
rebuilding of (447 BCE)
    76–81
seventeenth-century
    visitors to 293–4
statues of Athena 76, 163,
    169, 232
temple of Athena 45, 78,
    280, 281, 318, 319, 360
Paruyr (Prohaeresius) 209,
    210, 212
PASOK (Panhellenic
    Socialist Movement)
    478, 482–3, 485, 495,
    500, 503
Patriarchate/Patriarchs *see
    under* Orthodox
    Church
Paul the Apostle 188–92,
    217, 366, 369
Paul, king of Greece 463,
    466
Pausanias 196–7, 527
Pedro IV, king of Aragon
    253, 253–4
Peisistratus, tyrant 27–30,
    34, 41, 195
Pella 157
Peloponnesian War 82, 92,
    97, 103, 105, 111, 112,
    115–19, 120–22, 147,
    357, 389, 528
pensions 502
Pentelikon, Mount 137, 328,
    348, 375
Percy, Thomas 302
Pergamon 175–8

Pericles 70–2, 73–6, 79, 81,
    93, 94, 101, 104, 132,
    190, 298
  achievements of 146–7
  and Alcibiades 104,
    109, 111
  and Aspasia 91, 100–1
  building of the Parthenon
    119–20
  and Demosthenes 160
  funeral oration for the war
    dead 82, 83–8, 95–8,
    100, 422
  grave of 97
  legacy of the Periclean
    age 359
  and Plato 149
Pericles the younger 121
Peripatetics 179
Peristeri 452
Persephone, goddess 532
Persia
  Achaemenid dynasty
    24–5
  and Alcibiades 116
  and the Peloponnesian
    War 120, 122, 142, 144
  wars with Greece 37–55,
    56–7, 60–1, 75, 115,
    138–40, 141
Petraki monastery 296
Petrakis, Dionysios 308
Phaedo (Plato) 126, 127
Pharnabazus 122
Pheidias, sculptor 77, 80,
    262
Pheidippides 43, 44, 375
Philip of Macedon 150,
    152–9, 160, 162
  Demosthenes' speech
    on 161
  and the oracle of Delphi
    155–6
Philip V, king of Macedonia
    176, 177
Philippides, Chrysanthos
    439
Philokles 177
Philopappos mausoleum
    263
philosophy 147, 148–9,
    163–6, 178–9
  neo-Platonism 219–23
  see also Plato; Socrates
Phoenicians 52, 55

Phokians 156, 157–8
Phormio 92
photography 423–4
Piano, Renzo 530
Piraeus 48, 73, 181, 521
  Konon Walls 142
  and maritime fraud 147–8
  refugee community 417
  and Shia Muslims 524
Pittakis, Kyriakos 356–7
plague
  in ancient Athens 88–90,
    91, 92, 93–4, 95, 97
  in Ottoman Athens 306
Plaka 107, 277, 283, 360,
    429, 434, 475, 482,
    525–6
Plastiras, Nikolaos 421, 449
Plataea, Battle of 56–7,
    60, 209
Plato 148–9, 218, 369
  Academy 69, 148–9, 158,
    165, 176, 179, 181, 182,
    219, 526
  on Alcibiades 135
  Apology 130–1
  Euthyphro 128
  First Alcibiades 110–11
  Menexenus 101
  neo-Platonism 218,
    219–23
  Phaedo 126, 127
  Phaedrus 202
  Symposium 106–11, 131,
    212
Pleistoanax, Spartan king
    75
Plutarch 60, 65, 68, 180
  on Alcibiades 104, 105
  on Cicero 182–3
  on Demetrius the Besieger
    168, 170, 171
  on Pericles 70, 71, 77–8
Pnyx (hill) 3, 94, 128, 174,
    280
political rallies 461
politics in ancient Athens
  constraints on power
    62–3
  ostracism 63–8
Pollini, John 232, 233–4
pollution 480–1, 531–2
Polytechnic 477
Pompeion 182
Pompey 184–5

population 522
  growth 272, 352, 377
Poros 162
Poseidon, sea-god 7, 8, 12,
    13, 14, 49, 85, 119, 311
  and Athenian democracy
    86
  temple to 162
Posidonius 180
Potidaea 105
pottery 11, 13, 49, 240
  the François vase 26–7
Proclus 217–19, 221, 222
Prohaeresius (Paruyr) 209,
    210, 212
Protagoras 70
Protestants 289, 293, 294
Protimo, Niccolò 265
Prytaneion 197
Psirri district 322
Ptolemy 166
Ptolemy XIII of Egypt 185
public-private divide
  and Athenian democracy
    86
Pydna 154
Pylos 99
Pythagoras 369

Rallis, Dimitrios 386
Randolph, Bernard 288
rap music 528, 534
refugees
  Anatolian 405–9, 413,
    414–18, 533
  see also migration
religion
  Ancient Greek 4, 114–15,
    130
  and the Olympic Games
    10
  polytheists 190, 219–20,
    221–3
  see also Catholicism;
    Christianity; deities;
    Orthodox Church;
    Protestants
rembetika (type of urban
    music) 425, 427,
    476, 529
Rendi, Maria 256
Rendis, Dimitrios 253–4
Reshid Mehmed Pasha
    339, 344
restaurants 519, 534

Revett, Nicholas 80, 300–2, 303–4
Rhodes 154, 167
riots (2008) 525
Roberts, Jennifer T. 93, 95
Rodenwaldt, Gerhard 233
Rogers, Dylan 181
Rogge, Jacques 289
Roman Athens 186–99, 200–23, 290
　barbarian raids 203–7
　building programmes 194–7, 200, 201, 217
　and Christianity 188–92
Roman Republic 176, 177, 178–88
　Sulla's siege of Athens 179–82, 184, 185, 195
Romania 299, 392
Royal Palace 348–9, 354, 397, 398
Royal Stoa 128–30
Rumeli 351
Russia 179, 535
　and the Crimean War 366, 368–9, 370
　and the Greek War of Independence 331, 332
　and the kingdom of Greece 361, 363–4
　women and the Chechnya war 96
Russia and the Greek War of Independence 344
Rust , Bernhard 426

Sacred Band 443
Sacred Way 532
Sakellaropoulou, Katerina 528
Salamis 21, 48, 285
　Battle of 50–5, 56, 57, 60, 61, 65, 142, 207
　and the Greek War of Independence 335, 336
Salamis (Cyprus) 74
Salem (super-tanker) 148
Samaras, Antonis 507, 509–10
Samos 100, 117–18, 158
Santas, Lakis 43
Santorini 24, 310

Sardis (city) 25, 39, 40, 41, 141
Sari Mouselimi 302
Sarkozy, Nicolas 503
Schaubert, Eduard 352–3, 354, 360
Schinkel, Karl Friedrich 354
Schliemann, Heinrich 378, 420
Scobie, General Ronald 444, 445–6, 447–8, 449
Scotland 145
sculpture
　memorial to Dexileos 137–8
　Severe Style 31
Scythians 42
Second Athenian League 144
Second Sophistic 201–2
Second World War
　Battle of Britain 87–8
　Nazi occupation of Athens 6, 46, 431–45, 515
Seferiades, George (Seferis) 428, 429–30, 450, 473–7, 478, 491–2
　funeral 475–7, 488
Segesta 112
Sepolia 522, 523, 533
Seraidari, Elli 423–4
Setton, Kenneth 251
Sèvres, Treaty of 410
Sfikas, George 438, 450
Sgouros, Leo 240, 241
ship-building 47–8, 62, 160
shipping fraud 147–8, 160
Sibilia, queen of Aragon 254
Sicily 17, 112–13, 115–16
　Sicilian Vespers 244–5
　Syracuse 112, 115, 148
Sicinnus 51, 55
Sigeum 34
Skouzes, Panagis 307, 308
Skyros 69
Slavs 224–5, 230, 384
Sligo, Lord 326–7
Smyrna 372, 383, 406, 409–10, 411
snakes 7
Sobiewolsky, Lieutenant 281–2

social classes
　in ancient Athens 22
Socrates 104–6, 125–35, 147, 166, 187, 323
　and Alcibiades 132, 134–5, 212
　in Aristophanes' The Clouds 108–9
　death of 125–32, 149
　and Demosthenes 160
　in Plato's dialogues 101–2, 126, 127, 130–1
　Symposium 108, 109–10, 131
　trial of 109, 127–35
　and Zeno 164
Solon 20–7, 34, 38, 147, 191, 297
Sophocles 93–4, 123, 129, 146, 162–3
Soteres, Gregorios 296
Souliotis-Nikolaides, Athanasios 385
South Stoa 182
Soviet Union 471, 479
Sparta 12, 32–5, 39, 60–1, 68, 69, 74, 155
　and Athenian democracy 138
　Battle of Tanagra 73
　defeat at Mantinea 145–6, 152
　and the Delphic oracle 155–6
　helots 33, 69
　and Macedonia 155, 157, 171
　Pericles' funeral oration for war dead 82, 83–8
　Persian wars 39, 40, 44, 45, 57
　wars with Athens 58–9, 75, 92, 94, 98–100, 105–6, 111–16, 118, 120–3, 135, 137, 138, 140–6, 514
　women 33
　see also Peloponnesian War
Sphakteria 99
Sphodrias 143, 144
Spon, Jacob 287–90, 297
Stalin, Joseph 442, 443, 450
Stathakopoulos, Dionysios 257

Stavros Niarchos
    Foundation  530, 534
Stead, William  494
Stegi (Roof)  530
Stoa of Attalos  174–5,
    178, 182
Stoa of Eumenes  205
*Stoa Poikile* (Painted Stoa)
    163–4
Stoics  164, 165, 179, 189, 191
Strangford, Viscount  333
Stratokles  169
Stratou, Danae  511
Stuart, James  80, 300–4,
    306, 314
Sulla's siege of Athens
    179–82, 184, 185, 195
*Symposium* (Plato)  106–11,
    131
Syngrou Avenue  417, 486,
    524, 530
Syntagma Square  348, 353,
    429, 494
Syracuse  112, 115, 148
Syria  168
Syriza  507, 516–17

Tamerlane  259
Tanagra, Battle of  73
taxes  155
technology sector  497–8
territorial expansion
    nineteenth-century
        Greece  362
terrorism  489–90
Thackeray, William  355–6
Thasos  142
theatre  30
theatres  146, 152
    Dionysus  162, 178
    Herodes Atticus  201
Thebes
    and Macedonia  153, 160–1
    the Sacred Band  158
    and the Spartan wars  75,
        140, 141, 143–6, 152
Themistoclean wall  526
Themistocles  47, 48, 50–1,
    55, 61, 65, 66, 71, 147,
    210
    ostracism of  65, 66, 67
Theodorakis, Mikis  470,
    476–7
Theodore of Epirus  243
Theodore of Tarsus  226

Theotokis, George  386
Theotokos mosaic  228
Thermopylae  156, 157
Theseus, mythical king  8–9,
    11, 26, 29, 69, 164,
    197, 201, 229–30
Thessaloniki  224, 308, 389,
    390, 396, 401, 439,
    440, 495, 498
Thessaly  156, 162
Thirty Tyrants  132, 149
Thrace  40, 46, 68–9, 142
Thrasyboulos  142, 527, 531
Thucydides  31, 60–1, 83,
    88, 92, 99, 202, 438,
    528, 534
    on Alcibiades  113
    on Athenian democracy
        89, 90–1
    on the Athenian plague
        88–90
    on the *Dimosion Sema*
        526–7
    on the Sicilian expedition
        115–16
Tissaphernes  116, 117
Titus Pomponius (Atticus)
    183
Tocco, Carlo  256
Tolias, George  273
Tolmides  75
tourism  423, 519–20
Tower of the Winds  263,
    288, 303, 304, 526
trade
    in ancient Athens  23
Trajan, Emperor  193–4, 198
transport  494–5, 497
travellers, seventeenth-
    century  286–94
tribes of Athens  35, 171, 197
Trikoupis, Charilaos  361–2,
    379
Tripolitsa  332
triremes  47–8, 72, 140, 273
Tritsis, Antonis  480–2,
    484, 488
    funeral of  484–5
Trojan War  141, 258
Trump, Donald  2, 517
Tsakolotos, General
    Thrasyvoulos  340
Tsaldaris, Panagis  420–1
Tsalikis, Father Iakovos  462
Tsarouchis, Yannis  493

Tsiodras, Sotiris  534
Tsipras, Alexis  507–8, 509,
    510–11, 517
Tsolakoglou, George  439
Turkey
    and Cyprus  471, 478
    Greco-Turkish war (1919-
        22)  405–6, 410, 411
    and the migrant crisis
        517, 518
    modern Greek relations
        with  498–9, 517
    Turks in Athens  521
    *see also* Ottoman Empire
Turks  252
    the Karasids  248
    and the Venetians  259–60
    *see also* Ottoman Empire
Turner, J. M. W.  313
twentieth-century
    dictatorship  117
tyranny  18, 28–32, 41, 132,
    149

Ulen, Henry  419
United States  364
    and Athenian democracy
        87, 88
    and Britain  183
    and Cyprus  471
    post-Cold War  73
    Reagan administration
        479
    relations with Greece  464
    Supreme Court  136
University of Athens  360–1,
    370, 381, 425–7

Valerian, Emperor  206
Valerian wall  206
Vamvakaris, Markos  425
Vangelis  589
Varoufakis, George  455–6
Varoufakis, Yanis  507–9,
    510, 511–12
vases  26–7, 29, 48
Vasiliki  272
Vassos, Timoleon  382
Velestinlis, Rigas  325–6
Venetians
    in Athens  257–9
    and the Catalans  251
    and the Ottomans  269
    sack of Constantinople
        243

Venetian–Ottoman War 277–86, 296, 357
Venezis, Ilias 428
Venizelos, Eleftherios 424–5, 429, 448
and the Balkan Wars 387–9, 390–1, 392, 393
and Bourchier 381, 387–8
and the First World War 393, 395–7, 401–2, 403, 404, 409
interwar government 411, 412, 419, 420–1
and the Paris Peace Conference 409–10
see also Athens International Airport
Venizelos, Evangelos 504
Vernon, Francis 287–9
Versailles, Treaty of 409–10
Victoria, Queen 113, 371
Vidal, Gore 212, 213
Virgin Mary 296
Akathist hymn to 236–7
in the Parthenon 227, 228, 230, 233, 234, 235, 236, 237, 254, 258
Visigoths 214–16
visitors to Athens American 380
nineteenth-century 367–70
seventeenth-century 286–94

see also Byron, George Gordon, Lord
Vratsanos 519

Waddington, George 334, 335–6, 337–8, 339
Walter V of Brienne, duke of Athens 248–9
Walter VI of Brienne 251
Warsaw Pact 487
water supply 419, 532
Waugh, Evelyn 111
weddings 466–9, 487
Wheler, George 287, 289–91, 293, 294, 297
Wilson, Sir David 480
women
Aspasia 91, 100–1
and Athenian democracy 87
funerals and ceremonial lamentation 96
in funerary monuments 97
houses in ancient Athens 107
and Plato's Academy 149
St Filothei 274–7
in Sparta 33
Wyse, Edward 368

Xanthippos 70–1, 465
Xenophon 122, 139, 164

on the trial of Socrates 133–4
Xerxes, Persian king 46, 49, 52, 55, 57, 207, 523
Xi Jinping 521

Yerakaris, Limberakis 285–6
Yinka, Manolis 528–9
Young Turk movement 385–6, 390
Yourcenar, Marguerite 450
Ypsilantis, Alexander 331

Zagan Pasha 267
Zappas, Evangelos 372–3, 376
Zappeion Palace 373, 397, 398, 400–1
Zay, Jean 426–7
Zeno of Elea 70
Zeno of Kition 150, 164–5, 172
Zeus, god 7, 10, 11, 13, 15, 191, 193, 201, 214
temple of 77, 195–6, 258, 263, 291, 407
Ziller, Ernst 378–9, 407, 527
Zorba the Greek (film) 470
Zorzi, Chiara 264
Zosimus 214–15
Zygomalas, Theodosius 273

# About the Author

Bruce Clark writes on culture and religion for *The Economist*. He has been diplomatic correspondent of the *Financial Times*, Moscow correspondent for *The Times* and Athens correspondent for Reuters. He is the author of *Empire's New Clothes*, an exploration of the rise of nationalism in post-Soviet Russia in the 1990s, and *Twice a Stranger: How Mass Expulsion Forged Modern Greece and Turkey*, a history of the population exchange between Greece and Turkey which took place in the early 1920s following the Treaty of Lausanne. *Twice a Stranger* won the Runciman Award in 2007.